GIANT PRINT NEW WEBSTER'S DICTIONARY

edited by
R. F. PATTERSON, M.A., D.Litt.

1991 Edition

New Expanded Webster's Dictionary is not associated with, or published by,
the original publishers of Webster's Dictionary or their successors.

Published by

P.S.I. & Associates, Inc.
13322 S.W. 128th Street
Miami, Florida 33186
305-255-7959

Giant Print New Webster's Dictionary

All entries are arranged in alphabetical order and appear in bold faced type. Following each entry are related words, derivations, and meanings. Each bold entry also includes a special simplified syllabic pronunciation help. Each entry also displays a symbol indicating the specific part of speech.

ABBREVIATIONS USED IN THIS DICTIONARY

a. adjective.
adu adverb.
conj. conjunction.
int. interjection.
n. noun.

n.pl. noun plural.
p.a. participial adjective.
pl. plural.
pp. past participle.
prep. preposition.

pret. preterit.
pron. pronoun.
vi. verb intransitive.
vt. verb transitive.

GUIDE TO PRONUNCIATION

ch, *ch*ain; g, *g*o; ng, si*ng*; ŦH, *th*en; th, *th*in; w, *w*ig; wh, *wh*ig; ah, azure; fāte, fär, fat, fạll; mē, met, her; pine, pin; nōte, not, möve; tūbe, tub, bụll; oil, pound.

Computer Terms and Definitions

The following is a list of some of the common terms, along with their definitions, used by the computer industry that are unique to that field.

Basic: A high-level interactive programming language that comes with most computers. Basic is relatively easy to learn to use if you want to try your hand at writing your own computer programs.

Bit: The smallest unit of information that the computer recognizes. A bit is represented in the computer by the presence or absence of an electronic pulse represented by humans as a zero or one.

Byte: A group of bits (usually 8 or 16) which stand for a single letter or number in the computer. Each byte is stored in its own address/location in memory.

CAD/CAM: Short for Computer-Aided-Design and Computer-Aided-Manufacturing—encompassing almost every computer-related design, manufacturing and business function.

Cassette: The cheapest and slowest way to store information when the computer's off. Cassettes transfer 30-120 bytes (characters) per second. That's slow.

Chip (Silicon): A microprocessor that is the complete computer on a single chip of silicon.

COBOL: Common Business Oriented Language—High-level programming language used for business applications.

CP/M: Control Program/Microcomputer. One of several "operating systems" for computers.

CPU: Abbreviation for Central Processing Unit. The portion of a computer, sometimes called the brain, that controls the interpretation/execution of the programs and processing instructions.

CRT: Abbreviation for Cathode Ray Tube. Another name for a picture tube, monitor or video display terminal (VDT).

Data base: Program that files information—names, addresses, amounts owed. Some programs allow the user to sort the information alphabetically, by zip code, etc.

Disk drive: A memory storage device that operates something like a record player, using removable, flexible diskettes (also called floppies or disks)

DOS: Disk Operating System. One of the most popular "operating systems" for computers.

File: A collection of organized records the computer treats as a unit.

Floppy Disk: Single flexible magnetic disk (about the size of a 45-RPM record) that is used with small computers and word processors.

Hardware: The physical components of a computer system.

IC: The abbreviation for Integrated Circuit. The small electronic components that work together on circuit boards to perform a designated task. These components are usually referred to as chips.

I/O: The abbreviation for Input/Output.

Interface: A circuit board (also called a card) that electronically connects a computer to its accessories via a cable.

K: One thousand (actually 1,024), usually referring to memory. A 64K computer has 64,000 (actually 65,536) characters of random access memory. One double-spaced, typed page needs about 2K of memory.

Kilobyte (K): Approximately one thousand bytes. This refers to the amount of computer memory in a system. For example: 512K memory equals approximately 512,000 bytes.

Languages: Programming languages. They include: Basic, COBOL, Pascal (business), Fortran (scientific), Forth.

LASER: Acronym for Light Amplification by Stimulated Emission of Radiation. A device that produces a very narrow beam of coherent light. Lasers are used to produce ultra high resolution images on advanced typesetting systems such as the CG 9600 and Scanner 2000.

Mainframes: Largest, fastest, and most expensive class of computers.

Megabyte (MB): Approximately one million bytes or one thousand kilobytes. Often used to measure disk, tape, or larger computer storage capacity. For example: 30 MB hard disk drive.

Microcomputers: Smallest and least expensive class of computers containing microprocessors on silicon chips.

Microprocessor: The miniature, integrated electronic circuit in the CPU that executes the instructions of a program task.

MODEM: The acronym for MOdulator/DEModulator. A device that uses a telephone hook-up to convert computer signals so that data can be sent or received over telephone lines.

Module: Set of logically related program statements.

Monitor: Video display that gives a higher quality picture than a TV set. Typical size is 12 inches diagonal. Monochrome monitors are available in green, amber, or white displays. Some have non-glare faces. Color monitors are either composite color (so-so for reading words and numbers, fine for graphics and games), or RGB (red-green-blue). Display quality depends heavily on quality of the computer signal.

Operating system: A program or procedure that tells the computer how to operate. The computer you buy determines the operating system you get or have to buy. To operate a computer with disk drives, you need DOS (pronounced doss), a disk operating system.

Pascal: Structured high-level programming language.

Peripheral: An input/output device directed from a controller or computer. Examples: disk drives, printers.

Program: Step-by-step set of instructions that directs the computer to perform certain operations to solve a problem preparing for the execution.

Programmer: Person trained to design, code and test computer programs.

RAM: Random Access Memory. The memory the computer uses to store data. The more the better. Most personal computers store up to 64K bytes (64,000 characters). You lose what's stored in RAM when the computer is turned off, which is why you need a cassette recorder or disk drive.

ROM: Read only memory. ROM provides permanent storage of the computer's operating system and the Basic programming language, and can't be altered. It isn't lost when the computer is off. Caution: some computer makers advertise "total memory" meaning RAM and ROM added up, while most just list RAM, which is more meaningful.

Semiconductor (Silicon): A crystalline substance that conducts electric current when it has been "doped" with chemical impurities shot into the lattice-like structure of the crystal.

Software: A term used to describe the programs, instructions and applications of a computer system.

System: Organized set of related components established to perform a certain task.

Terminal: The peripheral device used to enter or extract data from the computer. It is sometimes referred to as the workstation or human interface. It usually consists of a CRT and keyboard. Sometimes called a monitor.

Word Processing: Computer-based system for inputting, editing, storing and printing of documents.

A

A, the indefinite article, used before a consonant.

Abbreviate, ab-brē'vi-āt, *vt.* To shorten.

Abbreviation, ab-brē'vi-ā'shon, *n.* A shortening; contraction.

Abdicate, ab'di-kāt, *vt.* (abdicating, abdicated). To resign voluntarily; to relinquish. *vi.* To resign power.

Abdomen, ab-dō'men, *n.* The lower belly.

Abduct, ab-dukt', *vt.* To entice or lead away wrongly.

Aberrant, ab-e'rant, *a.* Wandering from; deviating from an established rule.

Ability, a-bil'li-ti, *n.* Power to do anything; talent; skill; in *pl.* the powers of the mind.

Abnegate, ab'nē-gāt, *vt.* To deny; to renounce.

Abnormal, ab-norm'al, *a.* Deviating from a fixed rule; irregular.

Aboard, a-bōrd', *adv.* or *prep.* On board; in a ship or vessel.

Abode, a-bōd', *n.* Residence; habitation.

Abolish, a-bol'ish, *vt.* To destroy; to abrogate.

Abortion, a-bor'shon, *n.* A miscarriage.

Abound, a-bound', *vi.* To be, or have, in great plenty.

About, a-bout', *prep.* Around; near to; relating to; engaged in.—*adv.* Around; round; nearly; here and there.

Above, a-buv', *prep.* To or in a higher place than; superior to; more than; beyond; before.—*adv.* To or in a higher place; chiefly.

Above-board, a-buv'bōrd, *adv.* Without concealment or deception.

Abrasion, ab-rā'zhon, *n.* A rubbing off; substance worn off by rubbing.

Abreast, a-brest', *adv.* In a line; side by side.

Abridge, a-brij', *vt.* To shorten; to condense.

Abroad, a-brad', *adv.* At large; away from home; in a foreign country.

Absent, ab'sent, *a.* Being away from; not present; wanting in attention.

Absentee, ab-sen-tē', *n.* One who absents himself.

Absinthe, ab'sinth, *n.* A liqueur consisting of spirit flavored with wormwood.

Absolute, ab'sō-lūt, *a.* Unlimited; unconditional; certain; despotic.

Absolve, ab-solv', *vt.* To free from, as from guilt or punishment; acquit; pardon.

Absorb, ab-sorb', *vt.* To drink in; to engross.

Absorbent, ab-sorb'ent, *a.* Imbibing; swallowing.—*n.* That which absorbs.

Absorption, ab-sorp'shon, *n.* Act or process of imbibing or swallowing up.

Abstain, ab-stān', *vi.* To keep back from; to refrain; to forbear.

Abundance, a-bun'dans, *n.* Plenteousness; copiousness; wealth.

Abundant, a-bun'dant, *a.* Abounding; plentiful; ample.

Abuse, a-būz', *vt.* (abusing, abused). To turn from the proper use; to ill-use; to deceive; to vilify; to violate.

Abuse, a-būs', *n.* Misuse; bad language addressed to a person; insulting words; violation.

Abut, a-but', *vi.* (abutting, abutted). To border; to meet. (With *upon*.)

Abutment, a-but'ment, *n.* That which abuts; solid support for the extremity of a bridge, arch, etc.

Abyss, a-bis', *n.* A bottomless gulf; a deep pit or mass of waters; hell.

Acacia, a-kä'shi-a, *n.* A genus of ornamental plants, yielding catechu, gum-arabic, etc.

Academic, Academical, ak-a-dem'ik, ak-a-dem'ik-al, *a.* Belonging to an academy or university.

Academy, a-kad'ē-mi, *n.* A seminary of arts or sciences; a society of persons for the cultivation of arts and sciences.

Acaridan, a-kar'i-dan, *n.* A mite, tick, or allied animal.

Accede, ak-sēd', *vi.* (acceding, acceded). To assent to; to comply with.

Accelerate, ak-sel'lė-rāt, *vt.* (accelerating, accelerated). To hasten; to quicken the speed of.

Accent, ak'sent, *n*. A tone or modulation of the voice; stress of the voice on a syllable or word; the mark which indicates this stress; manner of speaking.

Accent, ak-sent', *vt*. To express or note the accent of.

Accept, ak-sept', *vt*. To receive; to admit; to promise to pay, by attaching one's signature.

Acceptable, ak-sept'a-bl, *a*. That may be accepted; pleasing; gratifying.

Access, ak'ses, *n*. Approach; admission; means of approach; increase.

Accessible, ak-ses'i-bl, *a*. Easy of approach; affable.

Accession, ak-se'shon, *n*. The act of acceding; augmentation; succession to a throne.

Accessory, ak'ses-sō-ri, *a*. Additional, contributing to.—*n*. An accomplice; an adjunct.

Acclamation, ak-kla-mā'shon, *n*. A shout of applause, assent, or approbation.

Accolade, ak-kō-lād', *n*. A ceremony used in conferring knighthood, usually a blow on the shoulder with the flat of a sword.

Accommodate, ak-kom'mō-dāt, *vt*. (accommodating, accommodated). To make suitable; to adjust; to furnish with.

Accompaniment, ak-kum'pa-niment, *n*. That which accompanies; the subordinate part or parts, in music.

Accordion, ak-kord'i-on, *n*. A small melodious, keyed wind-instrument.

Accost, ak-kost', *vt*. To speak to first; to address.

Account, ak-kount', *n*. A reckoning; a register of facts relating to money; narration; advantage; end; importance.—*vt*. To reckon; to consider; to deem; to value.—*vi*. To give or render reasons; to explain (with *for*).

Accountant, ak-kount'ant, *n*. One skilled or employed in accounts; one whose profession is to examine accounts.

Accumulate, ak-kū'mū-lāt, *vt*. (ac-cumulating, accumulated). To heap up; to amass.—*vi*. To increase.

Accumulator, ak-kū'mū-lāt-ėr, *n*. A kind of battery which stores electric energy.

Accurate, ak'kū-rāt, *a*. Done with care; exact; without error.

Accursed, ak-kėrs'ed, *a*. Lying under a curse; doomed; wicked.

Accusation, ak-kū-zā'shon, *n*. Act of accusing; impeachment; that of which one is accused.

Accusative, ak-kūz'at-iv, *a*. or *n*. A case in grammar, in English the objective.

Accuse, ak-kūz', *vt*. (accusing, accused). To charge with a crime; to impeach; to censure.

Accustom, ak-kus'tum, *vt*. To inure to a custom; to make familiar with by use.

Ace, ās, *n*. A unit; a single point on cards or dice; a distinguished airman, who has destroyed many enemy planes.

Aching, āk'ing, *p.a*. Being in continued pain.—*n*. Pain.

Achromatic, ak-rō-mat'ik, *a*. Free from color.

Acid, as'id, *a*. Sharp, or sour to the taste.—*n*. A sour substance; a substance that with certain other substances forms salts.

Acoustic, a-kous'tik, *a*. Pertaining to the sense of hearing, or to the doctrine of sounds.

Acoustics, a-kous'tiks, *n*. The science of sound.

Acquaint, ak-kwānt', *vt*. To make to know; to make familiar; to inform.

Acre, ā'kėr, *n*. A quantity of land, containing 4840 square yards.

Acreage, ā'kėr-āj, *n*. A number of acres in a piece of land.

Acrid, ak'rid, *a*. Sharp; hot or biting to the taste; corroding; harsh.

Acrimony, ak'ri-mo-ni, *n*. Sharpness; harshness; severity.

Acrobat, ak'rō-bat, *n*. A rope-dancer; one who practices vaulting, tumbling, etc.

Acrocephalic, ak'rō-se-fal'ik, *a*. High-skulled.

Acrogen, ak'rō-jen, *n*. A plant increasing by extension of the stem at the top.

Acropolis, a-krop'o-lis, *n.* The citadel of a Greek city, as of Athens.

Across, a-kros', *prep.* or *adv.* From side to side; transversely; crosswise.

Acrostic, a-kros'tik, *n.* A composition in verse, in which the first (or other) letters of the lines form the name of a person, etc.

Act, akt, *vi.* To be in action; to exert power; to conduct oneself.—*vt.* To do; to perform, as an assumed part; to counterfeit.—*n.* A deed; power, or the effect of power, put forth; a state of reality; a part of a play; law, as an act of parliament.

Actinia, ak-tin'i-a, *n.*; pl. **-iae.** A sea-anemone.

Actinism, ak'tin-izm, *n.* The chemical action of the sun's rays.

Action, ak'shon, *n.* A deed; operation; a series of events; gesture; a suit or process; an engagement, battle.

Active, ak'tiv, *a.* That acts or is in action; busy; quick; denoting action.

Actor, akt'er, *n.* One who acts; an active agent; a stage-player.

Acute, a-kūt', *a.* Sharpened; sharp; ending in a sharp point; penetrating; having nice sensibility; sharp in sound.

Adage, ad'āj, *n.* A proverb; a maxim.

Adapt, a-dapt', *vt.* To fit; to adjust; to suit.

Add, ad, *vt.* To join to; to annex; to say further.

Addendum, ad-den'dum, *n.*; pl. **-da.** A thing to be added; an appendix.

Additive, ad'it-iv, *a.* That is to be or may be added.

Addle, ad'l, *a.* Rotten; barren.—*vt.* (addling, addled). To make corrupt or barren.

Address, ad-dres', *vt.* To direct; to apply to by words or writing; to speak to; to apply (oneself); to write a name and destination on.—*n.* Verbal or written application; speech or discourse to a person; tact; courtship (generally in *plural*); direction of a letter.

Adduce, ad-dūs', *vt.* (adducing, adduced). To bring forward; to cite.

Adhesion, ad-hē'zhon, *n.* Act or state of sticking to; adherence.

Adhibit, ad-hib'it, *vt.* To attach (one's signature).

Adhortatory, ad-hor'ta-tō-ri, *a.* Containing counsel or warning.

Adieu, a-dū', *interj.* Farewell.—*n.*; pl. **-us** or **-ux.** A farewell.

Adipose, ad'i-pōs, *a.* Consisting of or resembling fat; fatty.

Adit, ad'it, *n.* An approach; the horizontal opening into a mine.

Adjacent, ad-jā'sent, *a.* Lying near; adjoining; contiguous; neighboring.

Adjective, ad'jek-tiv, *n.* A word used with a noun, to express some quality or circumstance.

Adjoin, ad-join', *vt.* To join to.—*vi.* To lie or be next; to be contiguous.

Adjourn, ad-jėrn', *vt.* To put off to a future day; to postpone.—*vi.* To leave off for a future meeting.

Admeasure, ad-me'zhūr, *vt.* To ascertain the size or capacity of.

Adminicle, ad-min'i-kl, *n.* Support; aid.

Administer, ad-min'is-tėr, *vt.* To manage; to dispense; to distribute.

Administration, ad-min'is-trā'shon, *n.* Management; executive part of a government.

Admirable, ad'mi-ra-bl, *a.* Worthy of admiration; excellent.

Admonish, ad-mon'ish, *vt.* To warn; to reprove solemnly or quietly; to exhort.

Admonition, ad-mō-ni'shon, *n.* Gentle or solemn reproof; instruction; caution.

Ado, a-dö', *n.* Stir; bustle; difficulty.

Adobe, a-dō'be, *n.* A sun-dried brick.

Adolescent, ad-ō-les'ent, *a.* Advancing to manhood.

Adopt, a-dopt', *vt.* To take and treat as a child, giving a title to the rights of a child; to embrace.

Adorable, a-dōr'a-bl, *a.* Worthy to be adored.

Adoration, a-dōr-ā'shon, *n.* Worship paid to God; profound reverence.

Adore, a-dōr', *vt.* (adoring, adored). To address in prayer; to worship with reverence and awe; to love intensely.

Adorn, a-dorn', vt. To deck with ornaments; to embellish; to beautify.

Adrift, a-drift', adv. Floating at random; at the mercy of any impulse.

Adroit, a-droit', a. Dexterous; skilful; ready.

Adulation, ad-ū-lā'shon, n. Servile flattery; excessive praise.

Adult, a-dult', a. Grown to maturity.—n. A person grown to manhood.

Adultery, a-dul'tė-ri, n. Unfaithfulness to the marriage-bed.

Advent, ad'vent, n. Arrival; the coming of Christ; the four weeks before Christmas.

Adventitious, ad-ven-ti'shi-us, a. Accidental; casual; accessory; foreign.

Adventure, ad-ven'tūr, n. Hazardous enterprise; a bold undertaking.—vt. To risk or hazard.—vi. To dare; to venture.

Adventurous, ad-ven'tūr-us, a. Prone to incur hazard; daring; full of hazard.

Adverb, ad'vėrb, n. A word which modifies a verb, adjective, or another adverb.

Adversary, ad'vėr-sa-ri, n. An enemy; an antagonist.

Adversative, ad-vėrs'at-iv, a. Noting or causing opposition.—n. A word denoting opposition.

Adverse, ad'vėrs, a. Hostile; unprosperous.

Adversity, ad-vėrs'i-ti, n. Misfortune; affliction; calamity; distress.

Advise, ad-vīz', vt. (advising, advised). To counsel; to warn; to inform.—vi. To deliberate or consider.

Advised, ad-vīzd', p.a. Cautious; done with advice.

Advocate, ad'vō-kāt, n. One who pleads for another; an intercessor.—vt. (advocating, advocated). To plead in favor of; to vindicate.

Adze, adz, n. A kind of axe, with the edge at right angles to the handle.

Aegis, ē'jis, n. A shield; protection.

Aeolian, ē-ō'li-an, a. Pertaining to Aeolus, the god of the winds; played upon by the wind.

Aerate, ā'ėr-āt, vt. (aerating, aerated). To put air into; to combine with carbonic acid.

Aerial, ā-ē'ri-al, a. Belonging to the air; high; lofty.—n. The overhead structure of a wireless station, used for transmitting and receiving electrical oscillations.

Aerie, ē'rē, n. The nest of a bird of prey; a brood of such birds.

Affair, af-fār', n. That which is to do, or which is done; business.

Affect, af-fekt', vt. To act upon; to move the feelings of; to aim at; to pretend.

Affectation, af-fek-tā'shon, n. False pretense; an artificial air put on by a person.

Affectedly, af-fekt'ed-li, adv. In an affected manner; feignedly.

Affecting, af-fekt'ing, p.a. Pathetic; tender; exciting.

Affection, af-fek'shon, n. The state of being affected; fondness; love.

Affectionate, af-fek'shon-āt, a. Tender; loving; fond.

Afferent, af'fėr-ent, a. Carrying to or inwards.

Affiance, af-fī'ans, n. Faith pledged; marriage contract; reliance.—vt. (affiancing, affianced). To pledge one's faith to; to betroth.

Affidavit, af-fi-dā'vit, n. A written declaration upon oath.

Affiliate, af-fil'li-āt, vt. (affiliating, affiliated). To adopt; to assign to a father; to unite to a chief society or body.

Affiliation, af-fil'li-ā'shon, n. Act of affiliating; association.

Affinity, af-fin'i-ti, n. Relation by marriage; resemblance; chemical attraction.

Affirm, af-fėrm', vt. To assert; to declare; to ratify.—vi. To declare solemnly.

Affix, af-fiks', vt. To fasten to; to subjoin.—n. af'fiks. A syllable or letter added to a word.

Afield, a-fēld', adv. To or in the field.

Afloat, a-flōt', adv. or a. Floating; in circulation (as a rumor).

Afoot, a-fut', adv. On foot, in action.

After, äft'ėr, a. Later in time; subsequent.—prep. Later in time than; behind; according to; in imitation of.—adv. Later in time.

Afterbirth, äft'ėr-bėrth, n. That which is expelled from the uterus after the birth of a child.

Aftermath, äft´ėr-math, *n.* A second crop of grass in the same season; consequences; results.

Afternoon, äft´ėr-nön, *n.* The part of the day which follows noon.

Age, āj, *n.* A period of time; an epoch; number of years during which a person has lived; decline of life; oldness; legal maturity.—*vi.* and *t.* (aging, aged). To grow or make old; to show signs of advancing age.

Agency, ā´jen-si, *n.* Instrumentality; office or business of an agent.

Agenda, a-jen´da, *n.pl.* Memoranda; business to be transacted at a meeting.

Agent, ā´jent, *n.* One who acts; a deputy; an active cause or power.

Agglomerate, ag-glom´mė-rāt, *vt.* To gather into a mass.—*vi.* To grow into a mass.

Agglutinant, ag-glü´tin-ant, *n.* Any viscous or gluey substance.

Agglutinate, ag-glü´tin-āt, *vt.* To glue to; to cause to adhere.

Aggrandize, ag´gran-dīz, *vt.* To make great; to magnify.

Aggravate, ag´gra-vāt, *vt.* (aggravating, aggravated). To intensify; to exasperate.

Aggregate, ag´grė-gāt, *vt.* To bring together; to heap up.—*a.* Formed of parts collected.—*n.* A sum, mass, or assemblage of particulars.

Aggression, ag-gre´shon, *n.* The first act of hostility; attack.

Aggressor, ag-gres´or, *n.* The person who commences hostilities.

Aggrieve, ag-grēv´, *vt.* To pain, oppress, or injure.

Aghast, a-gast´, *a.* or *adv.* Amazed; stupefied. Also *agast.*

Agile, aj´il, *a.* Ready to act; nimble.

Ago, a-gō, *adv.* or *a.* Past; gone.

Agonize, ag´ō-nīz, *vi.* (agonizing, agonized). To writhe with extreme pain.—*vt.* To distress with extreme pain; to torture.

Agony, ag´ō-ni, *n.* Extreme pain of body or mind; anguish; the pangs of death.

Agrarian, a-grā´ri-an, *a.* Relating to lands.

Agree, a-grē´, *vi.* (agreeing,

agreed). To be in concord; to correspond; to suit.

Agreement, a-grē´ment, *n.* Harmony, conformity; stipulation.

Agriculture, ag´ri-kul-tūr, *n.* The art or science of cultivating the ground.

AIDS, ādz, *n.* Acquired Immune Deficiency Syndrome. A breakdown of the human body's immune system.

Ail, āl, *vt.* To pain; to affect with uneasiness.—*vi.* To be in pain or trouble.

Aim, ām, *vi.* To point with a missive weapon; to intend; to endeavor.—*vt.* To level or direct as a firearm.—*n.* That which is aimed at; direction; purpose; drift.

Air, ār, *n.* The fluid which we breathe; a light breeze; a tune; mien; *pl.* affected manner.—*vt.* To expose to the air; to ventilate; to dry.

Airplane, ār´o-plān, *n.* A heavier-than-air power-driven flying-machine having one or two pairs of wings (monoplane or biplane) which support it owing to the reaction of the air.

Airport, ār´pört, *n.* An area for landing airplanes, usually having customs houses, servicing facilities, etc.

Air-pump, ār´pump, *n.* A machine for pumping the air out of a vessel.

Air-shaft, ār´shaft, *n.* A passage for air into a mine.

Air-tight, ār´tīt, *a.* So tight or compact as not to let air pass.

Airy, ā´ri, *a.* Open to the free air; high in air; light; thin; vain; gay.

Aisle, īl, *n.* A wing or side of a church; a passage in a church.

Ajar, a-jär´, *adv.* Partly open, as a door.

Akimbo, a-kim´bō, *pred.a.* or *adv.* With the elbow outwards and the hand on the hip.

Akin, a-kin´, *a.* Of kin; related to; partaking of the same properties.

Alabaster, al´a-bas-tėr, *n.* A soft marble-like mineral.—*a.* Made of alabaster.

Alacrity, a-lak´ri-ti, *n.* Liveliness; cheerful readiness; promptitude.

Alarm, a-lärm´, *n.* A call to arms;

sudden surprise; fright; a notice of danger.—*vt.* To give notice of danger; to disturb.

Albumen, al-bū´men, *n.* The white of an egg; a substance of the same kind found in animals and vegetables.

Alburnum, al-bėr´num, *n.* Sapwood of a tree.

Alchemy, al´ke-mi, *n.* An obsolete science, aiming at changing metals into gold, etc.

Alcohol, al´kō-hol, *n.* Pure spirit of a highly intoxicating nature.

Alcoholic, al-kō-hol´ik, *a.* Pertaining to alcohol.

Alcoholism, al´kō-hol-izm, *n.* The condition of habitual drunkards.

Alcove, al´kov, *n.* A recess.

Alexandrine, al´legz-an´´drin, *n.* A line with six stresses.

Alga, al´ga, *n.*; pl. -**gae,** A sea-weed.

Algebra, al´je-bra, *n.* The science of computing by symbols.

Alias, ā´li-as, *adv.* Otherwise.—*n.*; pl. -**ses,** An assumed name.

Alibi, al´i-bī, *n.* The plea of a person who, charged with a crime, alleges that he was elsewhere when the crime was committed.

Alien, āl´yen, *a.* Foreign; estranged from.—*n.* A foreigner.

Aliquot, al´i-kwot, *a.* A part of a number which divides the whole without remainder.

Alive, a-līv´, *a.* Living; lively; susceptible.

Alkali, al´ka-li, *n.*; pl. -**ies** or -**is.** A substance, as potash and soda, which neutralizes acids and unites with oil or fat to form soap.

All, al, *a.* Every part; every one.—*n.* The whole; everything.—*adv.* Wholly; entirely.

Allah, al´la, *n.* The Arabic name of God.

Allay, al-lā´, *vt.* To repress; to assuage.

Allegation, al-lē-gā´shon, *n.* Affirmation; declaration.

Allege, al-lej´, *vt.* (alleging, alleged). To adduce; to assert; to plead in excuse.

Allegiance, al-lē´ji-ans, *n.* Loyalty.

Alley, al´i, *n.* A narrow walk or passage.

Alliance, al-lī´ans, *n.* State of being allied; confederacy; league.

Allied, al-līd´, *p.a.* United by treaty.

Allopathy, al-lop´a-thi, *n.* The ordinary mode of curing diseases, by using medicines which produce a condition contrary to that of the disease.

Allot, al-lot´, *vt.* (allotting, allotted). To give by lot; to apportion.

Allotrophy, al-lot´ro-pi, *n.* The capability of substances of existing in more than one form.

Allow, al-lou´, *vt.* To grant; to admit; to abate; to bestow, as compensation.

Alloy, al-loi´, *vt.* To mix with baser metals; to abate by mixture.—*n.* A baser metal mixed with a finer; a metallic compound.

All-spice, al-spīs, *n.* Pimento or Jamaica pepper, supposed to combine many different flavors.

Allude, al-lūd´, *vi.* (alluding, alluded). To refer to; to hint at.

Allure, al-lūr´, *vt.* (alluring, allured). To draw by some lure; to entice; to decoy.

Allusion, al-lū´zhon, *n.* The act of alluding; a hint; a reference.

Almost, al´most, *adv.* Nearly; wellnigh; for the greatest part.

Alms, ämz, *n.pl.* A charitable gift.

Aloe, al´ō, *n.* A succulent plant; *pl.* a bitter purgative medicine.

Aloft, a-loft´, *adv.* In the sky; on high.

Alone, a-lōn´, *a.* Solitary.—*adv.* Separately.

Along, a-long´, *adv.* Lengthwise; forward.—*prep.* By the side of; lengthwise.

Aloof, a-löf´, *adv.* At a distance; apart.

Aloud, a-loud´, *adv.* Loudly.

Alp, alp, *n.* A high mountain.

Alpaca, al-pak´a, *n.* A Peruvian animal, with long, soft, and woolly hair; cloth made of its hair, or a similar cloth.

Alpenstock, al´pen-stok, *n.* A long stick shod with iron, used in climbing mountains.

Alpha, al´fa, *n.* The first letter in the Greek alphabet; the first or beginning.

Alphabet, al´fa-bet, *n.* The letters of a language arranged in the customary order.

Alpine, al'pīn, *a*. Pertaining to high mountains.

Already, al-red'i, *adv*. Before or by this time; even now.

Also, al'sō, *adv*. Likewise; in the same manner, further.

Altar, al'tėr, *n*. An elevated place on which sacrifices were offered; the communion table.

Alternation, al-tėrn-ā'shon, *n*. Reciprocal succession; interchange.

Alternative, al-tėrn'at-iv, *n*. A choice of two things.

Although, al'THō', *conj*. Be it so; admit all that.

Altitude, al'ti-tūd, *n*. Height; eminence; elevation.

Alto, al'tō, *a*. High.—*n*. In *music,* contralto.

Altogether, al-tö-geTH'ėr, *adv*. Wholly; entirely; without exception.

Altruism, al'trö-izm, *n*. Devotion to others or to humanity; the opposite of selfishness.

Alum, al'um, *n*. An astringent salt of great use in medicine and the arts.

Aluminum, a-lu-mi-num, *n*. A very light metal of a silvery white color.

Alumnus, a-lum'nus, *n*.; pl. -**ni.** A pupil; a graduate of a university.

Amaranthine, am-a-ran'thin, *a*. Unfading.

Amass, a-mas', *vt*. To form into a mass; to accumulate; to heap up.

Amateur, am-a-tūr', *n*. A lover of any art or science, not a professor.

Amatory, am'a-tō-ri, *a*. Relating to love; causing love; amorous.

Amaze, a-māz', *vt*. (amazing, amazed). To astonish; to bewilder.

Amazon, am'a-zon, *n*. A warlike or masculine woman; a virago.

Ambassador, am-bas'sa-dor, *n*. A representative of a sovereign or state at a foreign court.

Ambiguous, am-big'ū-us, *a*. Of uncertain signification; doubtful.

Ambit, am'bit, *n*. Compass; scope.

Ambition, am-bi'shon, *n*. Desire of preferment or power.

Ambitious, am-bi'shus, *a*. Aspiring.

Amble, am'bl, *vi*. (ambling, ambled). To move, as a horse, by lifting the two legs on each side alternately; to go between a walk and a trot.—*n*. A peculiar motion of a horse; a pace between a walk and a trot.

Ambrosia, am-brō'zhi-a, *n*. The imaginary food of the gods, which conferred immortality.

Ambulance, am'bū-lans, *n*. An itinerant hospital; a wagon for the sick or wounded.

Ambulatory, am'bū-lā-tō-ri, *a*. Movable.—*n*. A part of a building to walk in.

Amends, a-mendz', *n.pl*. Compensation; satisfaction; recompense.

Amenity, a-men'i-ti, *n*. Pleasantness; agreeableness of situation.

American, a-me'ri-kan, *n*. A native of America.—*a*. Pertaining to America.

Amethyst, am'ē-thist, *n*. A variety of quartz, a precious stone of a violet or purple color.

Amiable, ā'mi-a-bl, *a*. Lovable; sweet-tempered.

Amicable, am'ik-a-bl, *a*. Friendly; kind.

Amnesty, am'nes-ti, *n*. A general pardon of offenses against a government.

Amnion, am'ni-on, *n*. The innermost membrane surrounding the fetus of mammals, birds, and reptiles.

Amoeba, a-mē'ba, *n*.; pl. -**bae.** A microscopic animal commonly found in fresh water.

Among, Amongst, a-mung', a-mungst', *prep*. Amidst; throughout; of the number.

Amorous, am'or-us, *a*. Inclined to love; enamored; fond; relating to love.

Amorphous, a-mor'fus, *a*. Without shape; of irregular shape.

Amount, a-mount', *vi*. To mount up to; to result in.—*n*. The sum total; effect or result.

Amphitheater, am-fi-thē'a-tėr, *n*. An edifice of an oval form, with rows of seats all round, rising higher as they recede from the area.

Ample, am'pl, *a*. Spacious; copious; rich.

Amplification, am'pli-fi-kā''shon, *n*. Act of amplifying; enlargement;

discussion.

Amplify, am'plif-ī, vt. (amplifying, amplified). To enlarge; to treat copiously.—vi. To speak copiously; to be diffuse.

Amplitude, am'pli-tūd, n. Ampleness; extent; abundance.

Amply, am'pli, adv. Largely; liberally; fully; copiously.

Amputate, am'pū-tāt, vt. (amputating, amputated). To cut off, as a limb.

Amuck, a-muk', n. or adv. Only in phrase to run amuck, to rush about frantically, to attack all and sundry.

Amulet, am'ū-let, n. A charm against evils or witchcraft.

Amuse, a-mūz', vt. (amusing, amused). To entertain; to beguile.

Anagram, an'a-gram, n. A transposition of the letters of a name or sentence, by which a new word or sentence is formed.

Anal, ā'nal, a. Pertaining to the anus.

Analogous, an-al'og-us, a. Having analogy; corresponding.

Analogy, an-al'o-ji, n. Likeness; similarity.

Analyze, an'a-līz, vt. (analysing, analysed). To subject to analysis; to resolve into its elements.

Ancestor, an'ses-tėr, n. A progenitor; forefather.

Anchor, ang'kėr, n. An iron instrument for holding a ship at rest in water. vt. To hold fast by an anchor.—vi. To cast anchor.

Anchorage, ang'ker-āj, n. A place where a ship can anchor; duty on ships for anchoring.

Anchorite, ang'kō-rīt, n. A hermit.

Anchovy, an-chō'vi, n. A small fish of the herring kind, furnishing a fine sauce.

Ancient, ān'shent, a. That happened in former times; old, antique.

Ancillary, an'sil-la-ri, a. Pertaining to a maid-servant; subservient or subordinate.

Aneroid, an'ē-roid, a. Dispensing with fluid, said of a kind of barometer.

Anesthetic, an-es-thet'ik, a. Producing insensibility.—n. A sub-

stance, as chloroform, which produces insensibility.

Aneurysm, an'ū-rizm, n. Dilatation of an artery.

Anew, a-nū', adv. On new; fresh.

Angel, ān'jel, n. A divine messenger; a spirit; an old English gold coin worth ten shillings.

Anger, ang'gėr, n. A violent passion, excited by real or supposed injury; resentment.—vt. To excite anger; to irritate.

Angina, an-ji'na, n. Angina pectoris, a fatal disease characterized by paroxysms of intense pain and a feeling of constriction in the chest.

Angle, ang'gl, n. The inclination of two lines which meet in a point but have different directions; a corner.

Angle, ang'gl, n. A fishing-hook, or hook with line and rod.—vi. (angling, angled). To fish with an angle.

Anglican, ang'glik-an, a. Pertaining to England, or to the English Church.

Angular, ang'gū-lėr, a. Having an angle; stiff.

Anile, an'īl, a. Aged; imbecile.

Aniline, an'i-lin, n. A substance obtained from coal-tar, used in dyeing.

Animadvert, an'i-mad-vėrt'', vi. To criticise; to censure (with upon).

Animal, an'i-mal, n. A living being having sensation and voluntary motion; a quadruped.—a. Belonging to animals; gross.

Animus, an'i-mus, n. Intention; hostile spirit.

Anise, an'is, n. An aromatic plant, the seeds of which are used in making cordials.

Ankle, ang'kl, n. The joint which connects the foot with the leg.

Annals, an'nalz, n.pl. A record of events under the years in which they happened.

Anneal, an'nēl', vt. To temper glass or metals by heat; to fix colors laid on glass.

Annelid, an'ne-lid, n. An invertebrate animal whose body is formed of numerous small rings, as the worm, leech, etc.

Annex, an-neks', *vt.* To unite at the end; to subjoin; to take possession of.

Annihilate, an-nī'hil-āt, *vt.* (annihilating, annihilated). To reduce to nothing; to destroy the existence of.

Anniversary, an-ni-vėrs'a-ri, *n.* A day on which some event is annually celebrated.

Annotate, an'nō-tāt, *vt.* (annotating, annotated). To write notes upon.

Announce, an-nouns', *vt.* (announcing, announced). To declare; to proclaim.

Annular, an'nū-lėr, *a.* Having the form of a ring; pertaining to a ring.

Annulose, an'nū-lōs, *a.* Having a body composed of rings; applied to annelids.

Annunciation, an-nun'si-ā''shon, *n.* The angel's salutation to the Virgin Mary, and its anniversary, the 25th of March.

Anode, an'ōd, *n.* The positive pole of a voltaic current.

Anodyne, an'ō-din, *n.* Any medicine which allays or mitigates pain.—*a.* Assuaging pain.

Anoint, a-noint', *vt.* To rub over with oil; to consecrate by unction.

Anomaly, a-nom'a-li, *n.* Irregularity; deviation from common rule.

Anonymous, a-non'im-us, *a.* Nameless; without the real name of the author.

Another, an-ụṬH'ėr, *a.* Not the same; different; any other.

Answer, an'sėr, *vt.* To reply to; to satisfy; to suit.—*vi.* To reply; to be accountable; to succeed.—*n.* A reply; a solution.

Antecedent, an-tē-sē'dent, *a.* Going before; prior.—*n.* That which goes before; the noun to which a relative refers; *pl.* a man's previous history, etc.

Antechamber, an'tē-chām-bėr, *n.* An apartment leading into a chief apartment.

Antedate, an'tē-dāt, *n.* Prior date.—*vt.* To date before the true time.

Anthem, an'them, *n.* A sacred song sung in alternate parts; a piece of Scripture set to music.

Anther, an'thėr, *n.* The summit of the stamen in a flower, containing the pollen.

Anthology, an-thol'o-ji, *n.* A collection of poems.

Anthracite, an'thra-sīt, *n.* A hard, compact coal which burns almost without flame.

Anthropoid, an'thrō-poid, *a.* Resembling man: applied to the higher apes.

Anthropology, an-thrō-pol'o-ji, *n.* The science of man and mankind; the study of the physical and mental constitution of man.

Anthropomorphism, an-thrō'pō-mor''fizm, *n.* The representation of a deity in human form, or with human attributes.

Antidote, an'ti-dōt, *n.* A remedy for poison or any evil.

Antimony, an'ti-mo-ni, *n.* A brittle, white-colored metal, used in the arts and in medicine.

Antinomian, an-ti-nō'mi-an, *n.* One who opposes the moral law.

Antipathy, an-tip'a-thi, *n.* Instinctive aversion; dislike; opposition.

Antiphlogistic, an'ti-flo-jis''tik, *a.* Counteracting inflammation.

Antiphrasis, an-tif'ra-sis, *n.* The use of words in a sense opposite to the proper one.

Antipodes, an-tip'o-dēz, *n.pl.* Those who live on opposite sides of the globe; the opposite side of the globe.

Antipyrin, an-ti-pī'rin, *n.* A drug used to reduce fever and relieve pain.

Antithesis, an-tith'e-sis, *n.*; pl. **-theses.** Opposition of thoughts or words; contrast.

Antitype, an'ti-tīp, *n.* That which is shadowed out by a type or emblem.

Antler, ant'lėr, *n.* A branch of a stag's horn.

Antonym, ant'ō-nim, *n.* A word of directly contrary signification to another: the opposite of a synonym.

Anus, ā'nus, *n.* The opening of the body by which excrement is expelled.

Anvil, an'vil, *n.* An iron block on which smiths hammer and shape

A

their work.

Apathy, ap'a-thi, n. Want of feeling; insensibility; indifference.

Ape, āp, n. A monkey; an imitator.— vt. (aping, aped). To imitate servilely; to mimic.

Aperture, ap'ėr-tūr, n. An opening; a hole.

Apex, ā'peks, n.; pl. -exes and -ices. The summit of anything.

Aphelion, a-fē'li-on, n.; pl. -lia. The point of a planet's orbit farthest from the sun.

Aphorism, af-or-izm, n. A precept expressed in few words; a maxim.

Apiary, ā'pi-a-ri, n. A place where bees are kept.

Apiece, a-pēs', adv. In a separate share; to each; noting the share of each.

Aplomb, a-plong, n. Self-possession.

Apocalypse, a-pok'a-lips, n. Revelation; the last book of the New Testament.

Apology, a-pol'ō-ji, n. That which is said in defense; vindication; excuse.

Apophthegm, Apothegm, ap'o-them, n. A terse, pointed saying.

Apoplexy, ap'ō-plek'si, n. A sudden privation of sense and voluntary motion.

Apostasy, a-pos'ta-si, n. Departure from one's faith; desertion of a party.

Apostle, a-pos'l, n. One sent to preach the gospel; one of the twelve disciples.

Apostrophe, a-pos'tro-fē, n. An addressing of the absent or the dead as if present; a mark (') indicating contraction of a word, or the possessive case.

Apothecary, a-poth'e-ka-ri, n. One who prepares and sells drugs or medicines.

Apotheosis, ap-o-thē'ō-sis or -thē-ō'sis, n. A deification; a placing among the gods.

Appal, ap-pal', vt. (appalling, appalled). To depress with fear; to dismay.

Apparatus, ap-pa-rā'tus, n.; pl. -tus, or -tuses, Set of instruments or utensils for performing any operation.

Apparel, ap-pa'rel, n. Equipment; clothing. vt. (apparelling, apparelled). To dress; to array.

Apparent, ap-pā'rent, a. That may be seen; evident; seeming, not real.

Apparition, ap-pa-ri'shon, n. An appearance; a specter; a ghost or phantom.

Appeal, ap-pēl', vi. To call; to refer to a superior court; to have recourse.—vt. To remove to a superior court.—n. The removal of a cause to a higher tribunal; a reference to another.

Appear, ap-pēr', vi. To be or become visible; to seem.

Appease, ap-pēz', vt. (appeasing, appeased). To pacify; to tranquilize.

Appetite, ap'pē-tīt, n. A desire or relish for food or other sensual gratifications.

Applaud, ap-plad', vt. To praise by clapping the hands, etc.; to extol.

Apple, ap'l, n. The fruit of the apple-tree; the pupil of the eye.

Appliance, ap-plī'ans, n. Act of applying; thing applied; article of equipment.

Applicable, ap'pli-ka-bl, a. That may be applied; suitable.

Apposition, ap-pō-zi'shon, n. In grammar, the relation of one noun to another, when it explains its meaning, while agreeing in case.

Appraise, ap-prāz', vt. (appraising, appraised). To fix or set a price on; to estimate.

Appreciate, ap-prē'shi-āt, vt. (appreciating, appreciated). To value; to estimate justly.

Apprehend, ap-prē-hend', vt. To take hold of; to arrest; to conceive; to fear.—vi. To think; to imagine.

Approbation, ap-prō-bā'shon, n. Approval; attestation; a liking.

Appropriate, ap-prō'pri-āt, vt. (appropriating, appropriated). To take to oneself as one's own; to set apart for.—a. Set apart for a particular use or person; suitable; adapted.

Appropriateness, ap-prō'pri-āt-nes, n. Peculiar fitness.

Approval, ap-pröv'al, n. Approbation.

Approve, ap-pröv', *vt.* (approving, approved). To deem good; to like; to sanction.—*vi.* To feel or express approbation (with *of*).

Approximate, ap-prok'si-māt, *a.* Near; approaching.—*vt.* (approximating, approximated). To bring near.—*vi.* To come near; to approach.

Aquarium, a-kwā'ri-um, *n.*; pl. - **iums** or **-ia.** A vessel or tank for aquatic plants and animals; a collection of such vessels.

Aquarius, a-kwā'ri-us, *n.* The water-bearer, a sign in the zodiac.

Aquatic, a-kwat'ik, *a.* Living or growing in water.—*n.* A plant which grows in water; *pl.* sports or exercises in water.

Aqueduct, ak'wē-dukt, *n.* A conduit made for conveying water.

Aqueous, ā'kwē-us, *a.* Watery.

Aquiline, ak'wil-īn, *a.* Belonging to the eagle; hooked like the beak of an eagle.

Arab, a'rab, *n.* A native of Arabia; a street urchin; an Arabian horse.

Arbiter, är'bit-ėr, *n.* A person appointed by parties in controversy to decide their differences; an umpire.

Arbitrary, är'bi-tra-ri, *a.* Depending on one's will; despotic.

Arbitrate, är'bi-trāt, *vi.* (arbitrating, arbitrated). To act as an arbiter; to decide.

Arbor, är'bėr, *n.* A bower; a shelter in a garden, formed of trees, etc.

Arboreous, är-bō'rē-us, *a.* Belonging to trees.

Arborescent, är-bor-es'sent, *a.* Growing like a tree; becoming woody.

Arboretum, är-bo-rē'tum, *n.* A place where trees are cultivated for scientific purposes.

Arbutus, är'bū-tus, *n.* An evergreen shrub, with berries like the strawberry.

Arc, ärk, *n.* A part of a circle or curve.

Arcade, är-kād', *n.* A walk arched above; an arched gallery; a covered passage containing shops.

Arcanum, är-kān'um, *n.*; pl. **-na.** Mystery.

Arch, ärch, *a.* Chief; cunning; sly; roguish.

Arch, ärch, *n.* A concave structure supported by its own curve; a vault.—*vt.* To cover with an arch; to form with a curve.

Archaic, är-kā'ik, *a.* Antiquated; obsolete.

Archaism, är'kā-izm, *n.* Obsolete word or expression.

Archangel, ärk-ān'jel, *n.* An angel of the highest order.

Archeology, är-kē-ol'o-ji, *n.* The science of antiquities; knowledge of ancient art.

Archipelago, är-ki-pel'a-gō, *n.* The Aegean Sea; a sea abounding in small islands.

Architect, är'ki-tekt, *n.* One who plans buildings, etc.; a contriver.

Architecture, är'ki-tek-tūr, *n.* The art or science of building; structure.

Ardent, är'dent, *a.* Burning; fervent; eager.

Ardor, är'dėr, *n.* Warmth; fervency; eagerness.

Ardous, är'dū-us, *a.* Difficult; laborios.

Are, är. The plural pres. indic. of the verb *to be.*

Area, ā'rē-a, *n.* Any open surface; superficial contents; any inclosed space.

Arena, a-rē'na, *n.* An open space of ground, strewed with sand or sawdust, for combatants; any place of public contest.

Argue, är'gū, *vi.* (arguing, argued). To offer reasons; to dispute.—*vt.* To show reasons for; to discuss.

Argument, är'gū-ment, *n.* A reason offered; a plea; subject of a discourse; heads of contents; controversy.

Argus, är'gus, *n.* A fabulous being with a hundred eyes; a watchful person.

Arian, ā'ri-an, *a.* Pertaining to Arius, who denied the divinity of Christ.—*n.* One who adheres to the doctrines of Arius.

Arid, a'rid, *a.* Dry; dried; parched.

Aries, ā'ri-ēz, *n.* The Ram, the first of the twelve signs of the zodiac.

Arise, a-rīz', *vi.* (arising, pret. arose, pp. arisen). To rise up; to proceed from.

Aristocracy, a-ris-tok'ra-si, *n.* Government by the nobility; the nobility.

Aristocrat, a'ris-to-krat, *n.* A noble; one who favors aristocracy.

Arithmetic, a-rith'met-ik, *n.* The science of numbering; the art of computation.

Ark, ärk, *n.* A chest; a large floating vessel.

Arm, ärm, *n.* The limb from the shoulder to the hand; anything extending from a main body; a weapon; *pl.* war; armor; armorial bearings.—*vt.* To furnish with arms; to fortify.—*vi.* To take up arms.

Armada, är-mä'da, *n.* A fleet of armed ships; a squadron.

Armadillo, är-ma-dil'lō, *n.* A quadruped of the southwestern U.S. with a hard bony shell.

Armament, ärm'a-ment, *n.* A force armed for war; war-munitions of a ship.

Armenian, är-mē'ni-an, *a.* Pertaining to Armenia.—*n.* A native of Armenia; the language of the country.

Armory, ärm'e-ri, *n.* A repository of arms.

Armpit, ärm'pit, *n.* The hollow place under the shoulder.

Army, är'mi, *n.* A body of men armed for war; a great number.

Aroma, a-rō'ma, *n.* Perfume; the fragrant principle in plants, etc.

Aromatic, a-rō-mat'ik, *a.* Fragrant; spicy.—*n.* A fragrant plant or drug.

Around, a-round', *prep.* About; on all sides of; encircling.—*adv.* On every side.

Arouse, a-rouz', *vt.* (arousing, aroused). To rouse; to stir up.

Arrest, a-rest', *vt.* To stop; to apprehend.—*n.* A seizure by warrant; stoppage.

Arrive, a-rīv', *vi.* (arriving, arrived). To come; to reach; to attain.

Arrogance, a'rō-gans, *n.* Assumption; haughtiness; insolent bearing.

Arson, är'son, *n.* The malicious setting on fire of a house, etc.

Art, ärt, *n.* Practical skill; a system of rules for certain actions; cunning; profession of a painter, etc.

Artery, är'te-ri, *n.* A tube which conveys blood from the heart.

Artesian, är-tē'zi-an, *a.* Designating a well made by boring till water is reached.

Artful, ärt'ful, *a.* Full of art; skilful; crafty.

Arthritis, är-thrī'tis, *n.* Gout.

Artichoke, är'ti-chōk, *n.* An esculent plant somewhat resembling a thistle.

Article, är'ti-kl, *n.* A separate item; stipulation; a particular commodity; a part of speech used before nouns, as *the.*—*vt.* To bind by articles.—*vi.* To stipulate.

Articulate, är-tik'ū-lāt, *a.* Distinct; clear.—*vi.* To utter distinct sounds, syllables, or words.—*vt.* To speak distinctly.

Articulation, är-tik'ū-lā''shon, *n.* Juncture of bones; joint; distinct utterance.

Artifice, ärt'i-fis, *n.* An artful device; fraud; stratagem.

Aryan, är-i-an or ā'ri-an, *a.* Indo-European; belonging to the Hindus, Persians, and most Europeans (except Turks, Hungarians, Finns, etc.), and to their languages.

As, az, *adv.* and *conj.* Like; even; equally; while; since; for example.

Asbestos, as-bes'tos, *n.* A mineral fibrous substance which is incombustible.

Ascend, as-send', *vi.* To rise; to go backward in order of time.—*vt.* To move upward upon; to climb.

Aseptic, a-sep'tik, *a.* Not liable to putrefy.

Ash, ash, *n.* A well-known timber tree.

Ashamed, a-shāmd', *a.* Affected by shame.

Ashes, ash'ez, *n.pl.* The dust produced by combustion; the remains of a dead body.

Ashlar, Ashler, ash'lèr, *n.* A facing of dressed stones on a wall; hewn stone.

Ashore, a-shōr', *adv.* or *pred.a.* On shore.

Askance, Askant, a-skans', a-skant', *adv.* Awry; obliquely.

Aslant, a-slant', *pred.a.* or *adv.* On

slant; obliquely; not perpendicularly.

Asleep, a-slēp', *pred.a.* or *adv.* Sleeping; at rest.

Aslope, a-slōp', *pred.a.* or *adv.* On slope; obliquely.

Asp, asp, *n.* A small venomous serpent of Egypt.

Asparagus, as-pa'ra-gus, *n.* A well-known esculent plant.

Aspect, as'pekt, *n.* Appearance; situation.

Aspen, asp'en, *n.* A species of the poplar.

Asperity, as-pe'ri-ti, *n.* Roughness; harshness.

Asperse, as-pėrs', *vt.* (aspersing, aspersed). To calumniate; to slander.

Asphalt, as-falt', *n.* A bituminous, hard substance, used for pavement, etc.

Asphodel, as'fō-del, *n.* A kind of lily.

Asphyxia, as-fik'si-a, *n.* Suspended animation from suffocation, etc.

Aspirant, as-pīr'ant, *n.* A candidate.

Aspirate, as'pi-rāt, *vt.* (aspirating, aspirated). To pronounce with an audible breath; to add an *h*-sound to.—*n.* An aspirated letter.

Aspire, as-pīr', *vi.* (aspiring, aspired). To aim at high things; to soar.

Asquint, a-skwint', *adv.* Out of the corner or angle of the eye; obliquely.

Ass, as, *n.* A well-known animal skin to the horse; a dolt.

Assail, as-sāl', *vt.* To attack; to assault.

Assemble, as-sem'bl, *vt.* (assembling, assembled). To bring together.—*vi.* To come together.

Assembly, as-sem'bli, *n.* An assemblage; a convocation.

Assent, as-sent', *n.* Act of agreeing to anything; consent.—*vi.* To agree; to yield.

Assert, as-sėrt', *vt.* To affirm; to maintain; to vindicate.

Assiduous, as-sid'ū-us, *a.* Constantly diligent.

Assign, as-sīn', *vt.* To designate; to allot; to make over to another.—*n.* A person to whom property or any right may be or is transferred.

Assignation, as-sig-nā'shon, *n.* An appointment to meet, as of lovers; a making over by transfer of title.

Assignment, as-sīn'ment, *n.* Act of assigning; thing assigned; a writ of transfer.

Assimilate, as-sim'il-āt, *vt.* (assimilating, assimilated). To make like to; to digest.—*vi.* To become similar or of the same substance.

Assist, as-sist', *vt.* To help.—*vi.* To lend help; to contribute.

Assistance, as-sist'ans, *n.* Help; aid.

Associate, as-sō'shi-āt, *vt.* (associating, associated). To join in company with; to combine.—*vi.* To keep company with.—*n.* A companion; friend.

Assuage, as-swāj', *vt.* (assuaging, assuaged). To allay; to calm.—*vi.* To abate or subside.

Assume, as-sūm', *vt.* (assuming, assumed). To take for granted; to usurp.—*vi.* To claim more than is due; to be arrogant.

Assumption, as-sum'shon, *n.* Act of assuming; the thing assumed; the taking up of any person into heaven.

Assurance, a-shör'ans, *n.* Act of assuring; secure confidence; impudence; positive declaration; insurance.

Assure, a-shör', *vt.* (assuring, assured). To make sure; to confirm; to insure.

Astern, a-stėrn', *adv.* In or at the hinder part of a ship.

Asteroid, as'tėr-oid, *n.* A small planet.

Asthma, as'ma or as'thma, *n.* A disorder of respiration, characterized by difficulty of breathing, cough, and expectoration.

Astigmatism, a-stig'mat-izm, *n.* A malformation of the eye, in which rays of light do not properly converge to one point.

Astonish, as-ton'ish, *vt.* To surprise; to astound.

Astound, as-tound', *vt.* To astonish; to stun; to strike dumb with amazement.

Astrology, as-trol'o-ji, *n.* The pretended art of foretelling future events from the stars.

Astronomy, as-tron'o-mi, *n.* The science of the heavenly bodies.

Astute, as-tūt´, a. Shrewd; crafty.

Asunder, a-sun´dèr, adv. or pred.a. Apart; into parts; in a divided state.

Asylum, a-sī´lum, n. A place of refuge; an institution for the care or relief of the unfortunate.

At, at, prep. Denoting presence or nearness; in a state of; employed in, on, or with; with direction towards.

Atavism, at´a-vizm, n. The resemblance of offspring to a remote ancestor.

Athlete, ath-lēt´, n. One skilled in exercises of agility or strength.

Athletics, ath-let´iks, n.pl. Athletic exercises.

Athwart, a-thwart´, prep. Across; from side to side.—adv. Crossly; wrong.

Atlantean, at-lan-tē´an, a. Gigantic.

Atlantic, at-lan´tik, a. Pertaining to the ocean between Europe, Africa, and America.—n. This ocean.

Atlas, at´las, n. A collection of maps.

Atmosphere, at´mos-fèr, n. The mass of gas around the earth; air; pervading influence.

Atoll, a-tol´, n. A ring-shaped coral island.

Atom, a´tom, n. A minute particle of matter; anything extremely small.

Atomic bomb, a-tom´ik bom, n. A bomb in which the splitting of atoms causes vast heating and explosion on a catastrophic scale.

Atomism, at´om-izm, n. Atomic philosophy; the doctrine that atoms of themselves formed the universe.

Atone, a-tōn´, vi. (atoning, atoned). To make satisfaction.—vt. To expiate.

Attaché, at-ta-shā´, n. One attached to the suite of an ambassador. **Attaché case,** n. A small oblong case of leather or fiber, for carrying documents, books, etc.

Attack, at-tak´, vt. To assault; to assail.—n. An assault; seizure by a disease.

Attain, at-tān´, vi. To come or arrive.—vt. To reach; to gain; to obtain.

Attention, at-ten´shon, n. Act of attending; heed; courtesy.

Attentive, at-tent´iv, a. Heedful.

Attenuate, at-ten´ū-āt, vt. (attenuating, attenuated). To make slender or thin (as liquids).—vi. To diminish.

Attest, at-test´, vt. To bear witness to; to certify; to call to witness.

Attestation, at-test-ā´shon, n. Testimony.

Attic, at´tik, a. Pertaining to Attica or to Athens; pure; elegant in style or language.—n. The dialect of Attica or Athens; the uppermost story of a building; garret.

Attire, at-tīr´, vt. (attiring, attired). To dress; to array.—n. Dress.

Attitude, at´ti-tūd, n. Posture.

Attorney, at-tèr´ni, n. One who acts in place of another; one who practices in law-courts.

Attract, at-trakt´, vt. To draw to; to entice.

Attractive, at-trakt´iv, a. Having the power of attracting; enticing.

Attribute, at-trib´ūt, vt. (attributing, attributed). To ascribe; to impute.—n. at´tri-būt. Inherent property; characteristic; an adjectival word or clause.

Attrition, at-tri´shon, n. Act of wearing, or state of being worn, by rubbing.

Audit, a´dit, n. An official examination of accounts.—vt. To examine and adjust, as accounts.

Auditory, a´di-tō-ri, a. Pertaining to the sense or organs of hearing.—n. An audience; an auditorium.

Augean, a-jē´an, a. Pertaining to Augeas, King of Elis, in Greece, whose stable for 3000 oxen, uncleaned for thirty years, was cleaned by Hercules in one day.

Auger, a´gèr, n. An instrument for boring holes.

August, a´gust, n. The eighth month of the year.

Auk, ak, n. A swimming bird found in the British seas, with very short wings.

Aunt, änt, n. The sister of one's father or mother.

Aureate, a-rē´āt, a. Golden.

Aurelia, a-rē´li-a, n. The chrysalis

of an insect.

Aureola, Aureole, a̯-rē'o-la, a̯'rē-ōl, *n.* An illumination represented as surrounding a holy person, as Christ; a halo.

Aurora Borealis, a̯-rō'ra bō-rē-ā'lis, *n.* The northern lights or streamers.—**Aurora Australis,** a similar phenomenon in the S. hemisphere.

Auscultation, a̯s-kul-tā'shon, *n.* A method of discovering diseases of the lungs, etc., by listening for the sounds arising there.

Auspice, a̯'spis, *n.* Augury from birds; protection; influence.

Auspicious, a̯-spi'shus, *a.* Fortunate; propitious.

Austere, a̯-stēr', *a.* Rigid; sour; stern; severe.

Autocracy, a̯-tok'ra-si, *n.* Absolute government by one man.

Auto-de-fe, au'tō-de-fā'', *n.*; pl. **Autos-de-fe.** The burning of heretics by authority of the Inquisition. **Auto-da-fe,** ou'tō-dä-fā'', is the Portuguese form.

Autograph, a̯'tō-graf, *n.* A person's own handwriting; signature.

Automatic, a̯-tō-mat'ik.—*a.* Self-acting; moving spontaneously.—*n.* A pistol which is reloaded by force of the recoil.

Automaton, a̯-tom'a-ton, *n.*; pl. **-ta.** A self-moving machine, or one which moves by invisible machinery.

Automobile, a̯'tō-mō-bēl'', *n.* A motor-car or similar vehicle.

Autonomy, a̯-ton'o-mi, *n.* The power or right of self-government.

Autopsy, a̯'top-si, *n.* Personal observation; post-mortem examination.

Autumn, a̯'tum, *n.* The third season of the year, between summer and winter.

Auxiliary, ag-zil'i-a-ri, *a.* Aiding.—*n.* One who aids; a verb which helps to form the moods and tenses of other verbs; *pl.* foreign troops employed in war.

Avail, a-vāl', *vt.* To profit; to promote.—*vi.* To be of use; to answer the purpose.—*n.* Advantage; use.

Avalanche, av'a-lansh, *n.* A large body of snow or ice sliding down a mountain.

Avarice, av'a-ris, *n.* Covetousness.

Average, av'er-āj, *n.* Medium; mean proportion.—*a.* Medial; containing a mean proportion.—*vt.* To find the mean of.—*vi.* To form a mean.

Avidity, a-vid'i-ti, *n.* Eager desire; greediness; strong appetite.

Avocation, av-ō-kā'shon, *n.* Business; occupation.

Avoid, a-void', *vt.* To shun; to evade; to make void.

Avoirdupois, av'er-dū-poiz'', *n.* or *a.* A system of weight, in which a pound contains sixteen ounces.

Avow, a-vou', *vt.* To declare with confidence; to confess frankly.

Await, a-wāt', *vt.* To wait for; to expect; to be in store for.

Awake, a-wāk', *vt.* (awaking, pret. woke, awaked, pp. awaked). To rouse from sleep or from a state of inaction.—*vi.* To cease from sleep; to rouse oneself.—*a.* Not sleeping; vigilant.

Award, a-ward', *vt.* To adjudge.—*vi.* To make an award.—*n.* A judgment; decision of arbitrators.

Aware, a-wār', *a.* Informed; conscious.

Away, a-wā', *adv.* Absent; at a distance; in motion from; by degrees; in continuance.—*exclam.* Begone!

Awe, a̯, *n.* Fear; fear mingled with reverence.—*vt.* (awing, awed). To strike with fear and reverence.

Awful, a̯'ful, *a.* Filling with awe; terrible.

Awhile, a-whil', *adv.* For some time.

Awkward, ak'werd, *a.* Inexpert; inelegant.

Awkwardly, ak'werd-li, *adv.* In a bungling manner; inelegantly.

Awl, a̯l, *n.* A pointed iron instrument for piercing small holes in leather.

Awn, a̯n, *n.* The beard of corn or grass.

Awning, a̯n'ing, *n.* A cover of canvas, etc., to shelter from the sun or wind.

Awry, a-rī, *pred.a.* or *adv.* Twisted toward one side; distorted; asquint.

Axe, aks, *n.* An instrument for hewing and chopping.

Axilla, aks-il'la, *n.* The arm-pit.

Axiom, aks'i-om, *n.* A self-evident

truth; an established principle.

Azoic, a-zō'ik, *a*. Destitute of organic life.

Azote, az'ōt, *n*. Nitrogen.

Azure, ā'zhūr, *a*. Sky-colored.—*n*. The fine blue color of the sky; the sky.

B

Baccarat, bak-ka-rä, *n*. A game of cards played by any number and a banker.

Bacchanal, bak'ka-nal, *n*. A votary of Bacchus; a revel.—*a*. Characterized by intemperate drinking.

Bachelor, bach'el-ėr, *n*. An unmarried man; one who has taken the university degree below that of Master or Doctor.

Bacillus, ba-sil'lus, *n*.; pl. -**illi**. A microscopic organism which causes disease.

Back, bak, *n*. The hinder part of the body in man and the upper part in beasts; the hinder part.—*vt*. To support; to cause to recede; to endorse.—*vi*. To move back.—*adv*. To the rear; to a former state; in return.

Backbite, bak'bīt, *vt*. To speak evil of secretly.

Backbone, bak'bōn, *n*. The spine; strength.

Bacon, bā'kn, *n*. Swine's flesh cured and dried.

Bacteriology, bak-tē'ri-ol''o-ji, *n*. The doctrine or study of bacteria.

Bacterium, bak-tē'ri-um, *n*.; pl. -**ia**. A disease germ.

Bad, bad, *a*. Not good; wicked; immoral; injurious; incompetent.

Badge, baj, *n*. A mark or cognizance worn.

Badger, baj'ėr, *n*. A burrowing quadruped, nocturnal in habits.—*vt*. To worry; to pester.

Bagnio, ban'yō, *n*. A bath; brothel; prison.

Bagpipe, bag'pīp, *n*. A musical wind-instrument.

Bail, bāl, *vt*. To liberate from custody on security for reappearance; to free (a boat) from water; to bale.—*n*. Security given for release; the person who gives such security.

Bailiff, bā'lif, *n*. A subordinate civil officer; a steward.

Bailiwick, bā'li-wik, *n*. The extent or limit of a bailiff's jurisdiction.

Balance, bal'ans, *n*. A pair of scales; equilibrium; surplus; difference of two sums; the sum due on an account.—*vt*. (balancing, balanced). To bring to an equilibrium; to weigh, as reasons; to settle, as an account.—*vi*. To be in equilibrium; to be equal when added up; to hesitate.

Balcony, bal'ko-ni, *n*. A platform projecting from a window.

Bald, bald, *a*. Wanting hair; unadorned; bare; paltry.

Bale, bāl, *n*. A bundle or package of goods.—*vt*. (baling, baled). To make up in a bale; to free from water; to bail. **Bale out,** *vi*. To leave aircraft by parachute.

Baleful, bāl'ful, *a*. Calamitous; deadly.

Balk, bak, *n*. A ridge of land left unploughed; a great beam; a barrier; a disappointment.—*vt*. To baffle; to disappoint.

Ball, bal, *n*. A round body; a globe; a bullet; an entertainment of dancing.—*vi*. To form, as snow, into balls, as on horses' hoofs.

Ballad, bal'lad, *n*. A short narrative poem; a popular song.

Ballot, bal'lot, *n*. A ball, paper, etc., used for voting in private; the system of voting by such means.—*vi*. To vote by ballot.

Balm, bäm, *n*. Balsam; that which heals or soothes; the name of several aromatic plants.—*vt*. To anoint with balm; to soothe.

Balsam, bal'sam, *n*. An oily, aromatic substance got from trees; a soothing ointment.

Band, band, *n*. That which binds; a bond; a fillet; a company; a body of musicians.—*vt*. To bind together; to unite in a troop or confederacy.—*vi*. To unite in a band.

Bandage, band'āj, *n*. A band; a cloth for a wound, etc.—*vt*. (bandaging, bandaged). To bind with a bandage.

Bandbox, band'boks, *n*. A slight

box for caps, bonnets, etc.

Bandit, ban'dit, *n.*; pl. **-itti, -its.** An outlaw; a robber; a highwayman.

Bandolier, ban-dō-lēr', *n.* A shoulder-belt for carrying cartridges.

Bandy, ban'di, *n.* A bent club for striking a ball; a play at ball with such a club.—*vt.* (bandying, bandied). To strike to and fro; to exchange (compliments, etc.).

Bank, bangk, *n.* Ground rising from the side of a river, lake, etc.; any heap piled up; a bench of rowers; place where money is deposited; a banking company.—*vt.* To fortify with a bank; to deposit in a bank.

Bankrupt, bangk'rupt, *n.* One who cannot pay his debts.—*a.* Unable to pay debts.

Banner, ban'nėr, *n.* A flag bearing a device or national emblem; a standard.

Banquet, bang'kwet, *n.* A feast; a sumptuous entertainment.—*vt.* To treat with a feast.—*vi.* To feast.

Banshee, ban'shē, *n.* An Irish fairy believed to attach herself to a house or family.

Bantam, ban'tam, *n.* A small breed of domestic fowl with feathered shanks.

Banter, ban'tėr, *vt.* To attack with jocularity; to rally.—*n.* Raillery; pleasantry.

Barb, bärb, *n.* The points which stand backward in an arrow, hook, etc.; a Barbary horse.—*vt.* To furnish with barbs or points.

Barbarian, bär-bā'ri-an, *a.* Belonging to savages; uncivilized.—*n.* A savage.

Barbarous, bär'bär-us, *a.* In a state of barbarism; cruel; inhuman.

Barbecue, bär-be-kū, *n.* A hog, etc., roasted whole; a feast in the open air.—*vt.* To dress and roast whole.

Barber, bär'bėr, *n.* One who shaves beards and dresses hair.

Barge, bärj, *n.* A boat of pleasure or state; a flat-bottomed boat of burden.

Baritone, ba'ri-tōn, *a.* Having a voice ranging between tenor and bass.—*n.* A male voice between tenor and bass.

Bark, bärk, *n.* The outer rind of a tree; a barque; the noise made by a dog, wolf, etc.—*vt.* To strip bark off; to treat with bark; to make the cry of dogs, etc.

Barley, bär'li, *n.* A species of grain used especially for making malt.

Barmaid, bär'mād, *n.* A woman who tends a bar where liquors are sold.

Barn, bärn, *n.* A building for grain, hay, etc.

Barnacle, bär'na-kl, *n.* A shell-fish, often found on ships' bottoms; a species of goose.

Barrel, ba'rel, *n.* A round wooden cask; the quantity which a barrel holds; a hollow cylinder.—*vt.* (barreling, barreled). To pack in a barrel.

Barren, ba'ren, *a.* Sterile; unfruitful; unsuggestive.

Barricade, ba-ri-kād', *n.* A temporary fortification to obstruct an enemy; a barrier.—*vt.* To obstruct; to bar.

Barrier, ba'ri-ėr, *n.* Fence; obstruction.

Barrister, ba'ris-tėr, *n.* A counselor at law; a lawyer whose profession is to speak in court on behalf of clients.

Barrow, ba'rō, *n.* A small hand or wheel carriage; a sepulchral mound.

Barter, bär'tėr, *vi.* To traffic by exchange.—*vt.* To exchange in commerce.—*n.* Traffic by exchange.

Basalt, ba-zalt', *n.* A dark volcanic rock, often found in columnar form.

Bascule, bas'kūl, *n.* An arrangement in bridges by which one part balances another.

Base, bās, *a.* Low in value or station; worthless; despicable.—*n.* Foundation; lower side; support; chief ingredient of a compound; the gravest part in music.—*vt.* (basing, based). To place on a basis; to found.

Basilisk, baz'il-isk, *n.* A fabulous serpent, lizard, or cockatrice; a genus of crested lizards; an old kind of cannon.

Basin, bā'sn, *n.* A broad circular dish; a reservoir; a dock; tract of country drained by a river.

Basis, bās'is, *n.*; pl. **-ses.** A base; foundation; groundwork.

Bask, bask, *vt.* To lie in warmth, or in the sun; to enjoy ease and prosperity.—*vt.* To warm by exposure to heat.

Basket, bas'ket, *n.* A domestic vessel made of twigs, etc.; the contents of a basket.—*vt.* To put in a basket.

Bass, bäs, *n.* The American linden; a mat made of bast; a fish allied to the perch.

Bass, bās, *n.* The lowest part in musical harmony; the lowest male voice.

Bastion, bas'ti-on, *n.* A large mass of earth or masonry standing out from a rampart.

Bat, bat, *n.* A flying mammal, like a mouse; a heavy stick; a club used to strike the ball in cricket, etc.—*vi.* (batting, batted). To play with a bat.

Batch, bach, *n.* Quantity of bread baked at one time; a quantity.

Bath, bäth, *n.* Place to bathe in; immersion in water, etc.; a Jewish measure.

Bathe, bāTH, *vt.* (bathing, bathed). To immerse in water, etc.—*vi.* To take a bath.

Battle, bat'l, *n.* Encounter of two armies; a combat.—*vi.* (battling, battled). To contend in fight.

Bayonet, bā'on-et, *n.* A dagger-like weapon fixed to a rifle.—*vt.* (bayoneting, bayoneted). To stab with a bayonet.

Be, bē, *vi. substantive* (being, been; pres. am, art, is, are; pret. was, wast or wert, were). To exist; to become; to remain.

Beach, bēch, *n.* The shore of the sea.—*vt.* To run (a vessel) on a beach.

Beacon, bē'kn, *n.* A light to direct seamen; a signal of danger.—*vt.* To afford light, as a beacon; to light up.

Beaker, bēk'ėr, *n.* A large drinking-cup.

Beam, bēm, *n.* A main timber in a building; part of a balance which sustains the scales; pole of a carriage; a ray of light.—*vt.* To send forth, as beams; to emit.—*vi.* To shine.

Bean, bēn, *n.* A name of several kinds of pulse.

Bear, bār, *vt.* (bearing, pret. bore, pp. borne). To carry; to suffer; to produce; to have; to permit; to behave (oneself).—*vi.* To suffer; to be patient; to produce; to take effect; to be situated as to the point of the compass; to refer (with *upon*).

Bear, bār, *n.* A large carnivorous plantigrade quadruped; one of two constellations, the Greater and Lesser; an uncouth person; one who tries to bring down the price of stock.

Beard, bērd, *n.* The hair on the chin, etc.; the awn of corn.—*vt.* To defy to the face.

Beast, bēst, *n.* Any four-footed animal; a brutal man.

Beat, bēt, *vt.* (beating, pret. beat, pp. beat, beaten). To strike repeatedly; to overcome; to crush; to harass.—*vi.* To throb, as a pulse; to sail against the wind.—*n.* A stroke; a pulsation; a course frequently trodden.

Beatify, bē-at'i-fī, *vt.* (beatifying, beatified). To make happy; to declare a person blessed.

Beating, bēt'ing, *n.* Act of striking; chastisement by blows; a conquering; defeat.

Beatitude, bē-at'i-tūd, *n.* Blessedness; bliss; one of the declarations of blessedness to particular virtues made by Christ.

Beauty, bū'ti, *n.* Loveliness; elegance; grace; a beautiful woman.

Beaver, bē'vėr, *n.* A rodent quadruped; beaver-fur, or a hat made of it; the face-guard of a helmet; a visor.—*a.* Made of beaver, or of its fur.

Because, bē-kaz', By cause; on this account that.

Bed, bed, *n.* Something to sleep or rest on; the channel of a river; place where anything is deposited; a layer; a stratum.—*vt.* (bedding, bedded). To lay in a bed; to sow; to stratify.—*vi.* To go to bed.

Bedchamber, bed'chäm-bėr, *n.* An apartment for a bed.

Bedizen, bē-dī'zn, *vt.* To adorn gaudily.

Bedouin, bed'ö-in, *n.* A nomadic

Arab living in tents in Arabia, Syria, Egypt, etc.

Bedraggle, bē-drag'l, *vt.* To soil by drawing along on mud.

Bedrid, Bedridden, bed'rid, bed'rid-n, *a.* Confined to bed by age or infirmity.

Bedroom, bed'röm, *n.* A sleeping apartment.

Bedstead, bed'sted, *n.* A frame for supporting a bed.

Bee, bē, *n.* The insect that makes honey.

Beech, bēch, *n.* A large smooth-barked tree yielding a hard timber and nuts.

Beef, bēf, *n.* The flesh of an ox, bull, or cow.—*a.* Consisting of such flesh.

Befit, bē-fit', *vt.* To suit; to become.

Before, bē-fōr', *prep.* In front of; in presence of; earlier than; in preference to.—*adv.* In time preceding; further; onward; in front.

Beforehand, bē-fōr'hand, *a.* In good pecuniary circumstances.—*adv.* In advance.

Beg, beg, *vt.* (begging, begged). To ask in charity; to ask earnestly; to take for granted.—*vi.* To ask or live upon alms.

Beget, bē-get', *vt.* (begetting, pp. begot, begotten, pret. begot). To procreate; to produce.

Beggar, beg'gėr, *n.* One who begs.—*vt.* To impoverish.

Begin, bē-gin', *vi.* (pp. begun, pret. began). To take rise; to do the first act; to commence.—*vt.* To enter on; to originate.

Beige, bāzh, *n.* A fabric made of unbleached or undyed wool; a greyish-brown color.

Being, bē'ing, *n.* Existence; a creature.

Belabor, bē-lā'bėr, *vt.* To beat soundly; to thump.

Belated, bē-lāt'ed, *p.a.* Made late; benighted.

Belch, belch, *vt.* To eject, as wind from the stomach; to cast forth violently.—*vi.* To eject wind from the stomach; to issue out, as by eructation.—*n.* Eructation.

Believe, bē-lēv', *vt.* (believing, believed). To give belief to; to credit; to expect with confidence.—*vi.* To

have a firm persuasion.

Belittle, bē-lit'l, *vt.* To make smaller; to speak disparagingly of.

Bell, bel, *n.* A metallic vessel used for giving sounds by being struck; anything in form of a bell.—*vi.* To flower.—*vt.* To put a bell on.

Belladonna, bel-la-don'na, *n.* A European plant yielding a powerful medicine.

Belle, bel, *n.* A lady of great beauty.

Belles-lettres, bel-let'tr, *n.pl.* Polite literature, including poetry, rhetoric, history, etc.

Bellicose, bel'li-kōs, *a.* Warlike; pugnacious.

Belligerent, bel-lij'ėr-ent, *a.* Waging war.—*n.* A nation or state waging war.

Bellow, bel'ō, *vi.* To make a hollow loud noise, as a bull; to roar.—*n.* A roar.

Bellows, bel'ōz, *n.sing.* and *pl.* An instrument for blowing fires, supplying wind to organ-pipes, etc.

Bell-wether, bel'weTH-ėr, *n.* A sheep which leads the flock with a bell on his neck.

Belly, bel'li, *n.* That part of the body which contains the bowels.—*vt.* and *i.* (bellying, bellied). To swell, bulge.

Belong, bē-long', *vi.* To be the property; to appertain; to be connected; to have original residence.

Below, bē-lō', *prep.* Under in place; beneath; unworthy of.—*adv.* In a lower place; beneath; on earth; in hell.

Belt, belt, *n.* A girdle; a band.—*vt.* To encircle.

Bemoan, bē-mōn', *vt.* To lament; bewail.

Bemused, bē-mūzd', *a.* Muddled; stupefied.

Bench, bensh, *n.* A long seat; seat of justice; body of judges.—*vt.* To furnish with benches.

Bend, bend, *vt.* (pp. and pret. bent and bended). To curve; to direct to a certain point; to subdue.—*vi.* To become crooked; to lean or turn; to yield.—*n.* A curve.

Beneath, bē-nēth', *prep.* Under; lower in place, rank, dignity, etc.; unworthy of.—*adv.* In a lower

B

place; below.

Benediction, ben-ē-dik'shon, n. Act of blessing; invocation of happiness.

Benefaction, ben-ē-fak'shon, n. The doing of a benefit; a benefit conferred.

Benefactor, ben-ē-fak'tėr, n. He who confers a benefit.

Benefit, ben'ē-fit, n. An act of kindness; a favor; advantage.—vt. To do a service to.—vi. To gain advantage.

Benevolent, bē-nev'ō-lent, a. Kind; charitable.

Benumb, bē-num', vt. To deprive of sensation; to make torpid; to stupefy.

Benzene, ben'zēn, n. A liquid used to remove grease spots, etc.

Beri-beri, ber'i-ber'i, n. A dangerous disease endemic in parts of India and Ceylon, characterized by paralysis, difficult breathing, and other symptoms.

Beset, bē-set', vt. (besetting, beset). To surround; to press on all sides.

Beside, Besides, bē-sīd', bē-sīdz', prep. By the side of; near; over and above; distinct from.—adv. Moreover; in addition.

Besiege, bē-sēj', vt. (besieging, besieged). To lay siege to; to beset.

Besom, bē'zum, n. A brush of twigs; a broom.

Besot, bē-sot', vt. (besotting, besotted). To make sottish.

Bespangle, bē-spang'gl, vt. To adorn with spangles.

Bespatter, bē-spat'tėr, vt. To spatter over.

Bespeak, bē-spēk', vt. (pp. bespoke, bespoken, pret. bespoke). To speak for beforehand; to indicate.

Bessemer-steel, bes'e-mėr-stēl, n. Steel made directly from molten cast-iron by driving through it air to carry off impurities.

Best, best, a.superl. Most good; having good qualities in the highest degree; exceeding all.—n. The utmost; highest endeavor.—adv. In the highest degree; beyond all others.

Bestial, bes'ti-al, a. Belonging to a beast; brutish; vile.

Bestiary, bes'ti-a-ri, n. A book of the middle ages treating fancifully of beasts.

Bestir, bē-stėr', vt. To stir up; to put into brisk action. (Usually with refl. pron.)

Bestow, bē-stō', vt. To lay up; to give; to confer; to dispose of; to apply.

Bestride, bē-strīd', vt. (pp. bestrid, bestridden, pret. bestrid, bestrode). To stride over; to place a leg on each side of.

Bet, bet, n. A wager; that which is pledged in a contest.—vt. (betting, betted). To wager.

Betray, bē-trā', vt. To disclose treacherously; to entrap.

Betroth, bē-trōṪH', vt. To affiance; to pledge to marriage.

Better, bet'tėr, a.comp. More good; improved.—adv. More excellently; in a higher degree.—vt. To make better; to advance.—n. A superior (generally in pl.).

Between, bē-twēn', prep. In the middle; from one to another of; belonging to two.

Bevel, be'vel, n. An instrument for taking angles; an angle not a right angle.—a. Slant; oblique.—vt. (beveling, beveled). To cut to a bevel angle.

Beverage, bev'ėr-āj, n. Drink; liquor.

Bevy, be'vi, n. A flock of birds; a company of females.

Bewail, bē-wāl', vt. To lament.—vi. To utter deep grief.

Beware, bē-wār', vi. To take care (with of).

Bewilder, bē-wil'dėr, vt. To confuse; to perplex.

Bewitch, bē-wich', vt. To enchant; to fascinate; to overpower by charms.

Beyond, bē-yond', prep. On the further side of; farther onward than; out of the reach of; above.—adv. At a distance.

Bible, bī'bl, n. The Holy Scriptures.

Bibliography, bib-li-og'ra-fi, n. A history of books and their editions; list of books by one author or on one subject.

Bicycle, bī'si-kl, n. A two-wheeled vehicle propelled by the rider.

Bid, bid, vt. (bidding, pp. bid, bidden,

pret. bid, bade). To ask; to order; to offer.—*n*. An offer, as at an auction.

Bidding, bid'ing, *n*. Invitation; order; offer.

Bide, bīd, *vi*. (biding, bode). To dwell; to remain.—*vt*. To endure; to abide.

Biennial, bī-en'ni-al, *a*. Continuing for two years; taking place once in two years.—*n*. A plant which lives two years.

Bier, bēr, *n*. A carriage or frame for conveying a corpse to the grave.

Bile, bīl, *n*. A yellowish bitter liquid secreted in the liver; spleen; anger.

Bilge, bilj, *n*. The protuberant part of a cask; the breadth of a ship's bottom.—*vi*. (bilging, bilged). To leak in the bilge.

Bilingual, bī-lin'gwal, *a*. In two languages.

Biliteral, bī-lit'ėr-al, *a*. Consisting of two letters.

Bilk, bilk, *vt*. To defraud; to elude.

Bill, bil, *n*. The beak of a bird; anything resembling a bird's beak; an instrument for pruning, etc.; a military weapon now obsolete; an account of money due; draught of a proposed new law; a placard.—*vi*. To join bills, as doves; to fondle.—*vt*. To announce by bill; to stick bills on.

Bimetallism, bī-met'al-izm, *n*. A system of currency which recognizes silver and gold as legal tender to any amount.

Bimonthly, bī-munth'li, *a*. Occurring every two months.

Bin, bin, *n*. A receptacle for corn, etc.; a partition in a wine-cellar.

Binary, bī'na-ri, *a*. Twofold.

Bind, bīnd, *vt*. (binding, bound). To tie; to confine; to oblige; to cover (a book); to render costive; to make firm.—*vi*. To grow hard; to be obligatory.

Biographer, bī-og'ra-fėr, *n*. A writer of biography.

Biography, bī-og'ra-fi, *n*. An account of one's life and character.

Biology, bī-ol'o-ji, *n*. The science of life.

Bioplasm, bī'ō-plazm, *n*. The germinal matter in plants and animals.

Bipartite, bī-pärt'īt, *a*. Having two parts.

Biped, bī'ped, *n*. An animal with two feet.

Birch, bėrch, *n*. A tree having small leaves, white bark, and a fragrant odor.

Bismuth, bis'muth, *n*. A brittle yellowish or reddish-white metal.

Bison, bī'zon, *n*. A quadruped of the ox family; the American buffalo.

Bisque, bisk, *n*. Unglazed white porcelain; odds given at tennis, etc.

Bit, bit, *n*. A morsel; fragment; the metal part of a bridle inserted in a horse's mouth; a boring tool.—*vt*. (bitting, bitted). To put the bit in the mouth.

Bitch, bich, *n*. A female dog; a name of reproach for a woman.

Bite, bīt, *vt*. (biting, pp. bit, bitten, pret. bit). To crush or sever with the teeth; to cause to smart; to wound by reproach, etc.; to corrode.—*n*. Act of biting; wound made by biting; a mouthful.

Biting, bīt'ing, *p.a*. Sharp; severe; sarcastic.

Bitter, bit'ėr, *a*. Sharp to the taste; severe; painful; calamitous; distressing.

Biweekly, bī-wēk'li, *a*. Occurring every two weeks.

Bizarre, bi-zär', *a*. Odd; fantastical.

Blab, blab, *vt*. (blabbing, blabbed). To tell indiscreetly.—*vi*. To talk indiscreetly.

Black, blak, *a*. Destitute of light; dark; gloomy; sullen; astrocious; wicked.—*n*. The darkest color; a negro.—*vt*. To make black.

Black-ball, blak'bal, *n*. A composition for blacking shoes; a ball used as a negative in voting.—*vt*. To reject by private voting.

Blackberry, blak'be-ri, *n*. A plant of the bramble kind, and its fruit.

Blackbird, blak'bėrd, *n*. A species of thrush.

Blackboard, blak'bōrd, *n*. A board for writing on with chalk for instruction.

Blacken, blak'n, *vt*. To make black; to defame.—*vi*. To grow black or dark.

Blackguard, blak'gärd or bla'gärd, *n*. A scoundrel.—*vt*. To revile in scurrilous language.

Black-sheep, blak´shēp, *n*. One whose conduct is discreditable.

Blacksmith, blak´smith, *n*. A smith who works in iron.

Blackthorn, blak´thorn, *n*. The sloe.

Bladder, blad´ėr, *n*. A thin sac in animals containing the urine, bile, etc.; a blister; anything like the animal bladder.

Blade, blād, *n*. A leaf; cutting part of a sword, knife, etc.; flat part of an oar.

Blame, blām, *vt*. (blaming, blamed). To censure; to reprimand.—*n*. Censure; fault.

Blanch, blansh, *vt*. To make white.—*vi*. To grow white; to bleach.

Blare, blār, *vi*. (blaring, blared). To give forth a loud sound.—*vt*. To sound loudly; to proclaim noisily.—*n*. Sound like that of a trumpet; roar.

Blarney, blär´ni, *n*. Excessively complimentary language; gammon.—*vt*. To flatter.

Blasé, blä-zā, *a*. Satiated; used up; bored.

Blaspheme, blas-fēm´, *vt*. (blaspheming, blasphemed). To speak irreverently of, as of God; to speak evil of.—*vi*. To utter blasphemy.

Blast, blast, *n*. A gust of wind; sound of a wind-instrument; violent explosion of gunpowder; pernicious influence, as of wind; blight.—*vt*. To blight; to strike with some sudden plague, etc.; to destroy; to blow up by gunpowder.—*vi*. To wither; to be blighted.

Blatant, blā´tant, *a*. Bellowing; noisy.

Blaze, blāz, *n*. A flame; brilliance; a bursting out; a white spot.—*vi*. (blazing, blazed). To flame; to send forth a bright light.—*vt*. To noise abroad; to proclaim.

Bleed, blēd, *vi*. (bleeding, bled). To emit blood; to die by slaughter; to feel agony, as from bleeding; to drop, as blood.—*vt*. To take blood from; to extort money from.

Blemish, blem´ish, *vt*. To mar; to tarnish.—*n*. A mark of imperfection; dishonor.

Blend, blend, *vt*. To mix together.—*vi*. To be mixed.—*n*. A mixture.

Blindfold, blīnd´fōld, *a*. Having the eyes covered.—*vt*. To cover the eyes of.

Blindness, blīnd´nes, *n*. Want of sight or discernment; ignorance.

Blink, blingk, *vi*. To wink; to twinkle.—*vt*. To shut the eyes upon; to avoid.—*n*. A twinkle; a glimpse or glance.

Blinker, bling´kėr, *n*. A flap to prevent a horse from seeing sideways.

Bliss, blis, *n*. Blessedness; perfect happiness.

Blister, blis´tėr, *n*. A thin bladder on the skin; a pustule; something to raise a blister.—*vi*. To rise in blisters.—*vt*. To raise a blister or blisters on; to apply a blister to.

Blithe, blīⲧн, *a*. Joyful; gay; mirthful.

Blockade, blok-ād´, *n*. A close siege by troops or ships.—*vt*. (blockading, blockaded). To besiege closely.

Blockhead, blok´hed, *n*. A stupid fellow.

Blond, Blonde, blond, *a*. Of a fair complexion.—*n*. A person of fair complexion.

Blood, blud, *n*. The fluid which circulates in animals; kindred; high birth; the juice of fruits.—*a*. Pertaining to blood; of a superior breed.—*vt*. To bleed; to stain with blood; to inure to blood.

Blood-heat, blud´hēt, *n*. The heat of the human blood, about 98° Fah.

Blood-horse, blud´hors, *n*. A horse of the purest breed.

Blood-hound, blud´hound, *n*. A hound of remarkably acute smell.

Bloom, blōm, *n*. A blossom; a flower; state of youth; native flush on the cheek; the powdery coating on plums, etc.; a lump of puddled iron.—*vi*. To blossom; to flourish; to show the freshness of youth.

Blossom, blos´om, *n*. The flower of a plant.—*vi*. To bloom; to flower; to flourish.

Blot, blot, *vt*. (blotted, blotting). To spot; to stain; to cancel (with *out*); to dry.—*n*. A spot or stain; an obliteration.

Blotch, bloch, *n.* Pustule upon the skin; an eruption; a confused patch of color.

Blotter, blot'ẽr, *n.* One who blots; a piece of blotting-paper.

Blouse, blouz, *n.* A light loose upper garment.

Blow, blō, *vi.* (blowing, pp. blown, pret. blew). To make a current of air; to emit air or breath; to pant; to sound by being blown; to bloom; to flourish.—*vt.* To impel by wind; to inflate; to sound by the breath; to infect with the eggs of flies.—*n.* A blast; a blossoming; bloom; a stroke; a calamitous event.

Bluebell, blü'bel, *n.* The wild hyacinth (in England), the harebell (in Scotland).

Blue-print, blü'print, *n.* A print obtained by the action of light on prepared paper over which a transparent drawing is laid. The exposed part of the paper becomes covered with Prussian blue, and the drawing is shown in white.

Blue-stocking, blü'stok-ing, *n.* A learned and pedantic lady.

Blue-stone, blü'stōn, *n.* Sulphate of copper.

Bluff, bluf, *a.* Steep; blustering; burly; hearty.—*n.* A steep projecting bank.—*vt.* and *i.* To impose on by a show of boldness or strength.

Blunder, blun'dẽr, *vi.* To err stupidly; to stumble.—*vt.* To confound.—*n.* A gross mistake; error.

Blunt, blunt, *a.* Dull on the edge or point; not sharp; dull in understanding; uneremonious.—*vt.* To make blunt or dull.

Blur, blẽr, *n.* A stain; a blot.—*vt.* (blurring, blurred). To stain; to obscure; to render indistinct.

Board, bōrd, *n.* A piece of timber broad and thin; a table; food; persons seated round a table; a council; the deck of a ship; a thick stiff paper.—*vt.* To cover with boards; to supply with food; to place as a boarder; to enter a ship by force.—*vi.* To live in a house at a certain rate.

Boarder, bōrd'ẽr, *n.* One who receives food and lodging at a stated charge; one who boards a ship in action.

Boarding-school, bōrd'ing-sköl, *n.* A school which supplies board as well as tuition.

Boast, bōst, *vi.* To brag; to talk ostentatiously.—*vt.* To brag of; to magnify.—*n.* A vaunting; the cause of boasting.

Boat, bōt, *n.* A small open vessel, usually impelled by oars; a small ship.—*vt.* To transport in a boat.—*vi.* To go in a boat.

Boatswain, bō'sn, *n.* A ship's officer who has charge of boats, sails, etc.

Bob, bob, *n.* A pendant; something that plays loosely; a short jerking motion; a docked tail; (slang) a shilling.—*vt.* (bobbing, bobbed). To move with a short jerking motion.—*vi.* To play backward and forward, or loosely.

Body, bo'di, *n.* The trunk of an animal; main part; matter; a person; a system; strength; reality; any solid figure.—*vt.* (bodying, bodied). To give a body to; to embody (with *forth*).

Boisterous, bois'tẽr-us, *a.* Stormy; noisy.

Bold, bōld, *a.* Daring; courageous; impudent; steep and abrupt.

Bole, bōl, *n.* The body or stem of a tree; a kind of fine clay.

Bolero, bō-lär'ō, *n.* A Spanish dance.

Bolshevik, bol'shev-ik, *n.* The Russian name for the majority party in the 1903 split of the Social Democrats; revolutionists; extreme Socialists.

Bolster, bōl'stẽr, *n.* A long pillow; a pad.—*vt.* To support with a bolster; to hold up; to maintain.

Bond, bond, *n.* That which binds; obligation; state of being bonded; a writing by which a person binds himself; in *pl.* chains; imprisonment.—*a.* In a servile state.—*vt.* To grant a bond in security for money; to store till duty is paid.

Bondage, bond'āj, *n.* Slavery; thraldom.

Bonded, bond'ed, *a.* Secured by bond; under a bond to pay duty; containing goods liable to duties.

Bone, bōn, *n.* A hard substance, forming the framework of an animal; something made of bone.—*vt.* (boning, boned). To take out bones from.

Bonfire, bon'fīr, *n.* A large fire in the open air expressive of joy.

Book-maker, buk'māk-ėr, *n.* One who compiles books; one who bets systematically.

Bookworm, buk'wėrm, *n.* A worm that eats holes in books; a close student of books.

Boom, bōm, *n.* A long pole to extend the bottom of a sail; a chain or bar across a river or mouth of a harbor; a hollow roar; briskness in commerce.—*vi.* To make a humming sound; to roar, as waves or cannon.

Boomerang, bōm'e-rang, *n.* An Australian missile of hard wood, which can return to hit an object behind the thrower.

Boon, bön, *n.* Answer to a prayer; a favor, gift, or grant.—*a.* Merry; pleasant.

Boor, bör, *n.* A rustic; an ill-mannered or illiterate fellow.

Boot, böt, *vt.* To benefit; to put on boots.—*n.* Profit; a covering for the foot and leg; *pl.* a male servant in a hotel.

Bore, bōr, *vt.* (boring, bored). To make a hole in; to weary.—*vi.* To pierce.—*n.* The hole made by boring; the diameter of a round hole; a person or thing that wearies; a sudden rise of the tide in certain estuaries.

Bosky, bosk'i, *a.* Woody or bushy.

Bosom, bö'zum, *n.* The breast; the seat of the affections.—*vt.* To conceal.—*a.* Much beloved; confidential.

Boss, bos, *n.* A knob; an ornamental projection; a master.

Botany, bot'a-ni, *n.* The science which treats of plants.

Botch, boch, *n.* A swelling on the skin; a clumsy patch; bungled work.—*vt.* To mend or perform clumsily.

Both, bōth, *a.* and *pron.* The two, taken by themselves; the pair.—*conj.* As well; on the one side.

Bother, boTH'ėr, *vt.* To annoy.—*vi.* To trouble oneself.—*n.* A trouble, vexation.

Bothersome, boTH'ėr-sum, *a.* Causing trouble.

Bott, Bot, bot, *n.* A maggot found in the intestines of horses, etc.: generally in *pl.*

Bottle, bot'l, *n.* A narrow-mouthed vessel of glass, leather, etc., for liquor; the contents of a bottle.—*vt.* (bottling, bottled). To put into a bottle or bottles.

Bounce, bouns, *vi.* (bouncing, bounced). To spring or rush out suddenly; to thump; to boast or bully.—*n.* A strong sudden thump; a rebound; a boast.

Bound, bound, *n.* A boundary; a leap.—*vt.* To limit; to restrain.—*vi.* To leap; to rebound.—*p.a.* Obliged; sure.—*a.* Ready; destined.

Boundary, bound'a-ri, *n.* A mark designating a limit; border.

Bountiful, boun'ti-fu̧l, *a.* Munificent; generous.

Bounty, boun'ti, *n.* Liberality; generosity; a gratuity; premium to encourage trade.

Bow, bō, *n.* An instrument to shoot arrows; the rainbow; a curve; a fiddlestick; an ornamental knot.

Bowel, bou'el, *n.* One of the intestines; *pl.* the intestines; the seat of pity; compassion.

Bower, bou'ėr, *n.* An anchor carried at the bow; a shady recess; an arbor.

Bowie-knife, bō'i-nīf, *n.* A knife from 10 to 15 inches long and about 2 inches broad.

Bowl, bōl, *n.* A large roundish cup; a ball, of wood, etc.; used for rolling on a level plat of ground; *pl.* the game played with such bowls.—*vi.* To play with bowls; to deliver a ball at cricket; to move rapidly.—*vt.* To roll as a bowl; to deliver (a ball) at cricket, etc.

Bowler, bōl'ėr, *n.* One who bowls; a round-shaped felt hat.

Bowling, bōl'ing, *n.* Act or art of playing with bowls; art or style of a bowler.

Bowman, bō'man, *n.* An archer.

Bowsprit, bō'sprit, *n.* A large spar which projects over the bow of a ship.

Box　　　　　　　　29　　　　　　Bric-à-brac

Box, boks, *n*. A case of wood, metal, etc.; quantity that a case contains; a seat in a playhouse, etc.; driver's seat on a coach; a sportsman's house; a blow on the ear; a tree or shrub, yielding a hard wood.—*vt*. To put in a box; to strike with the hand.—*vi*. To fight with the fists.

Boxwood, boks'wud, *n*. The hard-grained wood of the box-tree; the plant itself.

Boy, boi, *n*. A male child; a lad.

Bracket, brak'et, *n*. A support for something fixed to a wall; a mark in printing to enclose words, etc.—*vt*. To place within or connect by brackets.

Brackish, brak'ish, *a*. Salt; saltish.

Bract, brakt, *n*. An irregularly developed leaf at the base of a flower.

Brad, brad, *n*. A small nail with no head.

Brag, brag, *vi*. (bragging, bragged). To bluster; to talk big.—*n*. A boast.

Brake, brāk, *n*. A place overgrown with brushwood, etc.; a thicket; the bracken; an instrument to break flax; a harrow for breaking clods; a contrivance for retarding the motion of wheels; a large wagonette.

Bramble, bram'bl, *n*. A prickly shrub of the rose family; its berry.

Bran, bran, *n*. The husks of ground corn.

Branch, bransh, *n*. The shoot of a tree or plant; the offshoot of anything, as of a river, family, etc.; a limb.—*vi*. To spread in branches.—*vt*. To divide or form into branches.

Brand, brand, *n*. A burning piece of wood; a sword; a mark made with a hot iron; a note of infamy; a trade-mark; a kind or quality.—*vt*. To mark with a hot iron; to stigmatize as infamous.

Bravado, bra-vā'dō, *n*. A boast or brag; would-be boldness.

Brave, brāv, *a*. Daring; bold; valiant; noble.—*n*. A daring person; a savage warrior.—*vt*. (braving, braved). To challenge; to defy; to encounter with courage.

Brawl, brȧl, *vi*. To quarrel noisily.—*n*. A noisy quarrel; uproar.

Brawn, bran, *n*. The flesh of a boar; the muscular part of the body;

muscle.

Bray, brā, *vt*. To beat or grind small.—*vi*. To make a loud harsh sound, as an ass.—*n*. The cry of an ass.

Braze, brāz, *vt*. (brazing, brazed). To cover with brass; to solder with brass.

Break, brāk, *vt*. (breaking, pret. broke, pp. broke, broken). To sever by fracture; to rend; to open; to tame; to make bankrupt; to discard; to interrupt; to dissolve any union; to tell with discretion.—*vi*. To come to pieces; to burst; to burst forth; to dawn; to become bankrupt; to decline in vigor; to change in tone.—*n*. An opening; breach; pause; the dawn; a brake for vehicles; a large wagonette.

Breaker, brāk'ėr, *n*. One who or that which breaks; a rock; a wave broken by rocks.

Breakfast, brek'fast, *n*. The first meal in the day.—*vi*. To eat the first meal in the day.—*vt*. To furnish with breakfast.

Breakwater, brāk'wa-tėr, *n*. A mole to break the force of the waves.

Bream, brēm, *n*. A fish.—*vt*. To clean a ship's bottom by means of fire.

Breast, brest, *n*. The fore part of the body, between the neck and the belly; the heart; the conscience; the affections.—*vt*. To bear the breast against; to meet in front.

Breath, breth, *n*. The air drawn into and expelled from the lungs; life; a single respiration; pause; a gentle breeze.

Breathe, brēᴛʜ, *vi*. (breathing, breathed). To draw into the eject air from the lungs; to live; to take breath; to rest.—*vt*. To inspire and exhale; to infuse; to utter softly or in private; to suffer to take breath.

Breech, brēch, *n*. The lower part of the body behind; the hinder part of a gun, etc.—*vt*. To put into breeches.

Bribe, brīb, *n*. A gift to corrupt the conduct or judgment.—*vt*. (bribing, bribed). To gain over by bribes.

Bric-à-brac, brik-a-brak, *n*. Articles of interest or value from rarity, antiquity, etc.

Brick, brik, *n.* A rectangular mass of burned clay, used in building, etc.; a loaf shaped like a brick.—*a.* Made of brick.—*vt.* To lay with bricks.

Bridal, brīd'al, *n.* A wedding-feast; a wedding.—*a.* Belonging to a bride or to a wedding.

Bride, brīd, *n.* A woman about to be or newly married.

Bridegroom, brīd'gröm, *n.* A man about to be or newly married.

Bride's-maid, brīdz'mād, *n.* A woman who attends on a bride at her wedding.

Bridge, brij, *n.* A structure across a river, etc., to furnish a passage; the upper part of the nose.—*vt.* (bridging, bridged). To build a bridge over.

Brier, brī'ėr, *n.* A prickly shrub, species of the rose.

Brig, brig, *n.* A vessel with two masts, square-rigged.

Brigand, bri'gand, *n.* A freebooter.

Brigantine, brig'an-tīn, *n.* A light swift vessel, two-masted and square-rigged.

Bright, brīt, *a.* Clear; shining; glittering; acute; witty; lively; cheerful.

Brilliant, bril'yant, *a.* Shining; sparkling; spendid; of great talents.—*n.* A diamond of the finest cut; a small printing type.

Brim, brim, *n.* The rim of anything; the upper edge of the mouth of a vessel.—*vi.* (brimming, brimmed). To be full to the brim.

Brimstone, brim'stön, *n.* Sulphur.

Brindled, brind'ld, *a.* Marked with brown streaks.

Brine, brīn, *n.* Salt water; the sea.

Bring, bring, *vt.* (bringing, brought). To lead or cause to come; to fetch; to produce; to attract; to prevail upon.

Brink, bringk, *n.* The edge of a steep place.

Broach, brōch, *n.* A spit; a brooch.—*vt.* To pierce, as with a spit; to tap; to open up; to publish first.

Broad, brad, *a.* Having extent from side to side; wide; unrestricted; indelicate.

Broaden, brad'n, *vi.* To grow broad.—*vt.* To make broad.

Broadside, brad'sīd, *n.* A discharge of all the guns on one side of a ship; a sheet of paper printed on one side.

Brocade, brō-kād', *n.* A silk or satin stuff variegated with gold and silver.

Broccoli, brok'o-li, *n.* A kind of cauliflower.

Bronchial, brong'ki-al, *a.* Belonging to the tubes branching from the windpipe through the lungs.

Bronchitis, brong-kī'tis, *n.* Inflammation of the bronchial tubes.

Bronze, bronz, *n.* An alloy of copper and tin; a color to imitate bronze; a figure made of bronze.—*vt.* (bronzing, bronzed). To make appear on the surface like bronze.

Brother, bruᴛʜ'ėr, *n.*; pl. **Brothers, Brethren,** bruᴛʜ'ėrz, breᴛʜ'ren. A male born of the same parents; an associate; a fellow-creature.

Browse, brouz, *vt.* (browsing, browsed). To pasture or feed upon.—*vi.* To crop and eat food.

Bruin, brö'in, *n.* A familiar name of a bear.

Bruise, bröz, *vt.* (bruising, bruised). To crush; to make a contusion on.—*n.* A contusion; a hurt from a blow.

Brusque, brusk, *a.* Abrupt in manner; rude.

Brussels-sprouts, brus'elz-sprouts, *n.pl.* A variety of cabbage.

Brutal, bröt'al, *a.* Cruel; ferocious.

Brute, bröt, *a.* Senseless; bestial; uncivilized.—*n.* A beast; a brutal person.

Bubble, bub'bl, *n.* A small vesicle of fluid inflated with air; a vain project; a swindle.—*vi.* (bubbling, bubbled). To rise in bubbles.—*vt.* To cheat; to swindle.

Bubo, bū'bō, *n.*; pl. **-oes.** A swelling or abscess in a glandular part of the body.

Bubonic, bū-bon'ik, *a.* Pertaining to bubo.

Buccaneer, buk-a-nēr', *n.* A pirate.

Buck, buk, *n.* The male of deer, goats, etc.; a gay young fellow; a lye for steeping clothes in.—*vt.* To steep in lye.—*vi.* To leap, as a horse, so as to dismount the rider.

Bucket, buk'et, *n.* A vessel in which water is drawn or carried.

Buckle, buk'l, *n.* An instrument to fasten straps, etc.—*vt.* (buckling, buckled). To fasten with a buckle; to bend or warp.—*vi.* To apply with vigor (with *to*).

Buck-shot, buk'shot, *n.* A large kind of shot used for killing large game.

Buckwheat, buk'whēt, *n.* A plant bearing small seeds which are ground into meal.

Bucolic, bū-kol'ik, *a.* Pastoral.—*n.* A pastoral poem.

Bud, bud, *n.* The first shoot of a leaf, etc.; a germ.—*vi.* (budding, budded). To put forth buds or germs; to begin to grow.—*vt.* To graft by inserting a bud.

Buffalo, buf'fa-lō, *n.* A species of ox, larger than the common ox; the American bison.

Buffer, buf'ėr, *n.* An apparatus for deadening concussion.

Buffet, buf'et, *n.* A cupboard for wine, glasses, etc.; a place for refreshments (pron. bu-fe).

Buffet, buf'et, *n.* A blow; a slap.—*vt.* To beat; to box; to contend against.

Buffoon, buf-fön', *n.* One who makes sport by low jests and antic gestures; a droll.

Bug, bug, *n.* A name for various insects, particularly one infesting houses and inflicting severe bites.

Bulb, bulb, *n.* A round root; a round protuberance.

Bulbul, bul'bul, *n.* The Persian nightingale.

Bulge, bulj, *n.* A swelling; bilge.—*vi.* (bulging, bulged). To swell out; to be protuberant.

Bulk, bulk, *n.* Magnitude; the majority; extent.

Bull, bul, *n.* The male of cattle; a sign of the zodiac; one who raises the price of stock; a letter or edict of the pope; a ludicrous contradiction in language.

Bull-frog, bul'frog, *n.* A large species of frog in N. America, with a loud bass voice.

Bullion, bul'yon, *n.* Uncoined gold or silver.

Bull's-eye, bulz'ī, *n.* A circular opening for light or air; the centre of a target.

Bully, bul'i, *n.* An overbearing quarrelsome fellow.—*vt.* (bullying, bullied). To insult and overbear.—*vi.* To bluster or domineer.

Bulrush, bul'rush, *n.* A large, strong kind of rush.

Bulwark, bul'wėrk, *n.* A bastion; a fortification; a means of defense or safety.

Bumble-bee, bum'bl-bē, *n.* A large bee.

Bump, bump, *n.* A heavy blow, or the noise of it; a lump produced by a blow.—*vi.* To make a loud, heavy, or hollow noise.—*vt.* To strike heavily against.

Bumpkin, bump'kin, *n.* An awkward rustic; a lout.

Bun, bun, *n.* A kind of cake or sweet bread.

Bunch, bunsh, *n.* A knob or lump; a cluster.—*vi.* To swell out in a protuberance; to cluster.

Bundle, bun'dl, *n.* A number of things bound together; a package.—*vt.* (bundling, bundled). To tie in a bundle; to dispose of hurriedly.—*vi.* To depart hurriedly (with *off*).

Bung, bung, *n.* The stopper of a cask.—*vt.* To stop with a bung; to close up.

Bungalow, bung'ga-lō, *n.* A single-storied house.

Buoy, boi, *n.* A floating mark to point out shoals, etc.; something to keep a person or thing up in the water.—*vt.* To keep afloat; to bear up.—*vi.* To float.

Buoyant, boi'ant, *a.* Floating; light; elastic.

Burglar, bėrg'lėr, *n.* One who robs a house by night.

Burgundy, bėr'gun-di, *n.* A kind of wine, so called from Burgundy in France.

Burn, bėrn, *vt.* (burning, burnt or burned). To consume with fire; to scorch; to inflame; to harden by fire.—*vi.* To be on fire; to be inflamed with desire; to rage fiercely.—*n.* A hurt caused by fire; a rivulet.

Burnish, bėr'nish, *vt.* To polish.—*vi.* To grow bright or glossy.—*n.*

Gloss; luster.

Burr, bėr, *n.* A guttural sounding of the letter *r;* a rough or projecting ridge; bur.

Burrow, bu'rō, *n.* A hole in the earth made by rabbits, etc.—*vi.* To excavate a hole underground; to hide.

Burst, bėrst, *vi.* (bursting, burst). To fly or break open; to rush forth; to come with violence.—*vt.* To break by force; to open suddenly.—*n.* A violent disruption; a rupture.

Bury, be'ri, *vt.* (burying, buried). To put into a grave; to overwhelm; to hide.

Bush, bush, *n.* A shrub with branches; a thicket; the backwoods of Australia; a lining of hard metal in the nave of a wheel, etc.—*vi.* To grow bushy.

Bushel, bush'el, *n.* A dry measure containing eight gallons or four pecks.

Business, biz'nes, *n.* Occupation; concern; trade.—*a.* Pertaining to traffic, trade, etc.

Butt, but, *n.* The end of a thing; a mark to be shot at; the person at whom ridicule, etc., is directed; a cask holding 126 gallons of wine.—*vi.* To thrust the head forward.—*vt.* To strike with the head or horns.

Butter, but'tėr, *n.* An oily substance obtained from cream by churning; any substance resembling butter.—*vt.* To spread with butter; to flatter grossly.

Butterfly, but'tėr-flī, *n.* The name of a group of winged insects.

Buttermilk, but'ėr-milk, *n.* The milk that remains after the butter is separated.

Buttock, but'tok, *n.* The protuberant part of the body behind; the rump.

Button, but'n, *n.* A knob to fasten the parts of dress; a knob or stud; *pl.* a page-boy.—*vt.* To fasten with buttons.

Buttress, but'tres, *n.* A projecting support for a wall; a prop.—*vt.* To support by a buttress; to prop.

Buxom, buks'um, *a.* Gay; brisk; wanton.

Buy, bī, *vt.* (buying, bought). To acquire by payment; to purchase; to

bribe.—*vi.* To negotiate or treat about a purchase.

Buzz, buz, *vi.* To hum, as bees; to whisper.—*vt.* To whisper.—*n.* The noise of bees; a confused humming noise.

Buzzard, buz'ėrd, *n.* A species of hawk; a blockhead.

By, bī, *prep.* Used to denote the instrument, agent, or manner; at; near; beside; through or with; in; for; according to; at the rate of; not later than.—*adv.* Near; passing. In *composition,* secondary, side.

Byzantine, biz-an'tīn or biz', *a.* Pertaining to Byzantium or Constantinople and the Greek Empire of which it was the capital.

C

Cabal, ka-bal', *n.* An intrigue; persons united in some intrigue.—*vi.* (caballing, caballed). To combine in plotting.

Cabaret, kab'a-ret, ka-ba-rā, *n.* A tavern; a restaurant in which singing and dancing performances are given.

Cabbage, kab'āj, *n.* A culinary vegetable.—*vt.* (cabbaging, cabbaged). To purloin, especially pieces of cloth.

Cabin, kab'in, *n.* A hut; an apartment in a ship.—*vt.* To confine, as in a cabin.

Cabinet, kab'in-et, *n.* A closet; a small room; a set of drawers for curiosities; the ministers of state.

Cacophony, ka-kof'ō-ni, *n.* Unpleasant vocal sound; a discord.

Cactus, kak'tus, *n.;* pl. -tuses or -ti. A spiny shrub of numerous species.

Caisson, kās'son, *n.* An ammunition chest; a structure to raise sunken vessels; a structure used in laying foundations in deep water.

Cajole, ka-jōl', *vt.* (cajoling, cajoled). To coax; to court; to deceive by flattery.

Cake, kāk, *n.* A composition of flour, butter, sugar, etc., baked; a mass of matter concreted.—*vt.* (caking, caked). To form into a cake or mass.—*vi*. To form into a hard mass.

Caledonian, kal-i-dō'ni-an, *a*. Pertaining to Scotland.—*n*. A Scot.

Calends, ka'lendz, *n.pl*. Among the Romans, the first day of each month.

Calf, käf, *n*.; pl. **Calves,** kävz. The young of the cow; a kind of leather; the fleshy part of the leg below the knee.

Caliber, ka'li-bėr, *n*. Diameter of the bore of a gun; extent of mental qualities; a sort or kind.

Calico, ka'li-kō, *n*. Cotton cloth.

Calk, kak, *vt. See* CAULK.

Calkin, Calker, kak'in, kak'ėr, *n*. The part of a horse-shoe bent downwards and pointed.

Call, kal, *vt*. To name; to style; to summon; to ask, or command to come; to appoint; to appeal to; to utter aloud; to awaken.—*vi*. To utter a loud sound; to make a short visit.—*n*. A vocal utterance; summons; demand; divine vocation; a short visit.

Calligraphy, kal-lig'ra-fi, *n*. The art of beautiful writing; penmanship.

Calling, kal'ing, *n*. Vocation; profession.

Callipers, kal'i-pėrz, *n.pl*. Compasses for measuring caliber.

Callisthenics, kal-is-then'iks, *n*. Exercise for health, strength, or grace of movement.

Callosity, ka-los'i-ti, *n*. Hardness of skin; horny hardness.

Callous, kal'us, *a*. Hardened; unfeeling; obdurate.

Calm, käm, *a*. Still; free from wind; peaceable; composed.—*n*. Absence of wind; tranquillity.—*vt*. To make calm; to still; to assuage.—*vi*. To become calm.

Caloric, ka-lo'rik, *n*. The principle or simple element of heat; heat.

Calumet, kal'ū-met, *n*. The North American Indians' pipe of peace.

Camera, kam'e-ra, *n*. An arched roof; a council chamber; an apparatus for taking photographs.

Camomile, kam'ō-mīl, *n*. A bitter medicinal plant.

Camouflage, kam-ö-fläzh, *n*. The art of disguising; especially the art of disguising material in warfare.

Camp, kamp, *n*. The ground on which an army pitch their tents; an encampment.—*vi*. To pitch a camp; to encamp.

Campaign, kam-pān', *n*. The time an army keeps the field every year, during a war; its operations.—*vi*. To serve in a campaign.

Campanile, kam-pa-nē'lā or kam'pa-nīl, *n*.; pl. **-ili** or **-iles.** A bell-tower.

Camphor, kam'fėr, *n*. A whitish, bitter, strong-smelling substance used in medicine.

Campion, kam'pi-on, *n*. A popular name of certain plants of the Pink family.

Can, kan, *n*. A cup or vessel for liquors.

Can, kan, *vi*. (pret. could). To be able; to have sufficient moral or physical power.

Canal, ka-nal', *n*. A channel; an artificial water-course for boats; a duct of the body.

Canard, ka-när or ka-närd', *n*. An absurd story; a false rumor.

Canary, ka-nā'ri, *n*. Wine made in the Canary Isles; a finch from the Canary Isles.

Cancel, kan'sel, *vt*. (cancelling, cancelled). To obliterate; to revoke; to set aside.—*n*. Act of cancelling.

Cancer, kan'sėr, *n*. One of the signs of the zodiac; a malignant growth in the body.

Candelabrum, kan-de-lā'brum, *n*.; pl. **-ra.** A branched ornamental candlestick.

Candid, kan'did, *a*. Sincere; ingenuous.

Candidate, kan'di-dāt, *n*. One who proposes himself, or is proposed, for some office; one who aspires after preferment.

Candied, kan'did, *a*. Preserved with sugar, or incrusted with it.

Candle, kan'dl, *n*. A cylindrical body of tallow, wax, etc., surrounding a wick, and used for giving light.

Candlestick, kan'dl-stik, *n*. An instrument to hold a candle.

Candor, kan'dėr, *n*. Frankness; sincerity.

C

Candy, kan'di, vt. (candying, candied). To conserve with sugar; to form into crystals.—vi. To take on the form of candied sugar.—n. Crystallized sugar; a sweetmeat.

Cane, kān, n. A reed; a walking-stick.—vt. (caning, caned). To beat with a cane.

Canine, ka'nīn, a. Pertaining to dogs.

Cannon, kan'un, n. A great gun; the striking of a ball on two other balls successively.—vi. To strike with rebounding collision; to make a cannon at billiards.

Canny, Cannie, kan'i, a. Cautious; wary.

Canoe, ka-nö', n. A boat made of the trunk of a tree, or of bark or skins; a light boat propelled by paddles.

Cant, kant, vi. To speak in a whining tone; to sham piety.—vt. To tilt up; to bevel.—n. A whining hypocritical manner of speech; jargon; slang; inclination from a perpendicular or horizontal line; a toss or jerk.—a. Of the nature of cant or slang.

Cantankerous, kan-tang'kėr-us, a. Ill-natured; cross; contentious.

Cantata, kan-tä'ta, n. A short musical composition in the form of an oratorio.

Canteen, kan-tēn', n. A vessel used by soldiers for carrying liquor; a place in barracks where provisions, etc., are sold.

Canton, kan'ton, n. A division of territory or its inhabitants.—vt. To divide into cantons; to allot separate quarters to different parts of an army. (In milit. lan. pron. kan-tön'.)

Canvas, kan'vas, n. A coarse cloth; sailcloth; sails of ships; cloth for painting on; a painting.

Canvass, kan'vas, vt. To scrutinize; to solicit the votes of.—vi. To solicit votes or interest; to use efforts to obtain.—n. Scrutiny; solicitation of votes.

Cap, kap, n. A covering for the head; something used as a cover; a top piece.—vt. (capping, capped). To put a cap on; to complete; to crown; to excel.

Capable, kā'pa-bl, a. Having sufficient skill or power; competent; susceptible.

Capacious, ka-pā'shus, a. Wide; large; comprehensive.

Capacitate, ka-pas'i-tāt, vt. To make able; to qualify.

Capacity, ka-pas'i-ti, n. Power of holding; extent of space; ability; state.

Capital, kap'it-al, a. First in importance; metropolitan; affecting the head; punishable with death.—n. The uppermost part of a column; the chief city; the stock of a bank, tradesman, etc.; a large letter or type.

Capitalist, kap'it-al-ist, n. A man who has a capital or wealth.

Capsicum, kap'si-kum, n. The generic name of some tropical plants yielding chilies and cayenne pepper.

Capsize, kap-sīz', vt. (capsizing, capsized). To upset or overturn.

Capstan, kap'stan, n. An apparatus in ships to raise great weights, weigh anchors, etc.

Capsule, kap'sūl, n. A dry, many-seeded seed-vessel; an envelope for drugs.

Captain, kap'tin, n. A head officer; the commander of a ship, troop of horse, or company of infantry; a leader.

Caption, kap'shon, n. Seizure; arrest; heading or short title of a division of a book, or of a scene in a cinematograph film.

Captious, kap'shus, a. Ready to find fault; carping.

Captive, kap'tiv, n. One taken in war; one ensnared by love, beauty, etc.—a. Make prisoner; kept in bondage.

Capture, kap'tūr, n. Act of taking; the thing taken.—vt. (capturing, captured). To take by force or stratagem.

Caravan, ka'ra-van, n. A company of travelers associated together for safety; a large close carriage.

Caraway, ka'ra-wā, n. A biennial, aromatic plant whose seeds are used in baking, etc.

Carbide, kär'bīd, n. A compound of carbon with a metal.

Carbine, kär'bīn, *n.* A short-barreled rifle used by cavalry, police, etc.

Carbolic, kär-bol'ik, *a.* An antiseptic and disinfecting acid obtained from coal-tar.

Carbon, kär'bon, *n.* Pure charcoal; an elementary substance, bright and brittle.

Carbonate, kär'bon-āt, *n.* A salt formed by the union of carbonic acid with a base.

Carbuncle, kär'bung-kl, *n.* A fiery red precious stone; an inflammatory tumor.

Carburetor, kär'bū-ret-ėr, *n.* A device for vaporizing the light oil fuel used in the engines of motorcars, airplanes, etc.

Carcass, kär'kas, *a.* A dead body; anything decayed; a framework; a kind of bomb.

Card, kärd, *n.* A piece of pasteboard with figures, used in games; a piece of pasteboard containing a person's name, etc.; a printed invitation; a note; the dial of a compass; a large comb for wool or flax.—*vt.* To comb wool, flax, hemp, etc.

Care, kär, *n.* Solicitude; attention; object of watchful regard.—*vi.* (caring, cared). To be solicitous; to be inclined; to have regard.

Careen, ka-rēn', *vt.* To lay (a ship) on one side, for the purpose of repairing.—*vi.* To incline to one side.

Career, ka-rēr', *n.* A race; course of action.—*vi.* To move or run rapidly.

Careful, kär'ful, *a.* Solicitous; cautious.

Caress, ka-res', *vt.* To fondle; to embrace affectionately.—*n.* An act of endearment.

Caret, kā'ret, *n.* In writing, this mark, ʌ, noting insertion.

Carious, kā'ri-us, *a.* Ulcerated; decayed.

Carminative, kär'min-āt-iv, *n.* A medicine for flatulence, etc.

Carmine, kär'mīn, *n.* A bright crimson color.

Carnage, kär'nāj, *n.* Great slaughter in war; massacre; butchery.

Carnal, kär'nal, *a.* Fleshly; sensual.

Carotid, ka-rot'id, *a.* Pertaining to the two great arteries in the neck conveying the blood to the head.

Carouse, ka-rouz', *vi.* (carousing, caroused). To drink freely with noisy jollity.—*n.* A drinking bout.

Carrion, ka'ri-on, *n.* Dead and putrefying flesh.—*a.* Relating to putrefying carcasses; feeding on carrion.

Carrot, ka'rot, *n.* A yellowish or reddish esculent root of a tapering form.

Carry, ka'ri, *vt.* (carrying, carried). To bear, convey, or transport; to gain; to capture; to import; to behave.—*vi.* To convey; to propel.—*n.* Onward motion.

Cart, kärt, *n.* A carriage of burden with two wheels.—*vt.* To carry or place on a cart.

Carte-blanche, kärt-blänsh, *n.* A blank paper; unconditional terms.

Cartel, kär'tel, *n.* A challenge; an agreement for the exchange of prisoners.

Cartilage, kär'ti-lāj, *n.* Gristle; an elastic substance from which bone is formed.

Cartography, kär-tog'ra-fi, *n.* The art or practice of drawing up charts.

Cartoon, kär-tön', *n.* A drawing for a fresco or tapestry; a pictorial sketch relating to a prevalent topic.

Cartouch, kär-tösh', *n.* A cartridge or cartridge-box; a sculptured ornament.

Cartridge, kär'trij, *n.* A case containing the charge of a gun or any firearm.

Carve, kärv, *vt.* (carving, carved). To cut; to engrave; to shape by cutting.—*vi.* To cut up meat; to sculpture.

Cash, kash, *n.* Money; ready money; coin.—*vt.* To turn into money.

Cashier, kash-ēr', *n.* One who has charge of money.—*vt.* To deprive of office; to dismiss; to break.

Cashmere, kash'mēr, *n.* A rich kind of shawl; a fine woolen stuff.

Casino, ka-sē'nō, *n.* A public dancing, singing, or gaming saloon.

Cast, kast, *vt.* (casting, cast). To throw; to impel; to throw off; to let fall; to condemn; to compute; to model; to found; to scatter (seed); to bring forth immaturely.—*vi.* To revolve in the mind; to contrive (with *about*); to warp.—*n.* A throw; the thing thrown; manner of throwing; distance passed by a thing thrown; a squint; form; a tinge; manner; that which is formed from a mould; the actors to whom the parts of a play are assigned.

Castor, kas'tẻr, *n.* A small cruet; a small wheel on the leg of a table, etc.

Castor-oil, kas'tẻr-oil, *n.* A medicinal oil obtained from a tropical plant.

Castrate, kas'trāt, *vt.* (castrating, castrated). To geld; to emasculate; to expurgate.

Cast-steel, kast'stēl, *n.* Steel melted and cast into ingots and rolled into bars.

Casual, ka'zhū-al, *a.* Happening by chance; occasional; contingent.

Casualty, ka'zhū-al-ti, *n.* Accident, especially one resulting in death or injury; death or injury caused by enemy action.

Casuistry, ka'zū-is-tri, *n.* The science of determining cases of conscience; sophistry.

Cat, kat, *n.* A domestic animal of the feline tribe; a strong tackle; a double tripod; an instrument for flogging.

Cataclysm, kat'a-klizm, *n.* A deluge; a sudden overwhelming catastrophe.

Catapult, kat'a-pult, *n.* An apparatus for throwing stones, etc.

Cataract, kat'a-rakt, *n.* A great waterfall; a disease of the eye.

Catarrh, ka-tär', *n.* A flow of mucus from the nose, etc.; a cold.

Catastrophe, ka-tas'trō-fē, *n.* Calamity or disaster; final event.

Catch, kach, *vt.* (catching, caught). To lay hold on; to stop the falling of; to grasp; to entangle; to receive by contagion; to be seized with; to get.—*vi.* To lay hold; to be contagious.—*n.* Act of seizing; anything that takes hold; a sudden advantage taken; something desirable; a capture; a song.

Catechism, ka'tē-kizm, *n.* A manual of instruction by questions and answers, especially in religion.

Caterwaul, kat'ẻr-wạl, *vi.* To cry as cats.

Catgut, kat'gut, *n.* The intestines of a cat; intestines made into strings for musical instruments, etc.; a kind of linen or canvas.

Cathartic, ka-thär'tik, *a.* Purging.—*n.* A medicine that purges.

Cathedral, ka-thē'dral, *n.* The principal church in a diocese.

Catheter, kath'e-tẻr, *n.* A tubular instrument, to be introduced into the bladder.

Cathode, kath'ōd, *n.* The negative pole of an electric current.

Catholic, ka'thol-ik, *a.* Universal; liberal; pertaining to the universal Church; pertaining to the Roman Catholic Church.—*n.* A member of the universal Christian Church; an adherent of the Roman Catholic Church.

Cattle, kat'tl, *n.pl.* Domestic quadrupeds serving for tillage or food; bovine animals.

Caucus, kạ'kus, *n.* A private committee to manage election matters.

Caudal, kạ'dal, *a.* Pertaining to a tail.

Caul, kạl, *n.* A net for the hair; a membrane investing some part of the intestines.

Cauliflower, kạ'li-flou-ẻr, *n.* A variety of cabbage.

Caulk, kạk, *vt.* To drive oakum into the seams of (a ship) to prevent leaking.

Causative, kạz'a-tiv, *a.* That expresses a cause or reason that effects.

Cause, kạz, *n.* That which produces an effect; reason; origin; sake; purpose; a suit in court; that which a person or party espouses.—*vt.* (causing, caused). To effect; to bring about.

Causeway, Causey, kạz'wā, kạz'i, *n.* A raised road; a paved way.

Caustic, kạs'tik, *a.* Burning; corroding; cutting.—*n.* A substance which burns the flesh.

Cauterization, ka̤'tėr-īz-ā''shon, *n.* Act of cauterizing.

Cavern, ka'vėrn, *n.* A large cave.

Caviare, Caviar, ka-vi-är', *n.* The roe of the sturgeon salted and prepared for food.

Cavil, ka'vil, *vi.* (caviling, caviled). To carp; to find fault with insufficient reason.—*n.* A captious objection.

Cavity, ka'vi-ti, *n.* A hollow place.

Cayenne, kā-en', *n.* A pepper made from capsicum seeds.

Cease, sēs, *vi.* (ceasing, ceased). To leave off; to fail; to stop; to become extinct.—*vt.* To put a stop to.

Cedar, sē'dėr, *n.* A large coniferous tree.—*a.* Made of cedar; belonging to cedar.

Celery, se'le-ri, *n.* An umbelliferous plant cultivated for the table.

Celestial, sē-les'ti-al, *a.* Heavenly; pertaining to heaven.—*n.* An inhabitant of heaven.

Celibacy, se'li-ba-si, *n.* The unmarried state; a single life.

Celibate, se'li-bāt, *n.* One who intentionally remains unmarried.—*a.* Unmarried.

Cell, sel, *n.* A small room; a cave; a small mass of protoplasm forming the structural unit in animal tissues.

Cellar sel'lėr, *n.* An apartment underground used for storage.

Cemetery, se'mē-te-ri, *n.* A burial-place.

Cenotaph, sen'ō-taf, *n.* A monument to one who is buried elsewhere.

Censer, sens'ėr, *n.* A vase or pan in which incense is burned.

Censor, sen'sėr, *n.* One who examines manuscripts, etc., before they are published; one who censures; in war-time, an official who controls the public press, etc., and who also supervises private correspondence.

Censorious, sen-sō'ri-us, *a.* Addicted to censure.

Censure, sen'shūr, *n.* Severe judgment; reproof.—*vt.* (censuring, censured). To judge unfavorably of; to blame.

Census, sen'sus, *n.* An enumeration of the inhabitants of a country.

Cent, sent, *n.* A hundred; a copper coin in America, etc.; the hundredth part of a dollar. *Per cent,* a certain rate by the hundred.

Centipede, sen'ti-pēd, *n.* An insect having a great number of feet.

Central, sen'tral, *a.* Placed in the center; relating to the center.

Center, sen'tėr, *n.* The middle point; a nucleus.—*vt.* (centering, centered). To fix on a center; to collect to a point.—*vi.* To be collected to a point; to have as a center.

Centrifugal, sen-trif'ū-gal, *a.* Tending to fly from a center.

Centripetal, sen-trip'et-al, *a.* Tending toward the center.

Cereal, sē'rē-al, *a.* Pertaining to corn.—*n.* A grain plant.

Cerebral, se'rē-bral, *a.* Pertaining to the brain.

Ceremony, se'rē-mō-ni, *n.* Outward rite; form; observance; formality.

Cerise, se-rēz', *n.* Cherry-color.

Certain, sėr'tān, *a.* Sure; undeniable; decided; particular; some; one.

Certificate, sėr-tif'i-kāt, *n.* A written testimony; a credential.

Certify, sėr'ti-fī, *vt.* (certifying, certified). To give certain information; to testify to in writing.

Chafe, chāf, *vt.* (chafing, chafed). To make warm by rubbing; to fret by rubbing; to enrage.—*vi.* To be fretted by friction; to rage.—*n.* A heat; a fretting.

Chafer, chāf'ėr, *n.* A beetle that eats roots, leaves, and young shoots.

Chaff, chaf, *n.* The husk of corn and grasses; banter.—*vt.* To banter.

Chagrin, sha-grēn', *n.* Ill-humor; vexation.—*vt.* To vex; to mortify.

Chain, chān, *n.* A series of links; a line of things connected; that which binds; a line formed of links, 66 feet long; (*pl.*) bondage; slavery.—*vt.* To bind with a chain; to confine.

Chair, chār, *n.* A movable seat; an official seat; professorship.—*vt.* To place or carry in a chair.

Chairman, chār'man, *n.* The presiding officer of an assembly; a president.

Chalybeate, ka-lib'ē-āt, *a.* Impregnated with particles of iron.—*n*. A liquid into which iron or steel enters.

Chamber, chăm'bėr, *n*. An apartment; an office; a hall of justice or legislation; a legislative body.

Chameleon, ka-mē'lē-on, *n*. A species of lizard, whose color changes.

Chamfer, cham'fėr, *n*. A small furrow in wood, etc.; a bevel.—*vt*. To cut a chamfer in; to bevel.

Chamois, sham'i or sham'wạ, *n*. A species of antelope; a soft leather.

Champ, champ, *vt*. To devour with violent action of the teeth; to bite the bit, as a horse.—*vi*. To keep biting.

Champagne, sham-pān', *n*. A kind of brisk sparkling wine.

Champion, cham'pi-on, *n*. A combatant for another, or for a cause; a hero; one victorious in contest.—*vt*. To fight for.

Chance, chans, *n*. That which happens; accident; possibility of an occurrence; opportunity.—*vi*. (chancing, chanced). To happen.—*a*. Happening by chance; casual.

Change, chānj, *vt*. (changing, changed). To cause to turn from one state to another; to substitute; to give one kind of money for another.—*vt*. To be altered.—*n*. Variation; small money.

Changeling, chānj'ling, *n*. A child substituted for another; a fool; one apt to change.

Channel, chan'nel, *n*. A watercourse; a narrow sea; means of passing or transmitting.—*vt*. (channelling, channelled). To form into a channel; to groove.

Chant, chant, *vt*. and *i*. To sing; to sing after the manner of a chant.—*n*. Song; a kind of sacred music; a part of church srvice.

Chaplain, chap'lān, *n*. A clergyman of the army, navy, court, etc.

Chapter, chap'tėr, *n*. Division of a book; a society of clergymen belonging to a cathedral or collegiate church; an organized branch of some fratrnity.

Char, chär, *vt*. (charring, charred). To reduce to a carbon by burning; to burn slightly.—*n*. A charred

body; a lake fish or the salmon kind.

Character, ka'rak-tėr, *n*. A mark engraved; a letter or figure; manner of writing; distinctive qualities of a person or thing; certificate of qualifications; a person in fiction or drama; a peculiar person.

Charade, sha-räd', *n*. A species of riddle upon the syllables of a word.

Charcoal, chär'kōl, *n*. Coal made by charring wood; the residue of animal, vegetable, and many mineral substances, when heated to redness in close vessls.

Charge, chärj, *vt*. (charging, charged). To load; to put a price on; to entrust; to impute, as a debt or crime; to command; to confide; to attack.—*vi*. To make a charge or onset.—*n*. That which is laid on; that which loads a rifle, etc.; an assault or onset; order; instruction; person or thing committed to another's care; accusation; cost.

Charity, cha'ri-ti, *n*. A disposition to relieve the wants of others; benevolence; alms; a charitable institution.

Charlatan, shär'la-tan, *n*. A quack.

Charm, chärm, *n*. A spell; fascination; a locket, etc.—*vt*. To enthrall; to delight.

Chart, chärt, *n*. A map; delineation of coasts, etc.; tabulated facts.

Charter, chär'tėr, *n*. A writing given as evidence of a grant, contract, etc.—*vt*. To establish by charter; to hire or to let (a ship).

Chauffeur, shō'fėr, *n*. A person regularly employed to drive a private motor-car.

Chauvinism, shō'vin-izm, *n*. Absurdly exaggerated patriotism or military enthusiasm.

Cheap, chēp, *a*. Of a low price; common; not respected.

Cheat, chēt, *vt*. To defraud; to deceive.—*n*. A deceitful act; a swindler.

Check, chek, *vt*. To stop; to curb; to chide; to compare with corresponding evidence.—*vi*. To stop; to clash or interfere.—*n*. An attack made on the king in chess; a stop; control; a counterfoil; a token; a cheque; cloth with a square pattern.

Checkmate, chek'māt, *n.* A move in chess which ends the game; defeat.—*vt.* To give checkmate to; to frustrate; to defeat.

Cheddar, ched'ér, *n.* A rich English cheese.

Cheek, chēk, *n.* The side of the face below the eyes on each side; impudence.

Chemistry, kem'ist-ri, *n.* The science which treats of the properties and nature of elementary substances.

Cherish, che'rish, *vt.* To treat with tenderness; to encourage.

Cheroot, shē-röt', *n.* A kind of cigar with both ends cut square off.

Cherry, che'ri, *n.* A tree and its fruit, of the plum family.—*a.* Like a cherry in color.

Cherub, che'rub, *n.*; pl. -**ubs** and -**ubim.** An angel of the second order; a beautiful child.

Chess, ches, *n.* A game played by two, with 16 pieces each on a board of 64 squares.

Chest, chest, *n.* A large close box; the part of the body containing the heart, lungs, etc.—*vt.* To reposit in a chest.

Chicory, chik'o-ri, *n.* A common English plant, often used to mix with coffee.

Chide, chīd, *vt.* and *i.* (chiding, pret. chid, pp. chid, chidden). To reprove; to scold.

Chief, chēf, *a.* Being at the head; first; leading.—*n.* A principal person; a leader.

Chilblain, chil'blān, *n.* A blain or sore produced on the hands or feet by cold.

Child, chīld, *n.*; pl. **Children.** An infant; one very young; a son or daughter; offspring.

Childbirth, chīld'bérth, *n.* The act of bringing forth a child; travail; labor.

Chill, chil, *n.* A shivering with cold; a cold fit; that which checks or disheartens.—*a.* Cold; tending to cause shivering; dispiriting.—*vt.* To make cold; to discourage.

Chime, chīm, *n.* A set of bells tuned to each other; their sound; harmony; the brim of a cask.—*vi.* (chiming, chimed). To sound in consonance; to agree.—*vt.* To cause to sound in harmony; to cause to sound.

Chin, chin, *n.* The lower part of the face; the point of the under jaw.

China, chī'na, *n.* A species of fine porcelain.

Chinchilla, chin-chil'la, *n.* A genus of S. American rodent animals; their fur.

Chinese, chī-nēz', *n. sing.* and *pl.* A native of China; the language of China.

Chiropodist, kīr-op'od-ist, *n.* One who extracts corns, removes bunions, etc.

Chirp, chérp, *vi.* To make the lively noise of small birds.—*n.* A short, shrill note of birds.

Chisel, chiz'el, *n.* A cutting tool, used in wood-work, masonry, sculpture, etc.—*vt.* (chiselling, chiselled). To cut, gouge, or engrave with a chisel.

Chit, chit, *n.* A note; an order or pass.

Chivalry, shi'val-ri, *n.* Knighthood; customs pertaining to the orders of knighthood; heroic defense of life and honor.

Chlorophyll, klō'rō-fil, *n.* The green coloring matter of plants.

Chocolate, cho'kō-lāt, *n.* A preparation from the kernels of the cacaonut.—*a.* Dark, glossy brown.

Choice, chois, *n.* Act of choosing; option; the thing chosen; best part of anything; the object of choice.—*a.* Select; precious.

Chop, chop, *vt.* (chopping, chopped). To cut into small pieces; to barter or exchange.—*vi.* To change; to turn suddenly.—*n.* A piece chopped off; a small piece of meat; a crack or cleft; a turn or change; the jaw; the mouth.

Chopsticks, chop'stiks, *n.* Two sticks of wood, ivory, etc., used by the Chinese in eating.

Chord, kord, *n.* String of a musical instrument; the simultaneous combination of different sounds; a straight line joining the ends of the arc of a circle or curve.

Chorus, kō'rus, *n.* A company of

singers; a piece performed by a company in concert; verses of a song in which the company join the singer; any union of voices in general.

Chosen, chōz'n, a. Select; eminent.

Chrism, krizm, n. Consecrated oil.

CHRIST, krīst, n. THE ANOINTED; the Messiah; the Saviour.

Christen, kris'n, vt. To baptize; to name.

Christendom, kris'n-dum, n. The countries inhabited by Christians; the whole body of Christians.

Christian, kris'ti-an, n. A professed follower of Christ.—a. Pertaining to Christ or Christianity.

Christmas, kris'mas, n. The festival of Christ's nativity, observed annually on 25th December.—a. Belonging to Christmas time.

Chromatic, kō-mat'ik, a. Relating to color; proceeding by semitones.

Chrome, Chromium, krōm, krō'mi-um, n. A steel-gray, hard metal, from which colored preparations are made.

Chronic, kron'ik, a. Continuing a long time; lingering; continuous.

Chronicle, kron'i-kl, n. An historical account of events in order of time.—vt. (chronicling, chronicled). To record.

Chronology, kro-nol'o-ji, n. Arrangement of events according to their dates.

Chronometer, kro-nom'et-ėr, n. An instrument that measures time.

Chrysalis, kris'a-lis, n.; pl. -ides or -ises. The form of certain insects before they arrive at their winged state.

Chrysanthemum, kri-san'thē-mum, n. The name of numerous composite plants.

Chub, chub, n. A small river fish of the carp family.

Church, chėrch, n. A house consecrated to the worship of God among Christians; the collective body of Christians; a particular body of Christians; the body of clergy; eccelesiastical authority.—vt. To give or receive a service in church, as after childbirth.

Cider, sī'dėr, n. A fermented drink prepared from the juice of apples.

Cigar, si-gär', n. A roll of tobacco for smoking.

Cigarette, sig-a-ret', n. A little cut tobacco rolled up in rice paper, used for smoking.

Cilia, sil'i-a, n.pl.. Minute hairs on plants or animals.

Ciliary, sil'i-a-ri, a. Belonging to or of the nature of eyelashes.

Cimmerian, sim-mē'ri-an, a. Pertaining to the fabulous Cimmerians, who dwelt in perpetual darkness; extremely dark.

Cinnamon, sin'na-mon, n. The inner bark of a tree, a native of Ceylon; a spice.

Cipher, sī'fėr, n. The figure 0 or nothing; any numeral; a person or thing of no importance; a device; a secret writing.—vi. To use figures. —vt. To write in secret characters.

Circle, sėr'kl, n. A plane figure contained by a curved line, every point of which is equally distant from a point within the figure, called the center; the curved line itself; a ring; enclosure; a class; a coterie.—vt. (circling, circled). To move round; to enclose.—vi. To move circularly.

Circuit, sėr'kit, n. Act of going round; space measured by travelling round; the journey of judges to hold courts; the district visited by judges; path of an electric current.

Circular, sėr'kū-lėr, a. Round; addressed to a number of persons.—n. A paper addressed to a number of persons.

Circulate, sėr'kū-lāt, vi. (circulating, circulated). To move in a circle; to have currency.—vt. To spread; to give currency to.

Circumcise, sėr'kum-sīz, vt. (circumcising, circumcised). To cut off the foreskin, according to Jewish and Mohammedan law.

Circumference, sėr-kum'fē-rens, n. The bounding line of a circle.

Circumstance, sėr'kum-stans, n. Something attending, or relative to a main fact or case; event; (pl.) state of affairs; condition.

Circumvent, sėr-kum-vent', vt. To encompass; to outwit.

Circus, sėr'kus, *n.*; pl. **-ses.** Among the Romans, a place for horse-races; a place for feats of horsemanship and acrobatic displays.

Cirrus, sir'rus, *n.*; pl. **Cirri.** A tendril; a light fleecy cloud at a high elevation.

Cistern, sis'tėrn, *n.* An artificial receptacle for water, etc.; a natural reservoir.

Citadel, si'ta-del, *n.* A fortress in or near a city.

Citation, sī-tā'shon, *n.* Quotation; a summons.

Cite, sīt, *vt.* (citing, cited). To summon to appear in a court; to quote; to adduce.

Citizen, si'ti-zen, *n.* An inhabitant of a city; one who has full municipal and political privileges.—*a.* Having the qualities of a citizen.

Civil, si'vil, *a.* Relating to the government of a city or state; polite; political; lay; legislative, not military; intestine, not foreign.

Civilian, si-vil'i-an, *n.* One skilled in the civil law; one engaged in civil, not military or clerical pursuits.

Civility, si-vil'i-ti, *n.* Quality of being civil; good breeding; (*pl.*) acts of politeness.

Civilize, si'vil-īz, *vt.* (civilizing, civilized). To reclaim from a savage state.

Clamor, klam'ėr, *n.* Loud and continued noise; uproar.—*vi.* To call aloud; to make importunate demands.

Clamp, klamp, *n.* A piece of timber or iron, used to strengthen or fasten; a heavy footstep.—*vt.* To fasten or strengthen with clamps; to tread heavily.

Clan, klan, *n.* A family; a tribe; a sect.

Clandestine, klan-des'tin, *a.* Secret; underhand.

Clang, klang, *vt.* or *i.* To make a sharp sound, as by striking metallic substances.—*n.* A loud sound made by striking together metallic bodies.

Clank, klangk, *n.* The loud sound made by the collison of metallic bodies.—*vi.* or *t.* To sound or cause to sound with a clank.

Clap, klap, *vt.* (clapping, clapped or clapt). To strike together so as to make a noise; to strike with something broad; to shut hastily; to pat. —*vi.* To move together suddenly with noise; to strike the hands together in applause.—*n.* A noise made by sudden collision; a sudden explosive sound; a striking of hands in applause.

Clash, klash, *vi.* To make a noise by collision; to meet in opposition; to interfere.—*vt.* To strike noisily together.—*n.* Noisy collision; opposition.

Clasp, klasp, *n.* An embrace; a hook for fastening; a catch; a bar added to a military medal to commemorate a particular battle or campaign.—*vt.* To fasten together with a clasp; to inclose in the hand; to embrace closely.

Clasp-knife, klasp'nīf, *n.* A knife the blade of which folds into the handle.

Class, klas, *n.* A rank of persons or things; an order; a group.—*vt.* To arrange in classes.

Clause, klaz, *n.* A member of a sentence; a distinct part of a contract, will, etc.

Claustrophobia, klas'trō-fo''bē-a, *n.* Morbid fear of confined spaces.

Clavicle, klav'i-kl, *n.* The collarbone.

Claw, kla, *n.* The sharp hooked nail of an animal; that which resembles a claw.—*vt.* To scrape, scratch, or tear.

Clay, klā, *n.* A tenacious kind of earth; earth in general; the body. —*vt.* To cover with clay; to purify and whiten with clay, as sugar.

Clean, klēn, *a.* Free from dirt; pure. —*adv.* Quite; fully.—*vt.* To purify; to cleanse.

Cleat, klēt, *n.* A piece of wood or iron in a ship to fasten ropes upon; a wedge.

Clement, kle'ment, *a.* Mild; humane.

Clench, klensh, *vt.* To secure; to confirm; to grasp.

Clergy, klėr'ji, *n.pl.* The body or order of men set apart to the service of God, in the Christian church.

Clericalism, kle'rik-al-izm, *n.* Clerical power to influence; sacerdotalism.

Clerk, klärk, *n*. A clergyman; one who reads the responses in church; one who is employed under another as a writer.

Clever, kle'vèr, *a*. Adroit; talented; excuted with ability.

Cliché, klē'shä, *n*. A hackneyed phrase.

Click, klĭk, *vi*. To make a small sharp noise, or a succession of such sounds.—*n*. A small sharp sound.

Client, klī'ent, *n*. A person under patronage; one who employs a lawyer.

Clientele, klī'en-tēl, *n*. One's clients collectively.

Cliff, klif, *n*. A precipice; a steep rock.

Climacteric, kli-mak-te'rĭk, *n*. A critical period in human life.

Climate, klī'māt, *n*. The condition of a country in respect of temperature, dryness, wind, etc.

Climax, klī'maks, *n*. A figure of rhetoric, in which the language gradually rises in strength and dignity; culmination; acme.

Climb, klĭm, *vi*. To creep up step by step; to ascend.—*vt*. To ascent.

Clock, klok, *n*. An instrument which measures time.

Clod, klod, *n*. A lump of earth; a stupid fellow.—*vt*. (clodding, clodded). To pelt with clods.

Clog, klog, *vt*. (clogging, clogged). To hinder; to impede; to trammel.—*vi*. To be loaded.—*n*. Hindrance; a shoe with a wooden sole.

Cloister, klois'tèr, *n*. A monastery or nunnery; an arcade round an open court.—*vt*. To shut up in a cloister; to immure.

Close, klōz, *vt*. (closing, closed). To shut; to finish.—*vi*. To come close together; to end; to grapple; to come to an agreement.—*n*. End.

Close, klōs, *a*. Shut fast; tight; dense; near; stingy; trusty; intense; without ventilation; disposed to keep secrets.—*adv*. Tightly; in contact, or very near.—*n*. An inclosed place; precinct of a cathedral.

Clot, klot, *n*. A mass of soft or fluid matter concreted.—*vi*. (clotting, clotted). To become thick; to coagulate.

Cloth, kloth, *n*. A woven material or fabric; the covering of a table; the clerical profession.

Clothe, klōⱦH, *vt*. (clothing, clothed or clad). To put clothes on; to cover or spread over.

Cloud, kloud, *n*. A collection of visible vapor, suspended in the air; something similar to this; what obscures, threatens, etc.; a great multitude, a mass.—*vt*. To obscure; to darken; to sully; to make to appear sullen.—*vi*. To grow cloudy.

Cloy, kloi, *vt*. To glut; to fill to loathing.

Club, klub, *n*. A cudgel; a card of the suit marked with trefoils; a staff with a heavy head for driving the ball in golf, etc.; an association for some common object; the meeting-place of such an association.—*vt*. To beat with a club.—*vi*. To join for some common object.

Club-footed, klub'fut-ed, *a*. Having short, crooked, or deformed feet.

Cluck, kluk, *vi*. To make the noise of the hen when calling chickens.—*n*. Such a sound.

Clue, klö, *n*. A ball of thread; a thread serving to guide; something helping to unravel a mystery.

Coast, kōst, *n*. The sea-shore; the country near the sea.—*vi*. To sail along a shore; to sail from port to port.

Coat, kōt, *n*. An upper garment; vesture, as indicating office; hair or fur covering of animals; a layer; a covering; that on which ensigns armorial are portrayed.—*vt*. To cover; to spread over.

Coax, kōks, *vt*. To wheedle; to persuade by fondling and flattering.

Cob, kob, *n*. A round knob; the head of clover or wheat; a smallish thick-set horse; a male swan.

Cobalt, kō'balt, *n*. A mineral of grayish color, and a metal obtained from it yielding a permanent blue; the blue itself.

Cobble, kob'l, *vt*. (cobbling, cobbled). To mend coarsely, as shoes;

to botch.—*n*. A roundish stone.

Cock kok, *n*. The male of the domestic fowl; the male of other birds; a vane; a person or thing having resemblance to a cock; a chief man; a tap for drawing off liquids; the hammer of a gun; a small pile of hay.—*vt*. To set erect; to set on the head with an air of pertness; to draw back the cock of a gun.

Coco, Cocoa, kō'kō, *n*. A tropical palm-tree.

Cocoa, kō'kō, *n*. The seed of the cacao prepared for a beverage; the beverage itself.

Coco-nut, Cocoa-nut, kō'kō-nut, *n*. The fruit of the coco palm.

Cocoon, kō'kön', *n*. The silky case in which the silkworm involves itself when still a larva; the envelope of other larvae.

Cod, kod, *n*. A species of sea fish allied to the haddock; a husk; a pod.

Coddle, kod'l, *vt*. (coddling, coddled). To fondle.

Code, kōd, *n*. A digest of laws; a collection of rules; a system of signals, etc.

Codicil, ko'di-sil, *n*. A writing by way of supplement to a will.

Coeval, kō-ē'val, *a*. Of the same age; contemporary.—*n*. One of the same age.

Coexist, kō-egz-ist', *vi*. To live at the same time with another.

Coffee, kof'i, *n*. A tree and its fruit or berries; a beverage made from the seeds.

Coffee-house, kof'i-hous, *n*. A house where coffee and refreshments are supplied.

Coffer, kof'èr, *n*. A chest for holding gold, jewels, etc.

Coffer-dam, kof'èr-dam, *n*. A case of piling, water-tight, serving to exclude water in laying the foundations of piers, bridges, etc.

Coffin, kof'fin, *n*. The chest in which a dead human body is buried.—*vt*. To inclose in a coffin.

Cog, kog, *n*. The tooth of a wheel.—*vt*. (cogging, cogged). To furnish with cogs; to trick, deceive; to manipulate dice unfairly.—*vi*. To cheat; to lie.

Cogent, kō'jent, *a*. Forcible; convincing.

Cogitate, ko'jit-āt, *vi*. (cogitating, cogitated). To ponder; to meditate.

Cognac, kō'nyak, *n*. A kind of brandy.

Cognate, kog'nāt, *a*. Born of the same stock; akin; of the same nature.

Cognition, kog-ni'shon, *n*. Knowledge from personal view or experience.

Cohesion, kō-hē'zhon, *n*. Act of sticking together; the attraction by which bodies are kept together; coherence.

Coiffure, koif'ūr, *n*. Mode of dressing the hair in women.

Coil, koil, *vt*. To wind into a ring.—*n*. A ring or rings into which a rope, etc., is wound.

Coin, koin, *n*. A piece of metal stamped, as money; that which serves for payment.—*vt*. To stamp and convert metal into money; to mint; to invent; to fabricate.

Coincide, kō-in-sīd', *vi*. (coinciding, coincided). To agree in position; to happen at the same time; to concur.

Coition, kō-i'shon, *n*. Sexual intercourse.

Colitis, kō-lī'tis, *n*. Inflammation of the large intestine, especially of its mucous membrane.

Collaborator, kol-la'bo-rāt-èr, *n*. An associate in literary or scientific labor.

Collapse, kol-laps', *n*. A wasting of the body; a sudden and complete failure.—*vi*. (collapsing, collapsed). To fall together, as the sides of a vessel; to break down.

Collar, kol'èr, *n*. A part of dress that surrounds the neck; something worn round the neck.—*vt*. To seize by the collar; to put a collar on; to roll up and bind with a cord.

Colleague, kol'lēg, *n*. An associate in office.

Collect, kol'ekt, *n*. A short comprehensive prayer; a short prayer adapted to a particular occasion.

Collected, kol-lekt'ed, *p.a*. Cool; self-possessed.

Collectivism, kol-lek'tiv-izm, *n*. The doctrine that the state should own or control the land and all means of production.

College, kol'lej, n. A society of men, invested with certain powers, engaged in some common pursuit; a seminary of the higher learning; the building occupied for such purposes.

Collide, kol-līd', vi. (colliding, collided). To strike against each other; to meet in opposition.

Collie, kol'i, n. A dog common in Scotland, much used for sheep.

Collier, kol'yėr, n. A ship that carries coals.

Colloquy, kol'lō-kwi, n. A speaking together; mutual discourse; dialogue.

Collude, 'kol-lūd', vi. (colluding, colluded). To conspire in a fraud; to connive.

Colon, kō'lon, n. A mark of punctuation, thus (:); the largest of the intestines.

Colophon, ko'lo-fōn, n. An inscription or device formerly on the last page of a book, now usually in its preliminary pages.

Color, kul'ėr, n. That which gives bodies different appearances independently of form; a pigment; complexion; appearance to the mind; pretense; (pl.) a flag.—vt. To give some kind of color to; to give a specious appearance to; to exaggerate in representation.—vi. To show color; to blush.

Color-blindness, kul'ėr-blīnd-nes, n. Inability to distinguish colors.

Coloring, kul'ėr-ing, n. Act of giving a color; color applied; a specious appearance; fair artificial representation.

Colossal, kō-los'al, a. Huge; gigantic.

Colossus, kō-los'us, n.; pl. **-lossi.** A statue of gigantic size.

Colure, kō-lūr', n. Either of two great circles of the heavens, passing through the solstitial and the equinoctial points of the ecliptic.

Coma, kō'ma, n. Deep sleep; stupor; the hair-like envelope round the nucleus of a comet.

Comb, kōm, n. An instrument for separating hair, wool, etc.; the crest of a cock; honeycomb.—vt. To separate and adjust with a comb.

Combat, kom'bat, vi. To fight; to act in opposition.—vt. To oppose; to resist.—n. A fighting; an engagement; a duel.

Combine, kom-bīn', vt. (combining, combined). To cause to unite; to join.—vi. To come into union; to coalesce; to league together.—kom' bīn, n. A union.

Combustible, kom-bust'i-bl, a. Capable of catching fire; inflammable.—n. A substance easily set on fire.

Combustion, kom-bust'shon, n. A burning; chemical combination, attended with heat and light.

Come, kum, vi. (coming, pret. came, pp. come). To move hitherward; to draw nigh; to arrive; to happen; to appear; to rise; to result.

Comedian, ko-mē'di-an, n. An actor in or writer of comedies.

Coming, kum'ing, p.a. Future.—n. Approach.

Comity, ko'mi-ti, n. Courtesy; civility.

Comma, kom'ma, n. A mark of punctuation, thus (,); an interval in music.

Command, kom-mand', vt. To order; to govern; to have at one's disposal.—vi. To have chief power.—n. Order; control; power of overlooking; power of defending.

Commend, kom-mend', vt. To commit to the care of; to recommend; to praise.

Commensal, kom-men'sal, n. One that eats at the same table; one living with another.

Commensurate, kom-men'sūr-āt, a. Proportional; having equal measure.

Comment, kom-ment', vi. To make remarks or criticisms.—vt. To annotate.—n. kom'-ment. An explanatory note; criticism.

Commentary, kom'ment-a-ri, n. Book of comments; an historical narrative.

Commerce, kom'mėrs, n. Exchange of goods by barter or purchase; trade; intercourse.

Commercial, kom-mėr'shal, a. Pertaining to commerce; trading; mercantile.

Commission, kom-mi'shon, n. Trust; warrant; a written document, investing one with an office; allowance made to an agent, etc., for transacting business; a body of men joined in an office or trust, or their appointment; perpetration.—vt. To appoint; to depute.

Commissure, kom'mis-sŭr, n. A joint or seam; juncture.

Commit, kom-mit', vt. (committing, committed). To intrust; to consign; to send to prison; to perpetrate; to endanger or compromise (oneself).

Committee, kom-mit'tē, n. A body of persons appointed to manage any matter.

Commix, kom-miks', vt. To blend; to mix.

Commode, kom-mōd', n. A kind of small sideboard; a lady's headdress; a night-stool.

Commodious, kom-mō'di-us, a. Convenient; spacious and suitable.

Commodity, kom-mo'di-ti, n. Something useful; any article of commerce; (pl.) goods;; merchandise.

Commodore, kom'mo-dōr, n. A captain in the navy who is discharging duties rather more important than those usually assigned to a captain.

Common, kom'mon, a. Having no separate owner; general; usual; of no rank; of little value,—n. An open public ground; pl. the untitled people; the lower House of Parliament; food at a common table; food in general.

Communicable, kom-mū'ni-ka-bl, a. Capable of being imparted to another.

Communicant, kom-mū'ni-kant, n. One who communicates; a partaker of the Lord's supper.

Communicate, kom-mū'ni-kāt, vt. (communicating, communicated). To cause to be common to others; to impart, as news, disease, etc.; to bestow; to reveal.—vi. To share with others; to partake of the Lord's supper; to have intercourse; to correspond.

Communion, kom-mūn'yon, n. A mutual participation in anything; mutual intercourse; condord; celebration of the Lord's supper.

Communism, kom'mūn-izm, n. The doctrine of a community of property by which the state owns and controls all means of production.

Communist, kom'mūn-ist, n. One who holds the doctrines of communism; member of the communist party.

Community, kom-mū'ni-ti, n. Mutual participation; the public; a society of persons under the same laws.

Company, kum'pa-ni, n. Companionship; an assembly of persons; partners in a firm; a division of a battalion, consisting of four platoons, and commanded by a major or mounted captain, with a captain as second-in-command; the crew of a ship.—vi. To associate with.

Comparative, kom-pa'ra-tiv, a. Estimated by comparison; not positive or absolute.

Compare, kom-pār', vt. (comparing, compared). To bring together and examine the relations between; to estimate one by another; to inflect in the degrees of comparison.—vi. To hold comparison.

Comparison, kom-pa'ri-son, n. Act of comparing; state of being compared; relation; the formation of an adjective in its degrees of signification; a simile.

Compartment, kom-pärt'ment, n. A division or part of a general design.

Compatriot, kom-pā'tri-ot, n. One of the same country.

Compete, kom-pēt', vi. (competing, competed). To strive for the same thing as another; to contend.

Competent, kom'pē-tent, a. Suitable, sufficient; qualified; having adequate right.

Competition, kom-pē-ti'shon, n. Contest for the same object; rivalry.

Compile, kom-pīl', vt. (compiling, compiled). To gather from various sources; to draw up by collecting parts from different authors.

Complacence, Complacency, kom-plā'sens, kom-plā'sen-si, n. A feeling of quiet satisfaction; complaisance.

Complain, kom-plān', *vi.* to express grief or distress; to lament; to express dissatisfaction; to make a formal accusation.

Complaisance, kom'plā-zans, *n.* A pleasing deportment; courtesy; urbanity.

Complement, kom'plē-ment, *n.* That which fills up; full quantity or number.

Complete, kom-plēt', *a.* Having no deficiency; finished; total; absolute.—*vt.* (completing, completed). To make complete; to finish; to fulfil.

Complex, kom'pleks, *a.* Of various parts; involved; composite.—*n.* A series of emotionally accentuated ideas in a repressed state.

Complexion, kom-plek'shon, *n.* The color of the face; general appearance.

Comply, kom-plī', *vi.* (complying, complied). To yield; to assent; to acquiesce.

Component, kom-pōn'ent, *a.* Composing; forming an element of a compound.—*n.* A constituent part; ingredient.

Comport, kom-pōrt', *vi.* To agree; to suit.—*vt.* To bear or carry (oneself); to behave.

Compose, kom-pōz', *vt.* (composing, composed). To form by uniting; to constitute; to write; to calm; to set types in printing.

Composer, kom-pōz'er, *n.* An author, especially a musical author.

Composite, kom'po-zīt or -zit, *a.* Compound; noting a rich order of architecture; noting plants whose flowers are arranged in dense heads.

Compost, kom'pōst, *n.* A mixture for manure.

Compress, kom-pres', *vt.* To press together; to squeeze; to condense.—*n.* kom'pres. A soft mass or bandage used in surgery.

Compressible, kom-pres'i-bl, *a.* Capable of being compressed.

Comprise, kom-prīz', *vt.* (comprising, comprised). To embrace; to contain; to inclose.

Compromise, kom'prō-mīz, *n.* An amicable agreement to settle differences; mutual concession.—*vi.* To settle by mutual concessions; to involve; to endanger the interests of.

Comptroller, kon-trōl'er, *n.* A controller; an officer who examines the accounts of collectors of public money.

Compulsion, kom-pul'shon, *n.* Act of compelling; state of being compelled; force.

Compulsory, kom-pul'so-ri, *a.* Constraining; coercive; obligatory.

Compunction, kom-pungk'shon, *n.* Remorse; contrition.

Concave, kon'kāv, *a.* Hollow, as the inner surface of a sphere; opposed to convex.—*n.* A hollow; an arch or vault.

Conceal, kon-sēl', *vt.* To hide; to secrete; to disguise.

Concede, kon-sēd', *vt.* (conceding, conceded). To yield; to grant.—*vi.* To make concession.

Conceit, kon-sēt', *n.* Conception; fancy; self-flattering opinion; vanity.

Conceive, kon-sēv', *vt.* (conceiving, conceived). To form in the womb; to take into the mind; to comprehend.—*vi.* To become pregnant; to have or form an idea.

Concentrate, kon'sen-trāt, *vt.* (concentrating, concentrated). To bring together; to direct to one object; to condense.

Concentric, kon-sen'trik, *a.* Having a common center.

Concept, kon'sept, *n.* An object conceived by the mind; a general notion of a class of objects.

Concert, kon-sert', *vt.* To plan together; to contrive.—*n.* kon'sert. Agreement in a design; harmony; performance of a company of players, singers, etc.

Concise, kon-sīs', *a.* Brief; abridged; comprehensive.

Conclave, kon'klāv, *n.* A private apartment; the assembly of cardinals for the election of a pope; a close assembly.

Conclude, kon-klūd', *vt.* (concluding, concluded). To end; to decide; to deduce.—*vi.* To end; to form a final judgment.

Concoct, kon-kokt', *vt.* To devise; to

plot.

Concomitance, Concomitancy, kon-kom'i-tans, kon-kom'i-tan-si, *n.* A being together or in connection with another thing.

Concubine, kong'kū-bīn, *n.* A woman who cohabits with a man; a mistress.

Concupiscence, kon-kū'pis-ens, *n.* Lust.

Concur, kon-kėr', *vi.* (concurring, concurred). To unite; to agree; to assent.

Concussion, kon-ku'shon, *n.* A violent shock.

Concussive, kon-kus'iv, *a.* Having the power or quality of shaking; agitating.

Condemn, kon-dem', *vt.* To pronounce to be wrong; to censure; to sentence.

Condense, kon-dens', *vt.* (condensing, condensed). To reduce in compass; to reduce from a gaseous to a liquid or solid state.—*vi.* To become dense; to grow thick.

Conditionally, kon-di'shon-al-li, *adv.* With certain limitatons.

Condole, kon-dōl', *vi.* (condoling, condoled). To grieve with another; to sympathize.

Condone, kon-dōn', *vt.* (condoning, condoned). To pardon; to imply forgiveness of.

Condor, kon'dor, *n.* A S. American vulture.

Conduce, kon-dūs', *vi.* (conducing, conduced). To lead; to tend; to contribute.

Conduct, kon'dukt, *n.* Personal behavior; management; escort.—*vt.* kon-dukt'. To lead or guide; to escort; to manage; to behave (oneself); to transmit, as heat, etc.

Confection, kon-fek'shon, *n.* A mixture; a sweetmeat.

Confectioner, kon-fek'shon-ėr, *n.* One who makes or sells sweetmeats.

Confederacy, kon-fe'de-ra-si, *n.* A confederation; the parties united by a league.

Confederate, kon-fe'de-rāt, *a.* Allied by treaty.—*n.* One united with others in a league.—*vt.* and *i.* (confederating, confederated). To unite in a league.

Confederation, kon-fe'de-rā''shon, *n.* A league; alliance, particularly of states, etc.

Confer, kon-fėr', *vi.* (conferring, conferred). To consult together.—*vt.* To give or bestow.

Conference, kon'fėr-ens, *n.* A meeting for consultation, or for the adjustment of differences; bestowal.

Confess, kon-fes', *vt.* To own, as a crime, debt, etc.; to admit; publicly to declare adherence to; to hear a confession, as a priest.—*vi.* To make confession.

Confide, kon-fīd', *vi.* (confiding, confided). To trust wholly; to have firm faith (with *in*).—*vt.* To intrust; to commit to the charge of.

Confidence, kon'fi-dens, *n.* Firm belief or trust; self-reliance; boldness; assurance; a secret.

Confidential, kon-fi-den'shal, *a.* Enjoying confidence; trusty; private; secret.

Configuration, kon-fig'ūr-ā''shon, *n.* External form; contour.

Confine, kon'fīn, *n.* Boundary; territory near the end; border (generally in *pl.*).—*vt.* kon-fīn' (confining, confined). To restrain; to limit; to shut up; to imprison.—**To be confined,** to be in childbed.

Confirm, kon-fėrm', *vt.* To make firm or more firm; to establish; to make certain; to administer the rite of confirmation to.

Confirmation, kon-fėrm-ā'shon, *n.* Act of confirming; additional evidence; ratification; the laying on of a bishop's hands in the rite of admission to the privileges of a Christian.

Confiscate, kon'fis-kāt, *vt.* (confiscating, confiscated). To seize as forfeited to the public treasury.

Conflagration, kon-fla-grā'shon, *n.* A great fire.

Conflict, kon'flikt, *n.* a struggle; clashing of views or statements.—*vi.* kon-flikt'. To meet in opposition; to be antagonistic.

Confluence, kon'flū-ens, *n.* A flowing together; meeting, or place of meeting, of rivers; a concourse; a crowd.

Conform, kon-form', *vt.* To cause to be of the same form; to adapt.—*vi.*

To comply.

Conformation, kon-for-mā'shon, n. The act of conforming; structure; configuration.

Conformist, kon-for'mist, n. One who conforms; one who complies with the worship of the established church.

Confound, kon-found', vt. To confuse; to astound; to overthrow; to mistake.

Confuse, kon-fūz', vt. (confusing, confused). To mix without order; to derange; to confound; to disconcert.

Confute, kon-fūt', vt. (confuting, confuted). To prove to be false; to refute.

Congeniality, kon-jē'ni-al''i-ti, n. Natural affinity; suitableness.

Congenital, kon-jen'it-al, a. Pertaining to an individual from his birth.

Conger, kong'gėr, n. The sea-eel.

Congeries, kon-jē'ri-ēz, n. A heap or pile; a collection of several bodies in one mass.

Congest, kon-jest', vt. and i. To accumulate to excess, as blood, population, etc.

Congestion, kon-jest'shon, n. Excessive accumulation; undue fullness of blood-vessels in an organ.

Congregation, kong-grē-gā'shon, n. Act of congregating; an assembly; an assembly met for divine worhip.

Congregationalist, kong-grē-gā'shon-al-ist, n. One who adheres to the system in which each separate congregation or church forms an independent body.

Congress, kong'gres, n. An assembly; a meeting of ambassaors, etc., for the settlement of affairs between different nations; the legislature of the United States.

Congruence, Congruency, kong'grṵ-ens, kong'grṵ-en-si, n. Accordance; consistency.

Congruity, kon-grṵ'i-ti, n. Suitableness; accordance; consistency.

Conic, Conical, kon'ik, kon'ik-al, a. Having the form of a cone; pertaining to a cone.

Conjugate, kon'jū-gāt, vt. (conjugating, conjugated). To join together; to inflect (a verb) through

its several forms.—a. Joined in pairs; kindred in origin and meaning.

Conjunction, kon-jungk'shon, n. Act of joining; state of being joined; connection; a connecting word.

Connect, kon-nekt', vt. To conjoin; to combine; to associate.—vi. To unite or cohere together; to have a close relation.

Connection, kon-nek'shon, n. Act of connecting; state of being connected; a relation by blood or marriage; relationship.

Connective, kon-nekt'iv, a. Having the power of connecting; tending to connect.—n. A word that connects other words and sentences; a conjunction.

Connivance, kon-nīv'ans, n. Voluntary blindness to an act; pretended ignorance.

Connive, kon-nīv', vi. (conniving, connived). To wink; to pretend ignorance or blindness; to forbear to see (with at).

Conquer, kong'kėr, vt. To gain by force; to vanquish; to subjugate; to surmount,—vi. To overcome; to gain the victory.

Conquest, kong'kwest, n. Act of conquering; that which is conquered; a gaining by struggle.

Conscience, kon'shens, n. Internal knowledge or judgment of right and wrong; the moral sense; morality.

Conscionable, kon'shon-a-bl, a. Reasonable.

Conscious, kon'shus, a. Knowing in one's own mind; knowing by sensation or perception; aware; sensible; self-conscious.

Consciousness, kon'shus-nes, n. State of being conscious; perception of what passes in one's own mind; sense of guilt or innocence.

Consequence, kon'sē-kwens, n. That which follows as a result; inference; importance.

Consequent, kon'sē-kwent, a. Following, as the natural effect, or by inference.—n. Effect; result; inference.

Consequential, kon-sē-kwen'shal, a. Following as the effect; pompous.

Conservation, kon-sėrv-ā'shon, *n.* Preservation; the keeping of a thing entire.

Consider, kon-si'dėr, *vt.* To fix the mind on; to ponder; to have respect to; to regard to be.—*vi.* To think seriously; to ponder.

Considerable, kon-si'dėr-a-bl, *a.* Worthy of consideration; moderately large.

Considerate, kon-si'dėr-āt, *a.* Given to consideration; mindful of others; deliberate.

Considerately, kon-si'dėr-āt-li, *adv.* In a considerate manner.

Consideration, kon-si'dėr-ā''shon, *n.* Mental view; serious deliberation; importance; motive of action; an equivalent.

Considering, kon-si'dėr-ing, *prep.* Taking into account; making allowance for.

Consign, kon-sīn', *vt.* To deliver over to another by agreement; to intrust; to commit; to deposit.

Consist, kon-sist', *vi.* To be in a fixed state; to be comprised; to be made up; to be compatible; to agree.

Consolation, kon-sōl-ā'shon, *n.* A solace; alleviation of misery; what helps to cheer; what gives comfort.

Console, kon-sōl', *vt.* (consoling, consoled). To comfort; to soothe; to cheer.

Console, kon'sōl, *n.* A bracket to support a cornice, vase, etc.

Consolidate, kon-sol'id-āt, *vt.* (consolidating, consolidated). To make solid or firm; to unite into one; to compact.—*vi.* To grow firm and solid.

Conspiracy, kon-spi'ra-si, *n.* A plot; a treasonable combination.

Conspire, kon-spīr', *vi.* (conspiring, conspired). To plot; to combine for some evil purpose; to tend to one end.

Constable, kun'sta-bl, *n.* An officer of the peace; policeman.

Constant, kon'stant, *a.* Steadfast; perpetual; assiduous; resolute.— *n.* That which remains unchanged; a fixed quantity.

Constellation, kon-stel-lā'shon, *n.* A group of fixed stars; an assemblage of splendors or excellences.

Consternation, kon-stėr-nā'shon, *n.* Prostration of the mind by terror, dismay, etc.

Constipate, kon'sti-pāt, *vt.* (constipating, constipated). To make costive.

Constituent, kon-stit'ū-ent, *a.* Forming; existing as an essential part.—*n.* An elector; an essential part.

Constitute, kon'sti-tūt, *vt.* (constituting, constituted). To set up or establish; to compose; to appoint; to make and empower.

Constitution, kon-sti-tū'shon, *n.* The particular frame or character of the body or mind; established form of government; a system of fundamental laws; a particular law.

Constitutional, kon-sti-tū'shon-al, *a.* Adherent in the human constitution; consistent with the civil constitution; legal.—*n.* A walk for the sake of health.

Constrain, kon-strān', *vt.* To urge by force; to necessitate; to restrain.

Constructive, kon-strukt'iv, *a.* Having ability to construct; created or deduced by construction; inferred.

Construe, kon'strū, *vt.* (construing, construed). To arrange words so as to discover the sense of a sentence; to interpret.

Consult, kon-sult', *vi.* To seek the opinion of another; to deliberate in common; to consider.—*vt.* To ask advice of; to refer to for information; to have regard to.

Consume, kon-sūm', *vt.* (consuming, consumed). To reduce to nothing; to burn up; to squander.—*vi.* To waste away slowly; to be exhausted.

Consummate, kon'sum-āt, *vt.* To finish; to perfect.—*a.* kon-sum'āt. Complete; perfect.

Consumption, kon-sum'shon, *n.* Act of consuming; quantity consumed; a gradual wasting away of the body; phthisis.

Contact, kon'takt, *n.* A touching together; close union or juncture of bodies.

Contagion, kon-tā'jon, n. Communication of a disease by contact; poisonous emanation; infection.

Contain, kon-tān', vt. To hold; to be able to hold; to comprise; to restrain.

Contaminate, kon-tam'in-āt, vt. To corrupt; to taint; to vitiate.

Contemptible, kon-tem'ti-bl, a. Worthy of contempt; despicable; vile; mean.

Contemptuous, kon-tem'tū-us, a. Manifesting contempt; scornful; insolent.

Contend, kon-tend', vi. To strive; to vie; to dispute; to wrangle.

Content, kon-tent', a. Easy in mind; satisfied.—vt. To satisfy the mind of; to please or gratify.—n. State of being contented; contentment. Kon-tent' or kon'tent, things contained in a vessel, book, etc.: in these senses pl.; capacity; space occupied: in these senses sing.

Contest, kon-test', vt. To call in question; to strive for.—vi. To strive; to contend; to emulate.—n. kon'test. Struggle for victory; encounter; debate; competition.

Context, kon'tekst, n. The parts which precede or follow a passage quoted.

Contiguous, kon-tig'ū-us, a. Touching one another; in contact; adjacent.

Continence, Continency, kon'tinens, kona-ti-nen-si, n. Restraint of the desires and passions; chastity; temperance.

Continent, kon'ti-nent, a. Chaste; moderate.—n. A connected tract of land of great extent; the mainland of Europe.

Contingence, Contingency, kontin'jens, kon-tin'jen-si, n. Quality of being contingent; an event which may occur; chance; juncture.

Continue, kon-tin'ū, vi. (continuing, continued). To remain in a state or place; to be durable; to persevere; to be steadfast.—vt. To prolong; to extend; to persevere in.

Continuity, kon-ti-nū'i-ti, n. Close union of parts; unbroken texture; cohesion.

Continuous, kon-tin'ū-us, a. Joined

together closely; conjoined; continued.

Contort, kon-tort', vt. To twist; to writhe; to draw or pull awry.

Contortionist, kon-tor'shon-ist, n. An acrobat who practices contortions of the body.

Contour, kontör', n. The line that bounds a body; outline.

Contractile, kon-trakt'īl, a. Having the power of contracting, as living fibers.

Contraction, kon-trak'shon, n. Shrinking; shortening; abbreviation.

Contractor, kon-trakt'er, n. One who contracts to perform any work or service, or to furnish supplies, at a certain price or rate.

Contradict, kon-tra-dikt', vt. To assert to be the contrary; to deny; to oppose.

Contradiction, kon-tra-dik'shon, n. A contrary assertion; inconsistency with itself.

Contradictory, kon-tra-dik'to-ri, a. Implying contradiction; inconsistent.

Contradistinction, kon'tra-distingk''shon, n. Distinction by opposites.

Contrast, kon-trast', vt. To set in opposition; to show the difference or heighten the effect.—vi. To stand in contrast to.—n. kon'trast. Opposition or comparison of things; a person or thing strikingly different.

Contravene, kon-tra-vēn', vt. (contravening, contravened). To oppose; to trangress.

Contretemps, kong-tr-tong, n. An unexpected and untoward accident.

Contribute, kon-trib'ūt, vt. (contributing, contributed). To give in common with others.—vi. To give a part; to conduce.

Contribution, kon-tri-bū'shon, n. Act of contributing; that which is contributed; an article sent to a periodical, etc.

Contrite, kon'trīt, a. Brokenhearted for sin; penitent.

Contrition, kon-tri'shon, n. Grief of heart for sin.

Contrivance, kon-trīv'ans, n.

Scheme; invention; artifice.

Contrive, kon-trīv', *vt.* (contriving, contrived). To invent; to devise.—*vi.* To form or design.

Control, kon-trōl', *n.* Restraint; superintendence; authority.—*vt.* (controlling, controlled). To restrain; to regulate.

Controller, kon-trōl'ėr, *n.* An officer who checks the accounts of collectors of public moneys.

Controversy, kon'trō-vėr-si, *n.* A disputation, particularly in writing; litigation.

Controvert, kon'trō-vėrt, *vt.* To dispute by reasoning; to attempt to disprove or confute.

Contumacious, kon-tū-mā'shus, *a.* Opposing rightful authority; obstinate.

Conundrum, kō-nun'drum, *n.* A sort of riddle turning on some odd resemblance between things quite unlike.

Convalesce, kon-va-les', *vi.* (convalescing, convalesced). To recover health.

Convalescence, kon-va-les'ens, *n.* The state of one convalescent; gradual recovery after illness.

Convene, kon-vēn', *vi.* (convening, convened). To assemble.—*vt.* To cause to assemble; to convoke.

Convenience, Conveniency, kon-vē'ni-ens, kon-vē'ni-en-si, *n.* Ease; comfort; suitable opportunity; an appliance or utensil.

Convenient, kon-vė'ni-ent, *a.* Suitable; adapted; opportune.

Convent, kon'vent, *n.* A body of monks or nuns; a monastery; a nunnery.

Conventicle, kon-ven'ti-kl, *n.* A secret meeting; a meeting of religious dissenters; their meeting-place.

Convention, kon-ven'shon, *n.* An assembly; an agreement; recognized social custom.

Conventional, kon-ven'shon-al, *a.* Formed by agreement; tacitly understood; resting on mere usage.

Convergent, kon-vėrj'ent, *a.* Tending to one point or object; approaching.

Conversant, kon'vėrs-ant, *a.* Having intercourse or familiarity;

versed in; proficient; occupied or concerned.

Conversation, kon-vėr-sā'shon, *n.* Familiar intercourse; easy talk.

Converse, kon-vėrs', *vi.* (conversing, conversed). To hold intercourse; to talk familiarly; to commune.—*n.* kon'vėrs. Conversation; familiarity; something forming a counterpart.—*a.* Put the opposite or reverse way.

Conversion, kon-vėr'shon, *n.* Change from one state, religion, or party to another; interchange of terms in logic.

Convert, kon-vėrt', *vt.* and *i.* To change from one state, use, religion, or party to another; to turn from a bad life to a good; to interchange conversely.—*n.* kon'vėrt. One who has changed his opinion, practice, or religion.

Convict, kon-vikt', *vt.* To prove or decide to be guilty—*n.* kon'vikt. A person found guilty; one undergoing penal servitude.

Conviction, kon-vik'shon, *n.* Act of finding a person guilty; strong belief; state of being sensible of wrong-doing.

Convince, kon-vins', *vt.* (convincing, convinced). To persuade by argument; to satisfy by evidence or proof.

Convivial, kon-vi'vi-al, *a.* Festive; festal; jovial; social.

Convocation, kon-vō-kā'shon, *n.* Act of convoking; an assembly, particularly of clergy or heads of a university.

Convoke, kon-vōk', *vt.* (convoking, convoked). To call together; to summon to meet.

Convolution, kon-vō-lū'shon, *n.* Act of rolling together or on itself; a winding; a spiral.

Convolve, kon-volv', *vt.* To roll together or on itself; to coil up.

Convolvulus, kon-volv'ū-lus, *n.* Bind-weed; a genus of slender twining plants.

Cook, kuk, *vt.* To prepare food by fire or heat; to concoct; to tamper with.—*n.* One who prepares victuals for the table.

Cool, kōl, *a.* Moderately cold; dispassionate; self-possessed; impudent.—*n*. A moderate degree or state of cold.—*vt*. To make cool; to moderate; to calm; to render indifferent.—*vi*. To lose heat, ardor, affection, etc.

Cope, kōp, *n*. A sacerdotal cloak; the arch of the sky; the roof of a house; the arch over a door, etc.—*vt*. (coping, coped). To cover, as with a cope; to strive, or contend; to oppose with success (with *with*).

Copernican, kō-pèr'ni-kan, *a*. Pertaining to Copernicus, or to his astronomical system.

Copper, kop'èr, *n*. A reddish colored ductile and malleable metal; a large boiler; a copper coin.—*a*. Consisting of or resembling copper.—*vt*. To cover with sheets of copper.

Coptic, kop'tik, *a*. Pertaining to the descendants of the ancient Egyptians, called *Copts*.—*n*. The language of the Copts.

Copula, kop'ū-la, *n*. The word which unites the subject and predicate of a proposition, part of *to be*; a bond; a link.

Copulate, kop'ū-lāt, *vi*. (copulating, copulated). To come together, as different sexes.

Copulation, kop-ū-lā'shon, *n*. Coition.

Copulative, kop'ū-lāt-iv, *a*. That unites.—*n*. A conjunction.

Copy, ko'pi, *n*. An imitation; a transcript; a pattern; a single example of a book, etc.; matter to be set up in type.—*vt*. (copying copied). To imitate; to transcribe.

Copyright, kop'i-rīt, *n*. The exclusive right to print or produce, given for a limited number of years to an author, artist, etc., or his assignee.—*a*. Relating to, or protected by copyright.—*vt*. To secure by copyright.

Coralline, ko'ral-īn, *a*. Consisting of, like, or containing coral.—*n*. A sea-weed; an orange-red color; a coral zoophyte.

Corbel, kor'bel, *n*. A piece projecting from a wall as a support.—*vt*. (corbelling, corbelled). To support on corbels; to provide with corbels.

Cord, kord, *n*. A small rope; a band; a sinew; a pile of wood, 8 feet long, 4 high, and 4 broad.—*vi*. To bind with a cord.

Corduroy, kor-dė-roi', *n*. A thick cotton stuff corded or ribbed.

Core, kōr, *n*. The heart or inner part; the central part of fruit.

Co-respondent, kō-rē-spond'ent, *n*. A joint respondent; a man charged with adultery in a divorce case.

Corn, korn, *n*. Grain; the seeds of plants which grow in ears, and are made into bread; a horny excresence on a toe or foot.—*vt*. To preserve with salt in grains; to granulate.

Cornea, kor'nē-a, *n*. The horny transparent membrane in the fore part of the eye.

Corned, korned, *a*. Cured by salting.

Corneous, kor'nē-us, *a*. Horny; hard.

Corner, kor'nèr, *n*. A projecting extremity; angle; a secret or retired place; a nook.—*vt*. To buy up the whole stock of a commodity.

Corner-stone, kor'nèr-stōn, *n*. The stone which lies at the corner of two walls, and unites them; the principal stone.

Cornet, kor'net, *n*. A sort of trumpet; formerly a cavalry officer, of the lowest commissioned rank, who bore the standard.

Cornice, kor'nis, *n*. A molded projection crowning a part; uppermost molding of a pediment, room, etc.

Cornish, korn'ish, *a*. Pertaining to Cornwall.—*n*. The language of Cornwall.

Cornucopia, kor-nū-kō'pi-a, *n*. The representation of a horn filled with fruit, flowers, and grain, a symbol of plenty and peace.

Coronet, ko'rō-net, *n*. A small crown worn by peers and peeresses; an ornamental headdress; something that surmounts.

Corporal, kor'po-ral, *n*. A non-commissioned officer ranking below a sergeant.—*a*. Belonging or relating to the body; material.

Corporate, kor'po-rāt, *a*. Formed into a legal body, and empowered to act in legal processes as an individual.

Corporation, kor-po-rā'shon, *n.* A body corporate, empowered to act as an individual; the human body or frame.

Corporeal, kor-pō'rē-al, *a.* Having a body; material; opposed to spiritual.

Corps, kōr, *n.*; pl. **Corps,** kōrz. A body of troops. *Army Corps.* Two or more divisions.

Corpse, korps, *n.* The dead body of a human being; a carcass; remains.

Corpulence, Corpulency, kor'pū-lens, kor'-pū-len-si, *n.* The state of being corpulent; excessive fatness.

Corpuscle, kor'pus-l, *n.* A minute particle or physical atom; a minute animal cell.

Corral, kor-räl', *n.* A pen for cattle; an inclosure formed by wagons; a stockade for capturing elephants.

Correct, ko-rekt', *a.* Right; accurate; exact.—*vt.* To make right; to chastise; to counteract.

Correction, ko-rek'shon, *n.* Act of correcting; state of being corrected; discipline; chastisement; counteraction.

Correctness, ko-rekt'nes, *n.* Freedom from faults or errors; accuracy; exactness.

Correlate, kor'ē-lāt, *n.* A correlative.—*vi.* (correlating, correlated). To be reciprocally related.—*vt.* To place in reciprocal relation; to determine the relations between.

Correlative, ko-rel'at-iv, *a.* Having a mutual relation, as father and son.—*n.* One who or that which stands in reciprocal relation.

Correspond, ko-rē-spond', *vi.* To answer one to another; to be congruous; to fit; to hold intercourse by letters.

Correspondence, ko-rē-spond'ens, *n.* Act or state of corresponding; fitness; congruity; intercourse by letters; the letters interchanged.

Correspondent, ko-rē-spond'ent, *a.* Corresponding; suitable; congruous.—*n.* One who has intercourse by letters.

Corridor, ko'ri-dör, *n.* A passage in a building, or round a court.

Corrosion, ko-rō'zhon, *n.* Action of corroding; state of being corroded.

Corrosive, ko-rōs'iv, *a.* Having the power of corroding; vexing; blighting.—*n.* That which has the quality of corroding.

Corrugate, ko'rū-gāt, *vt.* To wrinkle; to contract into folds or furrows.

Corrugation, ko-rū-gā'shon, *n.* A wrinkling; contraction into wrinkles.

Corrupt, ko-rupt', *vt.* To make putrid; to deprave; to taint; to bribe; to infect with errors.—*vi.* To become putrid or vitiated.—*a.* Tainted; depraved; infected with errors.

Corruptible, ko-rupt'i-bl, *a.* That may be corrupted; subject to decay, destruction, etc.

Corruption, ko-rup'shon, *n.* Act or process of corrupting; depravity; pollution; taint of blood; bribe-taking; bribery.

Corset, kor'set, *n.* An article of dress laced closely round the body; stays.

Cortège, kor'tāzh, *n.* A train of attendants.

Cortex, kor'teks, *n.* The bark of a tree; a membrane enveloping part of the body.

Cortical, kor'tik-al, *a.* Belonging to, consisting of, or resembling bark; belonging to the external covering.

Coruscate, ko-rus'kāt, *vi.* (coruscating, coruscated). To flash intermittently; to glitter.

Cosmetic, koz-met'ik, *a.* Improving beauty.—*n.* An application to improve the complexion.

Cosmic, Cosmical, koz'mik, koz' mik-al, *a.* Relating to the whole frame of the universe.

Cosmopolitan, Cosmopolite, koz-mō-pol'i-tan, koz-mop'o-līt, *n.* One who is at home in every place.—*a.* Free from local prejudices; common to all the world.

Cosmos, koz'mos, *n.* The universe; the system of order and harmony in creation.

Cost, kost, *vt.* (costing, cost). To be

bought for; to require to be laid out or borne.—*n*. That which is paid for anything; expenditure; loss; (*pl*.) expenses of a lawsuit.

Cosy, kō'zi, *a*. Snug; comfortable.— *n*. Padded covering put over a teapot to keep in the heat after the tea has been infused.

Cotton, kot'tn, *n*. A soft, downy substance in the pods of several plants; cloth made of cotton.—*a*. Pertaining to, or consisting of cotton.—*vi*. To agree; to become friendly.

Cougar, kö'gär, *n*. A large carnivorous quadruped of the cat kind; the puma.

Cough, kof, *n*. A violent convulsive effort of the lungs to throw off offending matter.—*vi*. To make a violent effort, with noise, to expel the airs from the lungs, and throw off any offensive matter.—*vt*. To expel from the lungs by a violent effort with noise; to expectorate.

Could, kud, *pret*. of *can*. Was able.

Coulter, kōl'tér, *n*. The blade of a plow that cuts the earth in advance of the share.

Council, koun'sil, *n*. An assembly for consultation; a body of men designated to advise a sovereign or chief magistrate; a convocation.

Counsel, koun'sel, *n*. Deliberation; consultation; advice; design; a barrister.—*vt*. (counselling, counselled). To advise; to warn.

Count, kount, *vt*. To enumerate; to compute; to consider; to judge.— *vi*. To reckon; to rely; to be reckoned.—*n*. Reckoning; a particular charge in an indictment; a continental title of nobility, equivalent to the English earl.

Countenance, koun'ten-ans, *n*. The human face; air; aspect; favor; encouragement.—*vt*. To favor; to encourage; to vindicate.

Counter, kount'ér, *n*. One who or that which counts; anything used to reckon, as in games; a shop table.—*adv*. Contrary; in an opposite direction.—*a*. Adverse; opposing.

Counteract, koun-tér-akt', *vt*. To act in opposition to; to render ineffec-

tual.

Counterbalance, koun-tér-bal'ans, *vt*. To weigh against with an equal weight; to act against with equal power.—*n*. Equal weight, power, or agency, acting in opposition.

Countercheck, koun-tér-chek', *vt*. To oppose by some obstacle; to check.—*n*. Check; check that controls another check.

Counterfeit, koun'tér-fit, *vt*. and *i*. To forge; to copy; to feign.—*a*. Made in imitation; fraudulent.—*n*. An imposter; a forgery.

Counterpoint, koun'tér-point, *n*. The art, in music, of adding to a given melody one or more melodies.

Counterpoise, koun'tér-poiz, *vt*. To counterbalance.—*n*. A weight which balances another; equivalence of power or force; equilibrium.

Countryman, kun'tri-man, *n*. One born in the same country with another; one who dwells in the country; a rustic.

County, koun'ti, *n*. A particular portion of a state or kingdom; a shire.—*a*. Pertaining to a county.

Couple, ku'pl, *n*. A band or leash; a pair; a brace; a man and his wife.—*vt*. and *i*. (coupling, coupled). To join together; to unite.

Couplet, kup'let, *n*. Two lines that rhyme.

Coupling, kup'ling, *n*. The act of one who couples; that which couples; a hook, chain, or other contrivance forming a connection.

Coupon, kö'pon, *n*. An interest certificate attached to a bond; one of a series of tickets which guarantee the holder to obtain a certain value or service for each at different periods.

Courage, ku'rij, *n*. Intrepidity; dauntlessness; hardihood.

Courageous, ku-rā'jē-us. *a*. Bold; brave; heroic, fearless.

Courier, kö'rē-ér, *n*. A messenger sent express with dispatches; a travelling attendant.

Course, kōrs, *n*. A running; passage; route; career; ground run over; line of conduct; order of succession; series of lectures, etc.;

range of subjects taught; a layer of stones in masonry; part of a meal served at one time.—*vt.* (coursing, coursed). To hunt; to run through or over.—*vi.* To move with speed.

Courthouse, kōrt 'hous, *n.* A house in which established courts are held.

Cove, kōv, *n.* A small inlet or bay; a sheltered recess in the sea-shore; a concave molding; a man, fellow.—*vt.* To arch over.

Covenant, kuv 'en-ant, *n.* A contract; compact; a writing containing the terms of an agreement.—*vi.* To enter into a formal agreement; to stipulate.—*vt.* To grant by covenant.

Cover, kuv 'ėr, *vt.* To overspread; to cloak; to secrete; to defend; to wrap up; to brood on; to be sufficient for; to include.—*n.* Anything spread over another thing; disguise; shelter; articles laid at table for one person.

Coverlet, kuv 'ėr-let, *n.* The cover of a bed.

Covert, kuv 'ėrt, *a.* Kept secret; private; insidious.—*n.* A shelter; a thicket.

Coward, kou 'ėrd, *n.* A person who wants courage to meet danger; a craven; a dastard.—*a.* Destitute of courage; dastardly.

Cowardice, kou 'ėrd-is, *n.* Want of courage to face danger.

Cow-catcher, kou 'kach-ėr, *n.* A frame in front of locomotives to remove obstructions.

Cower, kou 'ėr, *vi.* To crouch; to sink by bending the knees; to shrink through fear.

Cowhide, kou 'hīd. *n.* The hide of a cow; a leather whip.—*vt.* To flog with a leather whip.

Crab, krab, *n.* A crustaceous fish with strong claws; a portable windlass, etc.; Cancer, a sign of the zodiac; a wild sour apple; a morose person.

Crabbed, krab 'ed, *a.* Perverse; peevish; perplexing.

Crack, krak, *n.* A chink or fissure; a sudden or sharp sound; a sounding blow; a chat.—*vt.* and *i.* To break with a sharp, abrupt sound; to break partially; to snap; to

boast of; to utter with smartness; to chat.

Cracked, krakt, *a.* Having fissures but not in pieces; impaired; crazy.

Cracker, krak 'ėr, *n.* One who or that which cracks; a small firework; a hard biscuit.

Crackle, krak 'l, *vi.* (crackling, crackled). To make small abrupt noises rapidly repeated.

Crackling, krak 'ling, *n.* The act or noise of the verb to crackle; the brown skin of roasted pork.

Cradle, krā 'dl, *n.* A small bed in which infants are rocked; a frame to support or hold together.—*vt.* (cradling, cradled). To lay or rock in a cradle.

Craft, kraft, *n.* Ability; skill; artifice; guile; manual art; trade; a vessel or ship.

Craftsman, krafts 'man, *n.* An artificer.

Crane, krān, *n.* A migratory bird with long legs and neck; a machine for raising great weights; a crooked pipe for drawing liquor out of a cask.—*vi.* To stretch out one's neck.

Craniology, krā-ni-ol 'o-ji, *n.* The knowledge of the cranium or skull.

Cranium, krā 'ni-um, *n.* The skull; the bones which inclose the brain.

Crank, krangk, *n.* A contrivance for producing a horizontal or perpendicular motion by means of a rotary motion, or the contrary; a bend or turn.—*a.* Liable to be overset; loose.

Crater, krā 'tėr, *n.* A bowl; the circular cavity or mouth of a volcano; hole in the ground caused by the explosion of a shell, bomb, or mine.

Cravat, kra-vat ', *n.* A neck-cloth.

Crave, krāv, *vt.* (craving, craved). To ask earnestly or submissively; to desire strongly.—*n.* Strong desire.

Craven, krā 'vn, *n.* A coward; a weak-hearted, spiritless fellow.—*a.* Cowardly.

Craw, krạ, *n.* The crop or first stomach of fowls.

Crawl, krạl, *vi.* To creep; to advance slowly, slyly, or weakly.

Crayfish, Crawfish, krā 'fish, krạ '

fish, n. A crustacean found in streams; also the spiny lobster, a sea crustacean.

Crayon, krā'on, n. A pencil of colored clay, chalk, or charcoal, used in drawing; a drawing made with crayons.—vt. To sketch.

Craze, krāz, vt. (crazing, crazed). To shatter; to impair the intellect of.—vi. To become crazy.—n. An inordinate desire.

Crazy, krāz'i, a. Decrepit; deranged; weakened or disordered in intellect.

Create, krē-āt', vt. (creating, created). To bring into being from nothing; to cause to be; to shape; to beget; to bring about; to invest with a new character; to constitute or appoint.

Creation, krē-ā'shon, n. Act of creating; the aggregate of created things; the universe; conferring of a title or dignity.

Creature, krē'tūr, n. Something created; a human being; something imagined; a person who owes his rise to another; a mere tool.

Credential, krē-den'shi-al, n. That which gives a title to credit; (pl.) documents showing that one is entitled to credit, or is invested with authority.

Credit, kred'it, n. Reliance on testimony; faith; reputed integrity; transfer of goods, etc., in confidence of future payment; reputation for pecuniary worth; time given for payment of goods sold on trust; side of an account in which payment is entered; money possessed or due.—vt. To trust; to believe; to sell or lend to, in confidence of future payment; to procure credit or honor to; to enter on the credit side of an account; to attribute.

Credulity, kred-dū'li-ti, n. A disposition to believe on slight evidence.

Creed, krēd, n. A system of principles believed or professed; a brief summary of the articles of Christian faith.

Creek, krēk, n. A small bay; a small harbor; a brook.

Creep, krēp, vi. (creeping, crept). To move as a reptile; to crawl; to grow along the ground, or on another body; to move secretly, feebly, or timorously; to be servile; to shiver.

Crescent, kres'ent, n. The moon in her state of increase; anything resembling the shape of the new moon; the Turkish standard; buildings in the form of a crescent.

Cress, kres, n. The name of various plants, mostly cruciferous, used as a salad.

Crib, krib, n. A child's bed; a small habitation; a rack; a stall for oxen; a framework; a literal translation.—vt. (cribbing, cribbed). To shut up in a narrow habitation; to pilfer.

Cribbage, krib'āj, n. A game at cards.

Crick, krik, n. A local spasm or cramp; a stiffness of the neck.

Cricket, krik'et, n. An insect which makes a creaking or chirping sound; an open-air game played with bats, ball, and wickets.

Crime, krīm, n. A breach of law, divine or human; any great wickedness.

Cringe, krinj, vi. (cringing, cringed). To bend; to bend with servility; to fawn.—n. A bow; servile civility.

Crinkle, kring'kl, vi. (crinkling, crinkled). To bend in little turns; to wrinkle.—vt. To form with short turns or wrinkles.—n. A winding or turn; a wrinkle.

Criterion, krī-tē'ri-un, n.; pl. **-ia.** Standard of judging; a measure; test.

Critic, kri'tik, n. One skilled in judging literary or artistic work; a reviewer; a severe judge.—a. Relating to criticism.

Critical, kri'tik-al, a. Relating to or containing criticism; nicely judicious; inclined to find fault; relating to a crisis; momentous.

Crochet, krō'shā, n. A species of knitting performed by means of a small hook.

Crockery, krok'e-ri, n. Earthenware; vessels formed of clay, glazed and baked.

Crop, krop, n. The first stomach of birds; the craw; harvest; corn, etc., while growing; act of cutting, as hair; a short whip without a lash.—*vt.* (cropping, cropped). To cut off the ends of; to cut close; to browse; to gather before it falls; to cultivate.

Crop-eared, krop'ērd, *a.* Having the ears cut short.

Croquet, krō'kā, *n.* An open-air game played with mallets, balls, hoops, and pegs.

Cross, kros, *n.* An instrument of death, consisting of two pieces of timber placed transversely; the symbol of the Christian religion; the religion itself; a monument or sign in the form of a cross; anything that thwarts; a hybrid.—*a.* Athwart; adverse; fretful.—*vt.* To draw a line or lay a body across; to mark with a cross; to cancel; to pass from side to side of; to thwart; to perplex; to interbreed.—*vi.* To be athwart; to move across.

Crossword puzzle, kros'wėrd puz'l, *n.* A diagram of squares, each of which, except certain blanks, is to be filled with a letter so that the words formed, when read down and across, correspond to definitions given.

Crotch, kroch, *n.* A fork or forking.

Crotchet, kroch'et, *n.* A note in music, half the length of a minim; a whim; a perverse conceit; a bracket in printing.

Crow, krō, *n.* A black bird of the genus Corvus, including the raven, rook, jackdaw, etc.; a crowbar; the sound which a cock utters.—*vi.* (crowing, *pret.* crew, crowed, *pp.* crowed). To cry as a cock; to exult; to boast.

Crowbar, krō'bär, *n.* A bar of iron with a bent or forked end, used as a lever.

Crowd, kroud, *n.* A number of persons or things; a throng; the populace.—*vt.* To fill by pressing together; to fill to excess.—*vi.* To press in numbers; to throng.

Crowded, kroud'ed, *a.* Filled by a promiscuous multitude.

Crown, kroun, *n.* An ornament for the head in the form of a wreath; a diadem; a badge of royalty; perfection; completion; the top of any-

thing, especially the head; a coin.—*vt.* To invest with a crown; to cover; to adorn; to finish; to perfect.

Crow's-feet, krōz'fēt, *n.pl.* The wrinkles at corners of the eyes, the effects of age.

Crucial, krö'shi-al, *a.* Relating to a cross; severe; searching; decisive.

Crucible, krö'si-bl, *n.* A melting pot, used by chemists and others.

Crucifix, krö'si-fiks, *n.* A cross with the figure of Christ crucified on it.

Crucifixion, krö-si-fik'shon, *n.* The act of crucifying; the death of Christ.

Crucify, krö'si-fī, *vt.* (crucifying, crucified). To put to death by nailing the hands and feet of to a cross, to mortify; to torment.

Crude, kröd, *a.* Raw; unripe; in its natural state; not brought to perfection.

Cruel, krö'el, *a.* Unmerciful; hardhearted; ferocious; brutal; severe.

Cruet, krö'et, *n.* A vial or small glass bottle for holding vinegar, oil, etc.

Cruise, kröz, *vi.* (cruising, cruised). To sail hither and thither.—*n.* A sailing to and fro in search of an enemy's ships, or for pleasure.

Cruiser, kröz'ėr, *n.* A person or a ship that cruises; a swift armed vessel to protect or destroy shipping.

Crumb, krum, *n.* A fragment; a small piece of bread broken off; the soft part of bread.—*vt.* To break into small pieces with the fingers; to cover with breadcrumbs.

Crusade, krö-sād', *n.* A military expedition against the infidels of the Holy Land; a romantic or enthusiastic enterprise.

Crush, krush, *vt.* To squeeze; to bruise; to pound; to overpower; to oppress.—*vi.* To be pressed; to force one's way amid a crowd.—*n.* A violent pressing or squeezing; a crowding.

Crust, krust, *n.* The hard outer coat of anything; the outside of a loaf; a piece of hard bread; a deposit from wine.—*vt.* and *i.* To cover with a crust or hard coat.

Cry, krī, *vi.* (crying, cried). To utter the loud shrill sounds of weeping, joy, fear, surprise, etc.; to clamor; to weep.—*vt.* To shout; to proclaim.—*n.* The loud voice of man or beast; a shriek or scream; acclamation; weeping; importunate call; a political catchword.

Crypt, kript, *n.* A subterranean cell for burying purposes; a subterranean chapel.

Ctenoid, ten'oid, *a.* Comb-shaped; having the posterior edge with teeth: said of the scales of fishes; having scales of this kind.

Cub, kub, *n.* The young of certain quadrupeds, as the bear and fox.—*vi.* (cubbing, cubbed). To bring forth cubs.

Cube, kūb, *n.* A regular solid body, with six equal square sides, the third power, or the product from multiplying a number twice by itself.—*vt.* To raise to the third power.

Cubicle, kū'bi-kl, *n.* A sleeping-place; a compartment for one bed in a dormitory.

Cubit, kū'bit, *n.* The forearm; the length from the elbow to the extremity of the middle finger, usually taken as 18 inches.

Cuckold, kuk'old, *n.* A man whose wife is false to his bed.—*vt.* To make a cuckold of.

Cuckoo, ku̱'kö, *n.* A migratory bird, so named from the sound of its note.

Cucumber, kū'kum-bėr, *n.* An annual plant of the gourd family.

Cud, kud, *n.* The food which ruminating animals bring up from the first stomach to chew.

Cuddle, kud'dl, *vi.* (cuddling, cuddled). To lie close and snug.—*vt.* To hug; to embrace; to fondle.

Cudgel, kuj'el, *n.* A short thick stick; a club.—*vt.* (cudgelling, cudgelled). To beat with a cudgel; to beat in general.

Cue, kū, *n.* The last words of an actor's speech; catch-word; hint; the part which any man is to play in his turn; humor; the straight rod used in billiards.

Cuff, kuf, *n.* A blow; slap; part of a sleeve near the hand.—*vt.* To beat; to strike with talons or wings, or with fists.

Culpable, kulp'a-bl, *a.* Blameworthy; guilty; criminal; immoral; sinful.

Culprit, kul'prit, *n.* A person arraigned in court for a crime, or convicted of a crime; a criminal; an offender.

Cult, kult, *n.* A system of belief and worship; a subject of devoted study.

Cultivate, kul'ti-vāt, *vt.* To till; to refine; to foster; to improve.

Culture, kul'tūr, *n.* Cultivation; the rearing of certain animals, as oysters; the application of labor, or other means of improvement; the result of such efforts; refinement.—*vt.* To cultivate.

Culvert, kul'vėrt, *n.* An arched drain under a road, railway, etc., for the passage of water.

Cumulation, kū-mū-lā'shon, *n.* A heaping up; a heap; accumulation.

Cumulus, kū'mū-lus, *n.*; pl. **-li.** A cloud in the form of dense convex or conical heaps.

Cuneiform, kū-nē'i-form, *a.* Wedge-shaped; applied to the arrow-headed characters on old Babylonian and Persian inscriptions.

Cunning, kun'ing, *a.* Astute; artful.—*n.* Faculty or act of using stratagem; craftiness; artifice.

Cup, kup, *n.* A small vessel to drink out of; anything hollow, like a cup; a glass vessel for drawing blood; liquor in a cup.—*vt.* (cupping, cupped). To apply a cupping-glass.

Cupboard, kup'bōrd, *n.* A case or inclosure for cups, plates, dishes, etc.

Curate, kū'rāt, *n.* One to whom the cure of souls is committed; a clergyman employed to assist in the duties of a rector or vicar.

Curative, kū'rāt-iv, *a.* Relating to the cure of diseases; tending to cure.

Curator, kū-rāt'ėr, *n.* A superintendent; custodian; guardian.

Curb, kėrb, *vt.* To control; to check; to restrain with a curb, as a horse; to strengthen by a curb-stone.—*n.* Check; restraint; part of a bridle; a curb-stone.

Curio, kū′ri-ō, *n.*; pl. **-os,** A curiosity; an interesting and curious article.

Curiosity, kū-ri-os′i-ti, *n.* Inquisitiveness; a thing unusual; a rarity.

Curl, kėrl, *vt.* To form into ringlets,—*vi.* To take a twisted or coiled form; to play at the game of curling.—*n.* A ringlet of hair, or anything of a like form; a waving; flexure.

Current, ku′rent, *a.* Running; circulating; general; present in its course.—*n.* A running; a stream; progressive motion of water; successive course; the passage of electricity from one pole of an apparatus to the other; often used for strength, amount, or intensity of current.

Curriculum, ku-rik′ū-lum, *n.* A course of study in a university, school, etc.

Currier, ku′ri-ėr, *n.* A man who dresses leather after it is tanned.

Curry, ku′ri, *n.* A highly spiced sauce or mixture; a dish cooked with curry.—*vt.* (currying, curried). To flavor with curry; to dress leather; to rub and clean (a horse) with a comb; to seek (favor).

Curse, kėrs, *vt.* (cursing, cursed). To utter a wish of evil against; a blight; to torment with calamities.—*vi.* To utter imprecations; to blaspheme.—*n.* Imprecation of evil; execration; torment.

Curve, kėrv, *a.* Bending; inflected.—*n.* A bending without angles; a bent line.—*vt.* (curving, curved). To bend.

Cushion, kush′on, *n.* A pillow for a seat; something resembling a pillow.—*vt.* To seat on a cushion; to furnish with cushions.

Cusp, kusp, *n.* The point of the moon, or other luminary; a point formed by the meeting of two curves.

Custard, kus′tėrd, *n.* A composition of milk and egg, sweetened, and baked or boiled.

Custodian, kus-tō′di-an, *n.* One who has care of a library, public building, etc.

Custody, kus′tō-di, *n.* A keeping; guardianship; imprisonment; se-

curity.

Custom, kus′tum, *n.* Habit; established practice; fashion; a buying of goods; business support; a tax on goods; *pl.* duties on merchandise imported or exported.

Customer, kus′tum-ėr, *n.* An accustomed buyer at a shop, etc., one who buys goods.

Custom-house, kus′tum-hous, *n.* The office where customs are paid.

Cut, kut, *vt.* (cutting, cut). To divide into pieces; to fell or mow; to clip; to carve; to affect deeply; to intersect; to castrate; to divide, as cards; to refuse to recognize.—*vi.* To make an incision; to be severed by a cutting instrument; to pass straight and rapidly.—*a.* Gashed; carved; intersected; deeply affected.—*n.* The action of an edged instrument; a wound; a stroke with a whip; a severe remark; a channel; any small piece; a lot; a near passage; a carving or engraving; act of dividing a pack of cards; form; fashion; refusal to recognize a person.

Cyanide, sī′an-id, *n.* A combination of cyanogen with a metallic base.

Cyanogen, sī-an′ō-jen, *n.* A poisonous gas of a strong and peculiar odor.

Cycle, sī′kl, *n.* An orbit in the heavens; a circle of years; a bicycle or tricycle.—*vi.* To recur in a cycle; to ride a bicycle.

Cylinder, si′lin-dėr, *n.* An elongated round body of uniform diameter.

Cymbal, sim′bal, *n.* A basin-shaped musical instrument of brass, used in pairs.

Cynic, sin′ik, *n.* One of a sect of Greek philosophers who professed contempt of riches, arts, etc.; a morose man.

Cypress, sī′pres, *n.* An evergreen tree; the emblem of mourning.

Cyst, sist, *n.* A bag in animal bodies containing matter.

Czar, tsär or zär, *n.* Formerly, the title of the Emperor of Russia.

Czech, chek, *n.* One of the Slavonic inhabitants of Bohemia; the language of the Czechs.

D

Dab, dab, *vt.* (dabbing, dabbed). To hit lightly with something soft or moist.—*n.* A gentle blow; a small mass of anything soft or moist; a small flat fish; an adept or expert.

Dabble, dab'bl, *vt.* (dabbling, dabbled). To wet; to sprinkle.—*vi.* To play in water; to do anything in a superficial manner; to meddle.

Dairy, dā'ri, *n.* The place where milk is converted into butter or cheese; a shop where milk, butter, etc., are sold.—*a.* Pertaining to the keeping of cows, managing of milk, etc.

Dais, dā'is, *n.* The high table at the upper end of the dining-hall; the raised floor on which the table stood; a canopy.

Damage, dam'āj, *n.* Hurt; injury; money compensation (generally in *pl.*).—*vt.* (damaging, damaged). To injure; to impair.

Damask, dam'ask, *n.* A fabric, of various materials, with figures of flowers, etc.; a pink color.—*a.* Pink or rosy.—*vt.* To form or imprint flowers or figures on.

Damn, dam, *vt.* To send to hell; to condemn.

Damnation, dam-nā'shon, *n.* Condemnation; sentence to punishment in the future state.

Dance, dans, *vi.* (dancing, danced). To move with measured steps, regulated by a tune; to leap and risk.—*vt.* To make to dance; to dandle.—*n.* A leaping or stepping to the measure of a tune; the tune itself.

Dandelion, dan'di-lī-un, *n.* A composite plant bearing a bright yellow flower.

Dandle, dan'dl, *vt.* (dandling, dandled). To shake on the knee; as an infant; to fondle; to trifle with.

Dandruff, dan'druff, *n.* A scurf on the head.

Danger, dān'jèr, *n.* Exposure to injury; jeopardy; risk.

Dangerous, dān'jèr-us, *a.* Perilous; causing risk of harm; unsafe; insecure.

Dangle, dang'gl, *vi.* (dangling, dangled). To hang loose; to follow officiously.—*vt.* To carry suspended loosely; to swing.

Dark, därk, *a.* Destitute of light; clouded; black or blackish; disheartening; involved in mystery; keeping designs in concealment.—*n.* Darkness; obscurity; secrecy; a state of ignorance.

Darkness, därk'nes, *n.* Absence of light; blackness; gloom; ignorance; privacy.

Darling, där'ling, *a.* Dearly beloved.—*n.* One much beloved; a favorite.

Darn, därn, *vt.* To mend by imitating the texture of the stuff with thread and needle; to sew together.—*n.* A place so mended.

Dart, därt, *n.* A pointed missile thrown by the hand; a sudden rush or bound.—*vt.* To throw with a sudden thrust; to shoot.—*vi.* To fly or shoot, as a dart; to start and run.

Darwinism, där'win-izm, *n.* The doctrine as to the origin and modifications of species taught by Darwin; evolution.

Dash, dash, *vt.* To cause to strike suddenly or violently; to throw or cast; to sprinkle; to mix slightly; to sketch out hastily; to obliterate; to frustrate; to abash.—*vi.* To rush with violence; to strike or be hurled.—*n.* A violent striking of two bodies; admixture; a rushing or onset; vigor in attack; bluster; a mark in writing or printing (—).

Daub, dab, *vt.* To smear; to cover with mud or other soft substance; to paint coarsely; to flatter grossly.—*n.* Coarse painting; a smear.

Dauby, dab'i, *a.* Viscous; glutinous.

Daughter, da'tèr, *n.* A female child or descendant.

Day, dā, *n.* The time between the rising and setting of the sun; the time of one revolution of the earth; or 24 hours; light; time specified; age; time; anniversary.

Daybreak, dā'brāk, *n.* The dawn; first appearance of light in the morning.

Day-dream, dā'drēm, *n.* A vision to

the waking senses; a reverie.

Daylight, dā′līt, *n.* The light of the day.

Daze, dāz, *vt.* (dazing, dazed). To stupefy; to stun.

Dazzle, daz′zl, *vt.* (dazzling, dazzled). To overpower with light or splendor.—*vi.* To be intensely bright; to be overpowered by light.—*n.* A dazzling light; glitter.

Deacon, dē′kon, *n.* A person in the lowest degree of holy orders; a church officer; the president of an incorporated trade.

Dead, ded, *a.* Without life; deceased; perfectly still; dull; cold; tasteless; spiritless; utter; unerring.

Deaden, ded′n, *vt.* To abate in vigor, force, or sensation; to darken, dull, or dim.

Deaf, def, *a.* Wanting the sense of hearing; not listening or regarding.

Deaf-mute, def′mūt, *n.* A deaf and dumb person.

Deal, dēl, *n.* A part; an indefinite quantity, degree, or extent; the distribution of playing cards; a board or plank; fir or pine timber.—*vt.* (dealing, dealt). to distribute.—*vi.* To traffic; to behave; to distribute cards.

Dean, dēn, *n.* A dignitary in cathedral and collegiate churches who presides over the chapter; an officer in a university or college.

Dear, dēr, *a.* Bearing a high price; valuable; expensive; a high estimation; beloved.—*n.* A darling.—*adv.* Dearly.

Dearth, dèrth, *n.* Scarcity; want; famine.

Death, deth, *n.* Extinction of life; decease; cause of decease; damnation.

Debate, dē-bāt′, *n.* Contention in words or arguments; discussion; controversy.—*vt.* (debating, debated). To dispute; to argue; to discuss.—*vi.* To examine different arguments in the mind; to deliberate.

Debauch, dē-bach′, *vt.* To corrupt; to pervert.—*vi.* To riot; to revel.—*n.* Excess in eating or drinking; lewdness.

Debit, deb′it, *n.* A recorded item of debt; the left-hand page or debtor side of a ledger or account.—*vt.* To charge with debt.

Debonair, de-bō-nār′, *a.* Gracious; courteous.

Debouch, dē-bösh′, *vi.* To issue or march out of a narrow place.

Debris, dē-brē′, *n.sing.* or *pl.* Fragments; rubbish.

Debt, det, *n.* That which is due from one person to another; obligation; guilt.

Début, dā-bụ′, *n.* First appearance in public.

Débutant, dā-bu-täng; *fem.* **Débutante,** dā-bu-tängt, *n.* One who makes a début.

Decade, de′kād, *n.* The number of ten; a period of ten years.

Decadence, Decadency, dē-kā′dens, dē-kā′-den-si or dek′a-, *n.* A falling off; decay.

Decapitate, dē-kap′it-āt, *vt.* (decapitating, decapitated). To behead.

Decapod, dek′a-pod, *n.* A crustacean having ten feet, as a crab; also a cuttle-fish with ten prehensile arms.

Decay, dē-kā′, *vi.* To pass from a sound or prosperous state; to waste; to wither; to fail.—*n.* Gradual loss of strength, excellence, etc.; corruption; putrefaction.

Decease, dē-sēs′, *n.* Departure from this life; death.—*vi.* (deceasing, deceased). To die.

Deceit, dē-sēt′, *n.* Fraud; guile; cunning.

Deceitful, dē-sēt′fụl, *d.* Fraudulent; delusive; false; hollow.

Deceive, dē-sēv′, *vt.* (deceiving, deceived). To mislead the mind of; to impose on; to delude; to frustrate (hopes, etc.).

December, dē-sem′bèr, *n.* The twelfth and last month of the year.

Decency, dē′sen-si, *n.* The state or quality of being decent; decorum; modesty.

Decennial, dē-sen′ni-al, *a.* Consisting of ten years; happening every ten years.

Decent, dē′sent, *a.* Becoming; seemly; respectable; modest; moderate.

Decentralize, dē-sen′tral-īz, *vt.* To

remove from direct dependence on a central authority.

Deception, dē-sep'shon, n. Act of deceiving; state of being deceived; artifice practiced; fraud; double-dealing.

Decide, dē-sīd', vt. (deciding, decided). To determine; to settle; to resolve.—vi. To determine; to pronounce a judgment.

Decision, dē-si'zhon, n. Determination of a difference, doubt, or event; final judgment; firmness of purpose or character.

Deck, dek, vt. To clothe; to adorn; to furnish with a deck, as a vessel.— n. The platform or floor of a ship.

Declaim, dē-klām', vi. To make a formal speech; to harangue; to inveigh.

Declamation, de-kla-mā'shon, n. The art or act of declaiming; a harangue.

Declaration, de-kla-rā'shon, n. Act of declaring; that which is declared; an explicit statement; a solemn affirmation.

Declarative, dē-klār'at-iv, a. Explanatory; making proclamation.

Declare, dē-klār', vt. (declaring, declared). To show clearly; to tell explicitly; to testify; to reveal.—vi. To make a declaration.

Decline, dē-klīn', vi. (declining, declined). To bend downwards; to serve; to fail; not to comply.—vt. To bend downward; to refuse; to change the termination of a noun, etc.—n. A falling off; decay; deterioration; consumption.

Decoration, dek'ō-rā'shon, n. Act of decorating; that which adorns; a badge or medal.

Decorum, dē-kō'rum, n. Propriety of speech or behavior; seemliness.

Decoy, dē-koi', n. An enclosure for catching ducks or wild fowls; a lure.—vt. To lure into a snare; to entice.

Decrease, dē-krēs', vi. (decreasing, decreased). To grow less.—vt. To cause to become less.—n. Gradual diminution; decay; the wane of the moon.

Decree, dē-krē', n. An edict; an order or law; predetermined purpose; judicial decision.—vt. (decreeing, decreed). To enact; to award; to determine judicially.— vi. To make an edict; to appoint by edict.

Decrement, de'krē-ment, n. Decrease; quantity lost by diminution or waste.

Decrepit, dē-krep'it, a. Broken down with age; being in the last stage of decay.

Dedicate, ded'i-kāt, vt. (dedicating, dedicated). To consecrate to a sacred purpose; to devote (often refl.); to inscribe to a friend.

Dedication, ded-i-kā'shon, n. Act of devoting to some person, use, or thing; inscription or address.

Deduce, dē-dūs', vt. (deducing, deduced). To draw or bring; to gather from premises; to infer; to derive.

Deed, dēd, n. That which is done; an act; feat; reality; a written agreement; an instrument conveying real estate.

Deem, dēm, vt. To judge; to think.— vi. To judge; to be of opinion; to estimate.

Deep, dēp, a. Being far below the surface; descending far downward; low in situation; not obvious; sagacious; designing; grave in sound; very still or solemn; thick; strongly colored; mysterious; heartfelt; absorbed.—n. The sea; the abyss of waters; any abyss.

Deer, dēr, n. sing. and pl. A quadruped of several species, as the stag, the fallow-deer, the roebuck, the reindeer, etc.

Deface, dē'fās', vt. To destroy or mar the surface of a thing; to disfigure; to erase.

Defeat, dē-fēt', n. Frustration; overthrow; loss of battle.—vt. To frustrate; to foil, to overthrow; to conquer.

Defecate, de'fē-kāt, vt. To clear from lees; to purify.—vi. To void excrement.

Defect, dē-fekt', n. Want; a blemish; fault; flaw.

Defective, dē-fekt'iv, a. Having a defect; deficient; faulty.

Defend, dē-fend', vt. To guard; to support; to resist; to vindicate; to act as defendant.—vi. To make defense or opposition.

Defendant, dē-fen'dant, *n*. A defender; in *law*, the person that opposes a charge, etc.

Defense, dē-fens', *n*. A guarding against danger; protection; fortification; vindication; apology; plea; method adopted by one against whom legal proceedings are taken; skill in fencing.

Defensive, dē-fens'iv, *a*. Proper for defense; carried on in resisting attack; in a state or posture to defend.—*n*. That which defends; state or posture of defense.

Defer, dē-fėr', *vt*. (deferring, deferred). To put off to a future time; to postpone.—*vi*. To yield to another's opinion; to submit courteously or from respect.

Deference, de'fėr-ens, *n*. A yielding in opinion; regard; respect; submission.

Deferment, dē-fėr-ment, *n*. Postponement.

Defiance, dē-fī'ans, *n*. Act of defying; a challenge to fight; contempt of opposition or danger.

Deficient, de-fī'shent, *a*. Defective; imperfect; not adequate.

Deficit, de'fī-sit, *n*. Deficiency of revenue.

Defile, dē-fīl', *vt*. (defiling, defiled). To make foul; to pollute; to violate the chastity of; to march off in a line, or file by file.—*n*. A narrow way in which troops may march only in a line, or with a narrow front; a long narrow pass.

Define, dē-fīn', *vt*. (defining, defined). To limit; to explain exactly.

Definite, de'fin-it, *a*. Having fixed limits; precise; exact; clear.

Definition, de-fi-ni'shon, *n*. The act of defining; a brief description of a thing by its properties; an explanation in words.

Defunct, dē-fungkt', *a*. Dead; deceased.—*n*. A dead person; one deceased.

Defy, dē-fī', *vt*. (defying, defied). To provoke to combat; to dare; to challenge; to set at nought.

Degeneracy, dē-jen'e-ra-si, *n*. a growing worse or inferior; decline in good qualities; departure from the virtue of ancestors.

Degenerate, dē-jen'ė-rat, *vi*. To become worse than one's kind; to decay in good qualities. —*a*. Fallen from primitive or natural excellence; mean; corrupt.

Degrade, dē-grād', *vt*. (degrading, degraded). To reduce to a lower rank; to strip of honors, to debase; to depose; to dishonor.

Degree, dē-grē', *n*. A step; step in relationship, rank quality, etc.; measure; extent; the 360th part of the circumference of a circle; a mark of distinction conferred by universities; divisions marked on scientific instruments.

Dehydration, dē-hī-drā'shon, *n*. Process of freeing a compound from water.

Delay, dē-lā', *vt*. To defer; to retard; to stop; to protract.—*vi*. To linger; to stop for a time.—*n*. A lingering; stay; hindrance.

Delectable, dē-lekt'a-bl, *a*. Delightful.

Deliberate, dē-lib'ė-rāt, *vi*. To weigh well in one's mind; to consider; to consult; to debate.—*vt*. To balance well in the mind; to consider.—*a*. Cautious; discreet; well advised.

Deliberation, dē-lib'ė-rā''shon, *n*. Thoughtful consideration; prudence; discussion of reasons for and against a measure.

Delicacy, de'li-ka-si, *n*. The quality of being delicate; fineness of texture; tenderness; minute accuracy; refined taste; a dainty.

Delicate, de'li-kāt, *a*. Pleasing to the taste or senses; choice; fine; soft; smooth; nice in forms; minute; easily hurt or affected; tender; not robust.

Delicious, dē-li'shus, *a*. Highly pleasing to the taste; delightful.

Delight, dē-līt', *n*. That which yields great pleasure; a high degree of pleasure; joy.—*vt*. To affect with great pleasure; to give high satisfaction to.—*vi*. To take great pleasure; to be rejoiced.

Deliver, dē-liv'ėr, *vt*. To free, as from danger or bondage; to disburden a woman of a child; to surrender; to commit; to give forth in words or in action.

Deliverance, dē-liv'ėr-ans, *n*. Release; rescue; an authoritative judgment.

Delivery, dē-liv'e-ri, *n*. Act of delivering; childbirth; rescue; surrender; distribution (of letters); manner of speaking.

Delusive, dē-lū'siv, *a*. Apt to deceive.

Delve, delv, *vt*. and *i*. (delving, delved). To dig.

Demagnetize, dē-mag'net-īz, *vt*. To deprive of magnetic polarity.

Demagogue, dem'a-gog, *n*. A leader of the people; a factious orator.

Demand, dē-mand', *vt*. To seek as due by right; to require; to interrogate.—*n*. A claim by virtue of a right; an asking with authority; debt; the calling for in order to purchase; desire to purchase or possess.

Demarcation, dē-mär-kā'shon, *n*. Act of setting a limit; a limit fixed.

Demean, dē-mēn', *vt*. To conduct; to behave; to debase (oneself).

Demeanor, dē-mēn'er, *n*. Manner of conducting oneself; behavior.

Demobilize, dē-mō'bil-īz, *vt*. To disband.

Democracy, dē-mok'ra-si, *n*. A form of government in which the supreme power is vested in the people.

Demolish, dē-mol'ish, *vt*. To pull down; to destroy.

Demon, dē'mon, *n*. A spirit, holding a place below the celestial deities of the pagans; an evil spirit; a devil; a fiend-like man.

Demonstration, de-mon-strā'shon, *n*. Act or process of demonstrating; proof; massing of troops to deceive the enemy; a gathering to exhibit sympathy with a person or cause.

Demoralize, dē-mo'ral-īz, *vt*. To corrupt the morals of; to deprave.

Demoralizing, dē-mo'ral-īz-ing, *p.a.* Tending to destroy morals or moral principles.

Demure, dē-mūr', *a*. Consciously grave; affectedly modest.

Den, den, *n*. A cave; a dell; a haunt.

Denary, dē-na-ri, *a*. Containing ten; proceeding by tens.—*n*. The number ten.

Dendriform, den'dri-form, *a*. Having the form or appearance of a tree.

Dendritic, Dendritical, den-drit'ik, den-drit'i-kal, *a*. Resembling a tree; marked by figures resembling shrubs, moss, etc.

Denial, dē-nī'al, *n*. Act of denying; contradiction; refusal to grant or acknowledge.

Denigrate, den'i-grāt, *vt*. To blacken; to sully.

Denim, den'im, *n*. A coarse cotton drill used for making aprons, overalls, etc.

Denizen, de'ni-zn, *n*. A stranger admitted to residence in a foreign country.

Denominate, dē-nom'in-āt, *vt*. (denominating, denominated). To name; to designate.

Denomination, dē-nom'in-ā''shon, *n*. Act of naming; title; class; religious sect.

Denominationalism, dē-nom'in-ā'' shon-al-izm, *n*. A class spirit; system of religious sects having each their own schools.

Denominative, dē-nom'in-āt-iv, *a*. That confers a distinct appellation.

Denominator, dē-nom'in-āt-er, *n*. One who or that which denominates; that number placed below the line in vulgar fractions.

Denote, dē-nōt', *vt*. To indicate; to imply.

Dénouement, dā-nö'mäng, *n*. The winding up of a plot in a novel or drama; solution of a mystery; issue; the event.

Denounce, dē-nouns', *vt*. (denouncing, denounced). To threaten; to accuse publicly; to stigmatize.

Dentition, den-ti'shon, *n*. The cutting of teeth in infancy; the system of teeth peculiar to an animal.

Denture, den'tūr, *n*. A set of false teeth.

Denude, dē-nūd', *vt*. (denuding, denuded). To make bare; to divest; to uncover.

Denunciation, dē-nun'si-ā''shon, *n*. Act of denouncing; public menace; arraignment.

Deny, dē-nī', *vt*. (denying, denied). To declare not to be true; to disavow; to refuse to grant or acknowledge; not to afford or yield.

Deodorize, dē-ō′dėr-īz, *vt.* (deodorizing, deodorized). To deprive of fetid odor.

Deoxidate, Deoxidize, dē-ok′sīd-āt, dē-ok′sīd-īz, *vt.* To reduce from the state of an oxide.

Depart, dē-pärt′, *vi.* To go away; to desist; to abandon; to deviate; to die.

Department, dē-pärt′ment, *n.* A separate part; a division of territory; a distinct branch, as of science, etc.

Depend, dē-pend′, *vi.* To hang from; to be contingent or conditioned; to rest or rely solely; to trust.

Dependant, Dependent, dē-pend′ant, dē-pend′ent, *n.* One who depends on another; a retainer. (The spelling with -*ant* is more common in the noun, with -*ent* in the adj.).

Deplorable, dē-plōr′a-bl, *a.* To be deplored; lamentable; grievous; pitiable.

Deplore, dē-plōr′, *vt.* (deploring, deplored). To feel or express deep grief for; to bewail.

Deploy, dē-ploi′, *vt.* To open out; to extend from column to line as a body of troops.—*vi.* To form a more extended front or line.

Deportation, dē-pōrt-ā′shon, *n.* Removal from one country to another; exile.

Deportment, dē-pōrt′ment, *n.* Carriage; demeanor; manner of acting.

Depose, dē-pōz′, *vt.* (deposing, deposed). To dethrone; to divest of office; to degrade.—*vi.* To bear witness; to give testimony in writing.

Deposit, dē-poz′it, *vt.* To lay down; to lodge in a place; to lay in a place for preservation; to intrust; to commit as a pledge.—*n.* Any matter laid down or lodged; anything intrusted to another; a thing given as security.

Depositary, dē-poz′it-a-ri, *n.* One to whom a thing is lodged in trust; a guardian.

Deposition, dē-pō-zi′shon, *n.* Act of depositing and of deposing; attested written testimony; declaration; act of dethroning a king, or degrading an official.

Depot, dep′ō, *n.* A place of deposit; headquarters of a regiment; a railway-station.

Deprave, dē-prāv′, *vt.* (depraving, depraved). To make bad or worse; to impair the good qualities of; to corrupt; to vitiate.

Depredate, de′prē-dāt, *vt.* To plunder; to waste.

Depress, dē-pres′, *vt.* To press down; to lower; to humble; to deject.

Depression, dē-pre′shon, *n.* Act of depressing; state of being depressed; a low state; a sinking of a surface; a hollow; abasement; dejection; a state of dulness.

Deprivation, de-pri-vā′shon, *n.* Act of depriving; state of being deprived; want; bereavement; deposition of a clergyman.

Derange, dē-rānj′, *vt.* (deranging, deranged). To disturb the regular order of; to displace; to disconcert; to disorder the mind of.

Derangement, dē-rānj′ment, *n.* A putting out of order; disorder; insanity.

Derelict, de′re-likt, *a.* Abandoned.—*n.* Anything forsaken or left, especially a ship.

Dereliction, de-re-lik′shon, *n.* Act of forsaking; state of being forsaken; neglect.

Deride, dē-rīd′, *vt.* (deriding, derided). To laugh at in contempt; to ridicule; to jeer.

Derision, dē-ri′zhon, *n.* Act of deriding; scorn; ridicule; mockery.

Derivation, de-ri-vā′shon, *a.* Act of deriving; the tracing of a word from its root; deduction.

Derivative, de-riv′āt-iv, *a.* Derived; secondary.—*n.* That which is derived; a word which takes its origin in another word.

Derive, de-rīv′, *vt.* (deriving, derived). To draw or receive, as from a source or origin; to trace the etymology of.—*vi.* To come from.

Derma, Dermis, Derm, dėr′ma, dėr′mis, dėrm, *n.* The true skin, or under layer of the skin.

Descant, des′kant, *n.* A discourse; discussion; a song or tune with various modulations.—*vi.* deskant′. To discourse or animadvert freely; to add a part to a melody.

Descend, dē-send´, vi. To pass or move down; to invade; to be derived; to pass to an heir.—vt. To pass or move down, on, or along.

Descry, dē-skrī´, vt. (descrying, descried). To espy; to discover from a distance.

Desecrate, de´sē-krāt, vt. (desecrating, desecrated). To divert from a sacred purpose; to profane.

Desert, de´zėrt, a. Waste; uncultivated.—n. An uninhabited tract; a vast sandy plain.

Desert, dē-zėrt´, vt. To leave, as service; to abandon; to quit.—vi. To run away; to quit a service without permission.—n. That which is deserved; merit or demerit; reward.

Desiccate, dē-sik´āt, vt. To exhaust of moisture; to dry.

Desiderate, dē-sid´ėr-āt, vt. To desire; to want; to miss.

Desideratum, dē-sid´ėr-ā´´tum, n.; pl. **-ata** That which is not possessed, but is desirable; something much wanted.

Design, dē-sīn´, vt. To delineate by drawing the outline of; to form in idea; to plan; to propose; to mean.—vi. To intend.—n. A representation of a thing by an outline; first idea represented by lines; a plan drawn out in the mind; purpose; aim; project.

Desire, dē-zīr´, n. Eagerness to obtain or enjoy; aspiration; longing; a request to obtain; the object of desire; love; lust.—vt. (desiring, desired). To wish for the possession or enjoyment of; to covet; to ask; to petition.

Desist, dē-sist´, vi. To cease to act or proceed; to forbear; to leave off. (With *from*.)

Desk, desk, n. An inclining table to write or read upon; a portable case for the same purpose; a lectern; a pulpit.

Desolate, de´sō-lāt, a. Destitute of inhabitants; waste; laid waste; afflicted; forlorn.—vt. (desolating, desolated). To deprive of inhabitants; to make desert; to ravage.

Despair, dē-spār´, n. A hopeless state; despondency; that which causes despair; loss of hope.—vi.

To give up all hope; to despond.

Despicable, des´pik-a-bl, a. Contemptible; vile; base; mean.

Despise, dē-spīz´, vt. (despising, despised). To hold in contempt; to scorn; to disdain.

Despite, dē-spīt´, n. Extreme malice; defiance with contempt; an act of malice.—vt. To despise; to spite.—prep. In spite of; notwithstanding.

Despoil, dē-spoil´, vt. To take from by force; to rob; to bereave; to rifle.

Despond, dē-spond´, vi. To be cast down or dejected; to lose heart, hope, or resolution.

Dessert, dē-zėrt´, n. That which is served at the close of a dinner, as fruits, etc.

Destination, des-tin-ā´shon, n. Act of destining; ultimate design; predetermined end.

Destine, des´tin, vt. (destining, destined). To set or appoint to a purpose; to design; to doom; to ordain.

Destiny, des´ti-ni, n. State appointed or predetermined; fate; invincible necessity.

Destitute, des´ti-tūt, a. Wanting; needy; comfortless; forlorn.

Destitution, des-ti-tū´shon, n. Want; poverty; indigence.

Destroy, dē-stroi´, vt. To pull down; to overthrow; to devastate; to annihilate.

Detachment, dē-tach´ment, n. Act of detaching; a body of troops, or number of ships, sent from the main army or fleet.

Detail, dē-tāl, vt. To relate in particulars; to specify; in military affairs, to appoint to a particular service.—n. dē-tāl´ or dē´tāl. An individual fact, circumstance, or portion; an item; a report of particulars.

Detain, dē-tān´, vt. To keep back or from; to withhold; to arrest; to check; to retard.

Detect, dē-tekt´, vt. To discover; to bring to light.

Detergent, dē-tėrj´ent, a. Cleansing; purging.—n. That which cleanses.

Deteriorate, dē-tē´ri-ō-rāt, vi. (deteriorating, deteriorated). To grow worse; to degenerate.—*vt*. To reduce in quality.

Determination, dē-tėr'min-ā'' shon, *n*. Act of determining; firm resolution; judgment; strong direction to a given point; end.

Determine, dē-tėr'min, *vt*. (determining, determined). To bound; to fix permanently; to decide; to establish; to give a direction to; to resolve on; to bring to an end.—*vi*. To resolve; to conclude.

Detest, dē-test', *vt*. To abhor; to loathe.

Detestable, dē-test'a-bl, *a*. Extremely hateful; abominable; odious.

Detestation, dē-test-ā'shon, *n*. Extreme hatred; abhorrence; loathing.

Dethrone, dē-thrōn', *vt*. (dethroning, dethroned). To divest of royal authority and dignity; to depose.

Detonate, de'tō-nāt, *vt*. (detonating, detonated). To cause to explode; to cause to burn with a sudden repot.—*vi*. To explode.

Detract, dē-trakt', *vt*. To draw away; to disparage.—*vi*. To take away from (especially reputation).

Detriment, de'tri-ment, *n*. Loss; damage; injury; prejudice; mischief; harm.

Devastate, de'vas-tāt, *vt*. (devastating, devastated). To lay waste; to ravage.

Develop, dē-vel'up, *vt*. To unfold; to lay open to view; to make to grow.—*vi*. To be unfolded; to become manifest; to grow or expand; to be evolved.

Deviate, dē'vi-āt, *vi*. (deviating, deviated). To stray; to wander; to swerve; to err.

Device, dē-vīs', *n*. That which is devised; contrivance; scheme; an emblem.

Devil, de'vil, *n*. An evil spirit; Satan; a very wicked person; a machine for cutting, tearing, etc.—*vt*. (devilling, devilled). To pepper excessively and broil; to tease or cut up.

Devote, dē-vōt', *vt*. (devoting, devoted). To set apart by vow; to consecrate; to addict (oneself); to apply closely to; to consign.

Devotee, dev-o-tē', *n*. One wholly devoted, particularly to religion; a votary.

Devotion, dē-vō'shon, *n*. Act of devoting or state of being devoted; prayer; devoutness; ardent love or affection; attachment; earnestness.

Devour, dē-vour', *vt*. To eat ravenously; to swallow up; to waste; to look on with keen delight.

Devout, dē-vout', *a*. Pious; expressing devotion; earnest; solemn.

Dew, dū, *n*. Moisture from the atmosphere condensed into drops on the surface of cold bodies, as grass, etc.; damp.—*vt*. To wet with dew; to moisten; to damp.

Diabetes, dī-a-bē'tēz, *n*. Disease characterized by a morbid discharge of urine.

Diabolic, Diabolical, dī-a-bol'ik, dī-a-bol'ik-al, *a*. Devilish; atrocious.

Diagnose, dī-ag-nōs', *vt*. To ascertain from symptoms the true nature of.

Diagnosis, dī-ag-nō'sis, *n*. The ascertaining from symptoms the true nature of diseases.

Diagonal, dī-ag'on-al, *a*. Extending from one angle to another of a quadrilateral figure; lying in an oblique direction.—*n*. A straight line drawn between opposite angles of a quadrilateral figure.

Diagram, dī'a-gram, *n*. A drawing to demonstrate the properties of any figure; an illustrative figure in outline.

Dial, dī'al, *n*. An instrument for showing the hour by the sun's shadow; face of a clock, etc.

Dialect, dī'a-lekt, *n*. The idiom of a language peculiar to a province; language; manner of speaking.

Diameter, dī-am'et-ėr, *n*. A straight line passing through the center of a circle, and terminated by the circumference; the distance through the center of any object.

Diamond, dī'a-mond, *n*. A valuable gem, remarkable for its hardness and transparency; a rhombus; a card of the suit marked with such figures in red; a very small printing type.—*a*. Resembling a diamond; set with diamonds.

D

Diapason, dī-a-pā′zon, *n.* The entire compass of a voice or instrument; an organ stop.

Diaper, dī′a-pėr, *n.* A figured linen or cotton cloth.—*vt.* To variegate or diversify with figures.—*vi.* To draw flowers or figures on.

Diaphanous, dī-af′an-us, *a.* Having power to transmit rays of light; transparent.

Diaphragm, dī′a-fram, *n.* The midriff, a muscular partition separating the thorax from the abdomen.

Diarrhea, dī-a-rē′a, *n.* A morbidly frequent evacuation of the intestines.

Diary, dī′a-ri, *n.* A register of daily events or transactions; a journal.

Dibble, dib′bl, *n.* A pointed instrument to make holes for planting seeds, etc.—*vt.* (dibbling, dibbled). To make holes for planting seeds, etc.

Dice, dīs, *n.*; pl. of **Die,** for gaming.—*vi.* (dicing, diced). To play with dice.

Dichotomous, dī-kot′o-mus, *a.* In *botany,* regularly divided by pairs from top to bottom.

Dickey, Dicky, dik′i, *n.* A false shirt-front; the driver's seat in a carriage.

Dicotyledon, dī′kot-i-lē′′don, *n.* A plant whose seeds contain a pair of cotyledons.

Dictaphone, dik′ta-fōn, *n.* Trade name for an instrument into which correspondence is dictated, to be transcribed afterwards.

Dictate, dik′tāt, *vt.* (dictating, dictated). To deliver, as an order or direction; to prescribe; to tell what to say or write; to instigate.—*n.* An order delivered; an authoritative precept or maxim; an impulse.

Dictator, dik-tāt′ėr, *n.* One invested with absolute authority.

Diction, dik′shon, *n.* Choice of words; mode of expression; style.

Dictionary, dik′shon-a-ri, *n.* A book containing the words of a language arranged alphabetically, with their meanings, etc.; a work explaining the terms, etc., of any subject under heads alphabetically arranged.

Die, dī, *vi.* (dying, died). To cease to live; to expire; to sink gradually; to vanish.

Die, dī, *n.*; pl: **Dice,** dīs, in first sense, in the others **Dies,** dīz. A small cube with numbered faces; any cubic body; the dado of a pedestal; a stamp used in coining money; an implement for turning out things of a regular shape.

Diet, dī′et, *n.* A person's regular food; food prescribed medically; a meeting of dignitaries or delegates for legislative or other purposes.—*vt.* To furnish provisions for.—*vi.* To eat according to rules prescribed.

Dietetics, dī-et-et′iks, *n.* Principles for regulating the diet.

Differ, dif′ėr, *vi.* To be unlike or distinct; to disagree; to be at variance.

Difference, dif′ėr-ens, *n.* State of being different; dissimilarity; that which distinguishes; dispute; point in dispute; remainder after a sum is subtracted.

Digest, di-jest′, *vt.* To arrange under proper heads; to think out; to dissolve in the stomach; to soften by a heated liquid; to bear with patience.—*vi.* To undergo digestion, as food.—*n.* dī′jest. A collection of laws; systematic summary.

Digestion, di-jest′yon, *n.* Act of digesting; process of dissolving aliment in the stomach; operation of heating with some solvent.

Digit, di′jit, *n.* A finger; three-fourths of an inch; the twelfth part of the diameter of the sun or moon; any integer under 10.

Dignify, dig′ni-fī, *vt.* (dignifying, dignified). To invest with dignity; to exalt in rank or office; to make illustrious.

Dignity, dig′ni-ti, *n.* Nobleness or elevation of mind; honorable place; degree of excellence; grandeur of mien; an elevated office; one who holds high rank.

Digress, di-gres′ or dī′gres, *vi.* To depart from the main subject; to deviate.

Dilapidation, di-la′pi-dā′′shon, *n.* Decay; ruin; destruction; ruining or suffering to decay of a church building.

Dilatation, Dilation, dil-at-ā'shon, dī-lā'shon, *n.* Act of dilating; expansion; state of being expanded or distended.

Diligence, di'li-jens, *n.* Steady application; assiduity; a four-wheeled stage-coach.

Diligent, di'li-jent, *a.* Steady in application; industrious; persevering; prosecuted with care and constant effort.

Dilute, di-lūt', *vt.* (diluting, diluted). To render liquid or more liquid; to weaken by admixture of water.— *vi.* To become attenuated or diluted.—*a.* Thin; reduced in strength.

Diluvium, di-lū'vi-um, *n.* A deluge or inundation; a deposit of sand, gravel, etc., caused by a flood.

Dim, dim, *a.* Not seeing clearly; not clearly seen; mysterious; tarnished.—*vt.* (dimming, dimmed). To dull; to obscure; to sully.

Dime, dīm, *n.* A silver coin the tenth of a dollar.

Dimension, di-men'shon, *n.* Extension in a single direction; measure of a thing, its size, extent, capacity, (usually in *pl.*).

Diminish, di-min'ish, *vt.* To reduce; to abate; to degrade.—*vi.* To become less.

Diminutive, di-min'ūt-iv, *a.* Small; little.—*n.* A word formed from another word to express a little thing of the kind.

Dingy, din'ji, *a.* Of a dusky color; soiled.

Dinner, din'nėr, *n.* The principal meal of the day.

Diocese, dī'ō-sēs, *n.* An ecclesiastical division of a state, subject to a bishop.

Dioptrics, dī-op-triks, *n.* The science of the refractions of light passing through mediums, as air, water, or lenses.

Diorama, dī-ō-rä'ma, *n.* A contrivance for giving a high degree of optical illusion to painted scenes.

Dip, dip, *vt.* (dipping, dipped). To plunge in a liquid; to baptize by immersion.—*vi.* To dive into a liquid and emerge; to engage in a desultory way; to look cursorily; to choose by chance; to incline.—*n.* Act of dipping; a bath; candle; downward slope.

Diphtheria, dif-thē'ri-a, *n.* An epidemic inflammatory disease of the throat.

Diphthong, dif'thong, *n.* A union of two vowels pronounced in one syllable.

Diploma, di-plō-ma, *n.* A document conferring some power, privilege, or honor.

Diplomacy, di-plō'ma-si, *n.* The art or practice of conducting international negotiations; skill in securing advantages.

Direct, di-rekt', *a.* Straight; right; in the line of father and son; not ambiguous; express.—*vt.* To point or aim at; to show the right course to; to conduct; to order; to instruct.

Directory, di-rek'to-ri, *n.* A rule to direct; a book containing directions for public worship; a book containing a list of the inhabitants of a place, with their addresses; a board of directors.

Disadvantage, dis-ad-van'tāj, *n.* Want of advantage; unfavorable state; detriment.

Disaffect, dis-af-fekt', *vt.* To make less faithful or friendly; to make discontented.

Disaffirm, dis-af-fėrm', *vt.* To deny; to annul.

Disagree, dis-a-grē', *vi.* To be of a different opinion; to dissent; to be unfriendly; to be unsuitable.

Disapprobation, dis-ap'prō-bā'' shon, *n.* Disapproval; censure, expressed or unexpressed.

Disapprove, dis-ap-pröv', *vt.* To censure as wrong; to regard with dislike; to reject.

Disarm, dis-ärm', *vt.* To take the arms or weapons from; to render harmless.—*vi.* To lay down arms; to disband.

Disarrange, dis-a-rānj', *vt.* To put out of arrangement or order; to derange.

Disarray, dis-a-rā', *vt.* To undress; to throw into disorder.—*n.* Disorder; undress.

Disaster, diz-as'tėr, *n.* An unfortunate event; mishap; catastrophe; reverse.

Disavow, dis-a-vou', *vt.* To deny to

be true; to reject; to dissent from.

Disband, dis-band´, *vt.* To dismiss from military service; to disperse.—*vi.* To retire from military service; to dissolve connection.

Disbar, dis-bär´, *vt.* To expel from being a member of the bar.

Discard, dis-kärd´, *vt.* To throw away; to cast off; to dismiss; to discharge.

Discern, dis-sėrn´ or di-zėrn´, *vt.* To distinguish; to discriminate; to descry.—*vi.* To see or understand difference; to have clearness of mental sight.

Discernment, dis-sėrn´ment, *n.* Act or power of discerning; judgment; sagacity.

Discharge, dis-chärj´, *vt.* To unload; to let fly or go, as a missile; to fire off; to give vent to; to clear off by payment; to perform; to acquit; to dismiss; to release.—*vi.* To get rid of or let out a charge or contents.—*n.* Act of discharging; unloading; a firing off; emission; dismissal; release from obligation, debt, or penalty; absolution from a crime; ransom; performance; release; payment, as of a debt.

Disciple, dis-sī´pl, *n.* A learner; a pupil; an adherent to the doctrines of another.

Disciplinarian, dis´si-plin-ā´´ri-an, *a.* Pertaining to discipline.—*n.* One who enforces discipline; a martinet.

Discipline, dis´si-plin, *n.* Training; method of government; order; subjection to laws; punishment; correction; execution of ecclesiastical laws.—*vt.* (disciplining, disciplined). To subject to discipline; to train up well; to chastise.

Disconsolate, dis-kon´sō-lāt, *a.* Comfortless; hopeless; gloomy; cheerless.

Discontent, dis-kon-tent´, *n.* Want of content; uneasiness of mind; dissatisfaction.

Discontinuance, dis-kon-tin´ū-ans, *n.* A breaking off; cessation.

Discontinue, dis-kon-tin´ū, *vt.* To leave off; to cause to cease; to cease to take or receive.—*vi.* To cease.

Discord, dis´kord, *n.* Want of concord; disagreement; disagreement of sounds.

Discordance, Discordancy, dis-kord´ans, dis-kord´an-si, *n.* Want of concord; disagreement; inconsistency; discord.

Discount, dis´kount, *n.* A sum deducted for prompt or advanced payment.—*vt.* dis-kount´. To advance the amount of, as of a bill, deducting a certain rate per cent; to make an allowance for supposed exaggeration; to disregard.

Discountenance, dis-koun´ten-ans, *vt.* To restrain by censure, cold treatment, etc.

Discourage, dis-ku´rāj, *vt.* (discouraging, discouraged). To dishearten; to dissuade.

Discouragement, dis-ku´rāj-ment, *n.* Act of discouraging; that which discourages.

Discourse, dis-kōrs´, *n.* A speech; treatise; sermon; conversation.—*vi.* (discoursing, discoursed). To talk; to converse; to treat of formally; to expatiate.—*vt.* To utter.

Discourtesy, dis-kōr´te-si, *n.* Incivility; rudeness; act of disrespect.

Discover, dis-kuv´ėr, *vt.* To lay open to view; to reveal; to have the first sight of; to find out; to detect.

Discovery, dis-kuv´ė-ri, *n.* Act of discovering; disclosure; that which is discovered.

Discredit, dis-kred´it, *n.* Want of credit; disrepute; disbelief; distrust.—*vt.* To give no credit to; to deprive of credit; to make less reputable; to bring into disesteem.

Discreet, dis-krēt, *a.* Prudent; wary; judicious.

Discrepance, Discrepancy, dis-krep´ans, dis-krep´an-si, *n.* Discordance; disagreement.

Discrete, dis´krēt, *a.* Separate; distinct.

Discriminate, dis-krim´in-āt, *vt.* (discriminating, discriminated). To distinguish; to select from.—*vt.* To make a distinction.—*a.* Having the difference marked; distinct.

Disease, diz-ēz´, *n.* Any state of a living body in which the natural functions are disturbed; illness; disorder.—*vt.* (diseasing, diseased). To afflict with disease; to infect; to derange.

Disembroil, dis-em-broil', *vt.* To disentangle; to free from perplexity.

Disentangle, dis-en-tang'gl, *vt.* To free from entanglement; to clear.

Disfavor, dis-fā'vėr, *n.* Want of favor; unfavorable regard.—*vt.* To withhold favor from; to discountenance.

Disfigure, dis-fi'gūr, *vt.* (disfiguring, disfigured). To mar the figure of; to impair the beauty, symmetry, or excellence of.

Disfranchise, dis-fran'chīz, *vt.* To deprive of the rights of a free citizen.

Disgorge, dis-gorj', *vt.* To vomit; to discharge violently; to surrender.

Disgrace, dis-grās', *n.* State of being deprived of grace or favor; cause of shame; dishonor.—*vt.* (disgracing, disgraced). To bring to shame; to degrade; to dishonor.

Disguise, dis-gīz', *vt.* (disguising, disguised). To conceal by an unusual habit or mask; to dissemble; to give an unusual appearance to.—*n.* A dress intended to conceal; an assumed appearance, intended to deceive.

Disgust, dis-gust', *n.* Distaste; loathing; repugnance.—*vt.* To cause distaste in; to offend the mind or moral taste of.

Dish, dish, *n.* A broad open vessel for serving up meat at table; the meat served; any particular kind of food.—*vt.* To put in a dish; to make (a wheel) hollow or concave.

Dishearten, dis-härt'n, *vt.* To discourage; to depress.

Dishevel, di-she'vel, *vt.* (disheveling, dishevelled). To put out of order, or spread loosely, as the hair.

Dishonest, dis-on'est, *a.* Void of honesty; fraudulent; knavish; perfidious.

Dishonor, dis-on'ėr, *n.* Want of honor; disgrace; ignominy.—*vt.* To deprive of honor; to treat with indignity; to violate the chastity of; to decline to accept or pay, as a draft.

Disjoint, dis-joint', *vt.* To separate, as parts united by joints; to put out of joint; to make incoherent.

Dislike, dis-līk', *n.* A feeling the opposite of liking; a moderate degree of hatred; aversion; antipathy.—*vt.* To regard with some aversion or displeasure.

Dislocate, dis'lō-kāt, *vt.* To displace; to put out of joint.

Dislodge, dis-loj', *vt.* To remove or drive from a place of rest or a station.—*vi.* To go from a place of rest.

Disloyal, dis-loi'al, *a.* Void of loyalty; false to a sovereign; faithless.

Dismal, diz'mal, *a.* Dark; gloomy; doleful; calamitous; sorrowful.

Dismantle, dis-man'tl, *vt.* To strip; to divest; to unrig; to deprive or strip, as of military equipment or defenses; to break down.

Disobedience, dis-ō-bē'di-ens, *n.* Neglect or refusal to obey.

Disobey, dis-ō-bā', *vt.* To neglect or refuse to obey; to violate an order.

Disoblige, dis-ō-blīj', *vt.* To fail to oblige; to be unaccommodating to.

Disorder, dis-or'dėr, *n.* Want of order; confusion; disease.—*vt.* To put out of order; to disturb; to produce indisposition; to craze.

Disorganize, dis-or'gan-īz, *vt.* To destroy organic structure or connected system in; to throw into confusion.

Disown, dis-ōn', *vt.* To refuse to acknowledge; to renounce; to repudiate.

Dispatch, dis-pach', *vt.* To send away in haste; to put to death; to perform quickly; to conclude.—*n.* Act of dispatching; communication on public business; speedy performance; due diligence.

Dispel, dis-pel', *vt.* (dispelling, dispelled). To scatter; to banish.—*vi.* To fly different ways; to disappear.

Dispensary, dis-pens'a-ri, *n.* A place where medicines are dispensed to the poor, and medical advice is given gratis; a place where medicines are compounded.

Dispensation, dis-pens-ā'shon, *n.* Act of dispensing; distribution; good or evil dealt out by providence; exemption.

Dispense, dis-pens', *vt.* (dispensing, dispensed). To deal out in portions; to administer; to apply; to exempt; to grant dispensation for.—*vi*. To do without (with *with*).

Disperse, dis-pėrs', *vt*. To scatter; to dispel; to diffuse; to distribute.—*vi*. To be scattered; to vanish.

Display, dis-plā', *vt*. To unfold; to spread before the eyes or mind; to show; to parade.—*vi*. To make a show; to talk without restraint.—*n*. An opening or unfolding; exhibition; parade.

Displease, dis-plēz, *vt*. To offend; to dissatisfy; to provoke.—*vi*. To disgust.

Displeasure, dis-ple'zhūr, *n*. Dissatisfaction; resentment.

Dispose, dis-pōz', *vt*. (disposing, disposed). To arrange; to apply to a particular purpose; to incline.—*vi*. To regulate; (with *of*) to part with, to employ.

Disproportionate, dis-prō-pōr'shon-āt, *a*. Not proportioned; unsymmetrical; inadequate.

Disprove, dis-pröv', *vt*. To prove to be false; to confute.

Disputant, dis-pūt-ant, *n*. One who argues in opposition to another.

Disputation, dis-pūt-ā'shon, *n*. Act of disputing; controversy in words; debate.

Dispute, dis-pūt', *vi*. (disputing, disputed). To contend in argument; to debate; to strive with.—*vt*. To attempt to prove to be false; to impugn; to contest; to strive to maintain.—*n*. Controversy in words; strife.

Disqualify, dis-kwo'li-fī, *vt*. To divest of qualifications; to incapacitate.

Disquiet, dis-kwī'et, *n*. Uneasiness; anxiety.—*vt*. To make uneasy or restless.

Disreputable, dis-re'pūt-a-bl, *a*. Discreditable; low; mean.

Disrepute, dis-rē-pūt', *n*. Loss or want of reputation; disesteem; disgrace.

Disrespect, dis-rē-spekt', *n*. Want of respect; incivility.—*vt*. To show disrespect to.

Disrobe, dis-rōb', *vt*. To undress; to uncover; to divest of any surrounding appendage.

Disroot, dis-röt', *vt*. To tear up the roots.

Disruption, dis-rup'shon, *n*. Act of rending asunder; breach; rent; rupture.

Dissatisfaction, dis-sa'tis-fak''shon, *n*. Want of satisfaction; discontent.

Dissatisfy, dis-sa'tis-fī, *vt*. To fail to satisfy; to render discontented.

Dissect, dis-sekt', *vt*. To cut up; to anatomize; to divide and examine minutely.

Dissent, dis-sent', *vi*. To disagree in opinion; to separate from an established church, in doctrines, rites, or government.—*n*. Disagreement; separation from an established church.

Dissentient, dis-sen'shi-ent, *a*. Declaring dissent; disagreeing.—*a*. One who declares his dissent.

Dissertation, dis-sėr-tā'shon, *n*. A formal discourse; treatise; disquisition.

Disservice, dis-sėr'vis, *n*. An ill-service; injury; harm; mischief.

Dissever, dis-sev'ėr, *vt*. To part in two; to disunite.

Dissident, dis'si-dent, *a*. Dissenting.—*n*. A dissenter.

Dissilient, dis-si'li-ent, *a*. Starting asunder; opening with an elastic force.

Dissimilitude, dis-si-mil'i-tūd, *n*. Unlikeness; want of resemblance.

Dissolution, dis-sō-lū'shon, *n*. Act of dissolving; a melting or liquefaction; separation of parts; decomposition; death; destruction; the breaking up of an assembly.

Dissolve, diz-zolv', *vt*. To melt; to break up; to put an end to; to cause to vanish.—*vi*. To be melted; to become soft or languid; to waste away; to perish; to break up.

Dissolvent, diz-zolv'ent, *a*. Having power to dissolve.—*n*. That which has the power of melting; a solvent.

Distance, dis'tans, *n*. Remoteness in place or time; extent of interval between two things; the remoteness which respect requires; reserve; coldness.—*vt*. (distancing, distanced). To leave behind in a race; to outdo or excel.

Distaste, dis-tāst', *n*. Aversion of

the taste or mind; dislike.—*vt*. To dislike.

Distemper, dis-tem'pér, *n*. Any morbid state of the body; disorder; a disease of young dogs; bad constitution of the mind; a kind of painting in which the pigments are mixed with size; a pigment so mixed.—*vt*. To disease; to derange; to ruffle.

Distemperature, dis-tem'pér-ā-tūr, *n*. Tumult; perturbation of mind.

Distend, dis-tend', *vt*. To stretch by force from within; to swell.—*vi*. To swell; to dilate.

Distinction, dis-tingk'shon, *n*. Act of distinguishing; that which distinguishes; difference; elevation of rank in society; eminence; a title or honor.

Distinguish, dis-ting'gwish, *vt*. To mark out by some peculiarity; to perceive; to make eminent; to signalize.—*vi*. To make a distinction; to find or show the difference.

Distort, dis-tort', *vt*. To twist; to pervert.

Distortion, dis-tor'shon, *n*. Act of distorting; a writhing motion; deformity; perversion of the true meaning of words.

Distract, dis-trakt', *vt*. To draw towards different objects; to perplex; to disorder the reason of; to render furious.

Distraught, dis-trat', *a*. Distracted.

Distress, dis-tres', *n*. Anguish of body or mind; affliction; state of danger or destitution; act of distraining.—*vt*. To afflict with pain or anguish; to perplex.

Distribute, dis-tri'būt, *vt*. (distributing, distributed). To divide among two or more; to apportion; to administer, as justice; to classify.

Distributive, dis-tri'būt-iv, *a*. That distributes; expressing separation or division.—*n*. A word that divides or distributes, as *each, every, either*.

District, dis'trikt, *n*. A limited extent of country; a circuit; a region.

Distrust, dis-trust', *vt*. To have no trust in; to doubt; to suspect.—*n*. Want of trust; doubt; suspicion; discredit.

Disturb, dis-térb', *vt*. To throw into disorder; to agitate; to hinder; to move.

Disturbance, dis-térb'ans, *n*. State of being disturbed; commotion; excitement; interruption of a right.

Ditch, dich, *n*. A trench in the earth for drainage or defense.—*vi*. To dig a ditch.—*vt*.To dig a ditch in; to drain by a ditch; to surround with a ditch.

Ditto, dit'tō, *n*. A word used in lists, etc., meaning same as above; often written *Do*.

Dive, dīv, *vi*. (diving, dived). To plunge into water head-foremost; to go under water to execute some work; to go deep.

Diverge, di-vérj', *vi*. (diverging, diverged). To proceed from a point in different directions; to deviate; to vary.

Diversion, di-vér'shon, *n*. Act of diverting; that which diverts; amusement; a feigned attack.

Diversity, di-vérs'i-ti, *n*. State of being diverse; contrariety; variety.

Divert, di-vért', *vt*. To turn aside; to amuse.

Divest, di-vest', *vt*. To strip of clothes; to deprive.

Divide, di-vīd', *vt*. (dividing, divided). To part asunder; to separate; to keep apart; to distribute, allot; to set at variance.—*vi*. To part; to be of different opinions; to vote by the division of a legislative house into parties.

Dividend, di'vi-dend, *n*. A number which is to be divided; share of profit; share divided to creditors.

Divination, di-vin-ā'shon, *n*. Act of divining; a foretelling future events, or discovering things secret, by magical means.

Divine, di-vīn', *a*. Of or belonging to God; excellent in the highest degree.—*n*. One versed in divinity; a clergyman.—*vt*. (divining, divined). To foretell; to presage; to guess.—*vi*. To practice divination; to have or utter presages; to guess.

Division, di-vi'zhon, *n*. Act of dividing; state of being divided; separation; partition; portion; a separate body of men; a process or rule in arithmetic; part of an army, comprising all arms and services in due proportion.

Divulsion, di-vul'shon, *n*. A pulling, tearing, or rending asunder, or separating.

Dizziness, diz'zi-nes, *n*. Giddiness; vertigo.

Dizzy, diz'zi, *a*. Having a sensation of whirling in the head; giddy; causing giddiness.—*vt*. (dizzying, dizzied). To make giddy.

Do, dö, *vt*. or *auxiliary* (doing, pret. did, pp. done). To perform; to bring about; to pay (as honor, etc.); to transact; to finish; to prepare; to cook.—*vi*. To act or behave; to fare in health; to succeed; to suffice; to avail.

Docile, dö'sīl, *a*. Easily taught; ready to learn; tractable; pliant.

Dock, dok, *n*. A troublesome weed; the tail of a beast cut short; the stump of a tail; an inclosed area on the side of a harbor or bank of a river for ships; the place where the accused stands in court.—*vt*. To cut off; to curtail; to deduct from; to put a ship in dock.

Docket, dok'et, *n*. A summary; a bill tied to goods; a list of cases in a court.—*vt*. To make an abstract of; to mark the contents of papers on the back; to attach a docket to.

Dockyard, dok'yärd, *n*. A yard near a dock for naval stores.

Doctor, dok'tèr, *n*. A person who has received the highest degree in a university faculty; one licensed to practice medicine; a physician.—*vt*. To treat medically; to adulterate.

Dodge, doj, *vt*. (dodging, dodged). To start aside; to quibble.—*vt*. To evade by a sudden shift of place.—*n*. An artifice; an evasion.

Dodo, dö'dö, *n*. An extinct bird of Mauritius, having a massive, clumsy body, short strong legs, and wings useless for flight.

Doe, dö, *n*. A female deer.

Dogmatism, dog'mat-izm, *n*. Positiveness in assertion; arrogance in opinion.

Dogmatize, dog'mat-īz, *vi*. (dogmatizing, dogmatized). To assert with undue confidence; to advance principles with arrogance.

Dog-star, dog'stär, *n*. Sirius, a star of the first magnitude.

Doily, doi'li, *n*. A small ornamental mat for glasses, etc.

Doldrums, dol'drumz, *n.pl*. The dumps.

Dole, döl, *n*. That which is dealt out; share; gratuity; grief; sorrow.—*vt*. (doling, doled). To deal out; to distribute.

Doleful, döl'ful, *a*. Full of pain, grief, etc.; expressing or causing grief; gloomy.

Dolomite, dol'o-mīt, *n*. A granular crystalline or schistose rock compounded of carbonate of magnesia and carbonate of lime.

Dolorous, dö'lèr-us, *a*. Sorrowful; doleful.

Dolor, dö'lèr, *n*. Sorrow; lamentation.

Dolphin, dol'fin, *n*. A small species of whale remarkable for gamboling in the water; a fish celebrated for its changes of color when dying.

Dolt, dölt, *n*. A blockhead.

Domain, dö-mān', *n*. Territory governed; estate; a demesne.

Dome, döm, *n*. A hemispherical roof of a building; a large cupola.

Domestic, dö-mes'tik, *a*. Belonging to the house or home; tame; not foreign.—*n*. A household servant.

Domesticate, dö-mes'tik-āt, *vt*. To accustom to remain much at home; to tame.

Domicile, do'mi-sīl, *n*. A habitation; family residence.—*vt*. (domiciling, domiciled). To establish in a residence.

Dominant, dom'in-ant, *a*. Governing; predominant; ascendant.

Dominate, dom'in-āt, *vt*. (dominating, dominated). To rule; to predominate over.

Don, don, *n*. A Spanish title, corresponding to Eng. Mr.; an important personage; a resident Fellow of a college at Oxford or Cambridge.—*vt*. (donning, donned). To put on; to invest with.

Donate, dö'nāt, *vt*. To bestow.

Donation, dö-nä'shon, *n*. Act of giving; that which is given; a gift; a present.

Donkey, dong'ki, *n*. An ass.

Donna, don'na, *n.* A lady; as, *prima donna,* the first female singer in an opera, etc.

Donor, dō'nėr, *n.* One who gives.

Doom, döm, *n.* Judicial sentence; fate; ruin.—*vt.* To condemn to punishment; to destine.

Doomsday, dömz'dā, *n.* The day of judgment.

Door, dōr, *n.* The entrance of a house or room; the frame of boards that shuts such an entrance; avenue; means of approach.

Dossier, dos'ē-ā, *n.* A collection of documents of information about a person or incident.

Dot, dot, *n.* A small point, as made with a pen, etc.; a speck.—*vt.* (dotting, dotted). To mark with a dot; to diversify with small objects.—*vi.* To make dots.

Dotage, dōt'āj, *n.* Feebleness of mind, particularly in old age; excessive fondness.

Dotal, dōt'al, *a.* Pertaining to dower.

Dotard, dōt'ėrd, *n.* One whose mind is impaired by age; one foolishly fond.

Dote, dōt, *vi.* (doting, doted). To have the intellect impaired by age; to be foolishly fond.

Double, du'bl, *a.* Twofold; forming a pair; of extra size, quality, etc.; deceitful.—*vt.* (doubling, doubled). To make twofold; to fold; to increase by adding an equal amount to; to sail round (a cape, etc.).—*vi.* To increase twofold; to turn or wind in running; to use sleights.—*n.* Twice as much; a turn in running; a shift; a duplicate; a wraith.

Doubling, du'bl-ing, *n.* Act of making double; a fold; a lining.

Doubloon, dub-lön', *n.* A Spanish gold coin.

Doubt, dout, *vi.* To waver in opinion or judgment; to question; to suspect.—*vt.* To deem uncertain; to distrust.—*n.* A wavering in opinion; uncertainty; suspicion.

Dovetail, duv'tāl, *n.* A mode of joining boards by letting one piece into another in the form of a dove's tail spread, or wedge reversed.—*vt.* and *i.* To unite by the above

method; to fit exactly.

Dowager, dou'ā-jėr, *n.* A title given to the widow of a person of title, provided that she is mother, grandmother, or stepmother of the successor.

Dowdy, dou'di, *n.* An awkward, ill-dressed woman.—*a.* Ill-dressed; vulgar-looking.

Dowel, dou'el, *n.* A pin of wood or iron to join boards, etc.—*vt.* (dowelling, dowelled). To fasten by dowels.

Dower, dou'ėr, *n.* That portion of the property of a man which his widow enjoys during her life; the property which a woman brings to her husband in marriage; dowry.

Down, doun, *n.* The fine soft feathers of birds; fine hair; the pubescence of plants; a hill; a dune; a tract of naked, hilly land.—*adv.* In a descending direction; on the ground; into less bulk; paid in ready money.—*prep.* Along in descent; toward the mouth of.—*a.* Downcast; dejected.

Downy, doun'i, *a.* Covered with, or pertaining to, down, soft; soothing.

Dowry, dou'ri, *n.* The property which a woman brings to her husband in marriage; a dower; gift.

Doxology, doks-ol'o-ji, *n.* A hymn or form of giving glory to God.

Doze, dōz, *vi.* (dozing, dozed). To sleep lightly; to be half asleep.—*vt.* To pass or spend in drowsiness.—*n.* A slight sleep; a slumber.

Dozen, du'zn, *n.* Twelve things regarded collectively.

Drab, drab, *n.* A sluttish woman; a strumpet; a thick woollen cloth of a dun color; a dull brownish color.—*a.* Of a dull brown color.

Draconic, Draconian, drā-kon'ik, drā-kō'ni-an, *a.* Relating to Draco, the Athenian lawgiver; extremely severe.

Draft, dräft, *n.* A detachment of men or things; an order for money; the first sketch of any writing; a sketch.—*vt.* To make a draft of; to sketch; to select.

Drag, drag, *vt.* (dragging, dragged). To draw along the ground by main force; to haul; to explore with a drag.—*vi*. To hang so as to trail on the ground; to move slowly.—*n*. A net drawn along the bottom of the water; an instrument to catch hold of things under water; a machine for dredging; a low cart; a long coach; a contrivance to stop a wheel of a carriage; whatever serves to retard.

Drake, drāk, *n*. The male of ducks.

Dram, dram, *n*. The eighth part of an ounce, or sixty grains apothecaries' measure; the sixteenth part of an ounce avoirdupois; as much spirituous liquor as is drunk at once.

Drama, drä'ma, *n*. A representation on a stage; a play; dramatic literature.

Dramatist, drä'mat-ist, *n*. The author of a dramatic composition.

Dramatize, drä'mat-īz, *vt*. To compose in the form of the drama.

Dramaturgy, dräm'a-tėr-ji, *n*. The science of dramatic composition and representation.

Drape, drāp, *vt*. (draping, draped). To cover with cloth or drapery.

Drapery, drāp'ė-ri, *n*. The occupation of a draper; fabrics of wool or linen; clothes or hangings.

Drastic, dras'tik, *a*. Acting with strength or violence.—*n*. A strong purgative.

Draw, dra, *vt*. (drawing, pret. drew, pp. drawn). To pull along or towards; to cause to come; to unsheathe; to suck; to attract; to inhale; to stretch; to lead, as a motive; to represent by lines drawn on a surface; to describe; to infer; to derive; to draft; to require a certain depth of water; to bend (a bow); to end indecisively.—*vi*. To pull; to shrink; to advance; to practice drawing; to make a written demand for money.—*n*. Act of drawing; the lot or chance drawn; a drawn game.

Drawer, dra'ėr, *n*. One who or that which draws; he who draws a bill; a sliding box in a case, etc.; *pl*. an under-garment for the lower limbs.

Drawing, dra'ing, *n*. Act of one who draws; representation of objects by lines and shades; delineation.

Drawl, dral, *vi*. To speak with slow, prolonged utterance.—*vt*. To utter in a slow tone.—*n*. A lengthened utterance.

Dread, dred, *n*. Fear, united with respect; terror; the person or the thing dreaded.—*a*. Exciting great fear; terrible; venerable.—*vt*. and *i*. To fear in a great degree.

Dress, dres, *vt*. To make straight; to put in good order; to cleanse and cover a wound; to prepare; to curry, rub, and comb; to clothe; to array; to trim.—*vi*. To arrange in a line; to put on clothes; to pay regard to dress.—*n*. Apparel; attire; a lady's gown.

Dribble, drib'l, *vi*. (dribbling, dribbled). To fall in a quick succession of drops; to trickle; to take a football up the field by means of a series of short kicks, keeping the ball near to the foot and under control.—*vt*. To throw down in drops.

Drift, drift, *n*. That which is driven by wind or water; impulse; tendency; aim; velocity of a current; the distance a vessel is driven by a current; rocks conveyed by glaciers and deposited over a country while submerged; in S. Africa, a ford.—*vi*. To move along like anything driven; to accumulate in heaps; to float or be driven by a current.—*vt*. To drive into heaps.—*a*. Drifted by wind or currents.

Drill, dril, *vt*. To pierce with a drill; to teach soldiers their proper movements, etc.; to teach by repeated exercise; to sow in rows; to furrow.—*vi*. To sow in drills; to muster for exercise.—*n*. A pointed instrument for boring holes; act of training soldiers; a row of seeds; a furrow.

Drill, dril, *n*. A kind of coarse linen or cotton cloth.

Drink, dringk, *vi*. (drinking, pret. drank, pp. drunk or drunken). To swallow liquor; to take spirituous liquors to excess.—*vt*. To swallow, as liquids; to absorb.—*n*. Liquor to be swallowed; any beverage; potion.

Drip, drip, *vi*. (dripping, dripped).

To fall in drops.—*vt.* To let fall in drops.—*n.* A falling in drops; the eaves; a projecting moulding.

Drive, drīv, *vt.* (driving, pret. drove, pp. driven). To impel; to hurry on; to impel and guide; to convey in a carriage; to carry on.—*vi.* To be impelled along; to aim at; to strike with force.—*n.* A journey in a vehicle; a road for driving on; a sweeping blow.

Dromedary, drom'ē-da-ri, *n.* A swift camel, usually the Arabian, with one hump, in distinction from the Bactrian, which has two.

Drone, drōn, *n.* The male or non-working bee; an idler; a low humming sound; a large tube of the bagpipe.—*vi.* (droning, droned). To give a low dull sound; to hum.

Droop, dröp, *vi.* To hang down; to languish; to fail; to be dispirited.—*vt.* To let sink or hang down.—*n.* A drooping position or state.

Drop, drop, *n.* A globule of any liquid; an earring; a small quantity; part of a gallows; a distance to fall.—*vt.* (dropping, dropped). To pour or let fall in drops; to let fall; to let down; to quit; to utter casually.—*vi.* To fall in drops; to fall; to cease; to come unexpectedly.

Drown, droun, *vt.* To deprive of life by immersion in water, etc.; to inundate; to overwhelm.—*vi.* To be suffocated in water, etc.

Drowse, drouz, *vi.* (drowsing, drowsed). To nod in slumber; to doze; to look heavy.—*vt.* To make heavy with sleep, or stupid.

Drug, drug, *n.* Any substance used in medicine; an article of slow sale.—*vt.* (drugging, drugged). To mix with drugs; to introduce a narcotic into; to dose to excess with drugs.

Drum, drum, *n.* A hollow cylindrical instrument of music beaten with sticks; something in the form of a drum; the tympanum of the ear.—*vi.* (drumming, drummed). To beat a drum; to beat with the fingers, as with drumsticks; to beat rapidly.—*vt.* To expel or summon by beat of drum.

Dry, drī, *a.* Destitute of moisture; arid; free from juice; thirsty; unin-

teresting; sarcastic; harsh; cold.—*vt.* (drying, dried). To free from moisture; to deprive of natural juice; to drain.—*vi.* To lose moisture; to evaporate wholly.

Dual, dū'al, *a.* Expressing the number two; existing as two; twofold.

Dub, dub, *vt.* (dubbing, dubbed). To tap with a sword and make a knight; to speak of as; to smooth; to trim.

Dubious, dū'bi-us, *a.* Wavering in opinion; doubtful; uncertain.

Due, dū, *a.* Owed; owing; suitable; proper; attributable; that ought to have arrived by the time specified.—*adv.* Directly.—*n.* That which law, office, rank, etc., require to be paid or done; fee; right; just title.

Duel, dū'el, *n.* A premeditated combat between two persons; single combat; contest.

Duet, dū'et, *n.* A piece of music for two performers, vocal or instrumental.

Dug-out, dug out, *n.* A rudely hollowed-out canoe from trunk of tree; an underground shelter from shells; an elderly officer recalled to duty from retirement.

Dull, dul, *a.* Stupid; slow; blunt; drowsy; cheerless; not bright or clear; tarnished; uninteresting.—*vt.* To make dull; to stupefy; to blunt; to make sad; to sully.—*vi.* To become dull, blunt, or stupid.

Dulness, Dullness, dul'nes, *n.* Stupidity; heaviness; slowness; dimness.

Duly, dū'li, *adv.* Properly; fitly.

Dumb, dum, *a.* Incapable of speech; mute; silent; not accompanied with speech.

Dump, dump, *n.* A heap of refuse; a place where refuse is deposited; a large concentration of military stores, especially of ammunition.

Dumpling, dump'ling, *n.* A pudding of boiled suet paste, with or without fruit.

Dumpy, dump'i, *a.* Short and thick.

Dun, dun, *a.* Of a dark dull color; swarthy.—*vt.* (dunning, dunned). To demand a debt from; to urge importunately.—*n.* An importu-

D

nate creditor; urgent demand for payment.

Dunce, duns, *n.* One slow at learning; a dullard; a dolt.

Dune, dūn, *n.* A sand-hill on the sea-coast.

Dung, dung, *n.* The excrement of animals.—*vt.* To manure; to immerse (calico) in cow-dung and water.—*vi.* To void excrement.

Dungeon, dun'jon, *n.* A strong tower in the middle of a castle; a deep, dark place of confinement.

Durable, dūr'a-bl, *a.* Having the quality of lasting long; permanent; firm.

Dust, dust, *n.* Fine dry particles of earth, etc.; powder; earth as symbolic of mortality; a low condition.—*vt.* To free from dust; to sprinkle, as with dust.

Dutch, duch, *a.* Pertaining to Holland, or to its inhabitants.—*n.pl.* The people of Holland; *sing.* their language.

Duty, dū'ti, *n.* That which a person is bound to perform; obligation; act of reverence or respect; business, service, or office; tax, impost or customs.

Dwarf, dwarf, *n.* A person or plant much below the ordinary size.—*vt.* To stunt; to make or keep small; to cause to appear small by comparison.—*a.* Below the common size; stunted.

Dwell, dwel, *vi.* (pret. and pp. dwelled). To live in a place; to reside; to hang on with fondness; to continue.

Dwindle, dwin'dl, *vi.* (dwindling, dwindled). To diminish gradually; to shrink; to sink.

Dye, dī, *vt.* (dyeing, dyed). To stain; to give a new and permanent color to.—*n.* A coloring liquid or matter; tinge.

Dying, dī'ing, *a.* Mortal; destined to death; uttered, given, etc., just before death; pertaining to death; fading away.

Dynamics, dī-nam'iks, *n.* The science which investigates the action of force.

Dynamite, din'a-mīt, *n.* An explosive substance consisting of some powdery matter impregnated with nitro-glycerine.

Dynamo, dī'na-mō, *n.* A machine for producing an electric current by mechanical power.

Dynasty, di'nas-ti, *n.* A race of kings of the same family.

Dyne, dīn, *n.* A unit of force, being that force which, acting on a gram for one second, generates a velocity of a centimeter per second.

Dysentery, dis'en-te-ri, *n.* A disorder of the intestines; a flux in which the stools consist chiefly of blood and mucus.

E

Each, ēch, *a.* and *pron.* Every one of any number considered individually.

Eager, ē'gėr, *a.* Sharp; ardent; keenly desirous; impetuous; earnest; intense.

Eagle, ē'gl, *n.* A large bird of prey, of great powers of flight and vision; a military standard.

Ear, ėr, *n.* The organ of hearing; power of distinguishing musical sounds; heed; regard; anything resembling an ear or ears; a spike, as of corn.—*vi.* To form ears, as corn.—*vt.* To plow or till.

Earnest, ėrn'est, *a.* Ardent in the pursuit of an object; eager; zealous; serious.—*n.* Seriousness; a reality; first-fruits; a part given beforehand as a pledge for the whole; indication; token.

Earnest-money, ėrn'est-mun-i, *n.* Money paid as earnest, to bind a bargain, etc.

Earnings, ėrn'ingz, *n.pl.* That which is gained or merited by labor or performance; wages; reward.

Earth, ėrth, *n.* The globe we inhabit; the world; the fine mold on the surface of the globe; dry land; the ground; the hiding hole of a fox, etc.—*vt.* To cover with earth.—*vi.* To retire underground; to burrow.

Ease, ēz, *n.* Freedom from toil, pain, anxiety, etc.; freedom from difficulty; freedom from stiffness or formality; unaffectedness.—*vt.* (easing, eased). To give ease to; to relieve; to calm; to alleviate; to shift a little.

East, ēst, *n.* That part of the heavens where the sun rises; the countries east of Europe.—*a.* In or toward the east; easterly.—*adv.* Eastwards.

Easter, ēs'tėr, *n.* A festival of the Christian church in March or April, in commemoration of Christ's resurrection.

Easy, ēz'i, *a.* Being at ease; free from pain or anxiety; not difficult; gentle; complying; affluent; not stiff or formal.

Easy-chair, ēz'i-chār, *n.* A large, padded armchair.

Eat, ēt, *vt.* (pret. ate, pp. eaten or eat). to chew and swallow, as food; to wear away; to gnaw; to consume.—*vi.* To take food; to taste or relish; to corrode.

Ebb, eb, *n.* The flowing back of the tide; decline; decay.—*vi.* To flow back; to decay; to decline.

Ebony, eb'on-i, *n.* A hard, heavy, dark wood admitting of a fine polish.

Ebullient, ē-bul'yent, *a.* Boiling over, as a liquor; over enthusiastic.

Eccentric, ek-sen'trik, *a.* Not having its axis in the center; not having the same center; deviating from usual practice, etc.; anomalous; whimsical.—*n.* An eccentric person; mechanical contrivance for converting circular into reciprocating rectilinear motion.

Ecclesiastes, ek-klē'zi-as''tēz, *n.* A canonical book of the Old Testament.

Ecclesiastical, ek-klē'zi-as''tik-al, *a.* Pertaining to the church; not civil or secular.

Echelon, esh'e-lon, *n.* The position of troops or ships in parallel lines, each line being a little to the right or left of the preceding one.

Echo, e'kō, *n.* A sound repeated or reverberated.—*vi.* To give out an echo.—*vt.* To reverberate or send back, as sound; to repeat with assent.

Eclat, e-klä', *n.* A burst of applause; renown; splendor.

Eclectic, ek-lek'tik, *a.* Proceeding by the method of selection; applied to certain philosophers who selected from the principles of various schools what they thought sound.—*n.* One who follows an eclectic method in philosophy, etc.

Eclipse, ē-klips', *n.* An interception of the light of the sun, moon, etc., by some other body; darkness; obscuration.—*vt.* (eclipsing, eclipsed). To cause an eclipse of; to excel.

Economic, Economical, ē-kon-om'ik, ē-kon-om'ik-al, *a.* Pertaining to economy or economics; frugal; careful.

Economics, ē-kon-om'iks, *n.* The science of the application of wealth; political economy.

Edge, ej, *n.* The cutting side of an instrument; an abrupt border or margin; sharpness; keenness.—*vt.* (edging, edged). To bring to an edge; to sharpen; to fringe; to exasperate; to move by little and little.—*vi.* To move sideways or gradually.

Edify, ed'i-fī, *vt.* (edifying, edified). To build up, in a moral sense; to instruct or improve generally.

Edit, ed'it, *vt.* To prepare for publication; to conduct, as regards literary contents.

Edition, ē-di'shon, *n.* A published book as characterized by form or editorial labors; the whole number of copies of a work published at once.

Editorial, ed-i-tō'ri-al, *a.* Pertaining to or written by an editor.—*n.* A leading article in a newspaper.

Educate, ed'ū-kāt, *vt.* (educating, educated). To teach; to cultivate and train; to enlighten.

Education, ed-ū-kā'shon, *n.* Act of educating; instruction and discipline; schooling.

Effect, ef-fekt', *n.* That which is produced; result; purpose; validity; striking appearance; impression produced by a work of art, etc.; *pl.* goods; movables; personal estate.—*vt.* To produce; to cause; to fulfil; to execute.

Efficacy, ef'fi-ka-si, *n.* Power to pro-

E

duce effects; production of the effect intended; virtue; force; energy.

Efficiency, ef-fi'shen-si, *n.* The state or character of being efficient; effectual agency.

Efficient, ef-fi'shent, *a.* Effecting; capable; qualified for duty.

Effigy, ef'fi-ji, *n.* The image or likeness of a person; portrait; figure.

Effusion, ef-fū'zhon, *n.* Act of pouring out; that which is poured out; in *pathology,* the escape of fluid out of its proper vessel into another part; cordiality of manner; a literary production.

Egg, eg, *n.* A roundish body produced by many female animals besides birds, from which their young is produced; something resembling an egg.—*vt.* To urge on; to instigate.

Egotism, eg'ot-izm or ē', *n.* The practice of too frequently using the word *I;* an exaggerated love of self; self-exaltation.

Egotist, eg'ot-ist or ē', *n.* One always talking of himself; one who magnifies his own achievements.

Eider, Eider-duck, ī'dėr, ī'dėr-duk, *n.* A species of sea-duck, producing down of the finest and softest kind.

Eight, āt, *a.* One more than seven and less than nine.—*n.* This number; the symbol representing this number; an eight-oared racing boat or its crew.

Eighteenth, āt'ēnth, *a.* and *n.* Next in order after the seventeenth; one of eighteen parts.

Eighth, ātth, *a.* and *n.* Next after the seventh; one of eight parts; an octave.

Either, ē'THėr or ī'THėr, *a.* or *pron.* One or the other; one of two; each;.—*conj.* or *adv.* Used disjunctively as correlative to *or.*

Elaborate, ē-lab'o-rāt, *vt.* (elaborating, elaborated). To produce with labor; to refine by successive operations.—*a.* Wrought with labor; studied; high-wrought.

Elaboration, ē-lab'o-rā''shon, *n.* Refinement by successive operations; the process in animal and vegetable organs by which something is produced.

Elapse, ē-laps', *vi.* (elapsing, elapsed). To slip or glide away.

Elastic, ē-las'tik, *a.* Having the power of returning to the form from which it is bent or distorted; rebounding.—*n.* Cord or ribbon made of cotton or silk, etc., with strands of rubber.

Elate, ē-lāt', *a.* Elevated in mind; flushed, as with success.—*vt.* (elating, elated). To exalt; to puff up; to make proud.

Elbow, el'bō, *n.* The bend or joint of the arm; an angle.—*vt.* To push with the elbow; to push, as through a crowd.—*vi.* To project; to push one's way.

Elder, eld'ėr, *a.* Older; having lived a longer time; senior.—*n.* One who is older; an office-bearer in the Presbyterian Church; a small tree with a spongy pitch and dark purple or red berries.

Elect, ē-lekt', *vt.* To pick or choose; to select for an office.—*a.* Chosen; chosen to an office, but not yet in office.—*n. sing.* or *pl.* One or several chosen; those favored by God.

Election, ē-lek'shon, *n.* Act of choosing; choice; voluntary preference; divine choice; predestination.

Electricity, ē-lek-tris'i-ti, *n.* The force that manifests itself in lightning and in many other phenomena; the science which deals with these phenomena.

Electrify, ē-lek'tri-fī, *vt.* (electrifying, electrified). To communicate electricity to; to thrill.—*vi.* To become electric.

Electrolyte, ē-lek'trō-līt, *n.* A compound decomposable by electricity.

Electron, ē-lek'tron, *n.* One of the extremely small particles of negative electricity, which form essential constituents of atoms, and by which, according to the electron theory, heat and electricity are conducted.

Eleemosynary, el-ē-mos'i-na-ri, *a.* Given in or relating to charity; founded to dispense some gratuity.—*n.* One who subsists on charity.

Elegance, Elegancy, el'ē-gans, el' ē-gan-si, n. Quality of being elegant; beauty resulting from propriety; refinement.

Elegiac, el'ē-jī'ak, a. Belonging to elegy; plaintive.—n. Elegiac verse.

Elegy, el'ē-ji, n. A poem or a song expressive of sorrow and lamentation.

Element, el'ē-ment, n. A fundamental part or principle; an ingredient; proper sphere; suitable state of things; pl. first principles of an art or science; data employed in a calculation; the bread and wine used in the Lord's supper.

Elementary, el-ē-ment'ar-i, a. Primary; uncompounded; teaching first principles or rudiments.

Elephant, el'ē-fant, n. A huge quadruped, having a long trunk and tusks.

Elevate, el'ē-vāt, vt. (elevating, elevated). To raise; to refine or dignify; to elate; to cheer.

Elevation, el-ē-vā'shon, n. Act of elevating; state of being elevated; an elevated station; a hill; representation of a building in vertical section.

Elevator, el'ē-vāt-ėr, n. One who or that which elevates; a hoist.

Eleven, ē-lev'n, a. Ten and one added.—n. The sum of ten and one; the symbol representing this number; a side of players in association football, cricket, etc.

Elf, elf, n.; pl. **Elves,** elvz. A fairy; a goblin; a mischievous person.

Elfin, elf'in, a. Relating to elves.—n. An elf; a little urchin.

Elicit, ē-lis'it, vt. To draw out by reasoning, discussion, etc.; to educe.

Elide, ē-līd', vt. (eliding, elided). To strike out; to cut off or suppress (a syllable).

Eligibility, el'i-ji-bil''i-ti, n. Worthiness or fitness to be chosen.

Elongation, ē-long-gā'shon, n. Act of lengthening; state of being extended; continuation; apparent distance of a planet from the sun.

Elope, ē-lōp', vi. (eloping, eloped). To escape privately; to run away with a lover.

Eloquence, e'lō-kwens, n. The quality or faculty of being eloquent; oratory.

Eloquent, e'lō-kwent, a. Having the power of fluent, elegant, or forcible speech; characterized by eloquence.

Else, els, a. or adv. Other; besides; in addition.—conj. Otherwise; in the other case.

Emaciate, ē-mā'shi-āt, vi. and t. (emaciating, emaciated). To become or make lean.

Emaciation, ē-mā'shi-ā''shon, n. Act of emaciating; leanness.

Emanate, em'a-nāt, vi. (emanating, emanated). To flow out; to issue; to spring.

Emancipate, ē-man'si-pāt, vt. (emancipating, emancipated). To set free from slavery; to liberate.

Emancipation, ē-man'si-pā''shon, n. Liberation; freedom; enfranchisement.

Emasculate, ē-mas'kū-lāt, vt. To castrate; to render effeminate; to expurgate.

Embark, em-bärk', vt. To put on board a ship; to engage in.—vi. To go on board of a ship; to engage in; to take a share.

Embarrass, em-ba'ras, vt. To involve in difficulties; to entangle; to disconcert.

Embarrassment, em-ba'ras-ment, n. Entanglement; trouble; abashment.

Embassy, em'bas-si, n. The mission, charge or residence of an ambassador; an important message.

Embezzlement, em-bez'l-ment, n. Act of fraudently appropriating money, etc., intrusted to one's care.

Embitter, em-bit'ėr, vt. To make bitter or more bitter; to exasperate.

Emblem, em'blem, n. A picture representing one thing and suggesting another; a symbol; type; device.

Embowel, em-bou'el, vt. To take out the bowels of; to eviscerate; to imbed.

Embower, em-bou'ėr, vt. To inclose in or cover with a bower; to shade.

Embrace, em-brās', vt. (embracing, embraced). To take within the arms; to press to the bosom; to seize ardently; to include; to accept.—*vi.* To join in an embrace.— *n.* Clasp with the arms; a hug; conjugal endearment.

Embryo, em'bri-ō, *n.* The first rudiments of an animal in the womb or of a plant in the seed; the first state of anything.—*a.* Pertaining to anything in its first rudiments.

Emerald, e'me-rald, *n.* A precious stone, akin to the beryl, usually green; a small printing type.—*a.* Of a bright-green color.

Emerge, ē-mėrj', *vi.* (emerging, emerged). To rise out of a fluid or other substance; to issue; to rise into view; to reappear.

Emergency, ē-mėrj'en-si, *n.* Act of emerging; unforeseen occurrence; pressing necessity.

Emeritus, ē-mer'i-tus, *a.* Discharged from duty with honor on account of infirmity, age, or long service.

Emersion, ē-mėr'shon, *n.* Act of rising out of a fluid or other substance; reappearance of a heavenly body after eclipse, etc.

Emery, e'me-ri, *n.* A hard mineral used in cutting gems and for polishing.

Emetic, ē-met'ik, *a.* Causing vomiting.—*n.* A medicine that provokes vomiting.

Emigrant, em'i-grant, *a.* Emigrating; pertaining to emigration or emigrants.—*n.* One who emigrates.

Emigrate, em'i-grāt, *vi.* (emigrating, emigrated). To remove from one country or state to another for the purpose of residence.

Eminence, em'in-ens, *n.* A rising ground; elevation; top; distinction; fame; a title of honor given to cardinals, etc.

Emotion, ē-mō'shon, *n.* Any agitation of mind; feeling.

Empale, em-pāl', *vt.* (empaling, empaled). To put to death by fixing on a stake.

Emperor, em'pėr-ėr, *n.* The sovereign of an empire.

Emphasis, em'fa-sis, *n.* A stress laid on a word or clause to enforce a meaning; impressiveness; weight.

Emphasize, em'fa-sīz, *vt.* (emphasizing, emphasized). To place emphasis on.

Empire, em'pīr, *n.* Supreme power in governing; sway; dominion of an emperor; region over which dominion is extended.

Employ, em-ploi', *vt.* To occupy; to engage in one's service; to keep at work; to make use of.—*n.* Business; occupation; engagement.

Employee, em-ploi'ē, *n.* One who works for an employer.

Employer, em-ploi'ėr, *n.* One who employs; one who keeps men in service.

Emporium, em-pō'ri-um, *n.*; pl. **-ia** or **-iums.** A commercial center; a warehouse or shop.

Empower, em-pou'ėr, *vt.* To give legal or moral power to; to authorize.

Empress, em'pres, *n.* The consort of an emperor; a female invested with imperial power.

Empty, em'ti, *a.* Containing nothing, or nothing but air; void; unsatisfactory; unburdened; hungry; vacant of head.—*vt.* (emptying, emptied). To make empty.—*vi.* To become empty.—*n.* An empty packingcase, etc.

Enamel, en-am'el, *n.* A substance of the nature of glass, used as a coating; that which is enamelled; a smooth glossy surface of various colors; the smooth substance on a tooth.—*vt.* (enamelling, enamelled). To lay enamel on; to paint in enamel; to form a surface like enamel; to adorn with different colors.—*vi.* To practice the art of enamelling.

Enamor, en-am'ėr, *vt.* To inspire with love; to charm; to fill with delight.

Encamp, en-kamp', *vi.* To take up position in a camp; to make a camp.—*vt.* To form into or place in a camp.

Enceinte, ang-sangt, *n.* The rampart which surrounds a fortress; the area thus surrounded.—*a.* Pregnant; with child.

Encircle, en-sėr'kl, *vt.* To inclose with a circle; to encompass; to embrace.

Encompass, en-kum'pas, *vt.* To encircle; to hem in; to go or sail round.

Encore, ang-kōr'. Again; once more; a call for a repetition of a performance.—*vt.* (encoring, encored). To call for a repetition of.

Encounter, en-koun'tėr, *n.* A meeting in contest; a conflict; a meeting; controversy; debate.—*vt.* To meet face to face; to meet suddenly; to strive against.—*vi.* To meet unexpectedly; to conflict.

Encourage, en-ku'rāj, *vt.* (encouraging, encouraged). To give courage to; to stimulate; to embolden; to countenance.

Encroach, en-krōch', *vi.* To trespass on the rights and possessions of another; to intrude; to infringe; with *on* or *upon.*

Encroachment, en-krōch-ment, *n.* Act of encroaching; invasion; inroad; that which is taken by encroaching.

Encumber, en-kum'bėr, *vt.* To impede the motion of with a load; to embarrass; to load with debts or legal claims.

End, end, *n.* The extreme point; the last part; final state; completion; close of life; death; issue; result; aim; drift.—*vt.* To bring to an end; to conclude; to destroy.—*vi.* To come to an end; to close; to cease.

Endanger, en-dān'jėr, *vt.* To bring into danger; to expose to loss or injury.

Endear, en-dēr', *vt.* To make dear; to make more beloved.

Endeavor, en-dev'ėr, *n.* Effort; attempt; exertion; essay; aim.—*vi.* To try; to strive; to aim.—*vt.* To try to effect; to strive after.

Endemic, Endemical, en-dem'ik, en-dem'ik-al, *a.* Peculiar to a people or region, as a disease,—*n.* A disease of endemic nature.

Ending, end'ing, *n.* Termination.

Endive, en'div, *n.* A plant allied to chicory; garden succory.

Endless, end'les, *a.* Without end; everlasting; infinite; incessant.

Endogen, en'dō-jen, *n.* A plant whose stem grows by additions developed from the inside, as palms and grasses.

Endogenous, en-doj'e-nus, *a.* Pertaining to endogens; developing from within.

Endorse, en-dors', *vt.* (endorsing, endorsed). To write on the back of, as one's name on a bill; to assign by endorsement; to ratify.

Endorsement, en-dors'ment, *n.* The act of endorsing; a docket; signature of one who endorses; sanction or approval.

Endure, en-dūr', *vi.* (enduring, endured). To continue in the same state; to last; to abide; to submit.—*vt.* To sustain; to bear; to undergo; to tolerate.

Enema, en'e-ma, *n.* A liquid or gaseous medicine injected into the rectum; a clyster.

Enemy, en'e-mi, *n.* One who is unfriendly; an antagonist; a hostile army.

Energetic, Energetical, en-ėr-jet'ik, en-ėr-jet'ik-al, *a.* Acting with energy; forcible; potent; active; vigorous.

Energy, en'ėr-ji, *n.* Inherent power to operate or act; power exerted; force; vigor; strength of expression; emphasis; in physics, power to do work; it may be mechanical, electrical, thermal, chemical, etc.

Enforcement, en-fōrs'ment, *n.* Act of enforcing; compulsion; a giving of force or effect to; a putting in execution, as law.

Enfranchise, en-fran'chīz, *vt.* (enfranchising, enfranchised). To set free; to admit to the privileges of a citizen; to endow with the franchise.

Engage, en-gāj', *vt.* (engaging, engaged). To bind by pledge or contract; to attach; to attract; to attack.—*vi.* To bind oneself; to embark on any business; to begin to fight.

Engineer, en-ji-nēr', *n.* One who constructs or manages engines; one who plans works for offense or defense; one who constructs roads, railways, etc.—*vt.* To direct the making of in the capacity of engineer.

English, ing'glish, *a.* Belonging to England, or to its inhabitants.—*n.* The people or language of England.—*vt*. To translate into English.

Engross, en-grōs', *vt*. To take up the whole of; to occupy, engage; to write a correct copy in legible characters; to take in undue quantities or degrees.—*vi*. To be employed in making fair copies of writings.

Engulf, en-gulf', *vt*. To ingulf; to swallow up.

Enhance, en-hans', *vt*. (enhancing, enhanced). To raise to a higher point; to increase; to aggravate.—*vi*. To grow larger.

Enigma, ē-nig'ma, *n*. An obscure statement or question; riddle; anything inexplicable.

Enjoin, en-join', *vt*. To order with urgency; to admonish; to prescribe.

Enjoy, en-joi', *vt*. To feel gladness in; to have, use, or perceive with pleasure.

Enjoyment, en-joi'ment, *n*. State of enjoying; pleasure; satisfaction; fruition.

Enlarge, en-lärj', *vt*. (enlarging, enlarged). To make large or larger; to set free.—*vi*. To grow large or larger; to expatiate.

Enlargement, en-lärj'ment, *n*. Act of enlarging; state of being enlarged; expansion; release; addition.

Enlighten, en-līt'en, *vt*. To make clear; to enable to see more clearly; to instruct.

Enlist, en-list', *vt*. To enter on a list; to engage in public service, especially military; to engage the services of.—*vi*. To engage voluntarily in public service; to enter heartily into a cause.

Enough, ē-nuf', *a*. That satisfies desire; that may answer the purpose.—*n*. A sufficiency; that which is equal to the powers or abilities.—*adv*. Sufficiently; tolerably.

Enrage, en-rāj', *vt*. To excite rage in; to incense.

Enrapture, en-rap'tūr, *vt*. To transport with rapture; to delight beyond measure.

Enrich, en-rich', *vt*. To make rich; to fertilize; to supply with an abundance of anything desirable; to adorn.

Enroll, Enrol, en-rōl', *vt*. To write in a roll or register; to record.

Ensign, en'sīn, *n*. A mark of distinction; the flag of a company of soldiers or a vessel; formerly the lowest rank of commissioned officer in the infantry.

Entail, en-tāl', *vt*. To cut off an estate from the heirs general; to settle, as the descent of lands by gift to a man and to certain heirs; to devolve as a consequence or of necessity.—*n*. The act of entailing; an estate entailed; rule of descent settled for an estate.

Entangle, en-tang'gl, *vt*. To knit or interweave confusedly; to involve; to hamper.

Enter, en'tėr, *vt*. To go or come into; to begin; to set down in writing; to register; to take possession of.—*vi*. To go or come in; begin; engage in; be an ingredient in.

Enteric, en-ter'ik, *a*. Belonging to the intestines.—*Enteric fever,* same as *Typhoid fever*.

Enterprise, en'tėr-prīz, *n*. That which is undertaken; a bold or hazardous attempt; adventurous spirit; hardihood.—*vt*. To undertake.

Entertain, en-tėr-tān', *vt*. To receive as a guest; to cherish; to treat with conversation; to please; to admit, with a view to consider.—*vi*. To give entertainments.

Entire, en-tīr', *a*. Whole; unshared; complete; sincere; hearty; in full strength.

Entirely, entīr'li, *adv*. Wholly; fully.

Entitle, en-tī'tl, *vt*. (entitling, entitled). To give a title to; to style; to characterize; to give a claim to; to qualify.

Entrail, en'trāl, *n*. One of the intestines; generally in *pl*.; the bowels.

Entrain, en-trān', *vt*. To put on board a railway train.—*vi*. To take places in a train.

Entrance, en'trans, *n*. Act or power of entering into a place; the door or avenue by which a place may be entered; beginning; act of taking possession.

Entrance, en-trans', *vt*. To put in a trance or ecstasy; to enrapture; to transport.

Enumerate, ē-nū′me-rāt, *vt.* (enumerating, enumerated). To count number by number; to reckon or mention a number of things, each separately.

Enunciate, ē-nun′si-āt, *vt.* (enunciating, enunciated). To utter; to pronounce; to proclaim.

Enunciation, ē-nun′si-ā′′shon, *n.* Act or manner of enunciating; expression; declaration; public attestation.

Envelop, en-vel′op, *vt.* To cover by wrapping or folding; to lie around and conceal.

Envelope, en′vel-ōp, *n.* That which infolds; a wrapper; a covering for a letter, etc.; an investing integument.

Environ, en-vī′ron, *vt.* To encompass; to encircle; to besiege; to invest.

Environment, en-vī′ron-ment, *n.* Act of environing; state of being environed; that which environs; conditions under which one lives.

Envisage, en-viz′āj, *vt.* To look in the face of; to apprehend directly or by intuition.

Envoy, en′voi, *n.* One sent on a mission; a person next in rank to an ambassador, deputed to transact business with a foreign power.

Envy, en′vi, *n.* Pain or discontent excited by another's superiority or success; malice; object of envy.— *vt.* (envying, envied). To feel envy towards or on account of; to begrudge.—*vi.* To be affected with envy.

Epic, ep′ik, *a.* Composed in a lofty narrative style; heroic.—*n.* A poem of elevated character, describing the exploits of heroes.

Epicure, ep′i-kūr, *n.* One devoted to sensual enjoyments; a voluptuary.

Epicurean, ep′i-kū-rē′′an, *a.* Luxurious; given to luxury.—*n.* A follower of Epicurus; a luxurious eater; an epicure.

Epidemic, Epidemical, ep-i-dem′ik, ep-i-dem′ik-al, *a.* Affecting a whole community, as a disease; prevalent.—**Epidemic,** ep-i-dem′ik, *n.* A disease which attacks many people at the same period.

Epidermis, ep-i-dėr′mis, *n.* The cuticle or scarf-skin of the body; the exterior coating of the leaf or stem of a plant.

Epiglottis, ep-i-glot′is, *n.* The cartilage at the root of the tongue that covers the glottis during the act of swallowing.

Epigram, ep′i-gram, *n.* A short poem, usually keenly satirical; a pointed or antithetical saying.

Epigraph, ep′i-graf, *n.* An inscription; quotation; motto.

Epilepsy, ep′i-lep-si, *n.* The falling-sickness; a disease characterized by spasms and loss of sense.

Epilogue, ep′i-log, *n.* A speech or short poem spoken by an actor at the end of a play.

Epiphany, ē-pif′a-ni, *n.* A church festival on January 6th, celebrating the manifestation of Christ to the wise men of the East.

Epitaph, ep′i-taf, *n.* That which is written on a tomb; an inscription, or a composition, in honor of the dead.

Epithalamium, ep′i-tha-lā′mi-um, *n.*; pl. **-iums** or **-ia.** A nuptial song or peom.

Epithet, ep′i-thet, *n.* Any word implying a quality attached to a person or thing.

Epitome, e-pit′o-mi, *n.* A brief summary; abridgment; compendium.

Epitomize, e-pit′om-īz, *vt.* To make an epitome of; to abstract; to condense.

Epoch, ē′pok, *n.* A fixed point of time from, which years are numbered; period; era; date.

Equable, ē-kwa-bl, *a.* Uniform; even; steady.

Equal, ē′kwal, *a.* The same in extent, number, degree, rank, etc.; same in qualities; uniform; proportionate; adequate; just.—*n.* One not inferior or superior to another.—*vt.* (equalling, equalled). To make equal to; to become or be equal to.

Equanimity, ē-kwa-nim′i-ti or ek-, *n.* Evenness of mind; steadiness of temper.

Equate, ē-kwāt, *vt.* (equating, equated). To make equal; to reduce to an equation; to reduce to mean time or motion.

E

Equation 86 **Esquire**

Equation, ē-kwā'shon, n. The act of equating; an expression asserting the equality of two quantities; a quantity to be taken into account in order to give a true result.

Equator, ē-kwā'tėr, n. The great circle of our globe which divides it into the northern and southern hemispheres; a circle in the heavens coinciding with the plane of the earth's equator.

Equilibrium, ē-kwi-li'bri-um or ek-, n. State of rest produced by the counteraction of forces; balance.

Equine, ē-kwīn,', a. Pertaining to a horse; denoting the horse kind.

Equinoctial, ē-kwi-nok'shal, or ek-, a. Pertaining to the equinoxes.—n. The celestial equator: when the sun is on it, the days and nights are of equal length.

Equinox, ē'kwi-noks or ek', n. The time when the day and night are of equal length, about March 21st and September 23rd.

Equip, ē-kwip', vt. (equipping, equipped). To fit out or furnish, as for war; to dress; to array.

Equipage, ek'wi-pāj, n. An equipment; retinue; carriage of state and attendants; accoutrements.

Equipment, ē-kwip'ment, n. Act of equipping; habiliments; warlike apparatus; necessary adjuncts.

Equitable, ek'wit-a-bl, a. Distributing equal justice; just; upright; impartial.

Equity, ek'wi-ti, n. The giving to each man his due; impartiality; uprightness; a system of supplementary law founded upon precedents and established principles.

Equivalent, ē-kwiv'a-lent or ek-, a. Equal in excellence, worth, or weight; of the same import or meaning.—n. That which is equal in value, etc.; compensation.

Equivocate, ē-kwiv'ō-kāt, vi. To use ambiguous expressions to mislead; to quibble.

Erect, ē-rekt', a. Upright; bold; undismayed.—vt. To raise and set upright; to build; to found; to cheer.

Erode, ē-rōd', vt. (eroding, eroded). To gnaw off or away; to corrode.

Erotic, ē-rot'ik, a. Pertaining to or prompted by love; treating of love.

Err, er, vi. To wander; to stray; to depart from rectitude; to blunder.

Errand, e'rand, n. A message; mandate; business to be transacted by a messenger.

Erratic, e-rat'ik, a. Wandering; irregular; eccentric.

Erratum, e-rā'tum, n.; pl. -ata. An error or mistake in writing or printing.

Error, e'rėr, n. A deviation from truth or what is right; a mistake; a blunder; fault; offense.

Escalator, es'ka-lā-tėr, n. A mechanism consisting of a series of steps which are carried up and down by means of a continuous chain; a moving stairway.

Escapade, es-ka-pād', n. A runaway adventure; a freak; a mad prank.

Escape, es-kāp', vt. (escaping, escaped). To get out of the way of; to pass without harm; to pass unobserved; to avoid.—vi. To be free; to avoid; to regain one's liberty.—n. Flight; to shun danger; an evasion of legal retraint or custody.

Escarpment, es-kärp'ment, n. A steep declivity; ground cut away nearly vertically.

Eschatology, es-ka-tol'o-ji, n. The doctrine of the last or final things, as death.

Eschew, es-chö', vt. To shun; to avoid.

Escort, es'kort, n. A guard attending an officer or baggage, etc.; persons attending as a mark of honor.—vt. es-kort'. To attend and guard.

Espionage, es'pi-on-āj, n. Practice or employment of spies; practice of watching others without being suspected.

Espousal, es-pouz'al, n. Betrothal; nuptials: in this sense generally in pl; the adopting of a cause.

Espouse, es-pouz', vt. (espousing, espoused). To give or take in marriage; to betroth; to wed; to embrace or adopt; to uphold.

Esprit, es-prē, n. Soul; spirit; mind; wit.

Esquire, es-kwīr', n. A shield-bearer; a title of dignity next to a knight; a title of courtesy.

Essential, es-sen'shal, *a.* Relating to or containing the essence; necessary to the existence of; indispensable; highly rectified; volatile; diffusible (oils).—*n.* Something necessary; the chief point; constituent principle.

Establish, es-tab'lish, *vt.* To make stable; to found permanently; to institute; to enact; to sanction; to confirm; to make good.

Esteem, es-tēm', *vt.* To set a value on; to regard with respect; to prize.—*n.* Judgment of merit or demerit; estimation; great regard.

Estimate, es'tim-āt, *vt.* (estimating, estimated). To form an opinion regarding; to calculate; to appraise; to esteem,—*n.* Valuation; calculation of probable cost.

Estrange, es-trānj', *vt.* (estranging, estranged). To alienate, as the affections.

Estuary, es'tū-a-ri, *n.* The mouth of a river where the tide meets the current; a firth.

Etch, ech, *vt.* To produce designs on a copper or other plate by lines drawn through a thin coating, and then eaten into the plate by a strong acid; to draw finely in ink.—*vi.* To practice etching.

Etching, ech'ing, *n.* The act or art of the etcher; a mode of engraving; the impression taken from an etched plate.

Eternal, ē-tėrn'al, *a.* Everlasting; without beginning or end of existence; unchangeable.—*n.* An appellation of God.

Eternity, ē-tėrn'i-ti, *n.* Continuance without beginning or end; duration without end; the state or time after death.

Ether, ē'thėr, *n.* The clear upper air; refined air; a hypothetical medium of extreme tenuity universally diffused, and the medium of the transmission of light, heat, etc.; a very light, volatile, and inflammable fluid obtained from alcohol, used as a stimulant and anesthetic.

Ethereal, ē-thē'rē-al, *a.* Formed of ether; heavenly; aerial; intangible.

Ethic, Ethical, eth'ik, eth'ik-al, *a.* Relating to morals; treating of morality; delivering precepts of morality.

Ethics, eth'iks, *n.* The doctrine of morals; moral philosophy; a system of moral principles.

Ethnic, Ethnical, eth'nik, eth'nik-al, *a.* Pertaining to the gentiles; pagan; ethnological.

Etymology, et-i-mol'o-ji, *n.* that part of philology which traces the origin of words; the derivation or history of any word.

Eulogy, ū'lo-ji, *n.* A speech or writing in commendation; praise; panegyric.

Eunuch, ū'nuk, *n.* A castrated man.

Eupepsia, Eupepsy, ū-pep'si-a, ū-pep'si, *n.* Good digestion.

Euphemism, ū'fem-izm, *n.* A mode of speaking by which a delicate word or expression is substituted for one which is offensive; a word or expression so substituted.

Evade, ē-vād', *vt.* (evading, evaded). To avoid by dexterity; to slip away from; to elude; to baffle.—*vi.* To practice evasion.

Evaluate, ē-val'ū-āt, *vt.* To value carefully; to ascertain the amount of.

Evanesce, ev-a-nes', *vi.* To vanish.

Evaporate, ē-va'pėr-āt, *vi.* (evaporating, evaporated). To pass off in vapor; to exhale; to be wasted.—*vt.* To convert into vapor; to disperse in vapors.

Evasion, ē-vā'zhon, *n.* Act of evading; artifice to elude; shift; equivocation.

Even, ē'vn, *a.* Level; smooth; equable; on an equality; just; settled; balanced; capable of being divided by 2 without a remainder.—*vt.* To make even or level; to equalize; to balance.—*adv.* Just; exactly; likewise; moreover.—*n.* The evening.

Evening, ē'vn-ing, *n.* The close of the day; the decline of anything.—*a.* Being at the close of day.

Event, ē'vent', *n.* That which happens; an incident; the consequence of anything; issue; result; conclusion.

Ever, ev'ėr, *adv.* At all times; at any time; continually; in any degree.

Evergreen, ev'ėr-grēn, *n.* A plant that always retains its greenness.—*a.* Always green.

Everlasting, ev-ėr-last'ing, *a.* Enduring forever; eternal.—*n.* Eternity; the Eternal Being; a plant whose flowers endure for many months after being plucked.

Evict, ē-vikt', *vt.* To dispossess by judicial process; to expel from lands, etc., by law.

Evidence, ev'i-dens, *n.* That which demonstrates that a fact is so; testimony; proof; witness.—*vt.* To make evident; to prove.

Evil, ē'vil, *a.* Not good; bad; wrong; unhappy; calamitious.—*n.* That which is not good; anything which produces pain, calamity, etc.; wrong; malady.—*adv.* Not well; ill.

Evince, ē-vins', *vt.* (evincing, evinced). To show in a clear manner; to manifest.

Evolve, ē-volv', *vt.* (evolving, evolved). To unfold; to develop; to open and expand.—*vi.* To open or disclose itself.

Exact, egz-akt', *a.* Strictly accurate; methodical; precise; true.—*vt.* To extort by means of authority; to demand of right; to compel.—*vi.* To practice extortion.

Exaggerate, egz-aj'ė-rāt, *vt.* (exaggerating, exaggerated). To increase beyond due limits; to depict extravagantly.

Exalt, egz-alt', *vt.* To raise high; to raise to power or dignity; to extol.

Examination, egz-am'in-ā''shon, *n.* Act of examining; inquiry into facts, etc., by interrogation; scrutiny by study.

Examine, egz-am'in, *vt.* (examining, examined). To inspect carefully; to inquire into; to interrogate, as a witness, a student, etc.; to discuss.

Example, egz-am'pl, *n.* A sample; pattern; model; precedent; instance.

Exasperate, egz-as'pė-rāt, *vt.* (exasperating, exasperated). To irritate; to enrage; to make worse; to aggravate.

Excavate, eks'ka-vāt, *vt.* (excavating, excavated). To hollow out.

Exceed, ek-sēd', *vt.* To go beyond, as any limit; to surpass; to outdo.—*vi.* To go too far; to bear the greater proportion.

Excel, ek-sel', *vt.* (excelling, excelled). To surpass; to transcend; to outdo.—*vi.* To be eminent or distinguished.

Except, ek-sept', *vt.* To take or leave out of any number specified; to exclude.—*vi.* to object; to make objection.—*prep.* Exclusively of; without.—*conj.* Unless.

Exception, ek-sep'shon, *n.* Act of excepting; state of being excepted; that which is excepted; an objection; offense.

Excerpt, ek-sėrpt', *n.* An extract; a passage selected from an author.—*vt.* To pick out from a book, etc.; to cite.

Excess, ek-ses', *n.* That which exceeds; super-abundance; intemperate conduct; that by which one thing exceeds another.

Exchange, eks-chānj', *vt.* To change one thing for another; to commute; to bargain.—*n.* Act of exchanging; interchange; barter; the thing interchanged; place where merchants, etc., of a city meet to transact business; a method of finding the equivalent to a given sum in the money of another country.

Excise, ek-sīz', *n.* A tax on certain commodities of home production and consumption, as beer, etc.; also for licenses to deal in certain commodities.—*vt.* (excising, excised). To impose a duty on articles produced and consumed at home; to cut out.

Exclamation, eks-klam-ā'shon, *n.* A loud outcry; a passionate sentence; a note by which emphatical utterance is marked, thus, !; an interjection.

Exclude, eks-klūd', *vt.* (excluding, excluded). To shut out; to thrust out; to debar; to prohibit; to except.

Excrement, eks'krē-ment, *n.* That which is separated from the nutriment by digestion, and discharged from the body; ordure; dung.

Excrescence, eks-kres'ens, *n.* Anything which grows out of something else and is useless or disfiguring; a troublesome superfluity.

Excrete, eks-krēt′, *vt.* (excreting, excreted). To separate and discharge from the body by vital action.

Excruciate, eks-krö′shi-āt, *vt.* To torture; to rack.

Exculpate, eks-kul′pāt, *vt.* To clear from a charge of fault or guilt; to absolve.

Execrable, ek′sē-kra-bl, *a.* Deserving to be execrated or cursed; hateful; detestable.

Execrate, ek′sē-krāt, *vt.* (execrating, execrated). To curse; to abominate.

Executant, eks-ek′ū-tant, *n.* A performer.

Execute, ek′sē-kūt, *vt.* (executing, executed). To effect; to achieve; to inflict capital punishment on; to make valid, as by signing and sealing; to perform.—*vi.* To perform.

Execution, ek-sē-kū′shon, *n.* Act of executing; act of signing and sealing a legal instrument; capital punishment; mode of performing a work of art; facility of voice or finger in music.

Executioner, ek-sē-kū′shon-ér, *n.* One who puts to death by law.

Executive, egz-ek′ūt-iv, *a.* That executes; carrying laws into effect, or superintending their enforcement.—*n.* The person or persons who administer the government.

Executor, egz-ek′ūt-ér, *n.* One who executes or performs; the person appointed by a testator to execute his will.

Exempt, egz-emt′, *vt.* To free from; to privilege; to grant immunity from.—*a.* Free by privilege; not liable.

Exemption, egz-em′shon, *n.* Act of exempting; state of being exempt; immunity.

Exercise, eks′ér-sīz, *n.* Practice; use; drill; act of divine worship; application; a lesson or example for practice.—*vt.* (exercising, exercise). To employ; to practice; to train; to give anxiety to; to afflict.—*vi.* To take exercise.

Exert, egz-ért, *vt.* To put forth, as strength; to put in action. (*refl.*) to use efforts; to strive.

Exfoliate, eks-fō′li-āt, *vt.* and *i.* To scale off.

Exhale, egz-hāl′, *vt.* (exhaling, exhaled). To breathe out; to cause to be emitted in vapor or minute particles; to evaporate.—*vi.* To fly off as vapor.

Exhaust, egz-a̱st′, *vt.* To drain off contents; to expend entirely; to treat thoroughly; to tire.

Exhibit, egz-ib′it, *vt.* To show; to display; to administer by way of remedy.—*n.* Anything exhibited.

Exhibition, eks-i-bi′shon, *n.* Act of exhibiting; display; any public show; a benefaction for students in English universities.

Exhilarate, egz-il′a-rāt, *vt.* (exhilarating, exhilarated). To make cheerful; to inspirit.

Exist, egz-ist′, *vi.* To be; to live; to endure.

Existence, egz-ist′ens, *n.* State of being; life; continuation; anything that exists.

Exit, eks′it, *n.* A going out; the departure of a player from the stage; death; a way out.

Exodus, eks′ō-dus, *n.* Way out; departure; the second book of the Old Testament.

Exogen, eks′o-jen, *n.* A plant whose stem grows by additions to the outside of the wood.

Exonerate, egz-on′ē-rāt, *vt.* To exculpate; to acquit; to justify.

Exorable, eks′ōr-a-bl, *a.* That can be persuaded; placable.

Exorbitant, egz-or′bit-ant, *a.* Excessive; extravagant.

Exorcise, eks′or-sīz, *vi.* (exorcising, exorcised). To purify from evil spirits by adjurations.

Expand, ek-spand′, *vt.* and *i.* To spread out; to enlarge; to distend; to dilate.

Expect, ek-spekt′, *vt.* To wait for; to look for to happen; to anticipate.

Expectance, Expectancy, ek-spek′tans, ek-spek′tan-si, *n.* Act or state of expecting; expectation; hope.

Expectation, ek-spek-tā′shon, *n.* Act or state of expecting; prospect of good to come; prospect of reaching a certain age.

Expectorate, eks-pek'tō-rāt, *vt.* (expectorating, expectorated). To expel, as phlegm, by coughing; to spit out.

Expeditious, eks-pē-di'shus, *a.* Speedy; prompt; nimble; active.

Expel, eks-pel', *vt.* (expelling, expelled). To drive out; to eject; to banish.

Expend, ek-spend', *vt.* To spend; to use or consume; to waste.

Expenditure, ek-spend'i-tūr, *n.* Act of expending; a laying out, as of money; money expended; expense.

Expense, ek-spens', *n.* That which is expended; cost; charge; price.

Experience, eks-pē'ri-ens, *n.* Personal trial; continued observation; knowledge gained by trial or observation; trial and knowledge from suffering or enjoyment; suffering itself.—*vt.* (experiencing, experienced). To try; to know by trial; to have happen; to undergo.

Experiment, eks-pe'ri-ment, *n.* A trial; an operation designed to discover something unknown, or to establish it when discovered.—*vi.* To make trial or experiment.

Expert, eks-pėrt', *a.* Skillful; dexterous; adroit.—*n.* eks'pėrt. An expert person; a scientific witness.

Explanation, eks-pla-nā'shon, *n.* Act of explaining; interpretation; clearing up of matters between parties at variance.

Expletive, eks'plēt-iv, *a.* Serving to fill out; superfluous.—*n.* A word or syllable inserted to fill a vacancy or for ornament; an oath or interjection.

Explicate, eks'pli-kāt, *vt.* To unfold the meaning of; to explain.

Explicit, eks-plis'it, *a.* Plain in language; express, not merely implied; open.

Explode, eks-plōd', *vt.* (exploding, exploded). To drive out of use or belief; to cause to burst with violence and noise.—*vi.* To burst with noise; to burst into activity or passion.

Exploit, eks-ploit', *n.* A deed; a heroic act; a deed of renown.—*vt.* To make use of; to work.

Exploitation, eks-ploi-tā'shon, *n.* Successful application of industry on any object, as land, mines, etc.

Exploration, eks-plō-rā'shon, *n.* Act of exploring; strict or careful examination.

Explore, eks-plōr', *vt.* (exploring, explored). To travel with the view of making discovery; to search; to examine closely.

Explosion, eks-plō'zhon, *n.* Act of exploding; a bursting with noise; a violent outburst of feeling.

Explosive, eks-plō'siv, *a.* Causing explosion; readily exploding.—*n.* Anything liable to explode, as gunpowder; a mute or non-continuous consonant, as k, t, b.

Exponent, eks-pō'nent, *n.* One who explains or illustrates; that which indicates; the index of a power in algebra.

Expound, eks-pound', *vt.* To explain; to interpret; to unfold.

Express, eks-pres', *vt.* To press out; to set forth in words; to declare; to make known by any means; *(refl.)* to say what one has got to say.—*a.* Clearly exhibited; given in direct terms; intended or sent for a particular purpose; traveling with special speed.—*n.* A messenger or vehicle sent on a particular occasion; a message specially sent; a specially fast railway train.—*adv.* For a particular purpose; with special haste.

Expression, eks-pre'shon, *n.* Act of expressing; a phrase or mode of speech; manner of utterance; a natural and lively representation in painting and sculpture; musical tone, grace, or modulation; play of features; representation of a quantity in algebra.

Expropriate, eks-prō'pri-āt, *vt.* To take for public use; to dispossess.

Extemporary, eks-tem'pō-ra-ri, *a.* Arising out of the time or occasion; extemporaneous.

Extemporize, eks-tem'pō-rīz, *vi.* To speak without preparation.—*vt.* To make without forethought; to prepare in haste.

Extend, eks-tend', *vt.* To stretch out; to spread; to prolong; to bestow on.—*vi*. To stretch; to reach; to become larger.

Extenuate, eks-ten´ū-āt, *vt*. To lessen; to weaken the force of; to palliate.

Exterior, eks-tē´ri-ėr, *a*. External; on the outside; foreign.—*n*. The outward surface; that which is external.

Exterminate, eks-tėr´min-āt, *vt*. To destroy utterly; to extirpate; to root out.

External, eks-tėr´nal, *a*. On the outside; exterior; not being within, as causes or effects visible; foreign.

Extirpation, eks-tėrp-ā´shon, *n*. Act of rooting out; eradication; total destruction.

Extol, eks-tol´, *vt*. (extolling; extolled). To exalt in eulogy; to magnify; to glorify.

Extort, eks-tort´, *vt*. To exact by force; to wrest or wring.

Extortion, eks-tor´shon, *n*. Act of extorting; illegal or oppressive exaction.

Extra, eks´tra, *a*. and *adv*. Additional; beyond what is usual, due, etc.—*n*. Something in addition.

Extract, eks-trakt´, *vt*. To draw out or forth; to select; to draw or copy out; to find the root of a number.—*n*. eks´trakt. That which is extracted; a quotation; an essence, tincture, etc.

Extraction, eks-trak´shon, *n*. Act of extracting; lineage; operation of drawing essences; tinctures; etc.; operation of finding the roots of numbers.

Extradite, eks´tra-dīt, *vt*. To deliver up (a criminal) to the authorities of the country from which he has come.

Extradition, eks-traạ-di´shon, *n*. The delivery, under a treaty, of a fugitive from justice by one government to another.

Extreme, eks-trēm´, *a*. Outermost; furthest; most violent; last; worst or best; most pressing.—*n*. The utmost point or verge of a thing; end; furthest or highest degree; *(pl.)* points at the greatest distance from each other.

Extremist, eks-trēm´ist, *n*. A supporter of extreme doctrines or practice.

Extremity, eks-trem´i-ti, *n*. That which is extreme; utmost point, part, or degree; utmost distress or violence.

Extricate, eks´tri-kāt, *vt*. (extricating, extricated). To disentangle; to set free.

Extrinsic, Extrinsical, eks-trin´sik, eks-trin´-sik-al, *a*. Being on the outside; extraneous; accessory.

Extrude, eks-tröd´, *vt*. (extruding, extruded). To thrust out; to expel.

Extrusion, eks-trö´zhon, *n*. Act of extruding; a driving out; expulsion.

Exuberant, eks-ū-bė-rant, *a*. Superabundant; ovrflowing; luxuriant.

Exude, eks-ūd´, *vt*. (exuding, exuded). To discharge through the pores; to let ooze out.—*vi*. To flow through pores; to ooze out like sweat.

Exult, egz-ult´, *vi*. To rejoice exceedingly; to triumph.

Exultation, egz-ult-ā´shon, *n*. Lively joy; triumph; rapture; ecstasy.

Eye, ī, *n*. The organ of vision; sight or view; power of perception; something resembling an eye in form; a small hole; a loop or ring for fastening.—*vt*. (eyeing, eyed). To fix the eye on; to observe or watch narrowly.

Eyrie, Eyry, ī´ri, *n*. An aerie; nest of a bird of prey.

F

Fable, fā´bl, *n*. A fictitious narrative to instruct or amuse, often to enforce a precept; falsehood; an idle story; the plot in a poem or drama.—*vi*. (fabling, fabled). To tell fables or falsehoods.—*vt*. To feign; to invent.

Fabric, fab´rik, *n*. Frame or structure of anything; a building; texture; cloth.

Fabricate, fab´rik-āt, *vt*. (fabricating, fabricated). To make or fashion; to form by art or labor; to devise falsely.

Fabulous, fa´bū-lus, *a*. Containing or abounding in fable; feigned;

mythical; incredible.

Façade, Facade, fa-säd', fa-säd', *n.* Front view or elevation of an edifice.

Face, fās, *n.* The front part of an animal's head, particularly of the human head; the visage; front; effrontery; assurance; dial of a watch, etc.—*vt.* (facing; faced). To meet in front; to stand opposite to; to oppose with firmness; to finish or protect with a thin external covering; to dress the face of (a stone, etc.).—*vi.* To turn the face; to look.

Facsimile, fak-sim'i-lē, *n.* An exact copy or likeness.

Fact, fakt, *n.* Anything done; a deed; event; circumstance; reality; truth.

Faction, fak'shon, *n.* A party in political society in opposition to the ruling power; a party unscrupulously promoting its private ends; discord; dissension.

Factor, fak'tėr, *n.* An agent, particularly a mercantile agent; in Scotland, one appointed to manage an estate; one of two or more numbers or quantities, which, when multiplied together, form a product; one of several elements which contribute to a result.

Factory, fak'to-ri, *n.* An establishment where factors in foreign countries reside to transact business for their employers; buildings appropriated to the manufacture of goods; a manufactory.

Fad, fad, *n.* A favorite theory; crotchet; hobby.

Fade, fād, *vi.* (fading, faded). To lose color, strength, or freshness; to wither; to perish; to become indistinct.—*vt.* To cause to wither.

Faggot, Fagot, fag'ot, *n.* A bundle of sticks or twigs; a bundle of pieces of iron or steel for remanufacture; one hired to take the place of another at the muster of a military company; a shriveled old woman.—*vt.* To tie up; to collect promiscuously.

Fahrenheit, fä'ren-hīt, *a.* The name of the thermometer in which the freezing point is 32° and the boiling 212°.

Fail, fāl, *vi.* To become deficient; to decline; to become extinct; not to produce the effect; to be unsuccessful; to be guilty of omission or neglect; to become bankrupt.—*vt.* To cease or omit to afford aid, supply, or strength to; to forsake.—*n.* Omission; failure; want.

Faint-hearted, fānt'härt-ed, *a.* Cowardly; timorous; dejected.

Fairy, fā'ri, *n.* An imaginary being of human form, supposed to play a variety of pranks.—*a.* Belonging to fairies; given by fairies.

Faith, fāth, *n.* Belief; trust; confidence; conviction in regard to religion; system of religious beliefs; strict adherence to duty and promises; word or honor pledged.

Falcon, fa'kn, or fal'kon, *n.* The name of various small or medium-sized raptorial birds; a hawk of any kind trained to sport.

Falconry, fa'kn-ri, *n.* The art of training hawks; hawking.

Fall, fal, *vi.* (pret. fell, pp. fallen). To sink to a lower position; to drop down; to empty or disembogue; to sink into sin, weakness, or disgrace; to come to an end suddenly; to decrease; to assume an expression of dejection, etc.; to happen; to pass or be transferred; to belong or appertain; to be uttered carelessly.—*n.* Descent; tumble; death; ruin; cadence; a cascade or cataract; extent of descent; declivity; autumn; that which falls; a kind of ladies' veil; lapse or declension from innocence or goodness; *naut.* the part of a tackle to which the power is applied in hoisting.

False, fals, *a.* Not true; forged; feigned; fraudulent; treacherous; inconstant; constructed for show or a subsidiary purpose.

Falsehood, fals'höd, *n.* Quality of being false; untruth; fiction; a lie.

Falsetto, fal-set'tō, *n.* A false or artifical voice; the tones above the natural compass of the voice.

Fame, fām, *n.* A public report or rumor; favorable report; celebrity; reputation.

Familiar, fa-mil'i-ėr, *a.* Well acquainted; intimate; affable; well known; free; unconstrained.—*n.* An intimate; one long acquainted;

a demon supposed to attend at call.

Family, fam´i-li, *n.* Household; the parents and children alone; the children as distinguished from the parents; kindred; line of ancestors; honorable descent; a group or class of animals or plants.

Famine, fam´in, *n.* Scarcity of food; dearth.

Famish, fam´ish, *vt.* To kill or exhaust with hunger; to starve; to kill by denial of anything necessary.—*vi.* To die of hunger; to suffer extreme hunger or thirst.

Famous, fām´us, *a.* Much talked of and praised; renowned; distinguished; admirable.

Fan, fan, *n.* An instrument for winnowing grain; an instrument to agitate the air and cool the face; something by which the air is moved; a wing.—*vt.* (fanning, fanned). To cool and refresh by moving the air with a fan; to winnow, to stimulate.

Fanatic, Fanatical, fa-nat´ik, fa-nat´ik-al, *a.* Wild in opinions, particularly in religious opinions; excessively enthusiastic.—**Fanatic,** fa-nat´ik, *n.* A person affected by excessive enthusiasm, particularly on religious subjects; an enthusiast; a visionary.

Fancier, fan´si-ėr, *n.* One who fancies; one who has a hobby for certain things.

Fancy, fan´si, *n.* A phase of the intellect of a lighter cast than the imagination; thought due to this faculty; embodiment of such in words; opinion or notion; liking; caprice; false notion.—*vi.* (fancying, fancied). To imagine; to suppose without proof.—*vt.* To imagine; to like; to be pleased with.—*a.* Fine; ornamental; adapted to please the fancy; beyond intrinsic value.

Fantasy, fan´ta-si, *n.* Fancy; a vagary of the imagination; a fanciful artistic production.—*vt.* To picture in fancy.

Far, fär, *a.* Remote; distant, *adv.* To a great extent or distance in space or in time; in great part; very much; to a certain point.

Farad, far´ad, *n.* The unit of quantity in the measurement of electricity.

Farce, färs, *n.* A play full of extravagant drollery; absurdity; mere show.—*vt.* To stuff with forcemeat or mingled ingredients.

Fare, fär, *vi.* (faring, fared). To go; to travel; to be in any state, good or bad; to be entertained with food; to happen well or ill.—*n.* Sum charged for conveying a person; person conveyed; food; provisions of the table.

Farm, färm, *n.* A portion of land under cultivation; ground let to a tenant for tillage, pasture, etc.—*vt.* To let out or take on lease, as lands; to cultivate; to lease, as taxes, imposts, etc.—*vi.* To cultivate the soil.

Fascinate, fas´si-nāt, *vt.* (fascinating, fascinated). To bewitch; to charm; to captivate.

Fashion, fa´shon, *n.* The make or form of anything; external appearance; form of a garment; prevailing mode; custom; genteel life—*vt.* To give shape to; to mold; to adapt.

Fast, fäst, *a.* Firmly fixed; closely adhering; steadfast; durable; swift; dissipated.—*adv.* Firmly; rapidly; durably; near; with dissipation.—*vi.* To abstain from eating and drinking, or from particular kinds of food.—*n.* Abstinence from food; a religious mortification by abstinence; the time of fasting.

Fasten, fäs´n, *vt.* To fix firmly, closely, or tightly; to hold together; to affix.—*vi.* To become fixed; to seize and hold on.

Fastidious, fas-tid´i-us, *a.* Squeamish; delicate to a fault; difficult to please.

Fat, fat, *a.* Fleshy; plump; unctuous; heavy; stupid; rich; fertile.—*n.* A solid oily substance found in parts of animal bodies; the best or richest part of a thing.—*vt.* (fatting, fatted). To make fat.

Fatal, fāt´al, *a.* Proceeding from fate; causing death; deadly; calamitous.

Fate, fāt, *n.* Destiny; inevitable necessity; death; doom; lot; *pl.* the three goddesses supposed to pre-

F

side over the birth and life of men.

Father, fä 'ᴛʜėr, *n*. A male parent; the first ancestor; the oldest member of a society or profession; the first to practice any art; a creator; a name given to God; a dignitary of the church; one of the early expounders of Christianity.—*vt*. To become a father to; to adopt; to profess to be the author of; to ascribe to one as his offspring or production.

Fathom, faᴛʜ 'um, *n*. A measure of length containing six feet.—*vt*. To try the depth of; to sound; to master; to comprehend.

Fatigue, fa-tēg´, *vt*. (fatiguing, fatigued). To employ to weariness; to tire; to harass with toil or labor.—*n*. Weariness from bodily or mental exertion; exhaustion; toil; labors of soldiers distinct from the use of arms.

Fatten, fat 'n, *vt*. To make fat; to feed for slaughter; to make fertile.—*vi*. To grow fat.

Fauna, fa̧ 'na, *n*. A collective term for the animals peculiar to a region or epoch.

Faux-pas, fō-pä, *n*. A false step; a breach of manners or moral conduct.

Favorite, fä 'vėr-it, *n*. A person or thing regarded with peculiar favor; a darling; a minion; one unduly favored.—*a*. Regarded with particular favor.

Fealty, fē 'al-ti, *n*. Fidelity to a superior; loyalty.

Fear, fär, *n*. Painful emotion excited by apprehension of impending danger; dread; the object of fear; filial regard mingled with awe; reverence.—*vt*. To feel fear; to apprehend; to dread; to reverence.—*vi*. To be in apprehension of evil; to be afraid.

Feasibility, fēz-i-bil 'i-ti, *n*. Quality of being feasible; practicability.

Feasible, fēz-i-bl, *a*. That may be done; practicable.

Feast, fēst, *n*. A festal day; a sumptuous enterainment; a banquet; a festival; that which delights and entertains.—*vi*. To partake of a feast; to eat sumptuously; to be highly gratified.—*vt*. To entertain

sumptuously.

Feat, fēt, *n*. An exploit, an extraordinary act of strength, skill, or cunning.

Feather, feᴛʜ 'ėr, *n*. One of the growths which form the covering of birds; a plume; projection on a board to fit into another board; kind of nature; birds collectively; a trifle.—*vt*. To cover or fit with feathers; to turn (an oar) horizonatally over the water.

Feature, fē 'tūr, *n*. The make or cast of any part of the face; any single lineament; a prominent part or characteristic.

Federal, fed 'ėr-al, *a*. Pertaining to a league or contract; confederated; founded on alliance between states which unite for national purposes.—*n*. One who upholds federal government.

Federalism, fed 'ėr-al-izm, *n*. The principles of federal government.

Federation, fed-ėr-ā 'shon, *n*. Act of uniting in a league; confederacy.

Fee, fē, *n*. A reward for services; recompense for professional services; a fief; a freehold estate held by one who is absolute owner.—*vt*. (feeing, feed). To pay a fee to; to engage in one's service by advancing a fee to.

Feeble, fē 'bl, *a*. Weak; impotent; deficient in vigor, as mental powers, sound, light, etc.

Feed, fēd, *vt*. (feeding, fed). To give food to; to furnish with anything of which there is constant consumption; to fatten.—*vi*. To take food; to eat; to prey; to graze; to grow fat.—*n*. That which is eaten; fodder; portion of provender given to a horse, cow, etc.

Feel, fēl, *vt*. (feeling, felt). To perceive by the touch; to have the sense of; to be affected by; to examine by touching.—*vi*. To have perception by the touch; to have the sensibility moved; to have perception mentally.—*n*. Act of feeling; perception caused by the touch.

Feign, fān, *vt*. To pretend; to counterfeit; to simulate.—*vi*. To represent falsely; to pretend.

Feint, fānt, *n*. A pretense; an appearance of aiming at one part when another is intended to be struck.—*vi*. To make a feigned blow or thrust.

Felicitate, fē-lis'it-āt, *vt.* To congratulate.

Felon, fe'lon, *n.* One who has committed felony; a culprit; a whitlow.—*a.* Fierce; malignant; malicious.

Felony, fe'lon-i, *n.* Any crime which incurs the forfeiture of lands or goods; a heinous crime.

Female, fē'māl, *n.* One of that sex which conceives and brings forth young.—*a.* Belonging to the sex which produces young; feminine; weak.

Feminine, fem'in-in, *a.* Pertaining to females; womanly; effeminate; denoting the gender of words which signify females.

Femoral, fem'o-ral, *a.* Belonging to the thigh.

Femur, fē'mėr, *n.* The thigh-bone.

Fen, fen, *n.* A marsh; bog; swamp where water stagnates.

Fence, fens, *n.* That which defends or guards; a wall, railing, etc., forming a boundary, etc.—*vi.* To practice the swordsman's art; to parry arguments; to prevaricate.

Fencing, fens'ing, *n.* The art of using a sword or foil in attack or defense; material used in making fences; that which fences.

Fend, fend, *vt.* To keep or ward off.—*vi.* To act on the defensive; to provide a livelihood.

Fenestration, fen-es-trā'shon, *n.* The arrangement of windows in a building.

Fennel, fen'el, *n.* A plant cutivated for the aromatic flavor of its seeds and for its leaves.

Feral, fē'ral, *a.* Having become wild after a state of domestication or cultivation.

Fermentation, fėr-ment-ā'shon, *n.* Decomposition or conversion of an organic substance into new compounds by a ferment, indicated by the development of heat, bubbles, etc.; process by which grape juice is converted into wine; agitaion; excitement.

Fern, fėrn, *n.* The name of many cryptogams producing leaves called fronds.

Ferocious, fē-rō'shus, *a.* Fierce; savage; cruel.

Ferocity, fē-ros'i-ti, *n.* Savage wildness; fury; fierceness.

Ferry, fe'ri, *vt.* (ferrying, ferried). To carry over a river or other water in a boat.—*n.* Place where boats pass over to convey passengers; regular conveyance provided at such a place; a boat that plies at a ferry.

Fertile, fėr'tīl, *a.* Fruitful; prolific; inventive; able to produce abundantly.

Fertility, fėr-til'i-ti, *n.* Fruitfulness; rickness; fertile invention.

Fertilize, fėr'til-īz, *vt.* To make fertile or fruitful; to enrich; to impregnate.

Fervent, fėr'vent, *a.* Burning; vehement; ardent; earnest.

Festoon, fes-tön', *n.* A string of flowers, foliage, etc., suspended in a curve or curves; carved work in the form of a wreath of flowers, etc. —*vt.* To form in festoons; to adorn with festoons.

Fetch, fech, *vt.* To bring or draw; to make; to heave, as a sigh; to obtain as its price.—*vi.* To move or turn; to bring things.—*n.* A stratagem or trick; a wraith.

Fetus, fē'tus, *n.*; **pl. -uses.** The young or an animal in the womb, or in the egg, after being perfectly formed.

Feud, fūd, *n.* Hostility; a hereditary quarrel; a fief.

Fever, Fē'vėr, *n.* A disease characterized by an accelerated pulse, heat, thirst, and diminished strength; agitation; excitement.—*vt.* To put in a fever.—*vt.* To be seized with fever.

Few, fū, *a.* Not many; small in number.

Fey, fā, *a.* On the verge of a sudden or violent death; fated soon to die and often showing this by unnatural gaiety.

Fez, fez, *n.* A close-fitting red cap with a tassel, worn in Turkey, Egypt, etc.

Fiancé, Fiancée, fē-äng-sā, *n.*, *masc.* and *fem.* An affianced or be-

F

trothed person.

Fiasco, fē-as'kō, *n.* An ignominious failure.

Fiat, fi'at, *n.* A decree; a command.

Fib, fĭb, *n.* A falsehood (a softer expression than *lie*).—*vi.* (fibbing, fibbed). To tell fibs.

Fiber, fībèr, *n.* A thread; a fine, slender body which constitutes a part of animals, plants, or minderals.

Fickle, fik'l, *a.* Of a changeable mind; vacillating; capricious.

Fiction, fĭk'shon, *n.* A feigned story; literature in the form of novels, tales, etc., a falsehood; fabrication.

Fidelity, fī-del'i-ti, *n.* Faithfulness; trustiness; loyalty; integrity.

Fidget, fij'et, *vi.* To move uneasily or in fits and starts.—*n.* An uneasy restless motion.

Fiduciary, fī-dū'shi-a-ri, *a.* Held in trust; having the nature of a trust.—*n.* One who holds a thing in trust; a trustee.

Field, fēld, *n.* A piece of land suitable for tillage or pasture; piece of enclosed land; place of battle; battle; open space for action; sphere; blank space on which figures are drawn; those taking part in a hunt or race.—*vi.* and *t.* To watch and catch the ball, as in cricket.

Fiend, fēnd, *n.* A demon; the devil; a wicked or cruel person.

Fierce, fērs, *a.* Wild; savage; outrageous; violent.

Fig, fig, *n.* The fruit of a tree of the mulberry family; the tree itself; a mere trifle; dress.

Fight, fit, *vi.* (fighting, fought). To strive for victory; to contend in arms.—*vt.* To war against; to contend with in battle; to win by struggle.—*n.* A struggle for victory; a battle; an encounter.

Fighter, fit'èr, *n.* One who fights; a combatant; a warrior; an aeroplane designed for aerial combat.

Figment, fig'ment, *n.* A fiction; fabrication.

Figure-head, fig'ūr-hed, *n.* The ornamental figure on a ship under the bowsprit.

Filament, fil'a-ment, *n.* A slender thread; a fine fiber.

Filatory, fil'a-to-ri, *n.* A machine which spins threads.

Filbert, fil'bèrt, *n* The fruit of the cultivated hazel.

Filch, filsh or filch, *vt.* To pilfer; to steal.

File, fil, *n.* A line or wire on which papers are strung; the papers so strung; a row of soldiers one behind another; a steel instrument for cutting and smoothing iron, wood, etc.—*vt.* (filing, filed). To arrange or place on or in a file; to bring before a court by presenting the proper papers; to rub or cut with a file; to polish.—*vi.* To march in a line one after the other.

Fill, fil, *vt.* To make full; to occupy; to pervade; to satisfy; to surfeit; to supply with an occupant; to hold; to possess and perform the duties of.—*vi.* To grow or become full.—*n.* As much as fills or supplies want.

Fillet, fil'et, *n.* A little band to tie about the hair; the fleshy part of the thigh in veal; meat rolled together and tied round; something resembling a fillet or band.—*vt.* (filleting, filleted). To bind with a little band.

Film, film, *n.* A thin skin; a pellicle; *(pl.)* a cinema-show; the pictures.—*vt.* To cover with a thin skin.

Filter, fil'tèr, *n.* A strainer; any substance through which liquors are passed.—*vt.* To purify by passing through a filter.—*vi.* To percolate; to pass through a filter.

Finance, fi-nans', *n.* The science of public revenue and expenditure; management of money matters; *pl.* public funds or resources of money; private income.—*vi.* (financing, financed). To conduct financial operations.—*vt.* To manage the financial affairs of.

Finch, finsh, *n.* A small singing bird.

Find, find, *vt.* (finding, found). To come upon; to discover; to recover; to get; to perceive; to supply; to declare by verdict.—*n.* A discovery; the thing found.

Finding, find'ing, *n.* Discovery; act of discovering; that which is found; a verdict.

Fine, fin, *a.* Slender; minute; keen; delicate; refined; elegant; amiable; noble; splendid.—*n*. Payment of money imposed as a punishment; conclusion *(in fine)*.—*vt*. (fining, fined). To make fine; to purify; to impose a pecuniary penalty on.

Finery, fīn'e-ri, *n*. Fine things; showy articles of dress; a furnace where cast-iron is converted into malleable iron.

Finesse, fi-nes', *n*. Artifice; stratagem.—*vi*. To use finesse or artifice.

Finger, fing'ger, *n*. One of the five members of the hand; something resembling a finger; skill in playing on a keyed instrument.—*vt*. To handle with the fingers; to touch lightly; to pilfer.—*vi*. To dispose the fingers aptly in playing on an instrument.

Finis, fī'nis, *n*. An end; conclusion.

Finish, fin'ish, *vt*. To bring to an end; to perfect; to polish to a high degree.—*vi*. To come to an end; to expire.—*n*. Completion; the last touch to a work; polish.

Finite, fī'nīt, *a*. Limited; bounded; circumscribed; not infinite.

Fire, fīr, *n*. Heat and light emanating from a body; fuel burning; a conflagration; discharge of firearms; splendor; violence of passion; vigor of fancy; animation; ardent affection; affliction.—*vt*. (firing, fired). To set on fire; to irritate; to animate; to bake; to cause to explode; to discharge (firearms).—*vi*. To take fire; to be inflamed with passion; to discharge firearms.

Firm, fėrm, *a*. Steady; stable; strong; dense; hard; not fluid; fixed; resolute.—*n*. A partnership or commercial house.—*vt*. To make firm or solid.—*vi*. To become firm.

Firmament, fėrm'a-ment, *n*. The sky or heavens; region of the air; an expanse.

First, fėrst, *a*. Foremost in time, place, rank, value, etc.; chief; highest; the ordinal of *one*.—*adv*. Before all others in time, place, etc.

First-born, fėrst'born, *a*. Eldest.

Fiscal, fis'kal, *a*. Pertaining to the public treasury.—*n*. A treasurer; a public prosecutor, as in Scotland.

Fish, fish, *n*. An animal that lives in water; the flesh of such animals used as food.—*vi*. To attempt to catch fish; to attempt to obtain by artifice.—*vt*. To catch or try to catch fish in; to draw out or up when in water.

Fisherman, fish'ėr-man, *n*. One whose occupation is to catch fish.

Fistular, fis'tū-lėr, *a*. Hollow like a pipe.

Fix, fiks, *vt*. To make fast or firm; to settle; to define; to appoint; to deprive of volatility.—*vi*. To settle or remain permanently; to cease to be fluid; to congeal.—*n*. A condition of difficulty; dilemma.

Fixation, fiks-ā'shon, *n*. Act of fixing; state in which a body resists evaporation.

Fixative, fiks'a-tiv, *a*. Tending or causing to fix.—*n*. A substance that causes something to be stable or not fleeting.

Fixture, fiks'tūr, *n*. That which is fixed; that which is permanently attached; an appendage.

Fizz, Fizzle, fiz, fiz'l, *vi*. To make a hissing sound. Also used as a noun.

Flabbergast, flab'ėr-gast, *vt*. To strike with astonishment or dismay.

Flabby, flab'i, *a*. Soft; yielding to the touch; languid; feeble.

Flaccid, flak'sid, *a*. Flabby; soft and weak; drooping; limber.

Flag, flag, *n*. A cloth, usually attached to a pole, and bearing devices expressive of nationality, etc.; a banner; a flat stone for paving; an aquatic plant with sword-shaped leaves.—*vi*. (flagging, flagged). To hang loose; to droop; to languish; to slacken.—*vt*. To lay with broad flat stones.

Flake, flāk, *n*. A loose, filmy mass of anything; a scale; a fleecy or feathery particle, as of snow; a flock, as of wool.—*vt*. (flaking, flaked). To form into flakes.—*vi*. To break in layers; to peel off.

Flamboyant, flam-boi'ant, *a*. Noting that style of gothic architecture characterized by wavy tracery in the windows; florid.

Flame, flām, *n*. Light emitted from fire; a blaze; fire; heat of passion; ardor of temper or imagination;

ardent love; rage; one beloved.—*vi.*
(flaming, flamed). To blaze; to
glow; to rage.

Flamingo, fla-ming´gō, *n.* A webfooted, long-necked bird about 5 to
6 feet high.

Flange, flanj, *n.* A projecting rim or
edge on any substance; a raised
edge on a wheel, etc.—*vt.* (flang-
ing, flanged). To furnish with a
flange.

Flank, flangk, *n.* The part of the
side of an animal, between the
ribs and the hip; the side of an
army; the extreme right or left; the
side of any building.—*vt.* To be situated at the side of; to place
troops so as to command or attack the flank; to pass round the
side of.

Flannel, flan´el, *n.* A soft, nappy,
woollen cloth of loose texture; garment made of flannel.

Flap, flap, *n.* Something broad and
flexible that hangs loose; the motion or sound of anything broad
and loose, or a stroke with it; tail of
a coat, etc.—*vt.* (flapping, flapped).
To beat with a flap; to move; as
something broad.—*vi.* To move, as
wings; to wave loosely.

Flask, flask, *n.* A kind of bottle; a
bottle for the pocket; a vessel for
powder.

Flat, flat, *a.* Having an even surface; level; fallen; tasteless; vapid;
depressed; dull; absolute; below
the true pitch, as a sound.—*n.* A
level; a shallow; the broad side of
something; a mark in music ♭ indicating lowering of pitch; a story or
floor of a house; a simpleton.

Flatten, flat´n, *vt.* To make flat; to
level; to render less acute or
sharp, as a sound.—*vi.* To grow or
become flat.

Flatter, flat´ėr, *vt.* To gratify by
praise; to compliment; to praise
falsely.

Flattery, flat´ė-ri, *n.* False praise;
sycophancy; cajolery.

Flatulent, flat´ū-lent, *a.* Affected
with gases in the stomach and intestines; generating wind in the
stomach; empty; puffy.

Flaunt, flant, *vi.* and *t.* To display ostentatiously.—*n.* Bold or impudent
parade.

Flavor, flā´vėr, *n.* The quality of a
substance which affects the smell
or taste; relish; zest.—*vt.* To give a
flavor to.

Flaw, fla, *n.* A crack; a defect; a
speck; a gust of wind.—*vt.* To
make a flaw in.

Flawless, fla´les, *a.* Without defect;
perfect.

Flee, flē, *vi.* (fleeing, fled). To run
away; to hasten from.—*vt.* To shun.

Flesh, flesh, *n.* The muscular part
of an animal; animal food; beasts
and birds used as food; the body,
as distinguished from the soul;
mankind; corporeal appetites;
kindred; family.—*vt.* To feed with
flesh; to initiate to the taste of
flesh.

Fleshly, flesh´li, *a.* Carnal; worldly;
lascivious; human; not spiritual.

Flick, flik, *n.* A sharp sudden
stroke, as with a whip; a flip.—*vt.*
To strike with a flick; to flip.

Flicker, flik´ėr, *vi.* To flutter; to
waver, as an unsteady flame.—*n.*
A wavering gleam.

Flight, flīt, *n.* Act of fleeing or flying;
power or manner of flying; a flock
of birds; a volley, as of arrows;
pace passed by flying; a soaring;
lofty elevation, as of fancy; extravagant sally; a series of steps or
stairs.

Flimsy, flim´zi, *a.* Thin; slight;
weak; without force; shallow.

Flinch, flinsh, *vi* to shrink; to withdraw; to wince; to fail.

Fling, fling, *vt.* (flinging, flung). To
cause to fly from the hand; to hurl;
to scatter; to throw to the
ground.—*vi.* To fly into violent and
irregular motions; to flounce; to
rush away angrily.—*n.* A throw; a
gibe; a lively Scottish dance.

Flint, flint, *n.* A very hard siliceous
stone, which strikes fire with steel;
anything proverbially hard.

Flirt, flėrt, *vt.* To throw with a jerk;
to make coquettish motions with
(a fan).—*vi.* To run and dart about;
to coquette; to play at courtship.—
n. A sudden jerk; one who plays at
courtship; a coquette.

Float, flōt, *n.* That which is borne on
water or any fluid; a raft.—*vi.* To be

borne on the surface of a fluid; to be buoyed up; to move with a light, irregular course.—*vt*. To cause to be conveyed on water; to flood; to get (a company, scheme, etc.) started.

Flock, flok, *n*. A lock of wool or hair; stuffing for mattresses, etc.; a company, as of sheep, birds, etc.; a Christian congregation in relation to their pastor.—*vi*. To gather in companies; to crowd; to move in crowds.

Floe, flō, *n*. A mass of ice floating in the ocean.

Flog, flog, *vt*. (flogging, flogged). To whip; to chastise with repeated blows.

Flood, flud, *n*. A great flow of water; a deluge; a river; the flowing of the tide; a great quantity; abundance.—*vt*. To overflow; to deluge; to overwhelm.

Floor, flōr, *n*. That part of a building on which we walk; bottom of a room; story in a building; a flat, hard surface of loam, lime, etc., used in some kinds of business, as in malting.—*vt*. To lay a floor upon; to strike down.

Flop, flop, *vt*. and *i* (flopping, flopped). To clap or flap; to let down suddenly; to plump down.— *n*. A sudden sinking to the ground.

Flounder, floun'der, *n*. A flat fish found in the sea near the mouths of rivers.—*vi*. To struggle, as in mire; to roll, toss, and tumble.

Flour, flour, *n*. Finely ground meal of wheat or other grain; fine powder of any substance.—*vt*. To convert into flour; to sprinkle with flour.

Flourish, flu'rish, *vi*. To grow luxuriantly; to thrive; to live; to use florid language; to make ornamental strokes in writing, etc.; to move in bold and irregular figures.—*vt*. To adorn with flowers or figures; to ornament with anything showy; to brandish.—*n*. Showy splendor; parade of words and figures; fanciful stroke of the pen; decorative notes in music; brandishing.

Flout, flout, *vt*. To mock or insult; to jeer at.—*n*. A mock; an insult.

Flow, flō, *vi*. To move, as water; to issue; to abound; to glide smoothly; to hang loose and waving; to rise, as the tide; to circulate, as blood.— *vt*. To flow over; to flood.—*n*. A moving along, as of water; stream; current; rise of water; fullness; free expression; feeling.

Flower, flou'er, *n*. The delicate and gaily-colored leaves or petals on a plant; a bloom or blossom; youth; the prime; the best part; one most distinguished; an ornamental expression; *pl*. a powdery substance.—*vi*. To blossom; to bloom.—*vt*. To embellish with figures of flowers.

Flowing, flō'ing, *p.a*. Moving as a steam; abounding; fluent; undulating.

Fluctuate, fluk'tū-āt, *vi*. To move as a wave; to waver; to hesitate; to experience vicissitudes.

Fluctuation, fluk-tū-ā'shon, *n*. A rising and falling; change; vicissitude.

Flue, flö, *n*. A passage for smoke or heated air; a pipe for conveying heat; light downy matter; fluff.

Fluent, flu'ent, *a*. Flowing; ready in the use of words; voluble; smooth.

Fluff, fluf, *n*. Light down or nap such as rises from beds, cotton, etc.

Fluid, flu'id, *a*. Capable of flowing; liquid or gaseous.—*n*. Any substance whose parts easily move and change their relative position without separation; a liquid.

Fluor-spar, flö'or-spär, *n*. A mineral exhibiting yellow, green, blue, and red tints.

Flurry, flu'ri, *n*. Bustle; hurry; a gust of wind; light things carried by the wind.—*vt*. (flurrying, flurried). To agitate or alarm.

Fluster, flus'ter, *vt*. To agitate; to make hot with drink.—*n*. Agitation; confusion; heat.

Flute, flöt, *n*. A small wind-instrument with holes and keys; a channel cut along the shaft of a column; a similar channel.—*vi*. (fluting, fluted). To play on a flute.—*vt*. To play or sing in notes like those of a flute; to form flutes or channels in.

F

Flutist, flöt'ist, *n*. A performer on the flute.

Flutter, flut'er, *vi*. To move or flap the wings rapidly; to be in agitation; to fluctuate.—*vt*. To agitate; to throw into confusion.—*n*. Quick, confused motion; agitation; disorder.

Fluvial, flö'vi-al, *a*. Belonging to rivers.

Flux, fluks, *n*. Act of flowing, any flow of matter; dysentery; flow of the tide; anything used to promote fusion; fusion; liquid state from the operation of heat.—*vt*. To melt; to fuse.

Fly, flī, *vi*. (flying, pret, flew, pp. flown). To move through air by wings; to move in air by the force of wind, etc.; to rise in air; to move rapidly; to pass away; to depart suddenly; to spring; to flutter.—*vt*. To flee from; to cause to float in the air.—*n*. A winged insect; a revolving mechanism to regulate the motion of machinery; a light carriage; a cab.

Foal, fōl, *n*. The young of a mare, she-ass, etc.; a colt or filly.—*vt*. To bring forth, as a colt or filly.—*vi*. To bring forth a foal.

Foam, fōm, *n*. Froth; spume.—*vi*. To froth; to show froth at the mouth; to rage.—*vt*. To cause to give out foam; to throw out with rage or violence.

Fob, fob, *n*. A little pocket for a watch in the waistband of the breeches.

Focus, fō'kus, *n*.; pl. -cuses or -ci. A point in which rays of light meet after being reflected or refracted; point of concentration.—*vt*. To bring to a focus.

Fodder, fod'er, *n*. Food for cattle, etc.—*vt*. To furnish with fodder.

Foe, fō, *n*. An enemy; an opposing army; one who opposes anything.

Fog, fog, *n*. A dense vapor near the surface of the land or water; mental confusion; dimness; second growth of grass; long grass that remains in pastures till winter.

Fogey, Fogy, fō'gi, *n*.; pl. -eys, -ies. A stupid fellow; an old-fashioned person.

Foible, foi'bl, *n*. A weak point in character; a failing; the weak part of a sword.

Folio, fō'li-ō, *n*. A book of the largest size, formed by sheets of paper once doubled; a page; number appended to each page; a written page of a certain number of words.

Folk, fōk, *n*. People in general; certain people discriminated from others, as old *folks*.

Follicle, fol'li-kl, *n*. A little bag or vesicle in animals or plants.

Follow, fol'ō, *vt*. To go or come after; to chase; to accompany; to succeed; to result from; to understand; to copy; to practice; to be occupied with; to be guided by.—*vi*. To come after another; to ensure; to result.

Folly, fol'i, *n*. Foolishness; imbecility; a weak or foolish act; criminal weakness.

Foment, fō-ment', *vt*. To apply warm lotions to; to abet; to stir up (in a bad sense).

Fond, fond, *a*. Foolish; foolishly tender and loving; doting; loving; relishing.

Fondle, fon'dl, *vt*. (fondling, fondled). To treat with fondness; to caress.

Font, font, *n*. A large basin in which water is contained for baptizing; a complete assortment of printing types of one size.

Food, föd, *n*. Whatever supplies nourishment to animals or plants; nutriment; provisions; whatever feeds or augments.

Fool, föl, *n*. One destitute of reason; a simpleton; a silly person; a buffoon.—*vi*. To play the fool; to trifle.—*vt*. To make a fool of; to deceive.

Foolish, föl'ish, *a*. Void of understanding; acting without judgment or discretion; silly; ridiculous; unwise.

Foot, fut, *n*.; pl. feet, fēt. The lower extremity of the leg; that on which a thing stands; the base; infantry; a measure of twelve inches; a measure of syllables in a verse.—*vi*. to dance; to tread to measure or music; to skip; to walk.—*vt*. To tread; to dance; to trip; to add a foot to, as to a stocking.

Football, fụt'bạl, n. An inflated leather ball to be driven by the foot; a game played with such a ball.

Footstep, fụt'step, n. A track; the mark of the foot; vestige; pl. example; course.

For, for, prep. In the place of; because of; in favor of; toward; during; in quest of; according to; as far as; notwithstanding; in proportion to.—conj. Because.

Forage, fo'rāj, n. Food for horses and cattle; act of providing forage.—vi. (foraging, foraged). To collect forage; to rove in search of food.—vt. To strip of provisions for horses, etc.; to supply with forage.

Forage cap, n. Undress cap worn by soldiers of all branches of the army.

Foray, fo'rā, vt. To ravage; to pillage.—n. A predatory excursion; a raid.

Forbear, for-bār', vi. To keep away; to cease; to delay; to refrain.—vt. To abstain from; to avoid doing.

Forbid, for-bid', vt. To prohibit; to oppose; to obstruct.—vi. To utter a prohibition.

Force, fōrs, n. Strength; active power; might; violence; coercion; cogency; efficacy; power for war; troops; a waterfall.—vt. (forcing, forced). To compel; to impel; to take by violence; to ravish; to twist or overstrain; to ripen by artificial means; to stuff; to farce.—vi. To use force or violence.

Forceps, for'seps, n. A surgical instrument on the principle of pincers for holding anything difficult to be held by the hand.

Forcible, fōrs'i-bl, a. Efficacious; potent; cogent; done by force; suffered by force.

Forcing, fōrs'ing, n. Art of raising plants or fruits, at an earlier season than the natural one, by artifical heat.

Ford, fōrd, n. A shallow place in a river or other water, where it may be passed on foot.—vt. To cross by walking; to wade through.

Fore, fōr, a. In front of; anterior; coming first in time; prior.—adv. In the part that precedes or goes first.

Foreign, fo'rin, a. Belonging to another nation or country; alien; not to the purpose; irrelevant.

Forensic, fō-ren'sik, a. Belonging to courts of justice, or to public debate; used in courts or legal proceedings.

Forest, fo'rest, n. An extensive wood; a district devoted to the purposes of the chase; a tract once a royal forest.—a. Relating to a forest; sylvan; rustic.—vt. To convert into a forest.

Forever, for-ev'ér, adv. At all times; through endless ages; eternally.

Forewarn, fōr-warn', vt. To warn beforehand, to give previous notice to.

Foreword, fōr'wérd, n. A preface.

Forfeit, for'fit, vt. To lose by a misdeed.—n. That which is forfeited; fine; penalty.

Forfeiture, for'fit-ūr, n. Act of forfeiting; loss of some right, estate, honor, etc., by a crime or fault; fine; penalty.

Forge, fōrj, n. A furnace in which iron is heated and wrought; a smithy.—vt. (forging, forged). To frame or fabricate; to form by heating and hammering; to counterfeit.—vi. To commit forgery; to move on slowly and laboriously; to work one's way.

Forgery, fōrj'é-ri, n. The crime of counterfeiting; that which is forged or counterfeited.

Forget, for-get', vt. (forgetting, pret, forgot, pp. forgot, forgotten). To lose the remembrance of; to slight; to neglect.

Fork, fork, n. An instrument with two or more prongs, used for lifting or pitching anything; a branch or division; a prong.—vi. To shoot into branches; to divide into two.—vt. To raise or pitch with a fork, as hay, etc.

Forlorn, for-lorn', a. Deserted; abandoned; miserable.—**Forlorn hope,** a body of men appointed to perform some specially perilous service.

Form, form, n. Shape; manner; pattern; order; empty show; prescribed mode; ceremony; schedule; a long seat; a bench; a class; the seat or bed of a hare.—*vt*. To shape or mold; to arrange; to invent; to make up.—*vi*. To take a form.

Formal, form'al, *a*. Relating to outward form; according to form; precise; ceremonious; having mere appearance.

Former, form'er, *n*. He who forms.— *a. comp. deg*. Before in time; long past; mentioned before another.

Formicary, for'mi-ka-ri, *n*. A colony of ants; an ant-hill.

Formidable, for'mid-a-bl, *a*. Exciting fear or apprehension; difficult to deal with or undertake.

Formula, for'mū-la, *n*.; pl. **-lae**. A prescribed form; a confession of faith; expression for resolving certain problems in mathematics; expression of chemical composition.

Formulate, for'mū-lāt, *vt*. To express in a formula; to put into a precise and comprehensive statement.

Fornicate, for'ni-kāt, *vi*. To have unlawful sexual intercourse.

Forte, fōrt, *n*. The strong portion of a swordblade; peculiar talent; strong point; chief excellence.

Forthcoming, fōrth-kum'ing, *a*. Coming forth; making appearance; ready to appear.

Fortification, for'ti-fi-kā''shon, *n*. The art or science of fortifying places; the works erected in defense; a fortified place; additional strength.

Fortify, for'ti-fī, *vt*. (fortifying, fortified). To make strong; to strengthen by forts, batteries, etc.; to invigorate; to increase the strength of.

Fortunate, for'tū-nāt, *a*. Having good fortune; successful; coming by good luck.

Fortune, for'tūn, *n*. Chance; luck; the good or ill that befalls man; means of living; estate; great wealth; destiny; the power regarded as determining the lots of life.

Forty, for'ti, *a*. and *n*. Four times ten.

Forum, fō'rum, *n*. A public place in ancient Rome, where causes were tried; a tribunal; jurisdiction.

Forward, for'werd, *adv*. Toward a place in front; onward.—*a*. Near or towards the forepart; in advance of something; ready; bold; pert; advanced beyond the usual degree; too ready.—*vt*. To help onward; to hasten; to send forward; to transmit.—*n*. In football, hockey, etc., one of the players in the front line.

Foster-child, fos'ter-chīld, *n*. A child nursed by a woman not the mother; or bred by a man not the father. (Also *foster-brother, -mother, -parent,* etc.).

Foul, foul, *a*. Covered with or containing extraneous matter which is offensive; turbid; obscene; rainy or tempestuous; unfair; loathsome; entangled or in collision.— *vt*. To defile; to dirty.—*vi*. To become dirty; to come into collision; to become clogged.—*n*. A colliding, or impeding due motion; an unfair piece of play.

Found, found, *vt*. To lay the base of; to establish; to institute; to form by melting metal and pouring it into a mold; to cast.—*vi*. To rest or rely (with *on* or *upon*). Pret. and pp. of *find*.

Foundation, found-ā'shon, *n*. Act of founding; base of an edifice; base; endowment; endowed institution.

Founder, found'er, *n*. One who lays a foundation; an originator; an endower; one who casts metal.—*vi*. To fill with water and sink; to miscarry; to go lame, as a horse.

Foundry, found'ri, *n*. An establishment for casting metals.

Fountain, fount'ān, *n*. A spring or source of water; an artificial jet or shower; head of a river; original; source.

Fox, foks, *n*. A carnivorous animal, remarkable for cunning; a sly cunning fellow.—*vt*. and *i*. To turn sour; to become marked with brown spots, as paper.

Fracas, fra-käs', *n*. An uproar; a brawl.

Fraction, frak'shon, *n*. A fragment; a very small part; one or more of the equal parts into which a unit or number is divided.

Fractious, frak'shus, *a.* Snappish; peevish; cross.

Fracture, frak'tūr, *n.* A breach or break; breaking of a bone; manner in which a mineral breaks.— *vt.* (fracturing, fractured). To break.

Fragility, fra-jil'i-ti, *n.* Quality of being fragile; delicacy of substance.

Fragment, frag'ment, *n.* A part broken off; an imperfect thing.

Fragrant, frā'grant, *a.* Sweet-smelling; spicy; balmy; aromatic.

Frail, frāl, *a.* Easily broken; weak; liable to fail and decay.—*n.* A kind of basket.

Frame, frām, *vt.* (framing, framed). To make; to construct; to devise; to adjust; to shape; to place in a frame.—*n.* Anything composed of parts fitted together; structure; bodily structure; framework; particular state, as of the mind; mood or disposition.

Framing, frām'ing, *n.* Act of constructing a frame; frame thus constructed; rough timber-work of a house.

Franchise, fran'chīz, *n.* Right granted by a sovereign or government; right of voting for a member of parliament.

Frank, frangk, *a.* Free in uttering real sentiments; candid; outspoken.—*n.* Signature of a privileged person formerly securing free transmission of a letter.—*vt.* To exempt from postage.

Fratricide, fra'tri-sīd, *n.* Murder of a brother; one who murders a brother.

Fraud, frad, *n.* Artifice by which the right or interest of another is injured; deception.

Fray, frā, *n.* An affray; a broil; a night; a frayed place in cloth.—*vt.* To rub; to fret, as cloth, by wearing.—*vi.* Top become worn by rubbing.

Freak, frēk, *n.* A sudden causeless turn of the mind; a caprice; a sport.—*vt.* To variegate.

Freckle, frek'l, *n.* A yellowish spot in the skin; any small spot or discoloration.—*vt.* or *i.* (freckling, freckled). To give or acquire freckles.

Free, frē, *a.* Being at liberty; instituted by a free people; not arbitrary or despotic; open; clear; disjoined; licentious; candid; generous; gratuitous; guiltless.—*vt.* (freeing, freed). To set free; to liberate; to disentangle; to exempt; to absolve from some charge.

Freedom, frē'dum, *n.* State of being free; liberty; particular privilege; facility of doing anything; frankness; undue familiarity.

Free-will, frē'wil, *n.* The power of directing our own actions, without restraint by necessity or fate.—*a.* Spontaneous.

Freeze, frēz, *vi.* (freezing, pret. froze, pp. frozen or froze). To be congealed by cold; to be hardened into ice; to be of that degree of cold at which water congeals; to stagnate; to shiver or stiffen with cold.—*vt.* To congeal; to chill; to make credits, etc., temporarily unrealizable.

Freight, frāt, *n.* The cargo of a ship; lading; hire of a ship; charge for the transportation of goods.—*vt.* To load with goods; to hire for carrying goods.

Frenzy, fren'zi, *n.* Madness; distraction; violent agitation of the mind.

Frequent, frē'kwent, *a.* That takes place repeatedly; often seen or done; doing a thing often.—*vt.* frē-kwent'. To visit often; to resort to habitually.

Fresh, fresh, *a.* Full of health and strength; vigorous; brisk; bright; not faded; in good condition; not stale; cool and agreeable; clearly remembered; new; not salt; unpracticed; unused.

Fret, fret, *vt.* (fretting, fretted). To eat into; to corrode; to wear away; to chafe; to vex; to ornament or furnish with frets; to variegate.—*vi.* To be vexed; to utter peevish expressions; to rankle.—*n.* Irritation; peevishness; an ornament of bands or fillets; a piece of perforated work; one of the crossbars on the finger-board of some stringed instruments.

Friction, frik'shon, *n.* A rubbing; effect of rubbing; resistance which a

F

moving body meets with from the surface on which it moves.

Friday, frī'dā, n. The sixth day of the week.—**Good Friday,** the Friday preceding Easter, sacred as the day of Christ's crucifixion.

Friend, frend, n. One attached to another by affection; a favorer; one who is propitious; a favorite; a Quaker.

Fright, frīt, n. Sudden and violent fear; terror; consternation; an ugly or ill-dressed person.—vt. To frighten.

Frighten, frīt'n, vt. To strike with fright or fear; to terrify; to scare; to alarm.

Frigid, fri'jid, a. Cold; wanting spirit or zeal; stiff; formal; lifeless.

Frigidity, fri-jid'i-ti, n. Coldness; coldness of affection; dullness.

Frill, fril, n. A crisp or plaited edging on an article of dress; a ruffle.—vt. To decorate with frills.

Fringe, frinj, n. An ornamental appendage to furniture or dress, consisting of loose threads; margin; extremity.—vt. (fringing, fringed). To border with fringe or a loose edging.

Frisk, frisk, vi. To dance, skip, and gambol in frolic and gaiety.—n. A frolic; a fit of wanton gaiety.

Frog, frog, n. An amphibious animal, remarkable for its activity in swimming and leaping; a kind of button or tassel on a coat or vestment; a loop used to support a sword or bayonet; horny growth on sole of horse's hoof.

Frolic, fro'lik, a. Joyous; merry; frisky; poetic.—n. A merry prank; merry-making.—vi. To play merry pranks; to gambol.

From, from, prep. Out of the neighborhood or presence of; by reason of; denoting source, distance, absence, departure, etc.

Frond, frond, n. The leaf of a fern or other cryptogamic plant.

Front, frunt, n. The forehead; the whole face; the fore part; boldness; impudence; the area of military operations.—a. Relating to the front or face.—vt. To stand with the front opposed to; to oppose; to face; to supply with a front.—vi. To

face; to look.

Frontage, frunt'āj, n. The front part of an edifice, quay, etc.

Frontal, frunt'al, a. Belonging to the forehead.—n. An ornament for the forehead; a frontlet; a small pediment.

Frontier, fron'tēr, n. That part of a country which fronts another country; extreme part of a country.—a. Bordering; conterminous.

Frontispiece, fron'tis-pēs, n. The principal face of a building; an illustration facing the title- page of a book.

Frost, frost, n. That temperature of the air which causes freezing; frozen dew; rime; coldness or severity of manner.—vt. To injure by frost; to ornament with anything resembling hoar-frost; to frunish with frost-nails.

Froward, frō'wērd, a. Perverse; ungovernable; disobedient; peevish.

Frown, froun, vi. To express displeasure by contracting the brow; to look stern; to scowl.—n. A wrinkling of the brow; a sour or stern look; any expression of displeasure.

Fruit, fröt, n. Whatever of a vegetable nature is of use to man or animals; the reproductive produce of a plant; such products collectively; the seed or matured ovary; that which is produced; offspring; effect; outcome.—vi. To produce fruit.

Frustrate, frus'trāt, vt. (frustrating, frustrated). To balk; to foil; to bring to nothing; to render of no effect.

Frustration, frus-trā'shon, n. Disappointment; defeat.

Fry, fri, vt. (frying, fried). To cook by roasting over a fire.—vi. To be cooked as above; to simmer; to be in agitation.—n. A dish of anything fried; state of mental ferment; young fishes at an early stage; swarm of small fishes, etc.; insignificant objects.

Fuchsia, fū'shi-a, n. A beautiful flowering shrub.

Fuddle, fud'l, vt. (fuddling, fuddled). To make stupid by drink; to spend in drinking.—vi. To drink to excess.

Fuel, fū'el, *n*. That which serves to feed fire, or to increase excitement. etc.—*vt*. To feed or furnish with fuel.

Fugitive, fū-jit-iv, *a*. Apt to flee away; volatile; fleeting; vagabond; temporary.—*n*. One who flees from duty or danger; refugee.

Full, ful, *a*. Having all it can contain; abounding; crowded; entire; strong; loud; clear; mature; perfect; ample.—*n*. Complete measure; the highest state or degree (usually with *the*). —*adv*. Quite; altogether; exactly; directly.—*vt*. To scour and thicken, as woolen cloth, in a mill.

Fumble, fum'bli, *vi*. (fumbling, fumbled). To grope about awkwardly; to attempt or handle something bunglingly.

Fume, fūm, *n*. Smoke; vapor; exhalation from the stomach, as of liquor; heat of passion.—*vi*. (fuming, fumed). To yield vapor or visible exhalations; to be hot with anger.—*vt*. To smoke; to perfume; to disperse in vapors.

Fumigate, fūm'i-gāt, *vt*. (fumigating, fumigated). To smoke; to purify from infection, etc.

Fun, fun, *n*. Sportive acts or words; merriment.

Function, fungk'shon, *n*. Performance; office; duty; proper office of any organ in animals or vegetables; a ceremonial; a mathematical quantity connected with and varying with another.

Fund, fund, *n*. A stock or capital; money set apart for any object more or less permanent; store; supply.—*vt*. To provide and appropriate a fund for paying the interest of, as a debt; to place in a fund, as money.

Fundamental, fun-da-ment'al, *a*. Pertaining to the foundation; essential; primary.—*n*. A leading principle which serves as the groundwork of a system; an essential.

Funeral, fū'ne-ral, *n*. Burial; ceremony of burying a dead body.—*a*. Used at the interment of the dead.

Funereal, fū-nē're-al, *a*. Suiting a funeral; dark; dismal; mournful.

Funny, fun'i, *a*. Making fun; droll; comical.

Fur, fer, *n*. The short, fine, soft hair of certain animals, growing thick on the skin; furred animals collectively; something resembling fur.—*a*. Pertaining to or made of fur.—*vt*. (furring, furred). To line or cover with fur.

Furnace, fer'nās, *n*. A structure in which a vehement fire may be maintained for melting ores, heating water, etc.; place or occasion of torture or trial.

Furnish, fer'nish, *vt*. To supply; to equip; to yield; to provide.

Furniture, fer'ni-tūr, *n*. That with which anything is furnished; equipment; outfit; movable wooden articles in a house.

Furor, fū'ror, *n*. Fury; rage.

Furrow, fu'rō, *n*. A trench made by a plough; a groove; a wrinkle.—*vt*. To make furrows in; to groove; to wrinkle.

Further, fer'THer, *adv*. More in advance; besides; farther.—*a*. More distant; farther.—*vt*. To help forward; to advance.

Furtive, fer'tiv, *a*. Stolen; sly; stealthy.

Fury, fū'ri, *n*. Rage; a violent rushing; frenzy; a goddess of vengeance, in mythology; a violent woman.

Fusion, fū'zhon, *n*. Act or operation of fusing; state of being melted or blended; complete union.

Fuss, fus, *n*. Bustle; much ado about trifles.—*vi*. To make a fuss or bustle.

Fusty, fus'ti, *n*. Tasting or smelling of a foul or moldy cask; moldy; ill-smelling.

Futile, fū'til *a*. Serving no useful end; trivial; worthless.

Futility, fū-til'i-ti, *n*. Quality of being futile; worthlessness; unimportance.

Future, fū'tūr, *a*. That is to be; pertaining to time to come.—*n*. The time to come; all that is to happen; the future tense.

Fuzz, fuz, *vi*. To fly off in particles.—*n*. Fine part; volatile matter.

F

G

Gab, gab, *vi.* (gabbling, gabbed). To talk much; to chatter.—*n.* Idle talk.

Gabble, gab'l, *vi.* (gabbling, gabbled). To talk fast, or without meaning.—*n.* Rapid talk without meaning; inarticulate sounds rapidly uttered.

Gadget, gad'jet, *n.* A tool, appliance, or contrivance.

Gain, gān, *vt.* To obtain; to get, as profit or advantage; to receive, as honor; to win to one's side; to conciliate; to reach, arrive at.—*vi.* To reap advantage or profit; to make progress.—*n.* Something obtained as an advantage; profit; benefit.

Gall, gal, *n.* A bitter fluid secreted in the liver; bile; rancor; malignity; an excrescence produced by the egg of an insect on a plant, especially the oak; a sore place in the skin from rubbing.—*vt.* To make a sore in the skin of by rubbing; to fret; to vex; to harass.

Gallant, gal'ant, *a.* Gay in attire; handsome; brave; showing politeness and attention to ladies (in this sense also pron. ga-lant').—*n.* A gay sprightly man; a daring spirit; (pron. also ga-lant') a man attentive to ladies; suitor; paramour.—*vt.* ga-lant'. To act the gallant towards; to be very attentive to (a lady).

Gallantry, gal'ant-ri, *n.* Show; bravery; intrepidity; polite attentions to ladies; vicious love or pretentions to love.

Gallery, gal'ė-ri, *n.* A long apartment serving as a passage of communication, or for the receptio of pictures, etc.; upper floor of a church, theatre, etc.; a covered passage; frame like a balcony projected from a ship.

Gallop, gal'up, *vi.* To move or run with leaps; to ride at this pace; to move very fast.—*n.* The pace of a horse, by springs or leaps.

Gallows, gal'ōz, *n. sing.* or *pl.*; also **Gallowses,** gal'ōz-ez, in *pl.* A structure for the hanging of crimi-

nals; one of a pair of braces for the trousers.

Gambit, gam'bit, *n.* An opening in chess incurring the sacrifice of a pawn.

Gamble, gam'bl, *vi.* (gambling, gambled). To play for money.

Gambling, gam'bl-ing, *n.* The act or practice of gaming for money or anything valuable.

Gambol, gam'bol, *vi.* (gamboling, gamboled). To skip about in sport; to frisk; to frolic.—*n.* A skipping about in frolic; a prank.

Game, gām, *n.* Sport of any kind; exercise for amusement, testing skill, etc.; scheme pursued; field-sports; animals hunted.—*vi.* (gaming, gamed). To play at any sport; to play for a stake or prize; to practice gaming. **To die game,** to maintain a bold spirit to the last.

Gamester, gām'stėr, *n.* A person addicted to gaming; a gambler.

Gamin, gam'in, *n.* A street arab; a neglected street-boy.

Gaming, gām'ing, *n.* The act or practice of gambling.

Gangrene, gang'grēn, *n.* An eating away of the flesh; first stage of mortification.—*vt.* (gangrening, gangrened). To mortify.—*vi.* To become mortified.

Gangster, gang'stėr, *n.* A member of a criminal organization.

Gap, gap, *n.* An opening; breach; hiatus; chasm.

Gape, gāp, *vi.* (gaping, gaped). To open the mouth wide; to yawn; to open in fissures; to stand open.—*n.* A gaping; the width of the mouth when opened, as of a bird, fish, etc.

Garage, gar'aj, *n.* A place for housing or repairing motor-cars.

Garb, gärb, *n.* Dress; clothes; mode of dress.—*vt.* To dress.

Garbage, gärb'āj, *n.* Waste matter; offal; vegetable refuse.

Garble, gär'bl, *vt.* (garbling, garbled). To pick out such parts as may serve a purpose; to falsify by leaving out parts; to corrupt.

Garlic, gär'lik, *n.* A plant allied to the onion, with a pungent taste and strong odor.

Garment, gär'ment, *n.* An article of

clothing, as a coat, a gown, etc.

Garner, gär'nėr, *n*. A granary; a store.—*vt*. To store in a granary; to store up.

Garnet, gär'net, *n*. A precious stone, generally of a red color.

Garnish, gär'nish, *vt*. To adorn; to embellish (a dish) with something laid round.—*n*. Ornament; an embellishment round a dish.

Garret, ga'ret, *n*. A room in a house on the uppermost floor, immediately under the roof.

Garrison, ga'ri-sn, *n*. A body of troops stationed in a fort or town.—*vt*. To place a garrison in.

Garrotte, ga-rot', *vt*. To rob by seizing a person and compressing his windpipe till he become helpless.

Garrulity, ga-rū'li-ti, *n*. Loquacity; practice or habit to talking much.

Garter, gär'tėr, *n*. A band to hold up a stocking; the badge of the highest order or knighthood in Great Britain; the order itself.—*vt*. To bind with a garter.

Gasp, gasp, *vi*. To open the mouth wide to catch breath; to labor for breath; to pant.—*vt*. To emit with a gasp.—*n*. Short painful catching of the breath.

Gasteropod, Gastropod, gas'tėr-o-pod, gas'trō-pod, *n*. A mollusc such as snails, having a broad muscular foot attached to the ventral surface.

Gastric, gas'trik, *a*. Belonging to the stomach.

Gastronomy, gas-tron'o-mi, *n*. The art or science of good eating; epicurism.

Gate, gāt, *n*. A large door or entrance; a frame of timber, iron, etc., closing an entrance, etc.; a way or passage; the frame which stops the passage of water through a dam, lock, etc.

Gate-crasher, gāt-krash'ėr, *n*. An uninvited guest; one who obtains admission to a public entertainment without a ticket.

Gateway, gāt'wā, *n*. A way through the gate of some enclosure; the gate itself.

Gather, gaTH'ėr, *vt*. To bring together; to collect; to acquire; to pucker; to deduce by inference.—

vi. To assemble; to increase.—*n*. A fold in cloth, made by drawing; a pucker.

Gazette, ga-zet', *n*. A newspaper, especially an official newspaper.—*vt*. (gazetting, gazetted). To insert in a gazette; to announce or public officially.

Gazetteer, ga-zet-tēr', *n*. A writer or publisher of news; a dictionary of geographical information.

Gear, gēr, *n*. Dress; ornaments; apparatus; harness; tackle; a train of toothed wheels.—*vt*. To put gear on; to harness.

Gelatine, jel'a-tin, *n*. A concrete transparent substance obtained by boiling from certain parts of animals; the principle of jelly; glue.

Geld, geld, *vt*. To castrate; to emasculate.

Gelding, geld'ing, *n*. Act of castrating; a castrated animal, but chiefly a horse.

Gelid, je'lid, *a*. Icy cold; frosty or icy.

Gem, jem, *n*. A precious stone of any kind; a jewel; anything remarkable for beauty or rarity.—*vt*. (gemming, gemmed). To adorn, as with gems; to bespangle; to embellish.

Gemini, jem'i-nī, *n.pl*. The Twins, a sign of the zodiac, containing the two stars Castor and Pollux.

General, jen'ė-ral, *a*. Of or belonging to a genus; not special; public; common; extensive, though not universal; usual; taken as a whole.—*n*. The whole; a comprehensive notion; a military officer of the highest rank.

Generous, jen'ė-rus, *a*. Noble; bountiful; liberal; full of spirit, as wine; courageous, as a steed.

Genesis, jen'e-sis, *n*. Act of producing; origin; first book of the Old Testament.

Genetic, Genetical, jen-net'ik, je-net'ik-al, *a*. Relating to origin or production.

Genial, jē'ni-al, *a*. Cordial kindly; contributing to life and cheerfulness.

Geniality, jē-ni-al'i-ti, *n*. Sympathetic cheerfulness or cordiality.

Genitals, jen'it-alz, *n.pl.* the parts of generation; sexual organs.

Genitive, jen'it-iv, *a.* and *n.* Applied to a case of nouns, pronouns, etc., in English called the possessive.

Genius, je'ni-us, *n.*; pl. **Geniuses,** jē'ni-us-ez; in first sense **Genii,** jē'ni-ī. A tutelary deity; aptitude of mind for a particular study or course of life; uncommon powers of intellect; a man with uncommon intellectual faculties; nature; peculiar character.

Genre, zhäng-r, *n.* A term applied to the department of painting which depicts scenes of ordinary life.

Genteel, jen-tēl, *a.* Having the manners of well-bred people; refined; elegant.

Gentle, jen'tl, *a.* Well-born; refined in manners; mild; placid; not rough, violent, or wild; soothing.— *n.* A person of good birth.

Gentleman, jen'tl-man, *n.* A man of good social position; technically any man above the rank of yeoman, comprehending noblemen; a man of good breeding or of high honor; a polite equivalent for 'man.'

Genuflection, jen-ū-flek'shon, *n.* The act of bending the knee, particularly in worship.

Genuine, jen'ū-in, *a.* Belonging to the original stock; real; pure; true.

Genus, jē'nus, *n.*; pl. **Genera** jen'ē-ra. A kind, class, or sort; an assemblage of species having distinctive characteristics in common.

Geometry, jē-om'e-tri, *n.* The science of magnitude; that branch of mathematics which treats of the properties and relations of lines, angles, surfaces, and solids.

Germinate, jėrm'in-āt, *vi.* (germinating, germinated). To sprout; to bud; to begin to vegetate or grow, as seeds.

Gerrymander, ge'ri-man-dėr, *vt.* To arrange so as to get an unfair result from the distribution of voters in political elections.

Gerund, je'rund, *n.* A kind of verbal noun in Latin; a verbal noun, such as 'teaching' in 'fit for teaching boys.'

Gestation, jest-ā'shon, *n.* The carrying of young in the womb from conception to delivery; pregnancy.

Gesticulate, jes-tik'ū-lāt, *vi.* To make gestures or motions, as in speaking.— *vt.* To represent by gesture; to act.

Gesture, jes'tür, *n.* A posture or motion of the body of limbs; action intended to express an idea or feeling; or to enforce an argument.

Get, get, *vt.* (getting, pret. got, pp. got, gotten). To obtain; to gain; to reach; to beget; to learn; to induce.— *vi.* To arrive at any place or state by degrees; to become; to make gain.

Geyser, gī'zėr, *n.* A hot-water spring, the water rising in a column.

Ghastly, gast'li, *a.* Deathlike in looks; hideous; frightful, as wounds.

Giant, jī'ant, *n.* A man of extraordinary stature; a person of extraordinary powers, bodily or intellectual.— *a.* Like a giant; extraordinary in size.

Gibberish, gib'bėr-ish, *n.* Rapid and inarticulate talk; unmeaning words.

Gibbet, jib'bet, *n.* A gallows; the projecting beam of a crane, on which the pulley is fixed.— *vt.* To hang on a gibbet; to expose to scorn, infamy, etc.

Gift, gift, *n.* Anything given; act of giving; power of giving; talent or faculty.— *vt.* To endow with any power or faculty.

Giggle, gig'l, *n.* A kind of laugh, with short catches of the voice or breath.— *vi.*(giggling, giggled). To laugh with short catches of the breath; to titter.

Gigot, jig'ot, *n.* A leg of mutton.

Gild, gild, *vt.* (pret. and pp. gilded or gilt). To overlay with gold in leaf or powder; to illuminate; to give a fair and agreeable appearance to.

Gill, gil, *n.* The organ of respiration in fishes; the flap below the beak of a fowl; the flesh on the lower part of the cheeks.

Gin, jin, *n.* A distilled spirit flavored

with juniper berries; a machine for driving piles, raising great weights, etc.; a machine for separating the seeds from cotton; a trap, snare.—*vt.* (ginning, ginned). To clear of seeds by a cotton-gin; to catch in a trap.

Ginger, jin'jèr, *n.* A tropical plant, the root of which has a hot, spicy quality.

Giraffe, ji-raf', *n.* The camelopard, the tallest of animals.

Gird, gèrd, *vt.* (pp. girded or girt). To bind; to make fast by binding; to invest; to encompass.—*vi.* To gibe; to sneer.—*n.* A stroke with a whip; a twitch; a sneer.

Girder, gèrd'èr, *n.* One who girds; a main beam supporting a superstructure.

Girdle, gèr'dl, *n.* That which girds; a band or belt; something drawn round the waist and tied or buckled.—*vt.* (girdling, girdled). To bind with a girdle; belt, or sash; to gird.

Girl, gèrl, *n.* A female child; young woman.

Girth, gèrth, *n.* That which girds; band fastening a saddle on a horse's back; measure round a person's body or anything cylindrical.

Gist, jist, *n.* The main point of a question; substance or pith of a matter.

Give, giv, *vt.* (giving, pret. gave, pp. given). To bestow; to deliver; to impart; to yield; to afford; to utter; to show; to send forth; to devote (oneself); to pledge; to allow; to ascribe.—*vi.* To make gifts; to yield to pressure; to recede.

Gizzard, giz'èrd, *n.* The muscular stomach of a bird.

Glacier, glā'shi-èr, *n.* An immense mass of ice formed in valleys above the snow-line, and having a slow movement downwards.

Glad, glad, *a.* Affected with pleasure; pleased; cheerful; imparting pleasure.—*vt.* (gladding, gladded). To make glad; to gladden.

Glance, gläns, *n.* A sudden shoot of light or splendor; a glimpse or sudden look.—*vi.* (glancing, glanced). To shine; to gleam; to dart aside; to look with a sudden rapid cast of the eye; to move quickly; to hint.—*vt.* To shoot or dart suddenly or obliquely; to cast for a moment.

Gland, gland, *n.* An acorn; any acorn-shaped fruit; a roundish organ in many parts of the body secreting some fluid; a secreting organ in plants.

Glare, glār, *n.* A bright dazzling light; a fierce piercing look.—*vi.* (glaring, glared). To shine with excessive luster; to look with fierce piercing eyes.

Glass, gläs, *n.* A hard transparent substance; a small drinking vessel of glass; a mirror; quantity of liquor that a glass vessel contains; a lens; a telescope; a barometer; *pl.* spectacles.—*a.* Made of glass; vitreous.

Glazier, glā'zhèr, *n.* One whose business is to set window-glass.

Gleam, glēm, *n.* A small stream of light; brightness.—*vi.* To shoot or dart, as rays of light; to shine; to flash.

Glider, glīd'èr, *n.* A modification of the airplane, which can travel through the air for a certain time without engine power.

Glimmer, glim'èr, *vi.* To shine faintly, and with frequent intermissions; to flicker.—*n.* A faint light; a twinkle.

Glimpse, glimps, *n.* A gleam or flash of light; short transitory view; faint resemblance; slight tinge.—*vi.* To appear by glimpses.

Globe, glōb, *n.* A round solid body; a sphere; the earth; an artificial sphere on whose surface is drawn a map of the earth or heavens.—*vt.* To gather into a round mass.

Globule, glob'ūl, *n.* A little globe; a small spherical particle; one of the red particles of the blood.

Globulin, glob'ū-lin, *n.* The main ingredient of blood globules and resembling albumen.

Gloom, glōm, *n.* Obscurity; thick shade; sadness; aspect of sorrow; darkness of prospect or aspect.—*vi.* To shine obscurely; to be cloudy or dark; to be sullen or sad.

Glorify, glō'ri-fī, *vt.* (glorifying, glorified). to make glorious; to ascribe glory or honor to; to extol.

Glorious, glō'ri-us, *a.* Full of glory; renowned; celebrated; grand; brilliant.

Glory, glō'ri, *n.* Praise, honor, admiration, or distinction; renown; magnificence; celestial bliss; the divine presence; the divine perfections; that of which one may be proud.—*vi.* (glorying, gloried). To boast; to rejoice; to be proud with regard to something.

Gloss, glos, *n.* Brightness from a smooth surface; sheen; specious appearance; an interpretation; comment.—*vt.* To give superficial luster to; to give a specious appearance to; to render plausible; to comment; to annotate.

Glossary, glos'a-ri, *n.* A vocabulary explaining antiquated or difficult words or phrases.

Glow, glō, *vi.* To burn with intense heat, especialy without flame; to feel great heat of body; to be flushed; to be ardent; to rage.—*n.* White heat; brightness of color; animation.

Glowworm, glō'werm, *n.* A wingless female beetle which emits a greenish light.

Glucose, glō'kōs, *n.* Grape-sugar, a sugar produced from grapes, starch, etc.

Glue, glō, *n.* A tenacious, viscid matter which serves as a cement.—*vt.* (gluing, glued). To join with glue; to unite.

Glum, glum, *a.* Sullen; moody; dejected.

Glycerine, glis'er-in, *n.* A transparent, colorless, sweet liquid obtained from fats.

Glyphic, glif'ik, *a.* Of or pertaining to carving or sculpture.

Glyptic, glip'tik, *a.* Pertaining to the art of engraving on precious stones.

Gnarl, närl, *n.* A protuberance on the outside of a tree; a knot.

Gnash, nash, *vt.* To strike together, as the teeth. —*vi.* To strike or dash the teeth together, as in rage or pain.

Gnat, nat, *n.* A small two-winged fly, the female of which bites.

Gnaw, nä, *vt.* To bite by little and little; to bite in agony or rage; to fret;

to corrode.—*vi.* To use the teeth in biting; to cause steady annoying pain.

Gneiss, nīs, *n.* A species of rock composed of quartz, feldspar, and mica, and having a slaty structure.

Gnome, nōm, *n.* A sprite supposed to inhabit the inner parts of the earth; a dwarf; a maxim, aphorism.

Go, gō, *vi.* (going, pret, went, pp. gone). To move; to proceed; to depart; to be about to do; to circulate; to tend; to be guided; to be alienated or sold; to reach; to avail; to conduce; to die; to fare; to become.

Goad, gōd, *n.* A pointed instrument to make a beast move faster; anything that stirs into action. *vt.* To drive with a goad; to instigate.

Goal, gōl, *n.* The point set to bound a race; a mark that players in some outdoor sport must attain; a success scored by reaching this; final purpose; end.

Goat, gōt, *n.* A ruminant quadruped with long hair and horns.

Gobble, gob'l, *vt.* (gobbling, gobbled). To swallow in large pieces or hastily.—*vi.* To make a noise in the throat, as a turkey.

Goggle, gog'l, *vi.* (goggling, goggled). To roll or strain the eyes.—*a.* Prominent, rolling, or staring (eyes).—*n.* A strained or affected rolling of the eye; *pl.* a kind of spectacles to protect the eyes or cure squinting.

Going, gō'ing, *n.* Act of one who goes; departure; way; state of roads.—**Goings-on,** actions; behavior.

Goiter, goi'ter, *n.* A morbid enlargment of the thyroid gland, forming a masss on the front of the neck.

Gold, gōld, *n.* A precious metal of a bright yellow color; money; something pleasing or valuable; a bright yellow color.—*a.* Made or consisting of gold.

Golden, gōld'n, *a.* Made of gold; like gold; splendid; most valuable; auspicious.

Gong, gong, *n.* A kind of metallic drum; a similar article used instead of a bell.

Good, gụd, *a.* The opposite of bad; wholesome; useful; fit; virtuous; valuable; benevolent; clever; adequate; valid; able to fulfil engagements; considerable; full or complete; immaculate.—*n.* What is good or desirable; advantage; welfare; virtue; *pl.* commodities, chattels, movables.—**For good,** to close the whole business; finally.—*interj.* Well; right.

Goose, gös, *n.*; pl. **Geese,** gēs. A swimming bird larger than the duck; a tailor's smoothing-iron; a silly person.

Gooseberry, gös'be-ri, *n.* The fruit of a prickly shrub, and the shrub itself.

Gopher, gō'fẻr, *n.* The name given in America to several burrowing animals.

Gordian knot, gor'di-an not. An inextricable difficulty; *to cut the Gordian knot,* to remove a diffculity by bold measures.

Gore, gōr, *n.* Blood that is shed; thick or clotted blood; a wedge-shaped piece of land or cloth; a gusset.—*vt.* (goring, gored). To cut in a triangular form; to pierce with a pointed instrument, or an animal's horns.

Gorge, gorj, *n.* The throat; the gullet; a narrow passage between hills or mountains; entrance into a bastion.—*vt.* and *i.* (gorging, gorged). To swallow with greediness; to glut; to satiate.

Gory, gō'ri, *a.* Covered with gore; bloody; murderous.

Gosling, goz'ling, *n.* A young goose.

Gospel, gos'pel, *n.* The history of Jesus Christ; any of the four records of Christ's life by his apostles; scheme of salvation as taught by Christ; any general doctrine.— *a.* Relating to the gospel; accordant with the gospel.

Gossamer, gos'a-mẻr, *n.* A fine, filmy substance, like cobwebs, floating in the air in calm, sunny weather; a thin fabric.

Gossip, gos'ip, *n.* An idle tattler; idle talk. *vi.* To prate; to run about and tattle.

Gourd, görd, *n.* The popular name of the family of plants represented by the melon, cucumber, etc.; a cup made from the rind of a gourd.

Gourmet, gör-mā or gör'met, *n.* A connoisseur in wines and meats; a nice feeder.

Gout, gout, *n.* A painful disease, affecting generally the small joints; a drop; a clot or coagulation.

Govern, gu'vẻrn, *vt.* To direct and control; to regulate; to steer; to affect so as to determine the case, etc., in grammar.—*vi.* To exercise authority; to administer the laws.

Governess, gu'vẻrn-es, *n.* A female who governs or instructs.

Government, gu'vẻrn-ment, *n.* Rule; control; administration of public affairs; system of polity in a state; territory ruled by a governor; executive power; the influence of a word in grammar in regard to construction.

Governor, gu'vẻrn-ẻr, *n.* One who governs; one invested with supreme authority; a tutor; a contrivance in machinery for maintaining a uniform velocity.

Gown, goun, *n.* A woman's outer garment; a long, loose garment worn by professional men, as divines.—*vt.* To put on a gown.

Grab, grab, *vt.* (grabbing, grabbed). To seize; to snatch.—*n.* A sudden grasp; implement for clutching objects.

Grace, grās, *n.* Favor; kindness; love and favor of God; state of reconciliation to God; pardon; license or privilege; expression of thanks before or after meals; title of a duke or archbishop; elegance with appropriate dignity; an embellishment; one of three ancient goddesses in whose gift were grace and beauty; in *music,* a trill, shake, etc.—*vt.* (gracing, graced). To lend grace to; to adorn; to favor.

Gracious, grā'shus, *a.* Full of grace; favorable; disposed to forgive offenses and impart blessings; benignant; condescending.

Gradation, gra-dā'shon, *n* rangement by grades; reg·· vance step by step; ra·

G

regular process by degrees.

Grade, grād, *n.* A step; degree; rank; gradient.—*vt.* (grading, graded). To arrange in order of rank, etc.; to reduce to a suitable slope.

Gradient, grā'di-ent, *a.* Moving by steps; rising or descending by regular degrees.—*n.* The degree of ascent or descent in a road, etc.; part of a road which slopes.

Graduate, grad'ū-āt, *vt.* (graduating, graduated). To divide into regular intervals or degrees; to mark with such; to arrange by grades; to confer a university degree on; to reduce to a certain consistency by evaporation.—*vi.* To receive a university degree; to change gradually.—*n.* One who has received a degree of a university, etc.

Graft, graft, *n.* A small scion of a tree inserted in another tree which is to support and nourish the scion; corrupt gains or practices in politics.—*vt.* To insert a graft on; to propagate by a graft; to join on as if organically; a part.

Grail, Graal, grāl, *n.* The holy vessel containing the last drops of Christ's blood, brought to England by Joseph of Arimathea, and, being afterwards lost, eagerly sought for by King Arthur's knights.

Grain, grān, *n.* A single seed of a plant; corn in general; a minute particle; a small weight; fibers of wood with regard to their arrangement; substance of a thing with respect to the size, form, or direction of the constituent particles; texture; dye.—*vt.* To paint in imitation of fibers; to granulate.

Gram, gram, *n.* The French unit of weight, equal to 15.43 grains troy.

Grammar, gram'ér, *n.* A system of principles and rules for speaking or writing a language; propriety of speech; an outline of any subject.

Grammatical, Grammatic, grammat'ik-al, gram-mat'ik, *a.* Belonging to grammar; according to the rules of grammar.

Granary, gra'na-ri, *n.* A storehouse for grain after it is thrashed.

Grand, grand, *a.* Great, figuratively; majestic; magnificent; noble.

Grandchild, grand'chīld, *n.* A son's or daughter's child.

Grand-daughter, grand'da-tér, *n.* The daughter of a son or daughter.

Grandeur, grand'yūr, *n.* Greatness; sublimity; splendor; magnificence.

Granulate, gran'ū-lāt, *vt.* and *i* (granulating, granulated). To form into grains; to make or become rough on the surface.

Granulation, gran-ū-lā'shon, *n.* Act of forming into grains; a process by which minute fleshy bodies are formed on wounds during healing; the fleshy grains themselves.

Grasp, gräsp, *vt.* To seize and hold by the fingers or arms; to take possession of; to comprehend.—*vi.* To make a clutch or catch.—*n.* Gripe of the hand; reach of the arms; power of seizing or comprehending.

Grass, gräs, *n.* Herbage; any plant of the family to which belong the grain-yielding and pasture plants.—*vt.* To cover with grass; to bleach on the grass.

Grasshopper, gräs'hop-ér, *n.* An insect that hops among grass, allied to the locusts.

Grate, grāt, *n.* A frame composed of parallel or cross-bars; grating; iron frame for holding coals used as fuel.—*vt.* (grating, grated). To furnish or make fast with crossbars; to wear away in small particles by rubbing; to offend. as by a discordant sound.—*vi.* To rub roughly on; to have an annoying effect; to sound harshly.

Grateful, grāt'ful, *a.* Pleasing; gratifying; feeling or expressing gratitude.

Grave, grāv, *vt.* (graving, pret. graved, pp. graven, graved). To make incisions on; to engrave; to impress deeply; as on the mind; to clean, as a ship's bottom, and cover with pitch.—*n.* A pit for the dead; a tomb.—*a.* Weighty; serious; staid; thoughtful; not gay; not tawdry; in *music,* low.

Gravel, gra'vel, *n.* Small pebbles; a

disease produced by small con-
cretions in the kidneys and bladder.—*vt.* (gravelling, gravelled). To
cover with gravel; to cause to stick
in the sand or gravel; to puzzle.

Gravely, gräv'li, *adv.* In a grave,
solemn manner; soberly; seriously.

Gravid, grav'id, *a.* Being with
young; pregnant.

Gravitate, grav'i-tāt, *vt.* To be affected by gravitation; to tend
towards the center.

Gravitation, grav-i-tā'shon, *n.* The
force by which bodies are drawn
towards the center of the earth;
tendency of all matter toward all
other matter.

Gravity, grav'i-ti, *n.* The tendency
of matter toward some attracting
body, particularly toward the center of the earth; state or character
of being grave; weight; enormity.

Gravy, grā'vi, *n.* The juice that
comes from flesh in cooking.

Gray, grā, *a.* Of the color of hair
whitened by age; white with a
mixture of black; having gray
hairs.—*n.* A gray color; a gray animal, as a horse; early morning
twilight.

Graze, grāz, *vt.* (grazing, grazed).
To rub or touch lightly in passing;
to feed with growing grass, as cattle; to feed on.—*vi.* to pass so as to
rub lightly; to eat grass; to supply
grass.—*n.* A slight rub or brush.

Grease, grēs, *n.* Animal fat in a soft
state; oily matter.—*vt.* (greasing,
greased). To smear with grease.

Great, grāt, *a.* Large in bulk or
number; long-continued; of vast
power and excellence; eminent;
majestic; pregnant; distant by one
more generation, as *great*-grandfa-
ther, etc.

Greet, grēt, *vt.* To salute; to meet
and address with kindness.—*vi.*
To meet and salute.

Gregarious, grē-gā'ri-us, *a.* Assembling or living in a flock; not habitually solitary.

Grenade, gre-nād', *n.* A small
bomb, thrown by hand or fired
from a rifle.

Greyhound, grā'hound, *n.* A tall,
slender, fleet dog kept for the
chase.

Griddle, grid'l, *n.* A circular plate
of iron, or a shallow pan, for baking cakes.

Grief, grēf, *n.* Pain of mind produced by loss, misfortune, etc.;
sorrow; cause of sorrow; trouble.

Grievance, grēv'ans, *n.* A wrong
suffered; cause of complaint; trouble.

Grieve, grēv, *vt.* (grieving, grieved).
To cause grief to; to deplore.—*vi.*
To feel grief; to sorrow; to lament.

Grim, grim, *a.* of a forbidding or
fear-inspiring aspect; stern; sullen; surly; ugly.

Grimace, gri-mās', *n.* A distortion
of the countenance; air of affectation.—*vi.* To make grimaces.

Grime, grīm, *n.* Foul matter.—*vt.*
(griming, grimed). To sully or soil
deeply.

Grin, grin, *vi.* (grinning, grinned).
To show the teeth, as in laughter,
scorn, or anguish—*n.* Act of showing the teeth; a forced smile or restrained laugh.

Grind, grīnd, *vt.* (grinding, ground).
To reduce to fine particles; to
sharpen or polish by friction; to
rub together; to oppress; to crush
in pieces.—*vi.* To turn a mill; to be
moved or rubbed together; to be
puverized by friction; to study
hard.—*n.* Act of one who grinds; a
laborious spell of work.

Grindstone, grīnd'stōn, *n.* A circular stone, made to revolve, to
sharpen tools.

Grip, grip, *n.* The act of grasping;
grasp; a fast hold; a hilt or handle.—*vt.* and *i* (gripping, gripped).
To grasp by the hand; to clutch; to
hold fast.

Groan, grōn, *vi.* To utter a mournful
voice, as in pain or sorrow; to
moan.—*n.* A deep, mournful
sound, uttered in pain, sorrow, or
disapprobation; any low rumbling
sound.

Groin, groin, *n.* The part of the human body between the belly and
thigh in front; the angular projecting curve made by the intersec-
tion of simple vaults at any ang'

Gross, grōs, *a.* Thick; coars'
scene; palpable; dense; s'

G

dull; whole.—*n*. Main body; bulk; the number of twelve dozen.

Grotesque, grō-tesk´, *a*. Wildly formed; extravagant; fantastic.— *n*. Whimsical figures or scenery.

Grotto, grot´tō, *n*. A natural cave; an artificial ornamented cave.

Ground, ground, *n*. Surface of the earth; soil; land; basis; reason; foil or background; predominating color; *pl*. dregs, sediment; ornamental land about a mansion—*vt*. To set on the ground; to found; to fix firmly; to instruct in first principles.—*vi*. To strike the bottom and remain fixed, as a ship.

Grove, grōv, *n*. A shady cluster of trees; a small wood.

Grovel, gro´vel, *vi*. (grovelling, grovelled). To lie prone, or creep on the earth; to be low or mean.

Grow, grō, *vi*. (pret, grew, pp. grown). To be augmented by natural process; to increase; to make progress; to become; to accrue; to swell.—*vt*. To raise from the soil; to produce.

Growl, groul, *vi*. To murmur or snarl, as a dog; to utter an angry, grumbling sound.—*vt*. to express by growling.—*n*. Angry sound of a dog; grumbling murmur.

Grown, grōn, *p.a*. Increased in growth; having arrived at full size or stature.

Growth, grōth, *n*. Act or process of growing; product; increase; advancement.

Grub, grub, *vi*.(grubbing, grubbed). To dig; to be employed meanly.— *vt*. To dig; to root out by digging.— *n*. The larva of an insect; caterpillar; maggot.

Grudge, gruj, *vi*. (grudging, grudged). To cherish ill-will; to be envious.—*vt*. To permit or grant with reluctance; to envy.—*n*. Reluctance in giving; secret enmity.

Gruel, grü´el, *n*. A light food made by boiling meal in water.

Gruesome, grö´sum, *a*. Causing one to shudder; frightful; horrible; repulsive.

Guarantee, ga-ran-tē´, *n*. An undertaking by a third person that a covenant shall be observed by the contracting parties or by one of them; one who binds himself to see the stipulations of another performed.—*vt*. (guaranteeing, guaranteed). To warrant; to pledge oneself for.

Guard, gärd, *vt*. To keep watch over; to secure against injury, loss, or attack.—*vi*. To watch, by way of caution or defense; to be in a state of caution or defense.—*n*. Defense; protector; sentinel; escort; attention; caution; posture of defense.

Guess, ges, *vt*. To conjecture; to form an opinion without certain means of knowledge; to surmise.—*vi*. To conjecture; to judge at random.—*n*. Conjecture; surmise.

Guest, gest, *n*. A visitor or friend entertained in the house or at the table of another.

Guffaw, guf-fa´, *n*. A loud burst of laughter.—*vi*. To burst into a loud laugh.

Guidance, gīd´ans, *n*. The act of guiding; direction; government; a leading.

Guide, gīd, *vt*. (guiding, guided). To lead; to direct; to influence; to regulate.—*n*. A person who guides; a director; a regulator; a guidebook.

Guise, gīz, *n*. External appearance; dress; mien; cast of behavior.

Guitar, gi-tär´, *n*. A musical instrument having six strings.

Gulch, gulch, *n*. A gully; dry bed of a torrent.

Gulf, gulf, *n*. An arm of the sea extending into the land; bay; chasm; whirlpool; anything insatiable; a wide interval.

Gull, gul, *vt*. To cheat.—*n*. One easily cheated; a simpleton; a marine swimming bird.

Gullet, gul´et, *n*. The passage in the neck of an animal by which food and liquor are taken into the stomach.

Gully, gul´i, *n*. A channel worn by water; a ravine.—*vt*. To wear into a gully.

Gulp, gulp, *vt*. To swallow eagerly.— *n*. Act of taking a large swallow.

Gum, gum, *n*. The fleshy substance of the jaws round the teeth; a juice which exudes from trees, etc., and thickens; a viscous substance.— *vt.* (gumming, gummed). To smear with or unite by a viscous substance.

Gunshot, gun'shot, *n.* Range of a cannon-shot; firing of a gun.—*a.* Made by the shot of a gun.

Gunwale, Gunnel, gun'wāl, gun' el, *n.* The upper edge of a ship's side.

Gurgle, gėr'gl, *vi.* (gurgling, gurgled). To run or flow in a broken noisy current.—*n.* Sound produced by a liquid flowing from or through a narrow opening.

Gush, gush, *vi.* To issue with violence and rapidity, as a fluid; to be effusively sentimental.—*n.* A sudden and violent issue of a fluid; the fluid thus emitted; effusive display of sentiment.

Gut, gut, *n.* The intestinal canal of an animal; *pl.* the entrails; a preparation of the intestines for various purposes; a channel.-*vt.* (gutting, gutted). To take out the entrails of; to plunder of contents; to destroy the interior of.

Gutter, gut'ėr, *n.* A channel at the side of a road, etc., for water.—*vt.* To cut or form gutters in.—*vi.* To become channelled.

Guttural, gut'tėr-al, *a.* Pertaining to the throat; formed in the throat.—*n.* A letter pronounced in the throat; any guttural sound.

Guy, gī, *n.* A rope to steady anything; a person of queer looks or dress.—*vt.* To steady or direct by means of a guy.

Guzzle, guz'l, *v.* and *t.* (guzzling, guzzled). To swallow greedily or frequently.—*n.* A debauch.

Gymnasium jim-nā'zi-um, *n.*; pl. **ia** or **-iums.** A place for athletic exercises; a school for the higher branches of education.

Gymnast, jim'nast, *n.* One who teaches or practices gymnastic exercises.

H

Haberdasher, ha'bėr-dash-ėr, *n.* A dealer in drapery goods, as woollens, silks, ribbons, etc.

Habilitate, ha-bil'i-tāt, *vi.* To qualify.

Habit, ha'bit, *n.* State of body, natural or acquired; mode of growth of a plant; aptitude acquired by practice; custom; manner; dress; outer dress worn by ladies on horseback.—*vt.* To dress; to clothe; to array.

Habitat, ha'bit-at, *n.* The natural abode or locality of a plant or animal.

Habitation, ha-bit-ā'shon, *n.* Occupancy; abode; residence.

Hades, hā'dēz, *n.* The abode of the dead; state of departed souls.

Haft, haft, *n.* A handle; that part of an instrument which is taken into the hand.—*vt.* To set in a haft.

Hag, hag, *n.* An ugly old woman; a witch; an eel-shaped fish that eats into other fishes.

Haggard, hag'ärd, *a.* Wild; intractable; having the face worn and pale; gaunt.—*n.* An untrained or refractory hawk.

Haggle, hag'l, *vt.* (haggling, haggled). To cut into small pieces; to mangle.—*vi.* To be difficult in bargaining; to stick at small matters; to chaffer.

Hail, hāl, *n.* Frozen drops of rain; a wish of health; a call.—*vi.* To pour down hail; to have as one's residence, or belong to (with *from*).—*vt.* To pour down in the manner of hail; to salute; to call to; to designate as.—*interj.* A salutation expressive of well-wishing.

Hailstone, hāl'stōn, *n.* A single pellet of hail falling from a cloud.

Hair, hār, *n.* A small filament issuing from the skin of an animal; the mass of filaments growing from the skin of an animal; anything similar; a very small distance.

Hale, hāl, *a.* Sound; healthy; robust.—*n.* A violent pull.—*vt.* (haling, haled). To take, pull, or drag by force.

Half, häf, *n.*; pl. **Halves,** hävz. One part of a thing divided into two equal parts.—*a.* Consisting of a half.—*adv.* In part, or in a equal part or degree.

H

Hall, hạl, *n.* A large room, especially a large public room; a large room at the entrance of a house; a manor-house; the name of certain colleges at Oxford and Cambridge.

Halleluiah, Hallelujah, hal-lē-lụ′ya, *n.* and *interj.* A word used in sacred songs of praise, signifying *praise ye Jehovah.*

Hallow-e'en, Hallow-even, hal′ō-ēn, hal′ō-ē-vn, *n.* The eve or vigil of All-Hallows' or All-Saints' Day.

Hallucination, hal-lū′si-nā′′shon, *n.* A mistaken notion; mere dream or fancy; morbid condition in which objects are believed to be seen and sensations experienced; object or sensation thus erroneously perceived.

Halo, hā′lō, *n.* A luminous ring round the sun or moon; any circle of light, as the glory round the head of saints; an ideal glory investing an object.—*vi.* To form itself into a halo.—*vt.* To surround with a halo.

Halt, hạlt, *vi.* To limp; to be lame; to hesitate; to cease marching.—*vt.* To stop; to cause to cease marching.—*a.* Lame; limping.—*n.* A limp; a stopping; stoppage on march.

Hammer, ham′ėr, *n.* An instrument for driving nails, beating metals, and the like.—*vt.* To beat or forge with a hammer; to contrive by intellectual labor.—*vi.* To work with a hammer; to labor in contrivance.

Hammock, ham′ok, *n.* A kind of hanging bed.

Hamper, ham′pėr, *n.* A large basket for conveying things to market, etc.; something that encumbers; a clog.—*vt.* To put into a hamper; to hinder or impede; to embarrass.

Hamstring, ham′string, *n.* One of the tendons of the ham.—*vt.* (pp. hamstrung or hamstringed). To cut the tendons of the ham, and thus to lame or disable.

Hand, hand, *n.* The extremity of the arm, consisting of the palm and fingers; a measure of four inches; side or direction; skill; manner of acting; power; cards held at a game; a game; an index; a male or female in relation to an employer; a person with some special faculty; style of penmanship.—*vt.* To give with the hand; to lead with the hand; to conduct; to handle.—*a.* Belonging to, or used by the hand.

Handcuff, hand′kuf, *n.* A fetter for the hands or wrists.—*vt.* To manacle with handcuffs.

Handful, hand′fụl, *n.* As much as the hand will grasp or hold; a small quantity or number.

Handicap, hand′i-kap, *n.* In racing, games, etc., an allowance to bring superior competitors to an equality with the others; a race or contest so arranged.—*vt.* To put a handicap on; to equalize by a handicap.

Handle, hand′dl, *vt.* (handling, handled). To feel, use, or hold with the hand; to discuss; to deal with; to treat or use well or ill.—*n.* That part of an instrument, etc., held in the hand; instrument for effecting a purpose.

Hang, hang, *vt.* (pret. and pp. hung and hanged). To suspend; to furnish with anything suspended; to cause to droop; to fit so as to allow of free motion; to put to death by suspending by the neck.—*vi.* To be suspended; to dangle; to adhere; to linger; to lean; to have a steep declivity; to be executed.

Hangar, hang′ar, *n.* A shed for housing airplanes.

Hanging, hang′ing, *n.* Act of suspending; death by the halter; *pl.* linings for rooms, of tapestry, paper, etc.

Happy, hap′i, *a.* Being in the enjoyment of agreeable sensations from the possession of good; fortunate; propitious; well suited; apt.

Harangue, ha-rang′, *n.* A noisy or pompous address; a declamatory public address; a tirade.—*vi.* (haranguing, harangued). To make a harangue.—*vt.* To address by a harangue.

Harass, ha′ras, *vt.* To vex; to tire with labor; to fatigue with importunity.

Harbinger, här′bin-jėr, *n.* A forerunner; that which precedes and gives notice of something else.— *vt.* To precede as harbinger.

Harbor, här'bėr, *n.* A shelter; a haven for ships; an asylum.—*vt.* To shelter; to entertain in the mind.— *vi.* To take shelter; to lodge or abide for a time.

Hard, härd, *a.* Not easily penetrated or separated; firm; difficult to understand; arduous; unfeeling; severe; unjust; harsh; stiff; grasping: applied to certain sounds, as sibilants contrasted with gutturals: applied to water not suitable for washing, from holding minerals.—*adv.* Close; diligently; with difficulty; fast; copiously; with force.

Harden, härd'n, *vt.* To make hard or more hard; to confirm in effrontery, obstinacy, wickedness, etc.; to make unfeeling; to inure; to render less liable to injury by exposure or use.—*vi.* To become hard or more hard; to become unfeeling; to become inured.

Hardy, härd'i, *a.* Bold; intrepid; full of assurance; inured to fatigue; capable of bearing exposure.

Harm, härm, *n.* Injury; hurt; evil.— *vt.* To hurt; to damage; to impair.

Harmless, härm'les, *a.* Free from harm; not causing harm; inoffensive; uninjured.

Harmonic, Harmonical, här-mon'ik, här-mon'ik-al, *a.* Pertaining to harmony; concordant; musical.— **Harmonic,** här-mon'ik, *n.* A less distinct tone accompanying a principal tone.

Harmony, här'mo-ni, *n.* The just adaptation of parts to each other; musical concord; agreement; peace and friendship.

Harness, här'nes, *n.* Armor; furniture of a carriage or draft horse.— *vt.* To dress in armor; to put harness on.

Harp, härp, *n.* A stringed musical instrument of triangular form played with the fingers.—*vi.* To play on the harp; to dwell on tediously.

Harpoon, här-pön', *n.* A spear or javelin, used to strike whales, etc.—*vt.* To strike, catch, or kill with a harpoon.

Harpy, här'pi, *n.* A fabulous winged monster with the face of a woman; any rapacious animal; an extortioner.

Harridan, ha'ri-dan, *n.* A hag; an odious old woman; a vixenish woman; a trollop.

Harrow, ha'rō, *n.* A frame set with spikes, to prepare plowed land for seed or to cover the seed.—*vt.* To draw a harrow over; to lacerate; to torment.

Harrowing, ha'rō-ing, *p.a.* Causing acute distress to the mind.

Harry, ha'ri, *vt.* (harrying, harried). To pillage; to plunder; to ravage.

Harsh, härsh, *a.* Grating to the touch, taste, or ear; jarring; rough; severe.

Hasp, hasp, *n.* A clasp that passes over a staple to be fastened by a padlock.—*vt.* To fasten with a hasp.

Hassock, has'ok, *n.* A thick mat or cushion used for kneeling on, etc.

Haste, hāst, *n.* Speed; hurry; sudden excitement of passion; precipitance.—*vt.* (hasting, hasted). To drive or urge forward; to hurry.— *vi.* To move with celerity; to be speedy.

Hate, hāt, *vt.* (hating, hated). To detest; to loathe; to abhor.—*n.* Great dislike; hatred.

Hateful, hāt'ful, *a.* Exciting hate; odious; loathsome; malignant.

Hatred, hāt'red, *n.* Great dislike or aversion; ill-will; rancor; abhorrence.

Haughty, hat'i, *a.* Proud and disdainful; lofty and arrogant.

Haul, hal, *vt.* To pull or draw with force; to drag; to compel to go.—*n.* A violent pull; draught of fish in a net; that which is taken or gained at once.

Have, hav, *vt.* (having, had). To possess; to accept; to enjoy; to hold in opinion; to be under necessity, or impelled by duty; to procure; to bring forth.

Haven, hā'vn, *n.* A harbor; port; shelter.

Haversack, hav'ėr-sak, *n.* A soldier's bag for provisions on the march.

Having, hav'ing, *n.* What one has;

possession; goods.

Havoc, hav'ok, n. Devastation; wide and general destruction; slaughter.

Hawk, hạk, n. A rapacious bird of the falcon family.—vi. To catch birds by means of hawks; to practice falconry; to take prey on the wing; to force up phlegm with noise.—vt. To carry about for sale from place to place.

Hazel, hā'zl, n. A small tree of the oak family that bears edible nuts.—a. Pertaining to the hazel; of a light-brown color.

Hazy, hāz'i, a. Thick with haze; mentally obscure or confused.

He, hē, pron. of the third person, nominative. A substitute for the third person masculine, representing the man or male named before; prefixed to names of animals to specify the male.

Head, hed, n. The anterior part of animals; uppermost part of the human body; seat of the brain; etc.; intellect; an individual; a chief; first place; top; chief part; principal source; crisis; height; promontory; division of discourse; headway.—vt. To form a head to; to behead; to lead; to go in front of in order to stop; to oppose.—vi. To form a head; to be directed, as a ship.

Headache, hed'āk, n. Pain in the head.

Heading, hed'ing, n. That which stands at the head; title of a section; passage excavated in the line of an intended tunnel.

Heal, hēl, vi. To make hale or sound; to cure; to reconcile.—vt. To grow whole or sound; to recover.

Health, helth, n. A sound state of body or mind; freedom from disease; bodily conditions; wish of health and happiness (used in drinking).

Healthy, helth'i, a. Being in health; sound; hale; salubrious; wholesome.

Heap, hēp, n. A mass; large quantity; pile.—vt. To raise in a heap; to amass; to pile.

Hear, hēr, vt. (hearing, heard). To perceive by the ear; to give audience to; to listen; to obey; to regard; to attend favorably; to try in a court of law; to learn; to approve.—vi. To enjoy the faculty of perceiving sound; to listen; to be told; to receive by report.

Hearing, hēr'ing, n. The faculty or sense by which sound is perceived; audience; opportunity to be heard; judicial trial; reach of the ear.

Hearsay, hēr'sā, n. Report; rumor.—a. Given at second hand.

Hearse, hērs, n. A carriage for conveying the dead to the grave; bier.

Heart, härt, n. The primary organ of the blood's motion; the inner, vital, or most essential part; seat of the affections, will, etc.; disposition of mind; conscience; courage; spirit; what represents a heart; one of a suit of playing cards marked with such a figure.

Hearty, härt'i, a. Warm; cordial; healthy; having a keen appetite; large to satisfaction.

Heat, hēt, n. The sensation produced by bodies that are hot; hot air; hot weather; high temperature; degree of temperature; a single effort; a course at a race; animal excitement; rage; ardor; animation in thought or discourse; fermentation.—vt. To make hot; to warm with passion or desire; to rouse into action.—vi. To grow warm or hot.

Heath, hēth, n. A small flowering shrub growing on waste or wild places; a place overgrown with heath; waste tract.

Heathen, hē'THen, n. A pagan; one who worships idols; a barbarous person.—a. Gentile; pagan.

Heathenism, hē'THen-izm, n. Paganism; idolatry.

Heather, heTH'ér, n. Common heath, a low shrub with clusters of rose-colored flowers.

Heave, hēv, vt. (heaving, pret. and pp. heaved, hove). To lift; to move upward; to cause to swell; to raise or force from the breast, as a groan; to throw; to turn in some direction.—vi. To rise; to swell, as the sea; to pant; to retch; *to heave in sight,* to appear, as a ship.—n. A rising or swell; an effort upward; a throw; a swelling, as of the breast.

Heaven, hev'n, *n*. The blue expanse surrounding the earth; the sky; the abode of God and of his angels; God or Providence; supreme felicity; bliss.

Heavenly, hev'n-li, *a*. Pertaining to heaven; divine; inhabiting heaven; enchanting.—*adv*. In a heavenly manner.

Heavy, he'vi, *a*. That is heaved or lifted with difficulty; weighty; sad; grievous; burdensome; drowsy; wearisome; not easily digested; soft and miry; difficult; large in amount; dense; abundant; forcible.

Hedge, hej, *n*. A fence consisting of thorns or shrubs.—*vt*. (hedging, hedged). To enclose with a hedge; to surround or restrain.—*vi*. To hide oneself; to bet on both sides; to skulk; to dodge or trim.—*a*. Pertaining to a hedge; mean; rustic.

Hedonism, hē'don-izm, *n*. The doctrine that the chief good of man lies in pursuit of pleasure.

Hedonist, hē'don-ist, *n*. One who professes hedonism.

Heed, hēd, *vt*. To look to or after; to regard with care; to notice.—*vi*. To mind; to consider.—*n*. Care; attention; regard.

Heedless, hēd'les, *a*. Inattentive; careless; remiss; negligent.

Heel, hēl, *n*. The hind part of the foot; a cant.—*vt*. To add a heel to; to furnish with heels, as shoes.—*vi*. To cant over from a vertical position.

Heft, heft, *n*. The act of heaving; effort; weight; gist.

Height, hīt, *n*. The condition of being high; distance of anything above its base or above the earth; eminence; any elevated ground; extent; degree; utmost degree.

Heighten, hīt'n, *vt*. To raise higher; to improve; to increase.

Heinous, hān'us, *a*. Hateful; characterized by great wickedness; flagrant.

Heir, ār, *n*. One who succeeds or is to succeed another in the possession of property.

Heirloom, ār'löm, *n*. Any personal chattel which, by law, descends to the heir or has belonged to a family for a long time.

Helium, hē'li-um, *n*. An inert gas present in the air in small quantities, the lightest element next to hydrogen.

Helix, hē'liks, *n*.; pl. **Helices,** hel'i-sēz. A spiral line, as of wire in a coil; something that is spiral.

Hell, hel, *n*. The place or state of punishment for the wicked after death; the abode of the devil and his angels; the infernal powers; a gambling-house.

Help, help, *vt*. To lend strength or means towards effecting a purpose; to aid; to relieve; to remedy; to prevent; to avoid.—*vi*. To lend aid.—*n*. Aid; remedy; an assistant.

Hem, hem, *n*. The border of a garment, doubled and sewed to strengthen it; edge; border.—*interj.* and *n*. A sort of half cough, suggested by some feeling.—*vt*. (hemming, hemmed). To form a hem or border on; to enclose and confine; to make the sound expressed by the word *hem*.

Hematite, he'ma-tit, *n*. A name of two ores of iron, red hematite and brown hematite.

Hemisphere, he'mi-sfēr, *n*. One half of a sphere; half the celestial or terrestrial sphere.

Hemlock, hem'lok, *n*. An umbelliferous plant whose leaves and root are poisonous.

Hemorrhage, he'mor-āj, *n*. A bursting forth of blood; any discharge of blood from the blood-vessels.

Hemorrhoids, he'mor-oidz, *n.pl.* Piles.

Hemp, hemp, *n*. An annual herbaceous plant of the nettle family, the fiber of which, also called hemp, is made into sail-cloth, ropes, etc.

Hen, hen, *n*. The female of the domestic fowl; any female bird.

Herald, he'rald, *n*. An officer whose business was to proclaim war or peace, bear messages, etc.; a forerunner; an officer who regulates matters relating to public ceremonies; one who records and blazons arms, etc.—*vt*. To introduce, as by

H

a herald; to proclaim.

Herb, hèrb, *n*. Any plant with a succulent stem which dies to the root every year.

Herbalist, hèrb'al-ist, *n*. One skilled in herbs, or who makes collections of them.

Herbarium, hèr-bā'ri-um, *n*.; pl. -iums and -ia. A collection of herbs or plants dried and preserved.

Herbivorous, hèrb-iv'or-us, *a*. Eating herbs; subsisting on herbaceous plants.

Herculean, hèr-kū'lē-an, *a*. Belonging to or resembling Hercules; of extraordinary strength; very great or difficult.

Herd, hèrd, *n*. A number of animals feeding or driven together; flock; crowd; rabble; a keeper of cattle or sheep.—*vi*. and *t*. To unite into a herd, as beasts; to congregate.

Herdsman, hèrdz'man, *n*. One employed in tending herds of cattle.

Here, hèr, *adv*. In this place; at this point; hither.

Hereafter, hèr-af'tèr, *adv*. After this time; in a future state.—*n*. The time after this; a future state.

Hereditary, he-red'it-a-ri, *a*. Relating to an inheritance; descending to an heir; that is or may be transmitted from a parent to a child.

Heredity, he-red'i-ti, *n*. Hereditary transmission of qualities; the doctrine that the offspring inherits parental characteristics.

Heresy, he're-si, *n*. A fundamental error in religion; error in doctrine; heterodoxy.

Heretic, he're-tik, *n*. One guilty of heresy.

Heritage, he'rit-āj, *n*. Inheritance; lot or portion by birth.

Hermit, hèr'mit, *n*. One who lives in solitude; a recluse.

Hernia, hèr'ni-a, *n*. A protrusion of some organ of the abdomen through an interstice; a rupture.

Hero, hē'rō, *n*.; pl. **Heroes,** hē'rōz. A man of distinguished valor; the person who has the principal share in some exploit, or in a play, novel, etc.

Heroic, he-rō'ik, *a*. Pertaining to a hero or heroes; intrepid and noble; reciting achievements of heroes; epic.

Heroin, her'o-in, *n*. A narcotic drug derived from morphia.

Heroine, he'rō-in, *n*. A female hero.

Heroism, he'rō-izm, *n*. The qualities of a hero; intrepidity; magnanimity.

Heron, her'un, *n*. A wading bird with a long bill, long slender legs and neck.

Herpes, hèr'pez, *n*. A skin disease characterized by eruption or inflamed vesicles.

Herpetology, hèr-pe-tol'o-ji, *n*. The natural history of reptiles.

Herring, he'ring, *n*. One of those small food fishes which go in shoals in northern seas.

Herring-bone, he'ring-bōn, *a*. Applied to masonry, sewing, etc., which bears resemblance to the backbone of a herring.

Hesitate, he'zi-tāt, *vi*. (hesitating, hesitated). To pause respecting decision or action; to stop in speaking; to stammer.

Hesitation, he-zi-tā'shon, *n*. Act of hesitating; doubt; a stopping in speech.

Hew, hū, *vt*. (pret. hewed, pp. hewed or hewn). To cut with an axe, etc.; to cut; to hack; to make smooth, as stone; to shape.

Hibernal, hī-bèr'nal, *a*. Belonging to winter; wintry.

Hibernate, hī-bèr'nāt, *vt*. To pass the winter in sleep or seculsion; to winter.

Hide, hīd, *vt*. (hiding, pret. hid, pp. hid, hidden). To withhold or withdraw from sight or knowledge; to screen; to secrete.—*vi*. To be or to lie concealed; to keep oneself out of view.—*n*. The skin of an animal, either raw or dressed; the human skin; an old measure of land of about 80 acres.

High, hī, *a*. Having a great extent from base to summit; elevated; lofty; far above the earth; elevated in rank or office; dignified; proud; violent; solemn; strong; vivid; dear; remote; sharp; far advanced; committed against the sovereign or state; tending towards putrefaction; strong-scented.—*adv*. In a high manner;

to a great altitude or degree; eminently; greatly.

High-pressure, hī'prē-shūr, *a*. Having or involving a pressure exceeding that of the atmosphere, or having a pressure greater than 50 lbs. to the square inch.

Highway, hī'wā, *n*. A public road; direct course; train of action.

Hike, hīk, *vi*. To tramp; to go on a long or fairly long walking expedition.

Hilarity, hi-la'ri-ti, *n*. Cheerfulness; merriment; good humor; jollity.

Hill, hil, *n*. A natural elevation of less size than a mountain; an eminence.

Hilt, hilt, *n*. A handle, particularly of a sword.

Himself, him-self', *pron*. The emphatic and reflexive form of *he* and *him*.

Hind, hīnd, *n*. The female of the red-deer or stag; a farm servant; a rustic.—*a*. Backward; back; pertaining to the backward part.

Hinder, hīnd'ėr, *a*. Posterior; in the rear; latter; after.

Hinder, hin'dėr, *vt*. To prevent from moving or acting; to obstruct; to thwart; to check.—*vi*. To interpose obstacles or impediments.

Hint, hint, *vt*. To suggest indirectly; to insinuate.—*vi*. To make an indirect allusion.—*n*. A distant allusion; a suggestion.

Hip, hip, *n*. The fleshy projecting part of the thigh; the haunch; the joint of the thigh; the fruit of the dog-rose or wild brier.—*interj*. Exclamation expressive of a call to anyone. *Hip, hip, hurrah!* the signal to cheer.

Hire, hīr, *vt*. (hiring, hired). To procure for temporary use, at a certain price; to engage in service for a stipulated reward; to let; to lease (with *out*).—*n*. Price paid for temporary use of anything; recompense for personal service; wages; pay.

Hirsute, hėr-sūt', *a*. Hairy; shaggy.

History, his'to-ri, *n*. An account of facts, particularly respecting nations or states; that branch of knowledge which deals with past events; narration; a story; an account of existing things, as animals or plants.

Histrionics, his-tri-on'iks, *n*. The art of theatrical representation.

Hit, hit, *vt*. (hitting, hit). To strike or touch with some force; to give a blow to; not to miss; to reach; to light upon; to suit.—*vi*. To strike; to come in contact; to reach the intended point; to succeed.—*n*. A stroke; a blow; a lucky chance; happy thought or expression.

Hitch, hich, *vi*. To move by jerks; to be entangled, hooked, or yoked.—*vt*. To fasten; to hook; to raise by jerks.—*n*. A catch; act of catching, as on a hook, etc.; knot or noose in a rope; a jerk; a temporary obstruction.

Hither, hiᴛн'ėr, *adv*. To this place.—*a*. Nearer; toward the person speaking.

Hive, hīv, *n*. A box or receptacle for honey-bees; the bees inhabiting a hive; a place swarming with busy occupants.—*vt*. (hiving, hived). To collect into a hive; to lay up in store.—*vi*. To take shelter together; to reside in a collective body.

Hoar, hōr, *a*. White or whitish; hoary.—*vi*. To become moldy or musty.

Hoard, hōrd, *n*. A store, stock, or large quantity of anything; a hidden stock.—*vt*. To collect; to store secretly.—*vi*. To form a hoard; to lay up in store.

Hoar-frost, hōr'frost, *n*. The white particles of frozen dew; rime.

Hoarse, hōrs, *a*. Having a grating voice, as when affected with a cold; discordant; rough; grating.

Hobby, hob'i, *n*. A small but strong British falcon; an active, ambling nag; a hobby-horse; any favorite object or pursuit.

Hod, hod, *n*. A kind of trough for carrying mortar and brick on the shoulder.

Hodge-podge, hoj'poj, *n*. A mixed mass; a medley of ingredients; a hotch-potch.

Hoe, hō, *n*. An instrument to cut up weeds and loosen the earth.—*vt*. (hoeing, hoed). To dig or clean with a hoe.—*vi*. To use a hoe.

Hog, hog, *n*. A swine; a castrated

H

boar; a sheep of a year old; a brutal or mean fellow.—*vi*. To bend, as a ship's bottom.

Hogshead, hogz'hed, *n*. A large cask; an old measure of capacity, containing about 52¹/₂ imperial gallons.

Hoist, hoist, *vt*. To heave up; to lift upward by means of tackle.—*n*. Act of raising; apparatus for raising goods, etc.; an elevator.

Hold, hōld, *vt*. (pret. held, pp. held,). To have in the grasp; to keep fast; to confine; to maintain; to consider; to contain; to possess; to withhold; to continue; to celebrate.—*vi*. To take or keep a thing in one's grasp; to stand as a fact or truth; not to give way or part; to refrain; to adhere; to derive title (with *of*).—*n*. A grasp; something which may be seized for support; power of keeping, seizing, or directing; influence; place of confinement; stronghold; interior cavity of a ship.

Hole, hōl, *n*. A hollow place in any solid body; a perforation, crevice, etc.; a den; a subterfuge.—*vt*. (holing, holed). To make a hole or holes in; to drive into a hole.

Holiday, ho'li-dā, *n*. A holy or sacred day; a festival; day of exemption from labor.—*a*. Pertaining to a festival.

Holiness, hō'li-nes, *n*. State or quality of being holy; moral goodness; sanctity.—**His Holiness,** a title of the pope.

Holometabolic, hol'o-met-a-bol''ik, *a*. Applied to insects which undergo a complete metamorphosis.

Holster, hōl'stėr, *n*. A leathern case for a pistol.

Holy, hō'li, *a*. Free from sin; immaculate; consecrated; sacred.

Homage, hom'āj, *n*. An act of fealty on the part of a vassal to his lord; obeisance; reverential worship.

Home, hōm, *n*. One's own abode; the abode of one's family; residence; one' own country; an establishment affording the comforts of a home.—*a*. Domestic; close; severe; poignant.—*adv*. To one's own habitation or country; to the point; effectively.

Homestead, hōm'sted, *n*. A house with the grounds and buildings contiguous; a home; native seat.

Homeward, hōm'wėrd, *adv*. Toward one's habitation or country.—*a*. Being in the direction of home.

Homicide, ho'mi-sīd, *n*. Manslaughter; a person who kills another.

Homiletics, ho-mi-let'iks, *n*. The art of preaching.

Homily, ho'mi-li, *n*. A sermon; a familiar religious discourse; a serious discourse or admonition.

Homologate, hō-mol'o-gāt, *vt*. To approve; to ratify.

Homologous, hō-mol'o-gus, *a*. Having the same relative position, proportion, or structure; corresponding.

Homonym, ho'mō-nim, *n*. A word which agrees with another in sound, and perhaps in spelling, but differs in signification.

Hone, hōn, *n*. A stone of a fine grit, used for sharpening instruments.—*vt*. (honing, honed). To sharpen on a hone.

Honest, on'est, *a*. Free from fraud; upright; just; sincere; candid; virtuous.

Honey, hun'i, *n*. A sweet viscous juice collected by bees from flowers; sweetness; a word of tenderness.—*vt*. To sweeten.

Honorary, on'ėr-a-ri, *a*. Relating to honor; conferring honor; possessing a title or place without performing services or without receiving a reward.

Honor, on'ėr, *n*. Respect; esteem; testimony of esteem; dignity; good name; a nice sense of what is right; scorn of meanness; a title of respect or distinction; one of the highest trump cards; *pl*. civilities paid; public marks of respect; academic and university distinction.—*vt*. To regard or treat with honor; to bestow honor upon; to exalt; to accept and pay when due, as a bill.

Honorable, on'ėr-a-bl, *a*. Worthy of honor; actuated by principles of honor; conferring honor; consistent with honor; performed with marks of honor; not base; honest; fair; a title of distinction.

Hood, hụd, *n*. A soft covering for the head; a cowl; a garment worn as part of academic dress, which indicates by its colors, material and shape the degree and University of its wearer; anything resembling a hood.—*vt*. To dress in a hood; to cover; to blind.

Hoodwink, hụd'wingk, *vt*. To blind by covering the eyes of; to impose on.

Hoof, höf, *n*.; pl. **Hoofs,** rarely **Hooves.** The horny substance that covers the feet of certain animals, as the horse.

Hook, hök, *n*. A bent piece of iron or other metal for catching; that which catches; a sickle.—*vt*. To catch with a hook; to ensnare.—*vi*. To bend; to be curving.

Hoot, höt, *vi*. To shout in contempt; to cry as an owl.—*vt*. To utter contemptuous cries at.—*n*. A cry or shout in contempt.

Hop, hop, *n*. A leap on one leg; a spring; a bitter plant of the hemp familyused to flavor malt liquors.—*vi*. To leap or spring on one leg; to skip; to limp; to pick hops.—*vt*. To impregnante with hops.

Hope, höp, *n*. A desire of some good, accompanied with a belief that it is attainable; trust; one in whom trust or confidence is placed; the object of hope.—*vi*. (hoping, hoped). To entertain hope; to trust.—*vt*. To desire with some expectation of attainment.

Horde, hörd, *n*. A tribe or race of nomads; a gang; migratory crew; rabble.—*vi*. (hording, horded). To live together like migratory tribes.

Horizon, ho-rī'zon, *n*. The circle which bounds tht part of the earth's surface visible from given point; the apparent junction of the earth and sky.

Hormones, hor'mōnz, *n.pl*. Products of the ductless glands, affecting other organs by way of the blood stream.

Horn, horn, *n*. A hard projection on the heads of certain animals; the material of such horns; wind-instrument of music; extremity of the moon; drinking-cup; powderhorn; something resembling a horn; the feeler of a snail, etc.

Horror, hor'rėr, *n*. A powerful feeling of fear and abhorrence; that which may excite terror; something frightful or shocking.

Horse, hors, *n*. A well-known quadruped, used for draft and carriage in war; the male animal; cavalry; a name of various things resembling or analogous to a horse.—*vt*. (horsing, horsed). To supply with a horse; to carry on the back; to bestride.

Horseradish, hors'rad-ish, *n*. A perennial plant, having a root of a pungent taste.

Horseshoe, hors'shö, *n*. A shoe for horses, commonly of iron shaped like the letter U; anything shaped like a horse-shoe.—*a*. Having the form of a horse-shoe.

Hortatory, hort'a-to-ri, *a*. Giving exhortation or advice; encouraging.

Horticulture, hor'ti-kul-tūr, *n*. The art of cultivating gardens.

Hosanna, hō-zan'na, *n*. An exclamation of praise to God, or an invocation of blessings.

Hose, höz, *n. sing*. or *pl*. A covering for the thighs, legs, or feet; close-fitting breeches; stockings; in these senses plural; a flexible pipe used for conveying water.

Host, höst, *n*. One who entertains a stranger or guest; an innkeeper; an army; any great number or multitude; the consecrated bread in the R. Catholic sacrament of the mass.

Hostage, host'āj, *n*. A person delivered to an enemy, as a pledge to secure the performance of conditions.

Hostel, Hostelry, hos'tel, hos'tel-ri, *n*. An inn; a lodging-house.

Hostile, hos'tīl, *a*. Belonging to an enemy; unfriendly; antagonistic; adverse.

Hostility, hos-til'i-ti, *n*. State or quality of being hostile; state of war between nations or states; the actions of an open enemy (in *pl*.); animosity; enmity; opposition.

Hot, hot, *a*. Having sensible heat; burning; glowing; easily exasper-

H

ated; vehement; eager; lustful; biting; pungent in taste.

Hour, our, *n.* The twenty-fourth part of a day, consisting of sixty minutes; the particular time of the day; an appointed time; *pl.* certain prayers in the R. Catholic Church.

House, hous, *n.*; pl. **Houses,** hou' zez. A building or erection for the habitation or use of man; any building or edifice; a dwelling; a household; a family; a legislative body of men; audience or attendance; a commercial establishment.—*vt.* (housing, housed). To put or receive into a house; to shelter.—*vi.* To take shelter; to take up abode.

Housing, houz'ing, *n.* A horsecloth; *pl.* the trappings of a horse.—*p.n.* Placing in houses; sheltering.

Hovel, ho'vel, *n.* A mean house; an open shed for cattle, etc.—*vt.* To put in a hovel.

Hover, ho'ver, *vi.* To hang fluttering in the air; to be in doubt; to linger near.

How, hou, *adv.* In what manner; to what extent; for what reason; by what means; in what state.

However, hou-ev'er, *adv.* In whatever manner or degree; in whatever state.—*conj.* Nevertheless; yet; still; though.

Howl, houl, *vi.* To cry as a dog or wolf; to utter a loud mournful sound; to roar, as the wind.—*vt.* To utter or speak with outcry.—*n.* A loud protracted wail; cry of a wolf, etc.

Hub, hub, *n.* The central cylindrical part of a wheel in which the spokes are set.

Hubbub, hub'bub, *n.* A great noise of many confused voices; tumult; uproar.

Huckster, huk'ster, *n.* A retailer of small articles; a hawker.—*vi.* To deal in small articles; to higgle.—*vt.* To hawk.

Huddle, hud'l, *vi.* (huddling, huddled). To crowd or press together promiscuously.—*vt.* To throw or crowd together in confusion; to put on in haste and disorder.—*n.* A confused mass; confusion.

Hue, hū, *n.* Color; tint; dye; a shouting; outcry; alarm.

Huff, huf, *n.* A fit of peevishness or petulance; anger.—*vt.* To treat with insolence; to bully; to make angry.—*vi.* To swell up; to bluster; to take offense.

Hug, hug, *vt.* (hugging, hugged). To press close in an embrace; to hold fast; to cherish; to keep close to.— *n.* A close embrace; a particular grip in wrestling.

Huge, hūj, *a.* Of immense bulk; enormous; prodigious.

Huguenot, hū'ge-not, *n.* A French Protestant of the period of the religious wars in France in the 16th century.

Hulk, hulk, *n.* the body of an old vessel; anything bulky or unwieldy.

Hull, hul, *n.* The outer covering of anything, particularly of a nut or of grain; husk; frame or body of a ship.—*vt.* To strip off the hull or hulls; to pierce the hull of a ship with a cannon-ball.

Hum, hum, *vi.* (humming, hummed). To utter the sound of bees; to make an inarticulate, buzzing sound.—*vt.* To sing in a low voice; to sing or utter inarticulately.—*n.* The noise of bees or insects; a low, confused noise; a low, inarticulate sound.—*interj.* A sound with a pause, implying doubt and deliberation.

Human, hū'man, *a.* Belonging to man or mankind; having the qualities of a man.

Humble, hum'bl, *a.* Of a low, mean, or unpretending character; lowly; modest; meek.—*vt.* (humbling, humbled). To make humble; to abase; to lower.

Humidity, hū-mid'i-ti, *n.* State of being humid; moisture.

Humiliate, hū-mil'i-āt, *vt.* To humble; to depress; to mortify.

Humility, hū-mil'i-ti, *n.* Humbleness of mind; modesty; sense of insignificance.

Humming-bird, hum'ing-bėrd, *n.* A family of minute but richly-colored birds that make a humming sound with their wings.

Hummock, hum'ok, *n.* A rounded

knoll.

Humorist, hū'mėr-ist or ū', *n.* One that makes use of a humorous style in speaking or writing; a wag.

Humor, hū'mėr or ū'mėr, *n.* Moisture or moist mater; fluid matter in an animal body, not blood; disposition; mood; a caprice; jocularity; a quality akin to wit, but depending for its effect less on point or brilliancy of expression.—*vt.* To comply with the inclination of; to soothe by compliance; to indulge.

Hundred, hun'dred, *a.* Ten times ten.—*n.* The sum of ten times ten; the number 100; a division or part of a county in England.

Hundredweight, hun'dred-wāt, *n.* A weight of a hundred and twelve pounds avoirdupois, twenty of which make a ton.

Hunger, hung'gėr, *n.* An uneasy sensation occasioned by the want of food; a craving of food; a strong or eager desire.—*vi.* To feel the uneasiness occasioned by want of food; to desire with great eagerness.

Hungry, hung'gri, *a.* Feeling uneasiness from want of food; having an eager desire; lean; barren.

Hunt, hunt, *vt.* To chase or search for, for the purpose of catching or killing; to follow closely; to use or manage, as hounds; to pursue animals over.—*vi.* To follow the chase; to search.—*n.* The chase of wild animals for catching them; pursuit; an association of huntsmen; a pack of hounds.

Hunter, hunt'ėr, *n.* One who hunts; a horse used in the chase; a kind of watch with a hinged case which protects the glass.

Hurdle, hėr'dl, *n.* A movable frame made of twigs or sticks, or of bars or rods.—*vt.* (hurdling, hurdled). To make up, cover, or close with hurdles.

Hurl, hėrl, *vt.* To send whirling through the air; to throw with violence; to utter with vehemence.—*n.* Act of throwing with violence.

Hurricane, hu'ri-kān, *n.* A violent storm of wind traveling over 75 miles per hour.

Hurry, hu'ri, *vt.* (hurrying, hurried). To drive or press forward with more rapidity; to urge to act with more celerity; to quicken.—*vi.* To move or act with haste; to hasten.—*n.* Act of hurrying; urgency; bustle.

Hurt, hėrt, *n.* A wound; bruise; injury; harm.—*vt.* (pret. and pp. hurt). To cause physical pain to; to bruise; to harm; to impair; to injure; to wound the feelings of.

Hurtle, hėr'tl, *vi.* (hurtling, hurtled). To meet in shock; to clash; to fly with threatening noise; to resound.

Husband, huz'band, *n.* A married man; the correlative of wife; a good manager; a steward.—*vt.* To manage with frugality; to use with economy.

Hush, hush, *a.* Silent; still; quiet.—*n.* Stillness; quiet.—*vt.* To make quiet; to repress, as noise.—*vi.* To be still; to be silent.

Husk, husk, *n.* The covering of certain fruits or seeds.—*vt.* To strip the husk from.

Hut, hut, *n.* A small house, hovel, or cabin; a temporary building to lodge soldiers.—*vt.* (hutting, hutted). To place in huts, as troops.—*vi.* To take lodgings in huts.

Hutch, huch, *n.* A chest or box; a corn bin; a box for rabbits; a low wagon used in coal-pits; a measure of 2 bushels.

Hyacinth, hī'a-sinth, *n.* A flowering, bulbous plant, of many varieties; a red variety of zircon, tinged with yellow or brown: also applied to varieties of garnet, sapphire, and topaz.

Hydrogen, hī'drō-jen, *n.* The gaseous elementary substance which combines with oxygen to form water.

Hydrophobia, hī-drō-fō'bi-a, *n.* A morbid dread of water; a disease produced by the bite of a mad animal, especially a dog.

Hydroponics, hī drō-pon'iks, *n.* The cultivation of plants in chemical solutions without soil.

Hyena, hī-ē'na, *n.* A carnivorous quadruped of Asia and Africa, feeding chiefly on carrion.

H

Hygiene, hī'ji-ēn, *n*. A system of principles designed for the promotion of health; sanitary science.

Hymnal, him'nal, *n*. A collection of hymns, generally for use in public worship.

Hyoid, hī'oid, *a*. Applied to a movable U-shaped bone between the root of the tongue and the larynx.

Hyperbola, hī-pėr'bō-la, *n*. A conic section, a curve formed by a section of a cone, when the cutting plane makes a greater angle with the base than the side of the cone makes.

Hyperbole, hī-pėr'bō-lē, *n*. Exaggeration; a figure of speech exceeding the truth.

Hyperborean, hī-pėr-bō'rē-an, *a*. Being in the extreme north; arctic; frigid.—*n*. An inhabitant of the most northern regions.

Hypercritic, hī-pėr-krit'ik, *n*. One critical beyond measure; a captious censor.

Hyphen, hī'fen, *n*. A character, thus (-), implying that two words or syllables are to be connected.

Hypnotism, hip'no-tizm, *n*. A sleep-like condition caused by artificial means.

Hypochondria, hī-pō-kon'dri-a, *n*. An ailment characterized by exaggerated anxiety, mainly as to the health; low spirits.

Hypocrisy, hi-pok'ri-si, *n*. A feigning to be what one is not; insincerity; a counterfeiting of religion.

Hypocrite, hi'pō-krit, *n*. One who feigns to be what he is not; a dissembler.

Hyssop, his'sop, *n*. An aromatic plant possessing stimulating, stomachic, and carminative properties.

Hysteria, Hysterics, his-tē'ri-a, his-ter'iks, *n*. A nervous affection chiefly attacking women, characterized by laughing and crying, convulsive struggling, sense of suffocation, etc.

I

I, ī, *pron*. The pronoun of the first person in the nominative case; the word by which a speaker or writer denotes himself.

Ibex, ī'beks, *n*. An animal of the goat family.

Ice, īs, *n*. Water or other fluid congealed; ice-cream.—*vt*. (icing, iced). To cover with ice; to convert into ice; to cover with concreted sugar; to freeze.

Iceberg, īs'bėrg, *n*. A vast body of ice floating in the ocean.

Ice-cream, īs'krēm, *n*. A confection of cream, sugar, etc., frozen.

Icicle, īs'i-kl, *n*. A pendent, conical mass of ice.

Iconoslast, ī-kon'o-klast, *n*. A breaker of images; one who attacks cherished beliefs.

Iconography, ī-ko-nog'ra-fi, *n*. The knowledge of ancient statues, paintings, gems, etc.

Icy, īs'i, *a*. Abounding with ice; made of ice; resembling ice; chilling; frigid; destitute of affection or passion.

Idea, ī-dē'a, *n*. That which is seen by the mind's eye; an image in the mind; object of thought; notion; conception; abstract principle; ideal view.

Ideal, ī-dē'al, *a*. Existing in idea or fancy; visionary; imaginary; perfect.—*n*. An imaginary model of perfection.

Idealism, ī'dē'al-izm, *n*. The system that makes everything to consist in ideas, and denies the existence of material bodies, or which denies any ground for believing in the reality of anything but percipient minds and ideas.

Idealize, ī-dē'al-iz, *vt*. To make ideal; to embody in an ideal form.

Identical, ī-den'tik-al, *a*. The same.

Identify, ī-den'ti-fi, *vt*. To make to be the same; to consider as the same in effect; to ascertain or prove to be the same.

Identity, ī-den'ti-ti, *n*. Sameness, as distinguished from similitude and diversity; sameness in every possible circumstance.

Idiopathy, id-i-op'a-thi, *n*. A morbid state not produced by any preceding disease.

Idiosyncrasy, id'i-o-sin''kra-si, *n*.

Peculiarity of temperament or constitution; mental or moral characteristic distinguishing an individual.

Idiot, i'di-ot, *n.* One void of understanding; one hopelessly insane.

Idle, I'dl, *a.* Not engaged in any occupation; inactive; lazy; futile; affording leisure; trifling; trivial.—*vi.* (idling, idled). To be idle; to lose or spend time in inaction.—*vt.* To spend in idleness.

Idleness, ī'dl-nes, *n.* Inaction; sloth; triviality; uselessness.

Idol, ī'dol, *n.* An image or symbol of a deity consecrated as an object of worship; a person honored to adoration; anything on which we set our affections inordinately.

Ignorance, ig-nō-rans, *n.* State of being illiterate, uninformed, or uneducated; want of knowledge.

Ignore, ig-nōr', *vt.* (ignoring, ignored). To pass over or overlook as if ignorant of; to disregard.

Iguana, ig-wä'na, *n.* An American reptile of the lizard family.

Iliac, il'i-ak, *a.* Pertaining to the lower bowels.

Ill, il, *a.* Bad or evil; producing evil, unfortunate; cross; crabbed; sick or indisposed; impaired; ugly; unfavorable; rude.—*n.* Evil; misfortune; calamity; disease; pain.—*adv.* Not well; badly; with pain or difficulty.

Illegal, il-lē'gal, *a.* Not legal; contrary to law; prohibited; illicit.

Illegible, il-le'ji-bl, *a.* Not legible; that cannot be read.

Illegitimate, il-lē-jit'i-māt, *a.* Not legitimate; born out of wedlock; illogical; not authorized.—*vt.* To render illegitimate.

Illicit, il-lis'it, *a.* Not permitted; unlawful; lawless.

Illuminate, il-lūm'in-āt, *vt.* (illuminating, illuminated). To light up; to adorn with festal lamps or bonfires; to enlighten intellectually; to adorn with colored pictures, etc., as manuscripts.

Illustrate, il-lus'trāt or il'lus-trāt, *vt.* (illustrating, illustrated). To make clear or obvious; to explain; to explain and adorn by means of pictures; drawings, etc.

Illustration, il-lus-trā'shon, Act of illustrating; that which illustrates; an example; design to illustrate the text of a book.

Illustrious, il-lus'tri-us, *a.* Renowned; celebrated; noble; conferring honor or renown; glorious.

Image, im'āj, *n.* A representative of any person or thing; a statue; an idol; embodiment; a picture drawn by fancy; the appearance of any object formed by the reflection or refraction of the rays of light.—*vt.* (imaging, imaged). To represent by an image; to mirror; to form a likeness of in the mind.

Imagery, im'āj-e-ri, *n.* Images in general; forms of the fancy; rhetorical figures.

Imaginary, im-aj'in-a-ri, *a.* Existing only in imagination; ideal; visionary.

Imagination, im-aj'in-ā''shon, *n.* The act of imagining; the faculty by which we form a mental image, or new combinations of ideas; mental image; a mere fancy; notion.

Imagine, im-aj'in, *vt.* (imagining, imagined). To picture to oneself; to fancy; to contrive; to think; to deem.—*vi.* To conceive; to have a notion or idea.

Imbroglio, im-brō'lyō, *n.* An intricate and perplexing state of affairs; a misunderstanding of a complicated nature.

Imbue, im-bū', *vt.* (imbuing, imbued). To tinge deeply; to dye; to inspire or impregnate (the mind).

Imitate, im'i-tāt, *vt.* (imitating, imitated). To follow as a model or example; to copy; to mimic; to counterfeit.

Imitation, im-i-tā'shon, *n.* Act of imitating; that which is made or produced as a copy; resemblance; a counterfeit.

Immaculate, im-ma'kū-lāt, *a.* Without spot; undefiled; pure.

Immediate, im-mē'di-āt, *a.* Without anything intervening; acting without a medium; direct; not acting by secondary causes; present; without intervention of time.

Immemorial, im-me-mō'ri-al, *a.* Beyond memory; extending beyond the reach of record or tradition.

Immense, im-mens', *a.* Immeasurable; huge; prodigious; enormous.

Immerge, im-merj', *vt.* (immerging, immerged). To dip or plunge; to immerse.—*vi.* To disappear by entering into any medium.

Immerse, im-mèrs', *vt.* (immersing, immersed). to plunge into water or other fluid; to overwhelm; to engage deeply.

Immesh, im-mesh', *vt.* To entangle in the meshes of a net, etc.

Immigrant, im'mi-grant, *n.* A person who immigrates into a country.

Immigrate, im'mi-grāt, *vi.* To come into a country for permanent residence.

Imminent, im'mi-nent, *a.* Hanging over; impending; threatening; near at hand.

Immolate, im'mō-lāt, *vt.* (immolating, immolated). To sacrifice; to kill, as a victim offered in sacrifice; to offer in sacrifice.

Immoral, im-mo'ral, *a.* Not moral; wicked; depraved; licentious.

Immunity, im-mū'ni-ti, *n.* Freedom from service or obligation; particular privilege or prerogative; state of not being liable.

Immure, im-mūr', *vt.* (immuring, immured). to inclose within walls; to imprison.

Immutable, im-mū'ta-bl, *a.* Unchangeable; unalterable; invariable.

Imp, imp, *n.* A young or little devil; a mischievous child.—*vt.* (imping, imped). To graft; to mend a deficient wing by the insertion of a feather; to strengthen.

Impact, im'pakt, *n.* A forcible touch; a blow; the shock of a moving body that strikes against another.

Impair, im-pār', *vt.* To make worse; to lessen in quantity, value, excellence, or strength.

Impale, im-pāl', *vt.* (impaling, impaled). To put to death by fixing on a stake; to join, as two coats of arms on one shield, with an upright line between.

Impalpable, im-pal'pa-bl, *a.* Not to be felt; so fine as not to be per-

ceived by the touch; not easily or readily apprehended by the mind.

Impassive, im-pas'iv, *a.* Not susceptible of pain or suffering; impassible; unmoved.

Impatient, im-pā'shent, *a.* Not patient; uneasy under given conditions and eager for change; not suffering quietly; not enduring delay.

Impeach, im-pēch', *vt.* To charge with a crime; to bring charges of maladministration against a minister of state, etc.; to call in question; to disparage.

Impeccable, im-pek'a-bl, *a.* Not peccable, or liable to sin.

Impecunious, im-pē-kū'ni-us, *a.* Not having money; without funds.

Impede, im-pēd', *vt.* (impeding, impeded). To entangle or hamper; to obstruct.

Impediment, im-ped'i-ment, *n.* That by which one is impeded; obstruction.

Impel, im-pel', *vt.* (impelling, impelled). To drive or urge forward; to press on; to instigate; to incite; to actuate.

Impend, im-pend', *vi.* To hang over; to threaten; to be imminent.

Imperceptible, im-pèr-sep'ti-bl, *a.* Not perceptible; not easily apprehended by the senses; fine or minute.

Imperfect, im-pèr'fekt, *a.* Not perfect; not complete; not perfect in a moral view; faulty; *imperfect tense,* a tense expressing an uncompleted action or state, especially in time past.

Imperforate, im-pèr'fo-rāt, *a.* Not perforated or pierced; having no opening or pores.

Imperial, im-pē'ri-al, *a.* Pertaining to an empire or emperor; supreme; suitable for an emperor; of superior excellence.—*n.* A tuft of hair beneath a man's lower lip; a size of paper measuring 30 by 22 inches.

Impersonal, im-pèr'son-al, *a.* Not having personal existence; not endued with personality; not referring to any particular person; *impersonal verb,* a verb (such as *it rains*) used only with an impersonal nominative.—*n.* That which wants personality; an impersonal verb.

Impersonate, im-pér'son-āt, *vt.* To invest with personality; to assume the character of; to represent in character; as on the stage.

Impertinent, im-pér'ti-nent, *a.* Not pertinent; irrelevant; petulant and rude; pert; intrusive.

Imperturbable, im-pér-térb'a-bl, *a.* That cannot be agitated; unmoved; calm.

Impervious, im-pér'vi-us, *a.* Not pervious; impassable; impenetrable.

Impetuous, im-pe'tū-us, *a.* Rushing with great force; forcible; precipitate; vehement of mind; hasty; passionate.

Impetus, im'pe-tus, *n.* The force with which any body is driven or impelled; momentum.

Impiety, im-pī'e-ti, *n.* Want of piety; irreverence toward the Supreme Being; ungodliness; an act of wickedness.

Impinge, im-pinj', *vi.* (impinging, impinged). To dash against; to clash.

Implicate, im'pli-kāt, *vt.* (implicating, implicated). To involve or bring into connection with; to prove to be connected or concerned, as in an offense.

Implication, im-pli-kā'shon, *n.* Act of implicating; state of being implicated; entanglement; a tacit inference; something to be understood though not expressed.

Implicit, im-pli'sit, *a.* Implied; fairly to be understood, though not expressed in words; trusting to another; unquestioning.

Implore, im-plōr, *vt.* and *i.* (imploring, implored). To call upon or for, in supplication; to beseech, entreat.

Imply, im-plī', *vt.* (implying, implied). To involve or contain in substance or by fair inference; to signify indirectly; to presuppose.

Importance, im-pōrt'ans, *n.* Quality of being important; weight; moment; rank or standing; weight in self-estimation.

Important, im-pōrt'ant, *a.* Full of

import; momentous; influential; grave; consequential.

Importune, im-por-tūn', *vt.* (importuning, importuned). To press with solicitation; to urge with frequent application.—*vi.* To solicit earnestly and repeatedly.

Impose, im-pōz', *vt.* (imposing, imposed). To place, set, or lay on; to lay on, as a tax, penalty, duty, etc.; to lay on, as hands; to obtrude fallaciously; to palm or pass off.—*vi.* Used in phrase *to impose on* or *upon,* to deceive; to victimize.

Impotent, im'pō-tent, *a.* Entirely wanting vigor of body or mind; feeble; destitute of the power of begetting children.

Impound, im-pound', *vt.* To confine in a pound or close pen; to confine; to take possession of for use when necessary.

Impoverish, im-po'vér-ish, *vt.* To make poor; to reduce to indigence; to exhaust the strength or fertility of, as of soil.

Impress, im-pres', *vt.* To press into; to imprint; to stamp on the mind; to inculcate; to compel to enter into public service, as seamen; to take for public use.—*n.* im'press. That which is impressed; mark made by pressure; impression; character; act of compelling to enter into public service.

Impression, im-pre'shon, *n.* Act of impressing; that which is impressed; mark; effect produced on the mind; an indistinct notion; idea; copy taken by pressure from type, etc.; edition; copies forming one issue of a book.

Impressionist, im-pre'shon-ist, *n.* One who lays stress on impressions; an artist who depicts scenes by their most striking characteristics as they first impress the spectator.

Impressive, im-pres'iv, *a.* Making an impression; solemn; awe-inspiring.

Imprimatur, im-pri-mā'tér, *n.* A license to print a book, etc.; mark of approval in general.

Impromptu, im-promp'tū, *n.* A saying, poem, etc., made off-hand; an extemporaneous composition.—*a.*

Off-hand; extempore.—*adv*. Off-hand.

Improper, im-pro'pėr, *a*. Not proper; unfit; not decent; erroneous; wrong.

Impropriety, im-prō-prī'e-ti, *n*. Quality of being improper; that which is improper; an unsuitable act, expression, etc.

Improvable, im-pröv'a-bl, *a*. That may be improved; susceptible of improvement.

Improve, im-pröv', *vt*. (improving, improved). To better; to ameliorate; to mend; to rectify; to use to good purpose; to apply to practical purposes.—*vi*. To grow better.

Improvement, im-pröv'ment, *n*. Act of improving; state of being improved; a change for the better; that which improves; a beneficial or valuable addition or alteration.

Improvident, im-pro'vi-dent, *a*. Not provident; wanting foresight or forethought; careless.

Improvise, im-pro-vīz', To form on the spur of the moment; to compose and recite, etc., without previous preparation.

Imprudence, im-pröadens, *n*. Want of prudence; indiscretion; a rash act.

Impudent, im'pū-dent, *a*. Offensively forward in behavior; bold-faced; impertinent.

Impugn, im-pūn', *vt*. To attack by words or arguments; to contradict; to call in question.

Impulse, im'puls, *n*. Force communicated instantaneously; effect of a sudden communication of motion; influence acting on the mind; motive; sudden determination.

In, in, *prep*. Within; inside of; surrounded by; indicating presence or situation within limits, whether of place, time, circumstances, etc.—*adv*. In or within some place, state, circumstances, etc.; not out.

Inadvertence, Inadvertency, in-ad-vėrt'ens, in-ad-vėrt'en-si, *n*. Quality of being inadvertent; any oversight or fault which proceeds from negligence or want of attention.

Inadvertent, in-ad-vėrt'ent, *a*. Not paying strict attention; heedless; unwary; negligent.

Inappreciable, in-ap-prē'shi-a-bl, *a*. Not appreciable; so small as hardly to be noticed.

Inapproachable, in-ap-prōch'a-bl, *a*. Not approachable; unapproachable.

Inappropriate, in-ap-prō'pri-āt, *a*. Not appropriate; unsuited; not proper.

Inaptitude, in-apt'ti-tūd, *n*. Want of aptitude; unsuitableness.

Inarticulate, in-är-tik'ū-lāt, *a*. Not articulate; not jointed or articulated; not uttered distinctly.

Inasmuch, in-az-much', *adv*. Seeing; seeing that; this being the fact.

Inattention, in-at-ten'shon, *n*. Want of attention; heedlessness; neglect.

Inaudible, in-a'di-bl, *a*. Not audible; that cannot be heard.

Inaugurate, in-a'gū-rāt, *vt*. To induct into an office with suitable ceremonies; to perform initiatory ceremonies in connection with.

Incalculable, in-kal'kū-la-bl, *a*. Not calculable; very great.

Incandescent, in-kan-des'ent, *a*. White or glowing with heat.—**Incandescent light,** a form of gas light; a form of electric light given forth from a filament of carbon inclosed in an airless glass globe.

Incantation, in-kan-tā'shon, *n*. The act of using certain words and ceremonies to raise spirits, etc.; the form of words so used; a magical charm or ceremony.

Incapable, in-kā'pa-bl, *a*. Not capable; possessing inadequate power or capacity; not susceptible; incompetent; unqualified or disqualified.—*n*. One physically or mentally weak.

Incarcerate, in-kär'sė-rāt, *vt*. To imprison; to shut up or inclose.

Incarnate, in-kär'nāt, *vt*. To clothe with flesh; to embody in flesh.—*a*. Invested with flesh; embodied in flesh.

Incense, in'sens, *n*. Aromatic substance burned in religious rites; odors of spices and gums, burned in religious rites; flattery or agreeable homage.—*vt*. (incensing, incensed). To perfume with incense.

Inceptive, in-sep'tiv, *a.* Pertaining to inception; beginning; applied to a verb which expresses the beginning of an action.—*n.* An inceptive verb.

Incessant, in-ses'ant, *a.* Unceasing; unintermitted; continual; constant.

Incest, in'sest, *n.* Sexual commerce between near blood relations.

Inch, insh, *n.* The twelfth part of a foot in length; a small quantity or degree.—*vt.* To drive or force by inches.

Incise, in-sīz', *vt.* (incising, incised). To cut in or into; to carve; to engrave.

Incite, in-sīt', *vt.* (inciting, incited). To move to action by impulse or influence; to instigate; to encourage.

Inclement, in-kle'ment, *a.* Not clement; harsh; stormy; rigorously cold.

Inclination, in-klin-ā'shon, *n.* The act of inclining; deviation from a normal direction; a leaning of the mind or will; tendency; bent; bias; predilection; liking.

Incline, in-klīn', *vi.* (inclining, inclined). To deviate from a direction regarded as normal; to slope; to be disposed; to have some wish or desire.—*vt.* To cause to lean or bend towards or away from; to give a leaning to; to dispose.—*n.* An ascent or descent; a slope.

Inclose, in-klōz', *vt.* (inclosing, inclosed). To shut up or confine on all sides; to environ; to cover with a wrapper or envelope.

Inclosure, in-klō'zhúr, *n.* Act of inclosing; what is inclosed; a space inclosed or fenced; something inclosed with a letter, etc.

Include, in-klöd', *vt.* (including, included). To hold or contain; to comprise; to comprehend.

Inclusive, in-klö'siv, *a.* Inclosing; comprehended in the number or sum; comprehending the stated limit.

Incognito, in-kog'ni-tō, *pred.a.* or *adv.* In disguise.—*n.* (fem. being **Incognita**). One passing under an assumed name; assumption of a feigned character.

Incognizance, in-kog'ni-zans or in-kon'i-zans, *n.* Failure to recognize or apprehend.

Incoherent, in-kō-hēr'ent, *a.* Not coherent; wanting rational connection, as ideas, language, etc.; rambling and unintelligible.

Incombustible, in-kom-bust'i-bl, *a.* Not combustible; that cannot be burned.

Income, in'kum, *n.* Receipts or emoluments regularly coming in from property or employment; annual receipts; revenue.

Income-tax, in'kum-taks, *n.* A tax levied on incomes according to their amount.

Incomparable, in-kom'pa-ra-bl, *a.* Not comparable; that admits of no comparison with others; matchless.

Incompatibility, in-kom-pat'i-bil''i-ti, *n.* State or quality of being incompatible; inconsistency; disposition or temper entirely out of harmony.

Incompatible, in-kom-pat'i-bl, *a.* Not compatible; inconsistent; irreconcilably different; that cannot be made to accord.

Incompetence, Incompetency, in-kom'pē-tens, in-kom'pē-ten-si, *n.* State or quality of being incompetent; want of suitable faculties, adequate means, or proper qualifications.

Incompetent, in-kom'pē-tent, *a.* Not competent; incapable; wanting legal qualifications; not admissible.

Incomplete, in-kom-plēt', *a.* Not complete; imperfect; defective.

Incondite, in-kon'dīt, *a.* Rude; unpolished; said of literary compositions.

Incongruity, in-kong-grų'i-ti, *n.* Want of congruity; inconsistency; absurdity.

Inconsistence, Inconsistency, in-kon-sist'ens, in-kon-sist'en-si, *n.* The condition or quality of being inconsistent; opposition or disagreement of particulars; self-contradiction; incongruity; discrepancy.

Inconsolable, in-kon-sōl'a-bl, *a.* Not to be consoled; grieved beyond consolation.

Inconspicuous, in-kon-spik'ū-us, *a.*

Not conspicuous; unobtrusive.

Inconstant, in-kon'stant, *a*. Not constant; subject to change of opinion or purpose; not firm in resolution; fickle.

Incontestable, in-kon-test'a-bl, *a*. Not contestable; not to be disputed; unquestionable.

Incontinent, in-kon'ti-nent, *a*. Not continent; not restraining the passions or appetites; unchaste; unable to restrain discharges.

Incontrovertible, in-kon'trō-vėrt''i-bl, *a*. Not controvertible; too clear to admit of dispute.

Inconvenience, in-kon-vē'ni-ens, *n*. The quality of being inconvenient; annoyance; molestation; trouble; disadvantage.—*vt*. To put to inconvenience; to trouble.

Inconvertible, in-kon-vėrt'i-bl, *a*. Not convertible; that cannot be changed into or exchanged for something else.

Incorporate, in-kor'pō-rāt, *vt*. To form into one body; to unite; to blend; to associate with another whole, as with a government; to form into a legal body or corporation.—*vi*. To unite; to grow into or coalesce.—*a*. Incorporated; united in one body.

Incorruptible, in-ko-rupt'i-bl, *a*. Not corruptible; that cannot corrupt or decay; inflexibly just and upright.

Increase, in-krēs', *vi*. (increasing, increased). To become greater; to augment; to advance in any quality, good or bad; to multiply by the production of young.—*vt*. To make greater or larger; to add to.—*n*. in'krēs. A growing larger in size, quantity, etc.; augmentation; addition; increment; profit; interest; offspring.

Incredible, in-kred'i-bl, *a*. Not credible; too improbable to admit of belief.

Incredulous, in-kred'ū-lus, *a*. Not credulous; refusing or withholding belief.

Increment, in'krē-ment, *n*. Act or process of increasing; increase; increase in the value of real property from adventitious causes.

Incriminate, in-krim'in-āt, *vt*. To bring an accusation against; to charge with a crime or fault.

Incubator, in'kū-bāt-ėr, *n*. One who or that which incubates; an apparatus for hatching eggs by artificial heat.

Incubus, in'kū-bus, *n*.; pl. **-buses** or **-bi.** A name of nightmare; something that weighs heavily on a person; burden or incumbrance; dead weight.

Inculcate, in-kul'kāt, *vt*. To press or urge forcibly and repeatedly; to teach.

Inculpate, in-kul'pāt, *vt*. To show to be in fault; to impute guilt to; to incriminate.

Incumbent, in-kum'bent, *a*. Lying on; resting on a person, as duty or obligation.—*n*. One in possession of an ecclesiastical benefice or other office.

Incurvate, in-kėrv'āt, *a*. Curved inward or upward.

Incuse, in-kūz', *vt*. To impress by stamping.—*a*. Impressed by stamping.

Indebted, in-det'ed, *a*. Being in debt; obliged by something received.

Indecency, in-dē'sen-si, *n*. The quality of being indecent; what is indecent in language, actions, etc.; indecorum; immodesty.

Indecipherable, in-dē-sī'fėr-a-bl, *a*. Incapable of being deciphered.

Indecision, in-dē-si'zhon, *n*. Want of decision; irresolution; hesitation.

Indeclinable, in-dē-klīn'a-bl, *a*. Not declinable; not varied by terminations of case, etc.

Indecorous, in-dē-kō'rus or in-de'kō-rus, *a*. Not decorous; unseemly; indecent; unbecoming.

Indeed, in-dēd', *adv*. In reality; in fact; really; truly.

Indelicate, in-de'li-kāt, *a*. Wanting delicacy; offensive to modesty or nice sense of propriety; somewhat immodest.

Indemnify, in-dem'ni-fī, *vt*. To make safe from loss or harm; to reimburse or compensate.

Indemnity, in-dem'ni-ti, *n*. Security given against loss, damage, or punishment; compensation for loss or injury sustained.

Indent, in-dent', *vt.* To notch; to cut into points or inequalities; to bind by indenture.—*n.* A cut or notch; an indentation.

Indenture, in-den'tūr, *n.* That which is indented; a deed under seal between two or more parties, each having a duplicate.—*vt.* To indent; to bind by indenture.

Independence, in-dē-pend'ens, *n.* State of being independent; complete exemption from control; self-reliance; political freedom.

Index, in'deks, *n.*; pl. **Indexes** or **Indices,** in'dek-sez, in'di-sēz. Something that points out; the hand ☞ used by printers, etc.; a table of contents; list of books disapproved of by R. Catholic authorities; the forefinger; the figure denoting to what power any mathematical quantity is involved.—*vt.* To provide with an index; to place in an index.

Indian, in'di-an, *a.* Pertaining to India, or to the Indies, East or West; pertaining to the aborigines of America.

Indicate, in'di-kāt, *vt.* To point out; to show; to intimate; to suggest.

Indication, in-di-kā'shon, *n.* Act of indicating; what points out; mark; token; sign.

Indicative, in-dik'a-tiv, *a.* That serves to point out; serving as an indication; designating a mood of the verb that declares directly or asks questions.—*n.* The indicative mood.

Indict, in-dīt', *vt.* To charge with a crime or misdemeanor in due form of law.

Indigestion, in-di-jest'yon, *n.* Incapability of or difficulty in digesting; dyspepsia.

Indignation, in-dig-nā'shon, *n.* A feeling of displeasure at what is unworthy or base; anger, mingled with contempt, disgust, or abhorrence; violent displeasure.

Indignity, in-dig'ni-ti, *n.* An insult; an affront; an outrage.

Indigo, in'di-go, *n.* A blue vegetable dye, from India and other places; the leguminous plant that produces the dye.

Indirect, in-di-rekt', *a.* Not direct; circuitous; not tending directly to a purpose or end; not straightforward; not resulting directly.

Indiscreet, in-dis-krēt', *a.* Not discreet; injudicious; inconsiderate.

Indissoluble, in-dis'sō-lū-bl, *a.* Not capable of being dissolved; perpetually binding or obligatory; not to be broken.

Indistinct, in-dis-tingkt', *a.* Not distinct; faint; confused; imperfect or dim.

Indistinguishable, in-dis-ting'gwish-a-bl, *a.* Incapable of being distinguished.

Indite, in-dīt', *vt.* and *i.* (inditing, indited). To compose or write; to direct or dictate.

Individual, in-di-vid'ū-al, *a.* Subsisting as one indivisible entity; pertaining to one only; peculiar to a single person or thing.—*n.* A being or thing forming one of its kind; a person.

Indocile, in-dō'sīl or in-dos'il, *a.* Not docile or teachable; intractable.

Indoctrinate, in-dok'trin-āt, *vt.* To imbue with any doctrine; to teach; to instruct.

Indolence, in'dō-lens, *n.* Habitual love of ease; laziness; idleness.

Indomitable, in-dom'it-a-bl, *a.* Not to be tamed or subdued; irrepressible.

Indoor, in'dōr, *a.* Being within doors; being within the house.— **Indoors,** in'dōrz, *adv.* Within doors; inside a house.

Indubitable, in-dū'bit-a-bl, *a.* Not to be doubted; too plain to admit of doubt; evident.

Induce, in-dūs', *vt.* (inducing, induced). To lead by persuasion or argument; to prevail on; to actuate; to produce or cause.

Induct, in-dukt', *vt.* To lead or bring into; to put in possession of an ecclesiastical living or office, with customary ceremonies.

Indulge, in-dulj', *vt.* (indulging, indulged). To give free course to; to gratify by compliance; to humor to excess.—*vi.* To indulge oneself; to practice indulgence.

Indulgence, in-dulj'ens, *n.* The act or practice of indulging; a favor;

intemperance; gratification of desire; tolerance; remission of the penance attached to certain sins.

Indurate, in'dū-rāt, *vi.* To grow hard.—*vt.* To make hard; to deprive of sensibility.

Industrious, in-dus'tri-us, *a.* Given to or characterized by industry; diligent; active.

Industry, in'dus-tri, *n.* Habitual diligence; steady attention to business; the industrial arts generally, or any one of them; manufacture; trade.

Inebriate, in-ē'bri-āt, *vt.* To make drunk; to intoxicate.—*n.* An habitual drunkard.

Inept, in-ept', *a.* Unsuitable; improper; foolish; silly; nonsensical.

Ineptitude, in-ept'i-tūd, *n.* Condition or quality of being inept; unfitness; silliness.

Inequality, in-ē-kwol'i-ti, *n.* Condition of being unequal; want of equality; an elevation or depression in a surface; diversity.

Inert, in-ėrt', *a.* Destitute of the power of moving itself, or of active resistance to motion impressed; lifeless; sluggish; inactive.

Inertia, in-ėr'shi-a, *n.* Passiveness; inactivity; the property of matter by which it tends to retain its state of rest or of uniform rectilinear motion.

Inexorable, in-eks'ōr-a-bl, *a.* Not to be persuaded by entreaty or prayer; unbending; unrelenting; implacable.

Inexpedient, in-eks-pē'di-ent, *a.* Not expedient; not advisable or judicious.

Inexperience, in-eks-pē'ri-ens, *n.* Want of experience.

Inexplicable, in-eks'pli-ka-bl, *a.* That cannot be explained or interpreted; unaccountable; mysterious.

Inexplicit, in-eks-plis'it, *a.* Not explicit; not clear in statement.

Infallible, in-fal'i-bl, *a.* Not fallible; not liable to fail; certain.

Infamous, in'fa-mus, *a.* Notoriously vile; detestable; branded with infamy.

Infamy, in'fa-mi, *n.* Total loss of reputation; public disgrace; qualities

detested and despised; extreme vileness.

Infancy, in'fan-si, *n.* State of being an infant; early childhood; period from birth to the age of twenty-one; first age of anything.

Infant, in'fant, *n.* A very young child; one under twenty-one years of age.—*a.* Pertaining to infants.

Infanticide, in-fant'i-sīd, *n.* Child murder; a slayer of infants.

Infantry, in'fant-ri, *n.* The soldiers or troops that serve on foot.

Infatuate, in-fa'tū-āt, *vt.* To make foolish; to inspire with an extravagant passion.

Infatuation, in-fa'tū-ā''shon, *n.* Act of infatuating; state of being infatuated; foolish passion.

Infect, in-fekt', *vt.* To taint with disease; to communicate bad qualities to; to corrupt.

Inferior, in-fē'ri-ėr, *a.* Lower in place, station, age, value, etc.; subordinate.—*n.* A person lower in rank, importance, etc.

Infernal, in-fėr'nal, *a.* Pertaining to the lower regions or hell; very wicked and detestable; diabolical.—**Infernal machine,** an explosive apparatus contrived for assassination or other mischief.

Infertile, in-fėr'tīl, *a.* Not fertile; barren.

Infertility, in-fėr-til'i-ti, *n.* Barrenness.

Infest, in-fest', *vt.* To attack; to molest; to annoy continually.

Infidel, in'fi-del, *n.* A disbeliever; a sceptic; one who does not believe in God or in Christianity.—*a.* Unbelieving; sceptical.

Infinitive, in-fin'it-iv, *a.* Designating a mood of the verb which expresses action without limitation of person or number, as, *to love.*—*n.* The infinitive mood.

Infinity, in-fin'i-ti, *n.* State or quality of being infinite; unlimited extent of time, space, quantity, etc.; immensity.

Infirmary, in-fėrm'a-ri, *n.* A place where the sick and injured are nursed; a hospital.

Infirmity, in-fėrm'i-ti, *n.* State of being infirm; unsound state of the body; weakness of mind or resolution; failing; malady.

Infix, in-fiks´, vt. To fix or fasten in; to implant, as principles, etc.

Inflame, in-flām´, vt. To set on fire; to kindle; to excite or increase; to incense; to make morbidly red and swollen.—vi. To grow hot, angry, and painful; to take fire.

Inflammation, in-flam-ā´shon, n. Act of inflaming; state of being inflamed; a redness and swelling attended with heat, pain, and feverish symptoms.

Inflection, in-flek´shon, n. Act of inflecting; state of being inflected; grammatical variation of nouns, verbs, etc.; modulation of the voice; deflection or diffraction.

Inflexed, in-flekst´, a. Curved; bent inward.

Inflexibility, in-fleks´i-bil´´i-ti, n. Firmness of purpose; unbending pertinacity or obstinacy.

Inflexible, in-fleks´i-bl, a. That cannot be bent; firm in purpose; pertinacious; inexorable.

Inflict, in-flikt´, vt. To cause to bear or suffer from; to impose, as pain, punishment, etc.

Inflow, in´flō, n. The act of flowing in or into; that which flows in; influx.

Influence, in´flų-ens, n. Agency or power serving to affect, modify, etc.; sway; effect; acknowledged ascendency with people in power.—vt. To exercise influence on; to bias; to sway.

Informal, in-form´al, a. Not in the usual form or mode; not with the official or customary forms; without ceremony.

Information, in-form-ā´shon, n. The act of informing; intelligence communicated or gathered; a charge or accusation before a magistrate.

Infrequent, in-frē´kwent, a. Not frequent; seldom happening; rare.

Infringe, in-frinj´, vt. (infringing, infringed). To break, as laws, agreements, etc.; to violate; to contravene.—vi. To encroach (with on or *upon*).

Infuriate, in-fū´ri-āt, vt. To madden; to enrage.—a. Enraged; mad; raging.

Infuse, in-fūz´, vt. (infusing, in-

fused). To pour in, as a liquid; to instil, as principles; to steep in liquor without boiling, in order to extract solutions, etc.

Infusion, in-fū´zhon, n. Act or process of infusing; that which is infused; liquor obtained by infusing or steeping.

Ingenious, in-jē´ni-us, a. Possessed of cleverness or ability; apt in contriving; contrived with ingenuity; witty or well conceived.

Ingenuity, in-jen-ū´i-ti, n. Quality of being ingenious; ready invention; skill in contrivance.

Ingratitude, in-grat´i-tūd, n. Want of gratitude; unthankfulness.

Ingredient, in-grē´di-ent, n. That which is a component part of any mixture; an element, component, or constituent.

Ingress, in´gres, n. Entrance; power of entrance; means of entering.

Inguinal, in´gwin-al, a. Pertaining to the groin.

Ingulf, in-gulf´, vt. To swallow up; to absorb; to overwhelm by swallowing.

Inhabit, in-ha´bit, vt. To live or dwell in; to occupy as a place of settled resident.—vi. To dwell; to live; to abide.

Inhalation, in-ha-lā´shon, n. Act of inhaling; that which is inhaled.

Inhale, in-hāl´, vt. (inhaling, inhaled). To draw into the lungs; to suck in.

Inharmonious, in-här-mō´ni-us, a. Not harmonious; unmusical; discordant.

Inherent, in-hēr´ent, a. Naturally pertaining; innate.

Inherit, in-he´rit, vt. To come into possession of as an heir; to receive by nature from a progenitor; to hold as belonging to one's lot.—vi. To take or have possession of property.

Inheritance, in-he´rit-ans, n. Act of inheriting; that which is or may be inherited; what falls to one's lot; possession.

Inhibit, in-hib´it, vt. To hold in or back; to restrain; to forbid; to interdict.

Inhospitable, in-hos´pit-a-bl, a. Not

hospitable; wanting in hospitality; affording no entertainment to strangers.

Inhuman, in-hū'man, *a.* Destitute of the kindness and tenderness that belong to a human being; cruel; merciless.

Initial, in-i'shal, *a.* Placed at the beginning; pertaining to the beginning; beginning.—*n.* The first letter of a word; *pl.* the first letter in order of the words composing a name.—*vt.* (initialling, initialled). To put one's initials to; to mark by initials.

Initiate, in-i'shi-āt, *vt.* To begin; to be the first to practice or bring in; to instruct in rudiments; to introduce into any society or set; to let into secrets; to indoctrinate.

Injure, in'jėr, *vt.* (injuring, injured). To do harm to; to hurt; to damage.

Injurious, in-jū'ri-us, *a.* Causing injury; tending to injure; hurtful; harmful.

Injury, in'jū-ri, *n.* The doing of harm; harm or damage; mischief; detriment.

Injustice, in-just'is, *n.* Want of justice or equity; iniquity; wrong.

Ink, ingk, *n.* A colored liquid, usually black, for writing, printing, etc.—*vt.* To black or daub with ink.

Inkling, ingk'ling, *n.* A hint or whisper; a slight notion or idea.

Inland, in'land, *a.* Interior; remote from the sea; domestic, not foreign; confined to a country.—*adv.* In or towards the interior of a country.—*n.* The interior part of a country.

Inn, in, *n.* A house for the lodging and entertainment of travellers.

Innate, in-nāt', *a.* Inborn; natural; native; inherent.

Inner, in'ėr, *a.* Interior; further inward than something else; internal.—*n.* A shot which strikes the target between the bull's-eye and the innermost ring.

Innocent, in'nō-sent, *a.* Not noxious or hurtful; free from guilt; simple-hearted; guileless.—*n.* One free from guilt or harm; a natural or simpleton.

Innocuous, in-nok'ū-us, *a.* Harmless; not injurious; producing no ill effect.

Innovate, in'nō-vāt, *vi.* To introduce novelties or changes.

Inoculate, in-ok'ū-lāt, *vt.* To graft by inserting a bud; to communicate a disease to by morbid matter introduced into the blood; to infect; to contaminate.

Inoffensive, in-of-fens'iv, *a.* Giving no offense or annoyance; harmless.

Inofficial, in-of-fi'shal, *a.* not official; not clothed with the usual forms of authority.

Inoperative, in-o'pe-rāt-iv, *a.* Not operative; not active; producing no effect.

Inopportune, in-op'por-tūn, *a.* Not opportune; inconvenient; unseasonable.

Inordinate, in-or'din-āt, *a.* Excessive; immoderate.

Inorganic, in-or-gan'ik, *a.* Not organic; devoid of the structure of a living being; pertaining to substances without carbon.

In-patient, in'pā'shent, *n.* A patient who is lodged as well as treated in a hospital.

Inquest, in'kwest, *n.* Inquiry; a judicial inquiry before a jury; the jury itself.

Inquietude, in-kwī'et-ūd, *n.* Want of quiet; uneasiness, either of body or mind.

Inquire, in-kwīr', *vi.* (inquiring, inquired). Often **enquire.** To ask a question; to seek for truth by discussion or investigation.—*vt.* To ask about; to seek by asking.

Inquiry, in-kwī'ri, *n.* Often **enquiry.** The act of inquiring; a question; research; investigation; examination.

Inquisition, in-kwi-zi'shon, *n.* The act of inquiring; inquiry; inquest; a R. Catholic court for the examination and punishment of heretics.

Insane, in-sān', *a.* Not sane; deranged in mind or intellect; intended for insane persons; senseless.

Insanity, in-san'i-ti, *n.* The state of being insane; derangement of intellect; lunacy.

Insatiable, in-sā'shi-a-bl, *a.* Not satiable; incapable of being satisfied or appeased.

Insatiate, in-sā'shi-āt, *a*. Not satisfied; insatiable.

Inscribe, in-skrīb', *vt*. (inscribing, inscribed). To write down; to imprint on, as on the memory; to address or dedicate; to mark with letters or words; to draw a figure within another.

Inscription, in-skrip'shon, *n*. The act of inscribing; words engraved; address of a book, etc., to a person.

Inscrutable, in-skrö'ta-bl, *a*. Unsearchable; that cannot be penetrated or understood by human reason.

Insect, in'sekt, *n*. One of those small animals that have three divisions of the body—head, thorax, and abdomen—and usually three pairs of legs and two pairs of wings, as flies, etc.; a puny, contemptible person.—*a*. Pertaining to insects; like an insect; mean.

Insensible, in-sens'i-bl, *a*. Not perceived or perceptible by the senses; void of feeling; unfeeling; callous; indifferent.

Inseparable, in-sep'a-ra-bl, *a*. Not separable; not to be parted; always together.

Insert, in-sėrt', *vt*. To put, bring, or set in; to thrust in; to set in or among.

Insertion, in-sėr'shon, *n*. Act of inserting; thing inserted; place or mode of attachment of a part or organ to its support.

Inset, in-set', *vt*. To set in; to implant.—*n*. in'set. That which is set in; insertion.

Inside, in'sīd, *n*. The interior side or part of a thing.—*a*. Interior; internal.—*prep*. In the interior of; within.

Insidious, in-sid'i-us, *a*. Treacherous; guileful; working evil secretly.

Insinuate, in-sin'ū-āt, *vt*. To introduce by windings or gently; to work gradually into favor; to introduce by gentle or artful means; to hint.—*vi*. To creep or wind; to make an insinuation; to wheedle.

Insipid, in-sip'id, *a*. Destitute of taste; vapid; flat; dull; heavy; spiritless.

Insist, in-sist', *vi*. To rest or dilate on; to be urgent or peremptory.

Insolvent, in-sol'vent, *a*. Not solvent; not having money, etc., sufficient to pay debts.—*n*. One unable to pay his debts.

Insomnia, in-som'ni-a, *n*. Want of sleep; morbid or unnatural sleeplessness.

Inspect, in-spekt', *vt*. To view or examine to ascertain the quality or condition, etc.

Inspiration, in-spi-rā'shon, *n*. The act of inspiring; the drawing in of breath; the divine influence by which the sacred writers were instructed; influence emanating from any object; the state of being inspired; something conveyed to the mind when under extraordinary influence.

Inspire, in-spīr', *vt*. (inspiring, inspired). To breathe in; to breathe into; to communicate divine instructions to; to infuse ideas or poetic spirit into; to animate in general.—*vi*. To draw in breath; to inhale air into the lungs.

Instant, in'stant, *a*. Pressing or urgent; immediate; making no delay; present or current.—*n*. A moment.

Instantaneous, in-stant-ā'nē-us, *a*. Done or occurring in an instant.

Instate, in-stāt', *vt*. (instating, instated). To set or place; to install.

Instead, in-sted', *adv*. In the place or room of; in place of that.

Instep, in'step, *n*. The fore part of the upper side of the foot, near its junction with the leg.

Instigate, in'sti-gāt, *vt*. To spur on; to urge; to incite; to impel.

Instil, in-stil', *vt*. (instilling, instilled). To pour in, as by drops; to infuse by degrees; to insinuate imperceptibly.

Instinct, in'stingkt, *n*. Spontaneous or natural impulse; the knowledge and skill which animals have without experience; intuitive feeling.—*a*. in-stingkt'. Animated or stimulated from within; inspired.

Institute, in'sti-tūt, *vt*. To set up or establish; to found; to begin; to appoint to an office; to invest with a benefice.—*n*. That which is instituted; established law; principle; a literary or scientific body; an institution; *pl*. a book of elements or principles.

Instruct, in-strukt', *vt*. To impart knowledge to; to teach; to advise or give notice to.

Insular, in'sū-lėr, *a*. Pertaining to an island; forming an island; narrow-minded.

Insulate, in'sū-lāt, *vt*. To make into an island; to detach; to separate, as an electrified body, by interposition of non-conductors.

Insulator, in'sū-lāt-ėr, *n*. One who or that which insulates; a body that interrupts the communication of electricity; non-conductor.

Insulin, ins'ū-lin, *n*. A substance extracted from the pancreas of animals, and found beneficial in diabetes.

Insult, in'sult, *n*. Any gross affront or indignity; act or speech of insolence or contempt.—*vt*. in-sult'. To treat with insult or insolence.—*vi*. To behave with insolent triumph.

Insure, in-shōr', *vt*. (insuring, insured). To make sure; to contract for the receipt of a certain sum in the event of loss, death, etc.

Insurgent, in-sėr'jent, *a*. Rising in opposition to lawful authority; rebellious.—*n*. One who rises in opposition to authority.

Insurrection, in-sėr-rek'shon, *n*. A rising against authority; rebellion.

Insusceptible, in-sus-sept'i-bl, *a*. Not susceptible; not capable of being affected.

Intact, in-takt', *a*. Untouched; unimpaired.

Intaglio, in-tal'yō, *n*. Any figure engraved or cut into a substance; a gem with a figure or device sunk below the surface.

Intangible, in-tan'ji-bl, *a*. That cannot be touched; not perceptible to the touch.

Integer, in'ti-jer, *n*. A whole; whole number, in contradistinction to a fraction.

Integral, in'ti-gral, *a*. Whole; forming a necessary part of a whole; not fractional.—*n*. A whole; an entire thing.

Integrate, in'ti-grāt, *vt*. To make or form into one whole; to give the sum or total of.

Integrity, in-teg'ri-ti, *n*. State of being entire; an unimpaired state; honesty; probity.

Intelligent, in-tel'i-jent, *a*. Endowed with the faculty of understanding or reason; endowed with a good intellect; well informed.

Intelligible, in-tel'i-ji-bl, *a*. Capable of being understood; comprehensible; clear.

Intemperate, in-tem'pėr-ēt, *a*. Not temperate; addicted to an excessive use of alcoholic liquors; excessive or immoderate.—*n*. One not temperate.

Intend, in-tend', *vt*. To design; to purpose; to mean.

Intended, in-tend'ed, *p.a.* Purposed; betrothed.—*n*. An affianced lover.

Intense, in-tens', *a*. Closely strained; strict; extreme in degree; violent; severe.

Intensify, in-ten'si-fī, *vt*. To render intense or more intense; to aggravate.—*vi*. To become intense.

Intercede, in-tėr-sēd', *vi*. (interceding, interceded). To mediate; to plead in favor of one; to make intercession.

Intercept, in-tėr-sept', *vt*. To take or seize on by the way; to stop on its passage; to obstruct the progress of; to cut or shut off.

Intercession, in-tėr-se'shon, *n*. Act of interceding; mediation; prayer or solicitation to one party in favor of another.

Interest, in'tėr-est, *vt*. To concern; to engage the attention of.—*n*. Concern or regard; advantage; profit; profit per cent from money lent or invested; influence with a person.

Interfere, in-tėr-fēr', *vi*. (interfering, interfered). To clash; to interpose; to take a part in the concerns of others.

Interim, in'tėr-im, *n*. The meantime; time intervening.—*a*. Belonging to an intervening time; temporary.

Interior, in-tē'ri-ėr, *a*. Internal; being within; inland.—*n*. The inner part of a thing; the inside; the inland part of a country, etc.

Interject, in-tèr-jekt´, *vt.* To throw in between; to insert.

Interlocution, in´tèr-lō-kū´´shon, *n.* Dialogue; interchange of speech; an intermediate act or decree before final decision.

Interlocutory, in-tèr-lo´kū-to-ri, *a.* Consisting of dialogue; not final or definitive.

Interlope, in-tèr-lōp´, *vi.* To traffic without proper license; to intrude.

Interlude, in´tèr-lūd, *n.* A short entertainment between the acts of a play, or between the play and the afterpiece; a piece of music between certain more important passages.

Interminable, in-tèr´min-a-bl, *a.* Admitting no limit; boundless; endless.

Interminate, in-tèr´min-āt, *a.* Unbounded; unlimited; endless.

Intermingle, in-tèr-ming´gl, *vt.* To mingle together.—*vi.* To be mixed or incorporated..

Intermission, in-tèr-mi´shon, *n.* Act or state of intermitting; pause; rest.

Internal, in-tèrn´al, *a.* Inward; not external; domestic; not foreign.

International, in-tèr-na´shon-al, *a.* Relating to or mutually affecting nations; regularing the mutual intercourse between nations.

Interpretation, in-tèr´pret-ā´´shon, *n.* Act of interpreting; explanation; representation of a character on the stage.

Interregnum, in-tèr-reg´num, *n.* The time between reigns; intermission or break in succession.

Interrelation, in´tèr-rē-lā´´shon, *n.* Mutual or corresponding relation; correlation.

Interrogate, in-te´rō-gāt, *vt.* To question; to examine by asking questions.

Interrogation, in-te´rō-gā´´shon, *n.* Act of interrogating; question put; a sign that marks a question, thus (?).

Interrupt, in-tèr-rupt´, *vt.* To break in upon the progress of; to cause to stop in speaking.

Interstellar, Interstellary, in-tèr-

stel´lèr, in-tèr-stel´la-ri, *a.* Intervening between the stars; situated beyond the solar system.

Interstice, in-tèrs´tis, *n.* A narrow space between things closely set; a chink.

Intertwine, in-tèr-twīn´, *vt.* To unite by twining or twisting.—*vi.* To be interwoven.

Interval, in´tèr-val, *n.* A space between things; amount of separation between ranks, degrees, etc.; difference in gravity or acuteness between sounds.

Intervene, in-tèr-vēn´, *vi.* (intervening, intervened). To come or be between; to interpose or interfere.

Interview, in´tèr-vū, *n.* A meeting between persons; a conference.— *vt.* To have an interview with to get information for publication.

Interweave, in-tèr-wēv´, *vt.* To weave together; to unite intimately; to interlace.

Intestate, in-test´āt, *a.* Dying without having made a will; not disposed of by will.—*n.* A person who dies without making a will.

Intestine, in-tes´tīn, *a.* Internal; domestic; not foreign. *n.* The canal extending from the stomach to the anus; *pl.* entrails or viscera in general.

Intimate, in´ti-māt, *a.* Inward or internal; close in friendship; familiar; close.—*n.* An intimate or familiar friend.—*vt.* (intimating, intimated). To hint or indicate; to announce.

Intimation, in-ti-mā´shon, *n.* Act of intimating; a hint; announcement.

Intimidate, in-tim´id-āt, *vt.* To put in fear or dread; to cow; to deter with threats.

Into, in´tö, *prep.* In and to: expressing motion or direction towards the inside of, or a change of condition.

Intolerable, in-tol´èr-a-bl, *a.* That cannot be borne; unendurable; insufferable.

Intolerant, in-tol´èr-ant, *a.* That cannot bear; not enduring difference of opinion or worship; refusing to tolerate others.

Intonate, in´tōn-āt, *vi.* To sound the notes of the musical scale; to mod-

I

ulate the voice.—*vt*. To pronounce with a certain modulation.

Intone, in-tōn', *vi*. To use a musical monotone in pronouncing.—*vt*. To pronounce with a muscial tone; to chant.

Intoxicate, in-toks'i-kāt, *vt*. To make drunk; to elate to enthusiasm or madness.—*vi*. To cause intoxication.

Intrepid, in-tre'pid, *a*. Undaunted; fearless; bold; daring; courageous.

Intricate, in'tri-kāt, *a*. Involved; complicated.

Intrigue, in-trēg', *n*. An underhand plot or scheme; plot of a play, etc.; an illicit intimacy between a man and woman.—*vi*. (intriguing, intrigued). To engage in an intrigue; to carry on forbidden love.

Intrinsic, Intrinsical, in-trin'sik, in-trin'sik-al, *a*. Being within; inherent; essential.

Introduce, in-trō-dūs', *vt*. To lead or bring in; to insert; to bring to be acquainted; to present; to make known; to import; to bring before the public.

Introduction, in-trō-duk'shon, *n*. Act of introducing; act of making persons known to each other; act of bringing something into notice; a preliminary discourse.

Introspect, in-trō-spekt', *vt*. To look into or within.

Introspection, in-trō-spek'shon, *n*. The act of looking inwardly; examination of one's own thoughts or feelings.

Introvert, in-trō-vėrt', *vt*. To turn inward.

Intrude, in-trōd', *vi*. (intruding, intruded). to thrust oneself in; to force an entry or way in without permission, right, or invitation; to encroach.—*vt*. To thrust in.

Intuition, in-tū-i'shon, *n*. A looking on; direct apprehension of a truth without reasoning.

Intuitive, in-tū'it-iv, *a*. Perceived by the mind immediately without reasoning; based on intuition; self-evident.

Inundate, in-un'dāt or in'-, *vt*. To spread or flow over; to flood; to overwhelm.

Invalid, in'va-lēd, *n*. One weak or infirm; a person disabled for active service.—*a*. In ill health; infirm; disabled.—*vt*. To render an invalid; to enrol on the list of invalids.

Invective, in-vek'tiv, *n*. Violent utterance of censure; railing language; vituperation.—*a*. Containing invectives; abusive.

Inveigh, in-vā', *vi*. To attack with invectives; to rail against; to reproach; to upbraid.

Inveigle, in-vē'gl, *vt*. To persuade to something evil; to entice; to seduce.

Invent, in-vent', *vt*. To devise or produce, as something new; to fabricate; to concoct.

Invention, in-ven'shon, *n*. Act of inventing; contrivance of that which did not before exist; device; power of inventing; ingenuity; faculty by which an author produces plots, etc.

Inventory, in'ven-to-ri, *n*. An account of catalogue of the goods and chattels of a deceased person; a catalogue of particular things.—*vt*. to make an inventory of.

Inverse, in'vėrs or in-vėrs', *a*. Opposite in order or relation; inverted.

Invest, in-vest', *vt*. To clothe; to array; to clothe with office or authority; to endow; to besiege; to lay out as money in some species of property.—*vi*. To make an investment.

Investigate, in-ves'ti-gāt, *vt*. To search into; to make careful examination of.

Invigorate, in-vi'gor-āt, *vt*. To give vigor to; to give life and energy to.

Invincible, in-vin'si-bl, *a*. Not to be conquered or overcome; insurmountable.—*n*. One who is invincible.

Inviolable, in-vī'ō-la-bl, *a*. Not to be violated; that ought not to be injured or treated irreverently; not susceptible or hurt.

Inviolate, in-vī'ō-lāt, *a*. Not violated; uninjured; unprofaned; unbroken.

Invisible, in-vi'zi-bl, *a*. Not visible; that cannot be seen; imperceptible.

Invitation, in-vi-tā'shon, *n.* Act of inviting; bidding to an entertainment, etc.

Invite, in-vīt', *vt.* (inviting, invited). To ask to do something; to ask to an entertainment, etc.; to allure or attract.—*vi.* To give invitation; to allure.

Involute, in'vō-lūt, *n.* A curve traced by any point of a tense string when it is unwound from a given curve.—*a.* Involved; rolled inward from the edges.

Involve, in-volv', *vt.* (involving, involved). To roll up; to envelop to imply; to include; to implicate; to complicate; in algebra, etc., to raise a quantity to any assigned power.

Invulnerable, in-vul'nėr-a-bl, *a.* That cannot be wounded; incapable of receiving injury.

Inward, in'wėrd, *a.* Internal; being within; intimate; in the mind, soul, or feelings.—*adv.* Toward the inside; into the mind.—*n.pl.* The inner parts of an animal; the viscera.

Iodide, ī'ō-dīd, *n.* A compound of iodine and metal.

Iota, ī-ō'ta, *n.* The name of Greek letter *i*; an insignificant amount.

I O U, ī' ō ū, *n.* A signed paper having on it these letters and a sum of money borrowed, serving an an acknowledgment of a debt.

Irascible, ī-ras'i-bl, *a.* Readily made angry; easily provoked; irritable.

Irate, ī-rāt', *a.* Angry; enraged; incensed.

Iron, ī'ėrn, *n.* The most common and useful metal; an instrument made of iron; a utensil for smoothing cloth; *pl.* fetters; chains; handcuffs.—*a.* Made of iron; consisting of or like iron; harsh; severe; binding fast; vigorous; inflexible.—*vt.* To smooth with an iron; to fetter; to furnish or arm with iron.

Ironware, ī'ėrn-wār, *n.* Iron worked up into utensils, tools, etc.

Irony, ī'ron-i, *n.* A mode of speech which expresses a sense contrary to that conveyed by the words; a subtle kind of sarcasm.

Irradiate, ir-rā'di-āt, *vt.* To send forth rays of light upon; to en-

lighten.—*vi.* To emit rays.

Irradiation, ir-rā'di-ā''shon, *n.* Act of irradiating; illumination; apparent enlargement of an object strongly illuminated.

Irregular, ir-re'gū-lėr, *a.* Not regular; not according to rule or custom; anomalous; vicious; crooked; variable; deviating from the common rules in its inflections.—*n.* A soldier not in regular service.

Irreparable, ir-rē'pa-ra-bl, *a.* Not reparable; irretrievable; irremediable.

Irrepressible, ir-rē-pres'i-bl, *a.* Not repressible; incapable of being repressed.

Irreproachable, ir-rē-prōch'a-bl, *a.* Incapable of being reproached; upright; faultless.

Irreprovable, ir-rē-pröv'a-bl, *a.* Not reprovable; blameless; upright; unblamable.

Irresistible, ir-rē-zist'i-bl, *a.* Not resistible; that cannot be resisted; resistless.

Irreversible, ir-rē-vėr'si-bl, *a.* Not reversible; not to be annulled.

Irrevocable, ir-re'vōk-a-bl, *a.* Not to be recalled, revoked, or annulled; irreversible.

Irrigate, ir'ri-gāt, *vt.* To bedew or sprinkle; to water by means of channels or streams.

Irritant, ir'rit-ant, *a.* Irritating; producing inflammation.—*n.* That which irritates; a medical application that causes pain or heat.

Irritate, ir'rit-āt, *vt.* To rouse to anger; to provoke; to inflame.

Irritation, ir-rit-ā'shon, *n.* Act of irritating; exasperation; annoyance; vital action in muscles or organs caused by some stimulus.

Irruption, ir-rup'shon, *n.* A bursting in; a sudden invasion or incursion.

Is, iz. The third pers, sing. of the verb *to be.*

Isolate, ī'sō-lāt, *vt.* To place in or as in an island; to place by itself; to insulate.

Isolationist, īs-ō-lā'shon-ist, *n.* One who favors keeping aloof from other countries politically.

Isometric, Isometrical, ī-sō-met'rik, ī-sō-met'rik-al, *a.* Pertaining to or

I

characterized by equality of measure.

Isosceles, ī-sos'e-lēz, *a.* Having two legs or sides only that are equal (an *isosceles* triangle).

Israelite, iz'ra-el-īt, *n.* A descendant of *Israel* or Jacob; a Jew.

Issuable, ish'ū-a-bl, *a.* That may be issued.

Issue, ish'ū, *n.* The act of passing or flowing out; delivery; quantity issued at one time; event; consequence; progeny; offspring; an artifical ulcer to promote a secretion of pus; matter depending in a lawsuit.—*vi.* (issuing, issued). To pass or flow out; to proceed; to spring; to grow or accrue; to come to an issue in law; to terminate.—*vt.* To send out; to put into circulation; to deliver for use.

Isthmus, ist'mus or is'mus, *n.* A neck of land connecting two much larger portions.

It, it, *pron.* A pronoun of the neuter gender, third person, nominative or objective case.

Italian, i-ta'i-an, *a.* Pertaining to Italy.—*n.* A native of Italy; the language of Italy.

Italic, i-ta'lik, *a.* Pertaining to Italy; the name of a printing type sloping towards the right.—*n.* An italic letter or type.

Itch, ich, *n.* A sensation in the skin causing a desire to scratch; a constant teasing desire—*vi.* To feel an itch; to have a teasing sensation impelling to something.

Item, ī'tem, *adv.* Also.—*n.* A separate particular; a scrap of news.—*vt.* To make a note of.

Iterate, it'ėr-āt, *vt.* To repeat; to utter or do a second time.

Itinerant, i- or ī-tin'ėr-ant, *a.* Passing or travelling from place to place; not settled.—*n.* One who travels from place to place.

Itinerary, i- or ī-tin'ėr-a-ri, *n.* A work containing notices of places of a particular line of road; a travel route; plan of a tour.—*a.* Travelling; pertaining to a journey.

Its, its, *pron.* The possessive case singular of *it.*

Itself, it-self', *pron.* The neuter reflexive pronoun corresponding to *himself.*

Ivory, ī'vo-ri, *n.* The substance composing the tusks of the elephants, etc. something made of ivory.—*a.* Consisting or made of ivory.

Ivy, ī'vi, *n.* A plant which creeps along the ground, or climbs walls, trees, etc.

J

Jabber, jab'ėr, *vi.* To gabble; to talk rapidly or indistinctly; to chatter.—*vt.* To utter rapidly with confused sounds.—*n.* Rapid and indistinct talk.

Jacket, jak'et, *n.* A short outer garment; a casing of cloth, felt, wood, etc.

Jade, jād, *n.* A mean or poor horse; a low woman; a huzzy; a hard tenacious green stone of a resinous aspect when polished.—*vt.* (jading, jaded). To ride or drive severely; to weary or fatigue.—*vi.* To become weary; to sink.

Jag, jag, *vt.* (jagging, jagged). To cut into notches or teeth; to notch.—*n.* A notch; a ragged protuberance.

Jaguar, ja-gwär', *n.* The American tiger, a spotted carnivorous animal, the most formidable feline quadruped of the New World.

Jail, jāl, *n.* A prison; place of confinement.

Jailer, Jailor, jāl'ėr, *n.* The keeper of a jail.

Jam, jam, *n.* A conserve of fruits boiled with sugar and water.—*vt.* (jamming, jammed). To crowd; to squeeze tight; to wedge in.

Jardinière, zhär-dēn-yär, *n.* An ornamental stand for plants and flowers.

Jargon, jär'gon, *n.* Confused, unintelligible talk; gibberish; phraseology peculiar to a sect, profession, etc.; a variety of zircon.

Jasmine, jas'min, *n.* A fragrant shrub, bearing white or yellow flowers.

Jaunt, jänt, *vi.* To ramble here and there; to make an excursion.—*n.* A trip; a tour; an excursion; a ramble.

Jaunty, jän'ti, *a*. Gay and easy in manner or actions; airy; sprightly; showy.

Javelin, jav'lin, *n*. A light spear thrown from the hand.

Jaw, ja, *n*. The bones of the mouth in which the teeth are fixed.

Jazz, jaz, *n*. Syncopated or rag-time music, originally of negro origin.

Jealous, je'lus, *a*. Uneasy through fear of, or on account of, preference given to another; suspicious in love; apprehensive of rivalry; anxiously fearful or careful.

Jehovah, je-hō'va, *n*. An old Hebrew name of the Supreme Being.

Jelly, je'li, *n*. Matter in a glutinous state; the thickened juice of fruit boiled with sugar; transparent matter obtained from animal substances by boiling.—*vi*. To become a jelly.

Jelly-fish, jel'i-fish, *n*. A gelatinous marine animal.

Jeopardy, je'perd-i, *n*. Hazard; risk; exposure to death, loss, or injury.

Jerk, jerk, *vt*. To give a sudden pull, thrust, or push to; to throw with a quick motion.—*vi*. to make a sudden motion.—*n*. A sudden thrust, push, or twitch; a sudden spring; a spasmodic movement.

Jesus, je'zus, *n*. The Savior of men; Christ.

Jet, jet, *n*. A shooting forth or spouting; what issues from an orifice, as water, gas, etc.; a compact and very black species of coal, used for ornaments.—*vt*. (jetting, jetted). To emit in a jet.—*vi*. To issue in a jet.

Jettison, jet'i-son, *n*. Jetsam.—*vt*. To throw overboard.

Jew, jū, *n*. A Hebrew or Israelite.

Jewel, jū'el, *n*. A personal ornament of precious stones; a precious stone.—*vt*. (jewelling, jewelled). To adorn with jewels.

Jilt, jilt, *n*. A woman who gives her lover hopes and capriciously disappoints him.—*vt*. To deceive in love.—*vi*. To play the jilt.

Jingle, jing'gl, *vi*. and *t*. (jingling, jingled). To sound with a tinkling metallic sound; to clink.—*n*. A rattling or clinking sound.

Job, job, *n*. A piece of work undertaken; a public transaction done for private profit.—*vt*. (jobbing, jobbed). To let out in separate portions or jobs; to let out for hire, as horses; to engage for hire; to peck or stab with something sharp.—*vi* To work at chance jobs; to buy and sell as a broker; to let or hire horses.

Jockey, jok'i, *n*. A man who rides horses in a race; a dealer in horses; one who takes undue advantage in trade.—*vt*. To play the jockey to; to ride in a race; to jostle by riding against; to cheat.

Join, join, *vt*. To bind, unite, or connect; to unite in league or marriage; to associate; to add; to couple.—*vi*. To unite; to be close, or in contact; to unite with in marriage, league, etc.—*n*. Place, act, etc., of joining.

Joiner, join'er, *n*. A mechanic who does the wood-work of houses; a carpenter.

Joint, joint, *n*. A joining; joining of two or more bones; articulation; a fissure in strata; part of an animal cut off by a butcher.—*a*. Joined; united; shared; acting in concert.—*vt*. To form with joints; to fit together; to divide into joints or pieces.—*vi*. To coalesce as by joints, or as parts fitted to each other.

Joist, joist, *n*. One of the pieces of timber to which the boards of a floor or the laths of a ceiling are nailed.—*vt*. To fit with joists.

Joke, jōk, *n*. A jest; something said to excite a laugh; raillery; what is not in earnest.—*vi*. (joking, joked). To jest; to sport.—*vt*. To cast jokes at; to rally.

Jot, jot, *n*. An iota; a tittle.—*vt*. (jotting, jotted). To set down in writing.

Journal, jer'nal, *n*. A diary; an account of daily transactions, or the book containing such; a daily or periodical paper; a narrative of the transactions of a society, etc.; that part of an axle which moves in the bearings.

Journalist, jer'nal-ist, *n*. The writer of a journal; a newspaper editor or contributor.

Journey, jėr'ni, *n.* A travelling from one place to another; tour; excursion; distance travelled.—*vi.* To travel from place to place.

Judaism, jū'dā-izm, *n.* The religious doctrines and rites of the Jews; conformity to the Jewish rites and ceremonies.

Judaize, jū'dā-īz, *vi.* and *t.* To conform to the religious doctrines and rites of the Jews.

Judas, jū'das, *n.* A treacherous person.

Judge, juj, *n.* A civil officer who hears and determines causes in courts; one who has skill to decide on anything; a critic; a connoisseur.—*vi.* (judging, judged). To act as an judge; to pass sentence; to form an opinion; to estimate.—*vt.* To hear and determine; to examine into and decide; to try; to esteem.

Judgment, juj'ment, *n.* Act of judging; good sense; discernment; opinion or estimate; mental faculty by which man ascertains the relations between ideas; sentence pronounced; a calamity regarded as a punishment of sin; final trial of the human race.

Jug, jug, *n.* A vessel for liquors, generally with a handle; a mug; a pitcher.—*vt.* (jugging, jugged). To put in a jug; to cook by putting into a jug, and this into boiling water (*jugged* hare).

Jumble, jum'bl, *vt.* (jumbling, jumbled). To mix in a confused mass.—*vi.* To meet, mix, or unite in a confused manner.—*n.* Confused mass; disorder; confusion.

Jump, jump, *vi.* To leap; to skip; to spring; to agree, tally, coincide.—*vt.* To pass over by a leap; to pass over hastily.—*n.* Act of jumping; leap; spring; bound.

Junction, jungk'shon, *n.* Act or operation of joining; state of being joined; point of union; place where railways meet.

Juncture, jungk'tūr, *n.* A joining or uniting; line or point of joining; point of time; point rendered critical by circumstances.

June, jūn, *n.* The sixth month of the year.

Jungle, jung'gl, *n.* Land covered with trees, brushwood, etc., or coarse, reedy vegetation.

Junior, jū'ni-ėr, *a.* Younger; later or lower in office or rank.—*n.* A person younger than another or lower in standing.

Juniper, jū'ni-pėr, *n.* A coniferous shrub, the berries of which are used to flavor gin.

Junket, jung'ket, *n.* Curds mixed with cream, sweetened and flavored; a sweetmeat; a feast.—*vi.* and *t.* To feast.

Juridical, jū-rid'ik-al, *a.* Relating to the administration of justice or to a judge.

Jurisdiction, jū-ris-dik'shon, *n.* Judicial power; right of exercising authority; district within which power may be exercised.

Jurisprudence, jū-ris-prö'dens, *n.* The science of law; the knowledge of the laws, customs, and rights of men necessary for the due administration of justice.

Jurist, jū'rist, *n.* A man who professes the science of law; one versed in the law, or more particularly, in the civil law.

Jury, jū'ri, *n.* A number of men selected according to law and sworn to declare the truth on the evidence; a body who jointly decides as to prizes.—*a.* In *ships,* applied to a temporary substitute, as a *jury*-mast.

Just, just, *a.* Right; acting rightly; upright, impartial; fair; due; merited; exact.—*adv.* Exactly; precisely; near or nearly; almost; merely; barely.

Justice, jus'tis, *n.* Quality of being just; rectitude; propriety; impartiality; fairness; just treatment; merited reward or punishment; a judge holding a special office.

Juxtapose, juks-ta-pōz', *vt.* To place near or next. Also **Juxtaposit,** juxta-poz'it.

Juxtaposition, juks'ta-pō-si''shon, *n.* A placeing or being placed near.

K

Kaleidoscope, ka-lī'dos-kōp, *n*. An optical instrument which exhibits an endless variety of colored figures.

Kangaroo, kang'ga-rö, *n*. An Australian marsupial quadruped that moves forward by leaps.

Keel, kēl, *n*. The principal timber in a ship, extending from stem to stern at the bottom; the corresponding part in iron vessels; the whole ship; something resembling a keel; a coal-barge.—*vi*. To capsize.

Keen, kēn, *a*. Acute of mind; shrewd; sharp; eager; piercing; severe; bitter.

Keep, kēp, *vt*. (keeping, kept). To hold; to preserve; to guard; to detain; to attend to; to continue any state, course, or action; to obey; to perform; to observe or solemnize; to confine to one's own knowledge; not to betray; to have in pay.—*vi*. To endure; not to perish or be impaired.—*n*. Care; guard; sustenance; a donjon or strong tower.

Kettle, ket'l, *n*. A vessel of iron or other metal, used for heating and boiling water, etc.

Key, kē,*n*. An instrument for shutting or opening a lock; a little lever by which certain musical instruments are played on by the fingers; fundamental tone in a piece of music; that which serves to explain a cipher, etc.—*vt*. To furnish or fasten with a key.

Kick, kik, *vt*. To strike with the foot; to strike in recoiling, as a gun.—*vi*. To strike with the foot or feet; to manifest opposition to restraint; to recoil.—*n*. A blow with the foot or feet; recoil of a firearm.

Kid, kid, *n*. A young goat; leather made from its skin; a small wooden tub.—*vt*. (kidding, kidded). To bring forth a kid.

Kidnap, kid'nap, *vt*. (kidnapping, kidnapped). To steal or forcibly abduct a human being.

Kidney, kid'ni, *n*. Either of the two glands which secret the urine; sort or character.

Kill, kil, *vt*. To deprive of life; to slay; to slaughter for food; to deaden (pain); to overpower.

Kiln, kil, *n*. A fabric of brick or stone, which may be heated to harden or dry anything.

Kin, kin, *n*. Race; family; consanguinity or affinity; kindred.—*a*. Kindred; congenial.

Kind, kīnd, *n*. Race; genus; variety; nature; character.—**In kind,** to pay with produce or commodities.—*a*. Humane; having tenderness or goodness of nature; benevolent; friendly.

Kindergarten, kin'dér-gär-tn, *n*. An infants' school in which amusements are systematically combined with instruction.

Kindle, kin'dl, *vt*. (kindling, kindled). To set on fire; to light; to rouse; to excite to action.—*vi*. To take fire; to be roused or exasperated.

Kindly, kīnd'li, *a*. Of a kind disposition; congenial; benevolent; mild.—*adv*. In a kind manner; favorably.

Kink, kingk, *n*. A twist in a rope or thread; a crotchet.—*vi*. To twist or run into knots.

Kinsfolk, kinz'fölk, *n*. People of the same kin; kindred; relations.

Kinsman, kinz'man, *n*. A man of the same kin; a relative.

Kipper, kip'ér, *n*. A salmon at the spawning season; a fish split open, salted, and dried or smoked.—*vt*. To cure (fish) by splitting open, salting, and drying.

Kismet, kis'met, *n*. Fate or destiny.

Kiss, kis, *vi*. To touch with the lips; to caress by joining lips; to touch gently.—*vi*. To join lips; to come in slight contact.—*n*. A salute given with the lips.

Kitchen, ki'chen, *n*. The room of a house appropriated to cooking.

Kitchen-garden, ki'chen-gär-dn, *n*. A garden for raising vegetables for the table.

Kite, kīt, *n*. A bird of the falcon family; a light frame of wood and paper constructed for flying in the air.

Kith, kith, *n.* Relatives or friends collectively.

Kitten, kit'n, *n.* A young cat.—*vi.* To bring forth young, as a cat.

Kleptomania, klep-tō-mā'ni-a, *n.* An irresistible mania for pilfering.

Knack, nak, *n.* Facility of performance; dexterity.

Knap, nap, *vt.* (knapping, knapped). To break short (as flints); to snap; to bite off.—*n.* A short sharp noise; a snap.

Knapsack, nap'sak, *n.* A bag for necessaries borne on the back by soldiers, etc.

Knave, nāv, *n.* A petty rascal; a dishonest man; a card with a soldier or servant on it.

Knead, nēd, *vt.* To work into a mass or suitable consistency for bread, etc.

Knee, nē, *n.* The joint connecting the two principal parts of the leg; a similar joint; piece of bent timber or iron used in a ship, etc.

Knife, nīf, *n.*; pl. **Knives,** nīvz. A cutting instrument consisting of a blade attached to a handle; cutting part of a machine.

Knob, nob, *a.* A hard protuberance; a boss; a round ball at the end of anything.

Knock, nok, *vt.* To strike with something thick or heavy; to strike against; to clash.—*vi.* To strike.—*n.* A stroke; a blow; a rap.

Knocker, nok'ėr, *n.* One who knocks; something on a door for knocking.

Knoll, nōl, *n.* A little round hill; ringing of a bell; knell.—*vt.* and *i.* To sound, as a bell.

Knot, not, *n.* A complication of threads or cords; a tie; ornamental bunch of ribbon, etc.; hard protuberant joint of a plant; a knob; bunch; group; a difficult question; a natutical mile (= 1.151 ordinary mile).—*vt.* (knotting, knotted). To tie in a knot; to unite closely.—*vi.* To become knotted; to knit knots.

Know, nō, *vt.* (pret. knew, pp. known). To perceive with certainty; to understand; to be aware of; to distinguish; to be acquainted with; to have experience of.—*vi.* To have knowledge; not to be doubtful.

Knowledge, nol'ej, *n.* The result or condition of knowing; clear perception; learning; information; skill; acquaintance.

L

Label, lā'bel, *n.* A slip of paper, etc., affixed to something and stating name, contents, etc.; a slip affixed to deeds to hold the seal.—*vt.* (labelling, labelled). To affix a label to.

Labor, lā'bėr, *n.* Exertion, physical or mental; toil; work done or to be done; laborers in the aggregate; the pangs and efforts of childbirth.—*vi.* To engage in labor; to work; to proceed with difficulty; to be burdened.—*vt.* To cultivate; to prosecute with effort.

Laborer, lā'bėr-ėr, *n.* One who labors; a man who does work that requires little skill, as distinguished from an artisan.

Labrum, lā'brum, *n.* An upper or outer lip.

Labyrinth, lab'i-rinth, *n.* A place full of intricacies; a maze; an inexplicable difficulty; a part of the internal ear.

Lace, lās, *n.* A cord used for fastening boots, etc.; ornamental cord or braid; a delicate fabric of interlacing threads.—*vt.* (lacing, laced). To fasten with a lace; to adorn with lace; to interlace; to mingle in small quantity.

Lack, lak, *vt.* To want; to be without; to need; to require.—*vi.* To be in want.—*n.* Want; deficiency; need; failure.

Ladder, lad'ėr, *n.* An article of wood, rope, etc., consisting of two long side-pieces connected by cross-pieces forming steps; means of rising to mienence; vertical flaw in stocking, etc.

Lag, lag, *a.* Coming behind; sluggish; tardy.—*n.* Quantity of retardation of some movement.—*vi.* (lagging, lagged). To loiter, tarry.

Laity, lā'i-ti, *n.* The people, as distinguished from the clergy; non-professional people.

Lake, lāk, *n.* A body of water wholly surrounded by land; a pigment of earthy substance with red (or other) coloring matter.

Lamb, lam, *n.* The young of the sheep; one as gentle or innocent as a lamb.—*vi.* To bring forth young, as sheep.

Lame, lām, *a.* Crippled in a limb or limbs; disabled; limping; defective; not satisfactory; not smooth.—*vt.* (laming, lamed). To make lame; to render imperfect and unsound.

Lamp, lamp, *n.* A vessel for containing oil to be burned by means of a wick; any contrivance for supply artificial light.

Lampoon, lam-pön', *n.* A scurrilous or personal satire in writing; a satiric attack.—*vt.* To write a lampoon against.

Lamprey, lam'prā, *n.* The name of eel-like, scaleless fishes with suctorial mouths, inhabiting fresh and salt waters.

Lance, lans, *n.* A weapon consisting of a long shaft with a sharp-pointed head; a long spear.—*vt.* (lancing, lanced). To pierce with a lance; to open with a lancet.

Land, land, *n.* The solid matter which constitutes the fixed part of the surface of the globe; soil; estate; country; people of a country or region.—*vt.* and *i.* To set or go on the land; to disembark.

Landscape, land'skāp, *n.* A portion of land which the eye can comprehend in a single view; a country scene; picture representing a piece of country.

Landslip, Landslide, land'slip, land'slīd, *n.* A portion of a hill which slips down; the sliding down of a piece of land.

Land-surveying, land'sėr-vā-ing, *n.* Act of surveying land; art of determining the boundaries and extent of land.

Lane, lān, *n.* A narrow way or street; a passage between lines of men.

Language, lang'gwāj, *n.* Human speech; speech peculiar to a nation; words especially used in any branch of knowledge; general style of expression; expresson of thought or feeling in any way.

Languid, lang'gwid, *a.* Wanting energy; listless; dull or heavy; sluggish.

Languish, lang'gwish, *vi.* To be or become faint, feeble or spiritless; to fade; to sink under sorrow or any continued passion; to look with tenderness.

Languor, lang'gėr, lang'gwėr, *n.* Languidness; lassitude; a listless or dreamy state.

Lank, langk, *a.* Loose or lax; not plump; gaunt.

Lanoline, lan'ō-lin, *n.* A greasy substance obtained from unwashed wool, used as an ointment.

Lantern, lan'tėrn, *n.* A case in which a light is carried; part of a lighthouse in which is the light; erection on the top of a dome, etc., to give light; a tower with the interior open to view.—*vt.* To provide with a lantern.

Lanyard, lan'yärd, *n.* A short piece of rope or line, used in ships.

Lap, lap, *n.* The loose lower part of a garment; the clothes on the knees of a person when sitting; the knees in this position; part of a thing that covers another; single round of a course in races; a lick, as with the tongue; sound as of water rippling on the beach.—*vt.* (lapping, lapped). To lap; to infold; to lick up; to wash gently against.—*vi.* To lie or be turned over; to lick up food; to ripple gently.

Larceny, lär'se-ni, *n.* Theft of goods or personal property.

Lard, lärd, *n.* The fat of swine, after being melted and separated from the flesh.—*vt.* To apply lard to; to fatten; to stuff with bacon; to interlard.

Large, lärj, *a.* Great in size, number, etc.; not small; copious; big; bulky; wide.—**At large,** without restraint; with all details.

Largely, lärj'li, *adv.* Widely; copiously; amply.

Largess, lärj-es', *n.* A present; a bounty bestowed.

Lariat, lä'ri-at, *n.* The lasso; a long

L

cord or thong of leather with a noose used in catching wild horses, etc.

Lark, lärk, *n.* A small song-bird; a frolic.

Larva, lär'va, *n.*; pl. **Larvae.** An insect in the caterpillar or grub state.

Larynx, la'ringks, *n.*; pl. **Larynxes, Larynges,** la'ringks-ez, la-rin'jēz. The upper part of the windpipe, a cartilaginous cavity serving to modulate the sound of the voice.

Lascivious, las-si'vi-us, *a.* Wanton; lewd; lustful.

Lash, lash, *n.* The thong of a whip; a whip; a stroke with a whip; a stroke of satire; a cutting remark.—*vt.* To strike with a lash; to satirize; to dash against, as waves; to tie with a rope or cord.—*vi.* To ply the whip; to strike at.

Lass, las, *n.* A young woman; a girl.

Lassitude, las'i-tūd, *n.* Faintness; languor of body or mind.

Lasso, las'sō, *n.* A rope with a running noose, used for catching wild horses, etc.—*vt.* To catch with a lasso.

Last, läst, *a.* That comes after all the others; latest; final; next before the present; utmost.—*adv.* The last time; in conclusion.—*vi.* To continue in time; to endure; not to decay or perish.—*vt.* To form on or by a last.—*n.* A mold of the foot on which boots are formed; a weight of 4000 lbs.

Latch, lach, *n.* A catch for fastening a door.—*vt.* To fasten with a latch.

Late, lāt, *a.* Coming after the usual time; slow; not early; existing not long ago, but not now; deceased; recent; modern; last or recently in any place, office, etc.—*adv.* At a late time or period; recently.

Latent, lā'tent, *a.* Not apparent; under the surface.

Latin, laītin, *a.* Pertaining to the Latins, a people of Latium, in Italy; Roman.—*n.* The language of the ancient Romans.

Latitude, la'ti-tūd, *n.* Breadth; width; extent from side to side; scope; laxity; distance north or south of the equator, measured on a meridian; distance of a star

north or south of the ecliptic.

Laud, lạd, *n.* Praise; a hymn of praise; *pl.* a service of the church comprising psalms of praise.—*vt.* To praise; to celebrate.

Laudanum, lạ'da-num, *n.* Opium prepared in spirit of wine; tincture of opium.

Laugh, läf, *vi.* To make the involuntary noise which sudden merriment excites; to treat with some contempt; to appear gay, bright, or brilliant.—*vt.* To express by laughing; to affect or effect by laughter.—*n.* The act of laughing; short fit of laughing.

Laughter, läf'tèr, *n.* Act or sound of laughing, expression of mirth peculiar to man.

Launch, länsh or lạnsh, *vt.* To throw; to cause to slide into the water; to put out into another sphere of duty, etc.—*vi.* To glide, as a ship into the water; to enter on a new field of activity; to expatiate in language.—*n.* Act of launching; the largest boat carried by a man-of-war.

Laundry, län'dri or lạn'dri, *n.* Place where clothes are washed and dressed.

Lavish, lav'ish, *a.* Profuse; liberal to a fault; extravagant; superabundant.—*vt.* To expend with profusion; to squander.

Law, lạ, *n.* A rule prescribed by authority; a statute; a precept; such rules or statues collectively; legal procedure; litigation; a principle deduced from practice or observation; a formal statement of facts observed in natural phenomena.

Lax, laks, *a.* Loose; flabby; soft; slack; vague; equivocal; not strict; remiss; having too frequent discharges from the bowels.

Laxative, laks'at-iv, *a.* Having the power of relieving from constipation.—*n.* A gentle purgative.

Laxity, laks'i-ti, *n.* State or quality of being lax; want of strictness; looseness.

Lay, lā, *vt.* (pret. and pp. laid). To place in a lying position; to set or place in general; to impose; to bring into a certain state; to settle; to allay; to place at hazard; to wager; to contrive.—*vi*. To bring forth eggs; wager.—*n*. A stratum; a layer; one rank in a series reckoned upward; a song; a narrative poem.—*a*. Not clerical; not professional.

Layer, lā'ėr, *n*. One who or that which lays; a stratum; a coat, as of paint; a row of masonry, etc.; a shoot of a plant, not detached from the stalk, partly laid underground for growth.—*vt*. To propagate by bending a shoot into the soil.

Lead, lēd, *vt*. (pret. and pp. led). To guide or conduct; to direct and govern; to precede; to entice; to influence; to spend; to begin.—*vi*. To go before and show the way; to be chief or commander; to draw; to have a tendency.—*n*. Guidance; precedence.

Leaden, led'n, *a*. Made of lead; like lead; heavy; inert; dull.

Leader, lēd'ėr, *n*. One who leads; a guide; captain; head of a party; editorial article in a newspaper.

Leaf, lēf, *n*.; pl. **Leaves,** lēvz. One of the thin, expanded, deciduous growths of a plant; a part of a book containing two pages; a very thin plate; the movable side of a table; one side of a double door.—*vi*. To shoot out leaves; to produce leaves.

League, lēg, *n*. A combination between states for their mutual aid; an alliance; a compact; a measure of three miles or knots.—*vi*. (leaguing, leagued). To form a league; to confederate.

Leak, lēk, *n*. A fissure in a vessel that admits water, or permits it to escape; the passing of fluid through an aperture.—*vi*. To let water in or out of a vessel through a crevice.

Lean, lēn, *vi*. (pret. and pp. leaned). To slope or slant; to incline; to tend; to bend so as to rest on something; to depend.—*vt*. To cause to lean; to support or rest.

Learn, lėrn, *vt*. (pret. and pp. learned). To gain knowledge of or skill in; to acquire by study.—*vi*. To gain knowledge; to receive instruction.

Least, lēst, *a*. Smallest.—*adv*. In the smallest or lowest degree.—**At least, at the least,** to say no more; at the lowest degree.

Leather, leTH'ėr, *n*. The skin of an animal prepared for use; tanned hides in general.—*a*. Leathern.

Leave, lēv, *n*. Permission; liberty granted; a formal parting of friends.—*vt*. (leaving, left). To let remain; to have remaining at death; to bequeath; to quit; to abandon; to refer.—*vi*. To depart; to desist.

Leaven, lev'n, *n*. A substance that produces fermentation, as in dough; yeast; barm.—*vt*. To mix with leaven; to excite fermentation in; to imbue.

Lecher, lech'ėr, *n*. A man given to lewdness.—*vi*. To practice lewdness; to indulge lust.

Lectern, lek'tėrn, *n*. A reading-desk in a church.

Lecture, lek'tūr, *n*. A discourse on any subject; a reprimand; a formal reproof.—*vi*. (lecturing, lectured). To deliver a lecture or lectures.—*vt*. To reprimand; to reprove.

Ledge, lej, *n*. A narrow shelf; a ridge or shelf of rocks.

Leer, lēr, *n*. A side glance; an arch or affected glance.—*vi*. To give a leer; to look meaningly.—*vt*. To turn with a leer; to affect with a leer.

Leeway, lē'wā, *n*. The drifting of a ship to the leeward.—**To make up leeway,** to overtake work in arrear.

Left, left, *a*. Denoting the part opposed to the right of the body.—*n*. The side opposite to the right.

Left-handed, left'hand-ed, *a*. Using the left hand and arm with more dexterity than the right; sinister; insincere; awkward.

Leg, leg, *n*. The limb of an animal; a lower or posterior limb; the long or slender support of anything.

Legacy, leg'a-si, *n*. A bequest; a particular thing given by last will.

Legal, lē'gal, *a*. According to, pertaining to, or permitted by law; lawful; judicial.

Legible, le'ji-bl, *a*. That may be read.

Legion, lē'jon, *n*. A Roman body of

L

infantry soldiers, in number from 3000 to above 6000; a military force; a great number.

Legislate, le'jis-lāt, *vi.* To make or enact a law or laws.

Legislation, le-jis-lā'shon, *n.* Act of making a law or laws; laws or statutes enacted.

Leisure, lē'zhūr or lezh'ūr, *n.* Freedom from occupation; vacant time.—*a.* Not spent in labor; vacant.

Lemma, lem'ma, *n.* A subsidiary proposition in mathematics.

Lemming, lem'ing, *n.* A small rodent mammal.

Lemon, le'mon, *n.* An acid fruit of the orange kind; the tree that produces this fruit.

Lemonade, le-mon-ād', *n.* A beverage, usually aerated, consisting of lemon-juice mixed with water and sweetened.

Lemur, lē'mėr, *n.* A quadrumanous mammal, allied to monkeys and rodents.

Lend, lend, *vt.* (lending, lent). To furnish on condition of the thing being returned; to afford or grant; *refl.* to accommodate.

Length, length, *n.* State or quality of being long; extent from end to end; extenstion; long duration; extent or degree.—**At length,** at full extent; at last.

Leprosy, lep'rō-si, *n.* A foul cutaneous disease, characterized by dusky red or livid tubercles on the face or extremities.

Lesion, lē'zhon, *n.* Injury; wound; derangement.

Less, les, *a.* Smaller; not so large or great.—*adv.* In a smaller or lower degree.—*n.* A smaller quantity.

Lessen, les'n, *vt.* To make less; to lower; to depreciate.—*vi.* To become less; to abate.

Lesson, les'n, *n.* Portion which a pupil learns at one time; portion of Scripture read in divine service; something to be learned; severe lecture; truth taught by experience.

Let, let, *vt.* (letting, let). To permit; to allow; to lease.—*vi.* To be leased or let.

Let, let, *vt.* To hinder; to impede.—*n.*

A hindrance; impediment.

Lethal, lēth'al, *a.* Deadly; mortal; fatal.

Lethargy, le'thär-ji, *n.* Morbid drowsiness; profound sleep; dulness.

Letter, let'ėr, *n.* A mark used as the representative of a sound; a written message; an epistle; the literal meaning; in *printing,* a single type; *pl.* learning; erudition.—*vt.* To impress or form letters on.

Lettuce, let'is, *n.* An annual composite plant, used in salads.

Level, le'vel, *n.* An instrument for detecting variation from a horizontal surface; an instrument by which to find a horizontal line; a horizontal line or plane; a surface without inequalities; usual elevation; equal elevation with something else; horizontal gallery in a mine.—*a.* Horizontal; even; flat; having no degree of superiority.—*vt.* (leveling, leveled). To make level; to lay flat on the ground; to reduce to equality; to point, in taking aim.—*vi.* To point a gun, etc.; to aim.

Lever, lē'vėr, *n.* A bar used for raising weights, etc.; a kind of watch.

Lewd, lūd, *a.* Lustful; sensual; vile.

Lexicographer, leks-i-kog'ra-fėr, *n.* The author or compiler of a dictionary.

Lexicography, leks-i-kog'ra-fi, *n.* The act or art of compiling a dictionary.

Lexicon, leks'i-kon, *n.* A word-book; a dictionary; a vocabulary containing an alphabetical arrangement of the words in a language, with the definition of each.

Liable, lī'a-bl, *a.* Answerable for consequences; responsible; subject; exposed: with *to.*

Liaison, lē-ā-zōng, *n.* A bond of union; an illicit intimacy between a man and woman.

Liar, lī'ėr, *n.* One who utters falsehood.

Libation, lī-bā'shon, *n.* Act of pouring a liquor, usually wine, on the ground or on a victim in sacrifice, in honor of some deity; the wine or other liquor so poured.

Libel, lī'bel, *n.* A defamatory writing; a malicious publication; the written statement of a plaintiff's ground of complaint against a defendant.—*vt.* (libelling, libelled). To frame a libel against; to lampoon; to exhibit a charge against in court.

Liberal, li'bėr-al, *a.* Generousl ample; profuse; favorable to reform or progress; not too literal or strict; free.—*n.* One who advocates great political freedom.

Liberty, li'bėr-ti, *n.* State or condition of one who is free; privilege; immunity; license; district within which certain exclusive privileges may be exercised; freedom of action or speech beyond civility or decorum; state of being disengaged.

Libidinous, li-bid'i-nus, *a.* Characterized by lust; lascivious; lewd.

Library, li'bra-ri, *n.* A collection of books; edifice or apartment for holding books.

Librate, li'brāt, *vt.* To poise; to balance.—*vi.* To move, as a balance; to be poised.

Libretto, li-bret'ō, *n.* The book of words of an opera, etc.

Lick, lik, *vt.* To draw the tongue over the surface of; to lap; to take in by the tongue; to beat.—*n.* A drawing of the tongue over anything; a slight smear or coat; a blow.

Licorice, lik'or-is, *n.* Liquorice.

Lid, lid, *n.* A movable cover of a vessel or box; eyelid.

Lie, lī, *vi.* (lying, lied). To utter falsehood with deceitful intention.—*n.* A falsehood; an intentional violation of truth.

Lie, lī, *vi.* (lying, pret. lay, pp. lain). To occupy a horizontal position; to rest on anything lengthwise; to be situated; to remain; to be incumbent; to exist; to depend; to be sustainable in law.—**To lie in,** to be in childbed.—**To lie to,** to stop and remain stationary.—*n.* Relative position of objects; general bearing or direction.

Life, lif, *n.*; pl. **Lives,** līvz. State of animals and plants in which the natural functions are performed; vitality; present state of existence; time from birth to death; manner of living; animal being; spirit; vivacity; the living form; exact resemblance; rank in society; human affairs; a person; narrative of a life; eternal felicity.

Lift, lift, *vt.* To raise to a higher position; to hoist; to elevate; to raise in spirit; to collect when due.—*vi.* To raise; to rise.—*n.* Act of lifting; assistance; that which is to be raised; an elevator or hoist.

Ligament, li'ga-ment, *n.* That which unites one thing to another; a band; a substance serving to bind one bone to another.

Ligature, li'ga-tūr, *n.* Anything that binds; a band or bandage.

Light, līt, *n.* That by which objects are rendered visible; day; that which gives or admits light; illumination of mind; knowledge; open view; explanation; point of view; situation; spiritual illumination.— *a.* Bright; clear; not deep, as color; not heavy; not difficult; easy to be digested; active; not laden; slight; moderate; unsteady; gay; trifling; wanton; sandy; having a sensation of giddiness; employed in light work.—*adv.* Lightly; cheaply.—*vt.* (pret. and pp. lighted or lit). To give light to; to enlighten; to ignite.—*vi.* To brighten; to descend, as from a horse, etc.; to alight; to come by chance.

Lignite, lig'nīt, *n.* Fossil wood or brown-coal.

Like, līk, *a.* Equal; similar; resembling; likely; feeling disposed.— *adv.* or *prep.* In the same manner; similarly; likely.—*vt.* (liking, liked). To be pleased with; to approve.— *vi.* To be pleased; to choose.—*n.* Some person or thing resembling another; a counterpart; a liking; a fancy.

Lilt, lilt, *vt.* and *i.* To sing cheerfully; to give musical utterance.—*n.* A song; a tune.

Lily, lil'i, *n.* A bulbous plant with showy and fragrant flowers.

Limb, lim, *n.* The arm or leg, especially the latter; a branch of a tree; graduated edge of a quadrant, etc.; border of the disc of the sun, moon, etc.—*vt.* To supply with limbs; to tear off the limbs of.

Limber, lim'bėr, *a.* Flexible; pliant.—*n.* A carriage with ammunition boxes attached to the gun-carriage.—*vt.* and *i.* To attach the limber to the gun-carriage.

Limbo, lim'bo, *n.* A supposed region beyond this world for souls of innocent persons ignorant of Christianity; any similar region; a prison of confinement.

Lime, līm, *n.* Any viscous substance; calcareous earth used in cement; mortar made with lime; the linden-tree; a tree producing an inferior sort of lemon.—*vt.* (liming, limed). To smear or manure with lime; to ensnare; to cement.

Line, līn, *n.* A small rope or cord; a threadlike marking; a stroke or score; a row of soldiers, ships, words, etc.; a verse; an outline; a short written communication; course of procedure, etc.; connected series, as of descendants; series of public conveyances, as steamers; the twelfth part of an inch; the equator; the regular infantry of an army; *pl.* works covering extended positions and presenting a front in only one direction to the enemy.—*vt.* (lining, lined). To draw lines upon; to set with men or things in lines; to cover on the inside; to put in the inside of.

Lineament, lin'ē-a-ment, *n.* One of the lines which mark the features; feature; form.

Linen, lin'en, *n.* Cloth made of flax; under clothing.—*a.* Made of flax; resembling linen cloth.

Linger, ling'gėr, *vi.* To delay; to loiter; to hesitate; to remain long.—*vt.* To spend wearily.

Link, lingk, *n.* A single ring of a chain; anything closed like a link; anything connecting; a measure of 7.92 inches; a torch.—*vi.* To be connected.—*vt.* To join or connect, as by links; to unite.

Linseed, lin'sēd, *n.* Flax-seed.

Lintel, lin'tel, *n.* The horizontal part of the door or window frame.

Lion, lī'on, *n.* A carnivorous animal of the cat family; a sign in the zodiac, Leo; an object of interest and curiosity.

Liquefy, lik'wē-fī, *vt.* To melt; to dissolve by heat.—*vi.* To become liquid.

Liqueur, li-kūr' or li-kör', *n.* An alcoholic beverage sweetened and containing some infusion of fruits or aromatic substances.

Liquid, lik'wid, *a.* Fluid; not solid; soft; smooth; devoid of harshness.—*n.* A fluid; a letter with a smooth flowing sound, as *l* and *r*.

Liquidate, lik'wid-āt, *vt.* To clear from obscurity; to adjust; to settle, adjust, and apportion, as a bankrupt's affairs.

Liquor, lik'ėr, *n.* A liquid; spirituous fluids; drink.

Lisp, lisp, *vi.* To pronounce the sibilant letters imperfectly, as in pronouncing *th* for *s*; to speak imperfectly, as a child.—*vt.* To pronounce with a lisp, or imperfectly.—*n.* The habit or act of lisping.

Lissom, lis'um, *a.* Supple; flexible; lithe; nimble; active.

List, list, *n.* The selvedge of cloth; a limit or border; a roll or catalogue; inclination to one side; *pl.* a field inclosed for a combat.—*vt.* To enroll; to enlist.—*vi.* To enlist, as in the army; to desire; to be disposed; to hearken.

Listen, lis'n, *vi.* To hearken; to give heed.—*vi.* To hear; to attend.

Literate, li'tėr-āt, *a.* Learned; literary.

Literature, li'tėr-a-tūr, *n.* Learning; literary knowledge; collective writings of a country or period; belles-lettres; the literary profession.

Lithe, līTH, *a.* Pliant; flexible; limber.

Lithium, lith'i-um, *n.* The lightest of all known solids.

Lithology, li-thol'o-ji, *n.* The knowledge of rocks; study of the mineral structure of rocks.

Litigant, li'ti-gant, *a.* Disposed to litigate; engaged in a lawsuit.—*n.* One engaged in a lawsuit.

Litigate, li'ti-gāt, *vt.* To contest in law.—*vi.* To carry on a suit by judicial process.

Little, lit'l, *a.* Small in size or extent; short in duration; slight; mean.—*n.*

A small quantity, space, etc.—**A little,** somewhat.—*adv.* In a small degree or quantity.

Liturgy, li'tėr-ji, *n.* A ritual or established formulas for public worship.

Live, liv, *vi.* (living, lived). To exist; to be alive; to dwell; to conduct oneself in life; to feed or subsist; to acquire a livelihood; to be exempt from spiritual death.—*vt.* To lead, pass, or spend.

Live, līv, *a.* Having life; alive; not dead, ignited; vivid, as color.

Load, lōd, *vt.* To charge with a load; to burden; to encumber; to bestow in great abundance; to charge, as a gun.—*n.* A burden; cargo; a grievous weight; something that oppresses.

Loaf, lōf, *n.*; pl. **Loaves,** lōvz. A mass of bread formed by the baker; a conical lump of sugar.—*vi.* To lounge.—*vt.* To spend idly.

Loam, lōm, *n.* A rich species of earth or mold.—*vt.* To cover with loam.

Loan, lōn, *n.* Lending; that which is lent; a sum of money lent at interest.—*vt.* and *i.* To lend.

Loath, Loth, lōth, *a.* Disliking; unwilling; averse; not inclined; reluctant.

Loathe, lōᴛʜ, *vt.* (loathing, loathed). To feel disgust at; to abhor; to abominate.—*vi.* To feel nausea or abhorrence.

Loathing, lōᴛʜ'ing, *n.* Extreme disgust or aversion; abhorrence; detestation.

Loathness, lōᴛʜ'sum, *a.* Exciting disgust; disgusting; detestable; abhorrent.

Lob, lob, *n.* A dolt; a lout.—*vt.* (lobbing, lobbed). To throw or toss slowly.

Lobby, lob'i, *n.* An apartment giving admission to others; an entrance-hall.

Lobe, lōb, *n.* A round projecting part of something; such a part of the liver, lungs, brain, etc.; the lower soft part of the ear.

Lobster, lob'stėr, *n.* A ten-footed crustacean with large claws, allied to the crab.

Local, lō'kal, *a.* Pertaining to a particular place; confined to a spot or definite district.—*n.* A local item of news; a local railway train.

Lock, lok, *n.* An appliance for fastening doors, etc.; mechanism by which a firearm is discharged; a fastening together; inclosure in a canal, with gates at either end; a tuft or ringlet of hair.—*vt.* To fasten with a lock and key; to shut up or confine; to join firmly; to embrace closely.—*vi.* To become fast; to unite closely by mutual insertion.

Locket, lok'et, *n.* A little case worn as an ornament, often containing a lock of hair.

Lodge, loj, *n.* A small country house; a temporary abode; place where members of a society, as freemasons, meet; the society itself.—*vt.* (lodging, lodged). To furnish with temporary accommodation; to set or deposit for keeping; to beat down (growing crops).—*vi.* To have a temporary abode; to settle; to reside.

Loft, loft, *n.* The space below and between the rafters; a gallery raised within a larger apartment or in a church.

Lofty, loft'i, *a.* Elevated in place; rising to a great height; proud; haughty; sublime; stately.

Log, log, *n.* A bulky piece of timber unhewed; a floating contrivance for measuring the rate of a ship's velocity; a log-book.

Loin, loin, *n.* The part of an animal on either side between the ribs and the haunch-bone.

Loiter, loi'tėr, *vi.* To be slow in moving; to spend time idly; to hang about.—*vi.* To waste carelessly; with *away.*

Loll, lol, *vi.* (lolling, lolled). To lean idly; to lie at ease; to hang out, as the tongue of a dog.—*vt.* To suffer to hang out.

Lone, lōn, *a.* Solitary; unfrequented; single.

Lonely, lōn'li, *a.* Unfrequented by men; retired; solitary.

Long, long, *a.* Drawn out in a line; drawn out in time; tedious; protracted; late; containing much verbal matter.—*n.* Something that is long.—*adv.* To a great extent in

L

space or in time; at a point of duration far distant.—*vi*. To desire eagerly; with *for*.

Longevity, lon-jev'i-ti, *n*. Great length of life.

Longhand, long'hand, *n*. Ordinary written characters, as distinguished from shorthand, etc.

Longitude, lon'ji-tūd, *n*. Length; distance on the surface of the globe east or west, measured by meridians.

Look, luk, *vi*. To direct the eye so as to see; to gaze; to consider; to expect; to heed; to face; to appear.—*vt*. To see; to express by a look.—*n*. Act of looking; sight; gaze; glance; mien; aspect.

Loose, lös, *a*. Not attached; untied; not dense or compact; vague; careless; having lax bowels; unchaste.—*vt*. (loosing, loosed). To untie or unbind; to detach; to set free; to relax; to loosen.

Loot, löt, *n*. Booty; plunder, especially such as is taken in a sacked city.—*vt*. To plunder.

Lop, lop, *vt*. (lopping, lopped). To cut off; to trim by cutting.—*n*. That which is cut from trees.

Lop-sided, lop'sīd-ed, *a*. Heavier at one side than the other; inclining to one side.

Loquacious, lo-kwā'shus, *a*. Talkative; garrulous; babbling.

Loquacity, lo-kwas'i-ti, *n*. Quality of being loquacious; garrulity.

Lord, lord, *n*. A master; a ruler; proprietor of a manor; a nobleman; a British title applied to peers, sons of dukes and marquises, and the eldest sons of earls; honorary title of certain high officials; (with *cap*.) the Supreme Being.—*vi*. To act as a lord; to rule with arbitrary or despotic sway.

Lore, lōr, *n*. Learning; erudition; space between the bill and the eye of a bird.

Lorgnette, lor-nyet', *n*. An operaglass.

Lose, löz, *vt*. (losing, lost). To cease to possess, as through accident; to fail to keep; to forfeit; not to gain or win; to miss; to cease or fail to see or hear; to misuse.—*vi*. To suffer loss; not to win.

Loss, los, *n*. Act of losing; failure to gain; that which is lost; failure to utilize.

Lost, lost, *p.a*. Gone from our hold, view, etc.; not to be found; ruined; wasted; forfeited; perplexed; alienated.

Lot, lot, *n*. A person's part or share; fate which falls to one; part in life allotted to a person; a distinct portion; a considerable quantity or number; something used to decide what is yet undecided.—*vt*. (lotting, lotted). To assign by lot; to sort; to portion.

Lounge, lounj, *vi*. (lounging, lounged). To loiter; to loll.—*n*. An idle gait or stroll; act of reclining at ease; a place for lounging.

Louse, lous, *n*.; pl. **Lice,** līs. A wingless insect, parasitic on man and other animals.

Lout, lout, *n*. A mean, awkward fellow.—*vt*. To bend or stoop down.

Lovable, luv'a-bl, *a*. Worthy of love; amiable.

Love, luv, *vt*. (loving, loved). To regard with affection; to like; to delight in.—*vi*. To be in love; to be tenderly attached.—*n*. Warm affection; fond attachment; the passion between the sexes; the object beloved; a word of endearment; Cupid, the god of love; the score of nothing at tennis, etc.

Low, lō, *a*. Depressed below any given surface or place; not high; deep; below the usual rate; not loud; wanting strength; mean; dishonorable; not sublime; plain.— *adv*. Not aloft; under the usual price; near the ground; not loudly.

Low, lō, *vi*. To bellow, as an ox or cow.

Lubricant, lū'brik-ant, *n*. A substance for oiling or greasing.

Luck, luk, *n*. That which happens to a person; chance; hap; fortune; success.

Lucky, luk'i, *a*. Meeting with good luck or success; fortunate; auspicious.

Lucrative, lū'krat-iv, *a*. Pertaining to gain; gainful; profitable.

Ludicrous, lū'di-krus, *a*. That serves for sport; laughable; droll; ridiculous.

Luggage, lug´āj, n. Anything cumbersome and heavy; a traveller's baggage.

Lugubrious, lū-gū´bri-us, a. Mournful; indicating sorrow; doleful.

Lukewarm, lūk´warm, a. Moderately warm; tepid; not zealous; indifferent.

Lull, lul, vt. To sing to, as to a child; to soothe.—vi. To subside; to become calm.—n. A season of quiet or cessation.

Lullaby, lul´a-bī, n. A song to lull or quiet babes; that which quiets.

Lumbago, lum-bā´gō, n. A rheumatic affection of the muscles about the loins.

Lumbar, lum´bar, n. Pertaining to or near the loins.

Lumber, lum´bėr, n. Anything useless and cumbersome; in America, timber sawed orsplit for use.—vt. To fill with lumber; to heap together in disorder.—vi. To move heavily, as a vehicle; in America, to cut and prepare timber.

Lump, lump, n. A small mass of matter; a mass of things.—vt. To throw into a mass; to take in the gross.

Lunge, lunj, n. A sudden thrust or pass, as with a sword.—vi. (lunging, lunged). To make a thrust.

Lunular, lū´nū-lėr, a. Having the form of a small crescent.

Lupine, lū´pin, n. A leguminous flowering plant.—a. lū´pīn. LIke a wolf; wolfish.

Lupus, lū´pus, n. A disease which eats away the flesh of the face.

Lurch, lėrch, vi. To lurk; to roll or sway to one side.—n. A sudden roll or stagger; a difficult or helpless position.

Lure, lūr, n. Something held out to call a trained hawk; a bait; any enticement.—vt. (luring, lured). To attract by a lure or bait; to entice.

Lurid, lū´rid, a. Pale yellow, as flame; ghastly pale; wan; gloomy; dismal.

Lurk, lėrk, vi. To lie hid; to lie in wait.

Luscious, lu´shus, a. Very sweet; delicious; sweet to excess.

Lush, lush, a. Fresh, succulent.

Lust, lust, n. Longing desire; carnal appetite; depraved affections.—vi. To desire eagerly; to have carnal desire.

Luster, lus´ter, n. Brightness; brilliancy; renown; a branched chandelier ornamented with cut glass; a glossy fabric for dress.

Luxurious, luks-ū´ri-us, a. Given to luxury; voluptuous; furnished with luxuries.

Luxury, luks´ū-ri, n. Extravagant indulgence; that which gratifies a fastidious appetite; anything delightful to the senses.

Lymphatic, lim-fat´ik, a. Pertaining to lymph; phlegmatic; sluggish.—n. A vessel in animal bodies which contains or conveys lymph.

Lynch, linsh, vt. To inflict punishment upon, without the forms of law, as by a mob.

Lynx, lingks, n. A carnivorous animal resembling the cat, noted for its keen sight.

Lyre, līr, n. A stringed instrument of the harp kind much used by the ancients.

Lyric, Lyrical, li´rik, li´rik-al, a. Pertaining to a lyre; designating that species of poetry which has reference to the individual emotions of the poet, such as songs.—**Lyric,** li´rik, n. A lyric poem; an author of lyric poems.

M

Macabre, mak-a´br, a. Gruesome; terrible.

Macerate, ma´se-rāt, vt. To steep almost to solution; to make lean or cause to waste away.

Machiavelian, ma´ki-a-vēl´´i-an, a. Pertaining to Machiavelli, or denoting his principles; cunning in political management.

Machinate, mak´i-nāt, vt. and i. To plot or plan; to form, as a plot or scheme.

Machine, ma-shēn´, n. Any contrivance which serves to regulate the effect of a given force or to produce or change motion; an organized system; a person who acts as the tool of another.—vt. To apply machinery to; to produce by machinery.

Mad, mad, *a*. Disordered in intellect; insane; crazy; frantic; furious; infatuated.—*vt*. (madding, madded). To make mad.

Madden, mad'n, *vt*. To make mad.—*vi*. To become mad; to act as if mad.

Madeira, ma-dē'ra, *n*. A rich wine made on the isle of Madeira.

Madness, mad'nes, *n*. Lunacy; frenzy; extreme folly.

Madonna, ma-don'na, *n*. The Virgin Mary; a picture representing the Virgin.

Madrigal, mad'ri-gal, *n*. A pastoral song; vocal composition in five or six parts.

Maestro, mä-es'trō, *n*. A master of any art; a musical composer.

Magazine, mag'a-zēn, *n*. A storehouse; a repository for ammunition or provisions; a serial publication.

Magenta, ma-jen'ta, *n*. A brilliant blue-red color derived from coaltar.

Maggot, ma'got, *n*. The larva of a fly or other insect; a grub; an odd fancy.

Magi, mā'jī, *n.pl*. The caste of priests among the ancient Medes and Persians; holy men or sages of the East.

Magic, ma'jik, *n*. The art of producing effects by superhuman means; sorcery; enchantment; power similar to that of enchantment.—*a*. Pertaining to magic; working or worked by or as if by magic.

Magician, ma-ji'shan, *n*. One skilled in magic; an enchanter.

Magisterial, ma-jis-tē'ri-al, *a*. Pertaining to a master or magistrate; imperious; haughty; authoritative.

Magistrate, ma'jis-trāt, *n*. A public civil officer, with executive or judicial authority.

Magnanimity, mag-na-nim'i-ti, *n*. Quality of being magnanimous; greatness of soul or mind.

Magnate, mag'nāt, *n*. A great man; a person of rank or wealth.

Magnesia, mag-nē'si-a, *n*. Oxide of magnesium, a white slightly alkaline powder.

Magnet, mag'net, *n*. The loadstone, which has the property of attracting iron; a bar of iron or steel to which the properties of the loadstone have been imparted.

Magnificence, mag-nif'i-sens, *n*. Grandeur of appearance; splendor; pomp.

Magnify, mag'ni-fī, *vt*. To make great or greater; to increase the apparent dimensions of; to extol; to exaggerate.—*vi*. To possess the quality of causing objects to appear larger.

Magnitude, mag'ni-tūd, *n*. Greatness; size; bulk; importance; consequence.

Maiden, mād'n, *n*. A maid or virgin; an old Scottish instrument of capital punishment resembling the guillotine.—*a*. Pertaining to maidens; unpolluted; unused; first.

Maidenhair, mād'n-hār, *n*. An elegant fern found growing on rocks and walls.

Maidenhead, mād'n-hed, *n*. Virginity; the hymen.

Mail, māl, *n*. A bag for conveying letters, etc.; letters conveyed; person or conveyance carrying the mail; armor of chain-work, etc.—*vt*. (mailing, mailed). To send by mail; to post; to arm with mail.

Maim, mām, *vt*. To mutilate; to disable.—*n*. An injury by which a person is maimed.

Main, mān, *a*. Chief, or most important; mighty; vast; directly applied; used with all one's might.—*n*. Strength; great effort; chief or main portion; the ocean; a principal gas or water pipe in a street; a hand at dice; a match at cockfighting.

Majestic, ma-jes'tik, *a*. Having majesty; august; sublime; lofty; stately.

Majesty, ma'jes-ti, *n*. Grandeur or dignity; a title of emperors, kings, and queens.

Majolica, ma-jol'i-ka, *n*. A kind of pottery richly colored and enameled.

Major, mā'jėr, *a*. The greater in number, quantity, or extent; the more important.—*n*. A military officer next above a captain; a person aged twenty-one years complete.

Majority, ma-jo'ri-ti, *n*. The greater number; excess of one number over another; full age; rank or commission of a major.

Make, māk, *vt*. (making, made). To produce or effect; to cause to be; to compose; to constitute; to perform; to cause to have any quality; to force; to gain; to complete; to arrive at; to have within sight.—*vi*. To act or do; to tend; to contribute; to flow toward land.—*n*. Form; structure; texture.

Maladroit, mal-a-droit', *a*. Awkward.

Malady, mal'a-di, *n*. Any disease of the human body; moral or mental disorder.

Malar, mā'lėr, *a*. Pertaining to the cheek or cheek-bone.

Malaria, ma-lā'ri-a, *n*. Noxious exhalations causing fever; fever produced by this cause.

Malcontent, mal'kon-tent, *n*. A discontented person.—*a*. Discontented with the rule under which one lives.

Male, māl, *a*. Pertaining to the sex that begets young; masculine.—*n*. One of the sex that begets young; a plant which has stamens only.

Malefactor, mal-e-fak'tėr, *n*. A criminal; a culprit; a felon.

Malevolence, ma-lev'ō-lens, *n*. Ill-will; personal hatred.

Malformation, mal-form-ā'shon, *n*. Ill or wrong formation; deformity.

Malice, mal'is, *n*. A disposition to injure others; spite; ill-will; rancor.

Malign, ma-līn', *a*. Of an evil nature or disposition; malicious; pernicious.—*vt*. To defame; to villify.

Mallet, mal'et, *n*. A wooden hammer; a long-handled mallet is used in polo, croquet, etc.

Malnutrition, mal-nū-tri'shon, *n*. Faulty feeding.

Malpractice, mal-prak'tis, *n*. Evil practice.

Malt, malt, *n*. Barley or other grain steeped in water till it germinates, then dried in a kiln and used in brewing.—*vt*. To make into malt.—

vi. To become malt.

Mammilla, mam-mil'la, *n*. A nipple, or something of this form.

Mammon, mam'on, *n*. A Syrian god of riches; riches; wealth.

Mammoth, mam'oth, *n*. An extinct species of elephant.—*a*. Very large; gigantic.

Man, man, *n*.; pl. **Men,** men. A human being; a male adult of the human race; mankind; the male sex; a male servant; a piece in a game, as chess, etc.—*vt*. (manning, manned). To furnish with men; to guard with men; *refl*. to infuse courage into.

Manacle, man'a-kl, *n*. An instrument of iron for fastening the hands; a handcuff; used chiefly in the *plural*.—*vt*. (manacling, manacled). To put manacles on; to fetter.

Manage, man'āj, *vt*. (managing, managed). To wield; to direct in riding; to conduct or administer; to have under command; to treat with judgment.—*vi*. To conduct affairs.

Mandatory, man'da-to-ri, *a*. Containing a command; preceptive; directory.

Mandible, man'di-bl, *n*. An animal's jaw.

Mange, mānj, *n*. A skin disease of horses, cattle, dogs, etc.

Manger, mān'jėr, *n*. A trough in which food is placed for cattle and horses.

Mangle, mang'gl, *vt*. (mangling, mangled). To mutilate; to lacerate; to smooth, as linen.—*n*. A rolling press, or small calender, for smoothing cotton or linen.

Manicure, man'i-kūr, *n*. One whose occupation is to trim the nails, etc., of the hand.

Manifest, man'i-fest, *a*. Clearly visible; evident; obvious.—*vt*. To make manifest; to display or exhibit.—*n*. A document stating a ship's cargo, destination, etc.

Manifesto, man-i-fest'ō, *n*. A public declaration; a proclamation.

Manifold, man'i-fōld, *a*. Numerous and various; of divers kinds.—*vt*. To multiply impressions of, as by a copying apparatus.

Manipulate, ma-nip'ū-lāt, *vt*. To

M

treat with the hands; to handle; to operate upon so as to disguise.

Manner, man´ėr, n. The mode in which anything is done; method; bearing or conduct; pl. carriage or behavior; civility in society; sort or kind.

Mannerism, man´ėr-izm, n. Adherence to the same manner; tasteless uniformity of style; peculiarity of personal manner.

Mannish, man´ish, a. Characteristic of or resembling a man; bold or masculin.

Maneuver, ma-nū´vėr or ma-nö´vėr, n. A regulated movement, particularly of troops or ships; management with address; stratagem.—vi. (maneuvering, maneuvered). To perform military or naval maneuvers; to employ stratagem; to manage with address.-vt. To cause to perform maneuvers.

Mantle, man´tl, n. A kind of cloak worn over other garments; something that covers and conceals; incandescent hood for gas jet.—vt. (mantling, mantled). To cloak; to cover as with a mantle.—vi. To become covered with a coating; to cream; to display superficial changes of hue.

Manual, man´ū-al, a. Performed by the hand; used or made by the hand.—n. A small book; a compendium; the service-book of the R. Catholic Church; keyboard of an organ.

Manufacture, man-ū-fak´tūr, n. The process of making anything by hand or machinery; something made from raw materials.—vt. (manufacturing, manufactured). To fabricate from raw materials; to fabricate without real grounds.—vi. To be occupied in manufactures.

Manumit, man-ū-mit´, vt. (manumitting, manumitted). To release from slavery.

Manure, man-ūr´, vt. (manuring, manured). To fertilize with nutritive substances.—n. Any substance added to soil to accelerate or increase the production of the crops.

Manuscript, man´ū-skript, n. A paper written with the hand: often contracted to MS., pl. MSS.—a. Written with the hand.

Many, me´ni, a. Forming or comprising a number; numerous.—**The many,** the great majority of people; the crowd.—**So many,** the same number of; a certain number indefinitely.

Marble, mär´bl, n. A calcareous stone of compact texture; a little hard ball used by boys in play; an inscribed or sculptured marble stone.—a. Made of or like marble.—vt. (marbling, marbled). To stain like marble.

March, märch, vi. To move by steps and in order, as soldiers; to walk in a stately manner; to progress; to be situated next.—vt. To cause to march.—n. The measured walk of a body of men; a stately walk; distance passed over; a musical composition to regulate the march of troops, etc.; a frontier or boundary (usually in pl.); the third month of the year.

Marine, ma-rēn´, a. Pertaining to the sea; found in the sea; used at sea; naval; maritime.—n. A soldier who serves on board of a man-of-war; collective shipping of a country; whole economy of naval affairs.

Marionette, ma´ri-o-net´´, n. A puppet moved by strings.

Maritime, ma´ri-tīm, a. Relating to the sea; naval; bordering on the sea; having a navy and commerce by sea.

Marjoram, mär´jō-ram, n. A plant of the mint family.

Mark, märk, n. A visible sign or impression on something; a distinguishing sign; indication or evidence; pre-eminence or importance; a characteristic; heed or regard; object aimed at; proper standard; extreme estimate; a German coin.—vt. To make a mark or marks on; to denote (often with out); to regard, observe, heed.—vi. To note; to observe critically; to remark.

Marked, märkt, p.a. Pre-eminent; outstanding; prominent; remarkable.

Market, mär'ket, *n.* An occasion on which goods are publicly exposed for sale; place in which goods are exposed for sale; rate of purchase and sale; demand for commodities; privilege of keeping a public market.—*vi.* To deal in a market.—*vt.* To offer for sale in a market.

Maroon, ma-rön, *n.* A fugitive slave in the W. Indies; a brownish crimson or claret color.—*vt.* To land and leave on a desolate island.

Marquetry, mär'ket-ri, *n.* Inlaid work.

Marriage, ma'rij, *n.* The act or ceremony of marrying; matrimony; wedlock.

Marrow, ma'rō, *n.* A soft substance in the cavities of bones; the best part; a kind of gourd, also called *vegetable marrow.*

Marry, ma'ri, *vt.* (marrying, married). To unite in wedlock; to dispose of in wedlock; to take for husband or wife.—*vi.* To take a husband or a wife.—*interj.* Indeed; forsooth.

Mars, märz, *n.* The god of war; a planet.

Marsh, märsh, *n.* A swamp; a tract of low wet land.—*a.* Pertaining to boggy places.

Marshal, mär'shal, *n.* One who regulates rank and order at a feast, procession, etc.; a military officer of the highest rank, generally called *field-marshal.*—*vt.* (marshalling, marshalled). To dispose in order; to array.

Masculine, mas'kū-lin, *a.* Male; manly; robust; bold or unwomanly; designating nouns which are the names of male animals, etc.

Mash, mash, *n.* A mixture of ingredients beaten or blended together; a mixture of ground malt and warm water yielding wort.—*vt.* To mix; to beat into a confused mass.

Mask, mask, *n.* A cover for the face; a masquerade; a sort of play common in the 16th and 17th centuries; pretense.—*vt.* To cover with a mask; to disguise; to hide.

Masquerade, mas-kėr-äd', *n.* An assembly of persons wearing masks; a disguise.—*vi.* To assemble in masks; to go in disguise.

Mass, mas, *n.* A body of matter; a lump; magnitude; an assemblage; collection; the generality; the communion service in the R. Catholic Church.—**The Masses,** the populace.—*vt.* and *i.* To form into a mass; to assemble in crowds.

Massacre, mas'sa-kėr, *n.* Ruthless, unnecessary, or indiscriminate slaughter.—*vt.* (massacring, massacred). To kill with indiscriminate violence; to slaughter.

Massage, ma-säzh' or mas'äj, *n.* A process of kneading, rubbing, pressing, etc., parts of a person's body to effect a cure.—*vt.* (massaging, massaged). To treat by this process.

Masseur, mas-ör, *n.* One who practices massage.

Masseter, mas-sē'tėr, *n.* Either of the pair of muscles which raise the under jaw.

Massive, mas'iv, *a.* Bulky and heavy; ponderous; pertaining to a mass; not local or special.

Mast, mäst, *n.* A long upright timber in a vessel, supporting the yards, sails, and rigging; the fruit of the oak, beech, etc. (no *pl.*).—*vt.* To supply with a mast or masts.

Master, mäs'tėr, *n.* One who rules or directs; an employer; owner; captain of a merchant ship; teacher in a school; a man eminently skilled in some art; a word of address for men (written *Mr.* and pron. mis'tėr) and boys (written in full); a vessel having masts.—*vt.* To bring under control; to make oneself master of.—*a.* Belonging to a master; chief.

Mat, mat, *n.* An article of interwoven rushes, twine, etc., used for cleaning or protecting; anything growing thickly or closely interwoven.—*vt.* (matting, matted'). To cover with mats; to entangle.—*vi.* To grow thickly together.

Matador, ma-ta-dōr', *n.* The man appointed to kill the bull in bullfights; a card in ombre and quadrille.

Match, mach, *n.* A person or thing

M

equal to another; union by marriage; one to be married; a contest; a small body that catches fire readily or ignites by friction.—*vt*. To equal; to show an equal to; to set against as equal in contest; to suit; to marry.—*vi*. To be united in marriage; to suit; to tally.

Mate, māt, *n*. A companion; a match; a husband or wife; second officer in a ship.—*vt*. (mating, mated). To equal; to match; to marry; to checkmate.

Material, ma-tē'ri-al, *a*. Consisting of matter; not spiritual; important; essential; substantial.—*n*. Anything composed of matter; substance of which anything is made.

Materialize, ma-tē'ri-al-īz, *vt*. To reduce to a state of matter; to regard as matter.

Maternal, ma-tėr'nal, *a*. Motherly; pertaining to a mother; becoming a mother.

Maternity, ma-tėr'ni-ti, *n*. The state, character, or relation of a mother.

Mathematics, ma-thē-ma'tiks, *n*. The science of magnitude and number, comprising arithmetic, geometry, algebra, etc.

Matron, mā'tron, *n*. An elderly married woman, or an elderly lady; head nurse or superintendent of a hospital, etc.

Matted, mat'ed, *p.a.* Laid with mats; entangled.

Matter, mat'ėr, *n*. Not mind; body; that of which anything is made; substance as distinct from form; subject; business; circumstance; import; moment; pus.—*vi*. To be of importance; to signify; to form pus.

Maw, ma, *n*. The stomach, especially of animals; paunch; crop of fowls.

Mawkish, mạk'ish, *a*. Apt to cause satiety or loathing; insipid; sickly.

Maxilla, mak-sil'la, *n*.; pl. **ae.** A jaw-bone; a jaw.

Maxim, mak'sim, *n*. An established principle; axiom; aphorism; a light machine-gun.

Maximum, mak'sim-um, *n*. The greatest degree or quantity.—*a*. Greatest.

May, mā, *n*. The fifth month of the year; hawthorn blossom.—*vi*. To celebrate the festivities of Mayday.—*v. aux*. (pret. might, mīt). Used to imply possibility, opportunity, permission, desire, etc.

Mead, mēd, *n*. A fermented liquor made from honey and water; a meadow: *poet*.

Meadow, me'dō, *n*. A low level tract of land under grass.—*a*. Belonging to a meadow.

Meager, mē'gėr, *a*. Thin; lean; poor; scanty.

Meal, mēl, *n*. Portion of food taken at one time; a repast; ground grain; flour.

Mealy-mouthed, mēl'i-mouᴛʜd, *a*. Unwilling to tell the truth in plain language; soft-spoken; inclined to hypocrisy.

Mean, mēn, *a*. Low in rank or birth; humble; base; comtemptible; occupying a middle position; middle; intermediate.—*n*. What is intermediate; average rate or degree; medium; *pl*. measure or measures adopted; agency (generally used as *sing*.); income or resources.—*vt*. (pret. and pp. *meant*). To have in the mind; to intend; to signify; to import.—*vi*. To have thought or ideas, or to have meaning.

Measure, me'zhúr, *n*. The extent or magnitude of a thing; a standard of size; a measuring rod or line; that which is allotted; moderation; just degree; course of action; legislative proposal; musical time; meter; a grave solemn dance; pl. beds or strata.—*vt*. (measuring, measured). To ascertain the extent or capacity of; to estimate; to value; to pass through or over; to proportion; to allot.—*vi*. To have a certain extent.

Measurement, me'zhúr-ment, *n*. Act of measuring; amount ascertained.

Meat, mēt, *n*. Food in general; the flesh of animals used as food; the edible portion of something (the *meat* of an egg).

Mechanic, me-kan'ik, *a*. Mechanical.—*n*. An artisan; an artisan employed in making and repairing machinery.

Mechanical, me-kan'ik-al, a. Pertaining to mechanism or machinery; resembling a machine; done by the mere force of habit; pertaining to material forces; physical.

Mechanics, me-kan'iks, n. The science which treats of motion and force.

Medical, med'i-kal, a. Pertaining to the art of curing diseases; tending to cure.

Medicate, med'i-kāt, vt. (medicating, medicated). To treat with medicine; to impregnate with anything medicinal.

Medicinal, me-dis'in-al, a. Pertaining to medicine; containing healing ingredients.

Medicine, med'sin, n. Any substance used as a remedy for disease; a drug; the science and art of curing diseases.

Medieval, mē-di-ēv'al, a. Pertaining to the middle ages.

Mediocre, mē'di-ō-kėr, a. Of moderate degree; middling.

Mediocrity, mē-di-ok'ri-ti, n. State of being mediocre; a moderate degree or rate; a person of mediocre talents or abilities.

Meditate, med'i-tāt, vi. (meditating, meditated). To dwell on anything in thought; to cogitate.—vt. To think on; to scheme; to intend.

Mediterranean, med'i-te-rā'nē-an, a. Surrounded by land: now applied exclusively to the *Mediterranean* Sea.

Medium, mē'di-um, n.; pl. -ia, -iums. Something holding a middle position; a mean; means of motion or action; agency of transmission; instrumentality.—a. Middle; middling.

Meet, mēt, vt. (meeting, met). To come face to face with; to come in contact with; to encounter; to light on; to receive; to satisfy.—vi. To come together; to encounter; to assemble.—n. A meeting, as of huntsmen.—a. Fit; suitable; proper.

Mellow, mel'ō, a. Soft with ripeness; soft to the ear, eye, or taste; toned down by time; half-tipsy.—vt. To make mellow; to soften.—vi. To become mellow.

Melodic, me-lod'ik, a. Of the nature of melody; relating to melody.

Melodrama, me-lō-dra'ma, n. Properly a musical drama; a serious play, with startling incidents, exaggerated sentiment, and splendid decoration.

Melody, me'lō-di, n. An agreeable succession of sounds; sweetness of sound; the particular air or tune of a musical piece.

Melon, me'lon, n. A kind of cucumber and its large, fleshy fruit.

Melt, melt, vt. To reduce from a solid to a liquid state by heat; to soften; to overcome with tender emotion.—vi. To become liquid; to dissolve; to be softened to love, pity, etc.; to pass by imperceptible degrees.

Member, mem'bėr, n. An organ or limb of an animal body; part of an aggregate; one of the persons composing a society, etc.; a representative in a legislative body.

Membrane, mem'brān, n. A thin flexible texture in animal bodies; a similar texture in plants.

Memento, mē-men'tō, n. That which reminds; a souvenir; a keepsake.

Memoir, mem'oir, mem'wär, n. A written account of events or transactions; a biographical notice; recollections of one's life (usually in the pl.).

Memorial, mē-mō'ri-al, a. Pertaining to memory or remembrance; serving to commemorate.—n. That which preserves the memory of something; a monument; memorandum; a written representation of facts, made as the ground of a petition.

Memorize, mem'or-īz, vt. To cause to be remembered; to record.

Memory, mem'ō-ri, n. The faculty of the mind by which it retains knowledge or ideas; remembrance; recollection; the time within which a person may remember what is past; something remembered.

Menace, men'ās, n. A threat; indication of probable evil.—vt. (menacing, menaced). To threaten.

Menage, men-äzh', n. A household;

M

housekeeping; household management.

Menagerie, me-naj'ér-i, *n.* A collection of wild animals kept for exhibition.

Mend, mend, *vt.* To repair; to restore to a sound state; to amend.— *vi.* To advance to a better state; to improve.

Meningitis, men-in-jī'tis, *n.* Inflammation of the membranes of the brain or spinal cord.

Menses, men'sēz, *n.pl.* The monthly discharge of a woman.

Menstrual, men'strụ-al, *a.* Monthly; pertaining to the menses of females.

Mensuration, men-sūr-ā'shon, *n.* The act, process, or art of measuring.

Mental, men'tal, *a.* Pertaining to the mind; performed by the mind; intellectual.

Mercenary, mér'se-na-ri, *a.* Hired; venal; that may be hired; greedy of gain; sordid.—*n.* One who is hired; a soldier hired into foreign service.

Merchandise, mér'chand-īz, *n.* The goods of a merchant; objects of commerce; trade.

Merchant, mér'chant, *n.* One who carries on trade on a large scale; a man who exports and imports goods.—*a.* Relating to trade; commercial.

Mercy, mér'si, *n.* Willingness to spare or forgive; clemency; pity; a blessing; benevolence; unrestrained exercise of authority.

Mere, mēr, *a.* This or that and nothing else; simple, absolute, entire, utter.—*n.* A pool or small lake; a boundary.

Meretricious, me-rē-tri'shus, *a.* Pertaining to prostitutes; alluring by false show; gaudy.

Merge, mérj, *vt.* (merging, merged). To cause to be swallowed up or incorporated.—*vi.* To be sunk, swallowed, or lost.

Meridian, mē-rid'i-an, *n.* Pertaining to midday or noon; pertaining to the acme or culmination.—*n.* Mid-day; point of greatest splendor; any imaginary circle passing through both poles, used in mark-

ing longitude; a similar imaginary line in the heavens passing through the zenith of any place.

Mermaid, mér'mād, *n.* A fabled marine creature, having the upper part like a woman and the lower like a fish.

Merriment, me'ri-ment, *n.* Mirth; noisy gaiety; hilarity.

Merry, me'ri, *a.* Joyous; jovial; hilarious; gay and noisy; mirthful; sportive.

Mesentery, me'sen-te-ri, *a.* A membrane retaining the intestines in a proper position.

Mesh, mesh, *n.* The space between the threads of a net; something that entangles; implement for making nets.—*vt.* To catch in a net.

Mess, mes, *n.* A dish of food; food for a person at one meal; a number of persons who eat together, especially in the army or navy; a disorderly mixture; muddle.—*vi.* To take meals in common with others.

Message, mes'āj, *n.* A communication, written or verbal; an official written communication.

Messenger, mes'en-jér, *n.* One who bears a message; a harbinger.

Messiah, mes-sī'a, *n.* The Anointed One; Christ, the Anointed.

Metabolism, me-tab'ol-izm, *n.* Change or metamorphosis; chemical change of nutriment taken into the body.

Metal, me'tal, *n.* An elementary substance, such as gold, iron, etc., having a peculiar luster and generally fusible by heat; the broken stone for covering roads.

Metallurgy, me'tal-ér-ji, *n.* Art of working metals; art or operation of separating metals from their ores by smelting.

Metamorphose, me-ta-mor'fōs, *vt.* To change into a different form; to transform.

Metamorphosis, me-ta-mor'fos-is, *n.*; pl. **-ses.** Change of form or shape; transformation.

Metaphor, me'ta-for, *n.* A figure of speech founded on resemblance, as 'that man is a fox.'

Metaphrase, me'ta-frāz, *n.* A verbal translation from one language into another.

Metaphysics, me-ta-fi'ziks, n. The science of the principles and causes of all things existing; the philosophy of mind as distinguished from that of matter.

Metathesis, me-ta'the-sis, n. Transposition, as of the letters or syllables of a word.

Mete, mēt, vt. (meting, meted). To measure; to measure out; to dole.

Meteor, mē'tē-ėr, n. An atmospheric phenomenon; a transient luminous body; something that transiently dazzles.

Meteoric, mē-tē-or'ik, a. Pertaining to or consisting of meteors; proceeding from a meteor; transiently or irregularly brilliant.

Meteorology, mē'tē-ėr-ol''o-ji, n. the science of atmospheric phenomena.

Meter, mē'tėr, n. One who or that which measures.

Method, me'thod, n. Mode or manner of procedure; system; classification.

Metric, met'rik, a. Pertaining to the decimal system.

Metric, Metrical, met'rik, met'rik-al, a. Pertaining to rhythm; consisting of verse.

Mettle, met'l, n. Moral or physical constitution; spirit; courage; fire.

Mew, mū, n. A sea-mew; a gull; moulting of a hawk; a coop for fowls; a place of confinement; the cry of a cat.—vt. To moult; to shut up, as in a cage.—vi. To moult; to cry as a cat.

Mezzo soprano, a treble voice between soprano and contralto.

Miasma, mī-az'ma, n.; pl. **Miasmata,** mī-az'ma-ta. The effluvia of any putrefying bodies; noxious emanation; malaria.

Mica, mī'ka, n. A mineral cleavable into thin shining elastic plates.

Microbe, mī'krōb, n. A microscopic organism such as a bacillus or bacterium.

Mid-day, mid'dā, n. The middle of the day; noon.—a. Pertaining to noon.

Middle, mid'l, a.; no compar.; superl. middlemost. Equally distant from the extremes; intermediate; intervening.—**Middle ages,** the period from the fall of the Roman Empire to about 1450.—n. Point or part equally distant from the extremities; something intermediate.

Mien, mēn, n. Look; bearing; carriage.

Might, mīt, n. Great power or ability to act; strength; force.—v. aux. Pret. of may.

Mighty, mīt'i, a. Having might; strong; powerful; potent; very great; vast.

Migrate, mī'grāt, vi. (migrating, migrated). To remove to a distant place or country.

Migration, mī'grā-shon, n. Act of migrating; removal from one place to another.

Milch, milsh, a. Giving milk, as cows.

Mild, mīld, a. Gentle in temper or disposition; merciful; soft; bland; mellow.

Mildew, mil'dū, n. A minute parastic fungus that causes decay in vegetable matter; condition so caused.—vt. and i. To taint with mildew.

Mile, mīl, n. A measure of length or distance equal to 1760 yards.

Militant, mil'i-tant, a. Serving as a soldier; fighting; combative.

Militarism, mil'i-ta-rizm, n. The system that leads a nation to pay excessive attention to military affairs.

Military, mil'i-ta-ri, a. Pertaining to soldiers or war; martial; soldierly; belligerent.—n. The whole body of soldiers; the army.

Militate, mil'i-tāt, vi. (militating, militated). To stand arrayed; to have weight or influence.

Militia, mi-li'sha, n. A body of soldiers not permanently organized in time of peace.

Milk, milk, n. A whitish fluid secreted in female animals, serving as nourishment for their young; what resembles milk; white juice of plants.—vt. To draw milk from.

Mill, mil, n. A machine for making meal or flour; a machine for grinding, etc.; building that contains

M

the machinery for grinding, etc.—
vt. To pass through a mill; to stamp in a coining press; to throw, as silk; to full, as cloth.

Milliard, mil-yärd', *n.* A thousand millions.

Milligram, mil'i-gram, *n.* The thousandth part of a gram.

Millimeter, mil-i-mā'tr, *n.* The thousandth part of a meter.

Milliner, mil'in-er, *n.* One who makes head-dresses, hats, etc., for females.

Milling, mil'ing, *n.* The process of grinding or passing through a mill; the transverse grooves on the edge of a coin.

Million, mil'yon, *n.* A thousand thousands; a very great number, indefinitely.

Millionaire, mil'yon-är, *n.* One worth a million dollars, etc.; a very rich person.

Mimic, mim'ik, *a.* Imitative; consisting of imitation.—*n.* One who imitates or mimics.—*vt.* (mimicking, mimicked). To imitate, especially for sport; to ridicule by imitation.

Mind, mīnd, *n.* The intellectual power in man; understanding; cast of thought and feeling; inclination; opinion; memory.—*vt.* To attend to; to observe; to regard.

Mindful, mīnd'ful, *a.* Bearing in mind; attentive; regarding with care; heedful.

Mine, mīn, *adj. pron.* My; belonging to me.—*n.* A pit from which coal, ores, etc., are taken; an underground passage in which explosives may be lodged for destructive purposes; a contrivance floating on or near the surface of the sea, to destroy ships by explosion; a rich source or store of wealth.—*vi.* (mining, mined). To dig a mine; to dig for ores, etc.; to burrow.—*vt.* To undermine; to sap.

Mineral, mi'ne-ral, *n.* An inorganic body existing on or in the earth.—*a.* Pertaining to or consisting of minerals; impregnated with mineral matter.

Mingle, ming'gl, *vt.* (mingling, mingled). To mix up together; to blend; to debase by mixture.—*vi.* To be mixed; to join.

Miniature, min'i-a-tūr, *n.* A painting of very small dimensions, usually in water-colors, on ivory, vellum, etc.; anything represented on a greatly reduced scale; a small scale.—*a.* On a small scale; diminutive.

Minion, min'yon, *n.* An unworthy favorite; a servile dependant; a minx; a small kind of printing type.

Minister, min'is-ter, *n.* A servant; attendant; agent; a member of a government; a political representative or ambassador; the pastor of a church.—*vt.* To give; to supply.—*vi.* To perform service; to afford supplies; to contribute.

Minnow, min'ō, *n.* A very small British fish inhabiting fresh-water streams.

Minor, mī'nor, *a.* Lesser; smaller; of little importance; petty; in *music,* less by a lesser semitone.—*n.* A person not yet 21 years of age.

Minority, mi-no'ri-ti, *n.* State of being a minor; period from birth until 21 years of age; the smaller number or a number less than half; the party that has the fewest vores.

Minus, mī'nus, *a.* Less; less by so much; wanting; the sign (-).

Minute, mi-nūt', *a.* Very small; precise; particular; exact.

Minute, mi'nit, *a.* The sixtieth part of an hour or degree; short sketch of an agreement, etc., in writing; a note to preserve the memory of anything.—*vt.* (minuting, minuted). To write down a concise state or note of.

Minutiae, mi-nū'shi-ē, *n.pl.* Small or minute things; minor or unimportant details.

Miracle, mi'ra-kl, *n.* A marvel; a supernatural event; a miracle-play.

Mirror, mi'rer, *n.* A looking-glass; any polished substance that reflects images; an exemplar.—*vt.* To reflect, as in a mirror.

Mirth, merth, *n.* The feeling of being merry; merriment; glee; hilarity.

Misadventure, mis-ad-ven'tūr, *n.* An unlucky accident; misfortune;

ill-luck.

Misalliance, mis-al-lī'ans, n. Improper association; an unequal marriage.

Misanthrope, Misanthropist, mis'an-thrōp, mis-an'thrōp-ist, n. A hater of mankind.

Misanthropy, mis-an'thrō-pi, n. Hatred or dislike to mankind.

Misapply, mis-ap-plī', vt. To apply amiss; to apply to a wrong purpose.

Misapprehend, mis-ap'prē-hend'', vt. To misunderstand; to take in a wrong sense. –

Misappropriate, mis-ap-prō'pri-āt, vt. To appropriate wrongly.

Misbecome, mis-bē-kum', vt. Not to become; to suit ill.

Misbegotten, mis-bē-got'n, p.a. Unlawfully or irregularly begotten.

Misbehave, mis-bē-hāv', vi. To behave ill; to conduct oneself improperly.

Misbelief, mis-bē-lēf', n. Erroneous belief; false religion.

Miscalculate, mis-kal'kū-lāt, vt. To calculate erroneously.

Miscarry, mis-ka'ri, vi. To fail to reach its destination; to fail of the intended effect; to bring forth young before the proper time.

Miscellaneous, mis-sel-lā'nē-us, a. Consisting of several kinds; promiscuous; producing written compositions of various sorts.

Miscreant, mis'krē-ant, n. A vile wretch; an unprincipled scoundrel.

Miser, mī'zėr, n. A niggard; one who in wealth acts as if suffering from poverty.

Miserable, miz'ėr-a-bl, a. Very unhappy; wretched; worthless; despicable.

Miserly, mī'zėr-li, a. Like a miser in habits; penurious; sordid; niggardly.

Misery, miz'ėr-i, n. Great unhappiness; extreme distress; wretchedness.

Misfeasance, mis-fē'zans, n. In law, a wrong done; wrong-doing in office.

Misfit, mis-fit', n. A bad fit.—vt. To make (a garment, etc.) of a wrong size; to supply with something not

suitable.

Misfortune, mis-for'tūn, n. Ill fortune; calamity; mishap.

Misgiving, mis-giv'ing, n. A failing of confidence; doubt; distrust.

Misguide, mis-gīd', vt. To guide into error; to direct to a wrong purpose or end.

Mishap, mis-hap', n. A mischance; an unfortunate accident.

Misinform, mis-in-form', vt. To give erroneous information to.

Misinterpret, mis-in-tėr'pret, vt. To interpret erroneously.

Misjudge, mis-juj', vt. To judge erroneously.—vi. To err in judgment.

Misplace, mis-plās, vt. To put in a wrong place; to set on an improper object.

Misprint, mis-print', vt. To print wrongly.—n. A mistake in printing.

Mispronounce, mis-prō-nouns', vt. or i. To pronounce erroneously.

Misquote, mis-kwōt, vt. To quote erroneously; to cite incorrectly.

Misshapen, mis-shāp'n, a. Ill-formed; ugly.

Missile, mis'īl, a. Capable of being thrown.—n. A weapon or projectile thrown with hostile intention, as an arrow, a bullet.

Mission, mi'shon, n. A sending or delegating; duty on which one is sent; destined end or function; persons sent on some political business or to propagate religion; a station of missionaries.

Missionary, mi'shon-a-ri, n. One sent to propagate religion.—a. Pertaining to missions.

Missive, mis'iv, a. Such as is sent; proceeding from some authoritative source.—n. A message; a letter or writing sent.

Misspell, mis-spel', vt. To spell wrongly.

Misspent, mis-spent', p.a. Ill-spent; wasted.

Misstatement, mis-stāt'ment, n. A wrong statement.

Mist, mist, n. Visible watery vapor; aqueous vapor falling in numerous but almost imperceptible drops; something which dims or darkens.

Mistake, mis-tāk', vt. To misunder-

M

stand or misapprehend; to regard as one when really another.—*vi*. To err in opinion or judgment.—*n*. An error in opinion or judgment; blunder; fault.

Mistress, mis'tres, *n*. The female appellation corresponding to *master*; a woman who has authority, ownership, etc.; a female teacher; a concubine; a title of address applied to married women (written *Mrs*. and pronounced mis'iz).

Mistrust, mis-trust', *n*. Want of confidence or trust; suspicion.—*vt*. To distrust; to suspect; to doubt.

Misunderstand, mis-un'der-stand' ', *vt*. To understand wrongly; to mistake.

Misuse, mis-ūz', *vt*. To use to a bad purpose; to abuse.—*n*. mis-ūs'. Improper use; misapplication.

Mite, mīt, *n*. A minute animal of the class Arachnida (cheese-*mite*, etc.); a very small coin formerly current; a very little creature.

Mitigant, mi'ti-gant, *a*. Softening; soothing.

Mixed, mikst, *p.a*. Promiscuous; indiscriminate; miscellaneous.

Mixture, miks'tūr, *n*. Act of mixing; state of being mixed; a compound; a liquid medicine of different ingredients.

Mnemonics, nē-mon'iks, *n*. The art of memory; rules for assisting the memory.

Moan, mōn, *vi*. To utter a low dull sound through grief or pain.—*vt*. To bewail or deplore.—*n*. A low dull sound due to grief or pain; a sound resembling this.

Moat, mōt, *n*. A deep trench round a castle or other fortified place.—*vt*. To surround with a ditch for defense.

Mob, mob, *n*. A crowd; disorderly assembly; rabble.—*vt*. (mobbing, mobbed). To attack in a disorderly crowd; to crowd round and annoy.

Mobile, mō'bil, *a*. Capable of being easily moved; changeable; fickle.

Moccasin, mok'a-sin, *n*. A shoe of deer-skin or soft leather, worn by N. American Indians; a venomous serpent of the United States.

Mock, mok, *vt*. To mimic in contempt or derision; to flout; to ridicule; to set at naught; to defy.—*vi*. To use ridicule; to gibe or jeer.—*n*. A derisive word or gesture; ridicule; derision.—*a*. Counterfeit; assumed.

Mockery, mok'e-ri, *n*. Derision; sportive insult; counterfeit appearance; vain effort.

Mode, mōd, *n*. Manner; method; fashion; custom.

Model, mo'del, *n*. A pattern; an image, copy, facsimile; standard, plan, or type; a person from whom an artist studies his proportions, postures, etc.—*vt*. (modelling, modelled). To plan after some model; to form in order to serve as a model; to mold.—*vi*. To make a model.

Moderate, mo'de-rāt, *vt*. To restrain from excess; to temper, lessen, allay.—*vi*. To become less violent or intense; to preside as a moderator.—*a*. Not going to extremes; temperate; medium; mediocre.— *n*. One not extreme in opinions.

Modicum, mod'i-kum, *n*. A little; a small quantity; small allowance or share.

Modify, mod'i-fī, *vt*. (modifying, modified). To qualify; to change or alter; to vary.

Modulus, mod'ū-lus, *n*. In *mathematics*, etc., a constant quantity used in connection with some variable quantity.

Modus, mō'dus, *n*. A way, manner, or mode.

Mohair, mō'hār, *n*. The hair of the Angora goat; cloth made of this hair; an imitation wool and cotton cloth.

Mold, mōld, *n*. Fine soft earth; mustiness or mildew; dust from incipient decay; form in which a thing is cast; model; shape; character.—*vt*. To cause to contract mold; to cover with mold or soil; to model; to shape; to fashion.—*vi*. To become moldy.

Molding, mōld'ing, *n*. Anything cast in a mold; ornamental contour or form in wood or stone along an edge or a surface.

Mole, mōl, *n*. A small discolored protuberance on the human body;

a mound or break-water to protect a harbor from the waves; a small burrowing insectivorous animal.

Molecule, mo'le-kūl, *n.* A very minute particle of matter.

Mole-hill, mōl'hil, *n.* A little hillock of earth thrown up by moles; a very small hill.

Molest, mō-lest', *vt.* To annoy; to disturb; to harass; to vex.

Mollify, mol'i-fī, *vt.* (mollifying, mollified). To soften; to assuage; to appease; to reduce in harshness; to tone down.

Mollusc, Mollusk, mol'usk, *n.* An animal whose body is soft, as mussels, snails, cuttle-fish, etc.; one of the *Mollusca*.

Molten, mōlt'n, old pp. of *melt.* Melted; made of melted metal.

Moment, mō'ment, *n.* A minute portion of time; a second; momentum; importance; gravity.

Momentary, mō-ment-a-ri, *a.* Done in a moment; continuing only a moment.

Momentous, mō-ment'us, *a.* Of moment; important; weighty.

Momentum, mō-ment'um, *n.*; pl. -**ta.** The force possessed by a body in motion; impetus.

Monachism, mon'ak-izm, *n.* The monastic life or system.

Monad, mon'ad, *n.* An ultimate atom.

Monadic, mon-ad'ik, *a.* Having the nature or character of a monad.

Monarch, mon'ärk, *n.* A supreme governor of a state; a sovereign; one who or that which is chief of its kind.—*a.* Supreme; ruling.

Monarchy, mon'är-ki, *n.* Government in which the supreme power is lodged in a single person, actually or nominally; a kingdom.

Monastery, mon'as-te-ri, *n.* A house for monks, sometimes for nuns; abbey; priory; convent.

Monatomic, mon-a-tom'ik, *a.* Said of an element one atom of which will combine with only one atom of another element.

Monday, mun'dā, *n.* The second day of the week.

Monetary, mo'ne-ta-ri, *a.* Relating to money; consisting in money.

Money, mun'i, *n.* Coin; pieces of gold, silver, or other metal, stamped by public authority and used as the medium of exchange; a circulating medium; wealth; affluence.

Mongol, Mongolian, mon'gol, mon-gō'li-an, *n.* A native of Mongolia.—*a.* Belonging to Mongolia.

Mongoose, mong' or mung'gös, *n.* A common ichneumon of India.

Mongrel, mung'grel, *a.* Of a mixed breed; hybrid.—*n.* An animal of a mixed breed.

Monitor, mo'ni-tėr, *n.* One who admonishes; one who warns of faults or informs of duty; a senior pupil in a school appointed to instruct and look after juniors; a lizard.

Monk, mungk, *n.* A male inhabitant of a monastery, bound to celibacy.

Monkey, mung'ki, *n.* A long-tailed quadrumanous animal; a playful or mischievous youngster.

Monochrome, mon'ō-krōm, *n.* A painting in one color, but with light and shade.

Monogamy, mon-og'a-mi, *n.* The practice or principle of marrying only once; the marrying of only one at a time.

Monogram, mon'ō-gram, *n.* A cipher composed of several letters interwoven.

Monograph, mon'ō-graf, *n.* An account of a single person, thing, or class of things.

Monolith, mon'ō-lith, *n.* A pillar, column, etc., consisting of a single stone.

Monologue, mon'ō-log, *n.* A speech uttered by one person alone; a soliloquy.

Monomania, mon-ō-mā'ni-a, *n.* Insanity in regard to a single subject or class of subjects; a craze.

Monopoly, mo-nop'o-li, *n.* An exclusive trading privilege; assumption of anything to the exclusion of others.

Monosyllabic, mon'ō-sil-lab''ik, *a.* Consisting of one syllable, or of words of one syllable.

Monotheism, mon'ō-thē-izm, *n.* The doctrine of the existence of one God only.

Monotone, mon'ō-tōn, *n.* A single

M

tone; unvaried pitch of the voice.

Monotony, mon-ot'o-ni, *n.* Uniformity of sound; a dull uniformity; an irksome sameness or want of variety.

Monsoon, mon-sön', *n.* The tradewind of the Indian seas, blowing from N.E. from November to March, and S.W. from April to October.

Monster, mon'stėr, *n.* An animal of unnatural form or of great size; one unnaturally wicked or evil.—*a.* Of inordinate size.

Monstrous, mon'strus, *a.* Unnatural in form; enormous; huge; horrible.—*adv.* Exceedingly.

Month, munth, *n.* The period measured by the moon's revolution (the lunar month, about 29½ days); one of the twelve parts of the year (the calendar month, 30 or 31 days).

Monthly, munth'li, *a.* Done or happening once a month, or every month.—*n.* A publication appearing once a month.—*adv.* Once a month; in every month.

Monument, mon'ū-ment, *n.* Anything by which the memory of a person or of an event is preserved; a memorial; a singular or notable instance.

Mood, möd, *n.* Temper of mind; disposition; a fit of sullenness; a form of verbs expressive of certainty, contingency, etc.; a form of syllogism.

Moon, mön, *n.* The changing luminary of the night; the heavenly body next to the earth, revolving round it in about 29½ days; a satellite of any planet; a month.

Moonlight, mön'līt, *n.* The light afforded by the moon.—*a.* Illuminated by the moon; occurring during moonlight.—**Moon-lit,** mön'lit, *a.* Illuminated by the moon.

Moonshine, mön'shīn, *n.* The light of the moon; show without substance; pretense; illegally distilled corn whiskey.

Moonstone, mön'stōn, *n.* A translucent variety of felspar used in trinkets, etc.

Moonstruck, mön'struk, *a.* Affected by the influence of the moon; lunatic.

Moor, mör, *n.* A tract of waste land, or of hilly ground on which game is preserved; a native of the northern coast of Africa.—*vt.* To secure a ship in a particular station, as by cables and anchors.—*vi.* To be confined by cables.

Mooring, mör'ing, *n.* Act of one who moors; *pl.* the anchor, etc., by which a ship is moored; the place where a ship is moored.

Moose, mös, *n.* The American variety of the elk.

Moot, möt, *vt.* To debate; to discuss.—*a.* Debatable; subject to discussion.

Moot-point, möt'point, *n.* A point debated or liable to be debated.

Mop, mop, *n.* A cloth or collection of yarns fastened to a handle, and used for cleaning; a grimace.—*vt.* (mopping, mopped). To rub with a mop; to wipe.—*vi.* To grimace.

Mope, mōp, *vi.* (moping, moped). To show a downcast air; to be spiritless or gloomy.—*n.* One who mopes.

Moral, mo'ral, *a.* Relating to morality or morals; ethical; virtuous; supported by reason and probability.—*n.* The practical lesson inculcated by any story; *pl.* general conduct as right or wrong; mode of life; ethics.

Morale, mō-räl', *n.* Mental condition of soldiers, etc., as regards courage, zeal, hope.

Moralist, mo'ral-ist, *n.* One who teaches morals; a writer or lecturer on ethics; one who inculcates or practices moral duties.

Morality, mō-ral'i-ti, *n.* The doctrine of moral duties; ethics; moral character or quality; quality of an action in regard to right and wrong; an old form of drama in which the personages were allegorical representations of virtues, vices, etc.

Morass, mō-ras', *n.* A tract of low, soft, wet ground; a marsh; a swamp; a fen.

Morbid, mor'bid, *a.* Diseased; sickly; not sound and healthful.

Moribund, mo'ri-bund, *a.* in a dying state.

Mormon, mor'mon, *n.* A member of a sect founded in the United States in 1830, who practice polygamy; a Latter-day Saint. Also **Mormonite, Mormonist.**

Morning, morn'ing, *n.* The first part of the day; the time between dawn and the middle of the forenoon; the first or early part. Often used as an *adj.*

Morocco, mŏrok'ō, *n.* A fine kind of leather prepared from goat skin.

Moron, mo'ron, *n.* A feeble-minded or degenerate person.

Morose, mō-rōs', *a.* Of a sour or sullen temper; gloomy; churlish; surly.

Morphia, Morphine, mor'fi-a, mor'fin, *n.* The narcotic principle of opium, a powerful anodyne.

Mortal, mor'tal, *a.* Subject to death; deadly; fatal; human.—*n.* A being subject to death; a human being.

Mortality, mor-tal'i-ti, *n.* State of being mortal; actual death of great numbers of men or beasts; death-rate.

Mortise, mor'tis, *n.* A hole cut in one piece of material to receive the tenon of another piece.—*vt.* To cut a mortise in; to join by a tenon and mortise.

Mortuary, mor'tū-a-ri, *n.* A place for the temporary reception of the dead.—*a.* Pertaining to the burial of the dead.

Mosaic, mō-zā'ik, *n.* Inlaid work of marble, precious stones, etc., disposed on a ground of cement so as to form designs.—*a.* Pertaining to or composed of mosaic.

Moslem, moz'lem, *n.* An orthodox Mohammedan.

Mosque, mosk, *n.* A Mohammedan place of worship.

Mosquito, mos-kē'tō, *n.* A sting gnat or fly.

Moss, mos, *n.* A small plant with simple branching stems and numerous small leaves; a bog; a place where peat is found,—*vt.* To cover with moss by natural growth.

Most, mōst, *a.* superl. of *more.* Greatest in any way.—*adv.* In the greatest degree, quantity, or extent; mostly; chiefly.—*n.* The greatest number; the majority; greatest amount; utmost extent, degree, etc.

Mote, mōt, *n.* A small particle; anything proverbially small.

Moth, moth, *n.* The name of numerous nocturnal insects allied to the butterflies.

Mother, muᴛʜ'er, *n.* A female parent; a woman who has borne a child; source or origin; an abbess or other female at the head of a religious institution; a slimy substance that gathers in vinegar, etc.—*a.* Native; natural; inborn; vernacular.

Mother-country, muᴛʜ'er-kun-tri, *n.* A country which has sent out colonies; a country as the producer of anything.

Mother-in-law, muᴛʜ'er-in-la, *n.* The mother of one's husband or wife.

Mother-of-pearl, muᴛʜ'er-ov-perl, *n.* The hard silvery brilliant internal layer of several kinds of shells.

Motile, mō'til, *a.* Having inherent power of motion.

Motion, mō'shon, *n.* Act or process of moving; power of moving; movement; internal impulse; proposal made; evacuation of the intestines.—*vi.* To make a significant gesture with the hand.

Motive, mō'tiv, *n.* That which incites to action; cause, inducement; purpose; theme in a piece of music; prevailing idea of an artist.—*a.* Causing motion.—*vt.* To supply a motive to or for; to prompt.

Motley, mot'li, *a.* Variegated in color; parti-colored; heterogeneous; diversified—*n.* A dress of various colors.

Motor, mō'tor, *n.* A moving power; force or agency that sets machinery in motion; a motor-car.—*a.* Imparting motion.

Mottle, mot'l, *n.* A blotched or spotted character of surface.—*vt.* (mottling, mottled). To mark with spots or blothes as if mottled.

Motto, mot'tō, *n.*; pl. **-oes,** or **-os.** A short sentence or phrase, or a single word, adopted as expressive of one's guiding idea.

Moult, mōlt, *vi.* and *t.* To shed or

cast the hair, feathers, skin, horns, etc., as birds and other animals.—*n*. Act or process of changing the feathers, etc.; time of moulting.

Mound, mound, *n*. An artificial elevation of earth; a bulwark, a rampart; the globe which forms part of the regalia.

Mount, mount, *n*. A hill; a mountain; that with which something is fitted; a setting, frame, etc.; opportunity or means of riding on horseback; a horse.—*vi*. To rise; to get on horseback or upon any animal; to amount.—*vt*. To raise aloft; to climb; to place oneself upon, as on horseback; to furnish with horses; to set in or cover with something; to set off to advantage.

Mountain, moun'tin, *n*. An elevated mass larger than a hill; anything very large.—*a*. Pertaining to a mountain; found on mountains.

Mountaineer, moun-tin-ēr', *n*. An inhabitant of a mountainous district; a climber of mountains.—*vi*. To practice the climbing of mountains.

Mountebank, moun'ti-bangk, *n*. One who mounts a bench or stage in a public place, and vends medicines or nostrums; a quack; any boastful and false pretender.

Mounting, mount'ing, *n*. Act of one who mounts; that with which an article is mounted or set off; trimming, setting, etc.

Mourn, mōrn, *vi*. To sorrow; to lament; to wear the customary habit of sorrow.—*vt*. To grieve for; to deplore.

Mourning, mōrn'ing, *n*. Lamentation; dress worn by mourners.—*a*.. Employed to express grief.

Mouse, mous, *n*.; pl. **Mice,** mīs. A small rodent quadruped that infests houses, fields, etc.—*vi*. mouz (mousing, moused). To hunt for or catch mice.

Moustache, mus-tash', *n*. The long hair on the upper lip.

Mouth, mouth, *n*.; pl. **Mouths,** mouᴛʜz. The opening in the head of an animal into which food is received, and from which voice is uttered; opening of anything hollow, as of a pitcher, or of a cave, pit,

etc.; the part of a river, etc., by which it joins with the ocean.—*vt*. mouᴛʜ. To take into the mouth; to utter with a voice affectedly big.—*vi*. To speak with a loud, affected voice; to vociferate.

Mouth-organ, mouth-or'gan, *n*. A small popular wind-instrument, flat in shape, with openings for the various notes, which are produced by inhalation and exhalation.

Mouth-piece, mouth'pēs, *n*. The part of a wind-instrument to which the mouth is applied; a tube by which a cigar, etc., is held in the mouth; one who believes the opinions of others.

Move, möv, *vt*. (moving, moved). To cause to change place, posture, or position; to set in motion; to affect; to rouse; to prevail on; to propose, as a resolution.—*vi*. To change place or posture; to stir; to begin to act; to shake; to change residence; to make a proposal to a meeting.—*n*. The act of moving; a movement; proceeding; action taken.

Movement, möv'ment, *n*. Act of moving; motion; change of position; manner of moving; gesture; an agitation to bring about some result desired; wheel-work of a clock.

Mow, mō, *vt*. (pret. mowed, pp. mowed or mown). To cut down, as grass, etc.; to cut the grass from; to cut down in great numbers.—*vi*. To cut grass; to use the scythe.

Much, much, *a*.; comp. *more,* superl. *most*. Great in quantity or amount; abundant.—*adv*. In a great degree; by far; greatly.—*n*. A great quantity; something strange or serious.

Mucilage, mū'si-lāj, *n*. A solution in water of gummy matter; a gummy substance found in certain plants.

Muck muk, *n*. Dung in a moist state; something mean, vile, or filthy.—*vt*. To manure with muck; to remove muck from.

Mucous, Mucose, mū'kus, *a*. Pertaining to mucus, or resembling it; slimy.—**Mucous membrane,** a membrane that lines all the cavities of the body which open externally, and secretes mucus.

Mucus, mū'kus, *n.* A viscid fluid secreted by the mucous membrane.

Mud, mud, *n.* Moist and soft earth; sediment from turbid waters; mire.—*vt.* (mudding, mudded). To soil with mud; to make turbid.

Muddle, mud'l, *vt.* (muddling, muddled). To make muddy; to intoxicate partially; to confuse; to make a mess of.—*vi.* To become muddy; to act in a confused manner.—*n.* A mess; confusion; bewilderment.

Muffin, muf'in, *n.* A light spongy cake.

Muffle, muf'l, *vt.* (muffling, muffled). To cover close, particularly the neck and face; to conceal; to deaden the sound of by wrapping cloth, etc., round.—*n.* The tumid and naked portion of the upper lip and nose of ruminants and rodents.

Muffler, muf'lėr, *n.* A cover for the face or neck; a stuffed glove for lunatics.

Mug, mug, *n.* A small vessel of earthenware or metal for containing liquor; a jug.

Muggy, Muggish, mug'i, mug'ish, *a.* Damp and close; moist; moldy.

Mulatto, mū-lat'tō, *n.* A person who is the offspring of a white and a negro.

Mulch, mulsh, *n.* Dungy material protecting the roots of newly-planted shrubs, etc.

Mulct, mulkt, *n.* A fine.—*vt.* To fine; to deprive.

Mule, mūl, *n.* The offspring of an ass and mare, or a horse and she-ass; a hybrid animal.

Mull, mul, *vt.* To heat, sweeten, and flavor with spices, as ale or wine.

Mullion, mul'yon, *n.* An upright division between the lights of windows, screens, etc., in Gothic architecture.

Multifarious, mul-ti-fā'ri-us, *a.* Having great diversity or variety.

Multiform, mul'ti-form, *a.* Having many forms, shapes, or appearances.

Multilateral, mul-ti-lat'ėr-al, *a.* Having many sides; many-sided.

Multipartite, mul'ti-pär-tīt, *a* Di-

vided into several or many parts.

Multiple, mul'ti-pl, *a.* Manifold; having many parts or divisions.—*n.* A number which contains another an exact number of times.

Multiplex, mul'ti-pleks, *a.* Manifold; complex.

Multiplicand, mul'ti-pli-kand'', *n.* A number to be multiplied by another.

Multiplication, mul'ti-pli-kā''shon, *n.* Act or process of multiplying; state of being multiplied; reproduction of animals.

Multiplicity, mul-ti-plis'i-ti, *n.* State of being multiplex or manifold; great number.

Multiplier, mul-ti-plī-ėr, *n.* One who or that which multiplies; the number by which another is multiplied.

Multiply, mul'ti-plī, *vt.* (multiplying, multiplied). To increase in number; to add to itself any given number of times.—*vi.* To increase in number, or to become more numerous by reproductive; to extend.

Multitude, mul'ti-tūd, *n.* State of being many; a great number, collectively or indefinitely; a crowd.— **The multitude,** the populace.

Mumble, mum'bl, *vi.* (mumbling, mumbled). To mutter; to speak with mouth partly closed; to eat with the lips close.—*vt.* To utter with a low, inarticulate voice.

Mummy, mum'i, *n.* A dead human body embalmed after the manner of the ancient Egyptians, with wax, balsams, etc.

Mumps, mumps, *n.* Silent displeasure; sullenness; a disease consisting in an inflammation of the salivary glands.

Munch, munsh, *vt.* and *i.* To chew audibly.

Mundane, mun'dān, *a.* Belonging to this world; worldly; earthly.

Municpal, mū-ni'si-pal, *a.* Belonging to a corporation or city.

Municipality, mū-ni'si-pal''i-ti, *n.* A town possessed of local self-government; community under municipal jurisdiction.

Munificence, mū-ni'fi-sens, *n.* A bestowing liberally; liberality; gener-

M

osity.

Munition, mū-ni'shon, *n.* Military stores; ammunition; material for any enterprise.

Murder, mėr'dėr, *n.* Act of killing a human being with premeditated malice.—*vt.* To kill (a human being) with premeditated malice; to mar by bad execution.

Muriatic, mū-ri-at'ik, *a.* Pertaining to or obtained from brine or sea-salt; hydrochloric.

Murky, mėr'ki, *a.* Dark; obscure; gloomy.

Murmur, mėr'mėr, *n.* A low continued or repeated sound; a hum; a grumble or mutter.—*vi.* To utter a murmur or hum; to grumble.—*vt.* To utter indistinctly; to mutter.

Murrain, mu'rān, *n.* A deadly and infectious disease among cattle, etc.

Muscadel, Muscatel, Muscadine, mus'ka-del, mus'ka-tel, mus'ka-dīn, *a.* and *n.* A sweet and strong Italian or French wine; the grapes which produce this wine; a delicious pear.

Muscle, mus'l *n.* A definite portion of an animal body consisting of fibers susceptible of contraction and relaxation, and thus effecting motion; a mussel.

Muscular, mus'kū-lėr, *a.* Pertaining to or consisting of muscle; performed by a muscle; strong; brawny; vigorous.

Muse, mūz, *n.* One of the nine sister goddesses of the Greeks and Romans presiding over the arts; poetic inspiration; a fit of abstraction.—*vi.* (musing, mused). To ponder; to meditate in silence; to be absent in mind.—*vt.* To meditate on.

Museum, mū-zē'um, *n.* A repository of interesting objects connected with literature, art, or science.

Mushroom, mush'röm, *n.* An edible fungus; an upstart,—*a.* Pertaining to mushrooms; resembling mushrooms in rapidity of growth.

Music, mū'zik, *n.* Melody of harmony; the science of harmonious sounds; the written or printed score of a composition.

Muster, mus'tėr, *vt.* To collect, as troops; to assemble or bring together—*vi.* To assemble; to meet in one place.—*n.* An assembling of troops; register of troops mustered; an array.

Musty, mus'ti, *a.* Moldy; sour; stale.

Mutable, mūta-bl, *a.* Changeable; inconstant; unstable; variable; fickle.

Mutation, mū-tā'shon, *n.* Act or process of changing; change; alteration, either in form or qualities; modification.

Mute, mūt, *a.* Silent; incapable of speaking; dumb; not pronounced, or having its sound checked by a contact of the vocal organs, as certain consonants (*t, p, k, etc.*).—*n.* A dumb person; a hired attendant at a funeral; a mute consonant.—*vi.* (muting, muted). To eject the contents of the bowels as birds.

Mutual, mū'tū-al, *a.* Reciprocal; interchanged; given and received on both sides.

Muzzle, muz'l, *n.* The projecting mouth and nose of an animal; the open end of a gun or pistol, etc.; a cover for the mouth which hinders an animal from biting.—*vt.* (muzzling, muzzled). To cover the mouth of to prevent biting or eating; to gag.

My, mī, *pron.* The possessive case sing. of *Iyopy; belonging to me.*

Myrtle, mėr'tl, *n.* An evergreen shrub.

Myself, mī-self', *compd. pron.*; pl. **Ourselves,** our-selvz'. As a nominative it is used, generally after I, to express emphasis—I, and not another; in the objective often used reflexively and without any emphasis.

Mysterious, mis-tē'ri-us, *a.* Containing mystery; beyond human comprehension; untelligible; enigmatical.

Mystery, mis'tėr-i, *n.* Something above human intelligence; a secret; an old form of drama in which the characters and events were drawn from sacred history; a trade craft, or calling.

Myth, mith, *n.* A tradition or fable

embodying the notions of a people as to their gods, origin early history etc.; an invented story.

Mythological, Mythologic, mith-o-loj'ik-al, mith-o-loj'ik, *a*. Relating to or proceeding from mythology; fabulous.

Mythology, mith-ol'o-ji, *n*. The science or doctrine of myths; the myths of a people collectively.

N

Nab, nab, *vt*. (nabbing, nabbed). To catch or seize suddenly or unexpectedly.

Nail, nāl, *n*. The horny substance at the end of the human finger and toes; a claw; a small pointed piece of metal, to be driven into timber, etc.; a stud or boss; a measure of 2¼ inches.—*vt*. To fasten or stud with nails; to hold fast or make secure.

Naïve, nä-ēv', *a*. Ingenuous; simple; artless.

Naïveté, nä-ēv'tā, *n*. Native simplicity; unaffected ingenuousness.

Naked, nā'ked, *a*. Not having clothes on; bare; nude; open to view; mere, bare, simple; destitute; unassisted.

Name, nām, *n*. That by which a person or thing is designated; appellation; title; reputation; eminence; sound only; not reality; authority; behalf; a family.—*vt*. (naming, named). To give a name to; to designate; to style; to nominate; to speak of or mention as.

Namely, nām'li, *adv*. By name; particularly; that is to say.

Nap, nap, *n*. The woolly substance on the surface of cloth, etc.; the downy substance on plants; a short sleep.—*vi*. (napping, napped). To have a short sleep; to drowse.

Nape, nāp, *n*. The prominent joint of the neck behind; the back part of the neck.

Nard, närd, *n*. An aromatic plant, usually called spikenard; an unguent prepared from the plant.

Narrate, na-rāt' or nar', *vt*. (narrat-ing, narrated). To tell or relate, orally or in writing.

Narrative, nar'a-tiv, *a*. Pertaining to narration.—*n*. That which is narrated or related; a relation orally or in writing.

Narrow, na'rō, *a*. Of little breadth; not wide or broad; very limited; straitened; not liberal; bigoted; near; close; scrutinizing.—*n*. A narrow channel; a strait: usually in *pl*.—*vt*. To make narrow.—*vi*. To become narrow; to contract in breadth.

Nasal, nā'zal, *a*. Pertaining to the nose; formed or affected by the nose, as speech.—*n*. An elementary sound uttered partly through the nose.

National, na'shon-al, *a*. Pertaining to a nation; public; attached to one's own country.

Nationality, na-shon-al'i-ti, *n*. Quality of being national; national character; strong attachment to one's own nation; a nation.

Native, nā'tiv, *a*. Pertaining to the place or circumstances of one's birth; indigenous; inborn; occurring in nature pure or unmixed.—*n*. One born in a place or country; an indigenous animal or plant; an oyster raised in an artificial bed.

Nativity, na-tiv'i-ti, *n*. Birth; time, place, and manner of birth.

Natty, nat'i, *a*. Neat; tidy; spruce.

Natural, na'tūr-al, *a*. Pertaining to nature; produced or effected by nature; consistent with nature; not artificial; according to the life; not revealed; bastard; unregenerated.—*n*. An idiot; a fool.

Naturalization, na'tūr-al-izā'' shon, *n*. Act of investing an alien with the privileges of a native citizen.

Nature, nā'tūr, *n*. The universe; the total of all agencies and forces in the creation; the inherent or essential qualities of anything; individual constitution; sort; natural human instincts; reality as distinct from that which is artificial.

Naughty, na̧'ti, *a*. Bad; mischievous.

Nausea, nā'shē-a, *n*. Sickness.

Navigate, na'vi-gāt, *vi*. To conduct

or guide a ship; to sail.—*vt*. To manage in sailing, as a vessel; to sail or guide a ship over.

Navy, nā'vi, *n*. All the ships of a certain class belonging to a country; the whole of the ships of war belonging to a mation.

Near, nēr, *a*. Not distant in place, time, or degree; intimate; affecting one's interest or feelings; parsimonious; narrow; on the left of a horse; not circuitous.—*prep*. Close to; nigh.—*adv*. Almost; within a little; close to the wind.—*vt*. and *i*. To approach; to come near.

Neat, nēt, *n*. Cattle of the bovine genus.—*a*. Pure; clean; trim; tidy; clever; smart; without water added.

Nebula, neb'ū-la, *n*. *pl*. **-ae.** Celestial objects like white clouds, generally clusters of stars.

Nebulous, neb'ū-lus, *a*. Cloudy; hazy.

Necessary, ne'ses-sa-ri, *a*. Such as must be; inevitable; essential; acting from necessity.—*n*. Anything indispensably requisite.

Necrology, nek-rol'o-ji, *n*. A register of deaths; a collection of obituary notices.

Necromancy, nek'rō-man-si, *n*. The revealing of future events through pretended communication with the dead; sorcery.

Necropolis, nek-rō'po-lis, *n*. A city of the dead, a cemetery.

Need, nēd, *n*. A state that requires supply or relief; urgent want; necessity; poverty; destitution.—*vt*. To have necessity or need for; to lack, require.—*vi*. To be necessary: used impersonally.

Needle, nē'dl, *n*. An instrument for interweaving thread; a small steel instrument for sewing; a magnetized piece of steel in a compass attracted to the pole; anything in the form of a needle.

Needless, nēd'les, *a*. No needed or wanted; unnecessary; not requisite; useless.

Needle-work, nē'dl-wėrk, *n*. Work done with a needle; business of a seamstress.

Needy, nēd'i, *a*. Being in need; necessitous; indigent; very poor.

Nefarious, nē-fā'ri-us, *a*. Wicked in the extreme; infamous; atrocious.

Negation, nē-gā'shon, *n*. A denial; contradiction or contradictory condition.

Negative, neg'at-iv, *a*. That denies; implying denial or negation; implying absence; the opposite of positive.—*n*. A word which denies, as *not, no*; a proposition by which something is denied; a veto; a photographic picture on glass or celluloid, in which the lights and shades are the opposite of those in nature.—*vt*. To prove the contrary of; to reject by vote.

Negotiate, nē-gō'shi-āt, *vi*. To treat with another respecting purchase and sale; to hold diplomatic intercourse; to conduct communications in general.—*vt*. To procure or bring about by negotiation; to pass into circulation (as a bill of exchange).

Neighborhood, nā'bėr-hud, *n*. Condition of being neighbors; neighbors collectively; vicinity; locality.

Neither, nē'ŦHėr or nī'ŦHėr, *pron*. and *pron*. *adj*. Not either; not the one or the other.—*conj*. Not either; nor.

Nematoid, nem'a-toid, *n*. A roundworm; one of an order of entozoa or intestinal worms.—*a*. Pertaining to or resembling the nematoids.

Nemesis, nem'e-sis, *n*. A female Greek divinity personifying retributive justice; just retribution or punishment.

Neptune, nep'tün, *n*. The god of the sea; a planet, the remotest from the sun except Pluto.

Nerve, nėrv, *n*. One of the fibrous threads in animal bodies whose function is to convey sensation and originate motion; fortitude; courage; energy; something resembling a nerve.—*vt*. (nerving, nerved). To give strength or vigor to; to steel.

Nervous, nėrv'us, *a*. Pertaining to the nerves; affecting the nerves; having the nerves easily affected; easily agitated; having nerve or bodily strength; vigorous; sinewy.

Nescience, nē'shi-ens. *n*. Want of

knowledge; ignorance.

Nest, nest, *n.* The place or bed formed by a bird for laying and hatching her eggs; a number of persons frequenting the same haunt; a snug abode.—*vi.* To build a nest; to nestle.

Nestle, nes'l, *vi.* (nestling, nestled). To make or occupy a nest; to lie close and snug.—*vt.* To shelter, as in a nest; to cherish.

Net, net, *n.* A texture of twine, etc., with meshes, commonly used to catch fish, birds, etc.; a snare.—*vt.* (netting, netted). To make into a net; to take in a net; to capture by wile.

Net, Nett, net, *a.* Being clear of all deductions; estimated apart from all expenses.—*vt.* (netting, netted). To gain as clear profit.

Neuter, nū'tėr, *a.* Neutral; neither masculine nor feminine; neither active nor passive, as a verb.—*n.* An animal or neither sex; a plant with neither stamens nor pistils; a noun of the neuter gender.

Neutral, nū'tral, *a.* Not siding with any party in a dispute; indifferent; neither acid nor alkaline.—*n.* A person or nation that takes no part in a contest between others.

Neutralize, nū'tral-īz, *vt.* To render neutral or inoperative; to counteract.

Neutron, nū'tron, *n.* An uncharged particle of the same mass as a proton.

Never, nev'ėr, *adv.* Not ever; at no time; in no degree; not at all.

Nevertheless, nev'ėr-ᴛʜė-les'', *adv.* Not the less; notwithstanding; yet; however.

New, nū, *a.* Recent in origin; novel; not before known; different; unaccustomed; fresh after any event; not second-hand.—*adv.* Newly; recently.

Newel, nū'el, *n.* The upright structure in a winding staircase supporting the steps.

Newfoundland, nū-found'land or nū'found-land, *n.* A large dog, remarkable for sagacity and swimming powers.

News, nūz, *n.* Recent intelligence or information; tidings; a newspaper.

Newspaper, nūz'pā-pėr, *n.* A sheet of paper printed periodically for circulating news.

Newt, nūt, *n.* A small amphibian of lizard-like appearance.

Next, nekst, *a.* superl. of *nigh*. Nearest in place, time, rank, or degree.—*adv.* At the time or turn nearest.

Niche, nich, *n.* A recess in a wall for a statue, a vase, etc.

Nick, nik, *n.* The exact point of time; the critical time; a notch; a score.—*vt.* To hit upon exactly; to make a nick in; to mark with nicks.

Nickel, nik'el, *n.* A valuable metal of a white color and great hardness, magnetic, and when pure malleable and ductile.

Nickel-silver, nik'el-sil-vėr, *n.* An alloy composed of copper, zinc, and nickel.

Nickname, nik'nām, *n.* A name given in contempt or jest.—*vt.* To give a nickname to.

Nicotine, nik'ō-tin, *n.* A volatile alkaloid from tobacco, highly poisonous.

Night, nīt, *n.* The daily period of darkness; the time from sunset to sunrise; a state or time of darkness, depression, etc.; ignorance; obscurity; death.

Nihilism, nī'hil-izm, *n.* Nothingness; the doctrine that nothing can be known; principles of a Russian secret society of communists.

Nil, nil, *n.* Nothing.

Nimble, nim'bl, *a.* Quick in motion; moving with ease and celerity; agile; prompt.

Nimbus, nim'bus, *n.* A rain-cloud; a halo surrounding the head in representations of divine or sacred personages.

Nit, nit, *n.* The egg of a louse, etc.

Niter, nī'tėr, *n.* Nitrate of potassium or saltpeter, used for making gunpowder, in dyeing, medicine, etc.

Nitrate, nī'trāt, *n.* A salt of nitric acid.

Nitric, nī'trik, *a.* Pertaining to neter; containing nitrogent and oxygen.

Nitrogen, nī'tro-jen, *n.* The elementary unflammable gas constituting about four-fifths of the atmospheric air.

Nitro-glycerine, nī-trō-glis'ėr-in, *n.* A powerful explosive produced by the action of nitric and sulphuric acids on glycerine.

Nitrous, nī'trus, *a.* Pertaining to niter; applied to compounds containing less oxygen than those called *nitric.*

Nival, nī'val, *a.* Snowy; growing among snow, or flowering during winter.

No, nō, *adv.* A word of denial or refusal; not in any degree; not.—*n.* A denial; a negative vote.—*a.* Not any; none.

Noble, nō'bl, *a.* Of lofty lineage; belonging to the peerage; illustrious; lofty in character; magnanimous; magnificent; stately.—*n.* A person of rank; a peer; an old English gold coin.

Nobody, nō'bo-di, *n.* No person; no one; a person of no standing or position.

Noctambulist, nok-tam'bū-list, *n.* A nightwalker or somnambulist.

Nocturn, nok'tėrn, *n.* A religious service formerly used in the R. Catholic Church at midnight, now a part of matins.

Nocturne, nok'tėrn, *n.* A painting or piece of music expressing some of the characteristic effects of night.

Nod, nod, *vi.* (nodding, nodded). To make a slight bow; to let the head sink from sleep; to incline the head, as in assent or salutation, etc.—*vt.* To incline; to signify by a nod.—*n.* A quick inclination of the head.

Node, nōd, *n.* A knot; a protuberance; a sort of knot on a stem where leaves arise; one of the two points in which two great circles of the celestial sphere intersect.

Nomenclature, no'men-kla-tūr, *n.* A system of names; vocabulary of terms appropriated to any branch of science

Nominal, no'mi-nal, *a.* Pertaining to a name; titular; not real; merely so called.

Nominate, no'mi-nāt, *vt.* To name;

to designate or propose for an office.

Nonagon, non'a-gon, *n.* A plane figure having nine sides and nine angles.

Nonchalance, non'sha-lans, *n.* Indifference.

Non-conductor, non-kon-dukt'ėr, *n.* A substance which does not conduct, or transmits with difficulty, heat, electricity, etc.

Nonconformist, non-kon-form'ist, *n.* One who does not conform to the established church.

Nonconformity, non-kon-form'i-ti, *n.* Neglect or failure of conformity; refusal to unite with an established church.

Nondescript, non'dē-skript, *a.* That has not been described; abnormal; odd; indescribable.—*n.* A person or thing not easily described or classed.

None, nun, *n.* or *pron.* Not one; not any; not a part; not the least portion.

Nonentity, non-en'ti-ti, *n.* Non-existence; a thing not existing; a person utterly without consequence or importance.

Nonesuch, nun'such, n. A person or thing that has not its equal or parallel.

Noology, nō-ol'o-ji, *n.* The science of intellectual facts or phenomena.

Noon, nön, *n.* The middle of the day; twelve o'clock; the prime.

Noonday, nön'dā, *n.* Mid-day; noon.—*a.* Pertaining to mid-day; meridional.

Noose, nös or nöz, *n.* A running knot, which binds the closer the more it is drawn.—*vt.* (noosing, noosed). To tie or catch in a noose; to entrap.

Nor, nor, *conj.* A word used to render negative a subsequent member of a clause or sentence; correlative to *neither* or other negative; also equivalent to *and not.*

Nordic, nor'dik, *a.* Of or belonging to those peoples of Northern Europe who are long-headed, tall, blue-eyed and fair-haired.

Norm, norm, *n.* A rule; a pattern; a type.

Normal, nor'mal, *a.* According to a

rule; conforming with a certain type or standard; regular; perpendicular.—**Normal school,** a training-college for teachers.—*n.* A perpendicular.

Nose, nōz, *n.* The organ of smell, employed also in respiration and speech; the power of smelling; scent; sagacity; a nozzle.—*vt.* and *i.* (nosing, nosed). To smell; to wange through the nose; to pry officiously.

Nosology, no-sol´o-ji, *n.* Arrangment or classification of diseases.

Nostalgia, nos-tal´ji-a, *n.* Vehement desire to revisit one's native country; home-sickness.

Nostril, nos´tril, *n.* One of the two apertures of the nose.

Nostrum, nos´trum, *n.* A quack medicine, the ingredients of which are kept secret.

Not, not, *adv.* A word that expresses negation, denial, or refusal.

Note, nōt, *n.* A mark, sign, or token; an explanatory or critical comment; a memorandum; a bill, account; a paper promising payment; a communication in writing; notice; reputation; distinction; a character representing a musical sound, or the sound itself.—*vt.* (noting, noted). To observe carefully; to mark; to set down in writing.

Noted, nōt´ed, *p.a.* Celebrated; famous.

Noteworthy, nōt´wer-ŦHi, *a.* Deserving notice; worthy of observation or notice.

Nothing, nu´thing, *n.* Not anything; non-existence; a trifle; a cipher.—*adv.* In no degree.

Notice, nōt´is, *n.* Act of noting; regard; information; order; intimation; civility; a brief critical review.—*vt.* (noticing, noticed). To take note of; to perceive; to make observations on; to treat with attention.

Noticeable, nōt´is-a-bl, *a.* That may be noticed; worthy of observation.

Notify, nōt´i-fī, *vt.* To make known; to declare; to give notice to; to inform.

Notion, nō´shon, *n.* A mental conception; idea; opinion; slight feel-

ing or inclination.

Notoriety, nō-tō-rī´e-ti, *n.* State of being notorious; discreditable publicity; one who is notorious.

Nous, nous, *n.* Intellect; mind; talent.

Novel, no´vel, *a.* Of recent origin or introduction; new and striking; unusual.—*n.* A fictitious prose narrative picturing real life.

Novelist, no´vel-ist, *n.* A writer of novels.

Noxious, nok´shus, *a.* Hurtful; pernicious; unwholesome; corrupting to morals.

Nozzle, noz´l, *n.* The projecting spout of something; terminal part of a pipe.

Nuance, nu-ängs, *n.* A gradation of color; delicate degree in transitions.

Nubile, nū´bīl, *a.* Marriageable (used only of a woman).

Nuciferous, nū-sif´er-us, *a.* Bearing or producing nuts.

Nucleus, nū´klē-us, *n.*; pl. **-lei.** A kernel or something similar; a mass about which matter is collected; body of a comet.

Nude, nūd, *a.* Naked; bare; undraped.

Number, num´ber, *n.* An aggregate of units, or a single unit; a numeral; many; one of a numbered series of things; part of a periodical; metrical arrangement of syllables; difference of form in a word to express unity or plurality.—*vt.* To reckon; to enumerate; to put a number on; to reach the number of.

Numeral, nū´mer-al, *a.* Pertaining to number; consisting of or representing number.—*n.* A figure used to express a number.

Numerate, nū´mer-āt, *vt.* (numerating, numerated). To count; to enumerate.

Numerator, nū´mer-āt-er, *n.* One who numbers; the number (above the line) in vulgar fractions which shows how many parts of a unit are taken.

Numerical, nū-me´rik-al, *a.* Belonging to number; consisting in numbers.

Numerous, nū´mer-us, *a.* Consist-

N

ing of a great number of individuals; many.

Numismatic, nū-mis-mat'ik, *a*. Pertaining to coins or medals.

Numismatist, nū-mis'mat-ist, *n*. One versed in numismatics.

Nuptial, nup'shal, *a*. Pertaining to marriage.

Nurse, nėrs, *n*. One who suckles or nourishes a child; one who tends the young, sick, or infirm; an attendant in a hospital; one who or that which nurtures or protects.— *vt*. (nursing, nursed). To act as nurse to; to suckle; to rear; to tend in sickness or infirmity; to foment; to foster.

Nursery, nėr'sė-ri, *n*. The place in which children are nursed and taken care of; a place where trees, plants, etc., are propagated.

Nurture, nėr'tūr, *n*. Upbringing; education; nourishment.—*vt*. (nurturing, nurtured). To nourish; to educate; to bring or train up.

Nut, nut, *n*. A fruit containing a seed or kernel within a hard covering; a small block of metal or wood with a grooved hole, to be screwed on the end of a bolt.—*vi*. (nutting, nutted). To gather nuts.

Nutation, nū-tā'shon, *n*. A nodding, a slight gyratory movement of the earth's axis.

Nutmeg, nut'meg, *n*. The aromatic kernel of the fruit of a tree of the Malay Archipelago.

Nutrient, nū'tri-ent, *a*. Nutritious.— *n*. Any substance which nourishes.

Nymph, nimf, *n*. A goddess of the mountains, forests, meadow, or waters; a young and attractive woman; a maiden; the chrysalis of an insect.

Nymphomania, nim-fō-mā'ni-a, *n*. Morbid or unnatural sexual desire in women.

O

O, ō. An exclamation used in earnest or solemn address; often distinguished from *Oh*, which is more strictly expressive of emotion.

Oaf, ōf, *n*. A fairy changeling; a dolt.

Obdurate, ob'dū-rāt, *a*. Hardened in heart; hardened against good; stubborn; inflexible.

Obedience, ō-bē'di-ens, *n*. Act of obeying; quality of being obedient; submission to authority.

Obeisance, ō-bā'sans, *n*. A bow or curtsy; act of reverence, deference, or respect.

Obelisk, o'be-lisk, *n*. A tall four-sided pillar, tapering as it rises, and terminating in a small pyramid; a mark (†) used in printing.

Obesity, ō-bēs'i-ti, *n*. State or quality of being obese; excessive corpulency.

Obey, ō-bā', *vt*. To comply with, as commands or requirements; to be ruled by; to yield to.—*vi*. To submit to authority.

Obfuscate, ob-fus'kāt, *vt*. To darken; to confuse.

Obituary, ō-bit'ū-a-ri, *n*. An account of a person or persons deceased; list of the dead.—*a*. Relating to the decease of a person.

Object, ob'jekt, *n*. That about which any faculty of the mind is employed; end; purpose; a concrete reality; the word, clause, etc., governed by a transitive verb or by a preposition.—*vt*. ob-jekt'. To oppose; to offer as an objection.—*vi*. To oppose in words or arguments.

Objective, ob-jek'tiv, *a*. Pertaining to an object; relating to whatever is exterior to the mind (also pron. ob'jek-tiv); belonging to the case which follows a transitive verb or preposition.—*n*. The objective case; object, place, etc., aimed at.

Oblige, ō-blīj', *vt*. (obliging, obliged). To constrain; to bind by any restraint; to lay under obligation of gratitude; to render service or kindness to.

Oblique, ob-lēk', *a*. Neither perpendicular nor parallel; slanting; indirect; sinister.

Obliterate, ob-lit'ė-rāt, *vt*. To blot out; to efface; to cause to be forgotten.

Oblivion, ob-li'vi-on, *n*. State of being forgotten; forgetfulness; act of forgetting.

Obscene, ob-sēn′, *a.* Indecent; offensive to chastity and delicacy; inauspicious.

Obscure, ob-skūr′, *a.* Darkened; dim; not easily understood; abstruse; unknown to fame; indistinct.—*vt.* (obscuring, obscured). To darken; to make less visible, legible, or intelligible; to tarnish.

Obsequies, ob′se-kwiz, *n.pl.* Funeral rites and solemnities.

Observe, ob-zėrv′, *vt.* (observing, observed). To take notice of; to behold with attention; to remark; to keep religiously; to celebrate; to comply with; to practice.—*vi.* To remark; to be attentive.

Obsession, ob-sesh′on, *n.* Act of besieging; persistent attack; state of being beset.

Obsolescent, ob-sō-les′ent, *a.* Becoming obsolete; passing into desuetude.

Obsolete, ob′sō-lēt, *a.* Antiquated; out of date; rudimentary.

Obstacle, ob′sta-kl, *n.* A stoppage; hindrance; obstruction; impediment.

Obstruction, ob-struk′shon, *n.* Act of obstructing; that which impedes progress; obstacle; impediment; check.

Obstruent, ob′strṳ-ent, *a.* Obstructing.—*n.* Anything that obstructs the natural passages in the body.

Obtain, ob-tān′, *vt.* To get possession of; to acquire; to earn.—*vi.* To be received in common use; to prevail; to hold good.

Obtuse, ob-tūs′, *a.* Not pointed or acute; greater than a right angle; dull; stupid.

Obverse, ob′vėrs, *n.* and *a.* That side of a coin or medal which has the face or head or principal device on it.

Obviate, ob′vi-āt, *vt.* (obviating, obviated). To meet, as difficulties or objections; to get over; to remove.

Obvious, ob′vi-us, *a.* Easily discovered, seen, or understood; evident; manifest.

Occupancy, ok′kū-pan-si, *n.* Act of occupying; a holding in possession; term during which one is oc-

cupant.

Occupation, ok-kū-pā′shon, *n.* Act of occupying; act of taking possession; tenure; business; employment; vocation.

Occupy, ok′kū-pī, *vt.* (occupying, occupied). To take possession of; to hold and use; to cover or fill; to employ; to engage: often *refl.*—*vi.* To be an occupant.

Occur, ok-kėr′, *vi.* (occurring, occurred). To come to the mind; to happen; to be met with; to be found here and there.

Occurrence, ok-ku′rens, *n.* The act of occurring or taking place; any incident or accidental event; an observed instance.

Ocean, ō′shan, *n.* The vast body of water which covers more than three-fifths of the globe; the sea; one of the great areas into which the sea is divided; any immense expanse.—*a.* Pertaining to the great sea.

Octopus, ok′tō-pus, *n.*; pl. -puses. A two-gilled cuttle-fish, having eight arms furnished with suckers.

Ocular, ok′ū-lėr, *a.* Pertaining to or depending on the eye; received by actual sight.

Oculist, ok′ū-list, *n.* One skilled in diseases of the eyes.

Odd, od, *a.* Not even; not exactly divisible by 2; not included with others; incidental; casual; belonging to a broken set; queer.

Oddity, od′i-ti, *n.* Singularity; a singular person or thing.

Odds, odz, *n. sing.* or *pl.* Inequality; excess; difference in favor of one; advantage; amount by which one bet exceeds another.

Ode, ōd, *n.* A song; a short poem; a lyric poem of a lofty cast.

Odious, ō′di-us, *a.* Hateful; offensive; disgusting.

Off, of, *adv.* Away; distant; not on; from; not toward.—**Well off, ill off,** in good or bad circumstances. *a.* Distant; farther away; as applied to horses; right hand.—*prep.* Not on; away from; to seaward from.— *interj.* Begone!

Offal, of′al, *n.* The parts of an animal butchered which are unfit for use; refuse.

Offense, of-fens', n. Injury; an affront, insult, or wrong; displeasure; transgression of law; misdemeanor.

Offend, of-fend', vt. To displease; to shock; to cause to sin or neglect duty.—vi. To sin; to commit a fault; to cause dislike or anger.

Offensive, of-fens'iv, a. Causing offense; causing displeasure or annoyance; disgusting; impertinent; used in attack; aggressive.—n. Act or posture of attack.

Offer, of'er, vt. To present for acceptance or rejection; to tender; to bid, as a price or wages.—vi. To present itself; to declare a willingness; to make an attempt.—n. Act of offering; act of bidding a price; the sum bid.

Offertory, of'er-to-ri, n. Sentences read or repeated in church while the alms or gifts are collecting; the alms collected.

Off-hand, of'hand, a. Done without thinking or hesitation; unpremeditated.—adv. On the spur of the moment; promptly.

Office, of'is, n. Special duty or business; high employment or position under government; function; service; a formulary of devotion; a place where official or professional business is done; persons intrusted with certain duties; persons who transact business in an office; pl. kitchens, outhouses, etc., of a mansion or farm.

Officer, of'is-er, n. A person invested with an office; one who holds a commission in the army or navy.—vt. To furnish with officers.

Official, of-fi'shal, a. Pertaining to an office or public duty; made by virtue of authority.—n. One invested with an office of a public nature.

Officiate, of-fi'shi-āt, vi. To perform official duties; to act in an official capacity.

Ogle, ō'gl, vt. (ogling, ogled). To view with side glances.—n. A side glance or look.

Ogre, ō'ger, n. A monster in fairy tales, who lived on human flesh; one like an ogre.

Oh, ō, exclam. (See O.) Denoting surprise, pain, sorrow, or anxiety.

Ohm, ōm, n. The unit of electric resistance.

Oil, oil, n. An unctuous inflammable liquid drawn from various animal and vegetable substances; a similar substance of mineral origin; an oil-color.—vi. To smear or rub over with oil.

Oleander, ō-lē-an'der, n. An evergreen flowering shrub.

Olfactory, ol-fak'to-ri, a. Pertaining to smelling; having the sense of smelling.—n. An organ of smelling.

Oligarchy, o'li-gär-ki, n. Government in which the supreme power is in a few hands; those who form such a class or body.

Olive, o'liv, n. An evergreen tree; its fruit, from which a valuable oil is expressed; the color of the olive; the emblem of peace.—a. Relating to, or of the color of the olive.

Olympiad, ō-lim'pi-ad, n. A period of four years reckoned from one celebration of the Olympic games to another, the first Olympiad beginning 776 B.C.

Omega, ō'me-ga or ō-me'ga, n. The last letter of the Greek alphabet, long o; the last, or the ending.

Omelet, o'me-let, n. A kind of pancake or fritter made with eggs, etc.

Omen, ō'men, n. An event thought to portend good or evil; an augury; presage.—vi. To augur; to betoken.—vt. To predict.

Ominous, o'min-us, a. Containing an omen, and especially an ill omen; inauspicious.

Omission, ō-mi'shon, n. Act of omitting; neglect or failure to do something required; failure to insert or mention; something omitted.

Omit, ō-mit', vt. (omitting, omitted). To pass over or neglect; not to insert or mention.

Omnivorous, om-niv'or-us, a. All-devouring; eating food of every kind.

Omphalic, om-fal'ik, a. Pertaining to the navel.

On, on, prep. Above and touching; by contact with the surface or upper part; in addition to; at or near;

immediately after and as a result; in reference or relation to; toward or so as to affect; at the peril of; among the staff of; pointing to a state, occupation, etc.—*adv.* Onward; in continuance; adhering; not off.

Once, wuns, *adv.* One time; formerly; immediately after; as soon as.—**At once,** all together; suddenly; forthwith.

Oncoming, on'kum-ing, *a.* Approaching; nearing.—*n.* Approach.

One, wun, *a.* Being but a single thing or a unit; closely united; forming a whole; single.—*n.* The first of the simple units; the symbol representing this (=1).—**At one,** in union or concord.—*pron.* Any single person; any man; any person; a thing; particular thing.

Only, ōn'li, *a.* Single; sole; alone.—*adv.* For one purpose alone; simply; merely; solely.—*conj.* But; excepting that.

Onomatopeia, on'o-ma-tō-pē''a, *n.* The formation of words by imitation of sounds.

Oology, ō-ol'o-ji, *n.* The study of birds' eggs.

Ooze, öz, *n.* A soft flow, as of water; soft mud or slime; liquor of a tanvat.—*vi.* (oozing, oozed). To flow or issue forth gently; to percolate.—*vt.* To emit in the shape of moisture.

Opal, ō'pal, *n.* A precious stone, which exhibits changeable reflections of green, blue, yellow, and red.

Opalescent, ō-pal-es'ent, *a.* Resembling opal; having the iridescent tints of opal.

Opaque, ō-pāk', *a.* Not transparent.

Open, ō'pn, *a.* Not shut, covered, or blocked; not restricted; accessible; public; spread out; free, liberal, bounteous; candid; clear; exposed; fully prepared; attentive; amenable; not settled; enunciated with a full utterance.—*n.* An open or clear space.—*vt.* To make open; to unclose; to cut into; to spread out; to begin; to make public; to declare open; to reveal.—*vi.* To un-

close itself; to be parted; to begin.

Opening, ō'pn-ing, *a.* First in order; beginning.—*n.* Act of one who or that which opens; an open place; aperture; beginning; vacancy; opportunity of commencing a business, etc.

Opera, o'pe-ra, *n.* A dramatic composition set to music and sung and acted on the stage; a theater where operas are performed.

Opinion, ō-pin'yon, *n.* A judgment or belief; notion; persuasion; estimation.

Opium, ō'pi-um, *n.* The inspissated juice of a kind of poppy, one of the most energetic of narcotics.

Opossum, ō-pos'um, *n.* The name of several marsupial mammals of America.

Opponent, op-pō'nent, *a.* Opposing; antagonistic; opposite.—*n.* One who opposes; an adversary; an antagonist.

Opportune, op-or-tūn', *a.* Seasonable; timely; well-timed; convenient.

Opposition, op-pō-zi'shon, *n.* Act of opposing; attempt to check or defeat; contradiction; inconsistency; the collective body of opponents of a ministry.

Oppress, op-pres', *vt.* To press or weigh down unduly; to harass; to overpower; to overburden.

Oppressive, op-pres'iv, *a.* Burdensome; unjustly severe; tyrannical.

Optics, op'tiks, *n.* The science which treats of the nature and properties of light and vision, optical instruments, etc.

Optimism, op'tim-izm, *n.* The opinion or doctrine that everything is for the best; tendency to take the most hopeful view.

Option, op'shon, *n.* Choice; free choice; power of choosing.

Opulence, op'ū-lens, *n.* Wealth; riches.

Or, or, *conj.* A particle that marks an alternative, and frequently corresponds with *either* and *whether.*—*adv.* Ere; before.—*n.* Heraldic name for gold.

Oracle, o'ra-kl, *n.* Among the Greeks and Romans, the answer of a god to an inquiry respecting some future event; place where the answers were given; the sanctuary of the ancient Jews; any person reputed uncommonly wise; a wise or authoritative utterance.

Oral, ō'ral, *a.* Pertaining to the mouth; spoken, not written.

Orange, o'ranj, *n.* An evergreen fruit-tree, and also its fruit; the color of this fruit, a reddish yellow.—*a.* Belonging to an orange; colored as an orange.

Orange-peel, o'ranj-pēl, *n.* The rind of an orange separated from the fruit; the peel of the bitter orange dried and candied.

Orate, ō'rāt, *vi.* (orating, orated). To make an oration; to talk loftily; to harangue.

Orchestra, or'kes-tra, *n.* That part of the Greek theater allotted to the chorus; that part of a theater, etc., appropriated to the musicians; a body of musicians.

Ordeal, or'dē-al, *n.* A trial by fire and water; severe trial or strict test.

Order, or'dėr, *n.* Regular disposition; proper state; established method; public tranquillity; command; instruction to supply goods or to pay money; rank, class, division, or dignity; a religious fraternity; division of natural objects; *pl.* clerical character, specially called holy orders.—**In order,** for the purpose.—*vt.* To place in order; to direct; to command; to give an order or commission for.—*vi.* To give command.

Ordinal, or'din-al, *a.* Expressing order or succession.—*n.* A number denoting order (as *first*); a book containing an ordination service.

Ordinance, or'din-ans, *n.* That which is ordained; law, statute, edict, decree.

Ordinary, or'din-a-ri, *a.* Conformable to order; regular; customary; common; of little merit.—*n.* An ecclesiastical judge; a judge who takes cognizance of causes in his own right; an eating-house where the prices are settled.—**In ordinary,** in actual and constant service; statedly attending, as a physician; but a ship *in ordinary* is

one laid up.

Ordinate, or'din-āt, *a.* Regular; methodical.—*n.* In *geometry,* a line of reference determining the position of a point.

Organ, or'gan, *n.* An instrument or means; a part of an animal or vegetable by which some function is carried on; a medium of conveying certain opinions; a newspaper; the largest wind-instrument of music.

Organization, or'gan-i-zā''shon, *n.* Act or process of organizing; suitable disposition of parts for performance of vital functions.

Organize, or'gan-īz, *vt.* To give an organic structure to; to establish and systematize; to arrange so as to be ready for service.

Orgasm, or'gazm, *n.* Immoderate excitement or action.

Orgy, or'ji, *n.* A wild or frantic revel; a drunken party.

Orient, ō'ri-ent, *a.* Rising, as the sun;; eastern; oriental; bright.—*n.* The East; luster as that of a pearl.—*vt.* To define the position of; to cause to lie from east to west.

Oriental, ō-ri-ent'al, *a.* Eastern; from the east.—*n.* A native of some eastern country.

Orientation, ōr'i-en-tā''shon, *n.* A turning towards the east; position east and west.

Orifice, o'ri-fis, *n.* The mouth or aperture of a tube, pipe, etc.; an opening; a vent.

Origin, o'ri-jin, *n.* Source; beginning; derivation; cause; root; foundation.

Original, ō-ri'jin-al, *a.* Pertaining to origin; primitive; first in order; having the power to originate; not copied.—*n.* Origin; source; first copy; model; that from which anything is translated or copied; a person of marked individuality.

Originate, ō-ri'jin-āt, *vt.* (originating, originated). To give origin to; to produce.—*vi.* To have origin; to be begun.

Orris, o'ris, *n.* A sort of gold or silver lace; a kind of iris.

Orthodox, or'thō-doks, *a.* Sound in opinion or doctrine; sound in religious doctrines; in accordance with sound doctrine.

Orthoepy, or'thō-e-pi or or-thō'e-pi, *n*. Correct pronunciation of words.

Orthography, or-thog'ra-fi, *n*. The art of writing words with the proper letters; spelling.

Orthopter, Orthopteran, or-thop'tėr, or-thop'tėr-an, *n*. One of an order of insects including cockroaches, grasshoppers, and locusts.

Oscillate, os'sil-lāt, *vi*. To swing; to vibrate; to vary or fluctuate.

Osculate, os'kū-lāt, *vt*. and *i*. To kiss; to touch, as curves.

Osmose, os'mōs, *n*. The tendency of fluids to pass through porous partitions and mix.

Osprey, os'prā, *n*. A kind of hawk or eagle which feeds on fish; one of its feathers.

Osteology, os-tē-ol'o-ji, *n*. The science which treats of the bones and bone-tissue.

Osteopathy, os-tē-op'a-thi, *n*. A system of medical treatment, based on the view that the proper adjustment of the vital mechanism is a more important factor than chemical intake in the maintenance of health.

Ostracize, os'tra-sīz, *vt*. To banish by ostracism; to expel; to banish from society.

Ostrich, os'trich, *n*. A large running bird of Africa, Arabia, and S. America, the largest of existing birds.

Other, uтн'ėr, *a*. and *pron*. Not the same; second of two; not this; opposite; often used reciprocally with *each*.

Ought, at, *n*. Aught.—*v*. To be held or bound in duty or moral obligation.

Ounce, ouns, *n*. The twelfth part of a pound troy, and the sixteenth of a pound avoirdupois; an Asiatic animal like a small leopard.

Our, our, *a*. or *pron*. Pertaining or belonging to us. **Ours** is used when no noun follows.

Oust, oust, *vt*. To eject; to turn out.

Out, out, *adv*. On or towards the outside; not in or within; forth; beyond usual limits; not in proper place; public; exhausted; deficient; not in employment; loudly; in error; at a loss; having taken her place as a woman in society.—*n*. One who is out; a nook or corner.—*vt*. To put out.—*interj*. Away! begone!

Outbreak, out'brāk, *n*. A breaking forth; eruption; sudden manifestation as of anger, disease, etc.

Outdo, out-dö', *vt*. To excel; to surpass.

Outdoor, out'dōr, *a*. In the open air; being without the house.

Outer, out'ėr, *a*. Being on the outside; external.—*n*. That part of a target beyond the circles surrounding the bull's-eye; a shot which hits this part.

Outermost, out'ėr-mōst, *a*. Being farthest out; being on the extreme external part.

Outfit, out'fit, *n*. A fitting out, as for a voyage; equipment of one going abroad.

Outflank, out-flangk', *vt*. To maneuver so as to attack in the flank; to get the better of.

Outgo, out-gō', *vt*. To go beyond; to excel.—*n*. out'gō. Expenditure.

Outgrow, out-grō', *vt*. To surpass in growth; to grow too great or old for anything.

Outing, out'ing, *n*. A short excursion; an airing; short time spent out-of-doors.

Outlandish, out-land'ish, *a*. Foreign; strange; uncouth; bizarre.

Outlaw, out'la, *n*. A person excluded from the benefit of the law.—*vt*. To deprive of the benefit and protection of law; to proscribe.

Out-of-the-way, out-ov-the-wā, *a*. Secluded; unusual; uncommon.

Out-patient, out'pā-shent, *n*. A patient not residing in a hospital, but who receives medical advice, etc., from the institution.

Outpost, out'pōst, *n*. A station at a distance from the main body of an army; troops placed at such a station.

Output, out'put, *n*. Quantity of material produced within a specified time.

Outrage, out'rāj, *vt*. (outraging, outraged). To do extreme violence

0

or injury to; to abuse; to commit a rape upon.—*n*. Excessive abuse; injurious violence.

Outskirt, out'skėrt, *n*. Parts near the edge of an area; border; purlieu; generally in *pl*.

Outspoken, out'spō-kn, *a*. Free or bold of speech; candid; frank.

Outspread, out-spred', *vt*. To spread out; to diffuse.—*a*. Extended; expanded.

Outstanding, out-stand'ing, *a*. Projecting outward; prominent; unpaid; undelivered.

Oval, ō'val, *a*. Shaped like an egg; elliptical.—*n*. A figure shaped like an egg or ellipse.

Ovariotomy, ō-vā'ri-ot''o-mi, *n*. The operation of removing a tumor in the ovary.

Ovary, ō'va-ri, *n*. The female organ in which ova are formed.

Ovate, ō'vāt, *a*. Egg-shaped; oval.

Ovation, ō-vā'shon, *n*. A lesser triumph among the ancient Romans; triumphal reception; public marks of respect.

Oven, uv'n, *n*. A place built in closely for baking, heating, or drying.

Over, ō'vėr, *prep*. Above; denoting motive, occasion, or superiority; across; throughout; upwards of.— *adv*. From side to side; in width; on all the surface; above the top or edge; in excess; completely; too.— *a*. Upper; covering.—*n*. *(cricket)* The number of balls (six or eight) which the bowler delivers in succession from one end of the pitch, before a change is made to the other side.

Overact, ō-vėr-akt', *vt*. To perform to excess.

Overcast, ō-vėr-käst', *vt*. To cloud; to darken; to sew coarsely over a rough edge.

Overcharge, ō-vėr-chärj', *vt*. To charge or burden to excess; to fill too numerously.—*n*. ō'vėr-chärj. An excessive charge.

Overcoat, ō'vėr-kōt, *n*. An upper coat; top-coat.

Overflow, ō-vėr-flō', *vt*. (pp. overflowed and overflown). To flow or spread over; to flood; to overwhelm.—*vi*. To be so full that the

contents run over; to abound.—*n*. ō'vėr-flō. An inundation; superabundance.

Overhang, ō-vėr-hang', *vt*. and *i*. To hang, impend, jut, or project over.

Overhaul, ō-vėr-hal', *vt*. To examine thoroughly with a view to repairs; to re-examine; to gain upon or overtake.—*n*. ō'vėr-hal. Examination; inspection; repair.

Overload, ō-vėr-lōd', *vt*. To load too much; to overburden.

Overlook, ō-vėr-luk', *vt*. To oversee; to superintend; to view from a higher place; to pass by indulgently.

Overnight, ō'vėr-nīt, *adv*. Through or during the night; in the night before.

Overpower, ō-vėr-pou'ėr, *vt*. To be too powerful for; to bear down by force; to overcome; to subdue; to crush.

Overrate, ō-vėr-rāt', *vt*. To rate at too much; to regard too highly.

Overreach, ō-vėr-rēch', *vt*. To reach over or beyond; to deceive by artifice; to outwit.

Override, ō-vėr-rīd', *vt*. To ride over; to supersede; to set at naught.

Overrule, ō-vėr-röl', *vt*. To control; to govern with high authority; to disallow.

Overrun, ō-vėr-run', *vt*. To run or spread over; to ravage; to outrun.—*vi*. To overflow; to run over.

Oversea, ō'vėr-sē, *a*. Foreign; from beyond sea.—**Overseas,** ō-vėr-sēz, *adv*. Abroad.

Oversee, ō-vėr-sē', *vt*. To see or look over; to overlook; to superintend.

Overshadow, ō-vėr-sha'dō, *vt*. To throw a shadow over; to shelter.

Overt, ō-vėrt, *a*. Open to view; manifest; not hidden; public; apparent.

Overtake, ō-vėr-tāk', *vt*. To come up with; to catch; to take by surprise.

Overthrow, ō-vėr-thrō', *vt*. To throw or turn over; to overset; to defeat; to destroy.—*n*. ō'vėr-thrō. Ruin; defeat.

Overtime, ō-vėr-tīm, *n*. Time during which one works beyond the regular hours.

Overture, ō'vėr-tūr, *n*. A proposal; offer; a musical introduction to oratorios, operas, etc.

Overturn, ō-vėr-tėrn', *vt.* To overset or overthrow; to capsize; to subvert; to ruin.

Overweening, ō-vėr-wēn'ing, *a.* Haughty; arrogant; proud; conceited.

Overweight, ō-vėr-wāt', *vt.* To overburden.—*n.* Excess of weight; preponderance.

Overwhelm, ō-vėr-whelm', *vt.* To whelm entirely; to swallow up; to submerge; to crush.

Overwork, ō-vėr-wėrk', *vt.* To work beyond strength; to tire with labor.—*n.* ō'vėr-wėrk. Work done beyond one's strength or beyond the amount required.

Overwrought, ō-vėr-rat', *p.a.* Wrought to excess; excited to excess; tasked beyond strength.

Owe, ō, *vt.* (owing, owed). To be indebted in; to be obliged or bound to pay; to be obliged for.

Owl, oul, *n.* A nocturnal bird of prey.

Own, ōn, *a.* Belonging to: used, distinctively and emphatically, after a possessive pronoun, or a noun in the possessive.—*vt.* To hold or possess by right; to acknowledge or avow; to concede.

Oxygen, oks'i-jen, *n.* A gaseous element, a component of atmospheric air and water, and essential to animal and vegetable life and combustion.

Oxygenate, oks'i-jen-āt, *vt.* To unite or cause to combine with oxygen.

Oyster, ois'tėr, *n.* A bivalve shellfish or mollusk.

Ozone, ō'zōn, *n.* A kind of gas with a peculiar odor, a modification of oxygen existing in the atmosphere.

P

Pabulum, pab'ū-lum, *n.* Food; that which feeds either mind or body.

Pace, pās, *n.* A step; space between the two feet in walking; distance of 2¹/₂ feet or 5 feet; gait; rate of progress.—*vi.,* (pacing, paced). To step; to walk slowly; to move by lifting the legs on the same side together; as a horse.—*vt.* To measure by steps; to accompany and set a proper rate of motion; to race.

Pacific, pa-sif'ik, *a.* Suited to make peace; pacifying; calm.—**The Pacific Ocean,** the ocean between America, Asia, and Australia.

Package, pak'āj, *n.* A bundle or bale; a packet; charge for packing goods.

Pack-horse, pak'hors, *n.* A horse employed in carrying goods and baggage on its back.

Pack-saddle, pak'sad-l, *n.* The saddle of a pack-horse, made for bearing burdens.

Pact, pakt, *n.* A contract; an agreement or covenant.

Pad, pad, *n.* An easy-paced horse; a robber who infests the road on foot; a soft saddle; a cushion; a quantity of blotting-paper.—*vi.* (padding, padded). To walk or go on foot; to rob on foot.—*vt.* To furnish with padding.

Padlock, pad'lok, *n.* A lock with a link to be fastened through a staple.—*vt.* To fasten or provide with a padlock.

Padre, päd'rä, *n.* A chaplain.

Paean, pē'an, *n.* A war-song; song of triumph.

Pagan, pā'gan, *n.* A heathen.—*a.* Heathenish; idolatrous.

Page, pāj, *n.* A young male attendant on persons of distinction; one side of a leaf of a book; a written record.—*vt.* (paging, paged). To number the pages of.

Pain, pān, *n.* A penalty; bodily suffering; distress; anguish; *pl.* The throes of childbirth; labor; diligent effort.—*vt.* To cause pain to; to afflict; to distress.

Painstaking, pānz'tāk-ing, *a.* Giving close application; laborious and careful.—*n.* The taking of pains; careful labor.

Paint, pānt, *vt.* To represent by colors and figures; to cover with color; to portray; to delineate.—*vi.* To practice painting.—*n.* A substance used in painting; a pigment; rouge.

Painting, pānt'ing, *n.* Art or employment of laying on colors; art of

P

representing objects by colors; a picture; colors laid on.

Pair, pār, *n.* Two things of like kind, suited, or used together; a couple; a man and his wife; two members on opposite sides in parliament, etc., who agree not to vote for a time.—*vi.* To join in pairs; to mate.—*vt.* To unite in pairs.

Pajamas, pā-jäm-az, *n.pl.* A sleeping-suit.

Palace, pa′läs, *n.* The house in which an emperor, king, bishop, etc., resides, a splendid residence.

Paleography, pal-ē-og′ra-fi, *n.* The art of deciphering ancient writing.

Paleolithic, pal′ē-ō-lith′′ik, *a.* Belonging to the earlier stone period, when rude unpolished stone implements were used.

Paleontology, pal′ē-on-tol′′o-ji, *n.* The science of fossil organic remains.

Paleozoic, pal′ē-ō-zō′′ik, *a.* In *geology,* applied to the lowest division of stratified groups.

Palatable, pa′lat-a-bl, *a.* Agreeable to the palate or taste; savory.

Palate, pa′lāt, *n.* The roof of the mouth; taste; relish; intellectual taste.

Palatial, pa-lā′shal, *a.* Pertaining to a palace; becoming a palace; magnificent.

Palaver, pa-la′vėr, *n.* A long or serious conference; idle talk.—*vt.* To flatter or humbug.—*vi.* To talk idly; to engage in a palaver.

Pale, pāl, *n.* A pointed stake; an inclosure; sphere or scope.—*vt.* (paling, paled). To inclose with pales; to fence in.—*vi.* To turn pale.—*a.* Whitish; wan; deficient in color; not bright; dim.

Pall, pal, *n.* An outer mantle of dignity; a cloth thrown over a coffin at a funeral; a linen cloth to cover a chalice; a covering.—*vt.* To cover with a pall; to shroud; to make vapid; to cloy.—*vi.* To become vapid or cloying.

Palladium, pal-lā′di-um, *n.* A statue of the goddess Pallas; bulwark; safeguard; a grayish-white hard malleable metal.

Pallet, pal′et, *n.* A palette; a tool used by potters, etc.; a small rude bed.

Palliate, pal′i-āt, *vt.* To extenuate; to mitigate; to lessen, abate, alleviate.

Pallid, pal′id, *a.* Pale; wan.

Pallor, pal′or, *n.* Paleness.

Palm, päm, *n.* The inner part of the hand; a measure of 3 or 4 inches; a name of plants constituting an order of endogens; a branch or leaf of such a plant; victory; triumph.—*vt.* To conceal in the palm of the hand; to impose by fraud.

Palpitate, pal′pi-tāt, *vi.* (palpitating, palpitated). To pulsate rapidly; to throb; to tremble.

Palpitation, pal-pi-tā′shon, *n.* Act of palpitating; violent pulsation of the heart.

Palsy, pal′zi, *n.* Paralysis, especially of a minor kind.—*vt.* (palsying, palsied). To affect with palsy; to paralyze.

Paltry, pal′tri, *a.* Mean and trivial; trifling; worthless; contemptible.

Paludal, pal′ū-dal, *a.* Pertaining to marshes. Also *paludine, palustral, palustrine.*

Pampas, pam′pas, *n.pl.* The immense grassy treeless plains of South America.

Pamper, pam′pėr, *vt.* To gratify to the full; to furnish with that which delights.

Pamphlet, pam′flet, *n.* A small book, stitched but not bound; a short treatise.

Pan, pan, *n.* A broad and shallow vessel, of metal or earthenware; a pond for evaporating salt water to make salt; part of a gun-lock holding the priming; the skull; the Greek and Roman god of flocks and herds.

Panacea, pan-a-sē′a, *n.* A remedy for all diseases; a universal medicine.

Pancake, pan′kāk, *n.* A thin cake fried in a pan or baked on an iron plate.

Panel, pa′nel, *n.* A surface distinct from others adjoining in a piece of work; a sunk portion in a door, etc.; a piece of wood on which a picture is painted; list of Health Insurance doctors for a district; a doctor's list of insured persons;

list of those summoned to serve on a jury; in Scotland, the accused.—*vt.* (panelling, panelled). To form with panels.

Pang, pang, *n.* A sharp and sudden pain; painful spasm; throe.

Panic, pan'ik, *n.* A sudden fright; terror inspired by a trifling cause.—*a.* Extreme, sudden, or causeless: said of fright.

Pant, pant, *vi.* To breathe quickly; to gasp; to desire ardently.—*n.* A gasp; a throb.

Pantaloons, pan'ta-lönz, *n.pl.* Tightly fitting trousers; trousers in general.

Pantheism, pan'thē-izm, *n.* The doctrine that the universe is God, or that all things are manifestations of God.

Pantheon, pan'thē-on, *n.* A temple dedicated to all the gods; all the divinities collectively worshipped by a people.

Papacy, pā'pa-si, *n.* The office and dignity of the pope; the popes collectively; papal authority or jurisdiction; popedom.

Paper, pā'pėr, *n.* A substance formed into thin sheets used for writing, printing, etc.; a leaf, or sheet of this; a journal; an essay or article; promissory notes, bills of exchange, etc.—*a.* Made or consisting of paper; appearing merely in documents without really existing; slight.—*vt.* To cover with paper; to inclose in paper.

Par, pär, *n.* State of equality; equality in condition or value; state of shares or stocks when they may be purchased at the original price.

Parable, pa'ra-bl, *n.* An allegorical representation of something real in life or nature, embodying a moral.

Parabola, pa-ra'bō-la, *n.* A conic section, shown when a cone is cut by a plane parallel to one of its sides; the curve described theoretically by a projectile.

Parachute, pa'ra-shöt, *n.* An apparatus like a large umbrella, enabling a safe drop to the ground from an aircraft.

Paraclete, pa'ra-klēt, *n.* One called to aid or support; the Holy Spirit.

Parade, pa-rād', *n.* Ostentation; show; military display; place where such display is held.—*vt.* (parading, paraded). To exhibit in ostentatious manner; to marshal in military order.—*vi.* To walk about for show; to go about in military procession.

Paragraph, pa'ra-graf, *n.* The character ¶ used as a reference, etc.; a distinct section of a writing, distinguished by a break in the lines; a brief notice.

Parallax, pa'ral-laks, *n.* The apparent change of position of an object when viewed from different points; the difference between the place of a heavenly body as seen from the earth's surface and its center at the same time.

Parallel, pa'ral-lel, *a.* Extended in the same direction, and in all parts equally distant, as lines or surfaces; running in accordance with something; equal in all essential parts.—*n.* A line which throughout its whole length is equidistant from another line; conformity in all essentials; likeness; comparison; counterpart.—*vt.* To place so as to be parallel; to correspond to; to compare.

Parallelogram, pa-ral-lel'ō-gram, *n.* A quadrilateral, whose opposite sides are parallel and equal.

Parapet, pa'ra-pet, *n.* A wall or rampart breast-high; a wall on the edge of a bridge, quay, etc.

Paraphernalia, pa'ra-fėr-nā''li-a, *n.pl.* That which a bride brings besides her dowry, as clothing, jewels, etc.; personal attire; trappings.

Paraphrase, pa'ra-frāz, *n.* A statement giving the meaning of another statement; a loose or free translation; a sacred song based on a portion of Scripture.—*vt.* To make a paraphrase of; to explain or translate with latitude.

Parasite, pa'ra-sīt, *n.* One who frequents the rich, and earns his welcome by flattery; a sycophant; an animal that lives upon or in another; a plant which grows on another.

Parasol, pa'ra-sol, *n*. A small umbrella used to keep off the sun's rays.

Parcel, pär'sel, *n*. A portion of anything; a small bundle or package; a collection.—*vt*. (parcelling, parcelled). To divide into portions; to make up into packages.

Parcel-post, pär'sel-pōst, *n*. Department of a post-office by which parcels are sent.

Parch, pärch, *vt*. To dry to extremity; to scorch.—*vi*. To become very dry; to be scorched.

Parenthesis, pa-ren'the-sis, *n*.; pl. -**theses**. A sentence or words inserted in another sentence, usually in brackets, thus, ( ).

Parhelion, pär-hē'li-on, *n*.; pl. -**lia**. A mock sun or meteor, appearing as a bright light near the sun.

Park, pärk, *n*. A piece of ground inclosed; ornamental ground adjoining a house; ground in a town for recreation; an assemblage of heavy ordnance.—*vt*. To inclose in a park; to bring together, as artillery; to draw up motorcars and leave them for a time in an inclosed space, or at the side of the road.

Parody, pa'rod-i, *n*. An adaptation of the words of an author, etc., to a different purpose; a burlesque imitation.—*vt*. (parodying, parodied). To imitate in parody.

Parole, pa-rōl', *n*. Words or oral declarations; word of honor; a promise by a prisoner of war not to bear arms against his captors for a certain period, or the like; a military countersign.

Paroxysm, pa'roks-izm, *n*. A violent access of feeling (as of rage); convulsion; spasm.

Parsimony, pär'si-mō-ni, *n*. The habit of being sparing in expenditure of money; excessive frugality; miserliness; closeness.

Parsley, pärs'li, *n*. A garden vegetable, used for flavoring in cooking.

Parsnip, pärs'nip, *n*. An umbelliferous plant with a fleshy esculent root.

Parson, pär'sn, *n*. The priest or incumbent of a parish; a clergyman.

Part, pärt, *n*. A portion or piece of a whole; a section; a constituent or organic portion; share; lot; party; duty; business; character assigned to an actor in a play; *pl*. faculties; superior endowments; regions; locality.—*vt*. To divide; to sever; to share; to distribute; to separate; to intervene.—*vi*. To become separated, broken, or detached; to quit each other; to depart.

Partake, pär-tāk', *vi*. (partaking, pret. partook, pp. partaken). To take or have a part with others; to share; to have something of the nature, claim, or right.—*vt*. To share.

Partial, pär'shal, *a*. Belonging to or affecting a part only; not general; biased to one party; having a fondness.

Partiality, pär'shi-al''i-ti, *n*. Unfair bias; undue favor shown; a liking or fondness.

Particularize, pär-tik'ū-lėr-īz, *vt*. To make particular mention of; to specify in detail.—*vi*. To be particular to details.

Parting, pärt'ing, *p.a.* Serving to part or divide; given at separation; departing.—*n*. Division; separation; leave-taking.

Partisan, pär'ti-zan, *n*. An adherent of a party or faction; a party man.—*a*. Adhering to a faction.

Partition, pär-ti'shon, *n*. Act of parting or dividing; division; a division-wall; part where separation is made.—*vt*. To divide by partitions; to divide into shares.

Partner, pärt'nėr, *n*. One who shares with another; an associate in business; a husband or wife.

Partnership, pärt'nėr-ship, *n*. Fellowship; the association of two or more persons in any business; joint interest or property.

Partridge, pär'trij, *n*. A game bird of the grouse family.

Parturition, pär-tū-ri'shon, *n*. The act of bringing forth young.

Pass, päs, *vi*. (pret. and pp. passed or past). To go by or past; to change; to die; to elapse; to be enacted; to be current; to thrust in fencing or fighting; to go successfully through an examination.—*vt.* To go past, beyond, or over; to cross; to live through; to undergo with success (as an examination); to circulate; to utter; to take no notice of; to enact; to thrust; to void, as feces.—*n.* A passage; a defile; a license to pass; a thrust; manipulation; condition; extremity.

Passage, pas'āj, *n.* Act of passing; transit; a journey, especially by a ship; road; channel; a gallery or corridor; access; episode; part of a book, etc., referred to; enactment; an encounter.

Passion-play, pa'shon-plā, *n.* A play representing scenes in the passion of Christ.

Passion-Sunday, pa'shon-sun-dā, *n.* The fifth Sunday in Lent.

Passive, pas'iv, *a.* Capable of feeling; suffering; not acting; unresisting; inert; in *grammar,* expressing that the nominative is the object of some action or feeling.

Passover, päs'ō-vėr, *n.* A feast of the Jews commemorative of the deliverance in Egypt, when the destroying angel passed over the houses of the Israelites; the sacrifice offered.

Passport, päs'pōrt, *n.* A license empowering a person to travel; that which enables one to reach some desired object.

Past, päst, *p.a.* Gone by or beyond; belonging to an earlier period; spent; ended.—*n.* Former time.—*prep.* Beyond; out of reach of; after.—*adv.* By; so as to pass.

Paste, päst, *n.* A mass of a semifluid state; a mixture of flour, etc., used in cookery, or to cause substances to adhere; a mixture of clay for pottery; a brilliant glassy substance, used in making imitations of gems.—*vt.* (pasting, pasted). To unite or fasten with paste.

Pastor, pas'tor, *n.* A minister of a church.

Pastoral, pas'tor-al, *a.* Pertaining to shepherds; rustic; rural; relating to the care of souls, or to a pastor.—*n.* A poem dealing with shepherds; a poem of rural life; a letter addressed by a bishop to the clergy and people of his diocese.

Patch, pach, *n.* A piece of cloth sewn on a garment to repair it; a small piece of silk stuck on the face for adornment; a small piece of ground.—*vt.* To mend by sewing on a patch; to repair clumsily; to make hastily without regard to forms (with *up*).

Patent, pā'tent or pa'tent, *n.* A writing (called *letters patent*) granting a privilege, as a title of nobility; a similar writing, securing exclusive right to an invention or discovery.—*a.* Open; manifest; secured by patent; lacquered (leather).—*vt.* To secure, as the exclusive right of a thing to a person.

Paterfamilias, pā'tėr-fa-mil''i-as, *n.* The head or father of a family.

Paternal, pa-tėr'nal, *a.* Fatherly; derived from the father; hereditary.

Paternoster, pa'tėr-nos-tėr, *n.* The Lord's prayer; a rosary; every tenth bead in a rosary.

Path, päth, *n.* A way beaten by the feet of man or beast; a footway; course or track; way or passage; course of life.

Pathetic, pa-thet'ik, *a.* Full of pathos; affecting; exciting pity, sorrow, etc.

Pathology, pa-thol'o-ji, *n.* That part of medicine which explains the nature of diseases, their causes and symptoms.

Pathos, pā'thos, *n.* Expression of strong or deep feeling; that quality which excites tender emotions, as pity, sympathy, etc.

Patience, pā'shens, *n.* Quality of being patient; endurance; composure; forbearance; a card game for one.

Patient, pā'shent, *a.* Enduring without murmuring; not easily provoked; persevering; not hasty.—*n.* A person or thing passively affected; a person under medical treatment.

Patriot, pā'tri-ot or pat', *n.* A person who loves his country, and zealously defends its interests.—*a.* Patriotic.

Patriotism, pā'tri-ot-izm or pat', *n.* The qualities of a patriot; love of one's country.

Patrol, pa-trōl', *n*. The marching round by a guard at night to secure the safety of a camp; the guard who go such rounds; on active service, a small party sent out to harass the enemy (fighting patrol), or to get information (reconnaissance patrol).—*vi*. (patrolling, patrolled). To go the rounds as a patrol.—*vt*. To pass round, as a guard.

Patron, pā'tron, *n*. A protector; one who supports or protects a person or a work; one who has the disposition of a church-living, professorship, or other appointment; a guardian saint.

Patronize, pat'ron-īz or pā', *vt*. To act as patron of; to countenance or favor; to assume the air of a superior to.

Paunchy, pansh'i, *a*. Big-bellied.

Pauper, pa'pėr, *n*. A poor person; one dependent on the public for maintenance.

Pause, paz, *n*. A temporary cessation; cessation proceeding from doubt; suspense.—*vi*. (pausing, paused). To make a short stop; to delay; to deliberate; to hesitate.

Pave, pāv, *vt*. (paving, paved). To cover with stone, brick, etc., so as to make a level and solid surface for carriages or foot-passengers.

Pavement, pāv'ment, *n*. The solid floor of a street, courtyard, etc.; paved part of a road used by foot-passengers; material with which anything is paved.

Pavilion, pa-vil'yon, *n*. A tent; a small building having a tent-formed roof; a building of ornamental character for entertainments; the outer ear.—*vt*. To furnish with pavilions; to shelter with a tent.

Pay, pā, *vt*. (paying, paid). To give money, etc., for goods received or service rendered; to reward; to discharge, as a debt; to give; to cover with tar or pitch.—*vi*. To make a payment; to be profitable or remunerative.—*n*. An equivalent for money due, goods, or services; salary; wages; reward.

Pea, pē, *n*.; pl. **Peas, Pease.** A well-known flowering plant cultivated for its seeds; one of the seeds of the plant.

Peace, pēs, *n*. A state of quiet; calm; repose; public tranquillity; freedom from war; concord.

Peak, pēk, *n*. A projecting point; the top of a mountain ending in a point; the upper corner of a sail extended by a yard; also, the extremity of the yard or gaff.—*vi*. To look sickly; to be emaciated.

Peal, pēl, *n*. A series of loud sounds, as of bells, thunder, etc.; a set of bells tuned to each other; chime.—*vi*. To give out a peal.—*vt*. To cause to ring or sound.

Pear, pār, *n*. A well-known fruit-tree; one of the fruits of the tree.

Pearl, pėrl, *n*. A smooth lustrous whitish gem produced by certain mollusks; something resembling a pearl; a small printing type; what is choicest and best.—*a*. Relating to or made of pearl or mother-of-pearl.—*vt*. To set or adorn with pearls.

Peck, pek, *n*. A dry measure of eight quarts.—*vt*. and *i*. To strike with the beak, or something pointed; to pick up, as food, with the beak.

Pectic, pek'tik, *a*. Having the property of forming a jelly.

Pectinate, pek'tin-āt, *a*. Toothed like a comb.

Pectoral, pek'to-ral, *a*. Pertaining to the breast.—*n*. A breastplate; a medicine for the chest and lungs.

Peculate, pe'kū-lāt, *vi*. To appropriate money or goods intrusted to one's care.

Peculiar, pē-kū'li-ėr, *a*. One's own; characteristic; particular; unusual; odd.

Peculiarity, pē-kū'li-a''ri-ti, *n*. Quality of being peculiar; something peculiar to a person or thing.

Pecuniary, pē-kū'ni-a-ri, *a*. Relating to or connected with money; consisting of money.

Pedagogue, ped'a-gog, *n*. A teacher of children; a schoolmaster.

Pedal, pēd'al, *a*. Pertaining to a foot or to a pedal.—*n*. pe'dal. A lever to be pressed by the foot; a part of a musical instrument acted on by the feet.

Peel, pēl, *vt*. To strip off, as bark or rind; to flay; to pare; to pillage.— *vi*. To lose the skin, bark or rind; to fall off, as bark or skin.—*n*. The skin or rind; a baker's wooden shovel.

Peep, pēp, *vi*. To chirp as a chicken; to begin to appear; to look through a crevice.—*n*. A chirp; a look through a small opening; first appearance.

Pelt, pelt, *n*. A raw hide; a blow; a heavy shower.—*vt*. To strike with something thrown.—*vi*. To throw missiles; to fall in a heavy shower.

Pelvis, pel'vis, *n*. The bony cavity forming the framework of the lower part of the abdomen.

Pen, pen, *n*. An instrument for writing with ink; style or quality of writing; a small inclosure for cows, etc.; a fold.—*vt*. (penning, penned). To write; to compose; to coop or shut up.

Penal, pē'nal, *a*. Relating to, enacting, or incurring punishment.

Penalty, pen'al-ti, *n*. Punishment for a crime or offense; forfeit for non-fulfilment of conditions; sum to be forefeited; a fine.

Penance, pen'ans, *n*. An ecclesiastical punishment imposed for sin; voluntary suffering as an expression of penitence.

Penchant, päng'shäng, *n*. Strong inclination; bias.

Pencil, pen'sil, *n*. A small brush used by painters; an instrument of black-lead, etc., for writing and drawing; a converging or diverging aggregate of rays of light.—*vt*. (pencilling, pencilled). To write or mark with a pencil.

Pend, pend, *vi*. To impend; to wait for settlement.

Pendant, pen'dant, *n*. Anything hanging down by way of ornament; a hanging apparatus for giving light, etc.; an appendix or addition; a flag borne at the mast-head.

Pendent, pen'dent, *a*. Hanging; pendulous; projecting.—*n*. Something hanging.

Pendulous, pen'dū-lus, *a*. Hanging;

hanging so as to swing; swinging.

Pendulum, pen'dū-lum, *n*. A body suspended and swinging; the swinging piece in a clock which regulates its motion.

Penetrable, pen'e-tra-bl, *a*. That may be entered or pierced; susceptible of moral or intellectual impression.

Penetrate, pen'e-trāt, *vt*. and *i*. To enter or pierce, as into another body; to affect, as the mind; to cause to feel; to understand.

Penitentiary, pe-ni-ten'sha-ri, *a*. Relating to penance.—*n*. One who does penance; an office or official of the R. Catholic church connected with the granting of dispensations, etc.; a house of correction.

Penumbra, pen-um'bra, *n*. The partial shadow on the margin of the total shadow in an eclipse; the point of a picture where the shade blends with the light.

Penurious, pe-nū'ri-us, *a*. Pertaining to penury; parsimonious; niggardly.

Penury, pe'nū-ri, *n*. Poverty; indigence; want of the necessaries of life.

Peon, pē'on, *n*. An attendant; a native constable; a day-laborer; a kind of serf.

Peony, pē'o-ni, *n*. A genus of plants of the ranunculus family, with large flowers.

People, pē'pl, *n*. The body of persons who compose a community, race, or nation; persons indefinitely.—*vt*. (peopling, peopled). To stock with inhabitants; to populate.

Pepper, pep'ėr, *n*.A plant and its aromatic pungent seed, much used in seasoning, etc.—*vt*. To sprinkle with pepper; to pelt with shot or missiles; to drub thoroughly.

Pepper-corn, pep'ėr-korn, *n*. The berry or fruit of the pepper plant.

Peppermint, pep'ėr-mint, *n*. A plant of the mint genus having a penetrating aromatic smell and a strong pungent taste.

Pepsin, Pepsine, pep'sin, *n*. The active principle of gastric juice.

Peptic, pep'tik, *a*. Promoting digestion; relating to digestion; digestive.

Per, pėr, *prep*. A Latin preposition used in the sense of *by* or *for*, chiefly in certain Latin phrases, as *per annum*, by or for the year.

Perceive, pėr-sēv', *vt*. (perceiving, perceived). To apprehend by the organs of sense or by the mind; to observe; to discern.

Percentage, pėr-sent'āj, *n*. The allowance duty, rate of interest, proportion, etc., reckoned on each hundred.

Perception, pėr-sep'shon, *n*. Act, process, or faculty of perceiving; discernment.

Perch, pėrch, *n*. A spiny fresh-water fish; a roost for fowls; an elevated place or position; 5¹/₂ yards, also called a rod or pole; 30¹/₄ square yards, a square rod.—*vi*. To sit on a perch; to light, as a bird.—*vt*. To place on a perch.

Percipient, pėr-sip'i-ent, *a*. Perceiving; having the faculty of perception.

Peregrinate, pe're-grin-āt, *vi*. To travel from place to place; to wander.

Peremptory, pe'remp-to-ri, *a*. Such as to preclude debate; decisive; absolute.

Perennial, pe-ren'i-al, *a*. Lasting through the year; perpetual; unceasing.—*n*. A plant whose root remains alive more years than two.

Perfect, pėr'fekt, *a*. Finished; complete; fully informed; completely skilled; faultless; in *grammar*, denoting a tense which expresses an act completed.—*vt*. To accomplish; to make perfect; to make fully skilful.

Performance, pėr-form'ans, *n*. Act of performing; deed; achievement; a literary work; exhibition on the stage; entertainment at a place of amusement.

Perfume, pėr'fūm or pėr-fūm', *n*. A pleasant scent or smell; fragrance.—*vt*. (perfuming, perfumed). To scent with perfume; to impregnate with a grateful odor.

Perfunctory, pėr-fungk'to-ri, *a*. Done carelessly or in a half-

hearted manner; negligent.

Perhaps, pėr-haps', *adv*. It may be; peradventure; perchance; possibly.

Perilous, pe'ril-us, *a*. Dangerous; hazardous; full of risk.

Perimeter, pe-rim'et-ėr, *n*. The outer boundary of a body or figure.

Period, pē'ri-od, *n*. The time taken up by a heavenly body in revolving round the sun; the time at which anything ends; end; an indefinite portion of any continued state or existence; a complete sentence; the point that marks the end of a sentence, thus (.).

Periodical, pē-ri-od'ik-al, *n*. A magazine, newspaper, etc., published at regular periods.—*a*. Periodic.

Peripatetic, pe'ri-pa-tet''ik, *a*. Walking about; itinerant; pertaining to Aristotle's system of philosophy, taught while walking.—*n*. One who walks; a follower of Aristotle.

Periphery, pe-rif'ėr-i, *n*. The boundary line of a figure.

Periscope, pe'ri-skōp, *n*. An apparatus or structure rising above the deck of a submarine vessel, giving by means of mirrors, etc., a view of outside surroundings, though the vessel itself remains submerged; a similar device used in trenches.

Perish, pe'rish, *vi*. To die; to wither and decay; to be destroyed; to come to nothing.

Peritoneum, pe'ri-tō-nē''um, *n*. A membrane investing the internal surface of the abdomen, and the viscera contained in it.

Peritonitis, per'i-tō-nī''tis, *n*. Inflammation of the peritoneum.

Perjure, pėr'jūr, *vt*. (perjuring, perjured). To forswear; wilfully to make a false oath when administered legally.

Permit, pėr-mit', *vt*. and *i*. (permitting, permitted). To allow; to grant; to suffer; to concede.—*n*. per'mit. A written permission or license given by competent authority.

Permutation, pėr-mū-tā'shon, *n*. Interchange; in *mathematics*, any of the ways in which a set of quantities can be arranged.

Pernicious, per-ni'shus, *a*. Having the quality of destroying or injuring; destructive; deadly; noxious.

Perorate, pe'rō-rāt, *vi*. To make a peroration; to speechify; to spout.

Perpetuate, per-pe'tū-āt, *vt*. To make perpetual; to preserve from oblivion.

Perpetuity, per-pe-tū'i-ti, *n*. State or quality of being perpetual; endless duration; something of which there will be no end.

Perplexity, per-pleks'i-ti, *n*. State of being puzzled, or at a loss; bewilderment; state of being intricate or involved.

Perquisite, per'kwi-zit, *n*. Something in addition to regulr wages or salary.

Persecute, per'se-kūt, *vt*. (persecuting, persecuted). To harass with unjust punishment; to afflict for adherence to a particular creed.

Persevere, per-se-vēr', *vi*. (persevering, persevered). To continue steadfastly in any business; to pursue steadily any design.

Persiflage, per'sē-fläzh, *n*. Idle bantering talk.

Persist, per-sist', *vi*. To continue steadily in any business or course; to persevere; to continue in a certain state.

Personal, per'son-al, *a*. Pertaining to a person; peculiar or proper to him or her; belonging to face and figure; denoting the person in a grammatical sense.

Personality, per-son-al'i-ti, *n*. State of being personal; that which constitutes an individual a distinct person; disparaging remark on one's conduct and character; in *law*, personal estate.

Perspective, per-spek'tiv, *n*. The art of representing objects on a flat surface so that they appear to have their natural dimensions and relations; a representation of objects in perspective; view.—*a*. Pertaining to the art of perspective.

Perspicacious, per-spi-kā'shus, *a*. Quick-sighted; of acute discernment.

Persuasive, per-swā'siv, *a*. Having the power of persuading; calcu-lated to persuade.—*n*. That which persuades; an incitement.

Pert, pert, *a*. Lively; brisk; saucy; bold.

Pertain, per-tān', *vi*. To belong; to relate; to concern; to regard.

Pertinacious, per-ti-nā'shus, *a*. Obstinate; inflexible; determined; persistent.

Pertinent, per'ti-nent, *a*. Related to the subject or matter in hand; apposite; fit.

Perturb, per-terb', *vt*. To disturb; to agitate; to disquiet; to confuse.

Peruse, pe-rūz', *vt*. (perusing, perused). To read through; to read with attention; to examine carefully.

Pervade, per-vād', *vt*. (pervading, pervaded). To pass or flow through; to permeate; to be diffused through.

Perverse, per-vers', *a*. Obstinate in the wrong; stubborn; untractable; petulant.

Perversely, per-vers'li, *adv*. Stubbornly; obstinately in the wrong.

Perversion, per-ver'shon, *n*. A diverting from the true intent or object; misapplication.

Pervert, per-vert', *vt*. To turn from truth or proper purpose; to corrupt; to misinterpret; to misapply.—*n*. per'vert. One who has been perverted.

Pestilence, pes'ti-lens, *n*. Any contagious disease that is epidemic and fatal; something morally evil or destructive.

Pestle, pes'l, *n*. An instrument for pounding substances in a mortar.—*vt*. and *i*. (pestling, pestled). To pound with a pestle.

Pet, pet, *n*. A darling; any little animal fondled and indulged; fit of peevishness.—*vt*. (petting, petted). To fondle; to indulge.

Petal, pe'tal, *n*. A flower leaf.

Petite, pe-tēt', *a*. Small in figure; tiny.

Petition, pē-ti'shon, *n*. An entreaty, supplication, or prayer; a written application in legal proceedings.—*vt*. To supplicate; to solicit.

Petrifaction, pet-ri-fak'shon, *n*. the process of changing into stone; a fossil.

P

Petrify, pet-ri-fī, *vt.* To turn into stone or a fossil; to paralyze or stupefy.—*vi.* To become stone, or of a stony hardiness.

Petulant, pe'tū-lant, *a.* Irritable; peevish; fretful; saucy; pert; capricious.

Pew, pū, *n.* An inclosed seat in a church.

Pewter, pū'tér, *n.* An alloy mainly of tin and lead; a vessel made of pewter.—*a.* Relating to or made of pewter.

Phalange, fa-lanj', *n.* One of the small bones of the fingers and toes.

Phallus, fal'lus, *n.* The emblem of the generative power in nature, especially in certain religious usages.

Pharmaceutic, Pharmaceutical, fär-ma-sū'tik, fär-ma-sū'tik-al, *a.* Pertaining to the knowledge or art of pharmacy.

Pharmacology, fär-ma-kol'o-ji, *n.* The science of drugs; the art of preparing medicines.

Pharmacopeia, fär'ma-kō-pē''a, *n.* A book describing the preparation of medicines.

Pharmacy, fär'ma-si, *n.* The art or practice of preparing medicines.

Pharynx, fā'ringks, *n.* The muscular sac between the mouth and the esophagus.

Phase, fāz, *n.* A particular stage of the moon or a planet in respect to illumination; state of a varying phenomenon; one of the various aspects of a question.

Pheasant, fe'zant, *n.* A bird commonly reared and preserved for sport and food.

Phenomenon, fē-no'me-non, *n.*; pl. -**mena.** An appearance; anything visible; an appearance whose cause is not immediately obvious; something extraordinary.

Phial, fī'al, *n.* A small glass bottle.

Philanthropist, fī-lan'throp-ist, *n.* One devoted to philanthropy; one who exerts himself in doing good to his fellowmen.

Philosopher, fi-los'o-fér, *n.* A person versed in philosophy; one who studies moral or mental science.

Philosophy, fi-los'o-fi, *n.* The sci-

ence which tries to account for the phenomena of the universe; metaphysics; the general principles underlying some branch of knowledge; practical wisdom.

Phonetics, fō-net'iks, *n.pl.* The doctrine or science of sounds, especially of the human voice; the representation of sounds.

Phonograph, fō'nō-graf, *n.* An instrument for registering and reproducing sounds; a predecessor of the gramophone.

Phosgene, fos'jēn, *n.* A poison gas, carbon oxychloride.

Phosphate, fos'fāt, *n.* A salt of phosphoric acid.

Photography, fō-tog'ra-fi, *n.* The art or practice of producing representations of scenes and objects by the action of light on chemically prepared surfaces.

Photology, fō-tol'o-ji, *n.* The doctrine or science of light.

Photometer, fō-tom'et-ér, *n.* An instrument for measuring the intensity of lights.

Phrase, frāz, *n.* A short sentence or expression; an idiom; style; diction.—*vt.* and *i.* (phrasing, phrased). To style; to express.

Phraseology, frā-zē-ol'o-ji, *n.* Manner of expression; peculiar words used in a sentence; diction; style.

Phrenetic, fre-net'ik, *a.* Having the mind disordered; frantic.—*n.* A frenzied person.

Phrenic, fren'ik, *a.* Belonging to the diaphragm.

Physician, fi-zi'shan, *n.* A person skilled in the art of healing; a doctor.

Physics, fi'ziks, *n.* That branch of science which deals with mechanics, dynamics, light, heat, sound, electricity, and magnetism; natural philosophy.

Physiognomy, fi-zi-og'no-mi, *n.* The art of perceiving a person's character by his countenance; particular cast or expression of countenance.

Physiography, fi-zi-og'ra-fi, *n.* The science of the earth's physical features and phenomena; physical geography.

Physiology, fi-zi-ol'o-ji, *n.* The science of the phenomena of life; the study of the functions of living beings.

Physique, fi-zēk´, *n.* A person's physical or bodily structure or constitution.

Phytology, fi-tol´o-ji, *n.* The science of plants; botany.

Pianist, pi´an-ist, *n.* A performer on the piano.

Pick, pik, *vt.* To strike at with something pointed; to peck at; to clean by the teeth, fingers, etc.; to select; to pluck; to gather.—*vi.* To eat slowly; to nibble; to pilfer.—*n.* A pointed tool; a pick-axe; choice; selection.

Pickaxe, pik´aks, *n.* A sharp-pointed iron tool used in digging, mining, etc.

Picket, pik´et, *n.* A pointed stake used in fortification; a pale; an advanced guard or outpost; a game at cards.—*vt.* To fortify with pickets; to post as a guard of observation.

Pickle, pik´l, *n.* Brine; a solution of salt and water for preserving flesh, fish, etc.; vegetables preserved in vinegar; a state of difficulty or disorder; a troublesome child.—*vt.* (pickling, pickled). To preserve in or treat with pickle.

Picture, pik´tūr, *n.* A painting, drawing, etc., exhibiting the resemblance of anything; any resemblance or representation; *pl.* the moving photographs shown in cinematography; the cinema.—*vt.* To represent pictorially; to present an ideal likeness of; to describe in a vivid manner.

Picturesque, pik-tūr-esk´, *a.* Forming, or fitted to form, a pleasing picture; abounding with vivid imagery; graphic.

Pie, pī, *n.* A paste baked with something in or under it; a mass of types unsorted; the magpie.

Piebald, pī´bald, *a.* Having spots or patches of various colors; pied; mongrel.

Piece, pēs, *n.* A portion of anything; a distinct part; a composition or writing of no great length; a separate performance; a picture; a coin; a single firearm.—*vt.* (piec-

ing, pieced). To patch; to join.—*vi.* To unite or join on.

Piety, pī´e-ti, *n.* Reverence or veneration towards God; godliness; devotion; religion.

Pig, pig, *n.* A young swine; a swine in general; an oblong mass of unforged metal.—*vt.* or *i.* (pigging, pigged). To bring forth pigs; to act like pigs.

Pigeon, pi´jon, *n.* A well-known bird of many varieties; a dove; a simpleton; a gull.

Pigeon-hole, pi´jon-hōl, *n.* A hole for pigeons to enter their dwelling; a division in a desk or case for holding papers.

Pig-iron, pig´ī-ėrn, *n.* Iron in pigs, as it comes from the blast-furnace.

Pigment, pig´ment, *n.* Paint; any preparation used by painters, dyers, etc., to impart colors to bodies; coloring matter.

Pig-skin, pig´skin, *n.* The skin of a pig, especially when prepared for saddlery, etc.

Pilgrim, pil´grim, *n.* A wanderer; one who travels to visit a holy place or relics.

Pilgrimage, pil´grim-āj, *n.* A journey to some holy place; the journey of human life.

Pill, pil, *n.* A medicine in the form of a little ball; anything nauseous to be accepted.—*vt.* To dose with pills; to form into pills; to rob; to plunder.

Pillow, pil´ō, *n.* A long soft cushion; something that bears or supports.—*vt.* To rest or lay on for support.

Pilot, pī´lot, *n.* One whose occupation is to steer ships; a guide; a director of one's course.—*vt.* To act as pilot of; to guide through dangers or difficulties.

Pimp, pimp, *n.* A man who provides gratifications for others' lusts; a procurer.—*vi.* To pander; to procure women for others.

Pimpernel, pim´pėr-nel, *n.* A little red-flowered annual found in British cornfields.

Pimple, pim´pl, *n.* A small elevation of the skin, with an inflamed base.

Pin, pin, *n.* A longish piece of metal,

P

wood, etc., used for a fastening, or as a support; a peg; a bolt.—*vt.* (pinning, pinned). To fasten with a pin or pins; to hold fast.—*vt.* To inclose, to pen or pound.

Pincers, pin'serz, *n.pl.* An instrument for gripping anything; nippers; prehensile claws.

Pinch, pinsh, *vt.* To press hard or squeeze; to nip; to afflict.—*vi.* To press painfully; to be sparing.—*n.* A close compression, as with the fingers; a nip; a pang; straits; a strong iron lever; as much as is taken by the finger and thumb; a small quantity.

Pinion, pin'yon, *n.* A bird's wing; the joint of a wing remotest from the body; a large wing-feather; a small toothed wheel; a fetter for the arms.—*vt.* To bind the wings of; to cut off, as the first joint of the wing; to fetter.

Pink, pingk, *n.* A garden flower; a light rose-color or pigment; the flower or something supremely excellent.—*a.* Of a fine light rose-color.—*vt.* To work in eyelet-holes; to scallop; to stab.—*vi.* To wink or blink.

Pinnacle, pin'a-kl, *n.* A rocky peak; the summit; a minor structure or turret above a building.

Pint, pint, *n.* The eighth part of a gallon.

Pioneer, pi-on-er', *n.* One whose business is to prepare the road for an army, make entrenchments, etc.; one who leads the way.—*vt.* To prepare a way for.—*vi.* To act as pioneer.

Pious, pi'us, *a.* Devout; godly; holy; proceeding from piety.

Pip, pip, *n.* The kernel or seed of fruit; a spot on cards; a disease of fowls.

Pipe, pip, *n.* A wind-instrument of music; a long tube; a tube with a bowl at one end for tobacco; the windpipe; a call of a bird; a wine measure containing about 105 imperial gallons.—*vi.* (piping, piped). To play on a pipe; to whistle.—*vt.* To utter in a high tone; to call by a pipe or whistle.

Piracy, pi'ra-si, *n.* The act or practice of robbing on the high seas; in-

fringement of the law of copyright.

Pirate, pi'rat, *n.* A robber on the high seas; a ship engaged in piracy; one who publishes others' writings without permission.—*vi.* (pirating, pirated). To rob on the high-seas.—*vt.* To take without right, as writings.

Pistachio, pis-ta'shi-o, *n.* The nut of a small tree cultivated in S. Europe for its fruit; the tree itself, also called *pistacia.*

Pistil, pis'til, *n.* The seed-bearing organ of a flower.

Pistol, pis'tol, *n.* A small firearm fired with one hand.—*vt.* (pistolling, pistolled). To shoot with a pistol.

Piston, pis'ton, *n.* a cylindrical piece of metal which fits exactly into a hollow cylinder, and works alternately in two directions.

Piston-rod, pis'ton-rod, *n.* A rod which connects a piston to some other piece, and either moved by the piston or moving it.

Pit, pit, *n.* A hollow in the earth; the shaft of a mine; a vat in tanning, dyeing, etc.' a concealed hole for catching wild beasts; a small cavity or depression; part of the floor of a theater.—*vt.* (pitting, pitted). To lay in a pit or hole; to mark with little hollows; to set in competition.

Pitch, pich, *vt.* To thrust, as a pointed object; to fix; to set; to throw; to set the key-note of; to set in array; to smear or cover with pitch.—*vi.* To settle; to fall headlong; to fix choice; to encamp; to rise and fall, as a ship.—*n.* A throw; degree of elevation; highest rise; descent; elevation of a note; (cricket) prepared ground between wickets; a thick dark resinous substance obtained from tar.

Pith, pith, *n.* The spongy substance in the center of exogenous plants; the spinal cord or marrow of an animal; strength or force; energy; cogency; essence.

Pity, pi'ti, *n.* Sympathy or compassion; ground of pity; thing to be regretted.—*vt.* (pitying, pitied). To feel pain or grief for; to sympathize with.—*vi.* To be compassionate.

Pivot, pi'vot, *n*. A pin on which something turns; a turning-point; that on which important results depend.—*vt*. To place on or furnish with a pivot.

Placable, pla'ka-bl, *a*. Readily appeased or pacified; willing to forgive.

Placard, plak'ėrd or pla-kärd', *n*. A written or printed bill posted in a public place; a poster.—*vt*. To post placards.

Place, plās, *n*. An open space in a town; a locality, spot, or site; position; room; an edifice; quarters; a passage in a book; rank; office; calling; ground or occasion; stead.—*vt*. (placing, placed). To put or set; to locate; to appoint or set in an office, rank, or condition; to invest; to lend.

Placenta, pla-sen'ta, *n*. The afterbirth; an organ developed in mammals during pregnancy, connecting the mother and fetus; the part of the seed-vessel to which the seeds are attached.

Placid, pla'sid, *a*. Gentle; quiet; mild; unruffled; calm.

Plagiarism, plā'ji-a-rizm, *n*. The act of plagiarizing; literary theft.

Plaintive, plänt'iv, *a*. Expressive of sorrow or grief; repining; mournful; sad.

Plait, plāt, *n*. A fold; a doubling of cloth, etc.; a braid, as of hair, etc.—*vt*. To fold; to double in narrow strips; to braid.

Plan, plan, *n*. The representation of anything on a flat surface; sketch; scheme; project; method; process.—*vt*. (planning, planned). To form a plan or representation of; to scheme.—*vi*. To form a scheme.

Plane, Plane-tree, plān, plān'trē, *n*. A forest tree with a straight smooth stem and palmate leaves; a kind of maple.

Planet, pla'net, *n*. A celestial body which revolves about the sun or other center.

Plank, plangk, *n*. A flat broad piece of sawed timber.—*vt*. To cover or lay with planks.

Plant, plant, *n*. One of the living organisms of the vegetable kingdom; a herb; a shoot or slip; the machinery, etc., necessary to carry on a business.—*vt*. To set in the ground for growth; to set firmly; to establish; to furnish with plants; to set and direct, as cannon.—*vi*. To set plants in the ground.

Plasma, plas'ma or plaz'ma, *n*. Formless matter; the simplest form of organized matter in the vegetable and animal body.

Plaster, pläs'tėr, *n*. An adhesive substance used in medical practice; a mixture of lime, water, sand, etc., for coating walls; calcined gypsum, used with water for finishing walls, for casts, cement, etc.—*vt*. To overlay with plaster; to lay on coarsely.

Plastic, plas'tik, *a*. Having the power to give form to matter; capable of being molded; applied to sculpture, as distinguished from painting, etc.—**Plastics,** plas'tiks, *n*. The science or craft of converting various resins into durable materials; the articles so made.

Plat, plat, *vt*. (platting, platted). To plait; to weave; to make a ground-plan of.—*n*. A plot of ground devoted to some special purpose.

Plate, plāt, *n*. A flat piece of metal; gold and silver wrought into utensils; a shallow flattish dish for eatables; an engraved piece of metal for printing; a page of stereotype for printing.—*vt*. (plating, plated). To cover with a thin coating of metal, as of silver.

Plating, plāt'ing, *n*. The art of covering articles with gold or silver; the coating itself.

Platinum, pla'tin-um, *n*. The heaviest of all metals, hard, ductile, malleable, and of a silvery color.

Player, plā'ėr, *n*. An actor; musician; gamester.

Playful, plā'ful, *a*. Full of play; sportive; given to levity; indulging a sportive fancy.

Playground, plā'ground, *n*. A piece of ground set apart for open-air recreation.

Playwright, plā'rīt, *n*. A maker of plays.

Plea, plē, *n*. A suit or action at law; that which is alleged in support,

P

justification, or defense; an excuse; a pleading.

Plead, plēd, *vi.* (pleading, pleaded or pled). To argue in support of or against a claim; to present an answer to the declaration of a plaintiff; to supplicate with earnestness; to urge.—*vt.* To discuss and defend; to argue; to offer in excuse; to allege in a legal defense.

Pleasant, ple'zant, *a.* Pleasing; agreeable; grateful; humorous; sportive.

Please, plēz, *vt.* (pleasing, pleased). To excite agreeable sensations or emotions in; to delight; to gratify; to seem good to.—*vi.* To give pleasure; to be kind enough.

Pleasurable, ple'zhūr-a-bl, *a.* Pleasing; giving pleasure; affording gratification.

Pleasure, ple'zhūr, *n.* The gratification of the senses or of the mind; agreeable emotion; delight; joy; approbation; choice; will; purpose; command; arbitrary will or choice.

Plebeian, ple-bē'an, *a.* Pertaining to the common people; vulgar; common.—*n.* One of the lower ranks of men; one of the common people of ancient Rome.

Plenipotent, ple-nip'o-tent, *a.* Possessing full power.

Plenipotentiary, ple'ni-pō-ten''shi-a-ri, *n.* A person with full power to act for another; an ambassador with full power.—*a.* Containing or invested with full power.

Plentiful, plen'ti-ful, *a.* Being in plenty or abundance; copious; ample; abundant.

Plenty, plen'ti, *n.* Abundance; copiousness; sufficiency.—*a.* Plentiful; abundant.

Pliant, plī'ant, *a.* Pliable; readily yielding to force or pressure without breaking; flexible; plastic; limber.

Pliers, plī'ėrz, *n.pl.* A small pair of pincers for bending wire, etc.

Plight, plīt, *vi.* To pledge, as one's word or honor; to give as a security; never applied to property or goods.—*n.* A pledge; a solemn promise; predicament; risky or dangerous state.

Plinth, plinth, *n.* A flat square slab, serving as the foundation of a column or pedestal.

Pliocene, plī'ō-sēn, *a.* and *n.* A term applied to the most modern division of the tertiary strata.

Plod, plod, *vi.* (plodding, plodded). To trudge or walk heavily; to toil; to drudge.—*vt.* To accomplish by toilsome exertion.

Plot, plot, *n.* A small piece of ground; a plan, as of a field, etc., on paper; a scheme; a conspiracy; the story of a play, novel, etc.—*vt.* (plotting, plotted). To make a plan of; to devise.—*vi.* To conspire; to contrive a plan.

Plow, plou, *n.* An instrument for turning up the soil.—*vt.* To turn up with the plow; to make grooves in; to run through, as in sailing.—*vi.* To turn up the soil with a plow; to use a plow.

Plum, plum, *n.* A fleshy fruit containing a kernel; the tree producing it; a raisin; a handsome sum or fortune generally.

Plumage, plöm'āj, *n.* The feathers of a bird.

Plumb, plum, *n.* A plummet; a perpendicular position.—*a.* Perpendicular.—*adv.* In a perpendicular direction.—*vt.* To set perpendicularly; to sound with a plummet; to ascertain the capacity of; to sound.

Plump, plump, *a.* Fat; stout; chubby.—*vt.* To make plump; to dilate.—*vi.* To plunge or fall like a heavy mass; to fall suddenly; to vote for only one candidate.—*adv.* Suddenly; at once; flatly.

Plunder, plun'dėr, *vt.* To deprive of goods or valuables; to pillage; to spoil.—*n.* Robbery; pillage; spoil; booty.

Plunge, plunj, *vt.* (plunging, plunged). To thrust into water or other fluid; to immerse; to thrust or push; to cast or involve.—*vi.* To dive or rush into water, etc.; to pitch or throw oneself headlong; to throw the body forward and the hind-legs up, as a horse.—*n.* Act of plunging into water, etc.; act of throwing oneself headlong, like an unruly horse.

Plunger, plunj´ėr, *n*. One who or that which plunges; a diver; a solid cylinder used as a piston in pumps.

Plus, plus, *n*. A character (+) noting addition.

Plush, plush, *n*. A textile fabric with a velvet nap on one side.

Plutocrat, plö´to-krat, *n*. A person possessing power on account of his riches.

Plutonium, plö-tōn´i-um, *n*. An element got from uranium by bombarding it with neutrons.

Pluvial, plö´vi-al, *a*. Relating to rain; rainy.

Ply, plī, *vt*. (plying, plied). To employ with diligence; to work at; to assail briskly; to beset; to press.—*vi*. To work steadily; to go in haste; to run regularly between any two ports, as a vessel.—*n*. A fold; a plait.

Pneumatic, nū-mat´ik, *a*. Pertaining to air; moved or played by means of air; filled with or fitted to contain air.

Pneumatics, nū-mat´iks, *n*. That branch of physics which treats of the mechanical properties of elastic fluids and particularly of air.

Pneumonia, nū-mō´ni-a, *n*. An inflammation of the lungs.

Poach, pōch,*vt*. To cook (eggs) by breaking and pouring among boiling water; to pierce; to tread or stamp.—*vt*. To encroach on another's ground to steal game; to kill game contrary to law; to be or become swampy.

Poetic, poetical, pō-et´ik, pō-et´ik-al, *a*. Pertaining or suitable to poetry; expressed in poetry or measure; possessing the peculiar beauties of poetry.

Poetry, pō´et-ri, *n*. The language of the imagination or emotions expressed rhythmically; the artistic expression of thought in emotional language; whatever appeals to the sense of ideal beauty; verse; poems.

Poignant, poin´ant, *a*. Sharp to the taste; pointed; keen; bitter; severe; piercing.

Point, point, *n*. The sharp end of anything; a small headland; sting

of an epigram; telling force of expression; exact spot; verge; stage; degree; a mark of punctuation; a mark or dot; end or purpose; characteristic; argument; (cricket) fielder square with wicket on off side; *pl*. The movable guiding rails at junctions on railways.—*vt*. To make pointed; to aim; to indicate; to punctuate; to fill the joints of with mortar.—*vi*. To direct the finger to an object; to indicate the presence of game, as dogs do; to show distinctly.

Point-blank, point-blangk, *a*. and *adv*. Having a horizontal direction; direct; express.

Poise, poiz, *n*. Weight; balance; that which balances.—*vt*. (poising, poised). To balance in weight; to hold in equilibrium.—*vi*. To be balanced or suspended; to depend.

Poison, poi´zn, *n*. Any agent capable of producing a morbid effect on anything endowed with life.—*vi*. To infect with poison; to taint, impair, or corrupt.

Polarize, pō-lėr-īz, *vt*. To communicate polarity or polarization to.

Pole, pōl, *n*. A long piece of wood; a measure of 5½ yards or 30¼ square yards; one of the extremities of the axis of the celestial sphere or the earth; the pole-star; one of the two points in a magnet in which the power seems concentrated; (with cap.) a native of Poland.—*vt*. (poling, poled). To furnish with poles; to impel by poles.

Police, pō-lēs´, *n*. The internal government of a community; a body of civil officers for enforcing order, cleanliness, etc.—*vt*. (policing, policed). To guard or regulate by police.

Policy, po´li-si, *n*. The governing a city, state, or nation; line of conduct with respect to foreign or internal affairs; dexterity of management; pleasure-grounds around a mansion; contract of insurance.

Politician, po-li-ti´shan, *n*. One versed in or occupying himself with politics.

Politics, po´li-tiks, *n*. The science of government; political affairs, or the contests of parties for power.

Pollute, pol-lūt', *vt.* (polluting, polluted). To defile; to profane; to taint morally; to debauch.

Pollution, pol-ū'shon, *n.* Act of polluting; defilement; uncleanness.

Polo, pō'lō, *n.* A game at ball resembling hockey, played on horseback.

Polytechnic, po-li-tek'nik, *a.* Comprehending many arts; designating a school teaching many branches of art or science.—*n.* A school of instruction in arts.

Polytheism, po'li-thē-izm, *n.* The doctrine of a plurality of gods.

Pomade, pō-'mäd', *n.* Perfumed ointment; pomatum.

Pomander, pom'an-dėr, *n.* A perfume ball.

Pomegranate, pōm'gran-āt, *n.* A fruit of the size of an orange, containing numerous seeds; the tree producing the fruit.

Pommel, pum'el, *n.* A knob or ball; the knob on the hilt of a sword; the protuberant part of a saddlebow.—*vt.* (pommelling, pommelled). To beat; to belabor.

Pomp, pomp, *n.* A showy procession; display; pageantry; splendor; parade.

Pomposity, pom-pos'i-ti, *n.* Ostentation; vainglorious show.

Pompous, pomp'us, *a.* Displaying pomp; showy; ostentatious; high-flown.

Pond, pond, *n.* A body of water less than a lake, artificial or natural.

Ponder, pon'dėr, *vt.* To weigh in the mind; to consider.—*vi.* To deliberate.

Ponderous, pon'dėr-us, *a.* Heavy; weighty; massive.

Pontiff, pon'tif, *n.* A high-priest; applied particularly to the pope.

Pontifical, pon-tif'ik-al, *a.* Belonging to a high-priest or to the pope.—*n.* A book containing rites performable by a bishop; *pl.* the dress of a priest or bishop.

Pontoon, pon-tön, *n.* A kind of boat for supporting temporary bridges; a water-tight structure to assist in raising submerged vessels.

Pop, pop, *n.* A small, smart sound.—

vi. (popping, popped). To make a small, smart sound; to enter or issue forth suddenly.—*vt.* To offer with a quick sudden motion; to thrust or push suddenly.—*adv.* Suddenly.

Popular, po'pū-lėr, *a.* Pertaining to the common people; familiar; plain; liked by people in general; prevalent.

Popularize, po'pū-lėr-īz, *vi.* To make popular or suitable to the common mind; to spread among the people.

Populate, po'pū-lāt, *vt.* To people; to furnish with inhabitants.

Population, po-pū-lā'shon, *n.* Act or process of populating; number of people in a country, etc.; the inhabitants.

Porcelain, pōr'se-lān, *n.* The finest species of pottery ware.

Porch, pōrch, *n.* A portico; covered approach at the entrance of buildings.

Porcine, pōr'sīn, *a.* Pertaining to swine; like a swine; hog-like.

Porcupine, por'kū-pīn, *n.* A rodent animal, about 2 feet long, with erectile spines.

Pore, pōr, *n.* A minute opening in the skin, through which the perspirable matter passes; a small interstice.—*vi.* (poring, pored). To look with steady attention; to read or examine with perseverance.

Pork, pōrk, *n.* The flesh of swine, fresh or salted, used for food.

Pornography, por-nog'ra-fi, *n.* Literature in which prostitutes figure.

Portable, pōrt'a-bl, *a.* That may be carried; not bulky or heavy.

Portage, pōrt'āj, *n.* Act of carrying; carriage; freight.

Portal, pōrt'al, *n.* A door or gate; the main entrance of a cathedral, etc.—*a.* Belonging to a vein connected with the liver.

Portend, por-tend', *vt.* To foretoken; to presage; to threaten.

Portent, pōr'tent, *n.* That which foretokens; an omen of ill.

Portentous, por-tent'us, *a.* Ominous; foreshowing ill; monstrous; wonderful.

Porter, pōr'tėr, *n.* A doorkeeper; a carrier; a dark brown malt liquor.

Portfolio, pŏrt-fō′li-ō, *n.* A case for drawings, papers, etc.; office and functions of a minister of state.

Portuguese, por′tū-gēz, *a.* Pertaining to Portugal.—*n.* The language of Portugal; the people of Portugal.

Pose, pōz, *n.* Attitude or position; an artistic posture.—*vi.* (posing, posed). To attitudinize; to assume characteristic airs.—*vt.* To cause to assume a certain posture; to state or lay down; to perplex or puzzle.

Position, pō-zi′shon, *n.* State of being placed; place; posture; rank; state; principle laid down; thesis.

Positive, poz′it-iv, *a.* Definitely laid down; explicit; absolute; actual; confident; dogmatic; affirmative; noting the simple state of an adjective; applied to the philosophical system of Auguste Comte, which limits itself to human experience; applied to electricity produced by rubbing a vitreous substance.—*n.* That which is positive; the positive degree.

Possess, po-zes′, *vt.* To have and hold; to own; to affect by some power or influence; to pervade; to put in possession; to furnish or fill.

Post, pōst, *n.* A piece of timber, etc., set upright; a place assigned; a military or other station; office or employment; a carrier of letters, messages, etc.; a system for the public conveyance of letters, etc.; a post-office; a size of paper, about 18 or 19 inches by 15.—*vt.* To travel with post-horses; to hasten on.—*vt.* To place; to place in the post-office; to transfer (accounts or items) to the ledger; to make master of full details; to fix up in some public place.—*a.* Used in travelling quickly.—*adv.* Travelling as a post; swiftly.

Postage, pōst′āj, *n.* The charge for conveying letters or other articles by post.

Post-date, pōst-dāt′, *vt.* To inscribe with a later date than the real one.

Poster, pōst′ėr, *n.* One who posts; a courier; a large printed bill for advertising.

Posterior, pos-tē′ri-or, *a.* Later or subsequent; hinder.—*n.* A hinder part; *pl.* the hinder parts of an animal.

Posterity, pos-te′ri-ti, *n.* Descendants; succeeding generations.

Post-office, pōst′of-is, *n.* An office where letters are received for transmission; a government department that has the duty of conveying letters, etc.

Postpone, pōst-pōn′, *vt.* (postponing, postponed). To put off to a later time; to set below something else in value.

Pot, pot, *n.* A metallic or earthenware vessel more deep than broad; the quantity contained in a pot; a sort of paper of small-sized sheets.—*vt.* (potting, potted). To put in a pot; to preserve in pots; to plant in a pot of earth.

Potent, pō′tent, *a.* Mighty; strong; powerful; efficacious.

Potentate, pō′ten-tāt, *n.* One who possesses great power or sway; a monarch.

Potential, pō-ten′shal, *a.* Possible; latent; that may be manifested.

Potter, pot′ėr, *n.* One who makes earthenware vessels or crockery.—*vi.* To busy oneself about trifles; to move slowly.

Pottery, pot′ė-ri, *n.* The ware made by potters; place where earthen vessels are made.

Pouch, pouch, *n.* A pocket; a small bag.—*vt.* To put into a pouch; to pocket.

Poultice, pōl′tis, *n.* A soft composition applied to sores.—*vt.* (poulticing, poulticed). To apply a poultice to.

Poultry, pōl′tri, *n.* Domestic fowls.

Pounce, pouns, *n.* A fine powder to prevent ink from spreading on paper; the claw or talon of a bird.—*vt.* (pouncing, pounced). To sprinkle or rub with pounce.—*vi.* To fall on and seize with the pounces or talons; to fall on suddenly.

Pound, pound, *n.* A standard weight of 12 ounces troy or 16 ounces avoirdupois; a money of account; an inclosure for cattle.—*vt.* To confine in a public pound; to beat; to pulverize.

Pour, pōr, *vt.* To flow or issue forth in

P

a stream.—*vt*. To let flow out or in; to emit; to throw in profusion.

Pout, pout, *vi*. To thrust out the lips; to look sullen; to be prominent.—*n*. Protrusion of the lips.

Poverty, po'vėr-ti, *n*. State of being poor; indigence; want; defect; insufficiency.

Powder, pou'dėr, *n*. A dry substance of minute particles; dust; gunpowder.—*vt*. To reduce to fine particles; to sprinkle with powder; to corn, as meat.—*vi*. To fall to dust; to use powder for the hair or face.

Power, pou'ėr, *n*. Ability to act or do; strength; influence; talent; command; authority; one who exercises authority; a state or government; warrant; a mechanical advantage or effect; product of the multiplication of a number by itself.

Practicable, prak'ti-ka-bl, *a*. That may be done or effected; feasible; passable.

Practical, prak'ti-kal, *a*. Pertaining to practice, action, or use; not merely theoretical; skilled in actual work.

Practice, prak'tis, *n*. A doing or effecting; custom; habit; actual performance; exercise of any profession; medical treatment; training; drill; dexterity.

Practice, prak'tis, *vt*. (practicing, practiced). To put in practice; to do or perform frequently or habitually; to exercise, as any profession; to commit; to teach by practice.—*vi*. To perform certain acts frequently for instruction or amusement; to exercise some profession.

Prance, prans, *vt*. (prancing, pranced). To spring, leap, or caper, as a horse; to strut about ostentatiously.

Prank, prangk, *vt*. To adorn in a showy manner; to dress up.—*vi*. To have a showy appearance.—*n*. A merry trick; a caper.

Prate, prāt, *vi*. (prating, prated). To babble, chatter, tattle.—*vt*. To utter foolishly.—*n*. Trifling talk; unmeaning loquacity.

Prattle, prat'l, *vi*. (prattling, prattled). To talk much and idly, like a child; to prate.—*n*. Trifling or puerile talk.

Pray, prā, *vi*. and *t*. To beg, supplicate, or implore; to address God.

Prayer, prā'ėr, *n*. One who prays; the act of praying; a petition; a solemn petition to God; a formula of worship, public or private; that part of a written petition whihc specifies the thing desired to be granted.

Preach, prēch, *vi*. To deliver a sermon; to give earnest advice.—*vt*. To proclaim; to publish in religious discourses; to deliver in public, as a discourse.

Precedent, prē-sēd'ent, *a*. Preceding; going before in time; anterior.

Precedent, prē' or pre'sē-dent, *n*. Something done or said, serving as an example or rule.

Precept, prē'sept, *n*. Anything enjoined as an authoritative rule of action; injunction; doctrine; maxim.

Precipitate, prē'si'pi-tāt, *vt*. and *i*. To throw or hurl headlong; to hasten excessively; to cause to sink or to fall to the bottom of a vessel, as a substance in solution.—*a*. Headlong; overhasty.—*n*. A substance deposited from a liquid in which it has been dissolved.

Precognition, prē-kog-ni'shon, *n*. Previous knowledge; preliminary examination, as of a witness befor a trial (*Scots law*).

Preconceive, prē-kon-sēv', *vt*. To form a conception or opinion of beforehand.

Precursor, prē-kėr'sėr, *n*. A forerunner; a harbinger.

Predestine, prē-des'tin, *vt*. To decree beforehand; to foreordain.

Predetermination, prē-dē-tėr'minā''shon, *n*. Purpose formed beforehand.

Predicable, pre'di-ka-bl, *a*. That may be attributed to something.—*n*. Anythng that may be affirmed of another.

Predicament, prē-dik'a-ment, *n*. Class or kind; condition; dangerous or trying state.

Predicate, pre'di-kāt, *vt*. and *i*. To affirm one thing of another; to assert.—*n*. In *logic*, that which is affirmed or denied of the subject; in *grammar*, the word or words which express what is affirmed or denied of the subject.

Predict, prē-dikt´, *vt.* To foretell; to prophesy.

Predominate, prē-dom´i-nāt, *vi.* and *t.* To have surpassing power or authority; to rule.

Pre-eminent, prē-em´i-nent, *a.* Eminent above others; surpassing or distinguished.

Pre-emption, prē-em´shon, *n.* The act or right of purchasing before others.

Preen, prēn, *vt.* To trim with the beak: said of birds dressing their feathers.

Pre-exist, prē-egz-ist´, *vi.* To exist beforehand, or before something else.

Prefabricate, prē-fab´ri-kāt, *vt.* To manufacture separately parts, of a building, etc., designed to be easily fitted together afterwards.

Preface, pre´fās, *n.* Introduction to a discourse or book, etc.—*vt.* (prefacing, prefaced). To introduce by preliminary remarks.

Prefect, prē´fekt, *n.* One placed over others; a governor, chief magistrate; a senior pupil entrusted with the maintenance of discipline.

Prefer, prē-fėr´, *vt.* (preferring, preferred). To bring or lay before; to present, as a petition, etc.; to exalt; to set higher in estimation; to choose rather.

Preference, pre´fėr-ens, *n.* Act of preferring; state of being preferred; choice.

Prehensible, prē-hen´si-bl, *a.* That may be seized.

Prehensile, prē-hen´sīl, *a.* Fitted for seizing or laying hold; grasping.

Prehistoric, prē-his-tor´ik, *a.* Relating to a time anterior to written records.

Prejudge, prē-juj´, *vt.* To judge beforehand; to condemn unheard.

Prejudice, pre´jū-dis, *n.* An unwarranted bias; prepossession; detriment; injury.—*vt.* To blas the mind of; to do harm to.

Preliminary, prē-lim´in-a-ri, *a.* Introductory; preparatory; prefac-

tory.—*n.* Something introductory; preface; prelude.

Prelude, prel´ūd or prē-lūd´, *vt.* (preluding, preluded). To introduce; to preface.—*vi.* To form a prelude.—*n.* prel´ūd or prē´lūd. Something preparatory; a musical introduction.

Premium, prē´mi-um, *n.* A reward or prize; a bonus; a bounty; sum paid for insurance; increase in value.

Premonition, prē-mō-ni´shon, *n.* Previous warning, notice, or information.

Preoccupation, prē-ok´kū-pā´´shon, *n.* Act of preoccupying; prior possession; state of being preoccupied.

Preoccupy, prē-ok´kū-pī, *vt.* To occupy before another; to engross before another; to engross beforehand.

Preordain, prē-or-dān´, *vt.* To appoint beforehand; to foreordain.

Preparation, pre-pa-rā´shon, *n.* Act or operation of preparing; that which is prepared; state of being prepared.

Prepare, prē-pār´, *vt.* and *i.* (preparing, prepared). To make ready; to adjust; to provide; to procure as suitable.

Preposterous, prē-pos´tėr-us, *a.* Absurd; irrational; monstrous; utterly ridiculous.

Prerogative, prē-ro´ga-tiv, *n.* A prior claim or title; an exclusive privilege; an official and hereditary right.

Presage, prē´sāj or pres´āj, *n.* a presentiment; a prognostic, omen, or sign.—*vt.* and *i.* prē-sāj´, (presaging, presaged). To betoken; to forebode; to predict.

Prescribe, prē-skrīb´, *vt.* (prescribing, prescribed). To lay down authoritatively for direction; to appoint; to direct to be used as a remedy.—*vi.* To give directions; to give medical directions; to become of no validity through lapse of time.

Prescription, prē-skrip´shon, *n.* Act of prescribing; that which is prescribed; a claim or title based on long use; the loss of a legal right by lapse of time.

Prescriptive, prē-skrip'tiv, *a.* Consisting in or acquired by long use.

Presence, pre'zens, *n.* State of being present; existence in a certain place; company; sight; port; mien; the person of a great personage; an appearance or apparition; readiness.

Present, pre'zent, *a.* Being at hand, in view, or in a certain place; now existing; ready at hand; quick in emergency.—*n.* Present time; *pl.* term used in a legal document for the document itself.

Present, prē-zent', *vt.* To introduce to or bring before a superior; to show; to give or bestow; to nominate to an ecclesiastical benefice; to lay before a public body for consideration; to point or aim, as a weapon.—*n.* pre'zent. A donation; a gift.

Preside, prē-zīd', *vi.* (presiding, presided). To exercise authority or superintendence; to have the post of chairman.

President, pre'zi-dent, *n.* One who presides; the head of a province or state; the highest officer of state in a republic.

Press, pres, *vt.* To bear or weigh heavily upon; to squeeze; to urge; to enforce; to emphasize; to solicit earnestly; to force into service.—*vi.* To bear heavily or with force; to crowd; to push with force.—*n.* A pressing; a crowd; an instrument for squeezing or crushing; a machine for printing; the art or business of printing; periodical literature; an upright cupboard; urgency.

Presume, prē-zūm', *vt.* (presuming, presumed). To take for granted; to take the liberty; to make bold.—*vi.* To infer; to act in a forward way.

Presumptuous, prē-zum'tū-us, *a.* Taking undue liberties; arrogant; overweening.

Presuppose, prē-sup-pōz', *vt.* To suppose or imply as previous; to take for granted.

Pretend, prē-tend', *vt.* To feign; to simulate; to assume or profess to feel; use as a pretest.—*vi.* To assume a false character; to sham;

to put in a claim.

Prevail, prē-vāl', *vi.* To gain the victory or superiority; to be in force; to succeed; to gain over by persuasion.

Prevalent, pre'va-lent, *a.* Prevailing; predominant; extensively existing.

Prevaricate, prē-va'ri-kāt, *vi.* To act or speak evasively; to shuffle; to quibble.

Prey, prā, Property taken from an enemy; spoil; booty; a victim.—*vi.* To take prey or booty; to get food by rapine; to cause to pine away; with *on.*

Price, prīs, *n.* The value which a seller sets on his goods; cost; value; worthy.—*vt.* (pricing, priced). To set a price on; to ask the price of.

Priceless, prīs'les, *a.* Too valuable to admit of a price; invaluable; inestimable.

Prick, prik, *n.* A slender pointed thing that can pierce; a thorn; a puncture by a prick; a sting; tormenting thought.—*vt.* To pierce with a prick; to erect, as ears; to spur; to sting with remorse; to trace by puncturing.—*vi.* To spur on; to ride rapidly; to feel a prickly sensation.

Prickle, prik'l, *n.* A small sharp-pointed shoot; a thorn; a small spine.—*vt.* To prick; to cause a prickly feeling in.

Pride, prīd, *n.* State or quality of being proud; inordinate self-esteem; a cause of pride; glory or delight; highest pitch; splendid show.—*vt.* To indulge pride; to value (oneself).

Priest, prēst, *n.* A man who officiates in sacred offices; a clergyman above a deacon and below a bishop.

Prima facie, prī'ma fā'shi-ē. At first view or appearance.

Primal, prī'mal, *a.* Primary; primitive.

Primary, prī'ma-ri, *a.* First; chief; first in time; original; elementary; radical.—*n.* That which stands first or highest in importance; a large feather of a bird's wing.

Primate, prī'māt, *n.* A chief ecclesiastic; an archbishop.

Prime, prīm, *a.* Foremost; first; original; first in rank, excellence, or importance; not divisible by any smaller number.—*n.* The earliest stage; full health; strength; or beauty; the best part.—*vt.* (priming, primed). To make ready for action; to supply with powder for communicating fire to a charge; to instruct or prepare beforehand; to lay on the first color in painting.

Primeval, prīm-ē'val, *a.* Being of the earliest age or time; original; primitive.

Priming, prīm'ing, *n.* The powder used to ignite a charge; a first layer of paint; water carried over with the steam into the cylinder.

Primitive, prim'it-iv, *a.* Being the first or earliest of its kind; original; antiquated; primary; radical; not derived.—*n.* That which is original; an original word.

Principal, prin'si-pal, *a.* First; chief; most important or considerable.—*n.* A chief or head; the president, governor, or chief in authority; one primarily engaged; a capital sum lent on interest.

Principality, prin-si-pal'i-ti, *n.* Sovereignty; territory of a prince; a prince.

Principally, prin'si-pal-li, *adv.* Chiefly; mainly.

Principle, prin'si-pl, *n.* Cause or origin; a general truth; a fundamental law; a rule of action; uprightness; an element.

Print, print, *vt.* To mark by pressure; to stamp; to form or copy by pressure; as from types, etc.—*vi.* To use or practice typography; to publish.—*n.* A mark made by pressure; an engraving, etc.; state of being printed; a newspaper; printed calico.

Printer, print'ėr, *n.* One who prints; more especially, the printer of letterpress.

Prison, pri'zn, *n.* A place of confinement; a jail.—*vt.* To imprison.

Pristine, pris'tīn, *a.* Original; first; earliest.

Private, prī'vat, *a.* Separate from others; solitary; personal; secret; not having a public or official character.—**In private,** secretly.—

n. A common soldier.

Privy, pri'vi, *a.* Private; assigned to private uses; secret; privately knowing (with *to*).—*n.* A water-closet or necessary house.

Prize, prīz, *n.* That which is seized; that which is deemed a valuable acquisition; a reward.—*vt.* (prizing, prized). To value highly.

Prize-fight, prīz'fīt, *n.* A boxing-match for a prize.

Probability, pro-ba-bil'i-ti, *n.* Likelihood; appearance of truth.

Probate, prō'bāt, *n.* The proceeding by which a person's will is established and registered; official proof of a will.

Probity, prō'bi-ti, *n.* Uprightness; honesty; rectitude; integrity.

Problem, prob'lem, *n.* A question proposed for solution; a knotty point to be cleared up.

Proboscis, prō-bos'is, *n.*; pl. **Proboscides,** prō-bos'i-dēz. The snout or trunk of an elephant, etc.; the sucking-tube of insects.

Procedure, prō-sēd'ūr, *n.* Act or manner of proceeding; conduct; management.

Proceed, prō-sēd', *vi.* To go forth or forward; to issue, arise, emanate; to prosecute any design; to carry on a legal action; to take a university degree.

Proclamation, pro-kla-mā'shon, *n.* Act of claiming; an official public announcement.

Proclivity, prō-kliv'i-ti, *n.* Inclination; propensity; tendency.

Procrastinate, prō-kras'ti-nāt, *vt.* and *i.* To put off from day to day; to postpone.

Procreate, prō'krē-āt, *vt.* To beget; to generate; to engender.

Prod, prod, *n.* A pointed instrument, as a goad; a stab.—*vt.* (prodding, prodded). To prick with a pointed instrument; to goad.

Prodigal, prod'i-gal, *a.* Lavish; wasteful.—*n.* A waster; a spendthrift.

Prodigality, prod-i-gal'i-ti, *n.* Extravagance in expenditure; profusion; waste.

Prodigious, prō-dij'us, *a.* Portentous; extraordinary; huge; enormous.

P

Prodigy, prod'i-ji, *n.* A portent; a wonder or miracle; a monster.

Produce, prō-dūs'v, *vt.* (producing, produced). To bring forward; to exhibit; to bring forth, bear, yield; to supply; to cause; to extend, as a line.—*n.* prō'dūs, What is produced; outcome; yield; agricultural products.

Product, pro'dukt, *n.* That which is produced; result; effect; number resulting from multiplication.

Production, prō-duk'shon, *n.* Act or process of producing; product; performance; literary composition.

Productive, prō-duk'tiv, *a.* Having the power of producing; fertile; causing to exist; producing commodities of value.

Profane, prō-fān', *a.* Not sacred; secular; irreverent; blasphemous; impure.—*vt.* (profaning, profaned). To treat with irreverence; to desecrate.

Profanity, prō-fan'i-ti, *n.* Quality of being profane; profane language or conduct.

Profess, prō-fes', *vt.* To avow; to ackowledge; to declare belief in; to pretend; to declare oneself versed in.—*vi.* To declare openly.

Profession, prō-fe'shon, *n.* Act of professing; declaration; vocation; such as medicine, law; etc.; the body of persons engaged in such calling.

Professional, prō-fe'shon-al, *a.* Pertaining to a profession.—*n.* A member of any profession; one who makes a living by arts, sports, etc., in which amateurs engage.

Profit, pro'fit', *n.* Any advantage, benefit, or gain; pecuniary gain.—*vt.* To benefit; to advance.—*vi.* To derive profit; to improve; to be made better or wiser.

Profitable, pro'fit-a-bl, *a.* Bringing profit or gain; lucrative; beneficial; useful.

Profligate, pro'fli-gāt, *a.* Abandoned to vice; utterly dissolute.—*n.* A depraved man.

Profound, prō-found', *a.* Deep; deep in skill or knowledge; far-reaching; bending low; humble.—*n.* The ocean, the abyss.

Program, prō'gram, *n.* A plan of proceedings; statement of the order of proceedings in any entertainment.

Progress, prō'gres, *n.* A going forward; a journey of state; a circuit; advance; development.—*vi.* prō-gres'. To advance; to improve.

Progressive, prō-gres'iv, *a.* Making steady progress; advancing; advocating progress.

Prohibit, prō-hib'it, *vt.* To forbid; to interdict by authority; to prevent.

Projector, prō-jek'tor, *n.* One who plans; that which casts something forward.

Prolapse, Prolapsus, prō-laps', prō-lap'sus, *n.* A falling down of some internal organ from its proper position.

Prolegomenon, prō-le-gom'e-non, *n.*; pl. **-mena.** A preliminary observation; *pl.* an introduction.

Prolepsis, prō-lep'sis, *n.* Something of the nature of an anticipation; a rhetorical figure.

Proletarian, prō-le-tā'ri-an, *n.* and *a.* Applied to a member of the poorest class.

Promenade, pro-me-näd', *n.* A walk for pleasure; a place set apart for walking.—*vi.* (promenading, promenaded). To walk for pleasure.

Prominent, pro'mi-nent, *a.* Jutting out; protuberant; eminent.

Promiscuous, prō-mis'kū-us, *a.* Confused; indiscriminate; miscellaneous.

Promise, pro'mis, *n.* A statement binding the person who makes it; ground or basis of expectation; pledge.—*vt.* (promising, promised). To make a promise of; to afford reason to expect.—*vi.* To make a promise; to afford expectations.

Promissory, pro'mis-o-ri, *a.* Containing a promise or binding declaration.

Promontory, pro'mon-to-ri, *n.* A headland; a cape.

Promote, prō-mōt', *vt.* (promoting, promoted). To forward or further; to advance; to encourage; to exalt; to form (a company).

Pronoun, prō'noun, *n*. A word used instead of a noun.

Pronounce, prō-nouns', *vt.* and *i* (pronouncing, pronounced). To articulate by the organs of speech; to utter formally; to declare or affirm.

Pronounced, prō-nounst', *p.a.* Strongly marked or defined; decided; glaring.

Proof, pröf, *n*. Something which tests; trial; what serves to convince; evidence; firmness; a certain standard of strength in spirit; an impression in printing for correction; early impression of an engraving.—*a*. Impenetrable; able to resist.

Prop, prop, *n*. A body that supports a weight; a support.—*vt*. (propping, propped). To support by a prop; to sustain generally.

Propaganda, pro-pa-gan'da, *n*. An institution or system for propagating any doctrine.

Propagate, pro'pa-gāt, *vt*. To multiply by generation or reproduction; to diffuse; to increase.—*vi*. To have young or issue; to be multiplied by generation, etc.

Propel, prō-pel', *vt*. (propelling, propeled). To drive, push, or thrust forward.

Prophet, pro'fet, *n*. One who foretells future events.

Prophylactic, prō-fi-lak'tik, *a*. Preventive of disease.—*n*. A medicine which preserves against disease.

Propinquity, prō-pin'kwi-ti, *n*. Nearness; vicinity; kindred.

Propitiation, prō-pi'shi-ā''shon, *n*. Act of propitiating or what propitiates; atonement.

Propitiatory, prō-pi'shi-a-to-ri, *a*. Having the power to make propitious; conciliatory.—*n*. Among the Jews, the mercy-seat.

Propitious, prō-pi'shus, *a*. Favorable; disposed to be gracious or merciful.

Proportion, pro-pōr'shon, *n*. Comparative relation; relative size and arrangement; symmetry; just or equal share; lot; that rule which enables us to find a fourth proportional to three numbers.—*vt*. To adjust in due proportion; to form with symmetry.

Proprietary, prō-prī'e-ta-ri, *a*. Belonging to a proprietor.—*n*. A proprietor; a body of proprietors.

Proprietor, pro-prī'e-tor, *n*. An owner; one who has legal right to anything.

Prosecute, pro'se-kūt, *vt*. and *i* (prosecuting, prosecuted). To persist in; to carry on; to pursue at law.

Prosecution, pro-se-kū'shon, *n*. Act of prosecuting; the carrying on of a suit at law; the party by whom criminal proceedings are instituted.

Proselyte, pro'se-līt, *n*. A convert to the Jewish faith; a new convert.—*vt*. To make a convert of.

Prospect, pros'pekt, *n*. A distant view; sight; scene; outlook; exposure; expectation.—*vt*. and *i*. prospekt'. To make search for precious stones or metals.

Prostitute, pros'ti-tūt, *vt*. (prostituting, prostituted). To offer publicly for lewd purposes for hire; to devote to anything base.—*a*. Openly devoted to lewdness.—*n*. A female given to indiscrimate lewdness.

Prostitution, pros-ti-tū'shon, *n*. Practice of offering the body to indiscriminate intercourse with men; debasement.

Prostrate, pros'trāt, *a*. Lying with the body flat; lying at mercy.—*vt*. (prostrating, prostrated). To lay flat or prostrate; to bow in reverence; to overthrow; to ruin.

Protean, prō'tē-an, *a*. Assuming different shapes; variable; changeable.

Protect, prō-tekt', *vt*. To shield from danger, injury, etc.; to guard against foreign competition by tariff regulations.

Protection, prō-tek'shon, *n*. Act of protecting; shelter; defence; the system of favoring articles of home production by duties on foreign articles.

Protect, prō-test', *vi*. To affirm with solemnity; to make a formal declaration of opposition.—*vt*. To assert; to mark for non-payment, as a bill.—*n*. prō'test. A formal declaration of dissent; a declaration

P

that payment of a bill has been refused.

Protestant, pro'test-ant, n. One of the party who adhered to Luther at the Reformation; a member of a reformed church.—a. Belonging to the religion of the Protestants.

Protocol, prō'tō-kol, n. A diplomatic document serving as a preliminary to diplomatic transactions.

Protrude, prō-tröd', vt. and i (protruding, protruded). To thrust forward; to project.

Protuberance, prō-tū'bėr-ans, n. A swelling or tumor; a prominence; a knob.

Protuberant, prō-tū'bėr-ant, a. Swelling; bulging out.

Proud, proud, a. Having a high opinion of oneself; haughty; of fearless spirit; ostentatious; magnificent.—**Proud flesh,** an excessive granulation in wounds or ulcers.

Prove, pröv, vt. (proving, proved). To try by experiment; to test; to establish the truth or reaity of; to demonstrate; to obtain probate of.—vi. To be found by experience or trial; to turn out to be.

Provident, pro'vi-dent, a. Foreseeing and providing for wants; prudent; frugal.

Province, pro'vins, n. A territory at some distance from the metropolis; a large political division; sphere of action; department.

Provincial, pro-vin'shal, a. Pertaining to or forming a province; characteristic of the people of a province; rustic.—n. A person belonging to a province.

Provision, prō-vi'zhon, n. Act of providing; preparaton; stores provided; victuals; stipulation; proviso.—vt. To supply with provisions.

Provisional, prō-vi'zhon-al, a. Provided for present need; temporary.

Proviso, prō-vī'zō n. An article or clause in any statute or contract; stipulation.

Provocative, prō-vok'a-tiv, a. Serving to provoke; exciting.—n. A stimulant.

Provoke, prō-vōk', vt (provoking, provoked). To incite; to stimulate;

to incense; to irritate.—vi. To produce anger.

Prow, prou, n. The forepart of a ship.

Prowess, prou'es, n. Bravery; boldness and dexterity in war; gallantry.

Prowl, proul, vi. and t. To roam or wander stealthily.—n. Act of one who prowls.

Prune, prön, vt. (pruning, pruned). To trim; to cut or lop off; to clear from superfluities.—n. A plum, particularly a dried plum.

Prurient, prö'ri-ent, a. Itching after something; inclined to lascivious thoughts.

Pry, prī, vi. (prying, pried). To peep narrowly; to look closely; to peer.—n. A keen glance.

Psychic, Psychical, sī'kik, sī'kik-al, a. Belonging to the soul; psychological; pertaining to that force by which spiritualists aver they produce "spiritual" phenomena.

Psychology, sī-kol'o-ji, n. That branch of knowledge which deals with the mind; mental science.

Ptomaine, tō'mān, n. A name of certain substances generated during putrefaction or morbid conditions prior to death.

Puberty, pū'bėr-ti, n. The age at which persons can beget or bear children.

Pubescent, pū-bes'ent, a. Arriving at puberty; covered with fine soft hairs.

Public, pub'lik, a. Not private; pertaining to a whole community; open or free to all; common; notorious.—n. The people, indefinitely.—**In public,** in open view.

Publication, pub-li-kā'shon, n. Act of publishing; announcement; promulgation; act of offering a book, etc., to the public by sale; any book, etc., published.

Publicity, pub-lis'i-ti, n. State of being made public; notoriety; currency.

Publish, pub'lish, vt. To make public; to proclaim, promulgate; to cause to be printed and offered for sale.

Puerperal, pū-ėr'pėr-al, a. Pertaining to childbirth.

Puff, puf, n. A sudden emission of breath; a whiff; a short blast of wind; a puff-ball; piece of light pastry; a consciously exaggerated commendation.—vi. To give a quick blast with the mouth; to breathe hard after exertion.—vt. To drive with a blast; to inflate; to praise extravagantly.

Puff-adder, puf'ad-er, n. A venomous snake which swells out the upper part of its body.

Puff-ball, puf'bal, n. A ball-shaped fungus which when ripe discharges a fine powder.

Pull, pul, vt. To draw towards one; to tug; to rend; to pluck; to gather.—vi. To draw; to tug.—n. Act of pulling; a twitch; act of rowing a boat; a drink; a struggle.

Pullet, pul'et, n. A young hen.

Pulley, pul'i, A small wheel in a block, used in raising weights.

Pulse, puls, n. The beating of the heart or an artery; vibration; leguminous plants or their seeds, as beans, etc.—vi. (pulsing, pulsed). To beat or throb.

Pulverize, pul'ver-īz, vt. To reduce to dust or fine powder.

Puma, pū'ma, n. A carnivorous quadruped of the cat kind; the cougar.

Pumice, pū'mis or pum'is, n. A light and spongy stone, used for polishing.

Pump, pump, n. A machine for raising water or extracting air; a shoe used in dancing.—vi. To work a pump.—vt. To raise with a pump; to free from liquid by a pump; to put artful questions to extract information.

Pumpkin, pump'kin, n. A plant and its fruit; a kind of gourd or vegetable marrow.

Pun, pun, n. A play on words like in sound, but different in meaning; a kind of quibble.—vi. (punning, punned) To make a pun or puns.

Punch, punsh, n. An instrument for driving holes in metal, etc.; a blow or thrust; a beverage of spirits, lemon-juice, water, etc.; a buffoon; a short-legged, barrel-bodied horse; a short fat fellow.—vt. To stamp or perforate with a punch; to hit with the fist.

Punctual, pungk'tū-al, a. Exact; made or done at the exact time.

Punish, pun'ish, vt. To inflict pain or any evil on, as a penalty; to chastise; to hurt.

Punitive, pū-ni-tiv, a. Pertaining to, awarding, or involving punishment.

Punning, pun'ing, p.a. Given to make puns; containing a pun or puns.

Puny, pūn'i, a. Small and weak; petty.

Pup, pup, n. A puppy.—vi. (pupping, pupped). To bring forth whelps.

Pupil, pū'pil, n. A young person under the care of a tutor; the aperture in the iris through which the rays of light pass.

Pupilary, (or -ll-), pū'pil-a-ri, a. Pertaining to a pupil or ward, or to the pupil of the eye.

Puppet, pup'et, n. A small figure in the human form mechanically worked; a person who is a mere tool.

Puppy, pup'i, n. A whelp; a young dog; a conceited, foppish fellow.

Purchase, pèr'chās, vt. (purchasing, purchased). To buy; to obtain by labor, danger, etc.—n. Acquisition of anything by money; what is bought; mechanical advantage.

Pure, pūr, a. Clean; clear; unmixed; spotless; chaste; genuine; sincere; absolute.

Purify, pū'ri-fī, vt. (purifying, purified). To make pure or clear; to free from admixture; to free from guilt.—vi. To become pure or clear.

Purist, pūr'ist, n. One excessively nice in the use of words, etc.

Puritan, pūr'i-tan, n. One very strict in religious matters or in conduct; an early Protestant dissenter from the Church of England.—a. Pertaining to the Puritans.

Purple, pèr'pl, n. A color produced by mixing red and blue; a purple robe, the badge of the Roman emperors; regal power.—a. Of a color made of red and blue; dyed with blood.—vt. (purpling, purpled). To make purple.

P

Purport, pėr'pōrt, n. Meaning; import.—vt. To signify; to profess.

Purpose, pėr'pos, n. End or aim; design; intention; matter in question.—vt. and i. (purposing, purposed). To propose; to intend.

Purr, pėr, vi. To murmur, as a cat when pleased.—n. The sound of a cat when pleased.

Purse, pėrs, n. A small bag or receptacle for money; money collected as a prize or a present; finances.—vt. (pursing, pursed). To put in a purse; to pucker.

Pursuant, pėr-sū'ant, a. Done in prosecution of anything; conformable.

Pursue, pėr-sū', vt. (pursuing, pursued). To follow with a view to overtake; to chase; to use measures to obtain; to carry on.—vi. To go in pursuit; to act as prosecutor.

Pus, pus, n. The soft yellowish substance formed in suppuration; matter of a sore.

Push, push, vt. To press against with force; to thrust or shove; to enforce; to urge; to prosecute energetically.—vi. To make a thrust or effort; to force one's way.—n. Act of pushing; vigorous effort; emergency; enterprise.

Pusillanimous, pū-sil-lan'im-us, a. Without strength of mind; timid; cowardly.

Pustule, pus'tūl, n. A small blister; small elevation of the cuticle, containing pus.

Put, put, vt. (putting, put). To place in any position or situation; to apply; to propose or propound; to state in words.

Put, Putt, put, vt. (putting, putted). To throw (a heavy stone) from the shoulder; in golf, to play the ball into the hole.—n. A rustic; a silly fellow.

Putrefy, pū'trē-fī, vt. (putrefying, putrefied). To render putrid.—vi. To decay; to rot.

Putrescence, pū-tres'ens, n. State of becoming rotten; a putrid state.

Putrid, pū'trid, a. In a state of decay; rotten; corrupt.

Putter, put'ėr, n. One who puts, sets, or places; a kind of golfing club (pron. put'ėr).

Putting-green, put'ing-grēn, n. A smooth piece of sward round a hole in a gold course.

Putty, put'i, n. A paste made of whiting and linseed-oil.—vt. To cement or fill with putty.

Puzzle, puz'l, vt. (puzzling, puzzled). To perplex; to entangle.—vi. To be bewildered.—n. Perplexity; something to try ingenuity.

Puzzling, puz'ling, p.a. Such as to puzzle; perplexing; embarrassing; bewildering.

Pygmy, pig'mi, n. A dwarf; anything little.—a. Dwarfish; little.

Pylorus, pī-lō'rus, n. The lower orifice of the stomach.

Pyramid, pi'ra-mid, n. A solid body having triangular sides meeting in a point at the top.

Pyre, pīr, n. A heap of combustibles for burning a dead body; a funeral pile.

Pyrites, pi-rī'tēz, n. A mineral combining sulphur with iron, copper, cobalt, etc.

Q

Quack, kwak, vi. To cry like a duck; to boast; to practice quackery.—n. The cry of a duck; a pretender to skill or knowledge, especially medical.—a. Pertaining to quackery.

Quackery, kwak'ė-ri, n. Practice or boastful pretenses of a quack, particularly in medicine.

Quadragesima, kwod-ra-je'si-ma, n. Lent.

Quadrangle, kwod-rang-gl, n. A plane figure, have four angles and sides; an inner square of a building.

Quadrennial, kwod-ren'ni-al, a. Comprising four years; occurring once in four years.

Quadrilateral, kwod-ri-lat'ėr-al, a. Having four sides and four angles.—n. A plane figure having four sides and angles.

Quadrillion, kwod-ril'yon, n. The fourth power of a million; a number represented by a unit and 24 ciphers.

Quadruped, kwod'ru̞-ped, *n*. An animal with four legs or feet.

Quadruple, kwod'ru̞-pl, *a*. Fourfold.—*n*. Four times the sum or number.—*vt*. To make fourfold.—*vi*. To become fourfold.

Quaff, kwäf, *vt*. and *i*. To drain to the bottom; to drink copiously.

Qualification, kwo'li-fi-kā''shon, *n*. Act of qualifying; state of being qualified; suitable quality or characteristic; legal power; ability; modification; restriction.

Qualify, kwo'li-fi, *vt*. (qualifying, qualified). To give proper or suitable qualities to; to furnish with the knowledge, skill, etc., necessary; to modify or limit; to soften or moderate; to dilute.—*vi*. To become qualified or fit.

Quality, kwo'li-ti, *n*. Sort, kind, or character; a distinguishing property or characteristic; degree of excellence; high rank.

Qualm, kwäm, *n*. A sudden fit of nausea; a twinge of conscience; compunction.

Quandary, kwon-dā'ri or kwon'da-ri, *n*. A state of perplexity; a predicament.

Quarrel, kwo'rel, *n*. An angry dispute; a brawl; cause of dispute; a dart for a crossbow; a glazier's diamont.—*vi*. (quarrelling, quarelled). To dispute violently; to disagree.

Quarry, kwo'ri, *n*. A place where stones are dug from the earth; any animal pursued for prey; game killed.—*vt*. (quarrying, quarried). To dig or take from a quarry.

Quart, kwart, *n*. The fourth part of a gallon; two pints.

Quarter, kwar'ter, *n*. The fourth part of anything; 28 lbs; 8 bushels; any direction or point of the compass; a district; locality; division of a heraldic shield; proper position; mercy to a beaten foe; *pl*. shelter or lodging; encampment.—*vt*. To divide into four equal parts; to cut to pieces; to furnish with lodgings or shelter; to add to other arms on an heraldic shield.—*vi*. To lodge.

Quash, kwosh, *vt*. To subdue or quell; to suppress; to annul or make void.

Quasi, kwā'sī. A prefix implying appearance without reality; sort of; sham.

Quatercentenary, kwa-ter-sen'te-na-ri, *n*. A four hundredth anniversary.

Quaternary, kwa-ter'na-ri, *a*. Consisting of four; arranged in fours; applied to the strata above the tertiary.

Quaternion, kwa-ter'ni-on, *n*. A set of four; a quantity employed in mathematics.

Quaver, kwā'ver, *vi*. To have a tremulous motion; to vibrate.—*vt*. To utter with a tremulous sound.—*n*. A shake or rapid vibration of the voice, or on a musical instrument; a musical note equal to half a crotchet.

Quay, kē, *n*. A built landing-place for vessels; a wharf.

Querimonious, kwe-ri-mō'ni-us, *a*. Apt to complain; complaining; querulous.

Quern, kwern, *n*. A stone hand-mill for grinding grain.

Querulous, kwe'rū-lus, *a*. Complaining; murmuring; peevish.

Query, kwē'ri, *n*. A question; the mark of interrogation (?).—*vi*. (querying, queried). To ask a question or questions.—*vt*. To question; to mark with a query.

Quest, kwest, *n*. Act of seeking; search; pursuit; inquiry; solicitation.

Question, kwest'yon, *n*. Act of asking; an interrogation; inquiry; discussion; subject of discussion.—*vi*. To ask a question; to doubt.—*vt*. To interrogate; to doubt; to challenge.

Quick, kwik, *a*. Alive; brisk; swift; keen; sensitive; irritable.—*n*. A growing plant, usually hawthorn, for hedges; the living flesh; sensitiveness.—*adv*. Quickly; soon.

Quicken, kwik'n, *vt*. To revive or resuscitate; to cheer; to increase the speed of; to sharpen; to stimulate.—*vi*. To become alive; to move quickly or more quickly.

Quicksand, kwik'sand, *n*. A movable sandbank under water; sand yielding under the feet; something treacherous.

Quilt, kwilt, *n*. A padded bedcover.—*vt.* To form into a quilt; to sew pieces of cloth with soft substance between.

Quince, kwins, *n.* The fruit of a tree allied to the pear and apple; the tree itself.

Quintuple, kwin'tu̧-pl, *a.* Fivefold.—*vt.* To make fivefold.

Quip, kwip, *n.* A sharp sarcastic turn; a severe retort; a gibe.

Quirk, kwėrk, *n.* An artful turn for evasion; a shift; a quibble.

Quit, kwit, *a.* Discharged; released; free; clear.—*vt.* (quitting, quitted). To discharge; to rid; to acquit; to leave; to abandon.

Quite, kwīt, *adv.* Completely; wholly; entirely; altogether; very.

Quiver, kwi'vėr, *n.* A case or sheath for arrows.—*vi.* To shake with small rapid movements; to tremble; to shiver.

Quixotic, kwiks-ot'ik, *a.* Chivalrous to extravagance; aiming at visionary ends.

Quiz, kwiz, *n.* A hoax; a jest; one who quizzes; one liable to be quizzed; a game or test in which two or more persons or teams compete in answering questions.—*vt.* (quizzing, quizzed). To make fun of, as by obscure questions; to look at inquisitively; to tease; to test by questioning.

Quote, kwōt, *vt.* (quoting, quoted). To adduce or cite, as from some author; to name as the price of an article.

Quotient, kwō'shent, *n.* The number obtained by dividing one number by another.

R

Rabbi, rab'bī, *n.* A Jewish teacher or expounder of the law.

Rabbit, rab'it, *n.* A burrowing rodent allied to the hare.

Rabble, rab'l, *n.* A crowd of vulgar, noisy people; the mob; the lower class of people.

Rabid, ra'bid, *a.* Raving; furious; mad.

Rabies, rā'bi-ēs, *n.* A disease affecting certain animals, especially dogs, from which hydrophobia is communicated.

Raccoon, Racoon, ra-kön', *n.* An American carnivorous animal.

Race, rās, *n.* A body of individuals sprung from a common stock; a breed or stock; a running; a contest in speed; a course or career; a rapid current or channel.—*vi.* (racing, raced). To run swiftly; to contend in running.—*vt.* To cause to contend in speed.

Radar, rā'där, *n.* A method of finding the position of an object (ship, aircraft, etc.) by reflection of radio waves.

Radiance, rā'di-ans, *n.* Brightness shooting in rays; luster; brilliancy; splendor.

Radiate, rā'di-āt, *vi.* To emit rays of light; to shine; to spread about as in rays.—*vt.* To emit in divergent lines; to enlighten.—*a.* Having rays or lines resembling radii.

Radical, ra'di-kal, *a.* Pertaining to the root; original; thorough-going; native; underived; relating to radicals in politics.—*n.* A root; a simple, underived word; one who advocates extreme political reform.

Radix, rā'diks, *n.* A root, as of a plant or a word; source; origin.

Raffle, raf'l, *n.* A kind of lottery.—*vi.* (raffling, raffled). To engage in a raffle.—*vt.* To dispose of by raffle.

Raft, räft, *n.* Logs fastened together and floated; a floating structure.

Raid, rād, *n.* A hostile incursion; a foray.—*vi.* To engage in a raid.—*vt.* To make a raid on.

Rail, rāl, *n.* A horizontal bar of wood or metal; a connected series of posts; a railing; one of the parallel iron bars forming a track for locomotives, etc.; a railway; a grallatorial bird.—*vt.* To inclose with rails; to furnish with rails.-*vi.* To use abusive language; to scold; to inveigh.

Rainbow, rān'bō, *n.* An arc of a circle, consisting of all the prismatic colors, appearing in the heavens opposite the sun.

Raise, rāz, *vt.* (raising, raised). To cause to rise; to lift upward; to excite; to recall from death; to stir up; to construct; to levy; to breed;

to originate; to give vent to; to inflate; to cause to be relinquished (a siege).

Raisin, rā'zn, *n.* A dried grape.

Rake, rāk, *n.* An implement for collecting hay or straw, smoothing earth, etc.; a dissolute, lewd man; slope.—*vt.* (raking, raked). To apply a rake to; to gather with a rake; to ransack; to enfilade.—*vi.* To use a rake; to search minutely; to incline; to slope, aft, as masts.

Rally, ral'i, *vt.* (rallying, rallied). To reunite, as disordered troops; to collect, as things scattered; to attack with raillery; to banter.—*vi.* To recover strength or vigor.—*n.* A stand made by retreating troops; recovery of strength.

Ram, ram, *n.* The male of the sheep; a battering-ram; the loose hammer of a pile-driving machine; a heavy steel beak of a war-vessel; an iron-clad ship with such a beak; one of the signs of the zodiac.—*vt.* (ramming, rammed). To strike with a ram; to batter; to cram.

Ramble, ram'bl, *vi.* (rambling, rambled). To roam carelessly about; to talk incoherently; to have parts stretching irregularly.—*n.* An irregular excursion.

Rampant, ram'pant, *a.* Rank in growth; exuberant; unrestrained; in *heraldry,* standing up on the hind-legs.

Ranch, ranch, *n.* In North America, a farming establishment for rearing cattle and horses.

Rancid, ran'sid, *a.* Having a rank or stinking smell; strong-scented; sour; musty.

Rancor, rang'kor, *n.* Deep-seated enmity; malice; malignity.

Random, ran'dum, *n.* Action without definite object; chance; caprice.—**At random,** in a haphazard manner.—*a.* Left to chance; done without previous calculation.

Range, rānj, *vt.* (ranging, ranged). To set in a row; to dispose systematically; to wander through or scour.—*vt.* To rank; to rove about; to fluctuate.—*n.* A row; a rank; compass or extent; a kitchen

grate; distance to which a projectile is carried; a place for gun practice.

Rank, rangk, *n.* A row; a line; a social class; comparative station; titled dignity.—*vt.* To place in a line; to classify.—*vi.* To belong to a class; to put in a claim against a bankrupt.—*a.* Luxuriant in growth;; strong-scented; utter; coarse; disgusting.

Rap, rap, *n.* A quick smart blow; a knock.—*vi.* (rapping, rapped). To strike a quick, sharp blow.—*vt.* To strike with a quick blow.

Rapacious, ra-pā'shus, *a.* Greedy of plunder; subsisting on prey; extortionate.

Rape, rāp, *n.* A seizing by violence; carnal knowledge of a woman against her will; a plant of the cabbage kind, whose seeds yield an oil.—*vt.* (raping, raped). To carry off violently; to ravish.

Rapid, ra'pid, *a.* Very swift; speedy; hurried.—*n.* A swift current in a river.

Rash, rash, *a.* Precipitate; hasty; overbold; incautious.—*n.* An eruption on the skin.

Ratchet, rach'et, *n.* A catch which abuts against the teeth of a wheel to prevent it running back.

Rate, rāt, *n.* Proportion; standard; degree; degree of speed; price; a tax; assessment.—*vt.* (rating, rated). To fix the value, rank, or degree of; to appraise; to reprove; to scold.—*vi.* To be classed in a certain order.

Rather, räтн'ėr, *adv.* More readily; preferably; more properly; somewhat.

Ratify, ra'ti-fī, *vt.* (ratifying, ratified). To confirm; to approve and sanction.

Ratio, rā'shi-ō, *n.* Relation or proportion; rate.

Rattle, rat'l, *vi.* and *t.* (rattling, rattled). To clatter; to chatter fluently.—*n.* A rapid succession of clattering sounds; an instrument or toy which makes a clattering sound; one who talks much and rapidly.

Rattlesnake, rat'l-snāk, *n.* A venomous American snake, with

R

horny pieces at the point of the tail which rattle.

Raucous, ra̲'kus, *a.* Hoarse; harsh.

Ravage, ra̲'vāj, *n.* Devastation; havoc.—*vt.* (ravaging, ravaged). To lay waste; to pillage.

Rave, rāv, *vi.* (raving, raved). To be delirious; to speak enthusiastically; to dote.

Raw, ra̲, *a.* Not cooked or dressed; not manufactured; unfinished; not diluted; bare, as flesh; galled; sensitive; inexperienced; cold and damp.

Ray, rā, *n.* A line of light; a gleam of intellectual light; one of a number of diverging radii; a flat-fish.—*vt.* and *i.* (raying, rayed). To shine forth; to radiate; to streak.

Rayon, rā'on, *n.* Artificial silk, made from cellulose.

Raze, rāz, *vt.* (razing, razed). To graze; to lay level with the ground; to efface.

Razor, rā'zor, *n.* A knife for shaving off hair.

Reach, rēch, *vt.* To extend; to hand; to extend or stretch from a distance; to arrive at; to gain.—*vi.* To extend; to stretch out the hand in order to touch; to make efforts at attainment.—*n.* Act or power of extending to; straight course of a river; scope.

React, rē-akt', *vi.* To act in return; to return an impulse; to act reciprocally upon each other.—*vt.* To perform anew.

Reaction, rē-ak'shon, *n.* A reacting; reciprocal action; tendency to revert to a previous condition; exhaustion consequent on activity, and *vice versa.*

Read, rēd, *vt.* (reading, read). To peruse; to utter aloud, following something written or printed; to explain.—*vi.* To peruse; to study; to stand written or printed; to make sense.—*a.* red. instructed by reading; learned.

Reality, rē-al'i-ti, *n.* State or quality of being real; actuality; fact; truth.

Realize, rē'al-īz, *vt.* (realizing, realized). To make real; to convert into money; to impress on the mind as a reality; to render tangible or effective; to acquire; to gain.

Realm, relm, *n.* The dominions of a sovereign; a region, sphere, or domain.

Realty, rē'al-ti, *n.* The fixed nature of property termed *real*; real property.

Ream, rēm, *n.* A package of paper, consisting generally of 20 quires, or 480 sheets.

Reanimate, rē-an'i-māt, *vt.* To animate again; to revive; to infuse new life into.

Reap, rēp, *vt.* and *i.* To cut with a scythe, etc., as grain; to gather; to clear of a grain crop; to receive as a reward of labor, etc.

Rear, rēr, *n.* The part behind; the part of an army behind the rest; the background.—*vt.* To raise; to bring up, as young; to breed, as cattle; to build up.—*vi.* To rise on the hind-legs, as horse; to become erect.

Reasonable, rē'zn-a-bl, *a.* Having the faculty of reason; rational; conformable to reason; moderate; fair; tolerable.

Reasoning, rē'zn-ing, *n.* The act or process of exercising the faculty of reason; arguments employed.

Reassurance, rē-a-shör'ans, *n.* Act of reassuring; a second assurance against loss.

Reassure, rē-a-shör', *vt.* To assure anew; to free from fear or terror; to reinsure.

Rebuff, rē-buf', *n.* A sudden check; a repulse; refusal.—*vt.* To beat back; to check; to repel the advances of.

Rebuke, rē-būk', *vt.* (rebuking, rebuked). To reprimand; to reprove sharply.—*n.* A direct and severe reprimand; reproof.

Rebus, rē'bus, *n.* A set of words represented by pictures of objects; a kind of puzzle made up of such pictures.

Rebut, rē-but', *vt.* (rebutting, rebutted). To repel; to refute; in *law,* to oppose by argument, plea, or countervailing proof.

Recalcitrant, rē-kal'si-trant, *a.* Not submissive; refractory.

Recede, rē-sēd', *vi.* (receding, receded). To go back; to withdraw.—*vt.* To cede back.

Receipt, rē-sēt′, *n.* Act of receiving; that which is received; a written acknowledgment of something received; a recipe.—*vt.* To give a receipt for; to discharge, as an account.

Receive, rē-sēv′, *vt.* (receiving, received). To take, as a thing offered; to admit; to entertain; to contain; to be the object of; to take stolen goods.

Recess, rē-ses′, *n.* A withdrawing; place or period of retirement; time during which business is suspended; a niche in a wall; an alcove.

Recipe, re′si-pē, *n.* A medical prescription; a statement of ingredients for a mixture.

Recipient, rē-si′pi-ent, *n.* One who or that which receives; a receiver.

Reciprocal, rē-sip′rō-kal, *a.* Reciprocating; alternate; done by each to the other; mutual; interchangeable.

Reciprocate, rē-sip′rō-kāt, *vi.* To move backward and forward; to alternate.—*vt.* To exchange; to give in requital.

Reciprocity, re-si-pros′i-ti, *n.* Reciprocation; interchange; reciprocal obligation; equal commercial rights mutually enjoyed.

Reckoning, rek′n-ing, *n.* Calculation; a statement of accounts with another; landlord's bill; calculation of a ship's position.

Reclaim, rē-klām′, *vt.* To claim back; to reform; to tame; to recover; to reduce to a state fit for cultivation.

Recline, rē-klīn′, *vt.* and *i* (reclining, reclined). To lean; to rest or repose.

Recluse, rē-klōs′, *a.* Retired; solitary.—*n.* A person who lives in seclusion; a hermit.

Recognition, re-kog-ni′shon, *n.* Act of recognizing; avowal; acknowledgment.

Recognizance, rē-kog′niz-ans or rē-kon′i-zans, *n.* Recognition; an obligation, as to appear at the assizes, keep the peace, etc.

Recognize, re′kog-nīz, *vt.* (recognizing, recognized). To know again; to admit a knowledge of; to acknowledge formally; to indicate one's notice by a bow, etc.; to indicate appreciation of.

Recoil, rē-koil′, *vi.* To move or start back; to retreat; to shrink; to rebound.—*n.* A starting or falling back; rebound, as of a gun.

Recommend, re-kom-mend′, *vt.* To praise to another; to make acceptable; to commit with prayers; to advise.

Recompense, re′kom-pens, *vt.* (recompensing, recompensed). To compensate; to requite; to make amends for.—*n.* Compensation; reward; amends.

Reconcile, re′kon-sīl, *vt.* (reconciling, reconciled). To make friendly again; to adjust or settle; to harmonize.

Record, rē-kord′, *vt.* To preserve in writing; to register; to chronicle.—*n.* rek′ord. A written memorial; a register; a public document; memory; one's personal history; best results in contests.

Recount, rē-kount′, *vt.* To relate in detail; to count again.—*n.* A second counting.

Recoup, rē-köp′, *vt.* To recompense or compensate; to indemnify.

Recourse, rē-kōrs′, *n.* A going to with a request, as for aid; resort in perplexity.

Recover, rē-kuv′ėr, *vt.* To get back; to regain; to revive; to rescue; to obtain in return for injury or debt.—*vi.* To grow well; to regain a former condition.

Recriminate, rē-krim′in-āt, *vi.* To return one accusation with another.—*vt.* To accuse in return.

Recruit, rē-kröt′, *vt.* To repair; to supply with new soldiers.—*vi.* To gain new supplies of anything; to raise new soldiers.—*n.* A soldier newly enlisted.

Rectangle, rek′tang-gl, *n.* A quadrilateral having all its angles right angles.

Rectification, rek′ti-fi-kā′′shon, *n.* Act or operation of rectifying; process of refining by repeated distillation.

Rectify, rek′ti-fī, *vt.* (rectifying, rectified). To correct; to refine by repeated distillation

Recumbent, rē-kum'bent, *a.* Leaning; reclining; reposing; inactive.

Recuperate, rē-kū'pėr-āt, *vt.* and *i.* (recuperating, recuperated). To recover.

Recur, rē-kėr', *vi.* (recurring, recurred). To return; to be repeated at a stated interval.

Recurrent, rē-ku'rent, *a.* Recurring from time to time.

Recusancy, Recusance, re'kū-zan-si, re'kū-zans, *n.* Nonconformity.

Red, red, *a.* Of a color resembling that of arterial blood.—*n.* A color resembling that of arterial blood; a red pigment.

Redemption, rē-dem'shon, *n.* The act of redeeming; state of being redeemed; ransom; release; deliverance.

Redout, Redoubt, rē-dout', *n.* A small inclosed fortification.

Redraft, rē-dråft', *vt.* To draft anew.—*n.* A second draft; a second order for money.

Redraw, rē-dra', *vt.* To draw again.—*vi.* To draw a new bill of exchange.

Redress, rē-dres', *vt.* To set right; to adjust; to repair; to relieve.—*n.* Relief; deliverance; reparation.

Red-tape, red'tāp, *n.* Excessive official routine and formality.—*a.* Characterized by excessive routine or formality.

Reduce, rē-dūs', *vt.* (reducing, reduced). To bring down; to decrease; to degrade; to subdue; to bring under rules or within categories; to restore to its proper place.

Reduction, rē-duk'shon, *n.* Act of reducing; diminution; conversion into another state or form; subjugation.

Redundant, rē-dun'dant, *a.* Superfluous; having more words than necessary.

Reduplication, rē-dū'pli-kā''shon, *n.* Act of reduplicating; the repetition of a root or initial syllable.

Redwood, red'wud, *n.* A name of various reddish timbers.

Reed, rēd, *n.* A tall broad-leaved grass growing in marshy places, or its hollow stems; a musical instrument; a rustic pipe.

Reedy, rēd'i, *a.* Abounding with reeds; harsh and thin, as a voice.

Reef-point, rēf'point, *n.* One of the small pieces of line for tying up a sail when reefed.

Reek, rēk, *n.* Vapor; steam; exhalation; smoke.—*vi.* To smoke; to exhale.

Reel, rēl, *n.* A bobbin for thread; a revolving appliance for winding a fishing-line; a staggering motion; a lively Scottish dance.—*vt.* To wind upon a reel; to stagger.

Refer, rē-fėr', *vt.* (referring, referred). To trace or carry back; to attribute; to appeal; to assign.—*vi.* To respect or have relation; to appeal; to apply; to allude.

Referee, ref-ėr-ē', *n.* One to whom a matter in dispute is referred for decision; an umpire.

Reference, re'fėr-ens, *n.* Act of referring; allusion; relation; one of whom inquiries may be made.

Referendum, ref-ėr-en'dum, *n.* The referring of a measure passed by a legislature to the people for final approval.

Refine, rē-fīn', *vt.* (refining, refined). To increase the fineness of; to purify; to make elegant; to give culture to.—*vi.* To become purer; to indulge in hair-splitting.

Reflection, rē-flek'shon, *n.* Act of reflecting; that which is produced by being reflected; meditation; a censorious remark; reproach.

Reflective, rē-flekt'iv, *a.* Throwing back rays; meditating.

Reflex, rē'fleks, *a.* Bent or directed back; done involuntarily or unconsciously.—*n.* A reflection.

Reflexive, rē-flek'siv, *a.* Reflective; having respect to something past; in *grammar,* having for its object a pronoun which stands for the subject; also applied to such pronouns.

Reflux, rē'fluks, *n.* A flowing back; ebb.

Reform, rē-form', *vt.* and *i.* To change from worse to better; to amend; to form anew.—*n.* A beneficial change; amendment; a change in the regulations of parliamentary representation.

Refractory, rē-frak'to-ri, *a.* Sullen

in disobedience; tubborn; unmanageable; resisting ordinary treatment.

Refrain, rē-frān', *vt.* To restrain; to keep (oneself) from action.—*vi.* To forbear; to abstain.—*n.* The burden of a song; part repeated at the end of every stanza.

Refresh, rē-fresh', *vt.* To revive; to reanimate; to freshen.

Refuge, re'fūj, *n.* Protection from danger or distress; a retreat; a shelter; a device; contrivance; shift.—*vt.* and *i.* To shelter.

Refugee, re-fū-jē', *n.* One who flees for refuge; one who flees to another country or place for safety.

Refulgent, rē-ful'jent, *a.* Casting a bright light; shining; splendid.

Refund, rē-fund', *vt.* To pay back; to repay; to reimburse.

Refuse, rē-fūz', *vt.* (refusing, refused). To deny, as a request or demand; to decline; to reject.—*vi.* To decline a request or offer.

Refuse, re'fūz, *a.* Rejected; worthless.—*n.* Waste matter; dregs.

Refutation, re-fūt-ā'shon, *n.* Act or process of refuting; disproof.

Refute, rē-fūt', *vt.* (refuting, refuted). To disprove; to overthrow by argument.

Regain, rē-gān', *vt.* To gain anew; to recover; to retrieve; to reach again.

Regal, rē'gal, *a.* Kingly; royal.

Regale, rē-gāl', *vt.* and *i.* (regaling, regaled). To refresh sumptuously; to feast.—*n.* A splendid feast; a treat.

Regality, rē-gal'i-ti, *n.* Royalty; kingship.

Regard, rē-gärd', *vt.* To notice carefully; to observe; to respect; to heed; to view in the light of; to relate to.—*n.* Look or gaze; respect; notice; heed; esteem; deference; *pl.* good wishes.

Regeneration, rē-jen'e-rā''shon, *n.* Act of regenerating; that change by which love to God is implanted in the heart.

Regent, rē'jent, *a.* Ruling.—*n.* A ruler; one who governs during the minority or disability of the king.

Regicide, re'ji-sīd, *n.* One who kills a king; the murder of a king.

Registry, re'jis-tri, *n.* Registration; place where a register is kept; an entry.

Regress, rē'gres, *n.* Return; power of returning.—*vi.* rē-gres'. To go back.

Regret, rē-gret', *n.* Grief at something done or undone; remorse; penitence.—*vt.* (regretting, regretted). To be sorry for; to lament.

Regular, re'gū-lėr, *a.* Conformed to a rule, law, or principle; normal; methodical; uniform; having the parts symmetrical; thorough.—*n.* A monk who has taken the vows in some order; a soldier of a permanent army.

Regulate, re'gū-lāt, *vt.* (regulating, regulated). To adjust by rule; to put or keep in good order; to direct.

Regurgitate, rē-gėr'jit-tāt, *vt.* and *i.* To pour or cause to surge back.

Rehabilitate, rē-ha-bil'i-tāt, *vt.* To restore to a former capacity or position; to re-establish in esteem.

Rein, rān, *n.* The strap of a bridle, by which a horse is governed; an instrument for restraining; restrait.—*vt.* To govern by a bridle; to restrain.—*vi.* To obey the reins.

Reindeer, rān'dėr, *n.* A deer of northern parts, with broad branched antlers.

Reinforce, rē-in-fōrs', *vt.* To strengthen by new assistance, as troops.—*n.* An additional thickness given to an object to strengthen it.

Reinstate, rē-in-stāt', *vt.* To instate anew; to restore to a former position.

Reiterate, rē-it'ėr-āt, *vt.* To repeat again and again; to do or say repeatedly.

Reject, rē-jekt', *vt.* To cast off; to discard; to repel; to forsake; to decline.

Relation, rē-lā'shon, *n.* Act of relating; account; reference; connection; kindred; a relative; proportion.

Relative, re'lat-iv, *a.* Having relation or reference; not absolute or existing by itself; relevant.—*n.* Something considered in its relation to something else; one allied

R

by blood; a word which relates to or represents another word or sentence.

Relax, rē-laks', vt. To slacken; to loosen or weaken; to unbend.—vi. To become loose, feeble, or languid; to abate in severity.

Release, rē-lēs', vt. (releasing, released). To liberate; to disengage; to acquit.—n. Liberation; discharge; acquittance.

Relic, re'lik, n. A remaining fragment; the body of a deceased person (usually in pl.); a memento or keepsake.

Relief, rē-lēf', n. Ease or mitigation of pain; succor; remedy; redress; assistance given to a pauper; one who relieves another by taking duty; prominence of figures above a plane surface in sculpture, carving, etc.; prominence or distinctness.

Relieve, rē-lēv', vt. (relieving, relieved). To remove or lessen, as anything that pains; to ease; to succor; to release from duty; to give variety to; to set off by contrast; to give the appearance of projection to.

Religion, rē-li'jon, n. An acknowledgment of our obligation to God; practical piety; devotion; any system of faith and worship.

Reluctant, rē-luk'tant, a. Loath; averse; acting with slight repugnance.

Rely, rē-lī', vt. (relying, relied). To rest with confidence; to trust; with on or upon.

Remain, rē-mān', vi. To continue in a place or condition; to abide; to be left; to last.—n. That which is left; pl. a dead body; literary works of one who is dead.

Remainder, rē-mān'dėr, n. That which remains; residue; remnant; an estate limited so as to be enjoyed after the death of the present possessor or otherwise.—a. Left over.

Remand, rē-mand', vt. To call or send back; to send back to jail.

Remark, rē-märk', n. Notice; an observation in words; a comment.—vt. To observe; to utter by way of comment.

Remember, rē-mem'bėr, vt. To have in the memory; to think of; to observe; to give a gratuity for service done.—vi. To have something in remembrance.

Remembrance, rē-mem'brans, n. The keeping of a thing in mind; memory; what is remembered; a memorial; a keepsake.

Remind, rē-mīnd', vt. To put in mind; to cause to remember.

Remnant, rem'nant, n. That which is left; a scrap, fragment.—a. Remaining.

Remonstrance, rē-mon'strans, n. Act of remonstrating; expostulation; strong representation against something.

Remonstrate, rē-mon'strāt, vi. To present strong reasons against an act; to expostulate.

Remorse, rē-mors', n. Reproach of conscience; compunction for wrong committed.

Remorseless, rē-mors'les, a. Without remorse; ruthless; relentless; merciless.

Remote, rē-mōt', a. Distant in place or time; not immediate or direct; slight; inconsiderable.

Remove, rē-möv', vt. (removing, removed). To move from its place; to take away; to displace from an office; to banish or destroy.—vi. To be moved from its place; to change the place of residence.—n. A removal; departure.

Rend, rend, vt. (rending, rent). To force asunder; to tear away; to sever.—vi. To be or become torn; to split.

Render, ren'dėr, vt. To give in return; to give back; to present; to afford; to invest with qualities; to translate; to interpret; to clarify, as tallow.

Rendezvous, ren'de-vö, n. A place of meeting.—vi. To meet at a particular place.

Rendition, ren-di'shon, n. A rendering; interpretation; translation; surrender.

Renegade, re'nē-gād, n. An apostate; a deserter.

Renew, rē-nū', vt. To make new again; to repair; to repeat; to grant anew; to transform.—vi. To grow or begin again.

Reniform, rē'ni-form, *a.* Having the shape of the kidneys.

Rent, rent, *n.* Money, etc., payable yearly for the use of lands or tenements; a tear; a schism.—*vt.* To let on lease; to hold on condition of paying rent.—*vi.* To be leased or let for rent.

Renunciation, rē-nun'si-ā''shon, *n.* Act of renouncing; disavowal; abandonment.

Repair, rē-pār', *vt.* To restore; to refit; to mend; to retrieve.—*vi.* To betake oneself; to resort.—*n.* Restoration; supply of loss; state as regards repairing; a resorting; abode.

Repeat, rē-pēt', *vt.* To do or utter again; to recite; to recapitulate.—*n.* Repetition.

Repeating, rē-pēt'ing, *a.* Producing a like result several times in succession.

Repel, rē-pel', *vt.* (repelling, repelled). To drive back; to resist successfully.—*vi.* To cause repugnance; to shock.

Repellent, rē-pel'ent, *a.* Having the effect of repelling; repulsive; deterring.

Repent, rē-pent', *vi.* To feel regret for something done or left undone; to be penitent.—*vt.* To remember with self-reproach or sorrow.

Repentance, rē-pent'ans, *n.* Act of repenting; sorrow for sin; penitence; contrition.

Repercussion, rē-pėr-ku'shon, *n.* Act of driving back; reverberation.

Repertoire, rep'ėr-twär, *n.* The aggregate of pieces that an actor or company performs.

Repetition, re-pē-ti'shon, *n.* Act of repeating; recital; that which is repeated.

Replace, rē-plās', *vt.* (replacing, replaced). To put again in the former place; to put in the place of another; to take the place of.

Replenish, rē-plen'ish, *vt.* To fill again; to fill completely; to stock abundantly.

Report, rē-pōrt', *vt.* and *i.* To bring back, as an answer; to relate; to give an official statement of; to take down from the lips of a speaker, etc.; to lay a charge against.—*n.* An account; rumor; repute; noise of explosion; official statement; account of proceedings.

Reporter, rē-pōrt'ėr, *n.* One who reports; one of a newspaper staff who gives accounts of public meetings, events, etc.

Repose, rē-pōz', *vt.* (reposing, reposed). To lay at rest.—*vi.* To lie at rest; to rely.—*n.* A lying at rest; tranquillity; composure; absence of show of feeling.

Repoussé, rè-pös'sā, *a.* Embossed.

Reprehend, re-prē-hend', *vt.* To charge with a fault; to reprove; to censure.

Reprehension, re-prē-hen'shon, *n.* Act of reprehending; reproof; censure; blame.

Containing reprehension or reproof.

Represent, re-prē-zent', *vt.* To exhibit by a likeness of; to typify; to act the part of; to describe; to be a substitute for; to exemplify.

Reprieve, rē-prēv', *vt.* (reprieving, reprieved). To grant a respite to; to relieve temporarily.—*n.* Suspension of the execution of a criminal's sentence; respite.

Reprimand, rep'ri-mand, *n.* A severe reproof for a fault.—*vt.* rep-ri-mand'. To administer a sharp rebuke to.

Reprint, rē-print', *vt.* To print again.—*n.* rē'print. A second or new edition.

Reprisal, rē-prīz'al, *n.* Seizure from an enemy by way of retaliation; retaliation.

Reproach, rē-prōch', *vt.* To charge severely with a fault; to censure.—*n.* Censure; blame; source of blame; disgrace.

Reptile, rep'til, *a.* Creeping; grovelling.—*n.* An animal that moves on its belly, or by means of small short legs.

Republic, rē-pub'lik, *n.* A commonwealth; a state in which the supreme power is vested in elected representatives.

Repudiate, rē-pū'di-āt, *vt.* (repudiating, repudiated). To divorce; to reject; to disavow.

R

Repugnance, rē-pug'nans, n. Aversion; reluctance; dislike; inconsistency.

Repulse, rē-puls', n. Act of repelling; a check or defeat; refusal; denial.—vt. (repulsing, repulsed). To repel.

Repurchase, rē-pėr'chās, vt. To buy back.—n. Purchase again of what has been sold.

Reputable, re'pūt-a-bl, a. Held in esteem; estimable.

Reputation, re-pūt-ā'shon, n. Character derived from public opinion; repute; good name; honor; fame.

Repute, rē-pūt', vt. (reputing, reputed). To estimate; to deem.—n. Reputation; character; good character.

Request, rē-kwest', n. An expressed desire; a petition; thing asked for; a state of being asked for.—vt. To ask; to beg.

Rescind, rē-sind', vt. To abrogate; to annul; to repeal; to revoke.

Rescue, res'kū, vt. (rescuing, rescued). To deliver from confinement, danger, or evil.—n. Act of rescuing; deliverance.

Research, rē-sėrch', n. A diligent seeking of facts or principles; investigation.—vt. To search again.

Resemblance, rē-zem'blans, n. Likeness; similarity; something similar; similitude.

Resemble, rē-zem'bl, vt. (resembling, resembled). To be like; to liken; to compare.

Reservoir, re'zėr-vwar, n. A place where anything is kept in store; an artificial lake to supply a town with water.

Reside, rē-zīd', vi. (residing, resided). To have one's abode; to dwell; to inhere.

Residential, re-zi-den'shal, a. Pertaining to or suitable for residence.

Resilient, rē-si'li-ent, a. Inclined to resile; rebounding.

Resin, re'zin, n. An inflammable vegetable substance; the hardened juice of pines.

Resist, rē-zist', vt. and i. To withstand; to oppose; to struggle against.

Resistant, Resistent, rē-zis'tent, a. Making resistance.—n. One who or that which resists.

Resolute, re'zō-lūt, a. Having fixedness of purpose; determined; steadfast.

Resolution, re-zō-lū'shon, n. Character of being resolute; determination; a formal decision; operation of separating the component parts; solution.

Resolve, rē-zolv', vt. (resolving, resolved). To separate the component parts of; to analyze; to solve; to determine; to decide.—vi. To separate into component parts; to melt; to determine; to decide.—n. Fixed purpose of mind; resolution.

Resonant, re'zo-nant, a. Resounding; full of sounds.

Resort, rē-zort', vi. To have recourse; to go; to repair frequently.—n. Recourse; concourse; a haunt.

Resound, rē-zound', vt. To give back the sound of; to echo; to praise.—vi. To sound again; to echo; to be much praised.

Resource, rē-sōrs', n. Any source of aid or support; expedient; pl. funds; means.

Respite, res'pit, n. Temporary intermission; interval; a reprieve.—vt. (respiting, respited). To grant a respite to; to reprieve.

Responsive, rē-spons'iv, a. Making reply; answering; correspondent; suited.

Rest, rest, n. Cessation of action; peace; sleep; an appliance for support; a pause; remainder; the others.—vi. To cease from action; to lie for repose; to be supported; to be in a certain state; remain; to be left.—vt. To lay at rest; to place, as on a support.

Restaurant, res'tō-rong, n. An establishment for the sale of refreshments.

Restaurateur, res-tō'ra-tėr, n. The keeper of a restaurant.

Restitution, res-ti-tū'shon, n. Act of restoring; reparation; amends.

Restriction, rē-strik'shon, n. Act of restricting; limitation; a reservation.

Result, rē-zult', vi. To rise as a consequence; to issue; to ensue; to end.—*n*. Consequence; effect; issue; outcome.

Resume, rē-zūm´, *vt*. (resuming, resumed). To take up again; to begin again.

Résumé, rā´zö-mā, *n*. A recapitulation; a summary.

Resurgent, rē-sėr´jent, *a*. Rising again.

Resurrection, re-zėr-rek´shon, *n*. A rising again; the rising of the dead at the general judgment.

Resuscitate, rē-sus´i-tāt, *vt*. and *i*. To revive.

Retail, rē-tāl´, *vt*. To sell in small quantities; to tell to many.—*n*. rē´tāl. The sale of commodities in small quantities; used also as *adj*.

Retain, rē-tān´, *vt*. To hold back; to keep in possession; to detain; to hire; to engage.

Retainer, rē-tān´ėr, *n*. One who retains; an adherent or dependent; a fee to engage a counsel.

Retaliate, rē-ta´li-āt, *vi*. and *t*. To return like for like; to repay; to take revenge.

Retina, re´ti-na, *n*. One of the coats of the eye, where visual impressions are received.

Retinue, re´ti-nū, *n*. A train of attendants; a suite.

Retire, rē-tīr´, *vi*. (retiring, retired). To go back; to withdraw from business or active life; to go to bed.—*vt*. To remove from service; to pay when due, as a bill of exchange.

Retiring, rē-tīr´ing, *a*. Reserved; unobtrusive; granted to one who retires from service.

Retort, rē-tort´, *vt*. To retaliate; to throw back.—*vi*. To return an argument or charge.—*n*. A severe reply; a repartee; a chemical vessel for distilling.

Retouch, rē-tuch´, *vt*. To improve by new touches, as a picture, etc.

Retract, rē-trakt´, *vt*. To draw back; to recall.—*vi*. To unsay one's words.

Retributive, Retributory, rē-tri´būtiv, rē-tri´bū-to-ri, *a*. Making retribution; entailing justly deserved punishment.

Retrieve, rē-trēv´, *vt*. (retrieving, retrieved). To recover; to regain; to repair.

Retriever, rē-trēv´ėr, *n*. A dog that brings in game which a sportsman has shot.

Return, rē-tėrn´, *vi*. To come or go back; to recur.—*vt*. To send back; to repay; to report officially; to elect; to yield.—*n*. Act of returning; repayment; election of a representative; profit; an official statement; *pl*. tabulated statistics; a light tobacco.

Revelation, re-ve-lā´shon, *n*. Act of revealing; that which is revealed; divine communication; the Apocalypse.

Revenge, rē-venj´, *vt*. and *i*. (revenging, revenged). To take vengeance for; to avenge.—*n*. Act of revenging; retaliation; deliberate infliction of injury in return for injury; vindictive feeling.

Revenue, re´ve-nū, *n*. Income; the annual income of a state.

Reverberate, rē-vėr´bė-rāt, *vt*. and *i*. To return, as sound; to echo; to reflect, as heat or light.

Revere, rē-vēr´, *vt*. (revering, revered). To regard with awe and respect; to venerate.

Reverence, rev´er-ens, *n*. Awe combined with respect; veneration; an obeisance; a reverend personage; a title of the clergy.—*vt*. To revere; to pay reverence to.

Reverent, rev´er-ent, *a*. Expressing reverence; humble; impressed with reverence.

Reverie, re´ver-i, *n*. A loose train of thoughts; a day-dream; a visionary project.

Reverse, rē-vėrs´, *vt*. (reversing, reversed). To alter to the opposite; to annul.—*n*. A reversal; a complete change or turn; a check; a defeat; the contrary; the back or undersurface.—*a*. Turned backward; opposite.

Revert, rē-vėrt´, *vt*. To reverse.—*vi*. To return to a former position, habit, statement, etc.; to return to the donor.

Revetment, rē-vet´ment, *n*. A facing to a wall or bank; a retaining wall.

Review, rē-vū´, *vt*. To view again; to reconsider; to write a critical notice of; to inspect.—*vi*. To write reviews.—*n*. A re-examination; a

R

criticism; a periodical containing criticisms; official inspection of troops.

Revile, rē-vīl', vt. (reviling, reviled). To vilify; to upbraid; to abuse.

Revise, rē-vīz', vt. (revising, revised). To go over with care for correction.—n. A revision; a second proof-sheet in printing.

Revolt, rē-vōlt', vi. To renounce allegiance; to rebel; to be disgusted: with at.—vt. To shock.—n. Rebellion; mutiny.

Revolution, re-vō-lū'shon, n. Act o of revolving; rotation; a turn; circuit; a cycle of time; a radical change; overthrow of existing political institutions.

Revue, rē-vū', n. A loosely-constructed and spectacular theatrical exhibition, depending on music and scenic and staging effects.

Revulsion, rē-vul'shon, n. A violent drawing away; a violent change, especially of feeling.

Reward, rē-ward', n. What is given in return for good done; recompense; punishment.—vt. To repay; to requite.

Rhapsody, rap'so-di, n. A short epic poem, or portion of an epic; a confused series of extravagantly enthusiastic statements.

Rhetoric, re'to-rik, n. The art of using language effectively; the art which teaches oratory; eloquence; flashy oratory; declamation.

Rhomb, Rhombus, rom, rom'bus, n. A quadrilateral whose sides are equal, but the angles not right angles.

Rhomboid, rom'boid, n. A quadrilateral whose opposite sides only are equal, and whose angles are not right angles.

Rhubarb, rö'bärb, n. A plant of which the leaf-stalks are used in cookery, and the roots of some species in medicine.

Rhyme, rīm, n. A correspondence of sound in the ends of words or verses; a short poem; a word rhyming with another.—vi. (rhyming, rhymed). To make verses; to accord in sound.—vt. To put into rhyme.

Rhythm, rithm, n. Periodical emphasis in verse or music; metrical movement; harmony; rhyme; meter; verse.

Rib, rib, n. One of the curved bones springing from the backbone; something resembling a rib; a long ridge on cloth.—vt. (ribbing, ribbed). To furnish with ribs; to inclose with ribs.

Ribald, ri'bald, n. A low, lewd fellow.—a. Low; obscene.

Ricochet, rik'o-shet, n. A rebounding from a flat, horizontal surface.—vt. and i. rik-o-shet'. To operate upon by ricochet firing; to rebound.

Rid, rid, vt. (ridding, rid). To make free; to clear; to disencumber.—a. Free; clear.

Riddle, rid'l, n. A puzzling question; an enigma; a coarse sieve.—vt. (riddling, riddled). To solve; to sift; to make many holes in.

Ride, rīd, vi. (riding, pret. rode, pp. ridden). To be borne on horseback, in a vehicle, etc.; to have ability as an equestrian; to be at anchor.—vt. To sit on, so as to be carried; to go over in riding; to domineer over.—n. An excursion on horseback, or in a vehicle; a road for the amusement of riding.

Ridge, rij, n. A long narrow prominence; strip thrown up by a plow; a long crest of hills; upper angle of a roof.—vt. (ridging, ridged). To form into ridges.

Ridicule, ri'di-kūl, n. Laughter with contempt; mockery; satire.—vt. To treat with ridicule; to make sport of.

Rig, rig, vt. (rigging, rigged). To clothe; to accoutre; to fit with tackling.—n. Dress; style of the sails and masts of a ship.

Rigging, rig'ing, n. The ropes which support the masts, extend the sails, etc., of a ship.

Right, rīt, a. Straight; upright; just; suitable; proper; real; correct; belonging to that side of the body farther from the heart; to be worn outward; perpendicular; formed by one line perpendicular to another.—adv. Justly; correctly; very; directly; to the right hand.—n. What is right; rectitude; a just claim; authority; side opposite to the left.—*vt*. To put right; to do justice to; to restore to an upright position.—*vi*. To resume a vertical position.

Righteous, rīt'yus, *a*. Upright; pious; just; honest; virtuous; equitable.

Ring, ring, *n*. Anything in the form of a circle; a circle of gold, etc., worn on the finger; an area in which games, etc., are performed; a group of persons; sound of a bell; a metallic sound.—*vt*. To encircle; to cause to sound; to repeat often or loudly.—*vi*. To sound; to resound; to tingle.

Riotous, rī'ot-us, *a*. Indulging in riot or revelry; tumultuous; seditious; excessive.

Rip, rip, *vt*. (ripping, ripped). To tear or cut open; to take out by cutting or tearing.—*n*. A rent; a scamp.

Ripe, rīp, *a*. Brought to perfection in growth; mature; complete; ready for action or effect.—*vt*. and *i*. (riping, riped). To mature.

Ripple, rip'l, *vi*. (rippling, rippled). To show a ruffled surface, as water; to make a gentle sound, as running water.—*vt*. To clean the seeds from, as flax.—*n*. A ruffle of the surface of water; a comb for separating the seeds from flax.

Rise, rīz, *vi*. (rising, pret. rose, pp. risen). To pass to a higher position; to stand up; to bring a session to an end; to arise; to swell by fermentation; to slope upwards; to become apparent; to come into existence; to rebel.—*n*. Act of rising; ascent; elevation; origin; beginning; appearance above the horizon; increase; advance.

Risk, risk, *n*. Hazard; peril; jeopardy.—*vt*. To hazard; to dare to undertake.

River, ri'vėr, *n*. A large stream of water on land; a copious flow; abundance.

Rivet, ri'vet, *n*. A metallic bolt whose end is hammered broad after insertion.—*vt*. (riveting, riveted). To fasten with rivets; to clinch; to make firm.

Rivulet, ri'vū-let, *n*. A small stream.

Road, rōd, *n*. An open way or public passage; a highway; a means of approach; a roadstead (usually in *plural*).

Roast, rōst, *vt*. To cook by exposure to a fire; to parch by heat; to banter severely.—*vi*. To become roasted.—*n*. Roasted meat; part selected for roasting.—*a*. Roasted.

Rob, rob, *vt*. (robbing, robbed). To strip unlawfully and by force; to deprive by stealing; to deprive.

Robe, rōb, *n*. A gown, or long, loose garment, worn over other dress; an elegant dress.—*vt*. (robing, robed). To put a robe upon; to invest.

Robin, rob'in, *n*. The European bird called also redbreast.

Robot, rōb'ot, *n*. Any mechanical contrivance designed to perform work normally requiring the exercise of human intelligence.

Robust, rō-bust', *a*. Sturdy; vigorous; muscular.

Rock, rok, *vt*. To move backwards and forwards without displacing; to swing.—*vi*. To sway; to reel.—*n*. A large mass of stone; defense; source of peril or disaster; a kind of solid sweetmeat.

Rod, rod, *n*. A straight slender stick; a badge of office; an enchanter's wand; a fishing-rod; a measure of $5\frac{1}{2}$ lineal yards.

Rodent, rō'dent, *a*. Gnawing; belonging to the gnawing animals (Rodentia).—*n*. An animal that gnaws, as the squirrel.

Roll, rōl, *vt*. To turn on its surface; to wrap on itself by turning; to involve in a bandage or the like; to press with a roller.—*vi*. To turn over and over; to run on wheels; to be tossed about; to sound with a deep prolonged sound.—*n*. Act of rolling; something rolled up; an official document; a catalogue; a cake of bread; a roller; a prolonged deep sound.

Roller, rōl'ėr, *n*. One who or that which rolls; a cylinder for smoothing, crushing, etc.; that on which something may be rolled up; a long, heavy, swelling wave.

Rolling, rōl'ing, *p.a*. Revolving; making a continuous noise; undu-

R

lating.

Roman, rō'man, a. Pertaining to Rome or its people and to the Roman Catholic religion; applied to the common upright letter in printing.

Romance, rō-mans', n. A tale in verse in a Romance dialect; a popular epic or tale in prose or verse of some length; a tale of extraordinary adventures; tendency to the wonderful or mysterious; a fiction.—a. (with cap.). A term applied to the languages sprung from the Latin.—vi. To tell fictitious stories.

Roost, röst, n. The pole on which birds rest at night; a collection of fowls resting together.—vi. To occupy a roost; to settle.

Rooster, röst'èr, n. The male of the domestic fowl; a cock.

Root, röt, n. That part of a plant which fixes itself in the earth; lower part of anything; origin; a form from which words are derived.—vi. To fix the root; to be firmly fixed.—vt. To plant deeply; to impress durably; to tear up or out; to eradicate.

Rooted, röt'ed, a. Fixed; deep; radical.

Rope, rōp, n. A cord or line of some thickness; a row or string of things united.—vi. (roping, roped). To draw out in threads.—vt. To pull by a rope; to fasten or inclose with a rope.

Rosewood, rōz'wud, n. The wood of a tree used in cabinet-work, when freshly cut having a faint smell of roses.

Rosin, ro'zin, n. The resin left after distilling off the volatile oil from turpentine; resin in a solid state.—vt. To rub with rosin.

Roster, ros'tèr, n. A list showing the rotation in which individuals, regiments, etc., are called on to serve.

Rostrum, ros'trum, n.; pl. -tra. The beak or bill of a bird; the ram of an ancient ship; pl. a platform or pulpit.

Rot, rot, vi. (rotting, rotted). To become rotten; to decay.—vt. To make rotten.—n. Putrid decay; a fatal distemper of sheep; a disease injurious to plants; nonsense.

Rouge, rözh, n. A cosmetic to impart ruddiness to the complexion.—vt. and i (rouging, rouged). To paint with rouge.

Rough, ruf, a. Not smooth; rugged; boisterous; harsh; rude; cruel; vague; hasty.—vt. To make rough; to rough-hew.—**To rough it,** to submit to hardships.—n. State of being rough or unfinished; a rowdy.

Roulette, rö-let', n. A game of chance; an engraver's tool with a toothed wheel.

Round, round, a. Circular; spherical; large; open; candid; brisk, as a trot; not minutely accurate, as a number.—n. That which is round; rung of a ladder; a circular course or series; circuit made by one on duty; a vocal composition in parts; ammunition for firing once; a turn or bout.—vt. To make round; to encircle; to make full and flowing; to pass round.—vi. To become round or full; to make a circuit.—adv. In a circle; around; not directly.—prep. About; around.

Route, röt, n. A course or way.

Routine, rö-tēn', n. A round of business or pleasure; regular course.

Rove, rōv, vt. (roving, roved). To move about aimlessly; to roam; to ramble.—vt. To wander over; to card into flakes, as wool.

Row, rō, n. A series in a line; a rank; a line of houses; an excursion in a boat with oars.—vt. To impel by oars, as a boat; to transport by rowing.—vi. To work with the oar.

Row, rou, n. A noisy disturbance; a riot.—vt. To scold.

Rub, rub, vt. (rubbing, rubbed). To move something along the surface of with pressure; to scour; to remove by friction; to chafe.—vi. To move along with pressure; to fret.—n. Act of rubbing; friction; obstruction; difficulty; a gibe.

Rubber, rub'èr, n. One who rubs; thing used in polishing or cleaning; india-rubber; obstruction or difficulty; contest of three games in whist.

Rude, röd, a. Unformed by art or skill; rough; uncivilized; uncivil; impudent; violent.

Rudiment, rö′di-ment, *n*. The original of anything; a first principle; an undeveloped organ; *pl.* first elements of a science or art.

Rudimentary, rö-di-ment′a-ri, *a*. Pertaining to rudiments; consisting in first principles; initial; in an undeveloped state.

Rue, rö, *vt*. (ruing, rued). To repent of; to regret.—*vi*. To become sorrowful or repentant.—*n*. An acrid ill-smelling plant.

Ruffian, ruf′i-an, *n*. A boisterous brutal fellow.—*a*. Like a ruffian; brutal.

Ruffle, ruf′l, *vt*. (ruffling, ruffled). To rumple; to derange; to disturb.—*vi*. To bluster.—*n*. A plaited cambric, etc., attached to one's dress; frill; state of being agitated; low vibrating beat of a drum.

Rug, rug, *n*. A heavy fabric used to cover a bed, protect a carpet, etc.; a mat.

Rugby, rug′bi, *n*. One of the two principal varieties of football, played by fifteen men a side, with an oval ball, handling being permitted.

Rugged, rug′ed, *a*. Full of rough projections; rough; harsh; crabbed.

Ruin, rö′in, *n*. Destruction; fall; overthrow; anything in a state of decay; that which destroys; *pl.* remains of a city, house, etc.; state of being destroyed.—*vt*. To bring to ruin; to destroy; to impoverish.

Rule, röl, *n*. A ruler or measure; a guiding principle or formula; a precept, law, maxim; government; control; regulation; order; method.—*vt*. (ruling, ruled). To govern; to manage; to decide; to mark with lines by a ruler.—*vi*. To exercise supreme authority; to maintain a level, as the market price; to settle, as a rule of court.

Rumble, rum′bl, *vi*. (rumbling, rumbled). To make a dull, continued sound.—*n*. A low, heavy, continued sound; a seat for servants behind a carriage.

Run, run, *vi*. (running, pret. ran, pp. run). To move by using the legs more quickly than in walking; to take part in a race; to flee; to spread; to ply; to move or pass; to become fluid; to continue in operation; to have a certain direction; to have a certain purport; to be current; to continue in time.—*vt*. To cause to run; to pursue, as a course; to incur; to break through (a blockage); to smuggle; to pierce; to melt; to carry on.—*n*. Act of running; course or distance run; a trip; course, tenor, etc.; general demand, as on a back; place where animals may run; generality.

Rune, rön, *n*. One of a set of alphabetic characters peculiar to the ancient northern nations of Europe.

Rung, rung, *n*. A heavy staff; the round or step of a ladder.

Runner, run′ėr, *n*. One who runs; a messenger; a bird of the order Cursores; a stem running along the ground and taking root; that on which something runs or slides.

Rustic, rus′tik, *a*. Pertaining to the country; rural; homely; unpolished.—*n*. A country-man, a peasant; a clown.

Rustle, rus′l, *vi*. and *t*. (rustling, rustled). To make the noise of things agitated, as straw, leaves, etc.—*n*. The noise of things that rustle; a slight sibilant sound.

Rut, rut, *n*. The track of a wheel; a line cut with a spade; line of routine; time during which certain animals are under sexual excitement.—*vt*. (rutting, rutted). To cut in ruts.—*vi*. To be in heat, as deer.

Ruthless, röth′les, *a*. Cruel; pitiless.

Rye, rī, *n*. A cereal plant and it seed.

Rye-grass, rī′gräs, *n*. A kind of grass much cultivated for cattle and horses.

S

Sabbath, sa′bath, *n*. The day of rest; Sunday.

Sabbatic, Sabbatical, sa-bat′ik, sa-bat′ik-al, *a*. Pertaining to the Sabbath; pertaining to a recurrence by sevens.

Saber, sā′bėr, *n*. A sword with one

edge; a cavalry sword.—*vt.* (sabering, sabered). To strike or kill with a saber.

Sable, sā'bl, *n.* A small animal of the weasel family; the fur of the sable; black.—*a.* Black; dark.

Sabotage, sä-bō-täzh, *n.* Malicious destruction of employers, property or national plant by employees on strike or during war-time.

Sack, sak, *n.* A bag for flour, wool, etc.; that which a sack holds; a sort of jacket; a dry wine; pillage of a town.—*vt.* To put in sacks; to pillage, as a town.

Sacrament, sa'kra-ment, *n.* A solemn religious ordinance observed by Christians, as baptism or the Lord's Supper.

Sacred, sā'kred, *a.* Set apart for a holy purpose; consecrated; religious; set apart to some one in honor; venerable.

Sacrifice, sa'kri-fis, *n.* The offering of anything to God; anything offered to a divinity; surrender made in order to gain something else.—*vt.* (sacrificing, sacrificed). To make an offering or sacrifice of.—*vi.* To offer up a sacrifice to some deity.

Sacrilege, sa'kri-lej, *n.* Violation of sacred things.

Saddle, sad'l, *n.* A seat for a rider on a horse's back; something like a saddle in shape or use.—*vt.* (saddling, saddled). To put a saddle on; to burden.

Sadducee, sad'ū-sē, *n.* One of a sect among the Jews who denied the resurrection and the existence of angels or spirits.

Sadism, sād'ism, *n.* A form of sexual perversion, in which pleasure is taken in the cruel treatment of the companion.

Safe, sāf, *a.* Secure; free from danger; unharmed; no longer dangerous; trustworthy.—*n.* A strong box or chamber for securing valuables; a cool receptacle for meat.

Safeguard, sāf'gärd, *n.* One who or that which guards; a defense; protection; a passport.—*vt.* To guard.

Sagacious, sa-gā'shus, *a.* Quick of perception; shrewd; sage.

Sagacity, sa-gas'i-ti, *n.* Quickness of discernment; shrewdness; high intelligence.

Sage, sāj, *a.* Wise; sagacious; well-judged; grave.—*n.* A wise man; a man venerable for years, and of sound judgment; a labiate plant.

Sailing, sāl'ing, *p.a.* Moved by sails and not by steam.—*n.* Act of setting sail; art or rules of navigation.

Sailor, sāl'or, *n.* A seaman; a mariner.

Saint, sānt, *n.* One eminent for piety and virtue; one of the blessed; a person canonized—*vt.* To canonize.

Salicylic, sal-i-sil'ik, *n.* An acid used as an antiseptic, etc.

Salient, sā'li-ent, *a.* Springing; darting; projecting, conspicious.

Saline, sa-līn', *a.* Consisting of salt; salt.—*n.* A salt spring.

Saliva, sa-lī'va, *n.* The fluid secreted by certain glands, which moistens the mouth and assists digestion.

Salivate, sa'li-vāt, *vt.* To produce an unusual secretion and discharge of saliva.

Sallow, sal'ō, *a.* Having a pale, sickly, yellowish color.—*n.* A kind of willow.

Sally, sal'i, *n.* A leaping forth; a rush of troops from a besieged place; a dart of intellect, fancy, etc.; frolic.—*vi.* (sallying, sallied). To leap forth; to issue suddenly.

Salmon, sa'mun, *n.* A large fish highly valued as food.

Salon, sä-long, *n.* An apartment for the reception of company; a saloon.

Salsify, sal'si-fi, *n.* A plant cultivated for its edible root.

Salt, salt, *n.* A sbustance for seasoning and preserving food; a compound produced by the combination of a base with an acid; taste; savor; piquancy; an old sailor.—*a.* Impregnated with salt; pungent.—*vt.* To sprinkle or season with salt.

Salute, sa-lūt', *vt.* (saluting, saluted). To greet; to greet by a bow, etc.; to kiss; to honor.—*vi.* To perform a salutation; to greet each other.—*n.* Act of saluting; greeting; a kiss; a bow; discharge of artillery, etc.

Salvage, sal'vāj, n. Act of saving a ship or goods from shipwreck, fire, etc.; an allowance for the saving of property; goods thus saved.

Salvation, sal-vā'shon, n. Act of saving; redemption of man from sin; that which saves.

Salve, salv or säv, n. A healing ointment; remedy.—vt. (salving, salved). To apply salve to; to remedy.

Salver, sal'vėr, n. A tray on which articles are presented.

Sanatorium, san-a-tō'ri-um, n. A place to which people go for the sake of health.

Sanctification, sangk'ti-fi-kā'' shon, n. Act of sanctifying; consecration.

Sanctify, sangk'ti-fī, vt. (sanctifying, sanctified). To make holy; to hallow; to make pure from sin.

Sanctimonious, sangk-ti-mō'ni-us, a. Making a show of sanctity; hypocrtical.

Sanction, sangk'shon, n. Confirmation; ratification; authority.—vt. To ratify; to authorize; to countenance.

Sanctity, sangk'ti-ti, n. State of being sacred; holiness; inviolability.

Sanctuary, sangk'tū-a-ri, n. A sacred place; a place of worship; part of a church where the altar is placed; a place of protection to criminals, debtors, etc.; shelter.

Sandstone, sand'stōn, n. A stone composed of agglutinated grains of sand.

Sandwich, sand'wich, n. Slices of bread, with meat or something savory between.—vt. To insert like the meat in a sandwich; to fit between two other pieces.

Sane, sān, a. Sound in mind; discreet.

Sang-froid, sang'frwä, n. Coolness; imperturbable calmness.

Sanguine, sang'gwin, a. Consisting of blood; full of blood; of the color of blood; cheerful; confident.

Sanitary, san'i-ta-ri, a. Pertaining to or designed to secure health; hygienic.

Saponify, sa-pon'i-fī, vt. To convert into soap by combination with an alkali.

Sapphic, saf'fik, a. Pertaining to Sappho, a Grecian poetess, or to a kind of verse invented by her.—n. A Sapphic verse.

Sapphire, saf'fīr, n. A precious stone of very great hardness, and of various shades of blue; a rich blue color; blue.

Sarcasm, sär'kazm, n. A bitter cutting jest; a severe gibe; keen irony.

Sarcastic, sär-kas'tik, a. Containing sarcasm; scornfully severe; taunting.

Sarcode, sär'kōd, n. Structureless gelatinous matter forming the bodies of animals belonging to the protozoa.

Sarcoid, sär'koid, a. Resembling flesh.

Sash, sash, n. A long band or scarf worn for ornament; the frame of a window; a frame for a saw.—vt. To furnish with sashes or sash windows.

Sassafras, sas'a-fras, n. A kind of laurel, the root of which has medicinal virtues.

Satan, sā'tan, n. The devil or prince of darkness; the chief of the fallen angels.

Satchel, sa'chel, n. A little sack or bag; a bag for a school-boy's books.

Sate, sāt, vt. (sating, sated). To satiate; to satisfy the appetite of; to glut.

Satellite, sa'tel-līt, n. An attendant; an obsequious dependant; a small planet revolving round another.

Satiate, sā'shi-āt, vt. (satiating, satiated). To fully satisfy the desire of; to surfeit; to glut.—a. Filled to satiety.

Satisfy, sa'tis-fī, vt. and i. (satisfying, satisfied). To gratify fully; to content; to fulfil the claims of; to answer; to free from doubt.

Saturate, sa'tūr-āt, vt. To imbue till no more can be received; to soak thoroughly.

Saucy, sas'i, a. Showing impertinent boldness; pert; impudent; rude.

Saunter, san'tėr, vi. To stroll about idly; to loiter.—n. A stroll; a leisurely pace.

Saurian, sạ'ri-an, *a*. Pertaining to the lizards.—*n*. A scaly reptile, as the lizard.

Sausage, sạ'sāj, *n*. The prepared intestine of an ox, etc., stuffed with minced meat.

Savage, sa'vāj, *a*. wild; unculti-vated; barbarous; brutal.—*n*. One who is uncivilized; a barbarian.

Savant, sä-väng', A man of learn-ing; a man eminent for his scien-tific acquirements.

Save, sāv, *vt*. (saving, saved). To pre-serve; to protect; to rescue; to spare; to keep from doing or suf-fering; to reserve; to obviate.—*vi*. To be economical.—*prep*. Except.

Saving, sāv'ing, *a*. Thrifty; that se-cures from evil; containing some reservation.—*n*. What is saved; sums accumulated by economy: generally *pl*.—*prep*. Excepting.

Savior, sāv'yėr, *n*. One who saves from evil, destruction, or danger; Christ.

Savor, sā'vor, *n*. Taste; flavor; odor; distinctive quality.—*vi*. To have a particular taste; to partake of some characteristic of something else.—*vt*. To taste or smell with pleasure; to like.

Savory, sā'vo-ri, *a*. Having a good savor; palatable; agreeable.

Say, sā, *vt*. (saying, said). To utter in words; to speak; to declare; to as-sume.—*vi*. To speak; to relate.—*n*. A speech; statement.

Saying, sā'ing, *n*. Something said; speech; an adage; a maxim; a proverb.

Scab, skab, *n*. An incrusted sub-stance over a sore in healing; a disease of sheep; the mange in horses.

Scabbard, skab'ard, *n*. The sheath of a sword.

Scale, skāl, *n*. A thin flake on the skin of an animal; dish of a bal-ance; balance itself (generally *pl*.); anything graduated used as a measure; series of steps or ranks; relative dimensions; succession of notes; gamut.—*vt*. (scaling, scaled). To weigh, as in scales; to strip of scales; to clean; to climb, as by a ladder.—*vi*. To come off in thin layers.

Scalene, skā'lēn, *a*. A term applied to a triangle of which the three sides are unequal.

Scallion, skal'yun, *n*. A shallot.

Scallop, skal'op or skol'op, *n*. An edible bivalve of the oyster family; a curving on the edge of any-thing.—*vt*. To cut the edge of into scallops or segmets of circles.

Scalloped, skal'opt, *p.a*. Cut at the edge into segments of circles.

Scalp, skalp, *n*. The skin of the top of the head, with the hair on it.—*vt*. To deprive of the scalp.

Scapel, skal'pel, *n*. A knife used in anatomical dissections.

Scamp, skamp, *n*. A knave; swin-dler; rogue.—*vt*. To do in a perfunc-tory manner.

Scamper, skam'pėr, *vi*. To run with speed; to scurry.—*n*. A hurried run.

Scan, skan, *vt*. (scanning, scanned). To measure by the metrical feet, as a verse; to scrutinize; to eye.

Scandal, skan'dal, *n*. Public re-proach; shame; defamatory talk; slander.

Scandalize, skan'dal-īz, *vt*. To of-fend by some action deemed dis-graceful; to shock.

Scapula, skap'ū-la, *n*. The shoul-der-blade.

Scapular, Scapulary, skap'ū-lėr, skap'ū-la-ri, *n*. A monastic gar-ment resting on the shoulders, with a flap hanging down in front and another behind.

Scar, skär, *n*. The mark of a wound or ulcer; a cicatrix; a cliff; a bare place on the side of a hill.—*vt*. (scarring, scarred). To mark with a scar; to wound.

Scarce, skärs, *n*. Not plentiful; defi-cient; uncommon.

Scarcity, skärs'i-ti, *n*. State or con-dition of being scarce; deficiency; dearth.

Scare, skär, *vt*. (scaring, scared). To strike with sudden terror; to frighten.—*n*. A sudden fright, a causeless alarm.

Scarlet, skär'let, *n*. A bright-red color.—*a*. Of a bright-red color.

Scathe, skāth, *n*. Damage; injury.—*vt*. (scathing, scathed). To injure; to harm.

Scathing, skāth'ing, *p.a.* Injuring; harming; blasting.

Scatter, skat'ėr, *vt.* To disperse; to spread; to strew; to disunite.—*vi.* To be dispersed; to straggle apart.

Scatter-brain, skat'ėr-brān, *n.* A thoughtless person.

Scattered, skat'ėrd, *p.a.* Thinly spread; loose and irregular in arrangement.

Scavenger, ska'ven-jėr, *n.* One employed to clean the streets.

Scene, sēn, *n.* A stage; a distinct part of a play; a painted device on the stage; place of action or exhibition; general appearance of any action; a view; display of emotion.

Scenery, sēn'ė-ri, *n.* The painted representations on the stage; pictorial features; landscape characteristics.

Schedule, shed'ūl, sed'ūl, *n.* A paper containing a list, and annexed to a larger writing, as to a will, deed, etc.; an inventory.—*vt.* (scheduling, scheduled). To place in a schedule.

Scheme, skēm, *n.* A combination of things adjusted by design; a system; project; diagram.—*vt.* and *i.* (scheming, schemed). To plan, contrive, project.

Schemer, skēm'ėr, *n.* A contriver; plotter.

School, sköl, *n.* A place of instruction; a body of pupils; disciples; sect or body; a system or custom; a shoal (of fishes).—*a.* Relating to a school; scholastic.—*vt.* To instruct; to reprove.

Schooner, skön'ėr, *n.* A vessel with two or more masts, her chief sails fore-and-aft.

Sciatic, Sciatical, sī-at'ik, sī-at'ik-al, *a.* Pertaining to the hip or to sciatica.

Sciatica, sī-at'i-ka, *n.* Neuralgia or inflammation of the sciatic never or great nerve of the thigh.

Science, sī'ens, *n.* Knowledge reduced to a system; the facts pertaining to any department of mind or matter in their due connections; skill resulting from training.

Scientific, sī-en-tif'ik, *a.* Pertaining to science; versed in science; according to the rules or principles of science.

Scintilla, sin-til'la, *n.* A spark; glimmer; trace.

Scissors, siz'ėrz, *n.pl.* A cutting instrument consisting of two blades.

Scleroma, Sclerosis, sklē-rō'ma, sklē-rō'sis, *n.* Induration of the cellular tissue.

Scoff, skof, *n.* An expression of derision or scorn; a gibe.—*vi.* To utter contemptuous language; to jeer; to mock.—*vt.* To mock at.

Scold, skōld, *vi.* To find fault with rude clamor; to utter harsh, rude rebuke.—*vt.* To reprimand loudly; to chide.—*n.* A clamorous, foulmouthed woman.

Scorch, skorch, *vt.* To burn superficially; to singe; to parch.—*vi.* To be as hot as to burn a surface; to be dried up; to ride a cycle at excessive speed.

Score, skōr, *n.* A notch; a long scratch or mark; an account or reckoning; the number twenty; a debt; the number of points made in certain games; motive; ground; draft of a musical composition.—*vt.* (scoring, scored). To make scores or scratches on; to record; to get for oneself, as points, etc., in games.

Scoria, skō'ri-a, *n.*; pl. **-ae.** Dross; cinder; the cellular, slaggy lavas of a volcano.

Scorn, skorn, *n.* Extreme contempt; subject of contempt.—*vt.* To hold in extreme contempt; to despise.—*vi.* To feel or show scorn.

Scornful, skorn'ful, *a.* Filled with or expressing scorn; contemptuous.

Scorpion, skor'pi-on, *n.* An animal of the class Arachnida, with a jointed tail terminating with a venomous sting; a sign of the zodiac.

Scot, skot, *n.* A native of Scotland; a tax or contribution.

Scottish, skot'ish, *a.* Pertaining to Scotland, its inhabitants, or language.

Scoundrel, skoun'drel, *n.* A mean, worthless fellow; a rascal.—*a.* Base; unprincipled.

Scout, skout, *n.* A person sent to obtain intelligence regarding an enemy; a college servant.—*vi.* To act

S

as a scout.—*vt.* To watch closely; to treat with disdain.

Scout-master, skout-mäs'tėr, *n.* The leader of a troop of Boy Scouts.

Scow, skou, *n.* A flat-bottomed boat.

Scowl, skoul, *vi.* To wrinkle the brows, as in displeasure; to frown.—*n.* A deep angry frown; gloom.

Scrabble, skrab'l, *vi.* and *t.* To scrawl; to scribble.—*n.* A scribble.

Scrape, skrāp, *vt.* (scraping, scraped). To rub with something hard; to clean by a sharp edge; to act on with a grating noise; to erase; to collect laboriously.—*vi.* To roughen or remove a surface by rubbing; to make a grating noise.—*n.* Act of scraping; an awkward bow; an awkward predicament.

Scraper, skrāp'ėr, *n.* One who or that which scrapes; an instrument for scraping or cleaning.

Scratch, skrach, *vt.* and *i* To mark or wound with something sharp; to tear with the nails; to withdraw from the list of competitors.—*n.* A score in a surface; a slight wound; a line from which runners start, etc.; one most heavily handicapped in a contest.—*a.* Taken at random; hastily collected.

Scrawl, skral, *vt.* and *i* To write or draw carelessly or awkwardly.—*n.* Inelegant or hasty writing.

Scream, skrēm, *vi.* To shriek; to utter a shrill cry.—*n.* A sharp, shrill cry.

Screw, skrö, *n.* A cylinder with a sprial ridge which enables it when turned to enter another body; a screw-propeller; a twist or turn; a niggard.—*vt.* To fasten by a screw; to twist; to oppress.

Screw-driver, skrö'drīv-ėr, *n.* An instrument for turning screw-nails.

Screw-nail, skrö'nāl, *n.* A nail grooved like a screw.

Screw-propeller, skrö'prō-pel-ėr, *n.* An apparatus on the principle of the common screw, for propelling boats and ships.

Scribble, skrib'l, *vt.* and *i.* (scribbling, scribbled). To write with haste or without care; to tease coarsely, as cotton or wool.—*n.* Careless writing; a scrawl.

Scribe, skrīb, *n.* A writer; notary; copyist; doctor of the law among the Jews.

Scrimmage, skrim'āj, *n.* A tussle; a confused, close struggle in football.

Scrimp, skrimp, *vt.* To make too small or short; to scant; to limit.—*a.* Scanty.

Scrofula, skro'fū-la, *n.* A disease, a variety of consumption, often showing itself by glandular tumors in the neck which suppurate.

Scroll, skrōl, *n.* A roll of paper or parchment; a draft or first copy; a spiral ornament; a flourish added to a person's name.

Scrotum, skrō'tum, *n.* The bag which contains the testicles.

Scrub, skrub, *vt.* (scrubbing, scrubbed). To rub hard with something rough, to make clean or bright.—*vi.* To be diligent and penurious.—*n.* One who labors hard and lives sparingly; a mean fellow; a worn-out brush; low underwood.—*a.* Mean.

Scruple, skrö'pl, *n.* A weight of 20 grains; doubt; hesitation; backwardness.—*vi.* (scrupling, scrupled). To doubt; to hesitate.

Scuffle, skuf'l, *n.* A confused struggle.—*vi.* (scuffling, scuffled). To strive confusedly at close quarters.

Scull, skul, *n.* A short oar, used in pairs.—*vt.* To propel by sculls, or by moving an oar at the stern.

Sculptor, skulp'tor, *n.* One who works in sculpture; an artist who carves or models figures.

Sculpture, skulp'tūr, *n.* The art of carving wood or stone into images; an image in stone, etc.—*vt.* (sculpturing, sculptured). To carve; to form, as images on stone, etc.

Scum, skum, *n.* Impurities which rise to the surface of liquors; refuse.—*vt.* (scumming, scummed). To take the scum from.—*vi.* To throw up scum.

Scurvy, skėr'vi, *n.* A disease caused by insufficiency of vegetable food.—*a.* Vile; mean; malicious.

Scuttle, skut′l, *n*. A broad basket; a pail for coals; a hatchway in a ship's deck; a short run; a quick pace.—*vt*. (scuttling, scuttled). To sink by making holes in (a ship).—*vi*. To scurry.

Scythe, sīTH, *n*. An implement for mowing grass, etc.—*vt*. To cut with a scythe.

Sea, sē, *n*. The mass of salt water covering most of the earth; some portion of this; a name of certain lakes; a large wave; a surge; a flood.

Sea-anemone, sē′a-nem′o-nē, *n*. A beautiful sea-shore, plant-like animal.

Sea-breeze, sē′brēz, *n*. A wind or current of air blowing from the sea upon land.

Sea-calf, sē′käf, *n*. The common seal.

Seal, sēl, *n*. A hard substance bearing some device, used to make impressions; the wax stamped with a seal; assurance; that which makes fast; a carnivorous marine mammal.—*vt*. To set a seal to; to confirm; to fasten; to shut or keep close.

Seamanship, sē′man-ship, *n*. The art or skill of a seaman; art of managing a ship.

Seamstress, sēm′stres, *n*. A woman whose occupation is sewing; a sempstress.

Seamy, sēm′i, *a*. Having a seam; showing seams; showing the worst side; disagreeable.

Séance, sā-angs, *n*. A session, as of some public body; a sitting with the view of evoking spiritual manifestations.

Sea-port, sē′pōrt, *n*. A harbor on the seacoast; a town on or near the sea.

Sear, sēr, *n*. A catch in the mechanism of a rifle which holds back the cocking-piece.

Search, sėrch, *vt*. To look through to find something; to examine.—*vi*. To seek diligently; to inquire.—*n*. Act of searching; examination; inquiry.

Searching, sėrch′ing, *a*. Penetrating; trying; closely scrutinizing.

Sea-scape, sē′skāp, *n*. A picture representing a scene at sea; a sea-piece.

Sea-shore, sē′shōr, *n*. The shore of the sea; ground between high and low water mark.

Sea-sick, sē′sik, *a*. Affected with sickness caused by the motion of a vessel at sea.

Season, sē′zn, *n*. A division of the year; a suitable time; a time; time of the year marked by special activity; seasoning.—*vt*. To accustom; to acclimatize; to flavor.—*vi*. To become suitable by time.

Seasonable, sē′zn-a-bl, *a*. Natural to the season; opportune; timely.

Seasoning, sē′zn-ing, *n*. Something added to food to give it relish; relish; condiment.

Seat, sēt, *n*. That on which one sits; a chair; stool, etc.; place of sitting; a right to sit; residence; station.—*vt*. To place on a seat; to settle; to locate; to assign seats to; to fit up with seats.

Secessionist, sē-se′shon-ist, *n*. One who advocates or engages in a secession.

Seclude, sē-klöd′, *vt*. (secluding, secluded). To shut up apart; to separate; *refl*. to withdraw into solitude.

Seclusion, sē-klö′zhon, *n*. Act of secluding: retired mode of life; privacy.

Second, se′kund, *a*. Next after the first; repeated again; inferior; other.—*n*. One who or that which comes next a first; one who supports another; attendant in a duel; sixtieth part of a minute; a lower part in music; *pl*. a coarse kind of flour.—*vt*. To follow in the next place; to support; to join with in proposing some measure.

Secret, sē′kret, *a*. Hidden; concealed; private; unseen.—*n*. Something hidden or not to be revealed; a mystery.

Secretary, se′krē-ta-ri, *n*. A person employed to write orders, letters, etc.; an escritoire; one who manages the affairs of a department of government.

Secrete, sē-krēt′, *vt*. (secreting, secreted). To hide; to separate from the blood in animals or from the

S

sap in vegetables.

Section, sek'shon, *n.* Act of cutting; a distinct part; subdivision of a chapter, etc.; representation of an object as if cut asunder by an intersecting plane; a quarter of a platoon of infantry, the normal fire-unit.

Sector, sek'tor, *n.* A part of a circle between two radii; a mathematical instrument useful in making diagrams.

Secular, se'kū-lėr, *a.* Pertaining to things not spiritual or sacred; worldly; temporal; coming once in a century.

Secularism, sek'ū-lėr-izm, *n.* The elimination of the religious element from life.

Secure, sē-kūr', *a.* Free from care or danger; heedless; undisturbed; safe; confident.—*vt.* (securing, secured). To make safe or certain; to seize and confine; to guarantee; to fasten.

Security, sē-kū'ri-ti, *n.* Safety; confidence; protection; a guarantee; a surety; an evidence of property, as a bond, a certificate of stock, etc.

Sedate, sē-dāt', *a.* Composed in manner; staid; placid; sober; serious.

Sedition, sē-di'shon, *n.* A commotion in a state; insurrection; civic discord.

Seduce, sē-dūs', *vt.* (seducing, seduced).To lead astray; to corrupt; to entice to a surrender of chastity.

Seduction, sē-duk'shon, *n.* Act of seducing; allurement; the persuading of a female to surrender her chastity.

Sedulity, se-dū'li-ti, *n.* Unremitting industry; diligence; assiduity.

See, sē, *vt.* (seeing, pret, saw, pp. seen). To perceive by the eye; to notice; to discover; to understand; to receive; to experience; to attend.—*vi.* To have the power of sight; to understand; to consider.—*interj.* Lo! look!—*n.* A seat of episcopal power; a diocese.

Seed, sēd, *n.* That product of a plant which may produce a similar plant; seeds collectively; the semen; first principle; offspring.—*vi.* To produce seed; to shed the

seed.—*vt.* To sow; to supply with seed.

Seeming, sēm'ing, *p.a.* Appearing; specious.—*n.* Appearance; semblance.

Seemly, sēm'li, *a.* Becoming; suitable; decorous.—*adv.* In a suitable manner.

Seer, sēr, *n.* One who sees into futurity; a prophet.

See-saw, sē'sạ, *n.* A swinging movement up and down; a game in which children swing up and down on the two ends of a balanced piece of timber.—*vi.* and *t.* To move up and down or to and fro.

Seethe, sēTH, *vt.* (seething, seethed). To boil; to soak.—*vi.* To be in a state of ebullition; to be hot.

Segment, seg'ment, *n.* A part cut off; a section; a natural division of a body (as an orange).

Segregate, se'grē-gāt, *vt.* To set apart or separate.

Seize, sēz, *vt.* (seizing, seized). To lay hold of suddenly; to take by force or legal authority; to attack, as a disease, fear, etc.; to comprehend; to put in possession.—*vi.* To take hold or possession.

Seldom, sel'dom, *adv.* Rarely; not often.

Select, sē-lekt', *vt.* To choose; to pick out; to cull.—*a.* Chosen; choice; exclusive.

Selection, sē-lek'shon, *n.* Act of selecting; a collection of things selected.

Selenium, se-lē'ni-um, *n.* A non-metallic element akin to sulphur and tellurium.

Selenology, sel-ē-nol'o-ji, *n.* That branch of astronomy which treats of the moon.

Self, self, *n.*; pl. **Selves,** selvz. One's individual person; personal interest; a blossom of a uniform color (with *pl.* **Selfs**).—*a.* or *pron.* Same. Affixed to pronouns and adjectives to express emphasis or distinction, or reflexive usage.

Self-control, self-kon-trōl', *n.* Control exercised over oneself; self-command.

Self-denial, self-dē-nī'al, *n.* The forebearing to gratify one's own desires.

Self-denying, self-dē-nī'ing, a. Denying oneself; forbearing to indulge one's own desires.

Self-educated, self-ed'ū-kāt-ed, a. Educated by one's own efforts.

Self-esteem, self-es-tēm', n. The esteem or good opinion of oneself; vanity.

Self-evident, self-ev'i-dent, a. Evident in its own nature; evident without proof.

Self-government, self-gu'vėrn-ment, n. The government of oneself; government by rulers appointed by the people.

Self-important, self-im-pōrt'ant, a. Important in one's own esteem; pompous.

Self-imposed, self'im-pōzd, a. Imposed or voluntarily taken on oneself.

Selfish, self'ish, a. Devoted unduly to self; influenced by a view to private advantage.

Self-sufficient, self-suf-fi'shent, a. Having too much confidence in oneself; conceited; assuming; overbearing.

Self-willed, self'wild, a. Wilful; obstinate.

Sell, sel, vt. (selling, sold). To give in exchange for money, etc.; to betray.—vi. To practice selling; to be sold.

Selvedge, Selvage, sel'vej, sel'vāj, n. The edge of cloth; border of close work.

Semaphore, se'ma-för, n. An apparatus for signalling at a distance, usually a pole supporting a movable arm.

Semblance, sem'blans, n. Similarity; resemblance; image; appearance.

Seminary, se'min-a-ri, n. A school or academy; a place for educating for the priesthood.

Semination, se-min-ā'shon, n. Act of sowing; the natural dispersion of seeds.

Semite, sem'īt, n. A descendant of Shem; one of the Semitic race; a Shemite.

Semi-vowel, se'mi-vou-el, n. A sound partaking of the nature of both a vowel and a consonant, as

l, m, r.

Senescence, sē-nes'ens, n. State of growing old.

Senile, sē'nīl, a. Pertaining to old age; characterized by the failings of old age.

Senior, sē'ni-or, sēn'yor, a. Older; older or more advanced in office.—n. One older in age or office.

Senna, sen'na, n. The dried leaves of certain plants used as a purgative; the plant iself.

Sensation, sen-sā'shon, n. Impression made through the senses; feeling; power of feeling; what produces excited interest.

Sensational, sen-sā'shon-al, a. Relating to sensation; producing excited interest.

Sense, sens, n. The faculty of receiving impressions; a separate faculty of perception; sight; hearing, taste, smell, or touch; consciousness; discernment; understanding; good judgment; meaning.

Sensorium, sen-sō'ri-um, n. The common center at which all the impressions of sense are received; the brain.

Sensual, sens'ū-al, a. Pertaining to the senses, as distinct from the mind; carnal; voluptuous; indulging in lust.

Sentient, sen'shi-ent, a. Having the capacity of sensation; perceptive; sensible.

Sentiment, sen'ti-ment, n. Thought prompted by emotion; tenderness of feeling; sensibility; a thought or opinion.

Sentimental, sen-ti-men'tal, a. Having sentiment; apt to be swayed by emotional feelings; mawkishly tender.

Sentinel, sen'ti-nel, n. One who is set to keep watch; a sentry (now archaic or poetical).

Sentry, sen'tri, n. A soldier placed on guard; guard; watch; sentinel's duty.

Separate, se'pa-rāt, vt. (separating, separated). To put or set apart; to disjoin.—vi. To go apart; to cleave or split.—a. Detached; distinct; individual.

Separation, se-pa-rā'shon, n. Act of separating; disunion; incomplete

S

divorce.

Septuagenarian, sep'tū-a-jen-ā''ri-an, *n.* A person seventy years of age.

Septuagesima, sep'tū-a-jes''i-ma, *n.* The third Sunday before Lent.

Septuagint, sep'tū-a-jint, *n.* A Greek version of the Old Testament, finished about 200 B.C.

Septum, sep'tum, *n.*; pl. **-ta.** A wall separating cavities, as in animals or plants.

Sepulcher, se'pul-kėr, *n.* A tomb.—*vt.* To bury.

Sepulture, se'pul-tūr, *n.* Burial.

Sequacious, sē-kwā'shus, *a.* Following; logically consistent; consecutive.

Sequel, sē'kwel, *n.* That which follows; a succeeding part; result; issue.

Sequence, sē'kwens, *n.* A coming after; succession; arrangement; series.

Sequester, se-kwes'tėr, *vt.* To set apart; *refl.* to retire into seclusion; in *law,* to separate from the owner until the claims of creditors be satisfied; to appropriate.

Serene, sē-rēn', *a.* Clear; bright; calm; unruffled; formerly a form of address for princes, etc., in Germany and Austria.—*n.* Serenity; what is serene.

Serenity, sē-ren'i-ti, *n.* State of being serene; peace; calmness; coolness.

Serf, sėrf, *n.* A villein; a forced laborer attached to an estate; a bondman.

Sergeant, sär'jant, *n.* A noncommissioned officer above corporal; a police officer.

Serial, sē'ri-al, *a.* Pertaining to a series; forming a series.—*n.* A written composition issued in numbers.

Serous, sēr'us, *a.* Pertaining to serum; thin; watery; like whey; secreting serum.

Serpent, sėr'pent, *n.* A scaly reptile without feet; a bass musical instrument of wood; a firework.—*a.* Pertaining to a serpent.

Serpentine, sėr'pent-īn, *a.* Resembling or pertaining to a serpent; spiral.—*n.* A rock resembling a serpent's skin in appearance, used for decoration.—*vi.* To wind like a serpent.

Serrate, Serrated, ser'rāt, ser'rāt-ed, *a.* Notched on the edge like a saw; toothed.

Serration, ser-rā'shon, *n.* Formation in the shape of a saw.

Serried, se'rid, *a.* Crowded; in close order.

Serum, sē'rum, *n.* The watery part of curdled milk; whey; the thin part of the blood, etc.

Servant, sėrv'ant, *n.* One who serves; an attendant in a household; a drudge.

Serve, sėrv, *vt.* (serving, served). To work for and obey; to minister to; to set on a table for a meal; to conduce to; to be sufficient for; to manage or work; to deliver or transmit to; to perform the conditions of.—*vi.* To perform offices for another; to perform duties; to suffice; to suit.

Service, sėrv'is, *n.* Act of one who serves; employment; kind office; military or naval duty; period of such duty; usefulness; public religious worship; liturgy; set of dishes for the table; supply of things regularly provided.

Session, se'shon, *n.* The sitting of a court, etc., for business; time or term of sitting.—**Court of Session,** the hghest civil court of Scotland.

Set, set, *vt.* (setting, set). To put or dispose in a certain place or position; to fix; to appoint; to estimate; to regulate or adjust; to fit to music; to adorn; to intersperse; to incite.—*vi.* To disappear below the horizon; to solidify; to tend; to point out game; to apply oneself.—*p.a.* Placed, fixed, etc.; determined; established.—*n.* The descent of the sun, etc.; attitude, position; turn or bent; number of things combining to form a whole; a complete assortment; a clique.

Settle, set'l, *n.* A bench with a high back and arms.—*vt.* (settling, settled). To place in a more or less permanent position; to establish; to quit; to determine; to reconcile; to pay; to square or adjust; to colonize.—*vi.* To become fixed; to fix one's abode; to subside; to become calm; to adjust differences or accounts.

Settled, set'ld, *p.a.* Established; steadfast; stable; methodical.

Settlement, set'l-ment, *n.* Act of settling; establishment in life; colonization; a colony; adjustment; liquidation; arrangement; settling of property on a wife.

Severalty, se'ver-al-ti, *n.* A state of separation from the rest, or from all others.

Severance, se'ver-ans, *n.* Act of severing; separation.

Severe, se-vēr', *a.* Serious; grave; harsh; stern; austere; rigidly exact; keen.

Severity, se-ve'ri-ti, *n.* State or quality of being severe; rigor; intensity; austerity.

Sevres, sä-vr, *n.* A kind of beautiful porcelain, made of *Sèvres,* near Paris.

Sew, sō, *vt.* and *i.* To unite or make by needle and thread.

Sewage, sū'āj, *n.* The filthy matter which passes through sewers.

Sewer, sū'er, *n.* A subterranean drain, as in a city, to carry off water, filth, etc.

Sewer, sō'er, *n.* One who sews.

Sewing, sō'ing, *n.* Act of using a needle; that which is sewed; stitches made.

Sex, seks, *n.* That character by which an animal is male or female.

Sexual, seks'ū-al, *a.* Pertaining to, proceeding from, characterized by sex.

Shabby, shab'i, *a.* Poor in appearance; threadbare; mean; paltry; stingy.

Shackle, shak'l, *n.* A fetter; a manacle; that which obstructs free action.—*vt.* (shackling, shackled). To bind with shackles; to hamper.

Shade, shād, *n.* Obscurity caused by the interception of light; obscure retreat; twilight dimness; a screen; darker part of a picture; gradation of light; a scarcely perceptible degree or amount; a ghost.—*vt.* (shading, shaded). To screen from light; to obscure; to protect; to darken; to mark with

gradations of color.

Shadow, sha'dō, *n.* A figure projected by the interception of light; shade; an inseparable companion; an imperfect representation; a spirit; protection.—*vt.* To shade; to cloud; to screen; to represent faintly; to follow closely.

Shake, shāk, *vt.* (shaking, pret, shook, pp. shaken). To cause to move with quick vibrations; to agitate; to move from firmness; to cause to waver; to trill.—*vi.* To tremble; to shiver; to quake.—*n.* A wavering or rapid motion; tremor; shock; a trill in music; a crack in timber.

Shallow, shal'ō, *a.* Not deep; superficial; simple; silly.—*n.* A place where the water is not deep; a shoal.

Sham, sham, *n.* That which appears to be what it is not; imposture; humbug.—*a.* False; counterfeit.—*vt.* and *i.* (shamming, shammed). To feign, pretend.

Shame, shām, *n.* A painful sensation excited by guilt, disgrace, etc.; reproach; disgrace.—*vt.* (shaming, shamed). To make ashamed; to disgrace.

Shamefaced, shām'fāst, *a.* Easily put out of countenance; modest; bashful.

Shameful, shām'ful, *a.* Full of shame; disgraceful; scandalous; infamous.

Shameless, shām'les, *a.* Destitute of shame; immodest; unblushing.

Shampoo, sham-pö', *vt.* (shampooing, shampooed). To press and rub the body after a hot bath; to wash and rub thoroughly the head.

Shamrock, sham'rok, *n.* A trefoil plant, the national emblem of Ireland.

Shank, shangk, *n.* The leg; the shinbone; the part of a tool connecting the acting part with a handle; the stem of an anchor.

Shanty, shan'ti, *n.* A hut or mean dwelling; song sung by sailors working together.

Shape, shāp, *vt.* (shaping, shaped). To form; to mold; to adjust.—*vi.* To suit.—*n.* Form or figure; make; a model; a dish of blancmange, etc.

S

Shapeless, shāp'les, *a.* Destitute of any regular form; deformed.

Shard, shärd, *n.* A fragment of an earthen vessel; the wing-case of a beetle.

Share, shār, *n.* A part bestowed or contributed; lot or portion; a plow-share.—*vt.* (sharing, shared). To part among two or more; to participate in.—*vi.* To have part.

Shareholder, shär'hōld-ėr, *n.* One who holds shares in a joint property.

Shark, shärk, *n.* A voracious sea-fish; an unscrupulous person; a sharper.

Sharp, shärp, *a.* Having a very thin edge or fine point; keen; abrupt; not blurred; shrewd; acid; shrill; fierce; short and rapid; biting; barely honest; in *music,* raised a semitone.—*n.* A note raised a semitone, marked by the sign (#); the sign itself; *pl.* the hard parts of wheat.—*vt.* To sharpen.—*adv.* Sharply; exactly; rapidly.

Shave, shāv, *vt.* (shaving, shaved). To cut off the hair from the skin with a razor; to cut off thin slices from; to skim along; to fleece.—*vi.* To cut off the beard with a razor.—*n.* A cutting off of the beard; a thin slice; an exceedingly narrow escape.

Sheath, shēth, *n.* A case for a sword, etc.; a scabbard; wing-case of an insect.

Sheathe, shēTH, *vt.* (sheathing, sheathed). To put into a sheath; to protect by a casing.

Shed, shed, *vt.* (shedding, shed). To cast or throw off; to emit or diffuse; to let fall in drops; to spill.—*vi.* To let fall seed, a covering, etc.—*n.* A watershed; the opening betweem threads in a loom through which the shuttle passes; a penthouse; a hut; a large open structure.

Sheen, shēn, *n.* Brightness; splendor.—*a.* Bright; shining: *poetical.*

Sheep, shēp, *sing.* and *pl.* A ruminant animal valued for its wool and flesh; a silly or timid fellow.—**Sheep's eye,** a loving or wistful glance.

Sheet, shēt, *n.* A broad, thin piece of anything; broad expanse; piece of linen or cotton spread on a bed; piece of paper; a rope fastened to the lower corner of a sail.—*vt.* To furnish with sheets; to shroud.

Sheeting, shēt'ing, *n.* Linen or cotton cloth for making bed-sheets.

Shelf, shelf, *n.*; pl. **Shelves,** shelvz. A board fixed along a wall to support articles; a ledge; a ledge of rocks in the sea.

Shell, shel, *n.* A hard outside covering; an outside crust; framework; any slight hollow structure; a projectile contaiing a bursting charge.—*vt.* To strip off the shell of; to throw bomb-shells into or among.—*vi.* To cast the exterior covering.

Shellac, shel-lak', *n.* Lac melted and formed into thin cakes.

Shepherd, shep'ėrd, *n.* One who tends sheep.

Sherbet, sher'bet, *n.* An Eastern drink of water, the juice of fruits, and sugar.

Sheriff, she'rif, *n.* An officer in each county to whom is entrusted the administration of the law; in Scotland, the chief judge of a county.

Sherry, she'ri, *n.* A wine of southern Spain.

Shibboleth, shib'bō-leth, *n.* The watchword of a party; a cry or motto.

Shield, shēld, *n.* A broad piece of armor carried on the arm; protection; an escutcheon with a coat of arms.—*vt.* To cover, as with a shield; to protect.

Shift, shift, *vi.* To change; to change place or direction; to manage; to practice indirect methods.—*vt.* To remove; to alter; to dress in fresh clothes.—*n.* A change; expedient; evasion; an under garment; a squad of workmen; the working time of a relay of men; the spell of work.

Shingle, shing'gl, *n.* A thin piece of wood used in covering roofs; loose gravel and pebbles.—*vt.* To cover with shingles; to hammer so as to expel slag or scoriae from in puddling iron.

Shingles, shing'glz, *n.* An eruptive disease which spreads around the body.

Shining, shīn'ing, *a.* Bright; illustrious.

Shiny, shīn'i, *a.* Bright; brilliant; clear.

Ship, ship, *n.* A vessel of some size adapted to navigation; a three-masted, square-rigged vessel.—*vt.* (shipping, shipped). To put on board of a ship; to transport in a ship; to hire for service in a ship; to fix in its place.—*vi.* To engage for service on a ship; to embark.

Shipwreck, ship'rek, *n.* The wreck or loss of a ship; destruction; ruin.—*vt.* To wreck; to cast away; to ruin.

Shipwright, ship'rīt, *n.* A builder of ships or other vessels; a ship-carpenter.

Shirk, shėrk, *vt.* and *i* To avoid unfairly; to seek to avoid duty.

Shirt, shėrt, *n.* A man's loose under garment of linen, etc.; a lady's blouse.—*vt.* To clothe with a shirt.

Shiver, shi'vėr, *vt.* To shatter.—*vi.* To fall into many small pieces; to tremble, as from cold; to shudder.—*n.* A small fragment; a shaking fit; shudder.

Shoal, shōl, *n.* A multitude; a crowd; a sandbank or bar; a shallow.—*vi.* To become more shallow.—*a.* Shallow.

Shock, shok, *n.* A violent striking against; violent onset; a sudden disturbing emotion; a stook; a thick mass of hair.—*vt.* To give a shock to; to encounter violently; to disgust; to make up into shocks or stooks.

Shone, shon, pret. and pp. of *shine.*

Shook, shuk, pret. and pp. of *shake.*—*n.* The staves for a single barrel made into a package.

Shoot, shōt, *vt.* (shooting, shot). To cause to fly forth; to discharge; to hit or kill with a missile; to empty out suddenly; to thrust forward; to pass rapidly under, over, etc.—*vi.* To charge a missile; to dart along; to sprout; to project.—*n.* A shooting; a young branch; a sloping trough; a place for shooting rubbish.

Shooting, shōt'ing, *n.* Sport of killing game with firearms; tract over which game is shot; sensation of a darting pain.—*a.* Pertaining to one who shoots.

Shop, shop, *n.* A place where goods are sold by retail; a building in which mechanics work; one's special business.—*vi.* (shopping, shopped). To visit shops for purchasing goods.

Shot, shot, *n.* Act of shooting; a projectile; a bullet; bullets collectively; range or reach; a marksman; the number of fish caught in one haul; a reckoning.—*vt.* (shotting, shotted). To load with shot.—*a.* Having a changeable color, as silk; interwoven.

Should, shud, the pret. of *shall,* denoting present or past duty or obligation, or expressing a hypothetical case.

Shoulder, shōl'dėr, *n.* The joint by which the arm or the fore-leg is connected with the body; a projection; support.—*vt.* To push with the shoulder; to put upon the shoulder.—*vi.* To push forward.

Shoulder-blade, shōl'dėr-blād, *n.* The bone of the shoulder; scapula.

Shoulder-strap, shōl'dėr-strap, *n.* A strap worn on the shoulder, either to support dress, or as a badge of distinction.

Shout, shout, *vi.* To utter a loud and sudden cry.—*vt.* To utter with a shout.—*n.* A loud sudden cry.

Shove, shuv, *vt.* and *i* (shoving, shoved). To push forward; to press against; to jostle.—*n.* Act of shoving; a push.

Shovel, shu'vel, *n.* An instrument with a broad shallow blade, for lifting earth, etc.—*vt.* (shovelling, shovelled). To throw with a shovel.

Show, shō, *vt.* (pret. showed, pp. shown or showed). To display to the view of others; to let be seen; to make known; to prove; to bestow, afford.—*vi.* To appear.—*n.* Act of showing; exhibition; appearance; pretense; pageant; things exhibited for money.

Shrew, shrō, *n.* A peevish, ill-tempered woman; a scold; a shrew-mouse.

Shrewd, shröd, *a.* Astute; sagacious; discerning; sharp.

S

Shrine, shrīn, *n.* A case, as for sacred relics; a tomb; altar; a place hallowed from its associations.—*vt.* (shrining, shrined). To enshrine.

Shrink, shringk, *vi.* (pret. shrank or shrunk, pp. shrunk or shrunken). To contact spontaneously; to shrivel; to withdraw, as from danger; to flinch.—*vt.* To cause to contract.—*n.* Contraction.

Shrub, shrub, *n.* A woody plant less than a tree; a plant with several woody stems from the same root; a beverage containing the juice of fruit, etc.

Shrubbery, shrub'ėr-i, *n.* An ornamental plantation of shrubs; shrubs collectively.

Shrug, shrug, *vt.* and *i* (shrugging, shrugged). To draw up or to contract, as the shoulders.—*n.* A drawing up of the shoulders.

Shuck, shuk, *n.* A shell or husk.

Shudder, shud'ėr, *vi.* To tremble with fear, horror, etc.; to quake.—*n.* A tremor.

Shuffle, shuf'l, *vt.* (shuffling; shuffled). To shove one way and the other; to confuse; to change the position of cards.—*vi.* To change position; to quibble; to move with a dragging gait; to scrape the floor in dancing.—*n.* An evasion; mixing cards; scraping movement in dancing.

Shun, *vt.* (shunning, shunned). To avoid; to refrain from; to neglect.

Shunt, shunt, *vi.* and *t.* In railways; to turn from one line of rails into another; to free oneself of.

Shut, shut, *vt.* (shutting, shut). To close or stop up; to bar; to preclude; to exclude; to confine.—*vi.* To close itself; to be closed.—*a.* Made close; closed; not resonant.

Shutter, shut'ėr, *n.* One who shuts; a moveable covering for a window or aperture.

Shuttle, shut'l, *n.* An instrument used by weavers for shooting the thread of the woof between the threads of the warp.

Shuttle-cock, shut'l-kok, *n.* A cork stuck with feathers, and struck by a battledore.—*vt.* To throw backwards and forwards.

Sick, sik, *a.* Affected with disease of any kind; ill; inclined to vomit; disgusted or weary; pertaining to those who are sick.

Sick-bay, sik'bā, *n.* A ship's hospital.

Sicken, sik'n, *vt.* To make sick; to disgust.—*vi.* To become sick; to be disgusted; to languish.

Sickle, sik'l, *n.* An instrument for cutting grain, used with one hand; a reaping-hook.

Sickness, sik'nes, *n.* Disease; ill-health; illness; nausea.

Side, sīd, *n.* The broad or long surface of a body; edge, border; right or left half of the body; part between the top and bottom; any party or interest opposed to another.—*a.* Being on, from, or toward the side; indirect.—*vi.* (siding, sided). To embrace the opinions of one party.

Sidle, sīd'l, *vi.* (sidling, sidled). To go or move side foremost; to move to one side.

Siege, sēj, *n.* A regular attack on a fortified place; continued endeavor to gain possession.

Sienna, sē-en'na, *n.* An earth of a fine yellow color, used as a pigment.

Siesta, sē-es'ta, *n.* A sleep or rest in the hottest part of the day.

Sieve, siv, *n.* A utensil for separating the smaller particles of a loose substance.

Sift, sift, *vt.* To separate by a sieve; to examine minutely.—*vi.* To pass as if through a sieve.

Sigh, sī, *vi.* To make a long breath audibly, as from grief; to make a melancholy sound.—*n.* A long breath made audibly, as in grief.

Signal, sig'nal, *n.* A sign to communicate intelligence, orders, etc., at a distance.—*a.* Worthy of note; remarkable.—*vt.* or *i.* (signalling, signalled). To communicate by signals.

Signet, sig'net, *n.* A seal; seal used by the sovereign in sealing private letters.

Significant, sig-ni'fi-kant, *a.* Signifying something; indicative; important.

Signification, sig'ni-fi-kā''shon, *n.*

Act of signifying; meaning; import; sense.

Signify, sig'ni-fi, *vt.* (signifying, signified). To make known either by signs or words; to betoken; to mean; to imply; to import.

Silence, sī'lens, *n.* State of being silent; quiet; secrecy; absence of mention.—*vt.* To put to silence; to quiet; to cause to cease firing.

Silent, sī'lent, *a.* Not speaking; mute; dumb; taciturn; making no noise.

Silhouette, sil'ö-et, *n.* A profile portrait filled in with a dark color.

Sill, sil, *n.* The timber or stone at the foot of a door or window; the threshold; the floor of a gallery in a mine.

Silly, sil'li, *a.* Weak in intellect; foolish; unwise.

Silo, sī'lō, *n.* The pit in which green fodder is preserved in the method of ensilage.

Silt, silt, *n.* A deposit of fine earth from running or standing water.—*vt.* To fill with silt.

Silurian, sī-lū'ri-an, *a.* Applied to the lowest division of the paleozoic strata.

Silver, sil'ver, *n.* A precious metal of a white color; money; plate made of silver.—*a.* Made of silver; silvery.—*vt.* and *i.* To cover with a coat of silver; to tinge with gray.

Silversmith, sil'ver-smith, *n.* One whose occupation is to work in silver.

Simmer, si'mer, *vi.* To boil gently.

Simper, sim'per, *vi.* To smile in a silly manner.—*n.* A silly or affected smile.

Simple, sim'pl, *a.* Not complex; single; not involved; clear; artless; mere; plain; sincere; silly.—*n.* Something not mixed; a medicinal herb.

Simpleton, sim'pl-ton, *n.* A simple or silly person; one easily deceived.

Simplicity, sim-plis'i-ti, *n.* State or quality of being simple; singleness; artlessness; sincerity; plainness; foolishness.

Since, sins, *adv.* From that time; from then till now; ago.—*prep.* Ever from the time of; after.—*conj.*

From the time when; because that.

Sincere, sin-sēr', *a.* Pure; unmixed; real; genuine; guileless; frank; true.

Sincerity, sin-se'ri-ti, *n.* Honesty of mind or intention; freedom from hypocrisy.

Sinful, sin'ful, *a.* Full of sin; wicked; iniquitous; wrong.

Sing, sing, *vi.* (pret. sang, sung, pp. sung). To utter sounds with melodious modulations of voice; to have a ringing sensation.—*vt.* To utter with musical modulations of voice, to celebrate in song; to tell.

Singe, sinj, *vt.* (singeing, singed). To burn slightly; to burn the surface of.—*n.* A burning of the surface.

Single, sing'gl, *a.* Being one or a unit; individual; unmarried; performed by one person; simple; sincere.—*vt.* (singling, singled). To select individually; with *out.*

Singular, sing'gū-lėr, *a.* That is single; expressing one person or thing; remarkable; rare; odd.—*n.* The singular number.

Singularity, sing-gū-la'ri-ti, *n.* Peculiarity; eccentricity.

Sinister, si'nis-tėr, *a.* Left; evil; baneful; malign; unlucky.

Sink, singk, *vi.* (pret. sank or sunk, pp. sunk). To descend in a liquid; to subside; to enter; to decline in worth, strength, etc.—*vt.* To immerse; to submerge; to make by digging; to depress; to degrade.—*n.* A receptacle for liquid filth; a sewer; place where iniquity is gathered.

Sinker, singk'ėr, *n.* One who sinks; a weight on some body to sink it.

Sinless, sin'les, *a.* Free from sin; innocent.

Sinner, sin'ėr, *n.* One who sins; a transgressor; offender; criminal.

Sinology, si-nol'o-ji, *n.* The knowledge of the Chinese language, etc.

Sinter, sin'tėr, *n.* Stony matter precipitated by springs.

Sinuate, sin'ū-āt, *a.* Winding.

Sinuous, sin'ū-us, *a.* Bending or curving in and out; crooked.

Sinus, sī'nus, *n.* A curved opening; a bay; a cavity containing pus; a fistula.

S

Sinusitis, sī-nū-zī'tis, *n.* Inflammation of one of the air-cavities of the skull connecting with the nose.

Sip, sip, *vt.* (sipping, sipped). To drink in small quantities; to drink out of.—*vi.* To take a fluid with the lips.—*n.* A small quantity of liquid taken with the lips.

Siphon, sī'fon, *n.* A bent tube used for drawing off liquids, as from a cask, etc.

Sir, sėr, *n.* A word of respect used to men; title distinctive of knights and baronets.

Sire, sīr, *n.* A respectful word of address to a king; a father; male parent of a horse, etc.

Siren, sī'ren, *n.* A sea-nymph who enticed seamen by songs, and then slew them; a woman dangerous from her fascinations; a fog-signal; a signal used as an air-raid warning.—*a.* Bewitching.

Sit, sit, *vi.* (sitting, sat). To rest on the lower extremity of the body; to incubate; to remain; to be placed; to suit; to have a seat in Parliament, etc.; to hold a session.—*vt.* To keep the seat upon (a horse, etc.).

Site, sīt, *n.* Situation; a plot of ground for building on.

Sizable, Sizeable, sīz'a-bl, *a.* Of considerable bulk; of reasonable size.

Size, sīz, *n.* Comparative magnitude; bigness; bulk; a glutinous substance used by painters, etc.—*vt.* (sizing, sized). To arrange according to size; to take the size of; to cover with size.

Sizing, sīz'ing, *n.* Size or weak glue; act of covering with size.

Skein, skān, *n.* A small hank of thread.

Skeleton, ske'le-ton, *n.* The bony framework of an animal; general structure or frame; outline.—*a.* Resembling a skeleton.

Skeleton-key, ske'le-ton-kē, *n.* A thin light key that opens various locks.

Sketch, skech, *n.* An outline or general delineation; a first rough draft.—*vt.* To draw a sketch of; to give the chief points of; to plan.—*vi.* To practice sketching.

Skilful, skil'fúl, *a.* Skilled; dexterous; expert; clever.

Skill, skil, *n.* Ability; knowledge united with dexterity; aptitude.

Skillet, skil'et, *n.* A small vessel of metal, with a long handle, for heating water, etc.

Skim, skim, *vt.* (skimming, skimmed). To remove the scum from; to take off from a surface; to pass lightly over; to glance over superficially.—*vi.* To glide along.

Skim-milk, skim'milk, *n.* Milk from which the cream has been taken.

Skin, skin, *n.* The natural outer coating of animals; a hide; bark; rind.—*vt.* (skinning, skinned). To strip the skin from; to cover superficially.—*vi.* To be covered with skin.

Skirmish, skėr'mish, *n.* A slight battle; a brief contest.—*vi.* To fight in short contests or in small parties.

Skirt, skėrt, *n.* The lower and loose part of a garment; border; a woman's garment like a petticoat.—*vt.* To border.—*vi.* To be on the border.

Skit, skit, *n.* A satirical or sarcastic attack; a pasquinade; a squib.

Slab, slab, *n.* A thin flat piece of anything, as marlbe.—*a.* Thick and slimy.

Slack, slak, *a.* Not tight or tense; loose; remiss; backward; not busy.—*adv.* In a slack manner; partially; insufficiently.—*n.* The part of a rope that hangs loose; small broken coal.—*vt.* and *i.* To slacken; to slake.

Slacken, slak'n, *vi.* To become slack; to abate; to flag.—*vt.* To lessen the tension of; to relax.

Slag, slag, *n.* The scoria from a smelting furnace or volcano; fused dross of metal.

Slake, slāk, *vt.* (slaking, slaked). To quench, as thirst or rage; to extinguish.—*vi.* To abate; to become extinct.—*n.* A muddy tract adjoining the sea.

Slam, slam, *vt.* and *i.* (slamming, slammed). To shut with violence; to bang.—*n.* A violent shutting of a door.

Slander, slan'dėr, *n.* A false report maliciously uttered; defamation.—

vt. To defame; to calumniate.

Slang, slang, *n.* and *a.* A class of expressions not generally approved of, as being inelegant or undignified.—*vt.* To address with slang; to abuse vulgarly.

Slant, slant, *a.* Sloping.—*vt.* and *i.* To turn from a direct line; to slope; to incline.—*n.* A slope.

Slattern, slat'ern, *n.* A female who is not tidy; a slut.—*a.* Slatternly.

Slaughter, sla'ter, *n.* A slaying; carnage; massacre; a killing of beasts for market.—*vt.* To slay; to kill for the market.

Slavish, slāv'ish, *a.* Pertaining to slaves; servile; mean; oppressively laborious.

Slay, slā, *vt.* (pret. slew, pp. slain). To kill by violence; to murder; to destroy.

Sleazy, slē'zi, *a.* Thin; flimsy; wanting firmness of texture, as silk. Also *Sleezy.*

Sled, sled, *n.* A sledge.—*vt.* (sledding, sledded). To convey on a sled.

Sledge, Sledge-hammer, slej, slej'ham-ėr,*n.* A large, heavy hammer, used by iron-workers.

Sleek, slēk, *a.* Smooth and glossy.—*vt.* To make smooth and glossy.

Sleep, slēp, *vi.* (sleeping, slept). To take rest by a suspension of voluntary exercise of the powers of body and mind; to be dormant or inactive.—*vt.* To pass in sleeping; to get rid of by sleeping; with *off.*—*n.* That state in which volition is suspended; slumber; death; dormant state.

Sleight, slīt, *n.* A sly artifice; an artful trick; dexterity.

Slender, slen'dėr, *a.* Thin; slim; slight; feeble; meager; scanty.

Slice, slīs, *vt.* (slicing, sliced). To cut into thin pieces; to divide.—*n.* A thin, broad piece cut off; a broad flat utensil.

Slide, slīd, *vi.* (sliding, pret. slid, pp. slid, slidden). To move along a surface by slipping; to pass smoothly or gradually.—*vt.* To thrust smoothly along a surface.—*n.* A smooth and easy passage; that part of an apparatus which slides into place.

Slime, slīm, *n.* A soft or glutinous substance; moist earth or mud; viscous substance exuded by certain animals.—*vt.* (sliming, slimed). To cover with slime; to make slimy.

Sling, sling, *vt.* (slinging, slung). To throw; to hang so as to swing; to place in a sling.—*n.* An instrument for throwing stones; a bandage to support a wounded limb; a rope for raising heavy articles.

Slink, slingk, *vi.* (slinking, slunk). To sneak; to steal away.—*vt.* To cast prematurely.—*n.* A premature calf.

Slip, slip, *vi.* (slipping, slipped). To move smoothly along; to glide; to depart secretly; to have the feet slide; to err; to escape insensibly.—*vt.* To put or thrust secretly; to omit; to disengage oneself from; to make a slip of for planting.—*n.* A sliding of the feet; an unintentional error; a twig cut for planting or grafting; a long narrow piece; a leash by which a dog is held; a long strip of printed matter; a loose covering; an inclined plane upon which a ship is built.

Slipper, slip'ėr, *n.* One who slips or lets slip; a loose light shoe for household wear.

Slipshod, slip'shod, *a.* Shod with slippers; having shoes down at heel; slovenly.

Slit, slit, *vi.* (slitting, slit or slitted). To cut lengthwise; to cut into long strips.—*n.* A long cut or opening.

Slope, slōp, *n.* An oblique direction; a declivity.—*vt.* and *i.* (sloping, sloped). To form with a slope; to incline.

Sloppy, slop'i, *a.* Muddy; plashy; slovenly.

Slot, slot, *n.* A bolt or bar; an oblong hole; track of a deer.—*vt.* (slotting, slotted). To make a slot in.

Sloth, slōth or sloth, *n.* Indolence; laziness; idleness; a South American mammal.

Slouch, slouch, *n.* A stoop in walking; an ungainly gait; a droop.—*vi.* To hang down; to have a drooping gait.—*vt.* To cause to hang down.

Sludge, sluj, *n.* Mire; soft mud.

Slue, slö, *vt.* (sluing, slued). To turn

S

or swing round (as the yard of a ship).

Slug, slug, *n.* A sluggard; a shell-less snail injurious to plants; a piece of metal used for the charge of a gun.

Sluggish, slug'ish, *a.* Lazy; slothful; inert; not quick.

Slump, slump, *n.* The whole number taken in one lot; a sudden fall in prices or values.—*vt.* To throw into one lot.—*vi.* To sink in walking, as in snow.

Slur, slėr, *vt.* (slurring, slurred). To soil; to traduce; to pass lightly over; to pronounce in a careless indistinct manner.—*n.* A slight reproach; a stain or stigma.

Slush, slush, *n.* Sludge or soft mud; wet, half-melted snow.

Slut, slut, *n.* A woman negligent of tidiness and dress; a slattern.

Sly, slī, *a.* Cunning; crafty; wily; shrewd.

Smack, smak, *vi.* To make a sharp noise with the lips; to taste; to savor.—*vt.* To make a sharp noise with; to slap.—*n.* A loud kiss; a sharp noise; a smart blow; a slap; a slight taste; a smattering; a fishing-vessel.

Small, smạl, *a.* Little; petty; short; weak; gentle; not loud; narrow-minded; mean.—*n.* The small part of a thng; *pl.* small-clothes.

Smart, smärt, *n.* A quick, keen pain; pungent grief.—*a.* Keen; quick; sharp; brisk; witty; spruce; well dressed.—*vt.* To feel a sharp pain; to be acutely painful; to be punished.

Smell, smel, *vt.* (smelling, smelled). To perceive by the nose; to perceive the scent of; to detect.—*vi.* To give out an odor.—*n.* The faculty by which odors are perceived; scent; perfume.

Smelt, smelt, *vt.* To melt, as ore, to separate the metal.—*n.* A small fish allied to the salmon.

Smile, smīl, *vi.* (smiling, smiled). To show pleasure, sarcasm, pity, etc., by a look; to appear propitious.—*vt.* To express by a smile; to affect by smiling.—*n.* A set of the features expressing pleasure, scorn, etc.; favor.

Smock, smok, *n.* A chemise; a smock-frock.—*vt.* To clothe with a smock; to pucker diagonally.

Smocking, smok'ing, *n.* An ornamental diagonal puckering, in form of a honey-comb, and capable of being expanded.

Smoke, smōk, *n.* The exhalation from a burning substance; vapor; idle talk; nothingness; a drawing in and puffing out of tobacco fumes.—*vi.* (smoking, smoked). To emit smoke; to use tobacco.—*vt.* To apply smoke to; to befoul by smoke; to fumigate; to use in smoking.

Smooth, smōᴛH, *a.* Even on the surface; glossy; moving equably; not harsh; bland.—*n.* Smooth part of anything.—*vt.* To make smooth; to level; to make easy; to palliate; to soothe.

Smother, smuᴛH'ėr, *n.* Stifling smoke; suffocating dust.—*vt.* To stifle; to suffocate; to suppress.—*vi.* To be suffocated or suppressed; to smoulder.

Smoulder, smōl'dėr, *vi.* To burn and smoke without flame; to exist in a suppressed state.

Snack, snak, *n.* A small portion of food; a hasty repast; a bite; a share.

Snaffle, snaf'l, *n.* A bridle consisting of a slender bitmouth without a curb.—*vt.* To bridle; to manage with a snaffle.

Snag, snag, *n.* A short projecting stump; a shoot; the tine of a deer's antler; a tree in a river dangerous to vessels.

Snail, snāl, *n.* A slimy, slow-creeping mollusk; a slug; a sluggard.

Snake, snāk, *n.* A serpent.

Snap, snap, *vt.* (snapping, snapped). To bite or seize suddenly; to break with a sharp sound; to break short.—*vi.* To try to seize with the teeth; to break suddenly or without bending.—*n.* A quick eager bite; a sudden breaking; a sharp noise; a kind of biscuit.

Snare, snãr, *n.* A line with a noose for catching animals; anything that entraps.—*vt.* (snaring, snared). To catch with a snare; to ensnare.

Snarl, snärl, *vi*. To growl, as an angry dog; to talk in rude murmuring terms.—*vt*. To entangle.—*n*. A sharp angry growl; a knot; embarrassment.

Snatch, snach, *vt*. To seize hastily or abruptly.—*vi*. To make a grasp.—*n*. A hasty catch; a short fit or turn; a small portion; a snack.

Sneak, snēk, *vt*. To creep privately; to go furtively; to crouch.—*n*. A mean fellow; one guilty of underhand work.

Snip, snip, *vt*. (snipping, snipped). To cut off at a stroke with shears; to clip.—*n*. A single cut with shears; a bit cut off.

Snore, snōr, *vi*. (snoring, snored). To breathe with a rough, hoarse noise in sleep.—*n*. A breathing with a hoarse noise in sleep.

Snort, snort, *vi*. To force air with violence through the nose.—*n*. A loud sound produced by forcing the air through the nostrils.

Snout, snout, *n*. The projecting nose of a beast; muzzle; nozzle.

Snow, snō, *n*. Watery particles congealed in the air, and falling in flakes.—*vi*. To fall in snow; used impersonally.—*vt*. To scatter like snow.

Snow-plow, snō'plou, *n*. An implement for clearing away the snow from roads, etc.

Snow-shoe, snō'shö, *n*. A light frame worn on each foot to keep the wearer from sinking in snow; a snow-boot.

Snub, snub, *vt*. (snubbing, snubbed). To stop or rebuke with a tart, sarcastic remark; to slight designedly.—*n*. A check; a rebuke.

Snub-nose, snub'nōz, *n*. A flat nose.

Snuff, snuf, *vt*. To draw up through the nose; to smell; to crop, as the snuff of a candle.—*vi*. To draw up air or tobacco through the nose; to take offense.—*n*. A drawing up through the nose; resentment; burned wick of a candle; pulverized tobacco.

So, sō, *adv*. In this or that manner; to that degree; thus; extremely; very; the case being such;

thereby.—*conj*. Provided that; in case that; therefore; accordingly.

Soak, sōk, *vt*. To let lie in a fluid till the substance has imbibed all that it can; to steep; to wet thoroughly.—*vi*. To steep; to enter by pores; to tipple.

Soap, sōp, *n*. A compound of oil or fat with an alkali, used in washing.—*vt*. To rub or cover with soap.

Soar, sōr, *vi*. To mount upon the wing; to rise high; to tower.—*n*. A towering flight; a lofty ascent.

Sob, sob, *vi*. (sobbing, sobbed). To sigh or weep convulsively; to make a similar sound.—*n*. A convulsive catching of the breath in weeping or sorrow.

Sober, sō'bėr, *a*. Temperate; not drunk; calm; cool; staid; grave; dull-looking.—*vt*. To make sober.—*vi*. To become sober.

Society, sō-sī'e-ti, *n*. Fellowship; company; a body of persons united for some object; persons living in the same circle; those who take the lead in social life.

Sociology, sō-shi-ol'o-ji, *n*. The science which treats of society, its development, the progress of civilization, etc.

Sock, sok, *n*. The shoe of the ancient actors of comedy; a short woven covering for the foot.

Socket, sok'et, *n*. A cavity into which anything is fitted.

Sod, sod, *n*. That layer of earth which is covered with grass; piece of turf.

Soda, sō'da, *n*. The alkali carbonate of sodium used in washing, glass-making, etc., and extensively made from salt.

Soft, soft, *a*. Easily yielding to pressure; delicate; mild; effeminate; not loud or harsh; not strong or glaring.—*adv*. Softly.—*interj*. Be soft; stop; not so fast.

Soften, sof'n, *vt*. To make soft or more soft; to mollify; to alleviate; to tone down.—*vi*. To become soft; to relent; to become milder.

Soil, soil, *vt*. To sully; to tarnish; to manure; to feed (cattle) indoors with green fodder.—*vi*. To tarnish.—*n*. Dirt; ordure; tarnish; the upper stratum of the earth;

mould; loam; earth; land; country.

Solder, sol´dėr, *vt.* To unite metals by a fused metallic substance; to patch up.—*n.* A metallic cement.

Soldier, sōl´jėr, *n.* A man in military service; a man of distinguished valor.

Sole, sōl, *n.* The under side of the foot; the bottom of a shoe; a marine fish allied to the flounder.—*vt.* (soling, soled). To furnish with a sole, as a shoe.—*a.* Single; individual; only; alone.

Solid, so´lid, *a.* Resisting pressure; not liquid or gaseous; not hollow; cubic; sound; not frivolous.—*n.* A body that naturally retains the same shape.

Solidarity, so-li-dar´i-ti, *n.* Unity or communion of interests and responsibilities.

Soliloquy, sō-lil´ō-kwi, *n.* A speaking to oneself; discourse of a person alone.

Solitaire, so´li-tār, *n.* A solitary; an article of jewelry in which a single gem is set; a game for a single person.

Soluble, so´lū-bl, *a.* Susceptible of being dissolved in a fluid; capable of being solved, as a problem.

Solution, so-lū´shon, *n.* A dissolving; preparation made by dissolving a solid in a liquid; act of solving; explanation; termination or crisis of a disease.

Solve, solv, *vt.* (solving, solved). To explain; to make clear; to unravel; to work out.

Solvent, sol´vent, *a.* Having the power of dissolving; able to pay all debts.—*n.* A fluid that dissolves any substance.

Somatic, sō-mat´ik, *a.* Corporeal; bodily.

Somehow, sum´hou, *adv.* In some way not yet known; one way or another.

Somersault, Somerset, sum´ėr-salt, sum´ėr-set, *n.* A leap in which the heels turn over the head; a turn of the body in the air.

Something, sum´thing, *n.* A thing, quantity, or degree indefinitely; a person or thing of importance.—*adv.* Somewhat.

Sometime, sum´tīm, *adv.* Once; formerly; by and by.—*a.* Former; whilom.

Somewhat, sum´whot, *n.* Something; more or less.—*adv.* In some degree; a little.

Somite, sō´mīt, *n.* A single segment in the body of an articulated animal.

Somnambulism, som-nam´bū-lizm, *n.* The act or practice of walking in sleep.

Somniferous, som-nif´ėr-us, *a.* Bringing or causing sleep; soporific.

Somniloquence, Somniloquism, som-nil´ō-kwens, som-nil´ō-kwizm, *n.* The act of talking in sleep.

Sonorous, sō-nō´rus, *a.* Giving sound when struck; resonant; high-sounding.

Soon, sön, *adv.* In a short time; shortly; early; quickly; promptly; readily; gladly.

Soot, söt, *n.* A black substance formed from burning matter.—*vt.* To cover or foul with soot.

Soothe, sö͞тн, *vt.* (soothing, soothed). To please with soft words; to flatter; to pacify; to assuage; to soften.

Soothing, sö͞тн´ing, *p.a.* Serving to soothe, calm, or assuage; mollifying.

Soporiferous, sō-pō-rif´ik, *a.* Causing sleep.—*n.* A drug or anything that induces sleep.

Soprano, sō-prä´nō, *n.* The highest female voice; a singer with such a voice.

Sorcerer, sōr´sėr-ėr, *n.* A wizard; an enchanter; a magician.

Sorcery, sōr´sėr-i, *n.* Magic; enchantment; witchcraft.

Sordid, sor´did, *a.* Dirty; foul; vile; base; niggardly; covetous.

Sore, sōr, *a.* Painful; severe; distressing; tender; galled.—*n.* An ulcer, wound, etc.—*adv.* Severely; sorely.

Sorghum, sor´gum, *n.* A kind of millet.

Sorrel, so´rel, *n.* A plant allied to the docks; a reddish or yellow-brown color.—*a.* Of a reddish color.

Sorrow, so´rō, *n.* Affliction or distress of mind; grief; regret.—*vi.* To feel sorrow; to grieve.

Sorry, so'ri, *a*. Feeling sorrow; grieved; sorrowful; wretched; pitiful.

Sort, sort, *n*. Nature or character; kind; species; manner; a set.—*vt*. To assort; to arrange; to reduce to order.—*vi*. To consort; to agree.

Soul, sōl, *n*. The spiritual principle in man; the moral and emotional part of man's nature; elevation of mind; fervor; essence; an inspirer or leader; a person.

Sound, sound, *a*. Not in any way defective; healthy; valid; free from error; orthodox; just; heavy.—*n*. A narrow channel of water; a strait; air-bladder of a fish; that which is heard; noise.—*vt*. To measure the depth of; to examine medically; to try to discover the opinion, etc., of; to cause to give out a sound; to pronounce.—*vi*. To give out a sound; to appear on narration; to be spread or published.

Soundings, sound'ingz, *n.pl*. The depths of water in rivers, harbors, etc.

Soundless, sound'les, *a*. That cannot be fathomed; noiseless.

Soundness, sound'nes, *n*. Healthiness; solidity; validity; orthodoxy.

Soup, söp, *n*. A liquid food made generally from flesh and vegetables.

Sour, sour, *a*. Acid or sharp to the taste; tart; peevish; morose.—*vt*. To make sour; to make cross or discontented; to embitter.—*vi*. To become sour or peevish.

Source, sōrs, *n*. That from which anything rises; the spring, etc., from which a stream proceeds; first cause; origin.

Soviet, sov'i-et, *n*. The method of government in Russia since the Revolution, local soviets (elected councils) sending delegates to larger bodies, and these, in their turn, to the Supreme Congress, which elects the Supreme Council.

Sow, sou, *n*. The female of the swine.

Sow, sō, *vt*. (pret. sowed, pp. sowed or sown). To scatter seed over; to spread abroad.—*vi*. To scatter seed for growth.

Sower, sō'ér, *n*. One who sows.

Soy, soi, *n*. A sauce prepared in China and Japan from a bean; the plant producing the bean.

Spa, spạ, *n*. A place to which people go on account of a spring of mineral water.

Space, spās, *n*. Extension; room; interval between points or objects; quantity of time; a while.—*vt*. (spacing, spaced). To arrange at proper intervals; to arrange the spaces in.

Spacious, spā'shus, *a*. Roomy; widely extended; ample; capacious.

Spade, spād, *n*. An instrument for digging; a playing card of a black suit.—*vt*. (spading, spaded). To dig with a spade; to use a spade on.

Span, span, *n*. Reach or extent in general; space between the thumb and little finger; nine inches; a short space of time; the stretch of an arch; a yoke of animals.—*vt*. (spanning, spanned). To extend across; to measure with the hand with the fingers extended.

Spar, spär, *n*. A long piece of timber; a pole; a crystalline mineral; boxing-match; flourish of the fists.—*vi*. (sparring, sparred). To fight in show; to box; to bandy words.

Spare, spär, *a*. Scanty; thin; sparing or chary; superfluous; held in reserve.—*vt*. (sparing, spared). To use frugally; to dispense with; to omit; to use tenderly; to withhold from.—*vi*. To be frugal; to use mercy or forbearance.

Sparing, spär'ing, *a*. Saving; economical.

Spark, spärk, *n*. A particle of ignited substance, which flies off from burning bodies; a small transient light; a gay man; a lover.—*vi*. To emit particles of fire; to sparkle.

Sparkle, spär'kl, *n*. A little spark; luster.—*vi*. (sparkling, sparkled). To emit sparks; to glitter; to be animated.

Sparrow, spa'rō, *n*. A bird of the finch family.

Sparse, spärs, *a*. Thinly scattered; not thick or close together.

S

Speak, spēk, *vi.* (pret. spoke, spake, pp. spoken). To utter words; to talk; to deliver a speech; to argue; to plead; to be expressive.—*vt.* To utter with the mouth; to pronounce; to accost; to express.

Spear, spēr, *n.* A long, pointed weapon; a lance.—*vt.* To pierce or kill with a spear.

Special, spe'shal, *a.* Pertaining to a species; particular; distinctive; having a particular purpose or scope.

Specialist, spe'shal-ist, *n.* One who devotes himself to some particular subject.

Specialize, spe-shal-īz, *vt.* To assign a specific use to.—*vi.* To apply oneself to a particular subject.

Specialty, spe'shal-ti, *n.* Special characteristic; a special pursuit; a special product.

Specie, spē'shi, *n.* Metallic money; coin.

Species, spē'shēz, *n. sing.* and *pl.* Outward appearance; a kind, sort, or variety; a class.

Specific, spe-sif'ik, *a.* Pertaining to, designating or constituting a species; definite; precise.—*n.* A remedy which exerts a special action in the cure of a disease; an infallible remedy.

Specification, spe'si-fi-kā''shon, *n.* The act of specifying; details of particulars; particular mention; statement.

Specify, spe'si-fī, *vt.* (specifying, specified). To make specific; to state in detail.

Specimen, spe'si-men, *n.* A sample; a part intended to typify the whole.

Specious, spē'shus, *a.* Superficially correct; appearing well at first view; plausible.

Speck, spek, *n.* A small spot; a stain; a flaw; an atom.—*vt.* To spot.

Speckle, spek'l, *n.* A speck; a small colored marking.—*vt.* (speckling, speckled). To mark with small specks.

Spectacle, spek'ta-kl, *n.* A show; a sight; an exhibition; a pageant; *pl.* glasses to assist or correct defective vision.

Spectacular, spek-tak'ū-lèr, *a.* Pertaining to or of the nature of a show.

Speculate, spek'ū-lāt, *vi.* (speculating, speculated). To meditate; to engage in risky financial transactions with a view to profit.

Speculator, spek'ū-lāt-or, *n.* A theorizer; one who speculates in business.

Speech, spēch, *n.* The faculty of speaking; language; talk; a formal discourse; oration.

Speed, spēd, *n.* Success; velocity; haste.—*vi.* (speeding, sped). To make haste; to prosper.—*vt.* To dispatch in haste; to help forward; to dismiss with good wishes.

Spendthrift, spend'thrift, *n.* and *a.* One who spends improvidently; a prodigal.

Spent, spent, *p.a.* Wearied; exhausted; having deposited spawn.

Sphere, sfēr, *n.* An orb; a ball; a globe; a sun, star, or planet; circuit of motion, action, etc.; range; province; rank.—*vt.* (sphering, sphered). To place in a sphere or among the spheres.

Spheroid, sfēr'oid, *n.* A body like a sphere, but not perfectly spherical.

Sphincter, sfingk'tèr, *n.* A ring-like muscle closing the external orifices of organs, as the mouth or anus.

Sphygmograph, sfig'mō-graf, *n.* An instrument to indicate the nature of the pulse.

Spice, spīs, *n.* A vegetable production, aromatic to the smell and pungent to the taste; something piquant; flavor; smack.—*vt.* (spicing, spiced). To season with spice; to flavor.

Spill, spil, *vt.* (pret. and pp. spilled or spilt). To suffer to fall, flow over, etc.; to shed.—*vi.* To be shed; to be suffered to fall, be lost, or wasted.—*n.* A spigot; piece of wood or paper used to light a lamp, etc.; a fall.

Spin, spin, *vt.* (spinning, spun). To draw out and twist into threads; to protract; to whirl; to make threads, as a spider.—*vi.* To work at drawing and twisting threads; to rotate; to go quickly.—*n.* Act of spinning; a rapid run.

Spinach, Spinage, spin´āj, n. A culinary vegetable.

Spinal, spīn´al, a. Pertaining to the spine.

Spindle, spin´dl, n. A pin carrying a bobbin in a spinning machine; a small axis; a long, slender stalk; a measure of yarn.—vi. To grow in a long slender stalk.

Spine, spīn, n. A prickle; a thorn; a thin, pointed spike in animals; the backbone or spinal column.

Spire, spīr, n. A winding line like a screw; a spiral; a wreath; a convolution; a steeple; a stalk or blade of grass, etc.—vi. (spiring, spired). To taper up.

Spirit, spi´rit, n. The breath of life; the soul; a spectre; vivacity; courage; mood; essence; real meaning; intent; a liquid obtained by distillation; pl. alcoholic liquor.—vt. To infuse spirit into; to encourage.

Spirt, spért, vt. To force out in a jet; to squirt.—vi. To gush out in a jet.—n. A jet of fluid.

Spit, spit, n. A prong on which meat is roasted; low land running into the sea.—vt. (spitting, spitted). To put on a spit; to pierce.

Spit, spit, vt. and i. (spitting, spat). To eject from the mouth, as saliva.—n. What is ejected from the mouth; spittle.

Spite, spīt, n. A feeling of ill-will; malice; rancour—**In spite of,** notwithstanding.—vt. (spiting, spited). To mortify or chagrin; to thwart.

Spittle, spit´l, n. Saliva; the moist matter ejected from the mouth.

Splash, splash, vt. and i. To bespatter with liquid matter.—n. A quantity of wet matter thrown on anything; a noise from water dashed about; a spot of dirt.

Splice, splīs, vt. (splicing, spliced). To unite, as two ropes, by interweaving the strands; to unite by overlapping, as timber.—n. Union of ropes by interweaving; piece added by splicing.

Splint, splint, n. A splinter; piece of wood to confine a broken bone when set.

Splinter, splint´ėr, n. A piece of

wood, or other solid substance, split off.—vt. To split into splinters; to shiver.

Split, split, vt. (splitting, split). To divide lengthwise; to cleave; to rend; to burst.—vi. To part asunder; to burst; to crack; to differ in opinion.—n. A rent; fissure; breach or separation.—a. Divided; rent; deeply cleft.

Splutter, splut´ėr, n. A bustle; a stir.—vi. To speak confusedly; to sputter.

Spode, spōd, n. A material composed of calcined ivory, of which vases, etc., are made.

Spoil, spoil, n. Pillage; booty; plunder.—vt. To plunder; to impair; to ruin; to injure by over-indulgence.—vi. To grow useless; to decay.

Spoke, spōk, n. A bar of a wheel; the round of a ladder; a bar.—vt. (spoking, spoked). To furnish with spokes. Pret. of *speak*.

Spoken, spōk´n, p.a. Oral; speaking (as in fair-spoken).

Sponge, spunj, n. A soft porous marine substance which readily imbibes liquids; a mean parasite.—vt. (sponging, sponged). To wipe with a sponge; to wipe out completely; to harass by extortion; to get by mean arts.—vi. To imbibe; to act as a hanger-on.

Sponsor, spon´sor, n. A surety or guarantor; a godfather or godmother.

Spore, spōr, n. The reproductive germ of a cryptogamic plant; a germ of certain animal organisms.

Sport, spōrt, n. A game; a merrymaking; out-of-door recreation, as shooting, horse-racing, etc.; jest; object of mockery; a plant or animal that differs from the normal type.—vt. To divert (oneself); to wear in public.—vi. To play; to frolic; to practise the diversions of the field.

Sportsman, spōrts´man, n. One who engages in shooting, fishing, etc.

Spot, spot, n. A place discolored; a speck; a blemish; a flaw; a locality.—vt. (spotting, spotted). To

S

make a spot on; to stain; to catch
with the eye.—*vi*. To act as ob-
server of enemy's position, of effect of gunfire, or of approach of
hostile aircraft.

Sprain, sprān, *vt*. To overstrain, as
the muscles or ligaments of a
joint.—*n*. A violent strain of a joint
without dislocation.

Sprawl, sprạl, *vi*. To struggle or
show convulsive motions; to lie or
crawl with the limbs stretched.

Spray, sprā, *n*. A twig; collection of
small branches; water or any liquid flying in small drops or particles.—*vt*. To cause to take the form
of spray; to treat with spray.

Spring, spring, *vi*. (pret. sprang or
sprung, pp. sprung). To leap; to
start up; to dart; to warp; to become cracked; to originate.—*vt*. To
start or rouse; to propose on a sudden; to crack; to jump over.—*n*. A
leap; resilience; an elastic body,
made of various materials, especially steel; cause; an issue of water; source of supply; season of the
year when plants begin to grow; a
crack in timber.

Springy, spring'i, *a*. Elastic; light of
foot; abounding with springs; wet;
spongy.

Sprinkle, spring'kl, *vt*. and *i*. (sprin-
kling, sprinkled). To scatter in
small drops; to bedew.—*n*. A small
quantity scattered in drops.

Sprint, sprint, *n*. A short swift foot-
race; a spurt.

Spur, spėr, *n*. An instrument with
sharp points, worn on horsemen's
heels; incitement; stimulus; a
sharp outgrowth; a mountain
mass that shoots from another.—
vt. (spurring, spurred). To prick
with a spur; to incite; to put spurs
on.—*vi*. To travel with great expedition.

Spurious, spū'ri-us, *a*. Bastard; not
genuine; counterfeit; false.

Spurn, spėrn, *vt*. To drive away, as
with the foot; to reject with disdain; to treat with contempt.—*vi*.
To kick up the heels; to manifest
disdain.

Spurt, spėrt, *vt*. and *i*. To spirt.—*n*. A
gush of liquid; sudden effort for an
emergency; sudden increase of
speed.

Sputter, sput'ėr, *vi*. To emit saliva in
speaking; to throw out moisture;
to speak hastily and indistinctly.

Spy, spī, *vt*. (spying, spied). To gain
sight of; to gain knowledge of by
artifice; to explore.—*vi*. To pry.—*n*.
One who keeps watch on the
actions of others; a secret emis-
sary.

Squall, skwạl, *vi*. To cry out; to
scream violently.—*n*. A loud
scream; a violent gust of wind; a
brief storm of wind.

Squalor, skwol'ėr, *n*. Foulness; filthi-
ness.

Squander, skwon'dėr, *vt*. To spend
lavishly; to fling away; to waste.

Square, skwār, *a*. Having four
equal sides and four right angles;
forming a right angle; just; honest;
even; suitable.—*n*. A figure having
four equal sides and right angles;
any similar figure or area; an instrument having one edge at right
angles to another; product of a
number multiplied by itself; level;
equality.—*vt*. (squaring, squared).
To make square; to form to right
angles; to adjust; to fit; to settle
(accounts); to multiply a number
by itself.—*vi*. To suit; to spar (col-
loq.).

Squeamish, skwēm'ish, *a*. Having
a stomach easily turned; fastidious.

Squeeze, skwēz, *vt*. (squeezing,
squeezed). To subject to pressure;
to harass by extortion; to hug.—*vi*.
To press; to crowd.—*n*. An application of pressure; compression.

Squelch, skwelch, *vt*. To crush; to
destroy.—*vi*. To be crushed.—*n*. A
flat heavy fall.

Squid, skwid, *n*. A cuttle-fish.

Squint, skwint, *a*. Looking
obliquely or different ways.—*n*. An
oblique look; an affection in which
the optic axes do not coincide.—*vi*.
To look obliquely.

Stable, stā'bl, *a*. Firm; firmly established; steadfast.—*n*. A house for
horses, etc.—*vt*. (stabling, stabled).
To put or keep in a stable.—*vi*. To
dwell in a stable.

Stack, stak, *n*. A large, regularly
built pile of hay, grain, etc.; a num-

ber of chimneys standing together; a single tall chimney; a high rock detached.—*vt*. To build into a stack; to pile together.

Staff, stäf, *n*.; pl. **Staves** or **Staffs,** stävz, stäfs. A stick or rod; a prop or support; a baton; the five parallel lines on which musical characters are written; a body of officers attached to an army as a whole (pl. *staffs*); a body of persons assisting in any undertaking.

Stag, stag, *n*. A male animal, especially the male red-deer; a hart.

Stage, stäj, *n*. An elevated platform; the platform on which theatrical performances are exhibited; place of action; a halting-place; distance between two stopping-places; degree of progression; point reached.—*vt*. To put upon the theatrical stage.

Stagger, stag'ėr, *vi*. To reel; to totter; to waver.—*vt*. To cause to waver; to amaze; to arrange working hours so that employees enter and leave their place of work at intervals in batches, instead of simultaneously.—*n*. A sudden swaying of the body; *pl*. a disease of cattle, etc., attended with giddiness.

Stalk, stak, *n*. The stem of a plant; part that supports a flower, leaf, fruit, etc.; a stately step or walk.—*vi*. To walk in a dignified manner.—*vt*. To watch and follow warily, as game, for the purpose of killing.

Stall, stal, *n*. A place where a horse or ox is kept and fed; division of a stable; a bench or shed where anything is exposed to sale, etc.; the seat of a clerical dignitary in the choir; a seat in a theatre.—*vt*. To put into a stall; to plunge into mire.

Stallion, stal'yun, *n*. A horse not castrated.

Stalwart, Stalworth, stal'wėrt, stal'wėrth, *a*. Stout-hearted; tall and strong.

Stamina, sta'mi-na, *n.pl*. Whatever constitutes the principal strength; robustness; power of endurance.

Stammer, stam'ėr, *vt*. and *t*. To make involuntary breaks in utterance; to stutter.—*n*. Defective utterance; a stutter.

Stamp, stamp, *vt*. To strike by thrusting the foot down; to impress; to imprint; to affix a postage-stamp to; to coin; to form.—*vi*. To strike the foot forcibly downward.—*n*. Act of stamping; an instrument for crushing or for making impressions; mark imprinted; a postage-stamp; character; sort.

Stand, stand, *vi*. (standing, stood). To be upon the feet in an upright position; to be on end; to have locality; to stop; to endure; to persevere; to be as regards circumstances; to be equivalent; to become a candidate; to hold a certain course; to be valid.—*vt*. To set on end; to endure.—*n*. Act of standing; a stop; a halt; a station; a small table or frame; platform for spectators at gatherings.

Standard, stan'därd, *n*. A flag of war; a banner; a rule or measure; criterion; test; a certain grade in schools; an upright support.—*a*. Serving as a standard; satisfying certain legal conditions; not trained on a wall, etc., but standing by itself.

Star, stär, *n*. Any celestial body except the sun and moon; a heavenly body similar to our sun; a figure with radiating points; a badge of honor; an asterisk, thus *; a brilliant theatrical performer.—*vt*. (starring, starred). To adorn with stars; to bespangle.—*vi*. To shine as a star; to appear as an eminent actor among inferior players.

Starboard, stär'börd, *n*. and *a*. The right-hand side of a ship.

Start, stärt, *vi*. To move with sudden quickness; to wince; to deviate; to set out; to begin; to move from its place.—*vt*. To rouse suddenly; to startle; to originate; to dislocate.—*n*. A sudden motion; a twitch; outset; a handicap.

Startle, stärt'l, *vi*. (startling, startled). To move suddenly.—*vt*. To cause to start; to frighten.—*n*. A start, as from fear.

Starve, stärv, *vi*. (starving, starved). To perish with cold; to suffer from hunger; to be very indigent.—*vt*. To kill or distress with hunger or cold; to make inefficient through insufficient expenditure.

State, stāt, *n.* Condition; situation; rank; pomp; grandeur; an estate (of the realm); a commonwealth; a nation; civil power.—*a.* National; public; governmental.—*vt.* (stating, stated). To express the particulars of; to narrate.

Stately, stāt'li, *a.* Such as pertains to state; august; grand; lofty; dignified.

Statesman, stāts'man, *n.* A man versed in state affairs or in the arts of government.

Statistics, sta-tist'iks, *n.* A collection of facts, tabulated numerically; the science of subjects as elucidated by facts.

Statue, stat'ū, *n.* An image of a human figure or animal in marble, bronze, or other solid substance.

Stature, stat'ūr, *n.* The height of anyone standing; bodily tallness.

Stay, stā, *vt.* (pret. & pp. stayed or staid). To prop; to stop; to delay; to await.—*vi.* To remain; to reside; to delay; to forbear to act; to stop.—*n.* Sojourn; stop; obstacle; a prop; a rope to support a mast; *pl.* a stiffened bodice worn by females; a corset.—**To miss stays,** to fail in the attempt to tack about.

Stead, sted, *n.* Place or room which another had or might have; assistance: preceded by *in.*—*vt.* To be of use to.

Steadfast, sted'fäst, *a.* Firm; constant; resolute; steady.

Steady, sted'i, *a.* Firm; stable; constant; regular; equable.—*vt.* (steadying, steadied). To make or keep firm.

Steak, stāk, *n.* A slice of beef, etc., broiled or cut for broiling.

Steal, stēl, *vt.* (pret. stole, pp. stolen). To take feloniously; to pilfer; to gain by address or imperceptibly; to perform secretly.—*vi.* To pass silently or privily; to practice theft.

Stealth, stelth, *n.* A secret method of procedure; a proceeding by secrecy.

Steam, stēm, *n.* The vapor of water; aeriform fluid generated by the boiling of water.—*vi.* To give out steam; to rise in vaporous form; to sail by means of steam.—*vt.* To expose to steam; to apply steam to.

Steed, stēd, *n.* A horse; a horse of high mettle, for state or war.

Steel, stēl, *n.* A very hard form or iron, produced by addition of carbon; weapons, swords, etc.; a knife-sharpener; sternness; rigor.—*a.* Made of or like steel; unfeeling; rigorous.—*vt.* To furnish with steel; to harden.

Steep, stēp, *a.* Sloping greatly; precipitous.—*n.* A precipitous place; a cliff; process of steeping; liquid in which something is steeped.—*vt.* To soak; to imbue.

Stem, stem, *n.* The principal body of a tree, shrub, etc.; the stalk; stock or branch of a family; the prow of a vessel—*vt.* (stemming, stemmed). To make way against; to press forward through; to dam up; to check.

Step, step, *vi.* (stepping, stepped). To move the leg and foot in walking; to walk.—*vt.* To set (the foot); to fix the foot of, as of a mast.—*n.* A pace; a small space; a grade; a rise; footprint; gait; footfall; action adopted; something to support the feet in ascending; round of a ladder; *pl.* a step-ladder.

Stereography, ste-rō-og'ra-fi, *n.* The art of delineating solid bodies on a plane.

Stereotype, ste'rē-ō-tīp, *n.* and *a.* A metal plate presenting a facsimile of a page of type; an electrotype plate.—*vt.* To make a stereotype of; to fix unchangeably.

Sterile, ste'ril, *a.* Barren; unfruitful; incapable of reproduction; barren of ideas.

Sterling, stėr'ling, *a.* An epithet distinctive of English money; genuine; of excellent quality.

Stern, stėrn, *a.* Austere; harsh; rigid; stringent.—*n.* The hind part of a ship.

Stick, stik, *vt.* (sticking, stuck). To pierce or stab; to fasten by piercing, gluing, etc.; to fix; to set.—*vi.* To adhere; to abide firmly; to be brought to a stop; to scruple.—*n.* A rod or wand; a staff; a stiff, awkward person.

Stickler, stik'lėr, *n.* One who stick-les; an obstinate contender about trifles.

Stiff, stif, *a.* Rigid; tense; not moving easily; thick; not natural and easy; formal in manner; stubborn; difficult; strong.

Stiff-necked, stif'nekt, *a.* Stubborn; inflexibly obstinate; contumacious.

Stiffness, stif'nes, *n.* Want of pliancy; rigidity; viscidness; stubbornness; formality.

Stifle, stī'fl, *vt.* and *i.* (stifling, stifled). To suffocate; to smother; to suppress.—*n.* The joint of a horse next to the buttock.

Stigma, stig'ma, *n.*; pl. **-mas** or **-mata.** A brand made with a red-hot iron; any mark of infamy; part of a flower pistil which receives the pollen; pl. *stigmata,* bodily marks like Christ's wounds impressed supernaturally.

Stigmatize, stig'mat-īz, *vt.* To characterize by some opprobrious epithet.

Stiletto, sti-let'tō, *n.* A small strong dagger; a pointed instrument for making eyelet-holes.—*vt.* (stilettoing, stilettoed). To stab or pierce with a stiletto.

Still, stil, *a.* At rest; calm; silent; not loud; soft; not effervescing.—*vt.* To make still; to check; to appease or allay.—*adv.* To this time; always; nevertheless; yet.—*n.* A vessel or apparatus for distilling; a distillery.

Sting, sting, *vt.* (stinging, stung). To pierce, as wasps, etc.; to prick, as a nettle; to pain acutely.—*n.* A sharp-pointed defensive organ of certain animals; the thrust of a sting into the flesh; something that gives acute pain; the biting effect of words.

Stingily, stin'ji-li, *adv.* In a stringy or niggardly manner; meanly; shabbily.

Stingy, stin'ji, *a.* Very niggardly; meanly avaricious; scanty.

Stink, stingk, *vi.* (stinking, stunk). To emit a strong offensive smell; to be in disrepute.—*n.* A strong offensive smell.

Stirrup, sti'rup, *n.* A metal loop, suspended by a strap, to support the foot in riding.

Stitch, stich, *n.* A sharp pain; one complete movement of a needle in sewing; a complete turn or link in knitting, netting, etc.—*vt.* and *i.* To sew by making stitches in; to unite by stitches.

Stoat, stōt, *n.* The ermine in its summer fur.

Stock, stok, *a.* A post; a lifeless mass; stem of a tree; wooden piece of a rifle; a stiff cravat; an original progenitor; lineage; capital invested in any business; money funded in government securities; store; animals belonging to a farm; liquor used to form a foundation for soups and gravies; a sweet-smelling garden-plant; pl. an instrument of punishment confining the offender's ankles or wrists; timbers on which a ship is supported while building.—*vt.* To provide with a stock; to lay up in store.—*a.* Kept in stock; standing; permanent.

Stockade, stok-ād', *n.* A defense of strong posts stuck close to each other; an enclosure made with posts.—*vt.* (stockading, stockaded). To fortify with posts fixed in the ground.

Stocking, stok'ing, *n.* A close-fitting knitted covering for the foot and leg.

Stodgy, stoj'i, *a.* Crammed together roughly; crude and indigestible.

Stoicism, stō'i-sizm, *n.* Indifference to pleasure or pain.

Stone, stōn, *n.* A hard mass of earthy or mineral matter; a pebble; a precious stone; concretion in the kidneys or bladder; a testicle; the nut of a fruit; a measure of 14 lbs. avoirdupois.—*a.* Made of stone; like stone.—*vt.* (stoning, stoned). To pelt with stones; to free from stones; to provide with stones.

Stop, stop, *vt.* (stopping, stopped). To stuff up; to close; to arrest the progress of; to put an end to; to regulate the sounds of musical strings by the fingers, etc.—*vi.* To cease from any motion; to come to an end; to stay; to remain.—*n.* Obstruction; interruption; pause; a

S

series of pipes in an organ giving distinctive sounds; a point in writing.

Stop-watch, stop'woch, *n.* A watch one of the hands of which can be stopped instantaneously so as to mark with accuracy any point of time.

Store, stōr, *n.* A large quantity for supply; abundance; a place where goods are kept; a shop; *pl.* necessary articles laid up for use.—*a.* Pertaining to a store; kept in store.—*vt.* (storing, stored). To amass; to supply; to reposit in a store for preservation.

Storehouse, stōr'hous, *n.* A place in which things are stored; a repository.

Stork, stork, *n.* A large grallatorial or wading bird resembling the heron.

Storm, storm, *n.* A violent disturbance of the atmosphere; a tempest; an outbreak; assault on a strong position.—*vt.* To take by assault; to attack.—*vi.* To be in violent agitation; to rage.

Stowaway, stō'a-wā, *n.* One who hides himself on a ship to obtain a free passage.

Straddle, strad'l, *vt.* and *t.* (straddling, straddled). To spread the legs wide; to sit astride; to stride across; to drop bombs along or across a target so as to cover a large area.

Straggle, strag'l, *vi.* (straggling, straggled). To rove; to wander in a scattered way; to occur at intervals.

Straight, strāt, *a.* Stretched tight; direct; correct; upright.—*n.* A straight part or piece; straight direction.—*adv.* Immediately; directly.—*vt.* To straighten.

Straightforward, strāt'for-wėrd, *a.* Proceeding in a straight course; candid; honest; frank; open.—*adv.* Directly forward.

Strain, strān, *vt.* To stretch tightly; to exert to the utmost; to overtask; to sprain; to carry too far; to wrest; to filter.—*vi.* To exert oneself; to filter.—*n.* Violent effort; excessive stretching or exertion; tenor; theme; a lay; tune; race;

family blood; tendency.

Strange, strānj, *a.* Foreign; wonderful; odd; not familiar.

Stranger, strān'jėr, *n.* A foreigner; an alien; one unknown; a visitor.

Strangle, strang'gl, *vt.* (strangling, strangled). To choke; to throttle; to suppress or stifle.

Strangulate, strang'gū-lāt, *vt.* To strangle; to stop vital action in by compression.

Strap, strap, *n.* A long narrow slip of leather, etc.; a plate or strip of metal.—*vt.* (strapping, strapped). To beat with a strap; to fasten with a strap.

Strapping, strap'ing, *a.* Tall and well made; handsome.

Stratagem, stra'ta-jem, *n.* A piece of general-ship; an artifice in war; a wile.

Strategic, Strategical, stra-tej'ik, stra-tej'ik-al, *a.* Pertaining to strategy; effected by strategy.

Strategy, stra'te-ji, *n.* The science of military operations; generalship.

Stray, strā, *vi.* To go astray; to err; to roam.—*a.* Having gone astray; straggling.—*n.* Any domestic animal that wanders at large, or is lost.

Streak, strēk, *n.* A long mark; a stripe; appearance of a mineral when scratched.—*vt.* To form streaks in.

Stream, strēm, *n.* A river or brook; a current; drift.—*vi.* and *t.* To move in a stream; to stretch in a long line; to float at full length in the air.

Streamline, strēm-līn', *vt.* To shape so as to reduce resistance to air and water.

Street, strēt, *n.* A road in a town or village; the roadway and houses together.

Strength, strength, *n.* Property of being strong; force or energy; power; support; vigor; intensity; amount or numbers of an army, fleet, or the like.—**On the strength of,** in reliance upon, on the faith of.

Strenuous, stren'ū-us, *a.* Energetic; vigorous; zealous; ardent; earnest.

Stress, stres, *vt.* To put in difficulties; to subject to emphasis.—*n.* Constraint; pressure; weight; violence, as of weather; emphasis.

Strict, strikt, *a.* Tight; tense; exact; severe; rigorous; not loose or vague.

Stricture, strik'tūr, *n.* A contraction of any canal of the body; a critical remark; censure.

Stride, strīd, *vi.* (striding, pret. strode, pp. stridden). To walk with long steps; to straddle.—*vt.* To pass over at a step.—*n.* A long step; a measured tread.

Strident, strī'dent, *a.* Harsh; grating.

Strife, strīf, *n.* Act of striving; struggle; contest; discord; conflict; quarrel or war.

Strike, strīk, *vi.* (striking, pret. struck, pp. struck, stricken). To move or turn aside rapidly; to light (upon); to make a blow; to hit; to be stranded; to yield; to quit work to compel better terms.—*vt.* To smite; to mint; to thrust in; to notify by sound; to occur to; to impress strongly; to effect at once; to lower, as the flag or sails of a vessel.—*n.* Act of workmen who quit work to force their employer to give better terms; a strickle.

String, string, *n.* A small cord; a piece of twine; a line with the things on it; chord of a musical instrument; a series.—*vt.* (stringing, strung). To furnish with string; to put on a string; to make tense.

Stroke, strōk, *n.* A blow; calamity; attack; striking of a clock; touch; a masterly effort; a dash in writing or printing; a touch of the pen; a line; a gentle rub; the sweep of an oar; a stroke-oar.—*vt.* (stroking, stroked). To rub gently with the hand.

Stroll, strōl, *vi.* To ramble; to rove; to roam.—*n.* A short leisurely walk.

Strong, strong, *a.* Having power or force; robust; not easily broken; firm; effectual; earnest; containing much alcohol; glaring; forcible; tending upwards in price; effecting inflection by internal vowel change.

Strum, strum, *vi.* and *t.* (strumming, strummed). To play unskilfully on a stringed instrument; to thrum.

Strut, strut, *vi.* (strutting, strutted). To walk with affected dignity.—*n.* A lofty, proud step or walk; a strengthening piece placed diagonally in a framework.

Strychnia, Strychinine, strik'ni-a, strik'nīn, *n.* A vegetable alkaloid poison obtained from the seeds of nux-vomica.

Stubble, stub'l, *n.* The stumps of a grain crop left in the ground after reaping.

Stubborn, stub'orn, *a.* Not to be moved or persuaded; obstinate; intractable.

Studied, stu'did, *a.* Made the object of study; qualified by study; premeditated.

Studio, stū'di-ō, *n.* The work-place of a painter or sculptor.

Study, stu'di, *n.* Earnest endeavor; application to books, etc.; subject which one studies; apartment devoted to study; a reverie; a preparatory sketch.—*vt.* and *i.* (studying, studied). To apply the mind to; to investigate; to have careful regard to.

Stuff, stuf, *n.* Substance indefinitely; material; cloth; a light woollen fabric; goods; trash.—*vt.* To pack; to thrust in; to fill, as meat with seasoning; to fill, as an animal's skin to preserve the form.—*vi.* To cram; to feed gluttonously.

Stump, stump, *n.* The part of a tree, limb, etc., left after the rest is cut off or destroyed; a worn-down tooth; a wicket in cricket.—*vt.* To lop, as trees; to make a tour through, delivering speeches; to put out of play in cricket by knocking down a stump.—*vi.* To walk stiffly or noisily.

Stun, stun, *vt.* (stunning, stunned). To overpower the sense of hearing of; to stupefy; to make senseless with a blow; to surprise completely.

Stunt, stunt, *vt.* To stop the growth of; to dwarf.—*n.* A check in growth.

Stupefy, stū'pē-fī, *vt.* (stupefying, stupefied). To deprive of sensibility.

Stupendous, stū-pen'dus, *a.* Of astonishing magnitude; grand or awe-inspiring.

Stupid, stū'pid, *a*. Struck senseless; foolish; dull in intellect; nonsensical.

Style, stīl, *n*. A burin; pin of a sundial; manner of writing with regard to language; a characteristic mode in the fine arts; type; external manner, mode, or fashion; title; in *botany,* a slender prolongation of the ovary supporting the stigma.—*vt*. (styling, styled). To term; to designate.

Styptic, stip'tik, *a*. Able to stop bleeding.—*n*. A substance which stops a flow of blood.

Subject, sub'jekt, *a*. Ruled by another; liable; prone; submissive.—*n*. One who owes allegiance to a ruler or government; matter dealt with; theme; topic; the nominative of a verb; the thinking agent or principle.—*vt*. sub-jekt'. To subdue; to make liable; to cause to undergo.

Subjective, sub-jekt'iv or sub'jekt-iv, *a*. Relating to the subject; belonging to ourselves, the conscious subject; exhibiting strongly the personality of the author.

Subjugate, sub'jū-gāt, *vt*. To subdue; to conquer and compel to submit.

Subjunctive, sub-jungk'tiv, *a*. and *n*. Applied to a mood of verbs that expresses condition, hypothesis, or contingency.

Sublimate, sub'li-māt, *vt*. To raise by heat into vapor, as a solid, which, on cooling, returns again to the solid state; to refine; to elevate.—*n*. The product of sublimation.

Sublimation, sub-li-mā'shon, *n*. The process or operation of sublimating; exaltation; a highly refined product.

Sublime, sub-līm', *a*. High in place or excellence; affecting the mind with a sense of grandeur; noble; majestic.—**The sublime,** the grand in the works of nature or of art; grandeur of style; highest degree.—*vt*. (subliming, sublimed). To render sublime; to sublimate.—*vi*. To be susceptible of sublimation.

Submit, sub-mit', *vt*. (submitting, submitted). To yield or surrender; to refer; to state, as a claim.—*vi*. To surrender; to acquiesce; to suffer without complaint.

Subordinate, sub-or'din-āt, *a*. Inferior; occupying a lower position.—*n*. One who stands in rank, power, etc., below another.—*vt*. To place in a lower order or rank.

Suborn, sub-orn', *vt*. To bribe to commit perjury; to bribe to some wickedness.

Subpoena, sub-pē'na, *n*. A writ summoning a witness under a penalty.—*vt*. (subpoenaing, subpoenaed). To serve with a writ of subpoena.

Subscribe, sub-skrīb', *vt*. and *i*. (subscribing, subscribed). To append one's own signature to; to promise to contribute (money) by writing one's name; to assent.

Subsidize, sub'si-dīz, *vt*. (subsidizing, subsidized). To furnish with a subsidy; to purchase the assistance of another by a subsidy.

Subsidy, sub'si-di, *n*. A sum of money granted for a purpose; a sum given by a government to meet expenses.

Subsist, sub-sist', *vi*. To have existence; to live; to inhere.

Subsistent, sub-sist'ent, *a*. Having being or existence; inherent.

Subsoil, sub'soil, *n*. The bed or stratum of earth below the surface soil.

Substance, sub'stans, *n*. That of which a thing consists; material; a body; essence; purport; means and resources.

Substantial, sub-stan'shal, *a*. Actually existing; real; solid; strong; moderately wealthy.

Substantiate, sub-stan'shi-āt, *vt*. To give substance to; to prove.

Substantive, sub'stan-tiv, *a*. Expressing existence; independent; real; of the nature of a noun.—*n*. A noun.

Substitute, sub'sti-tūt, *vt*. (substituting, substituted). To put in the place of another; to exchange.—*n*. A person or thing in the place of another; a deputy.

Subterfuge, sub'tėr-fūj, *n*. An artifice to escape or justify; evasion; a dishonest shift.

Subterranean, Subterraneous, sub-te-rā'nē-an, sub-te-rā'nē-us, *a*. Being under the surface of the earth.

Subtle, sut'l, *a*. Thin or tenuous; acute; sly; cunning; artful.

Subway, sub'wā, *n*. An underground passage.

Succedaneum, suk-sē-dā'nē-um, *n*.; pl. **-nea.** A substitute.

Succeed, suk-sēd', *vt*. To follow in order; to take the place of; to come after.—*vi*. To follow in order; to ensue; to become heir; to obtain the end or object desired; to prosper.

Success, suk-ses', *n*. Issue; favorable result; good fortune; prosperity; something that succeeds.

Succession, suk-se'shon, *n*. A following of things in order; series of things; lineage; right of inheriting; act or right of succeeding to an office, rank, etc.

Successor, suk-ses'or, *n*. One who succeeds or follows another.

Succinct, suk-singkt', *a*. Compressed into few words; brief; concise.

Succor, suk'ėr, *vt*. To help when in difficulty; to aid; to relieve.—*n*. Aid; help; assistance given in distress; the person or thing that brings relief.

Succulent, suk'kū-lent, *a*. Full of sap or juice; sappy; juicy.

Succumb, suk-kum', *vt*. To yield; to submit; to sink unresistingly.

Such, such, *a*. Of like kind or degree; similar; like; the same as mentioned.

Suck, suk, *vt*. and *i*. To draw with the mouth; to draw milk from with the mouth; to imbibe; to absorb.— *n*. Act of sucking; milk drawn from the breast.

Sucker, suk'ėr, *n*. One who or that which sucks; an organ in animals for sucking; piston of a pump; shoot of a plant; the sucking-fish.

Suckling, suk'ling, *n*. A young child or animal nursed by the mother's milk.

Sucrose, sū'krōs, *n*. A name for the sugars identical with cane-sugar.

Suffer, suf'ėr, *vt*. To endure; to undergo; to be affected by; to permit.—*vi*. To undergo pain; to be injured.

Sufferance, suf'ėr-ans, *n*. Endurance; pain endured; passive consent; allowance.

Suffice, suf'fīs, *vi*. (sufficing, sufficed). To be sufficient.—*vt*. To satisfy; to content.

Sufficient, suf-fi'shent, *a*. Adequate; enough; competent; fit; able.

Sugar, shu̞'gėr, *n*. A sweet granular substance, manufactured from sugar-cane, maple, beet, etc.; something sweet like sugar.—*a*. Belonging to or made of sugar.— *vt*. To season, mix, etc., with sugar; to sweeten.

Suggest, su-jest' or sug-jest', *vt*. To hint; to insinuate; to propose; to intimate.

Suggestion, su-jest'yon, *n*. A hint; a tentative proposal; insinuation; intimation.

Suicide, sū'i-sīd, *n*. Self-murder; one guilty of self-murder.

Suit, sūt, *n*. Act of suing; a request; courtship; a suing at law; a set of things.—*vt*. and *i*. To adapt; to fit; to be agreeable to; to agree.

Sully, sul'i, *vt*. (sullying, sullied). To soil; to tarnish; to stain or pollute.—*vi*. To be soiled.—*n*. Soil; tarnish; spot.

Sulphate, sul'fāt, *n*. A salt of sulphuric acid.

Sulphide, sul'fīd, *n*. A combination of sulphur with another element.

Sulphur, sul'fėr, *n*. Brimstone; a simple mineral substance of a yellow color which burns with a pale-blue flame.

Summer, sum'ėr, *n*. The warmest season of the year; a lintel; a girder.—*a*. Relating to summer.— *vi*. To pass the summer.—*vt*. To keep or carry through the summer.

Summit, sum'it, *n*. The top; highest point; highest degree; acme.

Summon, sum'un, *vt*. To call by authority to appear at a place, especially a court of justice; to send for; to call up.

Sumptuary, sump'tū-a-ri, *a*. Relating to expense; regulating ex-

S

penditure.

Sumptuous, sump'tū-us, *a.* Very expensive or costly; splendid; magnificent.

Sun, sun, *n.* The self-luminous orb which gives light and heat to all the planets; sunshine or sunlight; sunny position; chief source of light, glory, etc.; a year.—*vt.* (sunning, sunned). To expose to the sun's rays.

Sunbeam, sun'bēm, *n.* A ray of the sun.

Sun-burn, sun'bėrn, *vt.* To discolor or scorch by the sun; to tan.

Sunstroke, sun'strōk, *n.* A bodily affection produced by exposure to the sun.

Supercilious, sū-pėr-sil'i-us, *a.* Lofty with pride; haughty; overbearing.

Supererogation, sū-pėr-e'rō-gā'' shon, *n.* Giving more than enough; performance of more than duty requires.

Superficial, sū-pėr-fi'shal, *a.* Being on the surface; shallow; not thorough.

Superfluous, sū-pėr'flu-us, *a.* Being more than is wanted; redundant; unnecessary.

Superhuman, sū-pėr-hū'man, *a.* Above or beyond what is human; divine.

Superimpose, sū'pėr-im-pōz'', *vt.* To lay or impose on something else.

Superinduce, sū'pėr-in-dūs'', *vt.* To bring in or on as an addition to something.

Superintend, sū'pėr-in-tend'', *vt.* To have the charge and oversight of; to direct or manage; to take care of with authority.

Superintendent, sū'pėr-in-tend'' ent, *n.* One who manages and directs; an overseer.—*a.* Overlooking others with authority.

Superior, sū-pē'ri-or, *a.* Higher; higher in rank or dignity; greater in excellence.—*n.* One who is superior to another; chief of a monastery, convent, or abbey.

Superlative, sū-pėr'lat-iv, *a.* Highest in degree; supreme.—*n.* That which is superlative; the highest degree of adjectives or adverbs.

Superscription, sū-pėr-skrip'shon, *n.* Act of superscribing; that which is written or engraved above or on the outside; address on a letter, etc.

Supersede, sū-pėr-sēd', *vt.* (superseding, superseded). To set aside; to take the place of; to supplant.

Supersonic, sū-pėr-son'ik, *a.* Faster than sound; above the audible limit.

Superstition, sū-pėr-sti'shon, *n.* Groundless belief in supernatural agencies; a popular belief held without reason.

Superstructure, sū-pėr-struk'tūr, *n.* Any structure raised on something else.

Supervene, sū-pėr-vēn', *vi.* (supervening, supervened). To come, as something extraneous; to happen.

Supervise, sū-pėr-vīz', *vt.* (supervising, supervised). To oversee and direct; to superintend; to inspect.

Suppliant, sup'li-ant, *a.* Supplicating; entreating earnestly; beseeching.—*n.* A supplicant; a humble petitioner.

Supplicant, sup'li-kant, *a.* Suppliant.—*n.* One who supplicates; a suppliant.

Supplicate, sup'li-kāt, *vt.* (supplicating, supplicated). To beg humbly for; to entreat; to address in prayer.—*vi.* To beg; to petition; to beseech.

Supply, sup-plī', *vt.* (supplying, supplied). To furnish; to provide; to satisfy.—*n.* Act of supplying; quantity supplied; store; *pl.* stores or articles necessary; money provided for government expenses.

Support, sup-pōrt', *vt.* To rest under and bear; to prop; to endure; to assist; to second; to maintain; to provide for.—*n.* Act of supporting; a prop; help; sustenance; maintenance.

Suppress, sup-pres', *vt.* To put down; to crush; to quell; to check; to conceal.

Sure, shör, *a.* Certain; positive; unfailing; stable; secure.—*adv.* Certainly.

Surety, shör'ti, *n.* State of being sure; certainty; security; one who gives security; a bail.

Surf, sėrf, *n*. The swell of the sea which breaks on the shore, rocks, etc.

Surface, sėr'fās, *n*. The exterior part of anything that has length and breadth; outside; external appearance.—*a*. Pertaining to the surface; superficial.

Surfeit, sėr'fit, *n*. An overloading of the stomach; disgust caused by excess; satiety.—*vt*. and *i*. To feed to excess; to nauseate; to cloy.

Surmise, sėr-mīz', *n*. A supposition; conjecture; speculation.—*vt*. (surmising, surmised). To guess; to imagine; to suspect.

Surmount, sėr-mount', *vt*. To mount or rise above; to overcome.

Surname, sėr'nām, *n*. The family name of an individual.—*vt*. To give a surname to.

Surpass, sėr-päs', *vt*. To go beyond; to excel; to outdo.

Surplus, sėr'plus, *n*. and *a*. Excess beyond what is required; balance.

Surtax, sėr'taks, *n*. A tax heightened for a particular purpose; an extra tax.

Surveillance, sėr-vāl'yans, *n*. A keeping watch over; superintendence; oversight.

Survey, sėr-vā', *vt*. To oversee; to examine; to measure and value, as land, etc.; to determine the boundaries, natural features, etc., of.—*n*. sėr'vā or sėr-vā'. A general view; examination; determination or account of topographical particulars.

Survive, sėr-vīv', *vt*. (surviving, survived). To outlive; to live beyond the life of; to outlast.—*vi*. To live after another or after anything else.

Suspense, sus-pens', *n*. State of being uncertain; indecision; cessation for a time.

Suspension, sus-pen'shon, *n*. Act of suspending; intermission; abeyance; deprivation of office or privileges for a time.

Suspicion, sus-pi'shon, *n*. Act of suspecting; fear of something wrong; mistrust.

Suspicious, sus-pi'shus, *a*. Mistrustful; inclined to suspect; apt to raise suspicion; doubtful.

Sustain, sus-tān', *vt*. To rest under and bear up; to support; to aid effectually; to undergo; to endure; to hold valid; to confirm; to continue.

Swallow, swol'ō, *vt*. To receive through the gullet into the stomach; to ingulf; to absorb; to believe readily; to put up with.—*n*. The gullet; voracity; capacity of swallowing; a small migratory bird.

Swamp, swomp, *n*. A piece of wet spongy land; a fen; a bog.—*vt*. To sink in a swamp; to overwhelm; to overset or fill, as a boat in water.

Swan, swon, *n*. A long-necked webfooted bird of the duck family.

Swap, swop, *vt*. (swapping, swapped). To barter; to exchange.—*n*. An exchange.

Swarm, swarm, *n*. A large body of small insects; a multitude.—*vi*. To depart from a hive in a body; to crowd; to abound; to climb a tree, pole, etc., by clasping it with the arms and legs.

Swathe, swāᴛн, *vt*. (swathing, swathed). To bind with a bandage; to swaddle.—*n*. A bandage.

Sway, swā, *vi*. To swing or vibrate; to incline; to govern.—*vt*. To swing; to wield; to bias; to influence; to rule.—*n*. Swing or sweep; preponderance; power; rule; ascendency.

Swear, swār, *vt*. and *t*. (swearing, pret. swore, pp. sworn). To make a solemn declaration, with an appeal to God for its truth; to make promise upon oath; to cause to take an oath; to curse.

Sweat, swet, *n*. The moisture which comes out upon the skin; labor; moisture resembling sweat.—*vi*. (pret. and pp. sweated or sweat). To emit sweat or moisture; to toil.—*vt*. To exude; to cause to perspire; to employ at starvation wages.

Sweater, swet'ėr, *n*. A heavy woollen jersey.

survey; a curve; one who sweeps chimneys.

Swell, swel, *vi*. (pp. swelled or swollen). To grow larger; to heave; to bulge out; to increase.—*vt*. To expand or increase; to puff up.—*n*. Act of swelling; gradual increase; a rise of ground; a wave or surge;

S

an arrangement in an organ for regulating the intensity of the sound; an important person; a dandy.

Swim, swim, *vi.* (swimming, pret. swam, swum, pp. swum). To float; to move through water by the motion of the limbs or fins; to be flooded; to be dizzy.—*vt.* To pass by swimming.—*n.* Act of swimming; distance swum; air-bladder of fishes.

Switch, swich, *n.* A small flexible twig or rod; a movable rail at junctions; a device for changing the course of an electric current.—*vt.* To strike with a switch; to shunt.

Swivel, swi'vel, *n.* A link in a chain partly consisting of a pivot turning in a hole in the next link; a fastening that allows the thing fastened to turn round freely.—*vi.* (swivelling, swivelled). To turn on a swivel.

Swoon, swön, *vi.* To faint.—*n.* A fainting fit; a faint; syncope.

Sword, sörd, *n.* A military weapon consisting of a long steel blade and a hilt, used for thrusting or cutting; the emblem of justice, authority, war, or destruction; the military profession.

Sworn, swörn, *p.a.* Bound by oath; having taken an oath; closely bound.

Sybarite, sib'a-rīt, *n.* A person devoted to luxury and pleasure.

Syllable, sil'la-bi, *n.* A sound or combination of sounds uttered with one effort; the smallest expressive element of language.—*vt.* To articulate.

Sylph, silf, *n.* A fabulous aerial spirit; a woman of graceful and slender proportions.

Sylvan, sil'van, *a.* Pertaining to a wood; wooded; rural.

Symbol, sim'bol, *n.* A sign; an emblem; a type; a figure; an attribute; a creed or summary of articles of religion.

Symbolize, sim'bol-īz, *vt.* To represent by a symbol; to typify; to treat as symbolic.—*vi.* To express or represent in symbols.

Symmetry, sim'me-tri, *n.* Due proportion of parts or elements; har-

mony; correspondence of arrangement.

Sympathy, sim'pa-thi, *n.* Fellowfeeling; compassion; agreement of inclinations; correspondence of sensations or affections.

Symphony, sim'fō-ni, *n.* Unison of sound; a musical composition for a full orchestra.

Symptom, sim'tom, *n.* That which indicates the existence and character of something else; a mark, sign, or token.

Synagogue, sin'a-gog, *n.* A congregation of Jews met for worship; a Jewish place of worship.

Syndic, sin'dik, *n.* A magistrate; one chosen to transact business for others.

Syndicate, sin'di-kāt, *n.* A body of syndics; office of a syndic; body of persons associated to promote some enterprise.—*vt.* To form a syndicate or body for the use of.

Syntax, sin'taks, *n.* The construction of sentences in grammar; due arrangement of words in sentences.

Synthesis, sin'the-sis, *n.*; pl. **-ses.** The putting of things together to form a whole; composition or combination.

Syphilis, sif'i-lis, *n.* A contagious and hereditary venereal disease.

Syringe, si'rinj, *n.* A tube and piston serving to draw in and expel fluid.—*vt.* (syringing, syringed). To inject by a syringe; to cleanse by injections from a syringe.

Systemic, sis-tem'ik, *a.* Pertaining to a system, or to the body as a whole.

Systole, sis'to-lē, *n.* The contraction of the heart and arteries for driving onwards the blood and carrying on the circulation.

Syzygy, siz'i-ji, *n.* The conjuction or opposition of any two heavenly bodies.

T

Tab, tab, *n.* A small flap or projecting piece.

Tabby, tab'i, *n.* A rich watered silk

or other stuff; a cat of a brindled color; a female cat.—*vt*. To water or cause to look wavy.

Tabernacle, tab´ér-na-kl, *n*. A booth; a temporary habitation; a place of worship; a repository for holy things.—*vi*. To sojourn.

Table, tā´bl, *n*. A thing with a flat surface; an article of furniture having a flat surface; fare or eatables; persons sitting at a table; a syllabus; index; list.—*vt*. (tabling, tabled). To tabulate; to lay on the table.—*a*. Appertaining to a table.

Tabor, tā´bor, *n*. A small drum.—*vt*. To play on a tabor.

Taboret, tā´bor-et, *n*. A small tabor; a frame for embroidery.

Tabular, ta´bū-lér, *a*. In form of a table; having a flat surface; set in columns.

Tabulate, ta´bū-lāt, *vt*. (tabulating, tabulated). To set down in a table of items.—*a*. Tabular.

Tacit, ta´sit, *a*. Implied, but not expressed in words; silent; unspoken.

Taciturn, ta´si-tèrn, *a*. Habitually silent; not apt to talk or speak.

Tack, tak, *n*. A small nail; a slight fastening; a rope for certain sails; course of a ship as regards the wind; in *Scots law*, a lease.—*vt*. To fasten by tacks; to attach slightly; to append.—*vi*. To change the course of a ship so as to have the wind acting from the other side.

Tackle, tak´l, *n*. Gear or apparatus; pulleys and ropes for moving weights; ropes and rigging, etc., of a ship.—*vt*. (tackling, tackled). To supply with tackle; to set vigorously to work upon; to seize.

Tact, takt, *n*. Touch; nice perception or discernment; adroitness in words or actions.

Tail, tāl, *n*. The projecting termination of an animal behind; the hinder or inferior part; the reverse of a coin; limited ownership.

Tailor, tā´lor, *n*. One who makes men's outer garments.—*vi*. To practice making men's clothes.

Taint, tānt, *vt*. To defile; to infect; to vitiate.—*vi*. To be infected or corrupted.—*n*. Infection; corruption; a stain; a blemish on reputation.

Take, tāk, *vt*. (taking, pret. took, pp. taken). To receive or accept; to capture; to captivate; to understand; to feel concerning; to employ; to need; to form or adopt; to assume; to note down; to be infected or seized with; to bear; to conduct, carry; to leap over.—*vi*. To direct one's course; to please; to have the intended effect; to admit of being made a portrait of.

Talc, talk, *n*. A magnesian mineral, unctuous to the touch.—*vt*. To rub with talc.

Tale, tāl, *n*. Number counted; reckoning; a story; a narrative.

Talent, ta´lent, *n*. An ancient weight and denomination of money; a special faculty; general mental power; people of high abilities collectively.

Tally, tal´i, *n*. A piece of wood on which notches are cut to keep accounts; anything made to suit another.—*vt*. (tallying, tallied). To record on a tally; to make to correspond.—*vi*. To correspond or agree exactly.

Talmud, tal´mud, *n*. The Hebrew civil and canonical laws, traditions, etc.

Talon, ta´lon, *n*. The claw of a bird of prey.

Tame, tām, *a*. Having lost its natural wildness; domesticated; spiritless; insipid.—*vt*. (taming, tamed). To make tame; to subdue; to depress.

Tamp, tamp, *vt*. To ram tight with clay, etc.; to stamp or make firm.

Tamper, tam´pèr, *vi*. To meddle or interfere; to influence secretly.

Tandem, tan´dem, *adv*. With two horses harnessed singly one before the other.—*n*. A wheeled carriage so drawn; a cycle for two persons, one behind the other.

Tangent, tan´jent, *n*. A straight line which touches a circle or curve, but which, when produced, does not cut it.

Tanner, tan´èr, *n*. One who tans hides, or converts them into leather by the use of tan.

Tantalize, tan´ta-līz, *vt*. (tantalizing, tantalized). To torment by presenting something desirable which cannot be attained; to excite by hopes that are never realized.

Tantamount, tan'ta-mount, *a.* Equal; equivalent in value, force, or effect.

Tantrum, tan'trum, *n.* A fit of ill-humor; display of temper; chiefly in *pl.*

Tape, tāp, *n.* A narrow strip of woven work, used for strings and the like.

Tapioca, tap-i-ō'ka, *n.* A farinaceous substance prepared from cassava meal.

Tap-root, tap'röt, *n.* Main root of a plant.

Tar, tär, *n.* A thick, dark, viscid substance obtained from pine or fir, coal, shale, etc.; a sailor.—*vt.* (tarring, tarred). To smear with tar.

Tarry, ta'ri, *vi.* (tarrying, tarried). To stay; to delay.—*vt.* To wait for.

Tarsus, tär'sus, *n.*; pl. **-si.** The ankle or ankle-joint.

Tart, tärt, *a.* Sharp to the taste; sour; acid; severe; snappish.—*n.* A species of pastry, consisting of fruit baked in paste.

Tartan, tär'tan, *n.* Cloth woven in colors in a checkered pattern; a Mediterranean vessel somewhat resembling a sloop.—*a.* Consisting of or resembling tartan.

Tartar, tär'tar, *n.* A native of Tartary; a very irascible or rigorous person; a shrew; a reddish crust deposited by wine on casks; a concretion formed on the teeth.

Task, täsk, *n.* A piece of work imposed by another or requiring to be done; burdensome employment; toil.—*vt.* To impose a task upon.

Tassel, tas'el, *n.* An ornament consisting of a knob with hanging threads.—*vi.* (tasseling, tasseled). To put forth a tassel or flower, as maize.—*vt.* To adorn with tassels.

Taste, tāst, *vt.* (tasting, tasted). To test by the tongue and palate; to perceive the flavor of; to experience; to partake of.—*vi.* To make trial by the tongue and palate; to have a flavor; to have experience.—*n.* Act of tasting; sense of tasting; flavor; intellectual relish or discernment; manner or style.

Taunt, tant, *vt.* To reproach with severe or sarcastic words; to upbraid.—*n.* A bitter or sarcastic reproach.

Tawdry, ta'dri, *a.* Tastelessly ornamental; cheap and showy.

Tax, taks, *n.* A contribution levied by authority; a rate, duty, or impost charged on income or property; a burdensome duty; an exaction.—*vt.* To impose a tax on; to put to a certain effort; to accuse.

Tea, tē, *n.* The dried leaves of plants cultivated in China, Assam, Ceylon, etc.; the plant itself; a decoction of tea leaves in boiling water; any decoction of vegetables.—*vi.* (teaing, teaed). To take tea.

Teach, tēch, *vt.* (teaching, taught). To instruct; to inform; to make familiar with.—*vi.* To practice giving instruction.

Teak, tēk, *n.* An E. Indian tree which furnishes hard and valuable timber.

Team, tēm, *n.* A brood; horses or other beasts harnessed together; a side in a game, match, etc.

Tea-pot, tē'pot, *n.* A vessel in which tea is infused.

Tear, tēr, *n.* A drop of the watery fluid appearing in the eyes; any transparent drop.

Tear, tār, *vt.* (pret. tore, pp. torn). To pull in pieces; to rend; to wound; to drag; to pull with violence; to make by rending.—*vi.* To be rent or torn; to rage.—*n.* A rent.

Tease, tēz, *vt.* (teasing, teased). To pull apart the fibers of; to annoy; to torment.

Tectonic, tek-ton'ik, *a.* Pertaining to building or construction.

Tedious, tē'di-us, *a.* Tiresome; wearisome; irksome; fatiguing; dilatory; tardy.

Tedium, tē'di-um, *n.* Irksomeness.

Telegraph, tel'e-graf, *n.* Any apparatus for transmitting messages to a distance; an apparatus for transmitting messages along a wire by electricity, but now also wireless.—*vt.* To convey or announce by telegraph.

Telemeter, te-lem'et-er, *n.* A rangefinder or similar instrument; an instrument to transmit variations marked by some physical instrument.

Telepathy, te-lep'a-thi or tel'e-path-i, *n.* Occult communication between persons at some distance.

Telescope, tel'e-skōp, *n.* An optical instrument for viewing distant objects.—*vt.* (telescoping, telescoped). To drive the parts of into each other, like the joints of a telescope.

Tell, tel, *vt.* (telling, told). To number; to relate; to disclose; to explain; to distinguish; to inform; to bid.—*vi.* To give an account; to take effect.

Temerarious, tem-ē-rā'ri-us, *a.* Reckless.

Temerity, tē-me'ri-ti, *n.* Contempt of danger; extreme boldness; rashness.

Temper, tem'pėr, *vt.* To proportion duly; to moderate; to form to a proper hardness.—*n.* Due mixture; disposition of the mind; temperament; irritation; state of a metal as to its hardness; medium.

Temperament, tem'pėr-a-ment, *n.* Due mixture of qualities; combined mental and physical constitution; disposition.

Temperance, tem'pėr-ans, *n.* Moderation in indulgence of the natural appetites; sobriety; abstinence from intoxicants.

Temperature, tem'pėr-a-tūr, *n.* State with regard to heat or cold; climatic heat.

Templet, Template, tem'plet, tem'plāt, *n.* A board whose edge is shaped so as to serve as a guide in making an article with a corresponding contour.

Tempo, tem'pō, *n.* The time of a piece of music; musical time.

Temporal, tem'pō-ral, *a.* Pertaining to time; pertaining to this life; not spiritual or ecclesiastical, secular; pertaining to the temples of the head.—*n.* Anything temporal or secular; a temporality.

Tenant, te'nant, *n.* One who occupies lands or houses for which he pays rent.—*vt.* To hold as a tenant.—*vi.* To live as a tenant; to dwell.

Tend, tend, *vi.* To move in or have a

certain direction; to conduce; to attend.—*vt.* To attend; to guard; to take care of.

Tendency, ten'den-si, *n.* Inclination; leaning; bent; proneness.

Tender, ten'dėr, *n.* One who attends; a small vessel employed to attend on a larger one; a carriage with fuel, etc., attached to a locomotive; an offer of money or service; an estimate; thing offered.—*vt.* To present for acceptance.—*a.* Fragile; delicate; compassionate; kind.

Tendon, ten'don, *n.* A sinew; a hard, insensible cord or bundle of fibers by which a muscle is attached to a bone.

Tennis, ten'is, *n.* A game in which a ball is driven against a wall, and caused to rebound; in ordinary use, lawn-tennis.

Tenor, ten'or, *n.* A prevailing course or direction; purport; substance, as of a discourse; the highest of the male adult chest voices; one who sings a tenor part.—*a.* Adapted for singing or playing the tenor.

Tense, tens, *n.* Inflection of a verb to express time.—*a.* Stretched; tight; strained to stiffness; rigid; not lax.

Tension, ten'shon, *n.* Act of stretching; state of being stretched; tightness; strain; intensity; elastic force.

Tensor, ten'sor, *n.* A muscle that extends or stretches the part to which it is fixed.

Tentacle, ten'ta-kl, *n. sing.* and *pl.* A filiform organ of various animals, used for prehension or as a feeler.

Tentative, ten'ta-tiv, *a.* Experimental; empirical.—*n.* An essay; a trial.

Tenure, ten'ūr, *n.* A holding or manner of holding real estate; condition of occupancy; manner of possessing in general.

Tepid, te'pid, *a.* Moderately warm; lukewarm.

Term, tėrm, *n.* A limit; boundary; time for which anything lasts; period of session, etc.; day on which rent or interest is paid; a word; a word having a technical meaning; *pl.* conditions; relative position or footing.—*vt.* To name; to call.

T

Terminal, tėr'min-al, *a.* Pertaining to or forming the end; terminating.—*n.* An extremity; the clamping screw at each end of a voltaic battery.

Terminate, tėr'min-āt, *vt.* and *i.* (terminating, terminated). To bound; to limit; to end.—*a.* Limited.

Terminology, tėr-min-ol'o-ji, *n.* The science or theory of technical or other terms; terms used in any art, science, etc.

Terminus, tėr'mi-nus, *n.*; pl. **-ni.** A boundary; a limit; station at the end of a railway, etc.

Termite, tėr'mīt, *n.* A neuropterous insect commonly called the white ant.

Terrace, te'räs, *n.* A raised level bank of earth; a raised flat area; a row of houses; flat roof of a house.—*vt.* (terracing, terraced). To form into or furnish with a terrace.

Terrify, te'ri-fī, *vt.* (terrifying, terrified). To cause or produce terror in; to alarm.

Territory, te'ri-to-ri, *n.* A definite piece of land under any distinct administration; a dominion; region; country.

Terror, te'ror, *n.* Such fear as agitates body and mind; dread; alarm; cause of fear.

Terrorism, te'ror-izm, *n.* A system of government by terror; intimidation.

Terse, tėrs, *a.* Free from superfluities of language; concise; forcible; pithy.

Tertiary, tėr'shi-a-ri, *a.* Third; applied to the third great division of stratified rocks, resting on the chalk.—*n.* The tertiary system of rocks.

Tessera, tes'e-ra, *n.*; pl. **-rae.** A small cube of marble, ivory, etc., used for mosaic work.

Test, test, *n.* A vessel used in trying or refining gold, etc.; a cupel; examination; means of trial; a standard; oath taken before admission to privileges; a hard outer covering.—*vt.* To put to a trial; to refine; to examine; to prove; to attest.

Testify, tes'ti-fī, *vi.* (testifying, testified). To bear witness; to give evidence.—*vt.* To bear witness to.

Tether, teᴛʜ'ėr, *n.* A rope confining a grazing animal with certain limits; scope allowed.—*vt.* To confine with a tether.

Tetrahedron, te-tra-hē'dron, *n.* A solid body having four equal triangles as its faces.

Teuton, tū'ton, *n.* A person of Germanic race in the widest sense of the term.

Text, tekst, *n.* An author's own work as distinct from annotations; a passage of Scripture selected as the subject of a discourse; a topic; a large kind of handwriting; particular kind of lettering.

Textile, teks'til, *a.* Woven; capable of being woven.—*n.* A fabric made by weaving.

Textual, teks'tū-al, *a.* Contained in the text; pertaining to the text.

Texture, teks'tūr, *n.* A web; that which is woven; a fabric; manner in which constituent parts are connected; the grain or peculiar character of a solid.

Thalamus, thal'a-mus, *n.*; pl. **-mi.** A large ganglion in the brain; the receptacle of a flower, or part on which the carpels are placed.

Thallus, thal'us, *n.* A solid mass of cells, forming the substance of the thallogens.

Than, ᴛʜan, *conj.* A particle used after certain adjectives and adverbs expressing compariosn or diversity, as *more, other,* etc.

Thanksgiving, thangks'giv-ing, *n.* Act of giving thanks; public celebration of divine goodness.

That, ᴛʜat, *a.* and *pron.*; pl. **Those,** ᴛʜōz. A pronominal adjective pointing to a person or thing mentioned or understood; a demonstrative pronoun; a relative pronoun equivalent to *who* or *which.*—*conj.* Introducing a reason, purpose, or result, a noun clause, or a wish.

Theater, thē'a-tėr, *n.* A house for the exhibition of dramatic performances; a place of action; a room for anatomical demonstrations, etc.

Theft, theft, *n.* Act of stealing; unlawful taking of another's goods;

thing stolen.

Their, THār, *pronominal* or *possessive adj.* Pertaining or belonging to them.—**Theirs,** possessive case of *they,* used without a noun.

Them, THem, *pron.* The dative and objective case of *they*; those persons or things.

Theme, thêm, *n.* A subject or topic; short dissertation by a student; leading subject in a musical composition.

Then, THen, *adv.* At that time, past or future; soon afterwards.—*conj.* In that case; therefore.

Theory, thē'ō-ri, *n.* Speculation; hypothesis to explain something; rules or knowledge of an art as distinguished from practice.

Therapeutics, the-ra-pūt'iks, *n.* That part of medicine which deals with the application and operation of remedies.

There, THār, *adv.* In or at that place; at that point; thither.

Thermal, Thermic, thėr'mal, thėr'mik, *a.* Pertaining to heat; warm; hot.

Thermometer, thėr-mom'et-ėr, *n.* An instrument for measuring temperature.

Thermotics, thėr-mot'iks, *n.* The science of heat.

Thesaurus, the-sạ'rus, *n.* A treasury; a lexicon.

They, THā, *pron. pl.* The plural of *he, she,* or *it*; sometimes used indefinitely.

Thick, thik, *a.* Having extent measured through; dense; foggy; crowded; close; stupid; gross.—*n.* The thickest part.—*adv.* In close succession; fast or close together.

Thicket, thik'et, *n.* A wood or collection of trees or shrubs closely set.

Thin-skinned, thin'skind, *a.* Having a thin skin; unduly sensitive; irritable.

Thirst, thėrst, *n.* The desire or distress occasioned by want of water; eager desire after anything.—*vi.* To feel thirst; to desire vehemently.

Thistle, this'l, *n.* A prickly composite plant, the national emblem of Scotland.

Thong, thong, *n.* A strap of leather, used for fastening anything.

Thorax, thōraks, *n.*; pl. **-races.** That part of the human body which contains the lungs, heart, etc.; the chest.

Thorn, thorn, *n.* A tree or shrub armed with spines or prickles; a prickle; anything troublesome.

Thorough, thu'rō, *a.* Passing through or to the end; complete; perfect.

Thorough-bred, thu'rō-bred, *a.* Bred from pure and unmixed blood, as horses; completely bred or accomplished; high-spirited.—*n.* An animal of pure blood.

Thoroughfare, thu'rō-fār, *n.* A passage through; unobstructed way; power of passing.

Those, THōz, *a.* and *pron.* Pl. of *that.*

Though, THō, *conj.* Granting it to be the fact that; notwithstanding that; if.—*adv.* However.

Thrashing, Threshing, thrash'ing, thresh'ing, *n.* Act of beating out grain; a sound drubbing.

Thread, thred, *n.* A fine cord; any fine filament; prominent spiral part of a screw; continued course or tenor; general purpose.—*vt.* To pass a thread through; to pass or pierce through.

Threadbare, thred'bār, *a.* Having the nap worn off; worn out; trite; hackneyed.

Threat, thret, *n.* A menace; declaration of intention to punish or hurt.

Threaten, thret'n, *vt.* To use threats towards; to menace; to show to be impending.—*vi.* To use threats.

Threshold, Thresh'ōld, *n.* The stone or piece of timber which lies under a door; a doorsill; entrance; outset.

Thrift, thrift, *n.* Frugality; economy; sea-pink.

Thrill, thril, *vt.* To send a quiver through; to affect with a keen tingling.—*vi.* To quiver; to move tremulously.—*n.* A warbling; thrilling sensation.

Throe, thrō, *n.* Extreme pain; anguish of travail in childbirth.—*vi.* (throeing, throed). To struggle in extreme pain.

Thrombosis, throm'bō-sis, *n.* The obstruction of a blood-vessel by a

T

clot of blood.

Throne, thrōn, *n*. The seat of a king or ruler; sovereign power and dignity.—*vt*. (throning, throned). To place on a royal seat; to enthrone; to exalt.

Throng, throng, *n*. A crowd; a great number.—*vi*. and *t*. To crowd or press together.

Throttle, throt'l, *n*. The windpipe or trachea; the throat; the gullet.—*vt*. (throttling, throttled). To choke; to strangle.

Through, thrö, *prep*. From end to end of; by means of; on account of; throughout.—*adv*. From end to end; to completion.—*a*. Going with little or no interruption from one place to another.

Thumb, thum, *n*. The short thick finger of the hand.—*vt*. To soil or handle awkwardly with the fingers.

Thump, thump, *n*. A dull, heavy blow; sound made by such a blow.—*vt*. and *i*. To strike with something thick or heavy.

Thwart, thwạrt, *a*. Transverse; being across.—*vt*. To cross; to frustrate or defeat.—*n*. The bench on which the rowers sit, athwart the boat.

Ticket, tik'et, *n*. A label; a card or paper enabling one to enter a place, travel in a railway, etc.—*vt*. To put a ticket on; to label.

Ticking, tik'ing, *n*. A striped closely-woven cloth containing the feathers, etc., of beds.

Tickle, tik'l, *vt*. (tickling, tickled). To touch and cause a peculiar thrilling sensation in; to please; to flatter; to puzzle.

Ticklish, tik'lish, *a*. Easily tickled; touchy; liable to be overthrown; difficult; critical.

Tide, tīd, *n*. Time; season; the rising and falling of the sea; flow; current.—*vt*. or *i*. (tiding, tided). To drive with the tide.—**To tide over,** to surmount.

Tidings, tī'dingz, *n.pl*. News; intelligence.

Tidy, tī'di, *a*. Clean and orderly; neat; trim; moderately large.—*vt*. (tidying, tidied). To make tidy.—*n*. A piece of fancy work to throw over a chair, etc.

Tie, tī, *vt*. (tying, tied). To bind; to fasten; to oblige; to constrain.—*n*. That which binds or fastens together; a fastening; a neck-tie; bond; obligation; an equality in numbers.

Tier, tēr, *n*. A row; a rank.

Tile, tīl, *n*. A slab of baked clay for covering roofs, floors, walls, etc.—*vt*. (tiling, tiled). To cover with tiles; to guard against the entrance of the unitiated.

Till, til, *n*. A money box or drawer for money in a shop, etc.—*prep*. To the time of; until.—*vt*. To cultivate; to plow and prepare for seed.

Tilt, tilt, *vi*. To run or ride and thrust with a lance; to joust; to lean or slope; to heel over.—*vt*. To set in a sloping position; to cover with an awning.—*n*. Inclination forward; a military contest with lances on horseback; a tilt-hammer; an awning.

Timber, tim'bėr, *n*. Wood suitable for building purposes; trees yielding such wood; one of the main beams of a fabric.—*vt*. To furnish with timber.

Timbre, tim'br or tam'br, *n*. Characteristic quality of sound.

Time, tīm, *n*. The measure of duration; a particular part or point of duration; occasion; season; epoch; present life; leisure; rhythm' rate of movement.—*vt*. (timing, timed). To adapt to the time or occasion; to regulate or measure as to time.

Tincture, tingk'tūr, *n*. A tinge, tint, or shade; slight quality added to anything; flavor; extract or solution of the active principles of some substance.—*vt*. (tincturing, tinctured). To tinge; to imbue.

Tinder, tin'der, *n*. An inflammable substance used for obtaining fire from a spark.

Tinkle, ting'kl, *vi*. (tinkling, tinkled). To make small, sharp sounds; to tingle; to clink. —*vt*. To cause to clink.—*n*. A sharp, ringing noise.

Tinkling, ting'kling, *n*. A small, sharp, ringing sound.

Tinsel, tin'sel, *n*. Thin, glittering metallic sheets; cloth overlaid with foil; something superficially showy.—a. Consisting of tinsel; showy to excess.—vt. (tinselling, tinselled). To adorn with tinsel.

Tint, tint, n. a tinge; a slight coloring; hue.—vt. To tinge.

Tiptoe, tip'tō, n. The tip or end of the toe.

Tirade, ti-rād', n. A violent declamation; an invective; a harangue.

Tissue, ti'shū, n. Any woven stuff; a textile fabric; a primary layer of organic substance; a fabrication.

Tissue-paper, ti'shū-pā-pėr, n. A very thin paper, used for protecting or wrapping.

Titanium, tī-tā'ni-um, n. A metallic element somewhat resembling tin.

Tithe, tīTH, n. The tenth part of anything; tenth part allotted to the clergy; any small part.—vt. (tithing, tithed). To levy a tithe on.—vi. To pay tithes.

Titter, tit'ėr, vi. To laugh with restraint.—n. A restrained laugh.

Titular, tit'ū-lėr, a. Holding a position by title or name only; nominal.

To, tụ or tō, prep. Denoting motion towards; indicating a point reached, destination, addition, ratio, opposition, or contrast; marking an object; the sign of the infinitive mood.—adv. Forward; on.

Toad, tōd, n. A reptile resembling the frog, but not adapted for leaping.

Tocsin tok'sin, n. An alarm-bell.

Today, tụ-dā', n. The present day; also, on this day, adverbially.

Toddle, tod'l, vi. (toddling, toddled). To walk with short, tottering steps.—n. A little toddling walk.

Toe, tō, n. One of the small members forming the extremity of the foot.—vt. (toeing, toed). To touch or reach with the toes.

Together, tụ-geTH'ėr, adv. In company; in concert; without intermission.

Toil, toil, vi. To labor; to work; to drudge. —n. Labor with fatigue; a string or web for taking prey.

Toilet, toi'let, n. A cloth over a table in a dressing room; a dressing-table; act or mode of dressing; attire.

Token, tō'kn, n. A mark; sign; indication; souvenir; keepsake; a piece of money current by sufferance, not coined by authority.

Tolerate, tol'ė-rāt, vt. (tolerating, tolerated). To allow or permit; to treat with forbearance; to put up with; to allow religious freedom to.

Tomato, tō-mä'tō, n.; pl. -toes. A tropical plant and its fruit, now widely cultivated.

Tomb, töm, n. A grave; a sepulchral structure,—vt. To bury; to entomb.

Tomboy, tom'boi, n. A wild, romping girl.

Tombstone, töm'stōn, n. A stone erected over a grave; a sepulchral monument.

Tone, tōn, n. Any sound in relation to its pitch, quality, or strength; sound as expressive of sentiment; timbre; healthy activity of animal organs; mood; tenor; prevailing character.—vt. (toning, toned). To give a certain tone to.—**To tone down,** to soften.

Tongs, tongz, n.pl. A metal instrument for taking hold of coals, heated metals, etc.

Tongue, tung, n. The fleshy movable organ in the mouth, of taste, speech, etc.; speech; a language; strip of land; a tapering flame; pin of a buckle.—vt. To utter; to scold; to modify with the tongue in playing, as in the flute.

Too, tö, adv. Over; more than sufficiently; very; likewise; also; besides.

Tool, töl, n. Any instrument to be used by the hands; a person used as an instrument by another.—vt. To shape or mark with a tool.

Toot, töt, vi. To make a noise like that of a pipe or horn.—vt. To sound, as a horn.—n. A sound blown on a horn.

Tooth, töth, n.; pl. **Teeth,** tēth. A bony growth in the jaws for chewing; any projection resembling a tooth.—vt. To furnish with teeth; to indent.

Top, top, n. The highest part of anything; highest rank; platform in ships surrounding the head of the lower masts; a whirling toy.—a. Being on the top; highest.—vi. (topping, topped). To rise aloft; to be eminent.—vt. To cap; to surmount; to rise to the top of.

Topaz, tō'paz, n. A transparent or translucent gem of various light colors.

Topography, to-pog'ra-fi, n. The description of a particular place, tract of land, etc.

Topple, top'l, vi. (toppling, toppled). To fall, as with the top first,—vt. To throw forward.

Torch, torch, n. A light to be carried in the hand; a flambeau.

Torrent, to'rent, n. A violent rushing stream.

Torrid, to'rid, a. Parched; violently hot; burning or parching.

Torsion, tor'shon, n. The act of twisting; the force with which a body, such as a wire, resists a twist; the twisting of the cut end of an artery to stop the flow of blood.

Torso, tor'sō, n. The trunk of a statue deprived of its head and limbs.

Toss, tos, vt. To pitch; to fling; to jerk, as the head; to agitate.—vi. To roll and tumble; to be in violent commotion.—n. A throw; pitch; throw of the head.

Toss-up, tos'up, n. The throwing up of a coin to decide something; an even chance.

Tot, tot, n. Anything small or insignificant.—vt. (totting, totted). To sum (with up).

Total, tō'tal, a. Pertaining to the whole; complete.—n. The whole; an aggregate.

Touch, tuch, vt. To perceive by the sense of feeling; to come in contact with; to taste; to reach or arrive at; to refer to; to affect.—vi. To be in contact; to take effect; to make mention; to call when on a voyage.—n. Act of touching; contact; sense of feeling; a trait; a little; a stroke; distinctive handling; in football, etc., part of the field beyond the flags.

Tough, tuf, a. Flexible and not brittle; tenacious; durable; viscous; stiff; stubborn.

Toughen, tuf'n, vi. To grow tough.—vt. To make tough.

Toupee, Toupet, tö-pē', tö'pē, n. A

curl or artificial lock of hair; a small wig or upper part of wig.

Tour, tör, n. A journey; a lengthy jaunt or excursion.—vi. To make a tour.

Tourist, tör'ist, n. One who makes a tour.

Tournament, tör'na-ment, n. A martial sport performed by knights on horseback; contest in which a number take part.

Tourniquet, tör'ni-ket, n. A bandage tightened by a screw to check a flow of blood.

Tousle, tou'zl, vt. (tousling, tousled). To dishevel.

Tout, tout, vi. To ply or seek for customers.—n. One who plies for customers.

Tow, tō, vt. To drag, as a boat, by a rope.—n. Act of towing; state of being towed; coarse part of flax or hemp.

Toward, Towards, tō'ērd, tō'ērdz, prep. In the direction of; regarding; in aid of; for; about.—adv. At hand; going on.

Towel, tou'el, n. A cloth for drying the skin after washing, or for domestic purposes.

Tower, tou'ér, n. A lofty narrow building; a citadel; a fortress.—vi. To soar; to be lofty; to stand sublime.

Toxicology, toks-i-kol'o-ji, n. That branch of medicine which treats of poisons and their antidotes.

Toxin, toks'in, n. A poisonous substance generated in an animal body.

Toy, toi, n. A plaything; a bauble; a trifle.—vi. To dally; to trifle.

Trace, trās, n. A mark left by anything; footstep; vestige; track; one of the straps by which a carriage, etc., is drawn.—vt. (tracing, traced). To track out; to follow by marks left; to draw or copy with lines or marks.

Tract, trakt, n. A region of indefinite extent; a short dissertation.

Tractable, trakt'a-bl, a. That may be easily managed; docile; manageable.

Trade, trād, n. Employment; commerce; traffic; those engaged in any trade.—a. Pertaining to

trade.—*vi*. (trading, traded). To traffic; to carry on commerce; to have dealings.—*vt*. To sell or exchange in commerce.

Tradition, tra-di'shon, *n*. The handing down of opinions, stories, etc., from father to son, by oral communication; a statement so handed down.

Tragedy, tra'je-di, *n*. A drama representing an important event generally having a fatal issue; a fatal and mournful event; a murderous or bloody deed.

Tragic, Tragical, tra'jik, tra'jik-al, *a*. Pertaining to tragedy; murderous; calamitous.

Trail, trāl, *n*. Something dragged behind; a train; the end of a field gun-carriage that rests on the ground in firing; a path; track followed by a hunter; the position of a rifle when carried horizontally at the full extent of the right arm.—*vt*. To draw behind or along the ground; to drag.—*vi*. To be dragged along a surface; to hang down loosely; to grow along the ground.

Trailer, trāl'ėr, *n*. One who trails; a plant which cannot grow upward without support; a carriage dragged by a motor vehicle; a series of excerpts advertising coming attractions at the cinema.

Train, trān, *vt*. To draw; to entice; to rear and instruct; to drill; to bring into proper bodily condition; to shape; to bring to bear, as a gun.—*vi*. To undergo special drill.—*n*. A trail; that part of a gown which trails; tail; a series; course; retinue; line of carriages and an engine on a railway; line to conduct fire to a charge or mine.

Trance, trans, *n*. A state of insensibility; ecstasy; catalepsy.—*vt*. (trancing, tranced). To entrance; to enchant.

Tranquil, tran'kwil, *a*. Quiet; calm; undisturbed; peaceful.

Transcribe, tran-skrīb', *vt*. (transcribing, transcribed). To write over again or in the same words; to copy.

Transcription, tran-skrip'shon, *n*. Act of transcribing; a copy; transcript.

Transept, tran'sept, *n*. The transverse portion of a church built in form of a cross.

Transfer, trans-fėr', *vt*. (transferring, transferred). To convey from one place or person to another; to make over.—*n*. trans'fėr. Act of trarnsferring; removal of a thing from one place or person to another; something transferred.

Transfuse, trans-fūz', *vt*. (transfusing, transfused). To transfer by pouring; to cause to pass from one to another.

Transition, tran-zi'shon, *n*. Passage from one place, state, or topic to another.—*a*. Pertaining to passage from one state, etc., to another.

Transitive, tran'sit-iv, *a*. In *grammar*, taking an object after it, as a verb.

Transitory, tran'si-to-ri, *a*. Passing away; fleeting; transient.

Translate, trans-lātụ', *vt*. (translating, translated). To remove from one place to another; to transfer; to render into another language.

Transmigration, trans-mi-grā' shon, *n*. Act of transmigrating; the passing of a soul into another body after death.

Transmissible, Transmittable, trans-mis'i-bl, trans-mit'i-bl, *a*. That may be transmitted.

Transmission, trans-mi'shon, *n*. Act of transmitting; transference; a passing through any body, as of light through glass, the gear box of an automobile by which engine power is transmitted to the wheels.

Transmit, trans-mit', *vt*. (transmitting, transmitted). To send from one person or place to another; to hand down; to allow to pass through.

Transom, tran'sum, *n*. A strengthening horizontal beam; a crossbar.

Transparent, trans-pā'rent, *a*. That can be seen through distinctly; not sufficient to hide underlying feelings.

Transpire, trans-pīr, *vt*. (transpiring, transpired). To emit through the pores of the skin; to send off in

T

vapor.—*vi.* To exhale; to escape from secrecy; to become public.

Transplant, trans-plant', *vt.* To remove and plant in another place.

Transport, trans-pōrt', *vt.* To carry from one place to another; to carry into banishment; to carry away by violence of passion; to ravish with pleasure.—*n.* trans' pōrt. Transportation; a ship employed to carry soldiers, warlike stores, etc.; passion; ecstasy.

Transverse, trans'vėrs or transvėrs', *a.* Lying or being across or in a cross direction.

Trap, trap, *n.* A contrivance for catching unawares; an ambush; a contrivance in drains to prevent effluvia rising; a carriage of any kind, on springs; a kind of movable ladder; an igneous rock.—*vt.* (trapping, trapped). To catch in a trap; to insnare; to adorn.—*vi.* To set traps for game.

Trap-door, trap'dōr, *n.* A door in a floor or roof, with which when shut it is flush.

Trapeze, tra-pēz', *n.* A sort of swing, consisting of a cross-bar suspended by cords, for gymnastic exercises.

Trashy, trash'i, *a.* Worthless; useless.

Traumatic, trạ-mat'ik, *a.* Pertaining to wounds.—*n.* A medicine useful in the cure of wounds.

Travail, tra'vāl, *vi.* To labor; to toil; to suffer the pangs of childbirth.— *n.* Labor; severe toil; childbirth.

Travel, tra'vel, *n.* Act of journeying; journey to a distant country; *pl.* account of occurrences during a journey.—*vi.* (travelling, travelled). To journey; to go to a distant country; to pass; to move.

Travelling, tra'vel-ing, *p.a.* Pertaining to, used in, or incurred by travel.

Traverse, tra'vėrs, *a.* Transverse.— *n.* Something that is transverse; something that thwarts; a denial.—*vt.* (traversing, traversed). To cross; to thwart; to cross in travelling; to deny.—*adv.* Athwart; crosswise.

Travertin, tra'vėr-tin, *n.* A white limestone deposited from the wa-

ter of springs holding carbonate of lime in solution.

Travesty, tra'ves-ti, *vt.* (travestying, travestied). To transform so as to have a ludicrous effect; to burlesque.—*n.* A burlesque treatment; parody.

Tread, tred, *vi.* (pret. trod, pp. trod, trodden). To set the foot on the ground; to step; to walk with a measured step; to copulate, as fowls.—*vt.* To plant the foot on; to trample; to dance; to walk on in a formal manner; to copulate with, as a bird.—*n.* A step; gait; horizontal part of the step of a stair.

Treason, trē'zon, *n.* A betrayal; breach of allegiance; treachery; disloyalty.

Treasure, tre'zhūr, *n.* Wealth accumulated; great abundance; something very much valued.—*vt.* (treasuring, treasured). To lay up or collect; to prize.

Treatise, trē'tiz, *n.* A written composition on some particular subject; a dissertation.

Treatment, trēt'ment, *n.* Act or manner of treating; management; usage.

Treaty, trē'ti, *n.* Negotiation; agreement between two or more nations.

Tremendous, trē-men'dus, *a.* Such as may cause trembling; terrible; extraordinary.

Tremor, tre'mor, *n.* An involuntary trembling; a shivering; vibration.

Tremulous, tre'mū-lus, *a.* Trembling; shaking; quivering; vibratory.

Trench, trensh, *vt.* To dig a ditch in; to turn over and mix, as soil.—*vi.* To cut a trench or trenches; to encroach (with *on* or *upon*).—*n.* A long narrow excavation; a deep ditch cut for defense.

Trenchant, tren'shant, *a.* Cutting; keen; severe.

Trepidation, tre-pid-ā'shon, *n.* Confused alarm; perturbation; involuntary trembling.

Trespass, tres'pas, *vi.* To enter unlawfully upon the land of another; to do wrong; to offend.—*n.* An offense; a sin; wrong done by entering on the land of another.

Tribe, trīb, *n.* A division or class of people; a family or race; a class of animals or plants.

Tribune, trī′būn, *n.* Among the ancient Romans, a magistrate chosen by the people, to protect them from the patricians; a platform; tribunal; throne of a bishop.

Tributary, tri′bū-ta-ri, *a.* Paying tribute to another; subject; contributing.—*n.* One that pays tribute; a stream which falls into another.

Tribute, tri′būt, *n.* A sum paid by one prince or nation to another; personal contribution.

Trick, trik, *n.* An artifice; a crafty device; fraud; a knack or art; a personal practice or habit; a prank; all the cards played in one round.—*vt.* To deceive; to impose on, to cheat; to draw in outline; to dress; to adorn (often with *out*).

Trickle, trik′l, *vi.* (trickling, trickled). To fall in drops; to flow gently.

Tricostate, trī-kos′tāt, *a.* Having three ribs or ridges.

Tricuspid, Tricuspidate, trī-kus′pid, trī-kus′pi-dāt, *a.* Having three cusps or points.

Tricycle, trī′si-kl, *n.* A cycle with three wheels.

Trident, trī′dent, *n.* Any instrument of the form of a fork with three prongs.

Tried, trīd, *p.a.* Tested by trial or experience; staunch; true.

Trifle, trī′fl, *n.* Something of no moment or value; a kind of fancy confection.—*vi.* (trifling, trifled). To act with levity; to play or toy; to finger lightly.—*vt.* To waste.

Triform, trī′form, *a.* Having a triple form or shape.

Trilateral, trī-lat′ėr-al, *a.* Having three sides, as a triangle.

Trilith, Trilithon, trī′lith, trī′lith-on, *n.* Three large blocks of stone placed together like door-posts and a lintel, and standing by themselves, as in sundry ancient monuments.

Trill, tril, *n.* A shake of the voice in singing; a quavering sound.—*vt.* To sing with a quavering voice; to sing sweetly or clearly.—*vi.* To sound with tremulous vibrations; to pipe; to trickle.

Trillion, tril′yon, *n.* The product of a million multiplied twice by itself.

Trilobate, trī-lō′bāt, *n.* Having three lobes.

Trilogy, tril′o-ji, *n.* A series of three connected dramas, each complete in itself.

Trim, trim, *vt.* (trimming, trimmed). To put in order; to embellish; to clip or pare; to adjust.—*vi.* To hold a middle course between parties.—*a.* Set in good order; properly adjusted; neat; tidy.—*n.* Condition; order; mood; dress.

Trio, trī′ō or trē′ō, *n.* Three united; musical composition for three voices or instruments; performers of a trio.

Trip, trip, *vi.* (tripping, tripped). To run or step lightly; to skip; to stumble; to err.—*vt.* To cause to fall or stumble; to loose an anchor.—*n.* A stumble; a light short step; an excursion or jaunt; a mistake.

Triplicate, tri′pli-kāt, *a.* Threefold.—*n.* A third thing corresponding to two others.

Tripod, trī′pod, *n.* A three-footed pot, seat, or stand.

Triptych, trip′tik, *n.* A picture or carving in three compartments side by side; a treatise in three sections.

Trisect, trī-sekt′, *vt.* To cut into three equal parts.

Trite, trīt, *a.* Hackneyed; threadbare; stale.

Triturate, tri′tū-rāt, *vt.* (triturating, triturated). To rub or grind to a very fine powder.

Troglodyte, trō′glod-īt, *n.* A cave-dweller; one living in seclusion.

Trojan, trō′jan, *a.* Pertaining to ancient Troy.—*n.* An inhabitant of ancient Troy; a jolly fellow; a plucky determined fellow.

Troop, tröp, *n.* A collection of people; a company; a body of soldiers; *pl.* soldiers in general; a troupe.—*vi.* To collect in numbers; to march in a body.

Trope, trōp, *n.* A word used figuratively; a figure of speech.

Trophy, trō′fi, *n.* A memorial of some victory; an architectural ornament representing the stem of a

T

tree, hung with military weapons.

Tropic, tro'pik, n. Either of two circles on the celestial sphere, limiting the sun's apparent annual path; either of two corresponding parallels of latitude including the torrid zone; pl. the regions between or near these.—a. Pertaining to the tropics.

Trot, trot, vi. (trotting, trotted). To run with small steps; to move fast.—vt. To cause to trot.—n. Pace of a horse more rapid than a walk.

Troubador, trö'ba-dör, n. one of a class of poets who flourished in S. Europe, especially in Provence, from the eleventh to the end of the thirteenth century.

Trouble, tru'bl, vt. (troubling, troubled). To disturb; to distress; to busy.—n. Distress; agitation; affliction; labor.

Trout, trout, n. A fresh-water fish of the salmon tribe.

Trow, trou or trō, vi. To believe; to suppose.

Trowel, trou'el, n. A hand-tool for lifting and dressing mortar and plaster, etc.; a gardener's tool.—vt. (trowelling, trowelled). To dress or form with a trowel.

Troy, Troy-weight, troi, troi'wāt, n. A weight used for gold and silver, divided into 12 ounces, each of 20 pennyweights, each of 24 grains, so that a pound troy = 5760 grains.

Truant, trö'ant, n. One who shirks duty; one who stays from school without leave.—a. Idle; wilfully absenting oneself.

Truce, trös, n. A temporary cessation of hostilities; armistice; short quiet.

Truck, truk, vi. and t. To barter.—n. Exchange of commodities; barter; payment of workmen's wages partly in goods; a small wheel; a barrow with two low wheels; an open railway wagon for goods; a motor driven vehicle used to carry heavy loads or general freight; the cap at the end of a flagstaff or topmast.

True, trö, a. Conformable to fact; truthful; genuine; constant; faithful; loyal; honest; exact; correct;

right.

Truism, trö'izm, n. A self-evident truth.

Trump, trump, n. A winning card; one of a suit for the time being superior to the others; a person upon whom one can depend; a trumpet.—vt. To take with a trump card; to concoct or forge.

Trunk, trungk, n. The woody stem of a tree; body of an animal without the limbs; main body; chest for containing clothes, etc.; a long wooden tube.

Truss, trus, n. A bundle, as of hay or straw; a bandage used in cases of rupture; a combination of timbers constituting an unyielding frame.—vt. To put in a bundle; to make tight or fast; to skewer.

Trust, trust, n. Reliance; confidence; hope; credit; that which is intrusted; safe-keeping; care; management.—vt. To rely on; to believe; to intrust; to sell to upon credit; to be confident.—vi. To have reliance; to confide readily.—a. Held in trust.

Trustee, trus-tē', n. One appointed to hold property for the benefit of those entitled to it.

Trustworthy, trust'wer-THi, a. Worthy of trust or confidence; faithful; reliable.

Truth, tröth, n. Conformity to fact or reality; integrity; constancy; exactness; reality; verified fact.

Truthful, tröth'ful, a. Closely adhering to truth; veracious; correct; true.

Try, trī, vt. (trying, tried). To test; to make trial of; to afflict; to examine judicially; to attempt.—vi. To endeavor.—n. The act of trying; a trial; experiment; in Rugby football, the right of trying to kick a goal, obtained by carrying the ball behind the opponents' goalline and touching it down.

Tub, tub, n. An open wooden vessel; a small cask; a clumsy boat; a vessel used as a bath.—vt. (tubbing, tubbed). To set in a tub.—vi. To make use of a bathing-tub.

Tuba, tü'ba, n. A large musical instrument of brass, low in pitch.

Tube, tüb, n. A pipe; a hollow cylinder; the underground electric railway system in London.—*vt.* (tubing, tubed) To furnish with a tube.

Tuck, tuk, *vt.* To gather into a narrower compass; to fold in or under.—*n.* A horizontal fold in a garment to shorten it.

Tumor, tū'mor, *n.* A morbid swelling in some part of the body.

Tumult, tū'mult, *n.* A commotion or disturbance; uproar; high excitement.

Tungsten, tung'sten, *n.* A heavy metal of a grayish-white color.

Tunic, tū'nik, *n.* A garment of various kinds; an ecclesiastical vestment worn over the alb; a full-dress military coat; a covering membrane; an integument.

Turbine, tér'bīn, *n.* A kind of waterwheel, usually horizontal, made to revolve under the influence of pressure derived from a fall of water; a similar contrivance driven by steam.

Turbulent, tér'bū-lent, *a.* Being in violent commotion; refractory; disorderly.

Turmeric, tér'mer-ik, *n.* An E. Indian plant of the ginger family yielding a condiment, a yellow dye, and a test for alkalies.

Turmoil, tér'moil, *n.* Disturbance; trouble; disquiet.—*vt.* To harass.

Turn, tern, *vt.* To cause to move round; to shape by a lathe; to direct; to alter in course; to blunt; to reverse; to change.—*vi.* To revolve; to depend; to change position or course; to return; to have recourse; to become; to become sour; to reel; to become nauseated; to result.—*n.* Act of turning; a revolution; a bend; a short walk; an alteration of course; occasion; occasional act of kindness or malice; purpose; character; short spell, as a work; nervous shock.

Turn-over, tern'ō-vér, *n.* The amount of money turned over or drawn in a business.

Turnstile, tern'stīl, *n.* A post at some passage surmounted by horizontal arms which move as a person pushes through.

Turpentine, tér'pen-tīn, *n.* A resinous substance flowing from trees,

as the pine, larch, fir, etc.; the oil distilled from this.

Turpitude, tér-pi-tūd, *n.* Inherent baseness or vileness; moral depravity.

Turquoise, tér'koiz, *n.* A greenish-blue or blue opaque precious stone.

Turret, tu'ret, *n.* A little tower on a larger building; a strong cylindrical iron structure on an iron-clad.

Turtle, tér'tl, *n.* A species of small pigeon; the sea-tortoise.

Tutor, tū'tor, *n.* A guardian; a private instructor; a fellow of an English college who superintends the studies of undergraduates.—*vt.* To instruct.

Tutorage, tū'tor-āj, *n.* Guardianship.

Twain, twān, *a.* Two.—*n.* A pair.

Twang, twang, *vi.* To make the sound of a string which is stretched and suddenly pulled.—*vt.* To make to sound sharply.—*n.* A sharp vibrating sound; a nasal sound.

Twice, twīs, *adv.* Two times; doubly.

Twig, twig, *n.* A small shoot or branch.—*vt.* and *i.* (twigging, twigged). To observe; to understand.

Twilight, twī'līt, *n.* The faint light of the sun reflected after sunset and before sunrise; dubious view or conditon.—*a.* Faint; seen or done by twilight.

Twinge, twinj, *vt.* and *i.* (twinging, twinged). To affect with or have a sharp, sudden pain.—*n.* A sudden, sharp, darting pain.

Twinkle, twingk'l, *vi.* (twinkling, twinkled). To sparkle; to shine with a quivering light.—*n.* A gleam or sparkle.

Twirl, twérl, *vt.* and *i.* To turn round with rapidity; to spin.—*n.* A rapid whirl.

Twist, twist, *n.* Something twined, as a thread, etc.; roll of tobacco; a spiral; contortion; mental or moral bent.—*vt.* and *i.* To form into a cord; to twine; to contort; to insinuate; to pervert.

Twitter, twit'ér, *vi.* To utter small, tremulous notes, as birds; to chirp.—*n.* A chirp or continued chirping.

T

Typesetter, tīp′set-ėr, *n*. One who sets up type; a compositor; a type-setting machine.

Typewriter, tīp′rīt-ėr, *n*. A machine used as a substitute for the pen, producing letters by inked types.

Typhoid, tī′foid, *n*. A fever characterized by abdominal pains and diarrhea; enteric fever.

Typhoon, tī-fön′, *n*. A violent hurricane on the coasts of China and Japan.

Typhus, tī′fus, *n*. A contagious or epidemic fever characterized by a deep livid eruption.

Typical, tip′ik-al, *a*. Pertaining to a type; emblematic; symbolic; representative.

Typify, tip′i-fī, *vt*. To serve as a type of; to represent; to exemplify.

Typographic, Typographical, tī-po-graf′ik, tī-po-graf′ik-al, *a*. Pertaining to typography or printing.

Typography, tī-pog′ra-fī, *n*. The art of printing; style of printing.

Typology, tī-pol′o-ji, *n*. A discourse on types; the doctrine of types in Scripture.

Tyranny, ti′ran-i, *n*. Rule of a tyrant; despotic exercise of power; oppression.

Tyrant, tī′rant, *n*. A despot; a cruel sovereign or master; an oppressor.

U

Ubiety, ū-bī′e-ti, *n*. The state of being somewhere.

Ubiquity, ū-bi′kwi-ti, *n*. Existence everywhere at the same time; omnipresence.

Udder, ud′ėr, *n*. The glandular organ of cows, etc., in which the milk is produced.

Ugly, ug′li, *a*. Repulsive; disagreeable in appearance; hateful; ill-omened.

Ukulele, ū′ku-lā′′lē, *n*. A small Hawaiian guitar.

Ulcer, ul′sėr, *n*. A sore that discharges pus.

Ultimatum, ul-ti-mā′tum, *n*.; pl. **-ta** or **-tums**. The last offer; a final proposition which being rejected

may be followed by war.

Ultra, ul′tra, *prefix, a*. Beyond due limit; extreme.—*n*. An ultraist.

Ultramarine, ul′tra-ma-rēn′′, *a*. Being beyond the sea.—*n*. A beautiful and durable sky-blue.

Umbrage, um′brāj, *n*. Shade; obscurity; jealousy; offense; resentment.

Umbrella, um-brel′la, *n*. A portable shade which opens and folds, for sheltering the person from the sun or rain.

Umlaut, um′lout, *n*. The change of a vowel in one syllable through the influence of a different vowel in the syllable immediately following.

Umpire, um′pīr, *n*. A person to whose decision a dispute is referred; a judge, arbiter, or referee.

Unable, un-ā′bl, *a*. Not able; not having sufficient ability; not equal for some task.

Unacceptable, un-ak-sept′a-bl, *a*. Not acceptable or pleasing; unwelcome.

Unadorned, un-a-dornd′, *a*. Not adorned; not embellished.

Unadvisable, un-ad-vīz′a-bl, *a*. Not advisable; not expedient; not prudent.

Unaffected, un-af-fekt′ed, *a*. Not affected; natural; simple; sincere; not moved.

Unalterable, un-al′tėr-a-bl, *a*. Not alterable; unchangeable; immutable.

Unanimous, ū-nan′i-mus, *a*. Being of one mind; agreeing in determination; formed by unanimity.

Unauthorized, un-a′thor-īzd, *a*. Not authorized; not warranted.

Unavailable, un-a-vāl′a-bl, *a*. Not available; vain; useless.

Unbroken, un-brōk′n, *a*. Not broken; not tamed; not interrupted.

Uncalled, un-kald′, *a*. Not called; not summoned; not invited.

Uncanny, un-kan′i, *a*. Not canny; mysterious; of evil and supernatural character.

Uncared, un-kārd′, *a*. Not regarded; not heeded; often with *for*.

Uncle, ung′kl, *n*. The brother of one's father or mother.

Unclean, un-klēn′ *a*. Not clean;

foul; dirty; morally impure; lewd.

Uncomfortable, un-kum´fort-a-bl, *a*. Not comfortable; uneasy; ill at ease.

Uncommon, un-kom´mon, *a*. Not common; rare; strange; remarkable.

Unconditional, un-kon-di´shon-al, *a*. Not limited by conditions; absolute.

Unconscious, un-kon´shus, *a*. Not conscious; not perceiving; unaware.

Unconstitutional, un-kon´sti-tū´´shon-al, *a*. Not agreeable to the constitution; against the law.

Uncover, un-ku´ver, *vt*. To divest of a cover; to disclose.—*vi*. To take off the hat.

Unction, ungk´shon, *n*. Act of anointing; an unguent; religious fervor; sham devotional fervor; oiliness.

Unctuous, ung´tū-us, *a*. Oily; greasy; nauseously emotional; oily; fawning.

Under, un´der, *prep*. Below; beneath; undergoing; affected by; subject to; inferior; during the time of; included in; in accordance with.—*adv*. In a lower condition or degree.—*a*. Lower; subject; subordinate.

Underclothes, Underclothing, un´der-klōᴛʜz, un´der-klōᴛʜ-ing, *n*. Clothes worn under others or next to the skin.

Undercurrent, un´der-ku-rent, *n*. A current below another; some movement or influence not apparent.

Undergo, un-der-gō, *vt*. To bear; to experience; to suffer.

Undergraduate, un-der-grad´ū-āt, *n*. A student who has not taken his first degree.

Underground, un´der-ground, *a*. and *adv*. Below the surface of the ground; operating in secret.

Undergrowth, un´der-grōth, *n*. Shrubs or small trees growing among large ones.

Underhand, un´der-hand, *a*. Working by stealth; secret; deceitful.—*adv*. In a clandestine manner.

Understand, un-der-stand´, *vt*. To comprehend; to see through; to

suppose to mean; to infer; to assume; to recognize as implied although not expressed.—*vi*. To comprehend; to learn.

Undertake, un´der-tāk, *vt*. To take in hand; to engage in; to attempt; to guarantee.—*vi*. To take upon oneself; to promise; to stand bound.

Undertaker, un´der-tāk-er, *n*. One who undertakes; one who manages funerals.

Underwear, un´der-wār, *n*. Underclothes.

Underworld, un´der-werld, *n*. The lower world; this world; the antipodes; the place of departed souls; Hades.

Underwrite, un-der-rīt, *vt*. To write under; to subscribe one's name and become answerable for a certain amount.

Undisturbed, un-dis-terbd´, *a*. Free from disturbance; calm; tranquil; not agitated.

Undivided, un-di-vīd´ed, *a*. Not divided; whole; entire.

Undo, un-dö´, *vt*. To reverse what has been done; annul; to loose; to take to pieces; to ruin.

Undying, un-dī´ing, *a*. Not dying; imperishable.

Unearned, un-ernd´, *a*. Not merited by labor or services.—**Unearned increment,** the increase in the value of property not due to any expenditure on the part of the owner.

Unearth, un-erth´, *vt*. To drive or bring from the earth; to uncover; to discover.

Unequal, un-ē´kwal, *a*. Not equal; inadequate; insufficient; not equable.

Unequivocal, un-ē-kwiv´ō-kal, *a*. Not equivocal; not doubtful; clear; evident.

Unerring, un-er´ing, *a*. Not erring; incapable of error; certain.

Uneven, un-ē´vn, *a*. Not even or level; rough; crooked; not fair or just; odd.

Unexpected, un-eks-pekt´ed, *a*. Not expected; not looked for; sudden.

Unexpired, un-eks-pīrd´, *a*. Not expired; not having come to the end of its term.

U

Unexplored, un-eks-plōrd', a. Not explored; not visited by any traveller.

Unfading, un-fād'ing, a. Not fading; not liable to wither or decay; ever fresh.

Unfailing, un-fāl'ing, a. Not liable to fail; that does not fail; certain.

Unfair, un-fār', a. Not honest or impartial; not just; inequitable; disingenuous.

Unfamiliar, un-fa-mil'i-ėr, a. Not familiar; not accustomed; strange.

Unfasten, un-fäs'n, vt. To loose; to unfix.

Unforgiving, un-for-giv'ing, a. Not forgiving; implacable.

Unfortunate, un-for'tū-nāt, a. Not fortunate; unlucky; unhappy.—n. One who is unfortunate; a prostitute.

Unfounded, un-found'ed, a. Having no real foundation; groundless; idle.

Ungrateful, un-grāt'ful, a. Not grateful; not thankful; unpleasing; harsh.

Ungrounded, un-ground'ed, a. Having no foundation or support; groundless.

Unguarded, un-gärd'ed, a. Not guarded; not cautious; negligent.

Unguent, un'gwent, n. An ointment.

Unhinge, un-hinj', vt. To take from the hinges; to unfix; to loosen; to derange.

Unholy, un-hō'li, a. Not holy; not sacred; unhallowed; profane; impious; wicked.

Unicorn, ū'ni-korn, n. A fabulous animal like a horse, with a long single horn on the forehead.

Unification, ū'ni-fi-kā''shon, n. The act of unifying or uniting into one.

Uniform, ū'ni-form, a. Having always one and the same form; equable; invariable; consistent.— n. A distinctive dress worn by the members of the same body.

Uniformity, ū-ni-for'mi-ti, n. State or character of being uniform; conformity to one type; agreement; consistency.

Unify, ū'ni-fī, vt. To form into one.

Unimaginable, un-im-aj'in-a-bl, a. Not imaginable; inconceivable.

Unimpaired, un-im-pārd', a. Not impaired; not diminished; uninjured.

Unimpassioned, un-im-pa'shond, a. Not impassioned; tranquil; not violent.

Unimpeachable, un-im-pēch'a-bl, a. Not impeachable; blameless; irreproachable.

Uninterrupted, un-in'tėr-rupt''ed, a. Not interrupted; unintermitted; incessant.

Uninviting, un-in-vīt'ing, a. Not inviting; unattractive; rather repellent.

Union, ūn'yon, n. Act of joining; combination; agreement; harmony; marriage; confederacy; a trades-union; a mixed fabric of cotton, flax, jute, silk, or wool, etc.; a certain kind of flag.

Uniparous, ū-nip'a-rus, a. Producing one at a birth.

Unique, ū-nēk', a. Without a like or equal; unmatched; unequalled.

Unison, ū-ni-son, n. Accordance; agreement; harmony; concord.

Unit, ū'nit, n. A single thing or person; an individual; the number 1; a dimension or quantity assumed as a standard.

Unitarian, ū-ni-tā'ri-an, n. One who ascribes divinity to God only, and denies the Trinity.—a. Pertaining to Unitarians.

Unite, ū-nīt', vt. (uniting, united). To combine; to connect; to associate.—vi. To become one; to combine; to concur.

Unlike, un-līk', a. Not like; dissimilar; having no resemblance; diverse.

Unmanageable, un-man'āj-a-bl, a. Not manageable; beyond control.

Unmerciful, un-mėr'si-ful, a. Not merciful; cruel; merciless.

Unmerited, un-mer'it-ed, a. Not deserved.

Unmindful, un-mīnd'ful, a. Not mindful; regardless.

Unnerve, un-nėrv', vt. To deprive of nerve, strength, or composure; to enfeeble.

Unnoticed, un-nōt'ist, a. Not observed.

Unobjectionable, un-ob-jek'shon-a-bl, a. Not liable to objection; unexceptionable.

Unobservant, Unobserving, un-ob-zėrv'ant, un-ob-zėrv'ing, *a.* Not observant.

Unobtrusive, un-ob-trö'siv, *a.* Not obtrusive; not forward; modest; retiring.

Unorthodox, un-ōr'tho-doks, *a.* Not orthodox; heterodox.

Unpleasant, un-ple'zant, *a.* Not pleasant.**Unpolished,** un-po'lisht, *a.* Not polished; rude; plain.

Unpopular, un-po'pū-lėr, *a.* Not popular.

Unprecedented, un-pre'sė-dent-ed, *a.* Having no precedent; unexampled.

Unprincipled, un-prin'si-pld, *a.* Not having settled principles; immoral.

Unqualified, un-kwo'li-fīd, *a.* Not qualified; not having the requisite qualifications; not modified by conditions.

Unquestionable, un-kwest'yon-a-bl, *a.* Not to be called in question; indubitable.

Unravel, un-ra'vel, *vt.* To disentangle; to disengage or separate; to solve.

Unreadable, un-rēd'a-bl, *a.* Incapable of being read; illegible; not worth reading.

Unreal, un-rē'al, *a.* Not real; not substantial.

Unreason, un-rē'zn, *n.* Want of reason; folly; absurdity.

Unrequited, un-rē-kwīt'ed, *a.* Not requited; not recompensed.

Unreserved, un-rē-zėrvd', *a.* Not reserved or restricted; full; free; open; frank.

Unrest, un-rēst', *n.* Disquiet; uneasiness.

Unrestrained, un-rē-strānd', *a.* Not restrained; licentious; loose.

Unrighteous, un-rīt'yus, *a.* Not righteous; not just; wicked.

Unripe, un-rīp', *a.* Not ripe; not mature; not fully prepared; not completed.

Unsavory, un-sā'vo-ri, *a.* Not savory; insipid; unpleasing; offensive.

Unscathed, un-skāᴛʜd', *a.* Not scathed; uninjured.

Unscrew, un-skrö', *vt.* To draw the screw from; to unfasten by screwing back.

Unscrupulous, un-skrö'pū-lus, *a.* Having no scruples; regardless of principle.

Unseasonable, un-sē'zn-a-bl, *a.* Not seasonable; ill-timed; untimely.

Unsound, un-sound', *a.* Not sound; erroneous; not orthodox.

Unsparing, un-spār'ing, *a.* Not sparing; profuse; severe; rigorous.

Unspeakable, un-spēk'a-bl, *a.* Incapable of being spoken or uttered; unutterable.

Unspoken, un-spō'kn, *a.* Not spoken.

Unstable, un-stā'bl, *a.* Not stable; inconstant; irresolute; wavering.

Unsteady, un-sted'i, *a.* Not steady; shaking; fickle; varying.

Unstop, un-stop', *vt.* To free from a stopper, as a bottle; to free from obstruction.

Unstrung, un-strung', *a.* Deprived of strings; having the nerves shaken.

Unsuccessful, un-suk-ses'fl, *a.* Not successful; not fortunate in the result.

Unsuitable, un-sūt'a-bl, *a.* Not suitable; ill adapted; unfit.

Unsung, un-sung', *a.* Not sung; not celebrated in song or poetry.

Untenable, un-ten'a-bl, *a.* Not to be maintained by argument; not defensible.

Unthinkable, un-thingk'a-bl, *a.* That cannot be made an object of thought.

Unthinking, un-thingk'ing, *a.* Not given to think; not heedful; inconsiderate.

Unthread, un-thred', *vt.* To draw or take out a thread from.

Untie, un-tī', *vt.* (untying, untied). To loosen, as a knot; to undo; to unfasten.

Untrue, un-trö', *a.* Not true; false.

Unwieldy, un-wēl'di, *n.* Movable with difficulty; unmanageable.

Unwilling, un-wil'ing, *a.* Not willing; loath; disinclined; reluctant.

Unwise, un-wīz', *a.* Not wise; injudicious.

Unwitting, un-wit'ing, *a.* Not knowing; unconscious; unaware.

U

Unwrap, un-rap´, *vt.* To open or undo, as what is wrapped up.

Unwritten, un-rit´n, *a.* Not written; blank; understood though not expressed.

Unyielding, un-yēld´ing, *a.* Stiff; firm; obstinate.

Up, up, *adv.* Aloft; in or to a higher position; upright; above the horizon; out of bed; in a state of sedition; from the country to the metropolis; quite; to or at an end.— *prep.* To a higher place or point on; towards the interior of.

Upland, up´land, *n.* Higher grounds; hillslopes.—*a.* Pertaining to uplands.

Uplift, up-lift´, *vt.* To lift up.—*n.* up´lift. A raising; rise; exaltation.

Upmost, up´mōst, *a.* Highest; uppermost.

Upon, up-on´, *prep.* Up and on; resting on; on.

Upper, up´ėr, *a.* Higher in place or rank.—*n.* The upper part of a shoe.

Upset, up-set´, *vt.* To overturn; to discompose completely.—*n.* up´set. Act of upsetting.—*a.* Fixed; determined.—**Upset price,** the price at which anything is exposed to sale by auction.

Upshot, up´shot, *n.* Final issue; end.

Upstairs, up´stärz, *a.* or *adv.* Ascending the stairs; in or pertaining to the upper part of a house.

Upstart, up-stärt´, *vi.* To start up suddenly.—*n.* up´stärt. A parvenu.

Upward, up´wėrd, *a.* Directed to a higher place; ascending.—*adv.* Upwards.

Uranium, ū-rā´ni-um, *n.* A rare metal, colored like nickel or iron.

Uranus, ū´ra-nus, *n.* The most distant of all the planets except Neptune and Pluto.

Urban, ėr´ban, *a.* Of or belonging to a city or town.

Urbane, ėr-bān´, *a.* Courteous; polite.

Urchin, ėr´chin, *n.* A hedgehog; a sea-urchin; a child or small boy.

Urine, ū´rin, *n.* An animal fluid secreted by the kidneys and stored in the bladder before being discharged.

Urn, ėrn, *n.* A vase swelling in the middle; a vessel for water.

Us, us, *pron.* The objective case of *we.*

Usable, ūz´a-bl, *a.* That may be used.

Usage, ūz´āj, *n.* Act or manner of using; treatment; practice; custom; use.

Use, ūs, *n.* Act of employing anything; employment; utility; need; practice; wont.—*vt.* ūz (using, used). To put to use; to employ; to accustom; to treat.—*vi.* To be accustomed.

Usher, ush´ėr, *n.* A door-keeper; an officer who introduces strangers, etc.; a subordinate teacher.—*vt.* To give entrance to; to introduce.

Usual, ū´zhū-al, *a.* Customary; common; frequent; ordinary; general.

Usurp, ū-zėrp´, *vt.* To seize and hold without right; to appropriate wrongfully.

Utmost, ut´mōst, *a.* Being farthest out; uttermost; extreme.—*n.* The greatest power, degree, or effort.

Utopia, ū-tō´pi-a, *n.* A place or state of ideal perfection.

Utter, ut´ėr, *a.* Complete; total; absolute.—*vt.* To give vent to; to put into circulation; to declare; to speak.

Uvula, ū´vū-la, *n.* The small fleshy body which hangs over the root of the tongue.

V

Vacant, vā´kant, *a.* Empty; void; unoccupied; leisure; thoughtless; inane.

Vacate, va-kāt´, *vt.* (vacating, vacated). To make vacant; to leave unoccupied; to annul.

Vacuum, va´kū-um, *n.* Empty space; a void; an enclosed space void of air.—**Vacuum cleaner,** *n.* An apparatus used for removing dust from carpets, etc., by means of suction.

Vagabond, va´ga-bond, *a.* Wandering to and fro; pertaining to a vagrant.—*n.* A wanderer; a vagrant; a rascal.

Vagina, va-jī′na, *n.* A sheath; the canal in females leading inwards to the uterus.

Vagrant, vā′grant, *a.* Wandering; unsettled.—*n.* A wanderer; a vagabond; a sturdy beggar; a tramp.

Vague, vāg, *a.* Indefinite; hazy; uncertain.

Vain, vān, *a.* Without real value; empty; worthless; ineffectual; light-minded; conceited.—**In vain,** to no purpose.

Valance, Valence, val′ans, val′ens, *n.* The drapery hanging round a bed, couch, etc.

Value, va′lū, *n.* Worth; utility; importance; import; precise signification.—*vt.* (valuing, valued). To rate at a certain price; to estimate; to esteem; to prize; to regard.

Valve, valv, *n.* A leaf of a folding door; a lid for an orifice, opening only one way and regulating the passage of fluid or air; a separable portion of the shell of a mollusk.

Vandal, van′dal, *n.* One who willfully or ignorantly destroys any work of art or the like.

Vane, vān, *n.* A weathercock; the broad part of a feather on either side of the shaft; blade of a windmill, etc.

Vanish, va′nish, *vi.* To disappear; to pass away.

Vanity, va′ni-ti, *n.* Quality or state of being vain; worthlessness; vain pursuit; desire of indiscriminate admiration; conceit; a trifle.

Vanquish, vang′kwish, *vt.* To conquer; to overcome; to confute.

Variable, vā′ri-a-bl, *a.* That may vary or alter; changeable; fickle; unsteady.

Varicose, va′ri-kōs, *a.* Exhibiting a morbid enlargement or dilation, as the veins.

Variety, va-rī′e-ti, *n.* State or quality of being varied or various; diversity; a varied assortment; a sort; a kind.

Various, vā′ri-us, *a.* Different; several; changeable; uncertain; diverse.

Varnish, vär′nish, *n.* A clear solution of resinous matter, for coating surfaces and giving a gloss; outside show; gloss.—*vt.* To lay varnish on; to gloss over.

Vary, vā′ri, *vt.* (varying, varied). To change; to diversify.—*vi.* To alter; to change; to differ; to swerve; to disagree.

Vascular, vas′kū-lėr, *a.* Pertaining to those vessels that have to do with conveying blood, chyle, etc.

Vase, väz, *n.* A vessel of some size and of various materials and forms, generally ornamental rather than useful.

Vast, väst, *a.* Of great extent; immense; mighty; great in importance or degree.—*n.* A boundless space; immensity.

Vat, vat, *n.* A large vessel for holding liquors; a tun; a wooden tank or cistern.—*vt.* (vatting, vatted). To put in a vat.

Vegetable, ve′je-ta-bl, *a.* Belonging to or like plants.—*n.* A plant; a plant for culinary purposes.

Vein, vān, *n.* A blood-vessel which returns impure blood to the heart and lungs; a blood-vessel; a sap tube in leaves; a crack in a rock, filled up by substances different from the rock; a streak; disposition; mood.—*vt.* To fill or variegate with veins.

Vellum, vel′um, *n.* A fine parchment made of calf's skin.

Velocity, vē-los′i-ti, *n.* Rate of motion; speed; rapidity.

Veneer, ve-nēr′, *n.* A thin facing of fine wood glued on a less valuable sort; any similar coating; fair outward show.—*vt.* To overlay with veneer; to put a fine superficial show on.

Venerate, ve′nė-rāt, *vt.* (venerating, venerated). To reverence; to revere; to regard as sacred.

Venereal, ve-nē′rē-al, *a.* Pertaining to sexual intercourse.

Venetian, vē-nē′shi-an, *a.* Belonging to Venice; denoting a window blind made of thin slats of wood.

Vengeance, venj′ans, *n.* Punishment in return for an injury; penal retribution.

Venial, vē′ni-al, *a.* That may be pardoned or forgiven; excusable.

Venison, ven′zn or ven′i-zn, *n.* The flesh of deer.

Venom, ve′nom, *n.* Poison; spite;

V

malice; malignity; virulency.

Vent, vent, *n.* A small opening; flue or funnel; an outlet; the anus; utterance; expression; sale; market.—*vt.* To let out; to publish.

Venter, ven'tẻr, *n.* The abdomen; in *law,* the uterus.

Ventilate, ven'ti-lāt, *vt.* (ventilating, ventilated). To winnow; to expose to the air; to supply with fresh air; to let be freely discussed.

Venture, ven'tūr, *n.* An undertaking which involves hazard or danger; a commercial speculation; thing put to hazard; chance.—*vi.* (venturing, ventured). To make a venture; to dare.—*vt.* To risk.

Venue, ven'ū, *n.* A thrust; the place where an action is laid or the trial of a cause takes place.

Venus, vē'nus, *n.* The Roman goddess of beauty and love; a planet.

Veracious, ve-rā'shus, *a.* Observant of truth; truthful; true.

Verbatim, vẻr-bā'tim, *adv.* Word for word; in the same words.

Verbose, vẻr-bōs', *a.* Wordy; prolix.

Verdant, vẻr'dant, *a.* Green with herbage or foliage; simple and inexperienced.

Verdict, vẻr'dikt, *n.* The answer of a jury; decision in general; opinion.

Verify, ve'ri-fī, *vt.* (verifying, verified). To prove to be true; to confirm; to fulfil.

Vermifuge, vẻr'mi-fūj, *n.* A medicine that expels intestinal worms.

Vermilion, vẻr-mil'yon, *n.* Cinnabar or red sulfide of mercury; a beautiful red color.—*vt.* To color with vermilion.

Vermin, vẻr'min, *n. sing.* and *pl.* A term for all sorts of small noxious mammals or insects.

Versatile, vẻrs'a-til, *a.* Readily turning; inconstant; having many accomplishments.

Versatility, vẻrs-a-til'i-ti, *n.* Aptness to change; facility in taking up various intellectual pursuits.

Verse, vẻrs, *n.* A line of poetry; meter; poetry; versification; a stanza; a short division of any composition.

Vertebrata, vẻr-te-brā'ta, *n.pl.* The highest division of animals, consisting of those which possess a backbone.

Vertebrate, vẻr'te-brāt, *a.* Having a backbone.—*n.* One of the Vertebrata.

Vertex, vẻr'teks, *n.*; pl. **-texes** or **-tices.** The highest point; top; apex; zenith.

Vertical, vẻr'ti-kal, *a.* Pertaining to the vertex; directly over the head; perpendicular to the horizon; upright.

Vertiginous, vẻr-ti'jin-us, *a.* Giddy or dizzy; affected with vertigo.

Vertigo, vẻr-tī'gō or vẻr'ti-gō, *n.* Dizziness or swimming of the head; giddiness.

Verve, verv, *n.* Spirit; energy.

Very, ve'ri, *a.* True; real; actual.—*adv.* Truly; in a great or high degree.

Vesical, ve'si-kal, *a.* Pertaining to the bladder.

Vesicate, ve'si-kāt, *vt.* To blister.

Vesicle, ve'si-kl, *n.* A small bladderlike structure or cavity; a little sac or cyst.

Vesper, ves'pẻr, *n.* The evening; the evening-star; *pl.* evening worship or service.—*a.* Relating to the evening or to vespers.

Vessel, ves'el, *n.* A hollow utensil for holding liquids or solids; a ship; a tube or canal for blood or sap; a person.

Vest, vest, *n.* Undergarment for the upper part of the body; a waistcoat.—*vt.* To clothe; to endow; to invest.—*vi.* To descend to; to devolve; to take effect, as a title or right.

Vested, vest'ed, *a.* Clothed or habited; robed; well settled or established.

Vestibule, ves'ti-būl, *n.* A passage or hall inside the outer door of a house.

Veterinary, ve'te-ri-na-ri, *a.* Pertaining to the art of healing the diseases of domestic animals.

Veto, vē'tō, *n.* The power or right of forbidding; any authoritative prohibition or refusal.—*vt.* (vetoing, vetoed). To forbid; to interdict.

Via, vī'a, *prep.* By way of.

Viable, vī'a-bl, *a.* Capable of living, applied to a new-born child.

Viaduct, vī'a-dukt, *n.* A long bridge for carrying a road or railway over a valley.

Vicarious, vī-kā′ri-us, *a.* Pertaining to a substitute; deputed, substituted or suffered for or in the place of another.

Vice, vīs, *n.* A blemish; fault; moral failing; profligacy; a fault or bad trick in a horse; an iron instrument which holds fast anything worked upon; a prefix denoting position second in rank.

Vicinity, vi-sin′i-ti, *n.* Neighborhood; proximity.

Vicious, vi′shus, *a.* Characterized by vice; faulty; depraved; immoral; spiteful.

Vicissitude, vi-sis′i-tūd, *n.* Change or alternation; one of the ups and downs of life.

Victim, vik′tim, *n.* A living being sacrificed; a person or thing destroyed; a person who suffers; a gull.

Victory, vik′to-ri, *n.* Conquest; a gaining of the superiority in any contest.

View, vū, *n.* A look; inspection; consideration; range of vision; power of perception; sight; scene; pictorial sketch; judgment; intention.— *vt.* To see; to survey; to consider.— *vi.* To look.

Vigil, vi′jil, *n.* Act of keeping awake; a devotional watching; the eve or day preceding a church festival.

Vigilant, vi′ji-lant, *a.* Watchful; circumspect; wary; on the outlook; alert.

Vignette, vin-yet′ or vi-net′, *n.* Flowers, head and tail pieces, etc., in books; a wood-cut without a definite border; a small photographic portrait; a small attractive picture.

Vigorous, vi′gor-us, *a.* Full of vigor; strong; lusty; powerful; energetic.

Vigor, vi′gor, *n.* Active force or strength; physical force; strength of mind.

Vincible, vin′si-bl, *a.* Conquerable.

Vindicate, vin′di-kāt, *vt.* (vindicating, vindicated). To prove to be just or valid; to maintain the rights of; to defend; to justify.

Vindictive, vin-dik′tiv, *a.* Revengeful.

Vine, vīn, *n.* A climbing plant producing grapes; the slender stem of any climbing plant.

Vinegar, vi′nē-gėr, *n.* Diluted and impure acetic acid, obtained from wine, beer, etc.; sourness of temper.

Vineyard, vin′yärd, *n.* A plantation of vines producing grapes.

Vintage, vint′āj, *n.* The gathering of the grape crop; the crop itself; the wine produced by the grapes of one season.

Vintner, vint′nėr, *n.* One who deals in wine; a wine-seller; a licensed victualler.

Viol, vī′ol, *n.* An ancient musical instrument like the violin.

Viola, vē-o′la, *n.* The tenor violin.

Violate, vī′ō-lāt, *vt.* (violating, violated). To injure; to outrage; to desecrate; to profane; to transgress.

Violation, vī-ō-lā′shon, *n.* Infringement; transgression; desecration; rape.

Violence, vī′ō-lens, *n.* Quality of being violent; vehemence; outrage; injury.

Violent, vī′ō-lent, *a.* Impetuous; furious; outrageous; fierce; severe.

Violin, vī-ō-lin′, *n.* A musical instrument with four strings, played with a bow; a fiddle.

Virgin, vėr′jin, *n.* A woman who has had no carnal knowledge of man; a maid; a sign of the zodiac.—*a.* Chaste; maidenly; unsullied.

Virgo, vėr′gō, *n.* The Virgin in the zodiac.

Virile, vi′rīl or vi′ril, *a.* Pertaining to a man; masculine; manly; strong.

Virility, vi-ril′i-ti, *n.* Manhood; the power of procreation; masculine action or vigor.

Virtual, vėr′tū-al, *a.* Being in essence or effect, not in name or fact.

Virtue, vėr′tū, *n.* Moral goodness; rectitude; morality; chastity; merit; efficacy.

Virtuoso, vėr-tū-ō′sō, *n.*; pl. **-osos** or **-osi.** A man skilled in the fine arts, or antiquities, curiosities, etc.

Virtuous, vėr′tū-us, *a.* Marked by virtue; morally good; pure or chaste.

V

Virulent, vi'rū-lent, *a.* Very poisonous or noxious; bitter in enmity; malignant.

Visé, vē-zā, *n.* An endorsation upon a passport denoting that it has been examined and found correct.

Visible, vi'zi-bl, *a.* Perceivable by the eye; apparent; open; conspicuous.

Vision, vi'zhon, *n.* Act of seeing; sight; that which is seen; an apparition; a fanciful view.

Visionary, vi'zhon-a-ri, *a.* Pertaining to visions; imaginative; imaginary; not real.—*n.* One who is visionary; one who upholds impracticable schemes.

Visit, vi'zit, *vt.* To go or come to see; to view officially; to afflict.—*vi.* To practice going to see others; to make calls.—*n.* Act of visiting; a call.

Vitalize, vī'tal-īz, *vt.* To give life to; to furnish with the vital principle.

Vitals, vī'talz, *n.pl.* Parts essential to life.

Vitamin, vī'ta-min, *n.* One of several substances necessary for animal nutrition, and occurring in minute quantities in natural foods; numerous types have been distinguished, and designated by the letters of the alphabet.

Vitriolic, vit'ri-ol'ik, *a.* Pertaining to vitriol; like vitriol; very biting or sarcastic.

Vituperative, vī-tū'pe-rāt-iv, *a.* Containing vituperation; abusive; railing.

Vivacious, vī-vā'shus or vi-, *a.* Lively; brisk; sprightly; tenacious of life.

Vivacity, vī-vas'i-ti or vi-, *n.* Animation; spirit; liveliness; briskness.

Vivid, vi'vid, *a.* Bright, clear, or lively; forcible; striking; realistic.

Vocal, vō'kal, *a.* Pertaining to the voice; uttered by the voice; endowed with a voice; having a vowel character.

Vocally, vō'kal-li, *adv.* With voice; with an audible sound; in words.

Vocation, vō-kā'shon, *n.* A calling; employment; profession; business.

Voice, vois, *n.* The sound uttered by the mouth; articulate human utterance; state of vocal organs; speech; sound emitted; right of expressing an opinion; vote; a form of verb inflection.—*vt.* (voicing, voiced). To utter or express; to declare.

Void, void, *a.* Empty; devoid; ineffectual; null.—*n.* An empty space.—*vt.* To make vacant; to quit; to nullify; to emit; to evacuate from the bowels.

Volant, vō'lant, *a.* Flying; nimble; rapid.

Volatile, vo-la-til, *a.* Readily diffusible in the atmosphere; flighty; airy; fickle; fugitive.

Volley, vol'i, *n.* A discharge of a number of missile weapons, as small-arms; emission of many things at once.—*vt.* and *i.* To discharge or be discharged in a volley; to sound like a volley; to strike and return a ball (in lawn-tennis, etc.) before it touches the ground.

Volt, vōlt, *n.* A sudden movement in fencing to avoid a thrust; the unit of electromotive force.

Volubility, vo-lū'bil'i-ti, *n.* Great readiness or fluency of speech.

Voluble, vo'lū-bl, *a.* Rolling round or revolving; glib in speech; over fluent.

Volume, vo'lūm, *n.* Something rolled up; a book; a coil; a convolution; mass or bulk; quantity or strength.

Voluntarily, vo'lun-ta-ri-li, *adv.* Spontaneously; of one's own free will.

Voluntary, vo'lun-ta-ri, *a.* Willing; free to act; spontaneous; regulated by the will.—*n.* A volunteer; a supporter of voluntaryism; an organ solo during a church service.

Volunteer, vo-lun-tēr', *n.* A person who enters into military or other service of his own free will.—*a.* Pertaining to volunteers.—*vt.* To offer or bestow voluntarily.—*vi.* To enter into any service voluntarily.

Vortex, vor'teks, *n.*; pl. **-tices** or **-texes.** A whirling motion in any fluid; a whirlpool or a whirlwind; an eddy.

Vortical, vor'tik-al, *a.* Pertaining to a vortex; whirling.

Votary, vō'ta-ri, *n.* One who is bound by a vow; one devoted to some particular service, state of life, etc.

Vote, vōt, *n*. Act or power of expressing opinion or choice; a suffrage; thing conferred by vote; result of voting; votes collectively.—*vi*. (voting, voted). To give a vote.—*vt*. To choose or grant by vote.

Votive, vōt'iv, *a*. Pertaining to a vow; promised or given, in consequence of a vow.

Vouch, vouch, *vt*. To attest; to affirm; to answer for.—*vi*. To bear witness; to stand surety.

Vowel, vou'el, *n*. A sound produced by opening the mouth and giving utterance to voice; the letter which represents such a sound.— *a*. Pertaining to a vowel; vocal.

Voyage, voi'āj, *n*. A journey by water to a distance.—*vi*. (voyaging, voyaged). To pass by water.

Vulcanize, vul'kan-īz, *vt*. To harden (india-rubber) by combining with sulphur, etc.

Vulgar, vul'gėr, *a*. Pertaining to the common people; vernacular; common; coarse.—**The vulgar,** the common people.

Vulture, vul'tūr, *n*. A bird of prey which lives chiefly on carrion.

W

Wad, wod, *n*. A soft mass of fibrous material, used for stuffing; material for stopping the charge in a gun.—*vt*. (wadding, wadded). To furnish with a wad or wadding.

Waddle, wod'l, *vi*. (waddling, waddled). To walk with a rolling gait; to toddle.

Wade, wād, *vi*. (wading, waded). To walk through a substance which hinders the lower limbs, as water; to move or pass with labor.—*vt*. To ford.

Wafer, wā'fėr, *n*. A thin cake, as of bread; a thin disc of paste for fastening letters.—*vt*. To seal with a wafer.

Wagon, Waggon, wag'on, *n*. A four-wheeled vehicle for heavy loads.

Waif, wāf, *n*. A stray article; a neglected, homeless wretch.

Wail, wāl, *vt*. To lament; to bewail.— *vi*. To weep.—*n*. A mournful cry or sound.

Wait, wāt, *vi*. To stay in expectation; to continue in patience; to attend; to serve at table.—*vt*. To await.—*n*. Act of waiting; ambush; a musician who promenades in the night about Christmas time.

Waiter, wāt'ėr, *n*. One who waits; a male attendant; a small tray or salver.

Waitress, wāt'res, *n*. A female waiter.

Waive, wāv, *vt*. (waiving, waived). To relinquish; to forgo.

Walk, wak, *vi*. To advance by steps without running; to go about; to behave.—*vt*. To pass over or through on foot; to lead about.—*n*. A short excursion on foot; gait; an avenue, promenade, etc.; sphere; way of living; tract of ground for grazing.

Wallow, wol'ō, *vi*. To tumble and roll in water or mire; to live in filth or gross vice.

Walnut, wal'nut, *n*. A valuable tree, a native of Persia; the edible nut of the tree.

Walrus, wol'rus, *n*. A hugh marine carnivorous mammal inhabiting the arctic seas.

Waltz, walts, *n*. A kind of dance for two persons; music for the dance.—*vi*. To dance a waltz.

Wan, won, *a*. Dark or gloomy; languid of look; pale.

Wand, wond, *n*. A long flexible stick; a rod; a staff of authority; a baton.

Wander, won'dėr, *vi*. To ramble here and there; to roam; to rove; to err; to be delirious.—*vt*. To traverse.

Wanton, won'ton, *a*. Not kept in due restraint; unprovoked; lustful; frolicsome; rank.—*n*. A lewd person; a trifler.—*vi*. To revel unrestrainedly; to sport lasciviously.

War, war, *n*. A contest between nations or parties carried on by force of arms; profession of arms; art of war; hostility; enmity.—*vi*. (warring, warred). To make or carry on war; to strive.

Wardrobe, ward'rōb, *n*. A piece of

furniture in which wearing apparel is kept; a person's wearing apparel collectively.

Warehouse, wār'hous, *n.* A storehouse for goods; a large shop.—*vt.* To deposit or secure in a warehouse.

Warn, warn, *vt.* To caution against; to admonish; to advise; to inform previously.

Warning, warn'ing, *n.* Act of one who warns; caution against danger, etc.; admonition; previous notice.

Warp, warp, *vt.* and *i.* To turn or twist out of shape; to contort; to pervert; to move, as a ship, by a rope attached to something.—*n.* The threads extended lengthwise in a loom; a rope used in moving a ship; deposit of rich mud; twist of wood in drying.

Warren, wo'ren, *n.* Ground appropriated for rabbits; a preserve in a river for fish.

Warrior, wa'ri-or, *n.* A soldier; a brave or able soldier.

Wart, wart, *n.* A hard dry growth on the skin.

Wary, wā'ri, *a.* Cautious; prudent.

Was, woz, *v.* The first and third person singular of the past tense of *to be.*

Wasp, wosp, *n.* An active, stinging, winged insect, resembling the bee.

Waspish, wosp'ish, *a.* Like a wasp; venomous; irritable; snappish.

Waste, wāst, *vt.* (wasting, wasted). To make desolate; to ravage; to wear away gradually; to squander.—*vi.* To decrease gradually.—*a.* Desolate; spoiled; refuse.—*n.* Act of wasting; prodigality; refuse matter; gradual decrease; a desert region.

Wasteful, wāst'ful, *a.* Causing waste; destructive; ruinous; lavish; prodigal.

Waste-pipe, wāst'pīp, *n.* A pipe for carrying off waste water, etc.

Wasting, wāst'ing, *a.* Such as to waste; desolating; enfeebling.

Watch, woch, *n.* A keeping awake to guard, etc.; vigilance; a guard; time during which a person is on guard or duty; a small pocket time-piece.—*vi.* To keep awake; to give heed; to act as a guard, etc.; to wait.—*vt.* To look with close attention at or on; to tend; to guard.

Water, wa'tèr, *n.* A transparent fluid; a fluid consisting of hydrogen and oxygen; the sea; rain; saliva; urine; color or luster of a diamond, etc.—*vt.* To wet or supply with water; to give a wavy appearance to, as silk.—*vi.* To shed liquid matter; to take in water; to gather saliva; to have a longing desire.

Water-level, wa'tèr-le-vel, *n.* The level at which water stands; a levelling instrument in which water is employed.

Watt, wot, *n.* The practical unit of power, or rate of conveying energy, used in electricity.

Wave, wāv, *vi.* and *t.* (waving, waved). To sway or play loosely; to undulate; to brandish; to beckon.—*n.* A swell or ridge on moving water; anything resembling a wave; an undulation; a signal made by waving the hand, a flag, etc.

Waver, wā'vèr, *vi.* To wave gently; to fluctuate; to be undetermined.

Wavy, wāv'i, *a.* Rising or swelling in waves; full of waves; undulating.

Wax, waks, *n.* A tenacious substance excreted by bees or in the ear; any similar substance; sealing-wax.—*vt.* To smear or rub with wax.—*vi.* To increase; to grow; to become.

Wax-work, waks'wèrk, *n.* Work in wax; figures of persons in wax as near reality as possible.

Weakness, wēk'nes, *n.* The state or quality of being weak; irresolution; want of validity; a failing.

Weal, wēl, *n.* Welfare; prosperity; happiness; mark of a stripe; wale.

Wealth, welth, *n.* Riches; affluence; opulence; abundance.

Wealthy, welth'i, *a.* Possessing wealth; rich; opulent; abundant; ample.

Wean, wēn, *vt.* To accustom to do without the mother's milk; to alienate; to disengage from any habit.

Weapon, we'pon, *n.* Any instrument of offense or defense.

Wear, wār, *vt*. (pret. wore, pp. worn).
To carry as belonging to dress; to
have on; to waste by rubbing; to
destroy by degrees; to produce by
rubbing; to exhibit.—*vi*. To last
well or ill; to waste gradually; to
make gradual progress.—*n*. Act of
wearing; diminution by friction,
use, time, etc.; fashion.

Weather, weᴛʜ'ėr, *n*. The general atmospheric conditions at any particular time. *a*. Turned towards
the wind; windward.—*vt*. To affect
by the weather; to sail to the windward of; to bear up against and
overcome.

Web, web, *n*. The whole piece of
cloth woven in a loom; a large roll
of paper; membrane which unites
the toes of water-fowl; the threads
which a spider spins; a cobweb;
anything carefully contrived.

Wedge, wej, *n*. A body sloping to a
thin edge at one end.—*vt*. (wedg-
ing, wedged). To drive as a wedge
is driven; to crowd or compress; to
fasten or split with a wedge.

Wedlock, wed'lok, *n*. The wedded
state; marriage.

Wednesday, wenz'dā, *n*. The fourth
day of the week.

Wee, wē, *a*. Small; little.

Week, wēk, *n*. The space of seven
days; space from one Sunday to
another.

Weep, wēp, *vi*. (pret. and pp. wept).
To manifest grief, etc., by shedding tears.

Weevil, wē'vil, *n*. An insect of the
beetle family, destructive to grain,
fruit, etc.

Weft, weft, *n*. The woof of cloth.

Weigh, wā, *vt*. To raise; to find the
heaviness of; to allot or take by
weight; to consider; to balance; to
burthen.—*vi*. To have weight; to
amount to in weight; to bear
heavily.

Weight, wāt, *n*. Heaviness; gravity;
the amount which anything
weighs; a metal standard for
weighing; a heavy mass; pressure; burden; importance; moment.—*vt*. To add to the heaviness
of.

Well, wel, *n*. A spring; a pit sunk for
water; perpendicular space in a
building in which stairs or a hoist
is place.—*vi*. To bubble up; to issue
forth.

Well, wel, *adv*. In a proper manner;
rightly; commendably; considera-
bly.—*a*. Being in health; comfortable; fortunate; convenient;
proper.

Wen, wen, *n*. A harmless fatty tumor.

Wench, wensh, *n*. A young woman;
a woman of loose character.—*vi*.
To frequent the company of
women of ill-fame.

Wend, wend, *vt*. To go; to direct.—*vi*.
To go; to travel.

Went, went. Used as the pret. of *go*.

Were, wer, *v*. The past tense plural
indicative and the past subjunctive of *be*.

Werwolf, wėr'wulf, *n*. A man trans-
formed into a wolf.

West, west, *n*. The point where the
sun sets, opposite to the east.—*a*.
Being in or towards the west; coming from the west.—*adv*. To the
west.

Whale, whāl, *n*. The largest of sea
animals, a mammal.

Wharf, wharf, *n*.; pl. **-fs** or **-ves**. A
quay for loading or unloading
ships.

What, whot, *pron*. An interrogative
pronoun used chiefly of things;
employed adjectively as equivalent to how great, remarkable,
etc.; substantively as equivalent
to the thing (or things) which.

Wheat, whēt, *n*. A cereal plant; its
seeds, which yield a white nutritious flour.

Whelp, whelp, *n*. A puppy; a cub; a
young man.—*vi*. To bring forth
whelps.—*vt*. To bring forth; to originate.

When, when, *adv*. and *conj*. At
what or which time; while;
whereas; used substantively with
since or *till*.

Where, whār, *adv*. and *conj*. At or in
what place; at the place in which;
whither.

Wherry, whe'ri, *n*. A light river boat
for passengers.

Whet, whet, *vi*. (whetting, whetted
or whet). To rub to sharpen; to

W

edge; to excite; to stimulate.—*n.* Act of sharpening; something that stimulates the appetite.

Whether, wheᴛʜ'ér, *pron.* Which of two.—*conj.* or *adv.* Which of two or more, introducing alternative clauses.

Whetstone, whet'stōn, *n.* A stone used for sharpening instruments by friction.

Whey, whā, *n.* The thin part of milk, from which the curd, etc., have been separated.

Which, which, *pron.* An interrogative pronoun, used adjectively or substantively; a relative pronoun, the neuter of *who;* an indefinite pronoun, any one which.

Whiff, whif, *n.* A puff of air; a puff conveying a smell.—*vt.* and *i.* To puff; to throw out whiffs; to smoke.

While, whīl, *n.* A time; short space of time.—*conj.* During the time that; though.—*vt.* whiling, whiled). To cause to pass pleasantly: usually with *away.*

Whim, *n.* A sudden fancy; a caprice.

Whimper, whim'pér, *vi.* To express grief with a whining voice.—*vt.* To utter in a low, whining tone.—*n.* A peevish cry.

Whirlwind, whérl'wind, *n.* A whirling wind; a violent wind moving as if round an axis, this axis at the same time progressing.

Whisker, whis'kér, *n.* Long hair growing on the cheek.

Whisky, Whiskey, whis'ki, *n.* An ardent spirit distilled generally from barley; a light one-horse chaise.

Whisper, whis'pér, *vt.* To speak with a low sibilant voice; to converse secretly.—*vt.* To utter in a whisper.—*n.* A low soft sibilant voice; a faint utterance.

Whistle, whis'l, *vi.* (whistling, whistled). To utter a clear shrill sound by forcing the breath through the lips; to warble; to sound shrilly.—*vt.* To utter or signal by whistling.—*n.* Sound produced by one who whistles; any similar sound; a small pipe blown with the breath; instrument sounded by steam.

White, whīt, *a.* Being of the color of pure snow; pale; pallid; pure and unsullied.—*n.* The color of snow; a white pigment; white of an egg, eye, etc., —*vt.* (whiting, whited). To make white.

Whittle, whit'l, *n.* A large knife.— *vt.* (whittling, whittled). To cut or pare with a knife.

Whiz, whiz, *vi.* (whizzing, whizzed). To make a humming or hissing sound.—*n.* A hissing and humming sound.

Who, hö, *pron.;* possessive **Whose,** höz; objective **Whom,** höm. A relative and interrogative pronoun always used substantively and with reference to persons.

Whoever, hö-ev'ér, *pron.* Any one without exception; any person whatever.

Whole, höl, *a.* Sound; healthy; healed; intact; entire.—*n.* An entire thing; total assemblage of parts.

Wholesale, höl'sāl, *n.* Sale of goods by the entire piece or in large quantities.—*a.* Pertaining to trade in large quantities; extensive and indiscriminate.

Whose, höz, *pron.* The possessive case of *who* or *which.*

Why, whī, *adv.* and *conj.* For what reason; wherefore.

Wick, wik, *n.* The loose spongy string or band in candles or lamps.

Widen, wīd'n, *vt.* To make wide or wider.—*vi.* To grow wide or wider.

Widow, wi'dō, *n.* A woman whose husband is dead.—*vt.* To bereave of a husband.

Widower, wi'dō-ér, *n.* A man whose wife is dead.

Widowhood, wi'dō-hud, *n.* The condition of being a widow or a widower.

Width width, *n.* Breadth; extent from side to side.

Wield, wēld, *vt.* To manage freely in the hands; to sway; to exercise.

Wildfire, wīld'fir, *n.* A kind of lightning unaccompanied by thunder; erysipelas.

Will, wil, *v. aux.* (past. would), expresses futurity in the second and third persons, and willingness, etc., or determination in the first.—*vt*. and *i*. To determine by choice; to wish; to bequeath.—*n*. Wish; choice; determination; purpose; legal declaration of a person as to what is to be done after his death with his property; faculty by which we determine to do or not to do something; volition.

Willful, wil'ful, *a*. Under the influence of self-will; obstinate; wayward; intentional.

Win, win, *vt*. (winning, won). To gain; to be victorious in; to allure; to reach; to attain.—*vi*. To gain the victory.

Wince, wins, *vi*. (wincing, winced). To shrink, as from pain; to start back.—*n*. A start, as from pain.

Wind, wind, in poetry often wīnd, *n*. Air in motion; a current of air; breath; power of respiration; empty words; flatulence.—*vt*. wind (pret. & pp. wound, sometimes winded). To blow, as a horn.—*vt*. wind (pret. & pp. winded). To follow by the scent; to render scant of wind; to let rest and recover wind.

Wind, wīnd, *vt*. (pret. & pp. wound). To bend or turn; to twist; to coil.—*vi*. To twine or twist; to crook; to bend; to meander.

Windmill, wind'mil, *n*. A mill driven by the wind.

Window, win'dō, *n*. An opening in a wall for the admission of light or air; the frame (usually fitted with glass) in this opening.

Windpipe, wind'pip, *n*. The cartilaginous pipe or passage for the breath; the trachea.

Wing, wing, *n*. One of the anterior limbs in birds; organ of flight; flight; a lateral extension; side; side division of an army, etc.—*vt*. To furnish with wings; to fly; to traverse by flying; to wound in the wing.

Wink, wingk, *vi*. To shut and open the eyelids; to give a hint by the eyelids; to connive; to be willfully blind (with *at*).—*n*. Act of shutting and opening the eyelids rapidly; a twinkling; a hint given by means of the eye.

Winnow, win'ō, *vt*. To separate the chaff from by wind; to fan; to sift;

to scrutinize.—*vi*. To separate chaff from corn.

Winsome, win'sum, *a*. Attractive; winning.

Winter, win'tėr, *n*. The cold season of the year; a year; any cheerless situation.—*a*. Belonging to winter—*vi*. To pass the winter.—*vt*. To keep or feed during winter.

Wiry, wīr'i, *a*. Made of or like wire; tough; lean and sinewy.

Wisdom, wiz'dom, *n*. Sound judgment and sagacity; prudence; learning or erudition.

Wit, wit, *vt*. and *i*. (pres. tense, wot, pret. wist, pres. part. witting and wotting). To know; to be aware.— **To wit,** namely; that is to say.—*n*. Understanding; sense; wisdom; intelligence; faculty of associating ideas cleverly and in apt language; a person possessing this faculty; cleverness.

Witch, wich, *n*. A woman who practises sorcery.—*vt*. To bewitch.

Witchcraft, wich'kraft, *n*. Sorcery; enchantment; fascination.

With, wiᴛʜ, *prep*. Against; in the company of; among; showing; marked by; immediately after; through; by.—*n*. With or with. A withe.

Withal, wiᴛʜ-al', *adv*. Moreover; likewise; at the same time.—*prep*. With: used after relatives at the end of a clause.

Withdraw, wiᴛʜ-dra, *vt*. To draw back or away; to retract; to cause to retire.—*vi*. To retire; to secede.

Witness, wit'nes, *n*. Testimony; attestation of a fact or event; one who knows or sees anything; one who gives evidence in a trial.—*vt*. To attest; to see the execution of a legal instrument, and subscribe it.—*vi*. To bear testimony.

Witticism, wit'i-sizm, *n*. A witty remark.

Wittingly, wit'ing-li, *adv*. Knowingly; by design.

Wolf, wulf, *n*.; pl. **Wolves,** wulvz. A carnivorous quadruped akin to the dog, crafty and rapacious; a cruel or cunning person.

Woman, wu'man, *n*.; pl. **Women,** wi'men. The female of the human race; the female sex; an adult fe-

W

male.

Womb, wŏm, *n.* The uterus; place where anything is produced; any deep cavity.

Wombat, wom'bat, *n.* A marsupial mammal about the size of a badger.

Wonder, wun'dėr, *n.* Something very strange; a prodigy or marvel; feeling excited by something strange.—*vi.* To be struck with wonder; to marvel; to entertain some doubt and curiosity.

Wood, wụd, *n.* A large collection of growing trees; the hard or solid substance of trees; timber.—*vi.* To take in or get supplies of wood.—*vt.* To supply with wood.

Woof, wŏf, *n.* The threads that cross the warp in weaving; the weft; texture in general.

Wool, wụl, *n.* That soft species of hair on sheep; any fleecy substance resembling wool.

Wool-gathering, wụl'gaᴛʜ-ėr-ing. *n.* Act of gathering wool; indulgence of idle fancies; a foolish or fruitless pursuit.

Word, wėrd, *n.* An articulate sound expressing an idea; a term; information; a saying; motto; order; assertion or promise; in *pl.,* talk; wrangle.—*vi.* To express in words.

Wording, wėrd'ing, *n.* The mode of expressing in words; form of stating.

Wordy, wėrd'i, *a.* Using many words; verbose.

Work, wėrk, *n.* Effort; labor; employment; a task; achievement; a literary or artistic performance; some extensive structure; establishment where labor of some kind is carried on; result of force acting.—*vi.* (pret. and pp. worked or wrought). To put forth effort; to labor; to take effect; to tend or conduce; to seethe; to ferment.—*vt.* To bestow labor upon; to bring about; to keep at work; to influence; to achieve; to fashion; to embroider; to cause to ferment.

World, wėrld, *n.* The whole creation; the earth; any celestial orb; a large portion of our globe; sphere of existence; a domain or realm; mankind; the public; great degree or quantity.

Worm, wėrm, *n.* A small creeping animal; an intestinal parasite; *pl.* the disease caused by such parasites; something vermicular or spiral.—*vi.* To wriggle; to work gradually and secretly.—*vt.* To effect by stealthy means; *refl.* to insinuate oneself; to extract cunningly.

Worm-eaten, wėrm'ēt-n, *a.* Gnawed by worms; having cavities made by worms.

Worn-out, wōrn'out, *a.* Useless from being much worn; wearied; exhausted.

Worry, wu'ri, *vt.* (worrying, worried). To tear with the teeth, as dogs; to harass; to annoy.—*vi.* To trouble oneself; to fret.—*n.* Trouble; care; anxiety.

Worse, wėrs, *a.* Bad or ill in a greater degree; inferior; more unwell; more ill off.—**The worse,** defeat; disadvantage.—*adv.* In a manner or degree more evil or bad.

Worsen, wėr'sn, *vi* and *t.* To grow or make worse.

Worship, wėr'ship, *n.* Dignity; honor; a title of honor; religious service; adoration; reverence.—*vt.* (worshipping, worshipped). To adore; to pay divine honors to; to idolize.—*vi.* To perform religious service.

Wound, wŏnd, *n.* A cut or stab, etc.; injury; hurt or pain to the feelings; damage.—*vt.* or *i.* To inflict a wound on; to pain.

Wraith, rāth, *n.* An apparition of a person about to die or newly dead.

Wrangle, rang'gl, *vi.* (wrangling, wrangled). To dispute angrily; to argue.—*n.* A dispute.

Wrap, rap, *vt.* (wrapping, wrapped or wrapt). To fold or roll; to cover by something wound; to envelop.—*n.* An outer article of dress for warmth.

Wrath, räth or rạth, *n.* Violent anger; rage; fury.

Wreck, rek, *n.* Ruin; overthrow; a ruin; destruction of a vessel at sea.—*vt.* To cause to become a wreck; to ruin.

Wrench, rensh, *n.* A violent twist;

injury by twisting; an instrument for screwing a bolt or nut.—*vt*. To pull with a twist; to distort.

Wrest, rest, *vt*. To twist; to take or force by violence; to distort.—*n*. Act of wresting; a wrench; an implement to tune stringed instruments with.

Wrestle, res'l, *vi*. (wrestling, wrestled). To contend by grappling and trying to throw down; to struggle.—*vt*. To contend with in wrestling.—*n*. A bout at wrestling.

Wrinkle, ring'kl, *n*. A small ridge or furrow; a crease; a hint; a notion.—*vt*. and *i*. (wrinkling, wrinkled). To form into wrinkles; to contract into furrows; to crease.

Wrist, rist, *n*. The joint by which the hand is united to the arm.

Writ, rit, *n*. That which is written; the Scriptures; a legal document commanding a person to do some act.

Write rit, *vt*. (writing, pret. wrote, pp. written). To form by a pen, etc.; to set down in letters or words; to cover with letters; to send in writing; to compose.—*vi*. To trace characters with a pen, etc.; to be engaged in literary work; to conduct correspondence.

Writhe, rīᴛʜ, *vt*. (writhing, writhed). To twist or distort, as the body or limbs.—*vi*. To twist and turn; to be distorted, as from agony.

Wrong, rong, *a*. Not right; not fit; not what ought to be; erroneous.— *n*. What is not right; an injustice; injury.—*adv*. In a wrong manner.—*vt*. To do wrong to; to treat with injustice.

X

Xanthin, Xanthine, zan'thin, *n*. A yellow coloring matter.

Xanthous, zan'thus, *a*. Fair-haired.

Xerotes, zē'ro-tēz, *n*. A dry habit of the body.

Xiphoid, zīf'oid, *a*. Shaped like a sword.

X-rays, eks'rāz, or **Röntgen rays**, runt'gen, *n*. Electromagnetic waves of high frequency, which penetrate most substances, except bones, metal, etc., and enable photographs to be taken of these in the living body.

Xyloid, zī'loid, *a*. Having the nature of wood; resembling wood.

Xylonite, zī'lō-nīt, *n*. Celluloid.

Xylophagous, zī-lof'a-gus, *a*. Wood-eating.

Xylophone, zī-lo-fōn, *n*. A musical instrument in which the notes are given by pieces of wood struck with hammers.

Xyst, Xystus, zist, zis'tus, *n*. A covered portico or open court for athletic exercises.

Y

Yacht, yot, *n*. A light vessel used for racing, pleasure, etc.—*vi*. To sail in a yacht.

Yard, yärd, *n*. A standard measure of 3 feet; a long beam slung crosswise to a mast and supporting a sail; piece of enclosed ground.

Yard-stick, yärd'stik, *n*. A stick 3 feet in length.

Yarn, yärn, *n*. Thread prepared from wool or flax for weaving; a story.

Yaw, ya, *vi*. To swerve suddenly in sailing.—*n*. The sudden temporary deviation of a ship.

Yawn, yan, *vi*. To have the mouth open involuntarily while a deep breath is taken; to gape.—*n*. A gaping; act of yawning; a chasm.

Yea, yā, *adv*. Yes: the opposite of *nay*.

Yean, yēn, *vi*. and *i*. To bring forth young, as a goat or sheep.

Year, yēr, *n*. The period of time during which the earth makes one revolution in its orbit; twelve months; *pl*. old age; time of life.

Yeast, yēst, *n*. A yellowish substance produced in alcoholic fermentation; barm.

Yell, yel, *vi*. To cry out with a loud piercing noise; to scream.—*n*. A loud, piercing outcry.

Yellow, yel'ō, *a*. Being of a bright golden color.—*n*. A bright golden color.

Y

Yelp, yelp, *vi.* To utter a sharp bark or cry, as a dog.—*n.* A sharp cry of a dog.

Yes, yes, *adv.* Even so; expressing affirmation or consent; opposed to *no.*

Yield, yēld, *vt.* To produce in return for labor, etc.; to afford; to grant; to give up.—*vi.* To submit; to comply; to produce.—*n.* Amount yielded; product; return.

Yodel, Yodle, yō'dl, *vt.* and *i.* (yodelling, yodling; yodelled, yodled). To sing like the Swiss and Tyrolese mountaineers by changing suddenly from the natural voice to the falsetto.

Yoke, yōk, *n.* Gear connecting draught animals by passing across their necks; a pair of draught animals; something resembling a yoke; shoulder-piece of a garment supporting the rest; servitude; burden; a bond; a tie.—*vt.* (yoking, yoked). To put a yoke on; to couple; to enslave.

Young, yung, *a.* Being in the early stage of life; youthful.—*n.* The offspring of an animal.

Youngster, yung'stėr, *n.* A young person.

Your, yör, possessive corresponding to *ye, you.* Pertaining or belonging to you.

Yours, yörz, *poss. pron.* That or those which belong to you. **Yourself,** Yör-self' *pron.*; pl. **-selves.** You, used distinctively or reflexively.

Youth, yöth, *n.* State or quality of being young; period during which one is young; a young man; young persons collectively.

Youthful, yöth'ful, *a.* Young; pertaining to youth; fresh or vigorous, as in youth.

Yowl, youl, *vi.* To give a long distressful or mournful cry, as a dog.—*n.* A mournful cry.

Yule, yöl, *n.* Christmas.

Z

Zany, zā'ni, *n.* A buffoon or merry-andrew.

Zeal, zēl, *n.* Eagerness; passionate ardour; enthusiasm.

Zealot, ze'lot, *n.* One who is zealous; a fanatical partisan; a bigot.

Zero, zē'rō, *n.* Number or quantity diminished to nothing: a cipher; lowest point.

Zest, zest, *n.* Orange or lemon peel, used to flavor liquor; relish; charm; gusto.

Zigzag, zig'zag, *n.* Something in the form of straight lines with sharp turns.—*a.* Having sharp turns or bends.—*vi.* (zigzagging, zigzagged). To move in a zigzag fashion; to form zigzags.

Zinc, zingk, *n.* A metal of bluish-white color, used for roofing, to form alloys, etc.

Zircon, zėr'kon, *n.* A hard lustrous mineral, one of the gems called also jargon.

Zither, Zithern, zith'ėr, zith'ėrn, *n.* A flat musical instrument with from twenty-nine to forty-two strings, played with the fingers.

Zodiac, zō'di-ak, *n.* An imaginary belt or zone in the heavens, within which the apparent motions of the sun, moon, and principal planets are confined, divided into twelve equal parts or signs.

Zoetrope, zō'ē-trōp, *n.* An optical contrivance by which, when the instrument revolves, certain painted figures inside appear to move in a lifelike manner.

Zone, zōn, *n.* A girdle or belt; one of the five great divisions of the earth, bounded by circles parallel to the equator; any well-defined belt.

Zoography, zō-og'ra-fi, *n.* The description of animals.

Zooid, zō'oid, *a.* Resembling or pertaining to an animal.—*n.* An organism, in some respects resembling a distinct animal.

Zoolite, zō'ol-līt, *n.* An animal substance petrified or fossil.

Zoology, zō-ol'o-ji, *n.* The science of the natural history of animals.

Zymotic, zi-mot'ik, *a.* Pertaining to fermentation; applied to epidemic and contagious diseases, supposed to be produced by germs acting like a ferment.